IN THE HIGHEST DE

In the Highest Degree Odious

DETENTION WITHOUT TRIAL
IN WARTIME BRITAIN

A. W. BRIAN SIMPSON

CLARENDON PRESS · OXFORD

This book has been printed digitally and produced in a standard specification in order to ensure its continuing availability

OXFORD
UNIVERSITY PRESS

Great Clarendon Street, Oxford OX2 6DP

Oxford University Press is a department of the University of Oxford.
It furthers the University's objective of excellence in research, scholarship,
and education by publishing worldwide in

Oxford New York

Auckland Cape Town Dar es Salaam Hong Kong Karachi
Kuala Lumpur Madrid Melbourne Mexico City Nairobi
New Delhi Shanghai Taipei Toronto
With offices in
Argentina Austria Brazil Chile Czech Republic France Greece
Guatemala Hungary Italy Japan South Korea Poland Portugal
Singapore Switzerland Thailand Turkey Ukraine Vietnam

Oxford is a registered trade mark of Oxford University Press
in the UK and in certain other countries

Published in the United States
by Oxford University Press Inc., New York

Oxford is a registered trade mark of Oxford University Press
in the UK and in certain other countries

Published in the United States
by Oxford University Press Inc., New York

© Brian Simpson 1992

The moral rights of the author have been asserted

Database right Oxford University Press (maker)

Reprinted 2005

ISBN 0-19-825949-2

The power of the Executive to cast a man into prison without formulating any charge known to the law, and particularly to deny him the judgement of his peers, is in the highest degree odious and is the foundation of all totalitarian government whether Nazi or Communist.

Winston S. Churchill

PREFACE

DURING the Second World War a very considerable number of people were detained by the British government without charge, or trial, or term set, on the broad ground that this was necessary for national security. Most were not British citizens, but technically enemy aliens—in fact most of these enemy aliens were refugees from Europe. A far smaller number of those detained were British citizens, and they were held under Regulation 18B of the Defence Regulations; it is with this regulation and those detained under it that this book is concerned. Although Winston Churchill was not responsible for the regulation itself, he was an enthusiast for its extensive use in the desperate days of 1940. But later in the war he came to feel increasingly unhappy over the gross violation of civil liberty over which he had presided, and the title to this book makes use of a quotation from a telegram of his on Regulation 18B which originated in Cairo in 1943.

During the war the executive imposed as much secrecy as it could get away with on the use of the regulation, and although a fair amount has been written on the subject there is in print no general account of the history of the regulation and the uses to which it was put. One reason for this is that since many of the detainees, but by no means all, were or had been fascists, they have not excited much public sympathy; the detained refugees have, and in part for this reason their story has been fully told. I have tried to write as full a history as is possible of the 18B detainees, but my account necessarily suffers from the fact that most of the relevant government records have been destroyed, and access to much of what has survived is still refused. In spite of this the quantity of material which is available is very considerable, and one of my chief problems has been that of keeping my account within a reasonable compass.

My own background is that of an academic lawyer, and, apart from

memories of the period, my own introduction to Regulation 18B began
with the study of the leading case of *Liversidge* v. *Anderson*, decided in
1941, which, I recall, we discussed in great detail. Subsequent work has
made it clear to me that, like the judges involved in that great case, we had
only a very shaky notion of what it was all about. In this book, as in other
writings, I have tried to give a general history of the regulation, and present the legal materials, the leading cases, and so forth as merely part of
that history. I hope that this may contribute to a better understanding of
the part legal and other institutions played, and can play, in the protection
of civil liberty. In general I have, however, deliberately avoided theoriz-
ing about the story, which I have tried to allow to speak for itself.

A large number of people have kindly replied to enquiries and helped in
the production of this book. I am particularly grateful to Professor De
Lloyd Guth, who played a large part in exciting my interest in the subject
in the first place, and to the legal firm of Ladner Downs who invited me
to lecture on the subject in Vancouver in the Leon Ladner Lecture Series.
I must also express thanks to Professor R. F. V. Heuston, whose work on
Liversidge v. *Anderson* places me in his debt. The University of Michigan
Law School has supported the research involved. Darlene Lentz has been
endlessly patient in helping the production of the manuscript. Mr John
Warburton has been exceptionally helpful in the research, and I must also
thank the Home Office Departmental Records Officer, D. J. Blackwood,
and his staff for putting up with my importunate demands. E. P. C.
Greene and H. Luttman-Johnson have kindly allowed me to use their late
fathers' papers. I have not kept a full list, but thanks are also due to
Rupert Allason, Lord Annan, A. M. Berrett, K. R. Bleach, Edward Burn,
P. Carter-Ruck Lord Dacre, Lord Denning, Dr Anthony Glees, Mrs
Jenifer Hart and Professor H. L. A. Hart, Professor Colin Holmes,
Professor Dafydd Jenkins, Professor R. V. Jones, Mrs Vivienne Jones, Sir
Frederick Lawton, R. W. Liversidge, W. K. Liversidge, Elizabeth
Longford, Group Captain I. Madelin, Sir Robert Mark, D. Massul,
Anthony Masters, Diana Mosley, Eric Newby, S. H. Noakes, P. Polden,
F. M. B. Reynolds, C. C. Ricketts, Colonel T. A. Robertson, Dr Albi
Rosenthal, R. Row, G. R. Rubin, Lord Selkirk, A. S. Swann, R. C.
Thurlow, J. H. Wallder, Sir Dick White, L. Wise, and D. C. Yalden-
Thomson.

A. W. B. S.

NOTE TO THE PAPERBACK EDITION

IN preparing this paperback edition the opportunity has been taken to incorporate some information which has come to light since the original edition appeared, and to correct some mistakes. In particular an unfortunately expressed footnote, which was principally concerned with R. C. Gordon-Canning,[1] quite unintentionally gave an unfair impression about the late Prince Henry of Pless, who was detained in 1940. Since then new information has come to light, which makes it clear that he was an innocent victim of 18B.[2] Since he was one of the very few top people detained, and a distant relative of Winston Churchill, his case is of some interest.

Hans Heinrich XVII, William Albert Edward, Prince Henry of Pless (2.2.1900–26.1.1984), was listed amongst the 'prominent persons' detained.[3] Known as Hansel, he was the son of His Serene Highness Hans Heinrich XVI of Pless, Baron Fürstenstein, of the house of Hochberg, and was born in Berlin. His mother, by a marriage dissolved in 1923, was Mary Theresa Olivia Cornwallis-West, known as Daisy. Her brother George married Jenny, widow of Lord Randolph Churchill, thus becoming Winston Churchill's stepfather, until this marriage too was dissolved in 1914. Prince Henry's godparents were the Kaiser and the Prince of Wales. The family was extremely wealthy, owning the Principality of Pless, comprising lands, forests, breweries and coal mines in Upper Silesia, which then formed part of Germany; thousands were dependent upon it for livelihood and employment. There were castles at Fürstenstein, and Pless, a smaller seat at Promnitz, Palast Pless on the Wilhelmstrasse in Berlin, and numerous other homes. Daisy von Hochberg published entertaining reminiscences of her life in this vanished world of the European aristocracy, for whom, before 1914, frontiers had little significance—*Daisy, Princess of Pless. By Herself* (1928), and *From my Private Diary* (1931).[4] The Prince spent some of his childhood at Eaton Hall (his maternal aunt Constance was Duchess

---

[1] 392 n.45. A correction slip was distributed as soon as this came to light.
[2] What follows is in part based upon reports of the advisory Committee on Pless' case, dated 9 January 1941 and 28 July 1942, to which the Home Office recently gave me a privileged access. Small passages, apparently, so far as I could judge, those directly referring to MI5's 'Statement of the Case', were blanked out in the photocopied pages I saw. What follows is not based upon information from the family or in any way authorized by them.
[3] See below 214.
[4] American edition in 1936 of the second book, also a selection from both in 1950.

of Westminster), and at Newnham in Hampshire with his grandfather, Colonel Cornwallis-West.

In the first war the Prince fought for Germany on the eastern front as an officer in the Life Guards Hussar Regiment. He won the Iron Cross (First Class) when seventeen or eighteen. After the war he commanded a Free Corps Company at Pless, fighting the communists. As a consequence of the Geneva Convention of 1922, and a plebiscite, the Principality of Pless became Polish, though the castle at Fürstenstein remained in Germany. The Prince was certified as of Polish nationality in 1924. From 1925 to 1935, when his father partially disinherited him in favour of his brother, Count Alexander von Hochberg, he administered the Principality. From 1930 he was involved, as administrator, and as chairman of the *Deutsche Volksbund*, in continuous disputes and delicate negotiations with the Polish and German governments over land reforms, and the protection of the interests of the German minorities in Poland:

he had in a sense to play German against Pole, Germany against Poland and *vice versa*, and strive to maintain a reasonable balance—and this not only from a selfish family point of view, and to secure the family revenues, but to protect the interests of all those who for generations had depended on the Pless estates for their livelihood.[5]

In about 1932 he married the Catholic Countess Marie Katherine Schönborn-Wiesentheid, the widow of a Baron Berckheim; she became an admirer of Hitler. In 1938 he inherited on the death of his father, but the family estates were by now heavily in debt, and subject to complex legal arrangements. Full details do not appear, but he was life tenant of Fürstenstein, and the entail on the Pless estates had been broken; his brother, Count Hochberg, had a share of the estate. He appears to have continued to live mainly in England, deriving an income from the property which remained. Hitler's invasion of Poland returned the Pless estates to Germany, but his citizenship would, so far as Britain was concerned, have been unaffected. During the war his wife lived at Pless; this marriage was in due course dissolved.

On 26 August 1939 he applied for naturalisation; he also offered his services in an intelligence capacity to Sir Robert Vansittart, who did not take to him. He also offered his services to the War Office, and in February 1940 volunteered for the 5th Battalion of the Scots Guards, destined for the support of Finland against Russia. He may have been accepted by the Colonel, but he was never commissioned into the regiment. Thereafter he attempted, without success, to join the air force, the navy, the R.N.V.R., the fire service, the special constabulary and a bomb disposal unit. He became a stretcher bearer at St. George's Hospital.

He was detained at 22 Hans Crescent as of 'hostile origin' on 19 August

---

[5] Report of 9.1.1941.

1940, and later supplied with a 'Reasons for Order' with nine paragraphs of particulars.

In January 1993, by an administrative error, some files on Nazi sympathizers under fifty year closure (HO 45/25568–25571) were released early. One, HO 45/25571, contained some information on his case. These files have since been withdrawn. Andrew Roberts, who saw one of them, has kindly allowed me access to his notes; he wrote an article based on the file for the *Spectator* for 23 January 1993. The file contains the 'invasion list' (called 'Suspect List Region III') for the South East Region based on Tunbridge Wells, and comprises a list of names dating from 1940, with later additions and notes on individuals. Prince Henry is not listed, but named in the notes as associated with a group organised by one Philip T. Farrer. Other members were Professor Robert Sencourt, General Fuller, George H. Drummond, and Sir Frederic H. Hamilton. Farrer had served in the first war and been in intelligence (1918–1919). He was involved in the British military mission to Albania in 1919–20; he then became private secretary to the 4th Marquess of Salisbury, sometime President of the Council, Lord Privy Seal, and Leader of the Lords; this employment ended in 1939. Drummond was of independent means and was High Sheriff of Northamptonshire in 1927, ending up after the war in the House of Keys. He was President of the Northampton section of the Link, and was a warden of the Right Club. Sencourt, formerly Indian Army, and the author of numerous books, was a right wing catholic. Hamilton was a mining magnate who had made his money in South Africa; 'Boney' Fuller was a fascist; the others had no connection with the British Union.

The meetings Pless is supposed to have attended appear merely to have discussed the possibility of peace negotiations with Germany. Mr. Roberts' impression of the file is that it contains a farrago of unchecked assertions. MI5 essentially operated a system based on guilt by association, parodied in a well known passage in Evelyn Waugh's war trilogy. The information in the file tallies with material in the reports of the advisory committee, which indicate that Prince Henry, as might be expected, had contacts with others of right wing aristocratic sympathies, such as Lord Tavistock and the Marquess of Londonderry (as well of course as the Duke of Westminster), had little sympathy for the Polish government and the British guarantee, and was interested in the possibility of peace negotiations. Paragraph VII of the particulars alleged that:

You have been active in England since the outbreak of war as a defeatist and an opponent of the war against Germany.

But there was so little evidential basis for this that both committees recommended that this should not be relied upon, though the Prince had made some indiscreet remarks.

As set out in the particulars MI5's real case against the Prince was that he was German by birth and tradition, was, with his wife, on good terms with the Nazis, hated the Poles and favoured their conquest by Germany, was materially interested in German victory so as to secure his estates again, was open to Nazi pressure, and was in England with Nazi approval, essentially as a potential agent. It was never alleged that he had engaged in any subversive conduct other than that specified in paragraph VII. MI5 also appears to have argued that his application for naturalisation was 'the grossest hypocrisy', being motivated not by a desire to become a loyal British subject but by a letter from his German lawyer which recommended this as a move in an attempt to recover his property.[6]

All this he vehemently denied.

He appeared before Birkett's committee on 3 and 4 December 1940.[7] The committee frankly conceded that:

no examination by an Advisory Committee could possibly ascertain all the precise facts . . . they cannot pretend to determine this case with the precision and with the accuracy they would desire. They can only record the general impression which the evidence has made upon them . . .

As was so typically the case[8] it all came down to an assessment of character in relation to his 'international' (i.e. in a sense stateless) position. The committee thought that so far from being:

the frank, straightforward reliable man whose word could be implicitly relied upon . . . he conveyed the impression of a man possessing rather a subtle and tortuous mind, who could be a clever schemer . . .

The report quoted a letter of his to his brother which was capable of sinister interpretation:

I am convinced that something can be done which will safeguard our common interests in the future and that, when the gale has blown over, people will say, 'He has trimmed his vessel and he has touched the rudder in such a masterly way that, in whichever direction the winds of Heaven may blow, they will fill his sails.'[9]

And so, applying the principle of resolving doubts in favour of security[10] the committee recommended his continued detention, whilst emphasising that:

no treasonable or dishonourable act has been alleged or suggested, much less proved.[11]

---

[6] The suggestion seems to have been made before the second committee hearing; the expression is quoted in the document I saw and must come from MI5's 'Statement of the Case'.   [7] With Clerk, Hazlerigg, and Russell. Report dated 9 January 1941.

[8] See below pp. 90–1.

[9] This comes from Halifax's pamphlet of 1688, 'Character of a Trimmer'.

[10] See below p. 86.

[11] The committee attached no importance to an allegation (Para. VI) that he had communicated with his wife since the war.

Morrison accepted this recommendation.

In detention he spent time in Brixton and Liverpool, and ended up on the Isle of Man. A fellow detainee, Mr. Leonard Wise, who at one time shared a room with him in a BU house there, tells me:

> my impression of Pless was that he was not really interested in politics. What interested him most was regaining his family's Silesian estates . . . he told me that he had been born in a six hundred room castle.[12] . . . His aristocratic friends sent him frequent food parcels (some came directly from Fortnum and Mason) and he handed these straight to the cook, John Charnley . . .

In 1942 he said that he disliked associating with fascists on the Isle of Man, and would have preferred a cell in Brixton.

In 1942 he appeared again before a committee chaired by Cockburn.[13] This took a much more favourable view of the evidence, such as it was. For example it accepted that his dislike was not of Poles generally, but of the Piłsudski Government; it accepted that he, though not his wife, disapproved of Hitler's regime. It also formed a much better view of his character; his apparent deviousness was simply born of long involvement in delicate negotiations. He was not a weak and shifty person who would give way to German pressure, though he had been less than candid over his motives for applying for naturalisation. At the end of the day it was, like the earlier committee, unable to come to any certain conclusion, and noted that the Polish Government in exile was suspicious of him. It recommended compromise—the suspension of the order with restrictions on his movements; he might for example live with the Duke of Westminster. MI5 must have opposed this recommendation, and Pless remained in detention. A curiosity of both reports is their failure to address at all a very obvious question—was the Prince, as were so many European aristocrats, more concerned over the communists than the fascists? So there is just no evidence one way or the other.

Pless' case interested his somewhat distant connection, Winston Churchill, who, on 22 March 1943, no doubt reacting to pressure from the establishment, probably the Duke of Westminster, sent a note to the Home Secretary protesting at his continued detention: 'I understand he has not been guilty of any subversive act.' This is published in the appendices to *The Hinge of Fate* but no papers are available which give the Home Office response. The papers I have seen do not provide any information on the review of his case which must have taken place in 1943, and which may well have involved a third committee hearing.

---

[12] In fact he was born in the Palast Pless in Berlin, not in Fürstenstein.

[13] On 12 and 15 June and 3 July.

Prince Henry's mother died in 1943, and he was allowed out to attend her memorial service in July.[14] His detention order was revoked on 8 October; revocation, as contrasted with suspension, implies exoneration. In an obituary notice in *The Times*[15] Sir Iain Moncreiffe of that Ilk claimed that he was 'released from internment with apologies through Churchill's personal intervention', but it is not probable that he received a formal apology. He joined the army as a private soldier on October 21, and on 18 November 1944 was commissioned as a 2nd. Lieutenant in the Pioneer Corps; in May 1945 he became a war substantive full lieutenant. This makes it very clear that he was indeed exonerated.

In December of 1943 *The Times* reports him suing Viscount Castlereagh, M.P., for defamation; his counsel was G.O. Slade, and Valentine Holmes appeared for the defence. The basis of the action was a letter sent by Castlereagh to his uncle, Major Cornwallis-West, suggesting that the Prince had been in improper contact with his then wife, and a statement made to Constance, Duchess of Westminster, that he had been forced to spy for Germany. Had he received a formal apology for detention his counsel would have mentioned this. The defendant admitted liability, paid substantial damages, and apologised for these falsehoods.

After the war, in April 1947, the Prince was naturalised as plain Mr. Pless. Again this is only compatible with his exoneration. He appears, therefore, to have been another unfortunate victim of MI5, though it would be unfair to say that there were no grounds for suspicion. The problem confronting the authorities was that it was impossible to obtain information which lay in Germany and Poland. Why the problem could not have been handled by allowing him liberty under restrictions is obscure.

Another development since the book was first published has been the discovery in the Home Office of the secret internal history of regulation 18B which was thought to have been destroyed. I asked about this back in March 1987 and was told the document was no longer extant in July; this was confirmed by letters the following year (see 422 n. 23)[16]. Mr J.M. Lloyd of the Home Office has kindly informed me of the survival of the history and given me access. It was with some trepidation that I travelled to London to inspect it. I shall for short refer to it in notes as SH (Secret History).

The document (Home Office file 863039/4) is a typescript carbon copy, with some hand-written amendments, titled *Home Office (G Division) War History*; the top copy does not survive. It is concerned

---

[14] *The Times* 21 July 1943.

[15] He died in London on 26 January 1984: the notice was published 23 February.

[16] There is a further reference to the history in HO 45/25758 (Home Office 863044). HO 45/25747 (HO 863001) containing material for a history has been devastated by weeding—for example subfiles 3–19 and 29–36 have been destroyed. It is of course impossible to tell what has gone.

only with regulation 18B, administered from 7 June 1940 by G2. It is not paginated but divided into 285 paragraphs. It dates from April 1949 and was written by C.D. Carew Robinson, who worked in the Home Office from 1912 to 1947, and from 1942 was an Assistant Under Secretary. He was acting chairman of the Prison Commission from 1939–41, then apparently head of G1 Division until 1943, when he became head of B Division (Aliens and Immigration)[17]. The text was checked by S.G. Gains of the Treasury Solicitor's Department. The document was classified as SECRET. Its function was to serve as a guide if emergency powers were taken again, and as a quarry to be used at some later date to produce a public Official History. Although a number of individual cases are mentioned Carew Robinson does not in general concern himself with them; at the time he wrote most personal files would still exist. He had general access to official files, but not apparently to those of MI5.

The Secret History has new information on a number of matters of detail; the more important information of this kind has been incorporated in the reprinted text where appropriate. Some points of detail are simply entertaining, such as the information that Frederick Bowman, the most difficult detainee, sued the Governor of Brixton for 12/6d. in the local county court for confiscating his headed writing paper.[18] Other detail is significant; for example the fact that the Home Office successfully opposed a proposal to deprive Captain Ramsay M.P., detained but never convicted, of his 70% war disability pension on the grounds of 'gross misconduct'. Had this not been resisted many other detainees might have been similarly mistreated.[19] It has valuable statistical information. I have accepted Carew Robinson's figures as likely to be more reliable than those I have compiled from available files, though I am a little sceptical of their precise accuracy[20].

With some relief I found that Carew Robinson's text does not require any significant revision of the account of detention set out by me before it came to light. In effect his history provides reassurance that it has been possible to reconstruct a reliable account without having had access to the Home Office's internal history.

[17] 1887–1958. Born Calcutta, the son of an Inner Temple Barrister. Educated Winchester and Balliol, and was a House of Commons Clerk in 1911 before joining the Home Office. A fly fisherman.
[18] Para. 253.
[19] Para. 77.
[20] Para.. 285 states that of the 1847 executed orders 971 were for British born persons, 805 for British of enemy origin, 35 for British of non-enemy alien origin, 3 for persons of doubtful nationality but enemy origin, 8 for aliens of enemy origin, 22 for aliens of non-enemy origin and 3 for aliens of doubtful origin. 1,756 cases went to the Advisory Committee, 1,616 reports were produced and 140 orders revoked or suspended before appearance. I have amended my figures on 222 to conform, but remain doubtful of the precise accuracy of the figures.

Before mentioning some matters of importance which it does however illuminate something needs to be said about the character of the history. It was written by a retired civil servant deeply loyal to the department he had served for thirty five years, and very much presents a Home Office rather than a detainees or civil libertarian's view of 18B. Sometimes it is impossible to fault this, as when the error in Greene's case is explained by 'a sudden and overwhelming burden of work on an already hard pressed staff'[21], it having already been explained that the division dealing with 18B, G2, had been formed on June 7, 1940 with a staff of one senior official and one clerk. At other times the history is less convincing. Thus it specifically identifies only one case of error, that of E.L. Diamond—'a disturbing case'[22]—and mentions one other[23]. Yet it does not claim that the cases mentioned were the only cases. So it plays down the fact that the regulation was grossly overused, something embarrassing to the Home Office, without in any way denying this[24]. Another example of its Home Office perspective is that in explaining the fact that Mosley, after release, was forced to leave Rignell House, the home of Derek and Pamela Jackson, it says that his residence there 'became embarrassing to the owner'. In reality Derek Jackson, so far from being embarrassed by Mosley's presence, was enraged when his brother-in-law was forced to leave.[25]

A number of other passages indeed appear at first sight to be disingenuous. But to read them in this way would be a mistake and unfair to the author. Carew Robinson is merely faithfully reproducing from the files the official 'Home Office View', that is the department's justification for action at the time, whether plausible or not. His text is not therefore a critical history, but an exercise in reportage. Many passages are probably in fact quotations from the files. Thus passages rationalising the Home Office resistance to a judicial review tribunal come not from the pen of Carew Robinson but that of Schuster, and are mentioned in this book.[26] His reproduction of the Home Office View does not necessarily mean that he personally was convinced by it.

There are numerous examples of this reporting of the official view. Thus the history rationalises the fact that male detainees were kept locked in cells during air raids, a terrifying way to treat anyone, as being in part protective of their safety. It was for their own good. For the stairs and

---

[21] Para. 79 note.

[22] Para. 130; see below 397.

[23] Para. 202, case of BU order when the individual belonged to the PPU and Fellowship of Reconciliation.

[24] See para. 193–8 on the Advisory Committee's view that many BU detainees were not dangerous.

[25] Para. 269; see below 390.

[26] Para. 171; see below 311, based on HO45/25114.

landings might be destroyed by bombing; unconstrained prisoners might rush out and fall into the void—better to keep them locked up—'experience showed that separation in cells was far safer'[27]. But the argument makes little sense, for women in Holloway were not locked in their cells. Presumably they were more cautious than the men and schooled to look before they leapt. To take another example—the refusal at first to allow letters to members of Parliament is rationalised thus:

It was felt that to allow letters to M.P.s as such was tantamount to recognising that an M.P. was entitled to inquire into the circumstances of the writer's detention and to try to satisfy himself that the Secretary of State had exercised his powers properly; and this could not be admitted.[28]

Another passage implausibly rationalises the refusal to make public the reasons for detention on the ground that on security grounds not all information could be released; hence any revalation would be 'misleading to the public *and unfair to the individual*' [my italics][29]. But Carew Robinson very fairly set out the fact that some members of Parliament were able to argue:

with some apparent show of reason that Parliamentary control over the Minister's action was largely illusory when he refused to disclose to members why any particular individual was detained.[30]

He replies by reporting the Home Office arguments that Parliamentary control was not illusory—members were given statistics, could attack the department twice each year on the Home Office vote or renewal of the Emergency Powers (Defence) Act, and the Home Secretary could only administer the regulation with the confidence of the House.[31] These arguments, perhaps taken from a ministerial brief, fail to meet the criticism, but they were nevertheless the best the Home Office mandarins could construct. So Carew Robinson reproduced them. That was what he conceived his job as official historian to be.

A somewhat comical example of Home Office rationalisation is presented in para. 115. This coyly reveals that some sort of public inquiry into errors and mistakes was considered after the first case brought by Captain Budd had brought the Home Office into some disrepute with the judges[32]. But the Home Office, no doubt horrified at this idea, thought 'the most satisfactory solution', which would restore its reputation with the judges, was to do nothing and leave the initiative with Captain Budd. He could bring a suit against the Home Office for false imprisonment; the Home Office could then call evidence to show how responsibly it always behaved. Thus would happy relationships be restored and the Reading

---

[27] Para. 236.   [28] Para. 239; see below 238.   [29] Para. 149.
[30] Para. 148; see below 414.   [31] Para. 150.   [32] See below 318–21.

Presumption of Executive Innocence recover from the battering it had received in 1941. Surely with his tongue in his cheek Carew Robinson wrote:

in fact Budd's advisers were obliging in due course to bring such an action.[33]

By the time the case came to trial the need to defend the Home Office had gone as a consequence of the House of Lords decisions in the cases of Greene and Liversidge. Executive Innocence no longer much mattered. So the evidence was never presented.

There are significant omissions in the history. The most curious is that in the discussion of the Arbon and de Laessoe action in 1942, and generally in passages dealing with the conditions of detention, Carew Robinson makes no mention of the secret Emergency Orders which in reality regulated conditions of detention, thereby misleading Parliament which had been led to think that the conditions were governed by the published White Paper[34]. Given the position he held in the Home Office this must, I fear, be a *suppressio veri*; he must have personally issued the orders. It was all too embarrassing to reveal them even in an internal secret document. Conceivably however it was the Treasury Solicitor's Department which was anxious to conceal the use made of Crown privilege. Another disappointing omission is that the history gives no information on what precisely triggered the action against the BU in May of 1940. The explanation will be that no material on the matter existed in Home Office files.

Turning now to points of real substance about which the Secret History provides new information the first involves another *suppressio veri*. Apparently it came to be accepted in the Home Office that Sir John Anderson never saw one of the schedules, containing 37 names, attached to the Italian omnibus order of 10 June, 1940[35]. This would mean that the document never passed over his desk. In litigation therefore he could not swear an affidavit saying, even somewhat mendaciously, that each case had been considered individually. Hence the order was invalid. Copies of the invalid order had been served on these detainees at the time of their detention. By the time the matter was considered in 1941, after the embarrassing Budd case, only seven of these persons remained, illegally, in detention. Morrison signed new detention orders, which made things legal for the future, but copies were not given to the detainees to inform them of the new detention order under which they were actually being held. To have done so would have drawn attention to the error and possibly provoked suits for false imprisonment, which the Home Office would

[33] Para. 115 referring to Home Office 840641/8; see below 329 n. 46.
[34] Para. 257 and following: see below 398-9.
[35] Appendix 2, based on Home Office 863035/5; see below 193-4, text to n. 134.

have lost, albeit paying only nominal damages. So the detainees, if they thought about the matter at all, continued to think they were being held under orders of 10 June, 1940, signed by Anderson, when in reality they were held under orders of 1941 signed by Morrison. The officials, or perhaps Morrison, convinced themselves that these detainees, illegally imprisoned for eleven months or so without their knowing it, had suffered no prejudice. One can well understand the reason for this. Scandal would have arisen if it has come to light that people had been locked up under 18B without the Home Secretary of the day considering their cases at all, though of course this must have happened in many other cases where the individual consideration was fictitious, amounting to no more than initialing a file. The fact that Carew Robinson honestly told this tale in his history may well explain why the top copy of the history was at some point thought to be better destroyed, though I have no direct evidence of this.

The history also sheds some further light on the question of judicial review and the words inserted in the amended regulation in 1939—'reasonable cause to believe'. Carew Robinson, using the same files as I have used, presents the Home Office view that it was always clear that these words did not introduce any power of judicial review except in cases of gross abuse of power.[36] He quotes a passage from an article by Dingle Foot in the *News Chronicle* for 29 November 1939 which is supposed to confirm that Foot was under no misunderstanding; in reality the passage does not show this, but merely points out that the Home Secretary was not bound by decisions of the Advisory Committee, and thus detention was an executive and not a judicial act. It is not concerned with review by the Courts.

However it is fairly clear that Carew Robinson was not himself wholly convinced. Not only does he concede the possibility of confusion[37], but he points out that five months later Dingle Foot attempted to have the expression included in the new regulation 2C (Corruption of Public Morale)[38]:

only to secure that the Home Secretary's action in issuing a warning . . . should be challengeable in the courts . . .

He also mentions the fact that Foot proposed, and Osbert Peake for the government accepted, an insertion of the expression 'has reasonable grounds to believe' to limit and make reviewable the power of a chief officer of police in the Official Secrets Bill during the committee stage in 1939. Osbert Peake did not dissent from Foot's understanding of the effect

[36] Paras. 23–7, relying on Home Office 863004/31A, 77 (claiming incorrectly that the issue first arose in Greene's case, whereas it arose in Lees) and 131–3 (adopting the implausible explanation advanced by Somervell, on which see 379 below); also below 61–6, 298–304.

[37] Para. 24.

[38] See below 100.

of this[39]. He notes too that the expression 'reasonably apprehends' was, at the instance of F. Kingsley Griffith, added to a provision in the Public Order Bill in 1936 to restrict the power of a chief constable to attach conditions to be the holding of a procession, and notes that the Attorney General, Sir John Simon, appeared to agree that this would introduce judicial review of his decision.[40] So fidelity to the Home Office and candour ended up a little at odds. Carew Robinson does not refer to the concession as to the existence of a power of judicial review made by the Solicitor General in the Lees case, which is critical to the issue[41].

The Secret History also sheds some important new light on the procedures followed. Over the drafting of the 'Reasons for Order' it says that the practice was for this document to be drafted by the Home Office, not by MI5, when an order was initiated by the police, and for the Home Office file to be provided to the Committee.[42] This appears to refer principally to practice followed in I.R.A. cases. It also states that in the case of new detention orders made after a date which is not specified, but was probably sometime in 1941, the procedures were altered so that in all cases thereafter the 'Reasons for Order' was prepared in the Home Office.[43] No explanation is given, but the reason may have been the inadequacy of the information provided when MI5 undertook this work.

So far as the production of agents before the Advisory Committee is concerned the history reveals a little more about the aftermath of the Kurtz affair[44]. Originally the agreement was that agents should be produced only in exceptional circumstances; the Advisory Committee had no power to compel any witness to attend. The Committee became unhappy about agents but, after discussion in September 1941, it was agreed that this rule should continue to be observed. But the Committee's anxiety was met by arranging that where an agent was not produced the Committee could question a responsible MI5 officer instead. After the Kurtz affair there was a conference between Anderson, Somervell and Swinton in January 1942, and out of this emerged a major change: a presumption in favour of the production of agents whenever the Advisory Committee thought this necessary in the interests of justice. There now had to be exceptional circumstances for an agent not to be produced. If MI5 thought there were then this was to be made clear at the outset when an application was made for a detention order, so that the problem was

---

[39] See *Hansard* HC Vol. 353 col. 1275–9. The same idea appealed to Lord Samuel in the Lords; see *Hansard* Vol. 112 cols. 40–50. The Lord Chancellor did not dissent from Samuel's understanding of the matter, though refusing to accept his amendment.

[40] The reference is to *Hansard* HC Vol. 317 cols. 141 and Vol. 318 cols. 147–9.

[41] See below 303.

[42] Para. 177. This differs from the account I originally gave at 87–9.

[43] Para. 179.

[44] Para. 182; see below 88, 91, 367–70. This is based on Home Office 863033/2.

faced at an early stage. The possibility of one member of the Committee meeting with the agent on neutral ground was also to be considered where there were reasons for the agent not visiting the Committee's premises. In one Scottish case the new system led to no order being made; there was a difficulty in the Home Secretary relying upon evidence which could not be put before his Advisory Committee.

The history sheds some additional light on Birkett's views and work. Thus in discussions with Lord Maugham and the Attorney General in November 1941[45] Birkett strongly opposed legal representation before the Committee which:

would introduce a barrier between the applicant and the committee. It would destroy the informal and friendly atmosphere . . . and would make it much more difficult to estimate his character and mentality, and his probable reactions if he were released from detention. In fact the Committee had had very few requests for legal representation.

On 30 January, 1941 he wrote of his quarrel with MI5:

The present procedure makes the Advisory Committee a mere body which reduces the frequently chaotic state of the information to something like order, but whose advisory function is in competition with MI5.[46]

Procedures were in fact changed to ensure that the Committee at least had the last word before Morrison made his decision.

The history also reveals that some difficulties were met over the interpretation of expressions used in the regulation. What did 'recently' mean in the expressions 'recently concerned in acts prejudicial . . .'? This arose over members of the I.R.A. who had served sentences—Walker, Ryan, and McCafferty, all convicted in 1939—whom it was wished to expel under the Prevention of Violence (Temporary Provisions) Act of 1939[47]. McCafferty, who had been sentenced to four and a half years for actions committed in 1939, was in 1942 expelled as having been 'recently engaged' in acts prejudicial. Under 18B the most extreme case is of an individual convicted in November 1940 under the Official Secrets Act and sentenced to three years. On release an 'acts prejudicial' 18B order was signed on 4 December, 1942, over two years after his actions had taken place, and he was detained late in that year or early in 1943. Although not named in the history this was the case of T.H. Beckett.[48] There was also difficulty over what sort of conduct fell foul of the 'acts prejudicial' limb of the regulation, which was very loosely drafted. Could vague talk of sabotage by I.R.A. members suffice? Must there be evidence which precisely

---

[45] Para. 186; see below 86, 363 n. 22.
[46] Paras. 191–2; see below 294.
[47] Paras. 210–13; below 47 and 65.
[48] Para. 214 based on Home Office file 860, 852; below 170, 381.

identified acts being prepared? The Attorney General was consulted and thought that active membership of an I.R.A. unit was enough, but mere vague talk by sympathisers of sabotage was not.[49] In another case, that of Lady Howard of Effingham, the making of contact with persons in the services and embassies with intention to transmit information to the enemy was viewed by the Attorney as 'acts prejudicial' rather than acts preparatory to such acts.[50] The text of the regulation blurred the distinction between act and preparation. These cases reflect both the Home Office respect for legality and the tendency to stretch the regulation where considerations of security appeared to justify this.

When he wrote his Secret History Carew Robinson supposed that it would itself never become public, a supposition which reflects the Home Office culture to which he belonged. It is now likely that the document will end up before long in the Public Record Office, though there has been no official decision about this yet so far as I am aware[51]. Had it not been mislaid I cannot myself see any reason of public as opposed to departmental interest why it should not have been released under the thirty year rule in 1979. Quite how it came to be mislaid, and what has become of the top and any other copies I do not know, but presumably MI5 would have been given a copy back in 1949, and there may indeed be a similar near contemporary document held by the Security Service giving an account of the part that organisation played in relation to detention, a document distinct that is from the published account by F.H. Hinsley and C.A.G. Simkins.

---

[49] Para. 216.

[50] Para. 216, relying on Home Office file 840, 784/5. She was detained about 10 February 1941 (*Evening Standard*). She was the wife of the 6th Earl, being by birth Hungarian. Her unmarried name was Manci Maria Malvina Gertler. The marriage was dissolved in 1946.

[51] Hence references given in this reprint may be of use.

CONTENTS

ABBREVIATIONS

ABBREVIATIONS for manuscript sources cited in footnotes are given in Appendix II, where they are printed in bold type.

AD/L	BU Assistant District Leader
Andrew	C. Andrew, *Her Majesty's Secret Service: The Making of the British Intelligence Community* (London, 1987)
BCAEC	British Council against European Commitments
BCCSE	British Council for Christian Settlement in Europe
BDBJ	Board of Deputies of British Jews
BEF	British Expeditionary Force
BPP	British People's Party
BU	British Union
BUF	British Union of Fascists
CID	Criminal Investigation Department
CPGB	Communist Party of Great Britain
CS	Chiefs of Staff
DD/L	BU Deputy District Leader
DI	BU District Inspector
D/L	BU District Leader
DORA	Defence of the Realm Act
DPP	Director of Public Prosecutions
D/T	BU District Treasurer
f.	file
Hinsley and Simkins	F. H. Hinsley and C. A. G. Simkins, *British Intelligence in the Second World War*, iv (London, 1990)
IFL	Imperial Fascist League
ILP	Independent Labour Party
IMHHTY	J. Wynn, *It Might Have Happened to You!* (Glasgow, 1943)
IP	*Information and Policy*
IRA	Irish Republican Army
JIC	Joint Intelligence Committee
MI5	Military Intelligence Section 5 (Secret Service Home Section)
MI6	Military Intelligence Section 6 (Secret Service Foreign Section)
NBBS	New British Broadcasting Station
NCCL	National Council for Civil Liberties
NKVD	Soviet secret police, 1934—53

NL	Nordic League
NSDAP	Nazi Party, Germany
NSL	National Socialist League
PPU	Peace Pledge Union
RC	Right Club
RFC	Royal Flying Corps
ROIA	Restoration of Order in Ireland Act 1920
sf.	subfile
SH	Secret History of 18B by C.D. Carew Robinson
SIS	Secret Intelligence Service (MI6)
WD/L	BU Women's District Leader

—○ I ○—

The Invention of Executive Detention

The Stable Door Principle

This book is a history of the use of executive detention during the war of 1939–45 under regulation 18B of the Defence (General) Regulations; this enabled the government to imprison citizens thought to be dangerous to national security without charge, trial, or term set, under what Herbert Morrison, who administered the system during most of the war, described as 'a terrible power'. Just under 2,000 individuals were so imprisoned in as gross an invasion of British civil liberty as could be conceived, only justifiable, if at all, by the grim necessity of the time.

Imprisonment is of course commonplace, and is indeed the typical punishment imposed for serious breaches of the criminal law; its use by the state is not normally regarded as in itself unjust. There are two basic distinctions, however, between imprisonment for criminal offences and imprisonment by way of executive detention; and in popular consciousness the distinctions are quite critical. The first is that imprisonment under the criminal law is acceptable because we are brought up to accept punishment for wrongdoing as just and proper. But the very idea of punishment entails the requirement that it be imposed after the event, as a reaction to it; only after the event is it deserved. We therefore wait until the horse has left the stable, and then punish the person responsible for leaving the door ajar. But executive detention is designed to be employed in advance, before the horse leaves the stable, since its very purpose and justification is to prevent future harm; hence detainees languish in prison not for what they have done, but for what they might do in the future if they remained at liberty. They, therefore, do not deserve their fate in the straightforward way in which a murderer does. The second is that imprisonment for crime is imposed after guilt of an offence is established at a public trial before a court, and the hope is that this provides the individual with a fair chance to establish innocence, and consequent immunity from punishment. Detention is typically imposed as a result of an administrative decision, taken in private, by state officials, without any form of prior trial. The typical complaint of detainees reflects these two distinctions: it is that it is wholly unjust to lock them up when they have never been proved to have done anything wrong. Their demand is always that they be released, or put on trial. The typical official reply is that they are not detained for having done anything wrong, but because the authorities have good reason to suppose that they might do something wrong in the future, and the conditions are such that no risks can be run. They are not being punished unjustly, because they are not being punished at all. The detainees remain unconvinced by this logic; being locked up certainly feels like being punished to them.

In reality the distinction between imprisonment as punishment for past crime and imprisonment by way of precautionary detention is never very clear-cut. Modern systems of criminal law are no longer purely retributive, that is to say based purely on the notion of just desert for past deliberate wrongdoing. For example long sentences of imprisonment may be preventive in character; some criminal 'offences', such as unlawful possession of explosives or drugs, enable imprisonment to be used in advance of harmful wrongdoing; not all trials are public, much less fair. Again detention may not be purely precautionary; it may be imposed for past wrongdoing, and continued as a punishment for wickedness, or symbolic condemnation, rather than a precaution. But these blurrings do not diminish the importance of the basic distinctions which exist between typical cases; there does seem to be all the difference in the world between locking someone up who has been convicted of murder, as a punishment, and locking someone up as a precaution because the authorities are convinced he has a murderous propensity, though he has to date never murdered anyone. The stable door principle of the criminal law, whatever may be said against it, and obviously much can be, clearly enhances liberty. It gives those thought to have a propensity to commit crimes an opportunity to remain free. It also seems in common sense to be easier to prove a wrongful action than a dangerous propensity. But enhanced liberty has its price.

In times of crisis British governments have been unwilling to pay this price where the security of the state is thought to be under threat, and have always locked up supposedly dangerous citizens, particularly in the colonies, before they have committed crimes. Detention is indeed one of the milder coercive mechanisms employed in conditions of emergency, in which individuals may be shot, or clubbed, or otherwise manhandled by the police or military.

Detention and the Irish Problem

Executive detention was therefore not invented in 1939; it has a long earlier history.[1] But the legalization of executive detention has taken differ-

[1] For a comparative account see C. L. Rossiter, *Constitutional Dictatorship: Crisis Government in the Modern Democracies* (New York, 1963).

ent forms. Once the favoured technique was Parliamentary legislation to emasculate the basic remedy which protected personal freedom, the writ of habeas corpus, by suspending the issuing of the writ; this conformed to a conception of the common law as essentially a scheme of remedies. Habeas Corpus Suspension Acts allowed the executive to hold individuals on treason charges without bringing them to trial.[2] The last use was in Ireland in 1866 and 1867. There might also be action under martial law, which did not require prior Parliamentary authorization, though for good measure it might be confirmed retrospectively by statute. But what powers martial law conferred, and when they arose, was never very clear.[3] Even the theory was not settled; one view based it on the royal prerogative, another viewed it as another name for the common law's licence to use any force reasonably necessary to restore the peace; the former view meant that emergency legislation would suspend the power.[4] In any crisis the executive tended to overdo things, and was normally exonerated retrospectively by Indemnity Acts. An attraction of legislation suspending habeas corpus, and retrospectively indemnifying the executive, was that it bypassed the practical uncertainties of applying the legal doctrines to real life.

The modern practice has been to pass legislation explicitly granting powers of detention in company with other emergency powers abridging civil liberty, and to attempt to exclude the regular courts from exercising any supervisory power over the executive. The early examples of this practice involve direct Parliamentary legislation; the first instance is The Protection of Life and Property (Ireland) Act of 1871, the 'Westmeath Act'.[5] Its object was 'to empower the Lord Lieutenant or other Chief Governor or Governors of Ireland to apprehend and detain for a limited period persons suspected of being members of the Ribbon Society in the County of Westmeath, or in certain adjoining portions of the County of Meath and the King's County'. This lapsed in 1875. Detention was by Lord-Lieutenant's warrants, which were conclusive evidence both as to what they stated and of the facts giving rise to the power to detain. This

[2] R. J. Sharpe, *The Law of Habeas Corpus* (Oxford, 1989), 94–5. W. Forsyth, *Cases and Opinions on Constitutional Law* (London, 1869), 452 lists such Acts. See also C. Townshend, *Political Violence in Ireland* (Oxford, 1983), 55 n. 3, 60–3, 131–7.

[3] Sharpe, *Habeas Corpus*, 110–15, provides an excellent account. For the obscurities see Rossiter, *Constitutional Dictatorship*, ch. 10 and literature cited; C. Townshend, 'Martial Law: Legal and Administrative Problems of Civil Emergency in Britain and the Empire 1800–1940', *Historical Journal*, 25 (1982), 167–95. Martial law was 'declared' in Ireland in 1798, 1803, 1916, and 1920 and elsewhere in the Empire on numerous occasions, for example Canada (1837–8), Cape of Good Hope (1835, 1849–51, 1899), Jamaica (1831–2, 1865), but surprisingly not in India during the Mutiny, though 'declaration' makes no legal difference. It was relied on in England in 1715, 1740, and 1780.

[4] *Egan v. Macready* [1921] 1 IR 265 and 280, criticized by D. L. Keir and F. H. Lawson, *Cases in Constitutional Law*, (Oxford, 1967), 233–7.

[5] 34 Vict. c. 25.

legislation predated the modern enthusiasm for secrecy; the names of those detained had to be published to Parliament.

This precedent was followed in March of 1881 by An Act for the Better Protection of Person and Property in Ireland.[6] A response to the violence of the land war, it permitted, in a prescribed district, detention of persons 'reasonably suspected' of involvement in high treason, treason felony, or any other crime 'being an act of violence or intimidation, and tending to interfere with or disturb the maintenance of law and order'. There could be successive periods of three months' detention. There were safeguards; in particular names, places of detention, and grounds stated for arrest had to be reported to Parliament, or published each month. This legislation again explicitly deprived the courts of any supervisory function; warrants were conclusive evidence of their own validity. Some 955 persons were detained.[7] The function of detention was to restore order by precautionary action; the mechanism employed was crippling a political organization, after an attempt to prosecute the leaders of the Land League for seditious conspiracy had failed in January 1881. Under this Act Members of Parliament were detained, including Parnell himself, which had not happened since the 1715 rising. The precedent was to be followed during both world wars.[8] However, a negotiated agreement, the Kilmainham 'treaty', ended the conflict, and detention ceased in 1882.[9]

Dicey commented on the incompatibility of such 'Coercion Acts', as they were called, with the ideals of liberty and the rule of law. The Act was 'in principle . . . thoroughly vicious . . . [it] in effect gave the Irish executive an unlimited power of arrest; it established in them a despotic government . . . [It] could not be made permanent, and applied to the whole United Kingdom, without depriving every citizen of security for his personal freedom'.[10] Dicey opposed such Acts which, politically, could only be temporary and confined to Ireland. If only jury power in Ireland was curbed vicious Acts would not be needed. He was suspicious of juries because they could nullify the law; hence in his account of the British constitution the right to jury trial receives little emphasis, though he thought that English juries usually followed judicial instructions, thereby avoiding any clash between the institution and the rule of law. Executive detention was indeed superseded in 1882 by Dicey's solution: power to try persons suspected of political violence by a Special

---

[6] 44 Vict. c. 4, to expire 30 Sept. 1882.

[7] C. Townshend, *Political Violence*, 137, citing 'Memo on Protection of Person and Property Act 1881' (9 Dec. 1887) in the Balfour MSS, BL Add. MSS 49808.

[8] In addition to Parnell four other members were detained. The numbers were 7 in the 1st World War and 2 in the 2nd, one being a member of the Ulster Parliament.

[9] F. S. L. Lyons, *Ireland Since the Famine*, (London, 1971), 151. ff

[10] A. V. Dicey, *The Case against Home Rule* (London, 1886), 117.

Commission Court of three judges, and no right to jury trial.[11] In Ulster at the present time the 'Diplock' courts follow the same model.

The difficulty of obtaining evidence from the native Irish, and the reluctance of Irish juries to convict even if it was obtained, provided the justification for using executive detention rather than regular criminal prosecution as a response to political violence in Ireland. There was no similar problem elsewhere in Britain, and therefore no requirement for executive detention.

The Defence of the Realm Acts

For some thirty-four years, in the high summer of Victorian liberalism, even Ireland was governed without the use of detention. The First World War ended that high summer, and executive detention was revived in 1915 by Regulation 14B of the wartime Defence of the Realm Act (DORA) regulations, and established throughout the United Kingdom. It persisted for nearly eight years, nearly twice as long as the hostilities with Germany, for the war was prolonged by legislation until 31 August 1921.[12] Even after that, for the power had been extended, as we shall see, by the Restoration of Order in Ireland Act (ROIA) of 1920, detention continued. Orders were still being executed in mainland Britain as late as 1923. Official experience in the use of detention between 1915 and 1923 provided the model followed in the Second World War.

There was no general breakdown in criminal proceedings during this period, except in Ireland. The use of detention was based on the more radically authoritarian belief that in a time of national emergency the executive ought not to be prevented by the requirements of regular criminal procedure from taking precautionary action against dangerous persons.

In both 1871 and 1882 executive detention had been openly and directly introduced by controversial Parliamentary legislation. But Regulation 14B was introduced in a much less straightforward way, as but one aspect of a general scheme of wartime government, 'a form of statutory martial law', created by delegated legislation.[13] This scheme derived from a bill drafted in 1888 by the military.[14] In earlier times there had been no bureaucracy to make advance plans for the conduct of war; now there existed both a professional Civil Service and a military general staff. Both conceived of forward planning as their function, and, during the period of heightened

---

[11] By The Prevention of Crime (Ireland) Act 45 and 46 Vict. c. 25, s. 1.

[12] By the Termination of the Present War (Definition) Act 1918.

[13] An expression quoted by Townshend, *Political Violence*, 183, from a memorandum of 19 July 1920, CAB 21/109.

[14] CAB 16/31 (Proceedings and Memoranda of a Subcommittee of the Committee of Imperial Defence, June 1914).

tension which preceded the war, a subcommittee of the Committee of Imperial Defence had considered what special powers, if any, would be needed in the event of war.[15] One view was none: the executive and military could rely simply upon the common law, or the prerogative, to take action necessary for the public safety, and later paper over any cracks by an Act of Indemnity. But what might be done at common law, or under the prerogative, was obscure: martial law had not been used in England since the eighteenth century, and its use would certainly be politically sensitive. Everyone concerned knew of the violent controversies, not so long before, over Governor Eyre's suppression of a supposed insurrection in Jamaica;[16] Governor Eyre had relied upon martial law, and lived to regret it.[17] Hence the military strongly favoured a code of emergency regulations, spelling out powers precisely; the model here again was Ireland, in particular an Irish Act of 1833. This view, though rejected as late as June 1914, prevailed.[18]

The scheme adopted did not involve Parliamentary legislation which directly conferred specific emergency powers. The regulations would become law through Orders in Council, authorized by a parent Act of Parliament, which would confer upon the executive a wide power to legislate in this way. So a code was prepared, and a hurriedly drafted parent *Defence of the Realm Bill* was rushed through Parliament on 8 August 1914, and a second on 28 August.[19] Apparently it was feared that these Acts merely clarified existing executive powers, without conferring new ones, but the Defence of the Realm (Consolidation Act) of 27 November 1914 dispelled this fear.[20] It declared that 'His Majesty in Council has power during the continuance of the present war to issue regulations for securing the public safety and defence of the realm, and as to the powers and duties for that purpose of the Admiralty and Army Council.' In effect the Defence of the Realm Acts 1914–1915 radically altered the British constitution for the duration of the emergency; the executive became the legislature, and Parliament declined into a relatively unimportant sounding

[15] G. R. Rubin, 'The Royal Prerogative or a Statutory Code? The War Office and Contingency Legal Planning, 1885–1914', in R. Eales and D. Sullivan, *The Political Context of Law* (London, 1986), 145–58.

[16] B. Semmel, *Jamaican Blood and the Victorian Conscience: the Governor Eyre Controversy* (Boston, 1963), and G. Dutton, *The Hero as Murderer: The Life of Edward John Eyre* (London, 1962). For Eyre's life see the second *Supplement to the Dictionary of National Biography* (Oxford, 1927), article by E. F. Im Thurn.

[17] See Townshend, cited 'Martial Law', 3 above.

[18] An Act for the more Effectual Suppression of Local Disturbances and Dangerous Associations in Ireland. 3 & 4 Will. IV c. 4. See C. P. Cotter, 'Constitutional Democracy and Emergency Powers Legislation in Great Britain since 1914' (Harvard D. Phil Thesis, 1953). For 1914 see 20ff. Cotter downplays the degree to which pre-war planning had prepared a full working system.

[19] 4 & 5 Geo. V, c. 21 and c. 63. See Sharpe, *Habeas Corpus*, 95–7.

[20] 5 Geo. V, c. 8. There were later amendments by 5 Geo. V, cc. 34, 37, and 42.

board for public opinion. The regulations made dramatic inroads into established liberties; the DORA of 27 November 1914, for example, made it possible to try any citizen by court martial for the more serious DORA offences, even capital offences, though the right to jury trial was in general restored by a DORA Amendment Act of March 1915.

In 1925, when it was all over, Sir Edward Troup, who was Permanent Under-Secretary of State in the Home Office from 1908 to 1922, wrote approvingly about the DORA system:

These regulations were, after all danger was over, subjected to a good deal of undeserved criticism; but while the war lasted they were essential to its successful prosecution. They took the place of legislation with the immense advantage that they could be altered from day to day as new demands arose, new difficulties had to be met, and new modes of evasion were detected.[21]

The 'immense advantage' was obtained at the expense of the ideal of the rule of law, for laws which can be altered from day to day lack that stability which the ideal requires. The law, here manifested as DORA, paradoxically erodes the rule of law, and Troup's enthusiasm marks a declining commitment to that ideal. It also reflects approval of a decline in the status of both Parliament and the courts. For the war occasioned a massive transfer of power to the new Civil Service, of which Troup was a distinguished member; with this professionalization of government older institutions, such as Parliament and the courts, came to play a lesser role.

Detention did not originally feature in the DORA scheme; it was introduced at the behest of the domestic security service on 10 June 1915.[22] This had by then become an established organ of government, with an ability to initiate policy. The security service also took a prominent part in its administration.

The Origin of the Security Service[23]

Today the domestic security service is usually called MI5; although I shall use this popular title its proper name is the Security Service, and it forms one part of a hybrid organization. The oldest part, the Special

---

[21] C. E. Troup, *The Home Office* (London, 1925), 239. The available Home Office papers which relate to DORA comprise HO 45/228849 (1912–14) and 45/11007 (1914–21); the latter oddly has nothing on 14B. Whether other papers have survived I do not know.

[22] Order in Council 551.

[23] See generally C. Andrew, *Her Majesty's Secret Service: The Making of the British Intelligence Community* (London, 1987), ch. 2 (hereafter cited as Andrew); B. Porter, *The Origins of the Vigilant State: The London Metropolitan Police Special Branch before the First World War* (London, 1987), esp. chs. 2–6; K. R. M. Short, *The Dynamite War: Irish American Bombers in Victorian Britain* (Atlantic Highlands, NJ 1979); S. T. Felstead, *German Spies at Bay* (New York, 1920); J. Bulloch, *MI5: The Origins and History of the British Counter-Espionage Service* (London, 1963).

Branch, is a subdivision of the detective branch of the Metropolitan Police, in its turn a department of the Home Office. Its members are plainclothes police officers, and their function, as originally conceived, was to prevent politically motivated terrorist crimes and detect their perpetrators.

Though primarily a counter to Irish nationalism, not to espionage, Special Branch was concerned with aliens, since some aliens might be terrorists. In the late nineteenth and early twentieth centuries xenophobic and racialist fears of immigrants, such as German gypsies, and Jews fleeing from persecution in Eastern Europe, led to the passing of the Aliens Act of 1905, designed to exclude undesirable and destitute aliens.[24] Its administration naturally fell to the Home Office. The Home Office had no reason to be worried about espionage, a purely military concern, and so Special Branch had no responsibility for detecting spies; and although an Official Secrets Act was passed in 1889 no special arrangements were made for enforcing it.

The Enemy in our Midst

The organization which came to be known as MI5, and which forms the other limb of the domestic security service, originated more recently. The nineteenth-century War Office had very little concern with domestic security or espionage; British security was largely taken for granted. But the developing rivalry between Britain and Germany added a new dimension to the fear and hostility towards aliens—anxiety over foreign invasion of Britain itself, facilitated by sabotage and espionage.[25] Though the name 'Fifth Column' dates from the Spanish Civil War, the conception itself existed well before 1914. There was even fear of airborne invasion, assisted by 'the enemy in our midst'; zeppelins, not the parachutists of the Second World War, were to be used.[26] There was alarmist fiction; the best-remembered example is Erskine Childers' *Riddle of the Sands* (1903),

---

[24] C. Holmes, *John Bull's Island: Immigration and British Society, 1871–1971* (Basingstoke, 1988), *passim*; V. Bevan, *The Development of British Immigration Law* (London, 1986), 68–72. The Act was a response to the *Report of the Royal Commission on Alien Immigration* of 1903 (Cd. 1741 and 1742).

[25] H. R. Moon in 'The Invasion of the United Kingdom: Public Controversy and Official Planning 1888–1918', Ph.D. Thesis, Univ. of London, 1968, esp. ch. 7: 'The Invasion Scare of 1909 and its Aftermath'. See also D. French, 'Spy Fever in Britain, 1900–1915', *Historical Journal*, 21 (1978), 364; and N. Hiley, 'The Failure of British Counter–Espionage against Germany 1907–1914', *Historical Journal*, 26 (1983), 835.

[26] The idea of using zeppelins was apparently developed by Rudolf E. Martin (1867–1916) in *Der Weltkrieg in den Luften*. The title *The Enemy in Our Midst: The story of a Raid on England* was used by Walter Wood for a book published in London in 1906.

which started a fashion.[27] More influential, however, were the writings of the ludicrous William Le Queux.[28]

There were three official enquiries into the risk of invasion; each one played down the risk.[29] All that existed was a handful of German spies, whose military significance was, as is so usual, negligible; there was no hidden army, or possibility of airborne invasion.[30] Nevertheless R. B. S. Haldane, Secretary of State for War, came to be concerned about spies, and in 1909 set up a subcommittee.[31] Its report is one of the more entertaining in the Public Records, rivalling in absurdity the file containing the Home Office rules for the keeping of pet mice in convict prisons.[32] The subcommittee was persuaded; it reported 'that an extensive system of German espionage exists in this country . . . ', and recommended establishing, in secret, a Secret Service Bureau. This recommendation was accepted. The existence of the bureau was first made public in November of 1914.[33] It is what is now called MI5.

The Secret Service Bureau

Its first head was Captain Vernon G. W. Kell.[34] Not long after its creation it was divided into a home and a foreign section, the latter becoming known as MI6 or SIS. The subcommittee also approved a new draft Official Secrets Bill, which became the basis for the Act of 1911; this was the principal legal counter to the threat of espionage. The home department was concerned with military policy in connection with the civil population, including aliens, and after 1914 with the administration of DORA regulations in so far as it concerned the military, and with counter-espionage; it was not concerned with political surveillance. Though an offshoot of the War Office, and ultimately perhaps under military control, it seems always to have operated independently as an interdepartmental organization; the nature of its work necessarily brought it into contact with both the Home Office and War Office, and it also had dealings with the Admiralty, the Post Office, and the Customs Service. This relative

[27] J. W. Cawelti and B. A. Rosenberg, The Spy Story (Chicago, 1987), ch. 2.
[28] (1864–1927). See Andrew, ch. 2.   [29] CAB 3/1/18A, 3/2/1/44a, and 3/2/5/62A.
[30] Andrew, ch. 2.
[31] CAB 16/8 (Report of Subcommittee on Foreign Espionage, established 25 Mar. 1909).
[32] PCOM 9/103.
[33] By Asquith on 18 Nov. (Parl. Deb. 5th ser. HC 68: 412) and by Lord Chancellor Haldane on 25 Nov. 1914 (Parl. Deb. HL 18: 129); see also HO 45/10756/267450.
[34] Vernon George Waldegrave Kell (1873–27 March 1942) was a professional soldier who joined the army in 1894. He achieved some prominence in the Boxer campaign and in 1904–9 served as a staff officer, from 1907 with the Imperial Defence Committee. For his early career see Bulloch, MI5. From 1924 to 1940 he was re-employed by the War Office as the Director–General of the Security Service.

independence had been recommended by the subcommittee in 1909, and is the source of the continual uncertainty over political responsibility for the security service.

Its first director became known, inevitably, as 'K'; in 1912 he acquired a deputy, another military officer, Eric E. B. Holt-Wilson.[35] It also recruited a barrister as legal officer, Walter H. Moresby.[36] The Moresby family were cousins of the Kells, and from this early date the system of recruitment operated through personal contacts.

MI5 during the War

The war naturally enlarged the bureau. By 4 August 1914 there were nine military officers, three civilian officers, four women clerks, and three policemen. Since then its officers have been partially military, and partially civilian. From 1915 Kell's responsibilities covered counter-espionage throughout the Empire, though not in India itself, which had its own Intelligence Bureau.[37] In January 1916 Kell's organization became Military Intelligence Section 5 (MI5). The existence of two security organizations produced a peculiar division of functions which has persisted to this day. Kell left the Irish to the police; aliens and enemy espionage were his concern. His staff collected information, but did not act upon it. If arrests, or searches, were needed, these were conducted by Special Branch; prosecutions were handled by the Director of Public Prosecutions and the Law Officers, as in case of other serious crimes. Interrogations were conducted by Basil Thomson, the head of Special Branch and the CID, assisted by Sir George Cave KC.[38] This whole untidy arrangement was attractive in that nobody was politically responsible for MI5; it also reflected the British class system, MI5 comprising officers and gentlemen and Special Branch the non-commissioned from the upper working class. Since Kell's officers did not themselves act upon the information they collected, there was in a sense nothing for which responsibility was required.

[35] Eric E. B. H. Wilson (1875–26 Mar. 1950), later hyphenated, was a Royal Engineer officer; he was placed on the retired list on 21 Dec. 1912, when he joined Kell, and became Chief Staff Officer to Kell in 1917. His *Who's Who* entry states that he was a GSO 1914–24 and 1939–40, and notes his involvement in drafting emergency legislation between 1924 and 1938. It also notes work in the Empire and India in 1929, 1930, and 1938.

[36] MA, LLB, and later CBE; an Inner Temple barrister, called 1888; son of Adm. John Moresby; still in practice from retirement in 1941.

[37] During the 1st World War under Sir Charles Raitt Cleveland, from 1919 to 1924 under Sir Cecil Kaye, and then under Sir David Petrie.

[38] See B. Thomson, *Queer People* (London, 1922), 134. Cave's name is given in *Parl. Deb.* HC 81: 427. His successors in this role were to be Walter Monckton and Helenus ('Buster') P. J. Milmo.

The Sacred Archive

Kell's principal weapon against espionage was archival—a card index of suspicious persons. Indeed the soul of counter-intelligence resides in such an archive, and in modern times Peter Wright, or his ghost-writer, has written feelingly of the religious awe which in his time surrounded the registry of MI5, where the nicely brought up registry queens, a legacy of Kell's days, attended upon the files and indexes.[39] The obsessive secrecy surrounding the work of MI5 meant that officers who compiled the archive never adopted the practice of interviewing suspects, and giving them a chance to rebut suspicion; consequently MI5's records were inherently unreliable, and the larger the archive grew the more this must have been true.

The most likely suspects were thought to be those of alien blood or connections. Hence the establishment, between 1910 and 1913, of a very incomplete secret register of aliens, which by July of 1913 covered 28,830 persons, 11,100 being German or Austrian, out of a total, according to the most recent census, of 284,830.[40] Kell would have liked to have kept a record of all aliens who entered the country, an immense undertaking; this idea was fought off by the Home Office, whose officials clearly regarded Kell and Holt-Wilson as somewhat foolish.[41] Holt-Wilson was much involved in the creation of the archive.[42] Constance Kell described him as 'a man of almost genius for intricate organization'.[43] The compilation of Kell's register necessarily involved the Home Office, since the police did most of the work, and it was responsible for aliens.[44] This helped to establish the curious relationship between the security service and the Home Office which has persisted to this day.

When war came the Aliens Restriction Act was passed by Parliament on 5 August 1914, even before the passing of the Defence of the Realm

[39] P. Wright, *Spycatcher: The Candid Autobiography of a Senior Intelligence Officer* (New York, 1988), 47, describes the system in his time, that is from 1955.

[40] J. C. Bird, *Control of Enemy Alien Civilians in Great Britain 1914–1918* (New York and London, 1986). WO 32/8873 and 8874 deal with aliens and special powers of control over them, and WO 32/8875 with the Register of Aliens.

[41] See French, 'Spy Fever' (n. 25 above), 360. CAB 17/90 contains a *Confidential Circular to Chief Constables* of Oct. 1912, cited by Bird, *Enemy Alien Civilians*, 38–9.

[42] (1875–26 March 1950). The claim is made in his *Who's Who* entry thus: 'inception and organization, through Home Office, of official registration by the police of alien residents in the UK', and in a document written by him in 1940, now in the US National Archives RG 84 London Embassy Confidential File 711.2–8202B, where he says that 'he had compiled . . . a Register with full biographical details of over thirty thousand aliens and others who were considered potentially dangerous in the event of a war with Germany and her potential allies'.

[43] 'Secret Well Kept' (Kell Papers in the Imperial War Museum), 136.

[44] HO 45/10629/199699. Up to 1911 Kell obtained information from the Chief Constables of County forces. In November he started to communicate with Borough Chief Constables.

Act, with virtually no opposition or discussion; its rationale was protection against subversion.[45] The British Nationality and Status of Aliens Act 1914 further weakened the position of aliens.[46] Enemy aliens, their names and addresses on the register, could be detained by the executive under the royal prerogative. Suspected spies, whatever their nationality, were also on file; they could be arrested and, if there was sufficient evidence against them, brought to trial. This at least was the ideal picture; in fact MI5's records were and remained very incomplete.[47] But by the outbreak of war some 30,000 aliens 'and others who were considered potentially dangerous' were on the secret list.[48] MI5 pressed for a fuller archive; in 1917 Holt-Wilson wanted the police to list all persons 'of enemy race by actual parentage in full or half blood' who were either British subjects or non-enemy aliens. The Home Office resisted this as a waste of police time. The ideal of a security service is of course to have absolutely everybody on file.

On 4 August 1914 some twenty-one supposed spies were arrested, though only one of them was ever brought to trial; whether the others were in fact spies is obscure, though the arrests were naturally claimed as a triumph by MI5. Only 342 enemy aliens were initially detained under the prerogative. The policy in the First World War was to try spies if there was sufficient evidence against them; thirty-five were caught, twenty-two convicted, and fourteen were executed, the last in April 1916.[49] If the evidence was lacking enemy alien spies could be detained.

The Order in Council of 1915

Disloyal British subjects, however, could not be detained, whether they had always been citizens since birth, or had acquired citizenship by marriage or naturalization; they enjoyed British liberty, and could not be imprisoned without charge or trial by the executive. Regulation 14B of 10 June 1915, as it came to be interpreted, altered the legal position for all British subjects. It provided that:

Where on the recommendation of a competent naval or military authority, or of one of the Advisory Committees hereinafter mentioned, it appears to the Secretary of State that for securing the public safety or for the defence of the realm it is expedient in view of the hostile origin or associations of any person that

[45] *Parl. Deb.* HC 65: 1990, 5 Aug. 1914.   [46] 4 & 5 Geo. V, c. 12 and c. 17.
[47] See HO 45/10881/338498.
[48] For further details of the system of classification see Andrew, ch. 5.
[49] Felstead, *German Spies*, 8–9, gives a list; 12 supposed spies had been arrested before the war. See Hiley, 'Failure of British Counter–Espionage' (n. 25 above). WO 32/4898 contains a list of 29 spies tried by court martial. In addition a number of persons were tried by the regular courts for offences of one kind or another, such as Eva de Bourneville (Central Criminal Court) 19 Jan. 1916, DPP 4/51 PCOM 8/245.

he shall be subjected to such obligations and restrictions as are hereinafter mentioned.

The Secretary of State could order his internment, or impose restrictions as to residence or movement, or order reporting to the police. This regulation was introduced soon after Sir John Simon became Home Secretary.[50] At the time there was violent feeling against persons with German connections, fanned by the sinking of the *Lusitania* on 7 May. On 13 May the government announced a decision to detain enemy aliens generally, and on the same day Prime Minister Asquith made it clear that the government intended to secure power to detain naturalized aliens as well.[51]

The impetus for the new regulation was the belief, formed in May and June of 1915, that the Germans were attempting to establish a new corps of agents, recruited from residents of German descent. Since the grounds for this belief were weak, it was also feared that those detected might be acquitted if tried by court martial.[52] The special function of the regulation was first explained to the Commons on 17 June by Simon as Home Secretary.[53] He argued that some individuals, though in law British subjects, were for practical purposes enemy aliens, and should therefore be denied the rights of *genuine* British subjects: 'it is reasonable that we should consider and deal with a certain number of cases where the individual is of hostile origin or hostile associations but is technically not an alien. I do not myself think that you ought to draw a strict line of legal division between persons who are naturalized and persons who are natural born citizens of this country.' Both, he argued, should be treated alike, being liable to internment if they were 'of hostile origin or associations'. In this way he justified the new regulation as no more than a modest and commonsensical extension of the existing law of alien control.

Nobody seriously committed to the rule of law could possibly accept Simon's argument. Law is just in the business of drawing firm lines of

---

[50] 1873–1954; see a *DNB* entry by R. F. V. Heuston. Immensely successful at the bar Simon became a Liberal MP, Solicitor-General in 1910 and Attorney in 1913. He had opposed the DORA scheme as unnecessary. He was Home Secretary from 1915 until January 1916, resigning over conscription. He was again at the Home Office 1935–7. With Churchill's accession to power in 1940 his political career was ended, and he became Lord Chancellor.

[51] *Parl. Deb.* HC 71: 1842. See also Simon on 9 June, ibid. 72: 247. See J. W. Garner, *International Law and the World War* (London, 1920), i. 73 ff.

[52] See Felstead, *German Spies*, 100ff. Felstead notes that 7 supposed spies were caught between the end of May and mid-June, and their detection caused anxiety: 'it was not easy to establish the suspects' connection with the German Secret Service and procure evidence sufficient to meet the requirements of a court martial. This difficulty was partially met by giving such people a long period of detention under the Defence of the Realm Act.' Bulloch, *MI5*, 116–21, lists them; 5 were shot, one died just before, and a Mrs Wertheim received 10 years' imprisonment.

[53] By Order 551 of 1915. See *Parl. Deb.* HC 72: 851.

demarcation—between mine and thine, between guilt and innocence, between citizens and non-citizens. Respect for the rule of law entails respect for these boundaries, even though, at the margins, they may seem artificial and technical, as indeed they are, and are bound to be. And this particular boundary was quite critical, for the right to a trial, if accused of disloyal conduct, had hitherto been quite fundamental to the conception of a British citizen's liberty, even though, as we have seen, it might be temporarily suspended.

Regulation 14B was thus both a reaction to a fear of a Fifth Column concealed within the population of citizens who were enemy aliens, or had enemy alien connections, and a reaction to the knowledge that the evidence for the actual existence of such dangerous persons was generally too weak to produce convictions in a regular court. Indeed belief in the enemy within, of alien blood or connections, underlies the invention of all the institutions of the vigilant state, such as MI5, the Special Branch, the Official Secrets Act, and Holt-Wilson's horrendous archive. In so far as fear of the nationalist Catholic Irish was a factor they tended to be viewed as if they were aliens too. Those responsible for the new Regulation 14B, including Simon himself, were no doubt perfectly honest in thinking of it as no more than a modest extension of the existing powers of alien control, and there is not the least reason to suppose that the officials involved had any concern except the efficient conduct of the war. But once government is, for one reason, empowered to bypass the tedious requirements of the rule of law, and lock up its citizens without charge, trial, or term set, the temptation to extend the use of so convenient a power seems to be quite irresistible. The threat to liberty comes not from some malevolent enthusiasm for tyranny, but from a professional concern for efficient government.

2

Regulation 14B and its Progeny

Administering the Regulation

It was the text of Regulation 14B, not its original limited purpose as an instrument of alien control, which lived on, and this text was drafted so as not to restrict the scope of the regulation to that purpose. The expression 'of hostile origin' clearly included former enemy citizens, and perhaps those whose parents were of enemy citizenship.[1] 'Of hostile associations' was much less precise. It might cover a British citizen who had lived in Germany, or had enemy friends, relatives, business contacts, or even mere acquaintances. It was unclear whether the *associations* had to be hostile or disloyal, or whether it was enough that the *associates* were now Britain's enemies. Furthermore the text did not require *recent* hostile associations. So the regulation, though ostensibly limiting the power of detention, left some rather alarming options open.

Although decisions to intern would be executive, and not judicial, there was a safeguard; detainees could appeal to an advisory committee, chaired by someone who held, or had held, 'high judicial office'—which means a judge of the High Court or above. The principal task of the committees (one for England and Wales, and one for Scotland) was to deal with appeals by enemy aliens; during the war just under 30,000 were detained.[2] Regulation 14B cases were a minor additional duty. The judges selected were fairly junior, being Sir John Sankey and Sir Robert Younger.[3] There were six other members.[4] They were Stanley Baldwin, Donald Maclean,[5] John J. Mooney,[6] the Lieutenant-Colonel A. R. M. Lockwood,[7] all members of Parliament, and two women, the Hon.

---

[1] After marriage or naturalization there would be dual nationality.

[2] Kell Papers. Lecture of 22 October 1935. J. C. Bird, *Control of Enemy Alien Civilians in Great Britain 1914–1918* (New York and London, 1986), gives a figure of 32,000. See also C. Holmes, *John Bull's Island: Immigration and British Society, 1871–1971* (Basingstoke, 1988), 96.

[3] Sankey (1866–1948), appointed to the bench 1914; later Lord Chancellor as Viscount Sankey. See R. F. V. Heuston, *Lives of the Lord Chancellors 1885–1940* (Oxford, 1964). Younger had just been made a judge in 1915; later became Baron Blanesburgh.

[4] *Parl. Deb.* HC 72: 4.

[5] 1864–1932. MP for Peebles and Selkirk.   [6] 1874–1934. MP for Newry.

[7] Later Lord Lambourne. Epping; much involved in raising hysteria about spies; see D. Hooper, *Official Secrets: The Use and Abuse of the Act* (London, 1987), 26.

Maude A. Lawrence[8] and a Miss Talbot.[9] The Scottish committee was chaired by Lord Dewar, assisted by Sir James H. Dalziel and Mr W. Watson.[10] No doubt the idea of involving judges was to legitimate executive action, the legitimacy being parasitic upon the respect accorded to the regular judicial system, which derives from its association with the ideal of the rule of law. Indeed Simon, in announcing the committee's membership and function, engaged in some revealing double-talk when he called it 'an advisory body of a judicial character'. Judicial bodies do not advise the executive; they decide, and do so within the formal framework of court procedure. The use of judges on the committee is an early example of a practice which has become increasingly common: judges come to be *used* by the executive, essentially cosmetically, to legitimate decisions they do not in fact control. Today judges seem prepared to take on virtually any non-judicial duty, however degrading to the judicial office.[11]

Very little is known about the administration of Regulation 14B.[12] By 21 February 1916 there were only thirty-six detainees in custody.[13] Of these seventeen were 'of hostile origin'. The seventeen 'hostile origin' detainees had acquired British citizenship by naturalization, or by marriage. The remaining nineteen detainees—more than 50 per cent—were natural-born British subjects who had been detained as being 'of hostile associations'.[14] Presumably they were suspected of espionage or sabotage. The regulations governing the conditions of detention are available; they were to be segregated from other prisoners, allowed free association and the use of their own clothes and property, given an option whether to work or not, allowed to buy food and tobacco, and have books and magazines sent in to them. They could send and receive three short letters each week, and receive visits twice a month.[15] These were slightly more generous rules than those officially adopted in the Second World War. The majority of 14B detainees were held in an old Poor Law institution, St Mary's Institute, in Cornwallis Road, Islington. A few men were held in Brixton Prison, and the remainder in Pentonville and Reading Prisons.[16] Women

---

[8] 1864–1933. Daughter of the first Baron Lawrence, Viceroy of India 1863–9; Chief Woman Inspector for the Board of Education.

[9] Possibly Emily Charlotte Talbot of Penrice Castle, or a civil servant, Muriel Lucy Talbot of the Board of Agriculture (D.B.E. 1920). In July 1918 the committee was reconstituted and comprised Sir John Butcher, Sir Donald Maclean, Mr J. J. Mooney, Lord Lambourne, Mr Thomas Richards, and Maj.-Gen. Lord Cheylesmore (1848–1925), one-time Chairman of the LCC. See Bird, *Enemy Alien Civilians*, 95 and 128.

[10] *Parl. Deb.* HC 72: 850, 17 June 1915.

[11] See my 'The Judges and the Vigilant State', *Denning Law Journal* (1989), 145.

[12] Conceivably records survive in HO 144, and with MI5.

[13] HO 45/25758/863044/4, memo of 12 October 1938.

[14] *Parl. Deb.* HC 80: 410 for 21 February 1916.   [15] HO 144/1496/362269.

[16] e.g. Louis F. Kehrbahn, who escaped from Islington with Graeme Scott and Hodgson. *Parl. Deb.* HC 99: 2208.

were normally held in the Aylesbury Inebriates Reformatory. The Islington camp, which mainly held aliens, was established in June 1915 and guarded by the police rather than by the military, and the Commandant, Sir Frederick Loch Halliday, was a former Indian police officer.[17]

By 2 March 1916 there were sixty-nine detainees, fifteen being British subjects by birth.[18] In February 1917 there were seventy-four, thirty-one British born.[19] By June 1917 there were 125, of whom seventy-three were British subjects; the others were non-enemy aliens thought to be danger-ous.[20] Numbers then began to fall, to sixty-seven by June of 1918, forty-nine being 'of hostile origin'.[21] The detainees were not all set free when fighting ceased on 11 November 1918; the DORA system continued until the war officially ended three years later. On 14 April 1919 there were still sixty-six detainees, of whom thirty-seven men and four women were British born.[22] The detainees languished until about the end of November of 1919, when the Islington camp was closed.[23] The total num-ber of orders made between 1915 and the armistice was not published, but the Islington camp received 135 persons in all; to this figure must be added a few women and persons held elsewhere, so the total was perhaps about 160.[24] Outside Ireland the regulation was thus used with restraint, and this at a time when enemy aliens were being detained on a very large scale. The veil of secrecy imposed by the Civil Service makes it impossi-ble to tell whether those who were detained ought to have been, or whether the advisory committee operated respectably. The executive never accounted publicly for its actions then and, with the destruction of records, it never will.

The Easter Rising

The war with Germany was not the only problem then confronting gov-ernment; there was, as always, the Irish question, and the authorities made extensive use of Regulation 14B to crush the Irish rebellion of 1916, thereby abandoning any claim that 14B was restricted to alien control. Some 3,430 men and seventy-nine women, were taken into custody in the weeks following the rising. Of these 1,836 men and five women were in

[17] HO 45/25758. Bird, *Enemy Aliens*, 139. In September 1918 Maj. R. F. Godfrey-Faussett took over (MEPO 2/1633).
[18] *Parl. Deb.* HC Vol. 80: 1236–72. There were also 4 detainees in Scotland.
[19] Ibid. 90: 1845 for 27 Feb. 1917.   [20] Ibid. 94: 1947.
[21] Ibid. 106: 1731 for 6 June 1918. Also ibid. 98: 1175.
[22] Ibid. 114: 2554 for 14 Apr. 1919.
[23] Ibid. 122: 251 for 2 December 1919 has them all released. MEPO 2/1633.
[24] *Parl. Deb.* HC Vol. 125 cc. 1489–90. A few files on Irish cases have been released and are discussed below.

due course moved to England, where most were sent to two camps at Frongoch in North Wales. Many were released not long afterwards.[25] But these Irish were not originally detained under Regulation 14B. They were prisoners taken in the course of military operations, and, although martial law had been proclaimed, it was not said that they were held or tried, as some were tried, under martial law.[26] The technical position was that they were held awaiting trial, either for regular criminal offences, or for offences under DORA. Since March 1915 it had been idle to charge serious DORA offences in political cases in Ireland; under an amendment to DORA civilians charged with such offences, previously triable by courts martial, became entitled to jury trial, and Irish juries could not be relied on to convict.[27] However, this right could be withdrawn in the event of a 'special military emergency', and in Ireland, but not elsewhere, it was so withdrawn on 26 April 1916 by proclamation. This enabled General J. H. Maxwell to have suspects tried by courts martial; over 2,000 persons were so tried, and numerous death sentences imposed; fourteen were carried out, and have never been forgotten.

But against many of the Irish prisoners there was no evidence of guilt which could be put to a court martial. Maxwell, for security reasons, did not want to hold a large number of unconvicted Irish men and women in Ireland, nor did he want to release them.[28] So in April and May he sent many of them, as prisoners, to England. Their legal position was uncertain. Troup thought Maxwell's action was legal under the common law conception of military necessity, but he favoured their rapid return to Ireland before his view might be challenged. The Irish authorities suggested that a new Regulation 14B should be introduced, specially drafted to cover those *suspected* of being involved in the Easter rebellion; this would have to be retrospective, and the Irish prisoners, as suspected rebels, could then be detained for the remainder of the war. Early in May this suggestion was discussed by the Home Secretary, the Law Officers, and the Prime Minister, and rejected. They thought the prisoners could

---

[25] See F. S. L. Lyons, *Ireland Since the Famine* (London, 1971), 374: E. Holt, *Protest in Arms: The Irish Troubles 1916–1923* (London, 1960), 136; C. Townshend, *Political Violence in Ireland: Government and Resistance Since 1848* (Oxford, 1983), 303–13. On 14 August 1916 there were 520 prisoners at Frongoch, and 30 in Reading (HO 144/1456/33106). The women must have been held elsewhere, presumably at Aylesbury. See CO 904/186 (List of internees 1916, correspondence 1917–20).

[26] See Townshend, *Political Violence*, 308–9. Martial law was proclaimed in 1916 but not 'put into force', the view of the Irish Law Officers being that, given DORA, the ordinary law was still operating. For Maxwell's formal instructions see *Parl. Deb.* HC Vol. 82 cc. 631 and 675 for 10 May 1916.

[27] The Defence of the Realm Amendment Act of 18 March 1915 (5 Geo. V, c. 34), discussed in W. B. Wells and N. Marlowe, *A History of the Irish Rebellion of 1916* (Dublin, 1916).

[28] HO 144/1455/313106.

be detained under the existing regulation as being 'of hostile associations': the 'hostile associations' involved could only have been associations with each other, not with foreign enemies. So the regulation was stretched and used for this entirely new purpose, for in no conceivable sense were the Irish detainees in effect enemy aliens, covered by Simon's explanation of the purpose of the regulation in June of the previous year.

The first Irish prisoners against whom 14B orders were made were five women, said to be 'of hostile associations' because they had 'favoured, promoted and assisted an armed insurrection against the King'. The text of Arthur Griffiths' order of July 1916 read: 'This order is made on the ground that he is of hostile associations and is reasonably suspected of having favoured, promoted, or assisted an armed insurrection against His Majesty.'[29] Somewhere between 1,800 and 1,900 men were similarly covered by orders and held in England. There was no way that the Home Secretary could personally consider each case before making an order, and this was conceded.[30] But their cases were reviewed by the committee, now afforced with an Irish judge, Mr Justice Jonathan Pim, and Sir James Dougherty.[31] Many were soon released, and on 14 June 1917 there was an amnesty.[32]

The legality of this use of the regulation seems never to have been challenged in court. The judges on the committee must have accepted it.

Secrecy and Detention without Trial

The names of these Irish exiles were published in the press. But this was not the practice for detainees in mainland Britain. Hence, as in the most odious of tyrannies, the executive could make people disappear; this became an issue, as we shall see over the detention of Miss Hilda M. Howsin.[33] Indeed DORA imposed no obligation even to disclose bare statistics. Figures were in fact given to Parliament from time to time, and occasionally, in response to pressure, other information. Apparently most requests for orders came from MI5, and presumably Home Office officials exercised some check over them.[34]

Executive secrecy meant that the very scope of the power of detention, which turned on the interpretation of the expression 'of hostile origin or associations', could be concealed. Thus in 1918 Sir George Cave, asked

---

[29] *Parl. Deb.* HC Vol. 83 c.513 for 26 June 1916. For Griffiths see HO 144/1458/316093.
[30] See *Parl. Deb.* HC Vol. 83 c.1357 for 4 July 1916, and 84: 11–14 for 10 July 1916. Names were published in the Irish press.
[31] (1844–1934); MP for Londonderry City 1914–18. *Parl. Deb.* HC Vol. 83 c.12 for 20 June 1916.
[32] R. Kee, *The Green Flag: The Turbulent History of the Irish Nationalist Movement* (New York, 1972), 600. CAB 24/14 GT 880, CAB 24/16 GT 1027.
[33] See below pp. 22, 25.   [34] HO 45/25758/863044/4.

for the definition of 'of hostile origin', replied that there was no definition, and the matter had to be determined on the facts of each particular case.[35] Again in a debate on 2 March 1916 C. P. Trevelyan pointed out that 'of hostile associations' 'may mean almost anything which the right honourable Gentleman [i.e. the Home Secretary] chooses to interpret it as meaning'.[36] No court offered guidance on the matter, nor were executive rulings, or decisions of the committee, ever published.[37] But some information was given to the Commons, for the first time, on 2 March 1916.[38] This made it clear that the power of detention had already been extended by executive action even before the Easter rebellion. Examples of cases were provided, without mentioning names. They included purely British born men who were suspected of espionage, detained as being 'of hostile associations'. So within a year Regulation 14B was no longer confined to persons who were by birth or assimilation, though not by law, enemy aliens. The regulation was also regularly used to detain aliens of non-enemy citizenship.[39] And in June, as we have seen, the regulation was stretched even further to legitimize the exile of the Irish at Frongoch.

Thus the security service, with the backing of the Home Office, appropriated a power to detain any citizen whatsoever, or any non-enemy alien, who was suspected of posing a danger through disloyalty or insurrection, even though the weakness of the evidence ruled out criminal charges. The committee's judges, Sankey, Younger, Dewar, and Pim, must have agreed with this, for we know that their advice for release was always accepted.[40] No Parliamentary authority was sought for this invasion of civil liberty, nor did it provoke any widespread protest.

The Advisory Committees

Little indeed is known about the committees; recommendations were never published, and there are no useful records available.[41] Seven days were apparently allowed for detainees to appeal.[42] The committees were not courts; they sat behind closed doors, and were in unfettered control over their procedures. Unlike their successors in the Second World War they did not sit in panels, at least in 14B cases. As senior judge, Sankey

---

[35] *Parl. Deb.* HC Vol. 106 c.67.   [36] Ibid. 80: 1236.
[37] Only one available file is relevant: HO 144/1494/360163.
[38] *Parl. Deb.* HC Vol. 80 c.1245ff.   [39] See ibid. 114: 2554 for 14 April 1919.
[40] Ibid. 104: 659 for 18 March 1918. The Home Office might order release even if the committee did not advise this. See ibid. 80: 1248 for 2 March 1916 mentioning one such case.
[41] HO 144/1458/316093 (Arthur Griffiths) is uninformative since he refused all co-operation.
[42] HO 144/1458/316093. A few other detainees refused to appeal; in 1917 it was said that there had been four cases. *Parl. Deb.* HC Vol. 99 c.13 for 12 November.

would preside.[43] The judges wholly failed to infuse into the procedures the quality which Dicey claimed to be basic to British constitutional arrangements, 'the predominance of the legal spirit'.[44] Instead the committees conformed to the popular vision of the Star Chamber. This was made clear by a Commons statement on 22 October 1917:

I understand that the proceedings are strictly private, no person whatsoever, other than the members of the Committee and their officers, being present. As the evidence given is often of an extremely confidential character, applicants are not present when it is taken, and are not supplied with copies, but care is taken to put to them in examination all points requiring explanation from them. Every applicant is entitled to have legal advice, but it is not the practice of the Committee to hear either counsel or solicitor as an advocate, although they allow any legal adviser an opportunity of tendering himself as a witness if he so desires . . .[45] They [i.e. the detainees] have a written statement of the case against them.[46]

To the question whether this statement meant in 'the most general terms . . . they have no particular instances of misconduct set forth in that statement', the reply given was that 'It depends upon the case. Some statements contain full details of their conduct.'[47] This statement suggests that witnesses were sometimes heard, though not on oath; to what extent is uncertain—for example it is unlikely that Kell's agents appeared. Hearings would take the form of interrogations, as was to be the case in the Second World War.

Critics of Regulation 14B

Naturally some deplored the extension of executive power under DORA generally, and Regulation 14B in particular. Opposition was encouraged by the Zadig case, which is more fully discussed later; indeed as a result of it Sir James H. Dalziel, a member of the Scottish committee, appears to have had serious misgivings.[48] On 2 March 1916 W. W. Ashley moved to reduce the Home Office vote by way of protest at 14B.[49] And on 23 March C. P. Trevelyan,[50] seconded by F. W. Jowett,[51] moved 'that the

---

[43] Statement on 2 March 1916 *Parl. Deb.* HC Vol. 80 c.1248.
[44] A. V. Dicey, *Introduction to the Study of the Law of the Constitution* (London, 1959), 195.
[45] Interviews with lawyers were supervised. *Parl. Deb.* HC Vol. 88 c.471.
[46] *Parl. Deb.* HC Vol. 98 c.482 for 22 October 1917. Originally detainees were given no written statement, but from March 1916 they were given a written statement 'showing on what grounds that internment order is made'. See ibid. 80: 1247 for 2 March 1916.
[47] Only one example of the grounds given is available in HO 144/1458/316093, quoted above, n. 41.
[48] See *Parl. Deb.* HC Vol. 80 c.224-5.
[49] 1867-1938. MP for Blackpool. *Parl.Deb.* HC Vol. 80 c.1236.
[50] MP for the Elland Division in the West Riding. *Parl. Deb.* HC Vol. 81 c.414.
[51] 1864-1944. MP for West Bradford.

administration of the Defence of the Realm Acts has often been more rig-
orous than the nature or seriousness of the cases justified and that . . . the
imprisonment without trial of any class of British citizens at the discretion
of the executive is dangerous to the liberty of the subject'.[52] The general
thrust of criticism was that 14B deprived citizens of their right to a regular
trial.

A case which focused opposition involved Miss Hilda M. Howsin,[53]
who, as we shall see, eventually applied for habeas corpus.[54] A Red Cross
nurse, she was the daughter of a retired surgeon, and was arrested on 1
September 1915 whilst her father was out shooting partridges.[55] Her
father did not discover where she was for seventeen days, and it was five
weeks before she appeared before the committee.[56] She was interrogated
by Sir George Cave[57] and, at the hearing, by Stanley Baldwin. On 23
March, under pressure in the debate, F. E. Smith, the Attorney-General,
gave an explanation for her arrest. She was, he claimed, a friend of a
person who fled from England in 1909, went to Berlin, and became a
German agent. He was involved in sedition and assassination. She had
visited him in Berlin before the war, and again in 1915 in Switzerland, acting as courier.

Elsewhere it was publicly suggested that her crime had been involvement with Indian British subjects.[58] According to her own later account
she was a friend of one Birendranath[59] Chattopadhyaya, a Hindu bar student, who had left England in 1909 for Paris, and then Berlin, after his Inn
refused to call him to the bar; there was a warrant out for his arrest. A
woman, whom she was later told was a spy, had urged her to go to
Switzerland where he was in some trouble; she had gone and carried an
innocent message back to a London friend of his.[60]

In 1909 Miss Howsin had published a book, now rare, sympathetic to
Indian nationalism, *The Significance of Indian Nationalism*,[61] and her
friend, who was later a member of the Communist Party in Germany, had
become the Vice-President of the India Independence Committee, an
organization based in Germany, and engaged in organizing insurrection

---

[52] The omitted passage deals with secret trials and the suppression of newspapers and
information.
[53] She was born 23 July 1877, the daughter of Edward A. Howsin.
[54] (1917) 33 TLR 527.
[55] She was arrested at her father's home in Reedness, Yorkshire.
[56] See *Parl. Deb.* HC 81: 427, 446, 1620, 2310; 84: 11–14; 88: 470; 96: 1093; 97: 566.
[57] He did not become Home Secretary until 1916.
[58] See *Parl. Deb.* HC Vol. 88 c.470.   [59] Also Virendranath.
[60] Possibly a Miss Brunner, a Swiss also detained because of associations with nationalists. *Parl. Deb.* HC Vol. 88 c.470 for 30 November 1916.
[61] I have used a reprint of 1922 published in Madras. In the same year she published
India's Challenge to Civilisation.

in India.[62] David Petrie, later head of MI5, in his *Communism in India*, described him as 'the doyen of Indian revolutionaries abroad' and as a 'notorious and dangerous revolutionary'; he was also known as Vincent Chatterton, A. Alfieri, and Mahomed Djafar.[63] He had come to England in 1902, and failed to secure admission to the Indian Civil Service; after leaving England he was prominent in Indian revolutionary circles, ending up in Russia, where he died in 1941.[64] In 1922 Howsin's book was reissued; she explained that she had been detained for four years, and that the 'innocuous opinions and arguments which it presents' were regarded by the committee as an indication that she was engaged in raising rebellion in India. Miss Howsin may have indeed been entirely innocent, but any contact with her friend would no doubt have raised grave suspicions, though had there been any solid evidence she would have been put on trial. In March 1918 attempts were made to secure her release with conditions of residence and bonds for good behaviour. She was apparently released in August 1919.[65]

Another case which caused some comment involved the Hungarian portrait painter, Philip de László.[66] He had long worked in England, but was not naturalized until 4 September 1914. He behaved indiscreetly during the war by illegally sending money to his family in Hungary, by using the Dutch diplomatic bag for correspondence, and by sympathetically giving an escaped Hungarian officer one pound, before repenting and reporting his escape to the police. He was arrested in August 1917, interrogated by Basil Thomson of the Special Branch, and interned as 'of hostile origin and associations' on the recommendation of the committee in the autumn of 1917. In 1919 a public hearing took place before another committee appointed to consider revocation of his naturalization. It recommended that his actions during the war had not entailed any disloyalty. He therefore retained his British citizenship.[67] His detention, though understandable perhaps, was thus thought unjustified, but seems to have done his career as a painter little harm. The only other detainees who attracted much attention were a group of Russian left-wingers, of whom

---

[62] Previously known as the German Union of Friendly India. See R. C. Majumdar (ed.), *Bharataya Vidya Bhavan's History and Culture of the Indian People*, xi. *Struggle for Freedom* (Bombay, 1969), 213–15 and 702. A rising was planned for 19 February 1915.

[63] D. Petrie's book *Communism in India* (Calcutta, 1972), covering 1924 to 1927, was originally an internal confidential intelligence report.

[64] C. Kaye, *Communism in India*, ed. M. Saha (Calcutta, 1972), has much material (see esp p. 1 nn.). He was a graduate of Calcutta University and the son of a professor of Nizam's College, Hyderabad. There is apparently a life in Russian by A. Volsky (1969).

[65] *Parl. Deb.* HC Vol. 104 c.1005.

[66] Philip Alexius László de Lombos (1869–1937). See *DNB.* 1931–40 and O. Rutter, *Portrait of a Painter: The Authorised Life of Philip de Laszlo* (London, 1939).

[67] *The Times* for 24–8 June 1919; Mr Justice Salter presided over the hearing under The British Nationality and Status of Aliens Act 1918.

the most prominent was Peter Petroff, a socialist activist originally held in Edinburgh Castle and later in Islington and Pentonville, before being deported; he had been organizing strikes in war industries.[68] Most appear to have been deported in 1918.[69]

But in spite of its critics, which after 1916 included Irish nationalists, regulation 14B does not seem to have been under any real political threat during the period of hostilities, and remarkably few individual detainees attracted any public comment.

The Role of the Courts[70]

Up to the date of the armistice Regulation 14B was challenged three times in the courts.[71] In the first two cases the validity of the regulation itself was in issue. One, *in re D.*, heard in December of 1915, was not reported. In habeas corpus proceedings it was argued that the regulation was *ultra vires*, that is to say outside the power of legislation delegated to the Privy Council by DORA.[72] The same argument was advanced in *R. v. Halliday ex parte Zadig*, which reached the Lords in March 1917, Halliday as Camp Commandant being the person who had custody of 'the body' of Arthur Zadig, a naturalized British subject of German origin. That there was some official doubt over the validity of some regulations, possibly including 14B, is evidenced by a proposal by J. J. Liddell, a Parliamentary draftsman, for legislation retrospectively confirming all previous regulations, though this was never acted upon.[73]

The issue in Zadig's case was simple: should the courts insist that major changes in the British constitution be explicitly authorized by Parliament, or should the executive be permitted to make such changes by delegated legislation, claiming it to be authorized by general words in a parent Act—here DORA—which said nothing at all about detention. Those who voted for DORA could never have envisaged anything so extreme as 14B, and it would undermine the sovereignty of Parliament, rather than respect it, to uphold the validity of the Order in Council which introduced it. Plausible or not, this argument was rejected by two judges in the first case, and by twelve judges in Zadig's case—five in the

---

[68] CAB 24/41 GT 3587, *Parl. Deb.* HC Vol. 80 c.1049; 81: 452, 2213 for 18 April 1916; 95: 13, 1595, 1653, 1686; 99: 1029.

[69] *Parl. Deb.* HC Vol. 85 c.2672 (Witkop); 92: 422 (the Petroffs, Sairo, Hasse); 92: 482 (Tchitcherine); 101: 643 (Mrs Petroff, Sairo, Hasse, and Natenbuk); 104: 1311 (Sairo).

[70] See C. P. Cotter, 'Constitutional Democracy and Emergency: Emergency Powers Legislation in Great Britain since 1914', Harvard Univ. D.Phil. Thesis, 1953, 50ff.

[71] J. W. Garner, *International Law and the World War* (London, 1920).

[72] For procedures see R. J. Sharpe, *The Law of Habeas Corpus* (Oxford, 1989), esp. ch. 10. Two hearings are normally involved, in the second of which a decision is given.

[73] [1916] 1 KB 738, 33 TLR. 245 and 301, [1917] AC 260. For Liddell's plan see HO 45/11007.

Divisional Court, three in the Court of Appeal, and four in the Lords, one of them being Atkin, whom we shall meet again. From 1917 onwards British judges have, with the rarest exceptions, consistently upheld the progressive erosion of British liberty in the name of good government; Zadig's case represents a sort of watershed between the world of Victorian liberalism and the world of the vigilant state.

Lord Shaw of Dunfermline alone dissented in an opinion described by the *Law Times* as 'an extraordinary tirade on the subject of what he calls British liberty'.[74] Shaw was never a popular judge with the profession. His view was that 'Parliament never sanctioned, either in intention or by reason of the statutory words employed in the Defence of the Realm Acts, such a violent exercise of arbitrary power.' But his was a lone voice. Arthur Zadig was in fact released from Reading Prison in 1918.[75]

So far as I am aware litigation only once challenged the particular exercise of the power to detain.[76] The one case again involved Hilda Howsin. In 1917 she applied for habeas corpus, and her counsel asked the court to investigate whether she really was 'of hostile associations', which she denied. The divisional court refused the application.[77] The Court of Appeal upheld this; so long as there was any evidence upon which the Home Secretary had acted the court would not intervene.[78] Counsel for the Crown only attended the hearing with a watching brief, and apparently no affidavit was put in from the Home Secretary. There was a suggestion in the opinion that she was entitled to be given at least some reason for her detention but, as she apparently had been, the point hardly arose. In the Zadig case Lords Atkinson and Wrenbury had suggested that the courts were at least entitled to determine whether the case against a detainee fell within the terms of the regulation.[79] In Howsin's case the Court of Appeal, presented with the opportunity of doing this, declined to exercise any supervisory role whatsoever. Two other cases challenging the exercise of the power to control residence under Regulation 14—*R. v. Denison*[80] and *Ronnfeldt v. Phillip and others*[81]—ruled that unless the applicant could show the power had not been honestly exercised, an all but impossible task, the court would not interfere.

Realistically Regulation 14B, never approved by Parliament, and extended in scope by executive decision, operated in a world largely disowned by the custodians of the regular law. But decisions in deportation cases, where the courts were again invited to review an analogous

---

[74] Vol. 143: 2.
[75] See *Parl. Deb.* HC Vol. 100 c.1513 for 14 December 1917 and 106: 1731 for 6 June 1918.
[76] Possibly there were other cases not publicly reported.
[77] Unreported.
[78] (1917) 33 TLR 527, decided 23 July 1917 by Pickford, and Scrutton L JJ, with Neville J.
[79] See Lord Atkinson at 308.   [80] (1916) 32 TLR 526.
[81] (1918) 34 TLR 153.

executive power exercised by the Home Office, did suggest that the judges reserved a right to intervene 'If that order is . . . practically a sham, if the purpose behind it is such as to show that the order is not a genuine or *bona fide* order', though in no case was this acted upon.[82]

The Irish Amendment of 1918

On 20 April 1918 the regulation was openly extended by adding a new category of potential detainees: 'any person who is suspected of acting or having acted or of being about to act in any manner prejudicial to the public safety or the defence of the Realm'.[83] This considerably extended the power of detention; for example it now became possible to detain individuals without charge, much less eventual trial, even though there had as yet been no insurrection, so long as they were suspected of planning one. But this amendment only applied where the proclamation of 1916 of a 'special military emergency' was in force, that is in Ireland, where the proclamation had never been revoked. This amendment first explicitly introduced detention on suspicion of 'acts prejudicial', though, as we have seen, detention based on mere suspicion of criminal wrongdoing appears in the Irish legislation of 1871 and 1881, and suspected spies could be detained as 'of hostile associations'. The conception employed, 'acts prejudicial', was to be revived in 1939.

The reluctance of Irish juries to convict in political cases was not the explanation for this change in the law, since in Ireland jury trial for DORA offences had been suspended. The reason was a desire to cripple Sinn Fein. The background was as follows. In February of 1918 the Irish Attorney-General had asked the Home Office a number of questions about the interpretation of the expression 'of hostile associations' in Regulation 14B, in order to see if it could be used against members of Sinn Fein.[84] The Home Office took the view that Sinn Feiners could be detained under the regulation if they had personally associated, directly or indirectly, with the enemy, or belonged to the executive of Sinn Fein at a time when the organization itself had associations with the enemy. But mere past involvement in the Easter rebellion, or advocating a new uprising, would not be enough. Soon after, in March of 1918, there was a crisis on the Western Front, and the British government decided to extend conscription to Ireland. So the War Cabinet, anticipating trouble, decided to

---

[82] The quotation is from Pickford LJ in *R. v. Chiswick Police Station (Superintendent) ex parte Sacksteder* [1918] 1 KB 378. Cf. *R. v. Brixton Prison (Governor) ex parte Sarno* [1916] 2 KB 742 *R. v. Home Secretary ex parte Chateau Thierry (Duke)* [1917] 1 KB 922. The name was an alias.

[83] SRO 1918 No. 462.

[84] HO 144/1494/360163. CAB 24/43 GT 3743 of 20 Feb. 1918, CAB 24/48 GT 4267. Memo by Cave of 18 April 1918.

exile the leaders of Sinn Fein to England under Regulation 14, but leave them at liberty. It was soon realized that it would be impossible to control them effectively in England, and by mid-April a new plan emerged: to intern around 150 of them. But under the existing Regulation 14B this was hardly possible—'at the present moment [i.e. 18 April] it is doubtful whether any connection with the enemy can be proved in the case of most of the Sinn Fein leaders'. The War Office, presumably advised by Kell, suggested a new regulation, giving a virtually unlimited power of detention. The Home Office resisted, proposing an 'acts prejudicial' Regulation 14B, confined to Ireland, and the Home Office view prevailed.

On 12 May a new Viceroy, Lord French, took office. Five days later he announced the discovery of a German plot involving Sinn Fein. It is now thought to have been wholly mythical, and, if contrived, its function was political, not legal, for under the amended regulation the Sinn Fein leaders could have been detained without it, though no doubt it strengthened the case. A hundred Sinn Fein leaders, including seven members of Parliament, were arrested.[85] They were dispersed in a number of prisons in England.[86] They included Eamon de Valera who, with others, escaped from Lincoln.[87] According to Kee, by the end of 1918 there were some 500 persons in custody in Ireland under DORA.[88] This figure, however, includes both persons convicted under DORA regulations and those awaiting trial; the number of 14B detainees, if indeed there were any in Ireland, seems to have been small.[89]

The Restoration of Order in Ireland Act

When the armistice came DORA regulations generally remained in force until the official end of the war in 1921, and detention continued.[90] The authorities were particularly reluctant to give up the new power to detain for suspicion of 'acts prejudicial'. Although the Sinn Feiners of 1918 were

[85] CAB 24/52 GT 4621 has the draft announcement of the plot, 23 May 1918. HO 144/1456/362269 sf. 179 has a nominal roll of 101 on 5 March 1919, of whom by then 12 or 13 had been released, one had died, and 7 had escaped. Others, at least 17, were out on parole. Sf. 184 has a warrant revoking 87 orders, and noting the earlier revocation of 11 orders.

[86] HO 144/1456/362269. The prisons used were Birmingham, Durham, Gloucester, Lincoln, Reading, Usk, and Holloway.

[87] See Lyons, *Ireland*, 393 and Holt, *Protest in Arms*, 162. The latter gives the number detained as over 1,000, but this must include persons in custody in Ireland under DORA. See also C. Younger, *Ireland's Civil War* (London, 1968), 65–6, CAB 23/6 and appendix 23 May 1918, CP 2392 of 31 Dec. 1920.

[88] Key, *Green Flag*, 622.

[89] Ibid. 618 ff. Townshend, *Political Violence*, 324–5, like Kee, is not clear on the legal basis for the mass arrests carried out under Lord French.

[90] SRO 1921 No. 1276, under the Termination of the Present War (Definition) Act 1918. Some DORA regulations were revoked earlier, and others incorporated in legislation to survive the war.

all released in March of 1919, a new group of nationalists, mainly suspected of conspiracy to murder, were interned in Wormwood Scrubs in London in 1919 and caused difficulty by going on hunger strike; after being moved to hospital many escaped, though a few were still there in May of 1920.[91] Legislation in 1920 provided that in Ireland the power of detention would be preserved for one year after the official end of the war, which was not yet fixed.[92]

The troubles in Ireland grew worse. This led the government, on 13 August 1920, to pass the Restoration of Order in Ireland Act (ROIA), a distinct parent act for a new scheme of Irish emergency regulations, which would survive the official ending of the war, and the lapsing of DORA regulations elsewhere. New Irish regulations were introduced on 13 August 1920.[93] Hence Regulation 14B lived on in Ireland in two forms—both as a DORA regulation until the war ended on 31 August 1921 and as one of the new ROIA regulations. In the latter form it covered suspicion of involvement in acts 'prejudicial to the restoration or maintenance of order in Ireland'. As a ROIA regulation it survived until the establishment of the Irish Free State.

Late in 1920 the authorities in Ireland adopted a policy of mass executive detention.[94] By 3 June 1921 there were over 3,000 detainees and a further 1,500 under arrest; there was pressure from the military to house up to 10,000 Irish detainees in England, but the British government, schooled by experience in attempting to hold Irish detainees, was reluctant to cooperate.[95] During this period Anderson, who was later to preside as Home Secretary and Minister for Home Security over executive detention in Britain from 1939 to 1940, was an Under-Secretary in Ireland.[96]

---

[91] HO 144/1496/362269 sf. 179. CAB 23/8 12 (199) App. IV (1), 8 (19) App. IV, CAB 23/21 27 (20) 8, 31 (20) 3, 33 (20) App. II, CAB 24 (98) CT 678, 695. By May of 1920 out of 225, 77 had escaped, and only 13 were left.

[92] The War Emergency Laws (Continuance) Act 10 & 11 Geo. V, c. 5.

[93] SR & O 1920 No. 1530. The first 66 regulations were DORA regulations in force in Ireland on 20 August 1920, subject to some modification (essentially substituting the function of restoring order in Ireland for that of protecting against foreign enemies). Regulations 67–84 were special to Ireland.

[94] See C. Townshend, *The British Campaign in Ireland 1919–1921* (Oxford, 1975).

[95] *Parl. Deb.* H.C. Vol. 138 c.2023, 1270; 143: 2316. CAB 23/6 47 (21) 3 2 June 1921, CAB 24/123 CP 2996. I suspect figures quoted by some writers.

[96] There are papers in CO 904/188. Sir John Anderson (1882–1958), later Lord Waverley, was one of the more remarkable administrators of the first half of this century. There is a saint's life by J. W. Wheeler-Bennett, *John Anderson, Viscount Waverley* (London, 1962). See also P. Hennessy, *Whitehall* (London, 1989), esp. 559–65. Originally from 1905 Colonial Office (concerned with West Africa); 1920 joint Under-Secretary in Dublin; 1922 Inland Revenue; 1922 Home Office as Permanent Under-Secretary; ran the Irish division (there are papers in CO 739); defeated the General Strike; 1932 Governor of Bengal; both in Ireland and in Bengal he became familiar with detention; those held under Regulation III of the Bengal Ordinance, and called at the time *détenus* rose to some 1,350; see *Parl. Deb.* HC Vol. 276 c.2182 for 10 April 1933. They were, unlike their equivalents nearer home, given an

Most of the Irish detainees were released under the Treaty of 6 December 1921 which established the Irish Free State, though the new Irish government continued to employ detention.[97]

The Reading Presumption of Executive Innocence

During the troubles the British authorities arrested suspects in England and Wales as well as in Ireland, and Irish detainees were also moved to English prisons.[98] These practices generated a number of remarkable cases, two in particular reflecting the strength of the British judicial tradition of faithfully supporting the executive in cases involving security.

R. v. *Governor of Wormwood Scrubs Prison* (1920) was a habeas corpus test case brought by Patrick Foy, a 20-year-old Dublin shop assistant detained in Dublin on 14 January by a DORA 14B order on suspicion of 'acts prejudicial to the public safety and defence of the realm', and held, with others, in Wormwood Scrubs Prison in London.[99] The peace treaty with Germany had been signed on 10 January, five days after the order. Two arguments were put to the court, ironically enough by Sir John Simon. The first was that 'The whole of the Defence of the Realm legislation . . . was directed to the protection of the country from foreign foes during the period of the war. It was not intended to be used for the suppression of rebellion or the preservation of internal order even during the war, and still less at a time when the war was over.' The second was that the 'acts prejudicial' limb of the regulation only applied where the proclamation of 1916 was in force, and since the Easter rebellion was long over and past, it had lapsed. English law does not have a doctrine under which legislation lapses through desuetude, but the position over proclamations is less clear, and this proclamation explicitly related to a particular emergency.

The court's reply was that the war was still officially in progress, and the proclamation had never been revoked. Lord Reading's opinion contains a frank statement of the attitude of mind he brought to the matter in hand: 'It is of course always to be assumed that the executive will act honestly and that its powers will be reasonably exercised.' The Reading

allowance both to cover their own expenses and the costs of maintaining their families. In 1938 MP for the Scottish Universities, and in 1939–40 Home Secretary and Minister for Home Security; from October 1940 Lord President of the Council; and from 1943 Chancellor of the Exchequer.

[97] CAB 23/27 76 (21) 8, J. M. Kelly, *Fundamental Rights in the Irish Law and Constitution* (New York, 1968), 77ff., describes Irish legislation continuing executive detention after independence.

[98] Thus on 31 March 1920 there were 102 DORA detainees in English prisons. *Parl.Deb.* HC Vol. 127 c.1237.

[99] [1920] 2 KB 305, 34 TLR 7, 36 TLR 432. The divisional court comprised the Lord Chief Justice, Lord Reading, Bray, and Avory JJ. See TS 27/85.

Presumption of Executive Innocence has continued to embody the attitude of the judiciary to executive power in such cases. Its application is regularly accompanied by ritual protestations of enthusiasm for civil liberty:

This Court has a sacred duty to preserve the liberty of the subject, and it always inquires into the facts when an application is made which shows an illegal arrest, or illegal detention. In ordinary circumstances, but for the war, it would have been our duty to inquire into and come to a conclusion upon the facts. But we are still in a state of war.

So, sacred duty notwithstanding, Patrick Foy did not secure his liberty.

Worse was to follow in *ex parte Brady* (1921).[100] Edward Brady had worked and lived in England since 1916. On the night of 7–8 June 1921 some telephone wires were cut in Cheshire. One of four men arrested, John Byrne, lodged with Brady.[101] Their room was searched; revolvers, masks, and cutters were found, but no clear evidence of complicity was found. Troup minuted: 'It is a case of suspicion, but I have no doubt the suspicion is well founded.'[102] Brady was the local secretary of the Self-Determination League, a Sinn Fein organization. An order was made under Regulation 14B of the ROIA regulations, and the intention was to move Brady to Ireland. He applied for habeas corpus.[103] His was a test case, for others had been arrested in England in similar circumstances. Behind the scenes there was some nervousness both over Brady's case and over the deportation to Ireland of one Father Dominic, because it was somewhat implausible to claim that shipping Irish revolutionaries back to Ireland could help to restore order in that troubled island. The courts might intervene if the order was a sham, its real purpose being to preserve order in England rather than Ireland.[104]

Surely, his counsel argued, an Act dealing with the restoration of order in *Ireland* could not be interpreted as permitting the detention of individuals in *England*.[105] But the court ruled that the Act did apply in England,

[100] TS 27/140, 37 TLR 854 and 975 as *Brady* v. *Gibb*. See also *The Times* 26 June 1921.

[101] Byrne was convicted and sentenced to 5 years' penal servitude at Birkenhead on 17 July. The other three men were also convicted and imprisoned.

[102] 15 June 1921.

[103] The case was determined on 27 June by the Lord Chief Justice with Shearman and Sankey JJ. The inclusion of the latter in the panel seems bizarre, given his involvement in the Advisory Committee's work.

[104] HO 45/19665 has a memorandum by Sir John Pedder of the Home Office expressing this view, which Anderson agreed; there was nervousness over a decision which might open up review of deportation orders (see note 82 above), especially as the Lord Chief Justice had reserved the right to do so in *ex parte Bressloff* on 23 April 1922. *Parl.Deb.* HC Vol.142 c.1074–5 for 1 June 1921 lists 22 other persons subject to orders at this time.

[105] A number of Parliamentary questions had been asked about the practice—on 8 March 1921 by Lt.-Com. Kenworthy (*Parl. Deb.* HC 139: 264), on 10 March by Mr T. Griffith (139: 682–4), on 6 March by Mr Briant (142: 289), and by Kenworthy on 21 June (142: 1107).

and was upheld by the Court of Appeal on 25 July, though not without a strongly expressed dissent by Lord Justice Scrutton. He acidly distinguished himself from his colleagues. They looked for clear language saying the Act did *not* apply outside Ireland, whereas he looked for clear words that it *did*. He pointed out that according to the view taken by his colleagues:

it is possible to take any person, who like this boy has lived five years in England, to shut him up for an indefinite time without telling him the charge against him, without bringing him to trial, at the uncontrolled discretion of an officer of the executive. In my view such a result should not follow unless the clearest words are used by Parliament. In this case Parliament has not used, in my opinion, clear words.[106]

Thus Scrutton joined the small group of judges whose commitment to liberty went beyond mere rhetoric.

There were two particularly disturbing aspects of this case. An attempt to prosecute Brady failed because the Wallasey Magistrates refused to commit him for trial; this refusal preceded the Court of Appeal hearing, and brought out the weakness of the case against him. Furthermore sending him to Ireland deprived him of the right of jury trial for the supposed offences.[107] In addition the Law Officers had given an opinion that the Act did not legitimate action outside Ireland, and this had been used as an argument against holding Irish prisoners detained under it in England.[108]

The Final Detentions

With the official end of the war on 31 August 1921 executive detention ceased to be possible in mainland Britain under DORA, and with the signing of the Anglo-Irish Treaty of 6 December 1921, and the establishment of the Irish Free State, it might be supposed that detention in *Britain* under ROIA might then have ceased too. But, incredibly, the arrests and detentions continued. Under an agreement with the Irish government the Home Office deported Irish republicans opposed to the Free State government to Ireland to be interned there. An account is given by Harold Scott, then an official at the Home Office. Summoned by the Under-Secretary, Sir John Anderson, 'known to us all as Ja Jehovah, the

---

[106] R. v. *Inspector of Cannon Row Police Station ex parte Brady* 125 LT 344, 126 LT 9, 37 TLR 854 and 975.

[107] He was indeed moved on 2 July and interned in Ballykinder; whether he was ever tried I do not know.

[108] A statement on 10 March (*Parl. Deb.* HC Vol.139: c.682–4) treated the application of the Act in England as obvious and said that the Law Officers had not been consulted. Material in the Treasury Solicitor's file makes it clear that the Attorney was consulted, and the opinion is referred to in CAB 24/125 CP 3082 and 3082A. I have not traced a text.

all wise, the all knowing, the all powerful . . . imperturbable, patient, decisive', he was told that

under orders from the Home Secretary [W. C. Bridgeman] the police had arrested at midnight about eighty Irish extremists who were suspected of plotting against the new Free State government, then only four months old. They had been packed into special trains, sent to Liverpool, where a destroyer was waiting, and deported to Dublin, where they were to be interned in Mountjoy Prison, under special warrants issued by the Home Secretary. 'There's bound to be a fuss over this,' said Sir John.[109]

Indeed there was, and it was not stilled by the fact that the detainees could appeal to a tribunal, presumably an advisory committee, chaired by Mr Justice Lawrence.[110] He was 77 years old, compliant, and about to be appointed Lord Chief Justice as a stopgap; he lasted only a year in the office. Scott, who acted as secretary, notes that the six or so who did appeal were lacking in suitable docility: 'The women in particular were irreconcilable, although the chairman exercised all his charm in an attempt to persuade them to a more reasonable attitude.' In effect what was involved was extradition, but the mechanism was a detention order under Regulation 14B (ROIA), coupled with an administrative instruction that internment was to be in Ireland. Anderson, to his credit, was dubious about the legality of this, but 'Sir Douglas Hogg (later Lord Hailsham) then Attorney-General pooh-poohed our fears and assured the Home Secretary that there was nothing to worry about.'[111]

This gross abuse of power was challenged in habeas corpus proceedings by a detainee, Art O'Brien, and actually upheld by the Divisional Court, where the new Lord Chief Justice, Lord Hewart, sat with the fearsome Avory, and Roche. They were reversed on appeal in *R. v. Secretary of State for Home Affairs ex parte O'Brien*.[112] The regulation had been impliedly repealed when the Irish Free State was established; more generally the Home Secretary could not order people to be detained outside the jurisdiction, where he had no control over what became of them.[113] The government, relying upon quite grotesque arguments, challenged this decision in the House of Lords, but failed. Once a release is ordered in habeas corpus proceedings there is no appeal, but the Crown tried to secure one by not releasing O'Brien.[114] O'Brien was then released, and at

---

[109] H. Scott, *Your Obedient Servant* (London, 1959), 49–52. The order was made on 11 March 1923 and involved about 100 persons; see CAB 23/45 26(23)1. Closed files exist in the Scottish records.   [110] *Parl. Deb.* HC Vol.161 c.1548 and 2097.

[111] 1872–1950. He gave a formal opinion; see *Parl. Deb.* HC Vol.164 c.656 for 17 May 1923. He succeeded Gordon Hewart as Attorney-General.

[112] The judges were Bankes, Scrutton, and Atkin LJJ.

[113] [1923] 2 KB 361, [1923] AC 603. See Sharpe, *Habeas Corpus* 198–9 and 176–7.

[114] By convention the Crown normally complies with court rulings in habeas corpus cases. CRIM 1/235 (closed) lists 7 accused with O'Brien.

once again arrested; he and five others were convicted at the Old Bailey on 4 July 1923 of seditious conspiracy, and he was eventually allowed to finish his term in conditions appropriate for a political prisoner, being released in 1924.[115] O'Brien and another detainee, Arthur Fitzgerald O'Hara, sued for damages, and in the end under the Restoration of Order in Ireland (Indemnity) Act of 1923 the Home Secretary was indemnified and a tribunal was set up, under Lord Justice Atkin, which paid the deportees compensation of over £43,000.[116] Consideration was given to the possible need to continue ROIA in force in England by new legislation, so that the detention of persons like O'Brien in England could continue. A committee under George Talbot KC recommended against this, but favoured modifying the criminal law by increasing powers of search, and setting up an inquisitorial procedure for interrogation. In the event nothing was done.[117] And on this inglorious note executive detention, at least for the time being, passed out of use in the United Kingdom, except of course in Northern Ireland.[118]

---

[115] *Parl.Deb.* HC Vol.176 c.1493 for 24 July 1924.

[116] See ibid. 164: 655 for 17 May 1923 and 169: 252 of 1924. Scott puts the figure at £85,000.

[117] CAB 23/45 26(23)1, 27(23) 3, 29(23)1 HO 45/9665, 9666. The report is Cmd. 2278 of 1924.

[118] The history of detention there is outside the scope of this book. The matter was governed by the Civil Authorities (Special Powers) Acts 1922–1943. Under Regulations 23A and 23B there could be both exclusion, residence, and internment orders. This legislation was supplanted by the Northern Ireland (Emergency Provisions) Act 1973.

3

Emergency Planning between the Wars

The Survival of MI5

For the next sixteen years the United Kingdom was free of executive detention. But MI5, the source of the demand for a power to detain citizens without trial in the name of national security, lived on, and its existence ensured that in any new crisis the practice would be revived.

During the war Kell's and Thomson's organizations had flourished mightily in pursuit of a phantom army of saboteurs and potential spies, and a very small number of real ones.[1] Both contracted once the fighting ended.[2] MI5 had originally been solely concerned with defence security; with the war won it might have seemed to have lost an obvious reason for existence. But in about 1917 new threats providentially arose: bolshevism and pacifism. Both MI5 and Special Branch began to investigate political subversion, principally from bolshevism. Kell called this activity civil security; it had not been a concern outside Ireland since the time of the Chartists.[3] Regular reports were prepared and feature in the Cabinet papers.[4] Since subversion was a domestic matter the institution directly concerned was the Home Office and its police, and from 1919 to 1921 civil security, mainly directed at bolshevism, was handled by Basil Thomson as head of a Home Office Special Intelligence Directorate.[5]

MI5's position improved in October 1921 when Thomson was dismissed.[6] In 1924 there was a reorganization of MI5 about which little is known; probably the Directorate was then disbanded.[7] In October 1931 Kell triumphed by becoming responsible for both defence and civil security. Special Branch became a mere tool of his secret organization, except

---

[1] See above, Ch. 2.

[2] F. H. Hinsley and C. A. G. Simkins, *British Intelligence in the Second World War*, iv (London, 1990), 9. (Hereafter Hinsley and Simkins.)

[3] C. Andrew, ch. 7.

[4] Weekly reports on revolutionary organizations will be found in CAB 24 until the practice of circulating them ended in 1924. See e.g. CAB 23/4 WC 245 (20) 4 Oct. 1917, WC 253 (1) 19 Oct. 1917.

[5] Hinsley and Simkins, 5, citing undisclosed papers; for a fuller account see Andrew, 332–8.   [6] Hinsley and Simkins, 6–7, Andrew, 282–3.

[7] Kell's *Who's Who* entry records him as leaving the Directorate of Military Intelligence as GSO1 in 1924, and being re-employed. Holt-Wilson's entry is similar. See Andrew, 359.

in relation to the Irish. A memorandum by Holt-Wilson says that although the security service, which covered the whole Empire apart from India, was established in 1915, it was not until 1931 that it was

expanded by the government to take over from the civil police forces, hitherto unco-ordinated for this purpose, the supervision of the civil side of the national security service also: thus forming the consolidated Imperial Security Service, with one Central Record Office and Registry for the whole Empire, exclusive of India, and achieving a goal towards which Kell and Holt-Wilson had been aiming for twenty years.[8]

The reason for this reorganization, suggested by Sir John Anderson, then Permanent Under-Secretary at the Home Office, can only be a matter for conjecture. It may have been designed to ensure that the Home Secretary did not become formally responsible for the security service. The official history implies that MI5, though retaining its name as a cover, now came under the Home Office, but this appears to be incorrect. As late as 1943 Anderson, who surely knew, took a different view; in a discussion with the Attorney-General he said 'he took no responsibility for MI5, who were a department of the War Office'.[9] Even this claim was then dubious; MI5's position in the constitutional scheme remained ambiguous, as I expect Anderson wanted it to be. Nobody owned it.

Kell's power was principally based on his archive. By 1925 he, or more directly Holt-Wilson, had card-indexed over 25,000 'suspicious' or 'dangerous' persons. Not all were aliens; in the same spirit as had inspired Regulation 14B, MI5 was not troubled by mere technicalities such as citizenship: 'It is not the nationality by place of birth, or by law, but nationality by blood, by racial interests, and by sympathy and friendship that is taken as the deciding factor in all classifications of possible enemy agents and dangerous persons.'[10] Over the years this sinister archive, indexed on punched cards, grew steadily in size, but surely not in reliability.

Countering Subversion

During the 1920s and early 1930s the activities of the Comintern, both in Britain and in India, continuously alarmed the authorities. Even before

[8] Hinsley and Simkins, 7–8, Andrew, 362 and US Archives Box 3 RG 84 London Embassy Confidential File 711.2–82002B.

[9] TS 27/522. Draft minute by H. C. Belk of a conference of 4 March 1943 on *Greene* v. *Anderson*. Many MI5 officers in wartime held military rank, and may have been paid through the War Office.

[10] Holt-Wilson, quoted Andrew, 241, noting that by the end of the war the Defence Black List comprised 13,500 names; it was after the war called the Precautionary Index. Relying on a document in the US National Archives (RG 165 9944-A-4/5) Andrew, 174, says that by 1917 the card index of Kell's registry contained 250,000 cards, and it held personal files on 27,000 chief suspects.

1931 Kell was putting 'penetration agents' into the Communist Party of Great Britain. According to his biographer it was to run such agents that Charles Maxwell-Knight, whom we shall meet again, was recruited to MI5 in 1925; more probably he was at first simply an agent. Maxwell-Knight joined the British Fascists Ltd. about this time, either as an anti-fascist 'mole', or through conviction, or to obtain information about communists.[11] He became its research officer and, by September 1926, a member of its council.[12] An interest in fascism might not then have caused any difficulty for him with MI5, which largely consisted of former army officers, of whom some could well have been sympathetic to fascism.[13]

In the 1930s MI5 continued to be interested in communists[14] and organizations in which they were influential; one such was the National Council for Civil Liberties, but there is no direct evidence of surveillance by MI5, though Special Branch did report on this organization.[15] It also watched pacifist movements, particularly the Peace Pledge Union, founded in October 1934 by Canon H. R. L. ('Dick') Sheppard, Vicar of St Martin-in-the-Fields.[16] In co-operation with Special Branch it also began to watch the political right; one reason was that clashes between the right and the left began to present serious problems of public order. The principal fascist group was Sir Oswald Mosley's British Union of

[11] See A. Masters, *The Man Who Was M: The Life of Maxwell Knight* (Oxford, 1984), 26–8; he says that Maxwell-Knight worked from 1920 to 1925 in a preparatory school in Putney, presumably Willington School at 5 Colinette Rd. Maxwell-Knight in 1943 (TS 27/522) stated that he had been involved in investigating fascism for 16 years, and an officer of MI5 for 12. See also W. J. West, *Truth Betrayed* (London, 1984), 233, based on HO 283/40.

[12] FO 371/113841/C9800. This lists the other members, who included, in addition to Miss R. Lintorn Orman and her mother, Miss Wedgwood OBE, Gen. Goady, Capt. Turner Coles (Chief of Staff) and Capt. R. Smith (Secretary). See also C108; the Foreign Office were anxious to discourage the formation of an Italian Branch of this organization. The Home Office was taking some interest in the organization, Harold Scott being the official concerned.

[13] Andrew cites PRO 30/69/221 (Ramsay MacDonald MSS letter of 2 Feb. 1924), which suggests some MI5 interest in the fascists in the 1920s.

[14] Hinsley and Simkins, 18–19. HO 45/24834 (1924–9) deals with Peace Organizations as Cover for Communist Activities.

[15] The NCCL was publicly formed in 1934 in response to the introduction of the Incitement to Disaffection Bill, the moving spirits being Robert H. Kidd, D. N. Pritt KC, Neil Lawson, and D. N. Thompson, solicitor to the CPGB; it was communist-inspired but attracted support from non-communists of the left. During the war Kenelm Digby, who had moved the 'King and Country' motion in the Oxford Union, was its legal officer, much assisted by Pritt; HO 45/25462–3 (1934–6, 1936–40); 25463 (1940–41) is under extended closure. Some records are in the University of Hull.

[16] See S. Morison, *I Renounce War: The Story of the Peace Pledge Union* (London, 1962). Prominent founder members included Storm Jameson, Ellen Wilkinson, Donald Soper, George Lansbury, and Siegfried Sassoon; later they were joined by, amongst others, Aldous Huxley, Laurence Housman, Vera Brittain, Bertrand Russell, and Cyril Joad. See Hinsley and Simkins, 20.

Fascists, formed in 1932.[17] Kell's first report was submitted in June of 1934.[18] By October 1935 there was suspicion of finance from Mussolini.[19] Various other small groups of the far right were also being watched, such as the Britons, the Imperial Fascist League, and the Nordic League.[20] Much surveillance simply involved officers of Special Branch openly or discreetly attending public meetings. Little is known about the extent to which MI5 had, by 1939, crossed the line which divides intelligence designed to prevent politically motivated crime on the one hand, and that designed to frustrate political 'subversion' (meaning non-criminal political activity of a radical character) on the other.[21]

Changes in the law may shift this difficult boundary, as some of the Defence Regulations did in the 1939–40 war. MI5 certainly had crossed it in the 1930s; it was then neither a crime nor an act of disloyalty for Mosley to receive finance from Mussolini, yet MI5 investigated this matter.[22] The extent to which MI5 engaged in work which is hard to reconcile with any liberal vision of society remains obscure, and the official history by Hinsley and Simkins does not address the question.

The Size and Structure of MI5

In the 1930s MI5 was a run-down organization on which little money was spent, and many of its problems in 1939 and 1940 stem from this fact. It must have been wholly incapable of checking the massive quantity of material in its archive. It also suffered from a foolish system of recruitment through personal contact, mainly employing retired army officers, none of whom seem to have achieved senior rank before joining. In 1930

---

[17] Hinsley and Simkins, 15, recording a formal decision in November 1933 which took effect in April 1934; the delay is not explained. See R. C. Thurlow, 'British Fascism and State Surveillance 1934–1945' *Intelligence and National Security*, 3 (1986), 79. See below, Ch. 7.

[18] Kell to Scott of the Home Office, 18 June 1934 HO 144/20141/300, cited Andrew, 371. A considerable number of reports on the BUF exist in the public records in classes HO 144, HO 45, and MEPO 2, indexed under 'Disturbances'. See e.g. HO 144/20140–7, 20154, 20710, 21040, 21060–4, 21381, 21429, 22454, HO 45/25385, 25386, 25393, 25895. See generally R. C. Thurlow, *Fascism in Britain: A History, 1918–1985* (Oxford, 1987).

[19] Memo of 27 November 1936 in HO 144/20144 and a Special Branch Report of 2 Nov. 1936 in HO 144/20162. Later material from 1940 is in TS 27/489 and HO 45/25393.

[20] Files on the Imperial Fascist League are in HO 45/24967 (1934–42), and have been devastated by weeding, leaving only 12 subfiles out of 105, and in HO 45/24968 (1945–54). HO 45/25482 (not available) deals with Branches of the Nazi Party and Fascists. HO 144/22454 deals with the Right Club, the Nordic League, the Pro-British Association, the National Citizens Union, and the Nationalist Association. On the Nordic League see also HO 144/21379, 21381. There is material on the Britons in HO 144/21377. See Thurlow, *Fascism in Britain*, ch. 4, who refers to the literature.

[21] See also B. Porter, *The Origins of the Vigilant State: The London Metropolitan Police Special Branch before the First World War* (London, 1987), 178.

[22] See below p. 280.

Kell commanded a staff of only six officers.[23] By 1935 there were fifteen, military or civil; the complete staff of eighty-five included thirty-nine female 'registry queens'.[24] In September 1938 the number of officers had doubled to thirty, and at the outbreak of war there were eighty-three officers and a supporting staff of 253.[25] In 1939 the branch concerned with 'investigating all threats to security' was in the charge of Brigadier O. A. Harker, known as Alan or 'Jasper', and all those who knew him have told me that he was an agreeable person of very limited attainments.[26] His deputy was Captain Guy M. Liddell.[27] It was then known as B division.[28] With the coming of war the organization expanded rapidly, and recruited a considerable number of lawyers, some very talented.[29] But, as we shall see, the service was not afforced soon enough to cope with the demands which were placed upon it.

[23] Andrew, 508; all were retired army officers. In addition there were 6 officers who ran the War Office Constabulary, and no doubt a number of supporting staff.

[24] Kell Papers.

[25] Hinsley and Simkins, 9.

[26] Described in Hinsley and Simkins as formerly of the Indian Police and Deputy Commissioner in Bombay during the war. He is said to have joined MI5 in 1920, but this does not tally with Andrew's account at 508.

[27] 1892–1958. R. Deacon [pseud.], *The Greatest Treason: The Bizarre Story of Hollis, Liddell and Mountbatten* (London, 1989), ch. 5, gives biographical information.

[28] Organizational charts with names of associated individuals are in N. West, *MI5* (London, 1983), and *Mole-Hunt: The Full Story of the Soviet Spy in MI5*, (London, 1987). These are not reliable, missing a reorganization in 1941. In 1939 (Hinsley and Simkins, 10) MI5 had four 'Branches' or 'Divisions'—A (personnel, finance, administration, and registry), B (all threats to security), C (vetting), and D (security of munitions industry and public utilities, and, in wartime, travel control). B branch was elaborately subdivided. The Hinsley and Simkins account tallies with file references on available letters. In 1941 B was confined to counter-espionage; alien control was passed to E, and F took over the fascists and communists, and probably 'counter-subversion' generally. Hinsley and Simkins, 69, note the change in 1941, and imply at 176 that there was another 'counter sabotage' division by 1943. This may have been called W.

[29] They included A. S. D. Albert (Lincoln's Inn), Edward J. P. Cussen (Inner Temple), A. A. Gordon-Clark (the novelist Cyril Hare) and later a County Court judge, James L. S. Hale (Middle Temple), Herbert L. A. Hart (Middle Temple and later Professor in Oxford), B. A. Hill (Gray's Inn), C. M. Hughes (Middle Temple), G. T. Martin (Lincoln's Inn), John C. Maude (Middle Temple and later a County Court judge), Helenus ('Buster') H. P. J. Milmo (later a High Court judge), Sydney H. Noakes (Lincoln's Inn, later a County Court judge), Gonne St C. Pilcher (later a High Court judge), John P. L. Redfern (Lincoln's Inn), A. W. Roskill (Inner Temple; later Chairman of the Monopolies and Mergers Commission), Thomas M. Shelford (Lincoln's Inn, later a bencher), E. Blanshard Stamp (Lincoln's Inn; later a High Court judge), R. W. Stevens (Inner Temple, identification dubious), T. F. Turner (Inner Temple), G. E. Wakefield (Gray's Inn), and W. E. Watson (Gray's Inn, identification dubious). Some other officers were legally qualified, such as Cecil F. J. Liddell (Middle Temple). In 1940 William C. Crocker, a solicitor of Wood Lord and Co., was appointed to carry out a reorganization of MI5, but failed. Andrew, 459, adds Patrick R. J. Barry KC and John F. E. Stephenson (Inner Temple), later judges.

The Imperial Security Service in 1940

In July 1940 an attaché in the US Embassy in London, Harvey Klemmer, briefed by Holt-Wilson, who had just retired, and by other MI5 officers, penned a somewhat credulous memorandum on the Fifth Column in Britain, and the steps being taken to counter it.[30] He recorded: 'One of the major activities of the Security Service is the maintenance in London of a central index of suspicious persons. This index contains the names of every person ever suspected in any part of the world of anti-British activity—a total of 4,500,000 names. The index is freely used by British industry and government departments.' The figure seems incredible; over twenty-eight years more than 3,000 names would have had to be added each week. It could, however, be genuine if it refers only to names indexed, rather than to personal files; even so much of the information can only have been rubbish.[31] There were then between 250 and 300 persons in the service, of whom a hundred were officers rather than supporting staff, organized in four divisions. Klemmer waxed lyrical over the low cunning with which it had been established:

Unknown to the British public, unknown to the newspapers, and unknown even to most of the government officials there has been in existence in this country for 31 years an elaborate organization for the detection and prevention of the activities of foreign governments . . .[32] Officials of the Security Service tell me that the success of the organization has been due primarily to the fact that they have operated in complete secrecy. They declare that no newspaperman has ever discovered the true scope of the organization.

Klemmer adds that the security service is not the same thing as MI5, which exists as a distinct organization: 'The only counter espionage activity which is ever mentioned in the newspapers is known as MI5, which is the Military Intelligence unit of the War Office. Apparently the public is completely unaware of the existence of the super machine of which MI5 is just a cog.'[33] The security service is thus presented as an imperial organization—'an ambitious collaboration of Chiefs of Police from all over the Empire, of representatives of the armed forces, and of officials from the

[30] Box 3 RG 84 London Embassy Confidential File 711.2 – 82002B. Holt-Wilson retired on 11 June 1940.

[31] Wright claimed that in 1955 the number of personal files was about 2 million, and the number in 1940 must have been very much smaller. Personal files used 5-figure numbers—for example the journalist Claud Cockburn's number was PF 41685, and Sir Oswald Mosley's file was PF 48909; repeated for each letter in the alphabet the total capacity would be 2,599,974. If numbers were allocated successively arithmetic suggests that by about 1935 there were over a million files.

[32] Probably a slip for 1931.

[33] Holt-Wilson is quoted—'we are not MI5'. See WO 32/35553 for a War Office intelligence unit which probably closed in 1926.

various government departments'. A set of lecture notes for a staff lecture by Kell, dating from the 1930s, takes the same line. The Defence Security organization is 'labelled for public and official purposes MI5', but the organization of which he was head was not MI5 but 'The Central Security Service', an anonymous organization of an interdepartmental character with no official existence. This had been created by amalgamating Defence Security and Civil Security in 1931 into an organization which was 'more than national, it is Imperial'.[34]

The Role of the Home Office

Although Kell's organization had never been a department of the Home Office, it had long been indirectly controlled by it. Troup's book *The Home Office* explained how the department acquired a supervisory role in spy-catching, Kell's original task; its officials co-ordinated the work of Special Branch, the County and Borough police forces, and MI5. MI5 possessed no executive police power; the Home Office, though claiming the contrary, did. What Troup urbanely called 'co-ordination' probably always involved some conflict between the mandarins of the Home Office and the endlessly suspicious military men of MI5, who were generally of lesser intellectual attainment. Indeed both Kell and Thomson seem to have been rather foolish people, who exaggerated the threats against which they claimed to be protecting the nation; there is evidence of Home Office scepticism and friction both before and during the war.[35] Out of this there developed a 'Home Office view' of its interest in the business. Troup explained this:

Every draft regulation or amendment to a regulation, before it was submitted to the Privy Council, was discussed fully by a standing Committee on which all the departments were represented, and in its deliberations *the Home Office took on itself the burden of defending individual liberty, and agreed, through its representative, to restrictions on liberty only when real necessity could be shown'*. [my italics][36]

This approach also coloured any decision to act or not act on the advice of MI5, so long as power, shared with the Law Officers and Director of Public Prosecutions, lay in the Home Office. The department's role was thus to guard British liberty against the threat presented by other agencies, principally the military men of the intelligence service.

Today when, whatever the reality, the Home Office contrives to appear an illiberal institution, this may appear implausible, but Troup's theory

---

[34] Kell Papers. Cf. notes of a lecture given to outsiders in the Imperial Defence College on 22 October 1935.
[35] See Ch. 2 and a memorandum by J. F. Moyle of 10 November 1917 HO 45/10881/338498.
[36] C. E. Troup, *The Home Office* (London, 1925), 239.

was both influential and persistent. In the Second World War Alexander Maxwell was Permanent Under-Secretary.[37] He inspired great affection in his staff; one well-placed informant has told me that 'it cannot be an offence to tell you about Maxwell [who] was a most humane, thoughtful and nice person—and a great believer in Mill's principles on all questions to do with liberty. He sometimes gave talks to officials about this, I seem to remember.' But the same informant recognized the element of contradiction, going on to say: 'You may say—if he was such a believer in liberty, how did he come to be involved in detaining all those BU people—many of whom were no danger to national security?'[38] It is a point to which we shall need to return. But much the same view of Maxwell is to be found in an article by Lord Allen of Abbeydale, who later succeeded him, and knew him well:

During the darkest days of the war he stuck up for liberal ideals and the rights of individuals in a way the world will never know. Heaven knows, enough people were locked up under Defence Regulation 18B and the Aliens Order, but the waves of panic which swept over Whitehall from time to time could have led to more arbitrary and sweeping measures if it had not been for Maxwell's gentle but firm powers of persuasion.[39]

Allen called the Home Office 'the last bastion of liberty'. A minute of February 1945, probably written by Maxwell, is quoted by Hinsley and Simkins: '[MI5] have arrived by different routes at a belief very like our own, namely that any interference with personal or political liberty must on grounds both of principle and expediency be regarded as an exceptional course.'[40] Maxwell was indeed the inheritor of a tradition. Newsam, who became Assistant Under-Secretary in charge of security in 1940, and succeeded Maxwell in 1948, appears also to have maintained the same tradition, though perhaps with less enthusiasm.[41] I am told by one who knew him that he had other preoccupations, including a commitment to keeping the minister out of trouble at all costs; given the nature of the work of the Home Office, this quality is much prized there. This tallies

[37] 1890–1963. Educated Plymouth College and Christ Church, Oxford; entered the Home Office 1904; private secretary to all Secretaries of State until 1924, when he became an assistant secretary. From 1928 with the Prison Commissioners, working with Alexander Patterson; 1932 Deputy Under-Secretary; Permanent Under-Secretary 1938–48. *DNB* entry by Duncan Fairn; *Times* obituary 2 July 1963; account in Viscount Templewood, *Nine Troubled Years* (London, 1954).
[38] Letter of 4 August 1988.
[39] 'In State Service: Reflections of a Bureaucrat', published by the Royal Institute of Public Affairs in *The Home Office: Perspectives on Policy and Administration. Bicentenary Lectures, 1982* (London, 1983), 27. Philip Allen succeeded to Maxwell's office 1966–74.
[40] p. 176.
[41] See below p.398.

with some of his views on Regulation 18B. He had a reputation amongst younger Civil Servants, however, as something of a reactionary.[42]

Preparation for Crisis

With the experience of the wartime system of government under DORA it was assumed that any future crisis would be handled in a similar way by a scheme of emergency powers, and not by relying upon either common law necessity or martial law.[43] Once Ireland ceased to be a problem a War Office committee began to prepare in a leisurely way for the next conflict.[44] In 1924 responsibility passed to the War Emergency Legislation Sub-Committee of the Committee of Imperial Defence, under Lord Chancellor Cave.[45] The Home Office was represented by Newsam, and MI5 by Holt-Wilson. By December 1923 a draft regulation reflected MI5's view, which was that the power of detention should be greatly expanded.[46] It added to the old 14B wide definitions of 'hostile origin' and 'hostile associations'. 'Hostile origin' was to include anyone whose parents had ever owed allegiance to a foreign state, or anyone who had habitually associated with such a person. 'Hostile associations' was to include those who had violated any of the general defence regulations, or even associated with those who had done so. The Home Office opposed this appalling proposal, preferring the categories used to remain undefined.[47] So the definitions were removed, but the draft was modified to include persons 'of hostile sympathies'.[48] This explicitly approved the interpretation earlier placed on the original 14B; first a power is covertly extended and, when the power is next conferred, the text is altered to legalize the extension for the future. A Home Office memorandum of rather later

---

[42] Newsam (1893–1964) was the subject of a notable clerihew by J. M. Ross of the Home Office: Sir Frank Newsam, | Affected to look gruesome, | Which carried great weight, | With successive Secretaries of State. Born in Barbados; *DNB* entry by Austin Strutt describes him as 'good looking in a rather Latin way', referring to his supposed partially African descent; MC in the war; entered Home Office 1920; private secretary to Anderson (then Permanent Under-Secretary) 1924–8. Much involved in the preparation of civil defence; regional officer; returned to the Home Office in 1940. A more decisive man than Maxwell, his desk was cleared by early each evening; Maxwell would worry away, surrounded with papers, until late at night.

[43] See W. K. Hancock and M. M. Gowing, *British War Economy* (London, 1949), 83–8.

[44] CAB 52/2 WEL 7.

[45] CAB 26/1 and 2 (Papers of the Home Policy Committee). See N. Stammers, *Civil Liberties in Britain during the Second World War: A Political Study* (London, 193), See CAB 52/1–7, in particular CAB 52/3 WEL (i.e. War Emergency Legislation), 99 ('Report of the Interdepartmental Committee on the Emergency Powers (Defence) Bill') of 21 April 1937. A note in CAB 52/4 summarizes the history, also in HO 45/20206.

[46] Numbered VI-8.

[47] CAB 52/2 WEL 25 (the Home Office observations on the draft). It was now regulation 26 (see WEL 17).

[48] CAB 52/2 WEL 40.

date, 11 December 1936, bluntly explained the new and of course secret policy: 'It would be necessary that the Defence Bill should confer on the Home Secretary an arbitrary power to intern, without trial and for an indefinite period, persons (whether British or alien) whose sympathies were such that if they were allowed to remain at large they would be likely to impede the war effort.'[49]

The 1924 subcommittee never presented a final report. When the Italian–Abyssinian conflict of 1935 suggested that war might not be so far away, a new *ad hoc* interdepartmental committee was established. Sir Claud Schuster, head of the Lord Chancellor's Department, was chairman.[50] Schuster's committee, though reporting to the Committee of Imperial Defence, was organized and serviced by the Home Office. Harold Kent has given an account of the committee; typically he presents MI5 in a ludicrous light.[51]

In March of 1936, in response to Hitler's move into the Rhineland, it was instructed to prepare a new code for a major emergency.[52] Its first report explained that even Regulation 31 did not satisfy MI5. In a future conflict it might be essential to detain citizens even though they did not sympathize with the enemy. For, the committee explained, 'there is a serious danger that attempts to impede the war effort of the nation might be made by persons actuated, not by sympathy with the enemy, but by "internationalist" affiliations or by disinterested opposition to the war'.[53] What MI5 now wanted was to be able to detain people simply as an instrument of political control, whether they were disloyal or not. But why should not such dangerous people be arrested and tried for criminal offences, either under regular law or under emergency regulations? The answer was air raids: 'if this country is subjected to frequent and large scale attacks from the air, the need for swift and effective action against persons who are suspected of mischievous activities will be far greater than in the last war'. In reality the German air force was quite incapable

[49] CAB 52/4. Probably by Newsam.
[50] 1869–1956. *DNB* article by Albert Napier; one of the most effective Civil Servants of his time; an alpinist and skier of ability. Educated Winchester and New College; barrister Inner Temple; joined Civil Service in 1895; the Lord Chancellor's Department 1915 as Clerk of the Crown, and Permanent Secretary to the Lord Chancellor. Sir Harold S. Kent in his *In on the Act: Memoirs of a Law Maker* (London, 1979), 35–6 describes him as 'a small puckish man, with bright eyes and the complexion of a russet apple acquired over many years as a leading light in the Alpine Club and the British Ski Club. He was a law unto himself and had acquired the status of a legend . . . Hewart would refer to Schuster as "the hidden hand".' After leaving the department in 1944 he became head of the legal branch of the Control Commission in Austria. Baron Schuster in 1944. Dr P. Polden's *Guide to the Records of the Lord Chancellor's Department* (London, 1989), 26–32 has an account of his work.
[51] Kent, *In on the Act*, ch. 10, recording that the draftsman involved was J. St C. Lindsay.
[52] CAB 52/5. In 1937 it was reconstituted as a standing War Legislation Subcommittee of the Committee of Imperial Defence.
[53] Para 5; HO 45/20206 and CAB 52/4.

of mounting such attacks, but it was then received truth that a future war would begin in this way, and fear was enhanced by accounts of the bombing of Guernica, much publicized by the left.[54]

The Genesis of Regulation 18B

In consequence Schuster's committee favoured an entirely unrestricted power of detention. The draft (now Regulation 20) read: 'The Secretary of State, if satisfied with respect to any particular person, that with a view to preventing him acting in any manner prejudicial to the public safety, or the defence of the realm, it is necessary to do so, may make and order:– . . .' The order might be that the person 'be detained in such place, and under such conditions, as the Secretary of State may from time to time determine'. Alternatively it might impose lesser restrictions: a prohibition or restriction on the possession or use of any specific article—presumably a weapon, a wireless set, a vehicle, a camera, a pigeon, or whatever—or a restriction on employment or business, or over association or communication with any other person, or even 'in respect of his activities in relation to the dissemination of news or the propagation of opinions'. Here indeed was 'an arbitrary power'.

This draft expressed the spirit of arrogant self-confidence which, as a consequence of the immense extension of bureaucratic power during the first war, had come to infect the higher Civil Service. Mainly it appears in the minutes and notes one can read on Civil Service files; it was publicly proclaimed in the evidence given by Civil Servants to the Committee on Ministers Powers, established in 1929.[55] All the public needed to do was to give the Civil Servants ample legal powers, and trust them in accordance with the Reading Presumption of Executive Innocence to act with good sense as benevolent despots. The function of law in this scheme of thought was simple enough: it was to be the instrument with which the rule of law was to be abolished, to be replaced by executive discretion, exercised by gentlemen, in secret, in pursuance of the public interest.

The Schuster Report was accepted by the Committee of Imperial Defence in July of 1937.[56] There was no further consideration of the scope of executive detention until after the outbreak of war, and it was essentially Schuster's Regulation 20 which was, by devious ways to be explained, to become law as Regulation 18B on 1 September 1939. But as originally accepted the regulation had made some concessions to the spirit of legality.[57] There was to be an advisory committee, chaired by a real judge, and a Home Office memorandum of 12 October 1938 proposed that

---

[54] See ch. 1, 'The Expected Holocaust', in T. Harrison, *Living through the Blitz* (London, 1976).
[55] Discussed in Ch. 4 below.   [56] HO 45/20206.   [57] HO 45/20206.

two Members of Parliament would serve with the judge. In addition the Secretary of State was to make procedural rules for the committee, and these were to provide a right to legal representation before it. But these concessions were to go by the time the regulation became law.

The care of the regulations now passed to a subcommittee of the War Legislation subcommittee, chaired by Sir Ernest Holderness, a baronet and, I am told, 'a lovely man', who was an Assistant Secretary at the Home Office; this asserted increased Home Office control.[58] Holderness and his colleagues met several times in 1938 and 1939, MI5 being represented by Holt-Wilson, and made a number of amendments to the code.[59] The express right to legal representation was removed; the impetus here surely came from MI5. This change was glossed over slightly disingenuously by saying that the committee ought to be allowed, as in the earlier war, to regulate its own procedure. A new right was conferred—to make objections to the committee. This was cosmetic; there would of course have been no point in having a committee unless objections could be made to it. A further cosmetic change was that the Home Secretary was given a *duty* to inform the detainee of this right. Regulation 20, together with the rest of the code, remained in storage, renumbered as Regulation 24 of the printed drafts of 1938 and of 31 March 1939.[60] In 1939, between the printings of 22 and 29 August, it was further modified.[61] The committee was no longer to be chaired by a real judge or former judge. No papers I have traced explain why this change was made, but later papers enable us to guess.[62] The status of judges was at odds with the advisory character of the committee. Less exalted chairmen would enhance the power of the Home Office in any case of conflict; possibly there had been problems in the earlier war. The change may have been in part *ad hominem*, for about this time it was decided to make Sir Walter Monckton chairman. Another development was a decision not to appoint Members of Parliament to the committee, again no doubt because they might be troublesome, as may have happened during the earlier war.[63] By selecting persons outside Parliament the secrecy of the system would be enhanced, and the Civil Service policy of providing that institution with as little information as possible furthered.

---

[58] Sir Ernest W. E. Holderness (1890–1968); son of an ICS official; the second baronet; uninformative entry in *Who Was Who*.

[59] CAB 52/7. The Subcommittee was interdepartmental with representatives of the Admiralty, War Office, Air Ministry, Scottish Office, and the Board of Trade. Parliamentary Counsel (J. St C. Lindsay) also attended, and the secretary was a Home Office official, J. M. Ross.

[60] In CAB 52/7.   [61] HO 45/25502.

[62] HO 45/25114 (difficulties over Birkett remaining Chairman after his appointment to the Bench). See also HO 45/25114/863686/23 (possible successor to Birkett).

[63] *Parl. Deb.* HC Vol. 80 c.224–5.

The Emergency Powers Bill

The parent Emergency Powers (Defence) Bill also remained in storage. Unlike DORA it explicitly spelt out the power to make regulations providing 'for the detention of persons whose detention appears to the Secretary of State to be expedient in the interests of public safety or the defence of the realm'. Schuster, respecting constitutional propriety, was not happy with *R. v. Halliday ex parte Zadig*, though it was a binding legal decision.[64] Consequently he thought that so severe a power should be expressly authorized by the parent Act.

This made it unlikely that Parliament would pass the bill in peacetime, except in conditions of crisis. There was a similar problem over the regulations. They could remain secret until the bill became law, and they could become law whilst still secret. But they then had to be published, and 'laid before' Parliament, where they could be annulled by a procedure known as 'moving a prayer'. Now many of the regulations made no serious inroads into civil liberty, but some certainly did, as did Regulation 24, and those which restricted industrial action and the expression of opinion.[65] Thus one regulation (eventually Regulation 39B) made it an offence 'to endeavour to influence, orally or otherwise, public opinion in a manner likely to be prejudicial to the efficient prosecution of the war or the defence of the realm', and another (Regulation 39A) made it an offence to 'endeavour to cause disaffection amongst persons engaged . . . in His Majesty's service', going even further than the highly controversial Incitement to Disaffection Act of 1934. The officials feared that such regulations might arouse opposition serious enough to imperil the whole scheme.

Yet it was the assumption in Whitehall that war could only be carried on in conditions in which civil liberty had, as a matter of law, been abolished, and the executive armed with even more draconian powers than had existed in the earlier war. I do not know of any paper setting out in a coherent form arguments in favour of this belief; it was simply taken for granted. Behind it presumably lay a fear that the horrors of the trenches had produced a state of affairs, symbolized by the celebrated King and Country motion in the Oxford Union in 1933, in which it might be extremely difficult for the government to conduct war at all. The solution was coercive powers to crush dissent, powers wholly incompatible with any vision of a democratic state. When war really came the official fears were found to be wholly misplaced, but by then it was too late to dismantle their legacy; hence the legal regime under which Britain fought the war was that of a totalitarian state.

[64] CAB 52/4 (Committee of Imperial Defence on 1 July 1937). The House of Lords regarded itself as being absolutely bound by its own decisions until 1966.
[65] For discussion see Stammers, *Civil Liberties*, 14–15.

The anxiety of the officials was particularly troubling because it was generally agreed that a number of emergency powers would be needed the very instant war broke out; thus Kell at a meeting on 5 November 1937 said that it might be essential for MI5 to act 'within a few hours after the outbreak of war'.[66] Nevertheless on 5 April 1938 the Committee of Imperial Defence, after some vacillation, decided against introducing the Emergency Powers Bill in time of peace; hence there could be no emergency regulations in force on the outbreak of war.[67]

Even dealing with the more immediate problems caused by the IRA was not a simple matter. On 12 January 1939 a bombing campaign began, and by 24 July there had been 127 incidents.[68] So in July 1939 the Prevention of Violence (Temporary Provisions) Act allowed the Home Secretary to expel IRA suspects, or prohibit them from entering the country; the Act did not, however, apply to those who had been long-term residents in the United Kingdom.[69] But since this legislation was introduced in peacetime and conferred powers directly, it is noticeable that they were quite strictly circumscribed in the bill itself. They had to be acceptable to the Commons, and contrast strikingly with the arbitrary detention power soon to be conferred on the Home Secretary under delegated legislative powers. And in spite of the care given to making the bill acceptable, there was considerable opposition in the Commons, led by Dingle Foot.[70]

The Management of Parliament

As the European situation deteriorated the problem of how to bring the emergency regulations into force became pressing, and in July of 1939 a special *ad hoc* Cabinet committee recommended that although the bill should not be introduced until an appropriate state of emergency existed, this would precede the actual outbreak of war; this was accepted.[71] But in a surprise attack, or if an emergency developed when Parliament was not sitting, or during an election, the code would still not be in force when hostilities began. Maxwell devised a partial solution, developing an idea mooted in 1938. This was to divide the regulations into those vitally needed the very moment hostilities began, and those which could wait. The Cabinet would authorize the first to be acted upon as if they were legally in force as soon as an emergency developed, and an appropriate

[66] CAB 52/4.   [67] CAB 52/5.
[68] T. P. Coogan, *The I.R.A.* (London, 1990), 158–73. This culminated in the Coventry bombing of 25 August, for which two men were executed on 7 February 1940. The campaign ended by March.
[69] 2 & 3 Geo. VI, c. 50. There could also be a registration order, requiring registration with the police.
[70] See below p. 58   [71] CAB 27/661, CAB 23/99 (22 (39) 3).

Order in Council would be passed at once; a session of the Privy Council could be organized at extremely short notice, though if the Monarch was away from London, say in Balmoral for the grouse, or Sandringham for the pheasants, some travelling would be needed. This would be coupled to a Royal Proclamation exhorting the populace to a willing obedience. Fourteen thousand copies of a poster were printed and supplied to the 181 police forces.[72] It read:

The King has made a Proclamation declaring that a state of imminent national danger exists and enjoining compliance with any regulations, orders, directions and instructions which may be issued by, or on behalf of, His Majesty for securing the public safety and the defence of the realm. It is therefore the duty of all persons concerned to comply with any such regulations, orders, directions and instructions, and to give every assistance within their power to persons acting on behalf of His Majesty in carrying out measures of national defence.

Then the parent Emergency Powers (Defence) Bill would be introduced, Parliament, if need be, being recalled. It would backdate its effect to before the passage of the Order in Council. Thus would the code be retrospectively validated, and for good measure there could also always be an Indemnity Act.

This ingenious perversion of legalism troubled the delicate conscience of the Lord Chancellor, Lord Maugham.[73] He suggested an alternative plan: a short, one-clause, widely drawn parent bill, to be presented in peacetime after all, which would authorize more or less anything. This silly idea was magisterially demolished by Sir Granville Ram, the First Parliamentary Counsel, who pointed out that it wholly failed to meet the difficulties which had generated the more elaborate plan in the first place. Maxwell's scheme was approved by the Cabinet on 17 May 1939.[74] But the Lord Chancellor dissented: 'As Lord Chancellor and as a Judge, he could not approve a procedure which was wholly illegal. He thought that only the most absolute necessity could excuse the King being advised to approve Orders in Council which were *ultra vires*. While certain circumstances might excuse wholly illegal acts, they did not, in his view, justify them.' It was agreed to ponder further in the hope of avoiding the problem, and there the matter rested for the moment.

So the code was divided. Code A comprised the regulations needed on the outbreak of war, but excluded the grosser violations of civil liberty. It was essential to conceal the fact that Code A was merely the first instalment; it was also necessary to avoid any administrative confusion arising

[72] Copies in HO 45/25012. See also CAB 24/286 CP 112 (39) referring to the 4th Report of the War Legislation Sub-Committee CID 1456–3.
[73] CAB 52/6 and 23/100, CM (39) 39, discussed in Stammers, *Civil Liberties*, 11.
[74] CAB 23/99 28 (39) Conc. 8 and CAB 23/100 36 (39) Conc. 1 of 5 July 1939.

from renumbering when the second code appeared.[75] So regulations in Code A were simply numbered in the normal way, as Regulation 18, or 19, or whatever. Code B contained the more sensitive provisions, and renumbering of Code A was avoided by numbering Code B regulations with a letter added to their numbers: an 'A', 'B' or 'C', and so on. Thus in the latest print of the draft regulations I have located Regulation 19 (in Code A) concerned control over the movement of ships and aircraft, an innocuous matter, but 19A (in Code B) concerned the more delicate matter of control over the movement of persons, and 19B (also in Code B) the even more delicate matter of internment. An incidental advantage of the scheme was that administrative circulars and forms dealing with Code A could be widely distributed in advance; even if information about Code A leaked out, no great harm would result.

There remained the problem of how Kell's immediate and supposedly essential arrests could be made. Anderson (and probably his predecessor) would have been prepared to authorize them illegally before the detention power existed. No doubt some would have been arrested on holding charges, and, given a little obstruction and the law's delays, a detainee would have found it impossible to secure release until a week or two had passed.

The Outbreak of War

As matters turned out the illegal Order in Council was never passed, the Home Secretary did not order illegal arrests, and the poster never saw the light of day.[76] On 22 August the Cabinet decided to recall Parliament, which had been adjourned from 4 August to 3 October. In the air of crisis then obtaining the Emergency Powers (Defence) Bill was passed on 24 August with little trouble.[77] Mr E. Harvey, Member for the English Universities, attempted but failed to make a High Court judge the final arbiter of decisions to intern. Sir Samuel Hoare, the Home Secretary, resisted: 'this must be an executive act'. So the bill became law. During its passage through the Commons Sir Samuel Hoare made it clear that the government felt it to be essential that some Defence Regulations should be in force before hostilities broke out, if indeed they were to do so. Hoare's speech on 24 August was much less than frank. It includes this

[75] HH 50/87 (Scottish Record Office) has a memo by Lindsay on the numbering difficulties.
[76] The only proclamation made at the outbreak of war was one specifying what articles would be treated as contraband of war.
[77] See *Parl. Deb*. HC Vol. 351 c.63–108 and HL Vol. 114 c.895–903. The Cabinet decision is in CAB 23/100 (41 (39) 5). The problem of likely opposition to the width of the powers is discussed by the Cabinet in CAB 23/99 (22 (39) 3 and 1). See also CAB 23/99 (28 (39) 8), CAB 23/100 (36 (39) 1), (39 (39) 13).

dishonest assurance: 'Neither I nor any member of the government can tell the House to-day what, supposing we were involved in war, would be the full powers that we should require to meet circumstances many of which we cannot at present define.' Nobody could guess from this that Codes A and B were already in print, the product of years of careful but secret deliberation in Whitehall. All that was said was that there was no intention to introduce regulations dealing with civil liberty, in particular detention, in peacetime, a discreet reference to the existence of Code B. The complete code was firmly labelled 'Secret', its existence known only to ministers and Civil Servants. Nothing so brings out the contempt for Parliament which, by 1939, had come to pervade the executive and Civil Service.

With the parent Act in force, Code A was brought into effect at a meeting of the Privy Council at 6 p.m. on 24 August.[78] On 26 August the Cabinet decided not to initiate the next step, called in the War Book the 'precautionary stage'.[79] So Code B remained in storage. In the last days of August hope of reaching some form of settlement with Germany rapidly faded away, and at about 10 a.m. on 1 September the Home Secretary decided that Code B should be brought into force; the Cabinet, which met at 11.30, agreed. It became law at a Privy Council held at 1 p.m. on the day Germany invaded Poland.[80] Last-minute modifications meant that Regulation 19B was renumbered as 18B. Its curious name thus reflects the devious operations of Parliamentary management which preceded its passage into law.

Kell's arrests could now, with no legal impropriety, be carried out. Indeed, for all the regulation had to say on the matter, anyone at all to whom the Home Secretary took exception could now be locked up for an indefinite period.

---

[78] SRO 1939 No. 927. Some regulations in the Code as most recently circulated internally were excluded; they do not here concern us.
[79] CAB 23/100 43 (39).   [80] CAB 23/100 (47 (39) 9).

4

The Commons Revolt

The Early Detentions

The Home Office division concerned with making detention orders was G2, under Holderness. Enemy aliens were the chief concern.[1] A few belonged to the Auslands Organization, the overseas organization of the Nazi Party, or were associated with such organizations as the German Labour Front. In 1937 the Auslands Organization had 300 members, and 2,000 'contacts', presumably persons on a mailing list.[2] For the 19,000 or so resident Italians there was the Fascio, with branches in towns with an Italian colony; it served in part as a social club, but MI5 viewed it and the Auslands Organization with suspicion, and wanted both closed down.[3] There were a number of German agents in Britain in the late 1930s, though by the time the war came the active numbers were not in double figures. Some Welsh Nationalists may have been approached in the hope that they would be prepared to assist Germany in return for independence, though it is hard to believe that they could have been gullible enough to take this seriously.[4] MI5 inevitably, though wrongly, suspected

---

[1] There are organizational charts in C. E. Troup, *The Home Office* (London, 1925) and F. Newsam, *The Home Office* (London, 1954), the second being barely intelligible; it is difficult to follow the changes. G division had originally dealt with the Irish, the Channel Islands, and the Isle of Man. On 13 March 1940 (Home Office Circular 11/40) responsibility for 18A and 18B and Irish deportations passed from G to B division (B1 and B2, with Prestige, Tudor, and Rumbelow) under Newsam, with Holderness retaining subversive organizations in G. Holderness handed over to A. S. Hutchinson on 16 May (HOC 24/40); E. N. Cooper ran B1 (detention of non-enemy aliens) and H. H. C. Prestige B2 (18B). B3 dealt with the administration of internment in camps. The increased use of detention caused confusion and on 10 June 1940 B division became concerned only with aliens, and 18B administration was passed back to G2, the principal officials being W. G. Jagelman, R. H. Rumbelow, R. F. Shepherd, and W. B. Lyon (HOC 40/40). Those involved over subversive organizations in G included C. Ross and R. S. Wells. See HO 333/4, incomplete collection of internal circulars.
[2] Hinsley and Simkins, 14 ff.   [3] HO 45/25385.
[4] N. West, *MI5* (London, 1983), 214–26, 401, J. C. Masterman, *The Double Cross System in the War of 1939 to 1945* (New Haven, Conn., 1972), 87. L. Mosley, *The Druid* (London, 1982), claims Gwyn Evans from the Welsh Patagonian Community was a successful agent with the code name DRUID. The book contains serious inaccuracies; I am indebted to Professor Daffyd Jenkins for advice on it. L. Farago, *The Game of the Foxes* (London, 1971), 163 has a similar story, and 'G.W.', in J. C. Masterman as a Welsh Nationalist saboteur

that there might be a considerable but unidentified espionage organization.[5]

A few active members of the Nazi Party were deported in April 1939; they included Dr R. G. Roesel, who ran the Anglo-German Information Service, and was the London representative for Goering's *National Zeitung*, O. G. Karlowa, leader of the Nazi Party in London, E. P. Himmelmann of the Auslands Organization and Fräulein Johanna Wolf, Secretary of the German Labour Front in Britain.[6] Pressure for this came from MI5, which suspected that Roesel was a Gestapo agent and acted as a link with Mosley's fascist party. At the same time Sir Robert Vansittart, official head of the Foreign Office and extreme Germanophobe, wanted to stop the import of propaganda in the form of *News from Germany*. Maxwell, typically liberal, opposed this: 'the view taken for the last 150 years in this country has been that in the long term it is better to allow freedom for the publication of poisonous lies than to give the government the power or the duty of deciding what is truth and what is falsehood and what is poisonous and what is medicinal'. But his advice was not followed by Hoare, then Home Secretary. Somewhat earlier, in 1937, five journalists suspected of spying for Germany had been expelled.[7] The Home Office possessed an executive power to deport aliens, and the propaganda was intercepted by the Post Office under a warrant issued on 6 July.

Once war came enemy aliens could be detained under the royal prerogative, and citizens, it was hoped, under 18B, which could also be used when citizenship was doubtful. The Home Office took the view that aliens who were stateless, but had long lived in Germany or Austria, and aliens who had long lived there, but recently acquired some other nationality, might also be detained with propriety under 18B.[8] From 1938 the settled Home Office policy was to oppose any plan for the general internment of enemy aliens if war came, but there was fear of public pressure against this policy. So accommodation for 18,000 detainees was earmarked in April of 1939.[9] MI5, under Home Office pressure, reduced its demands

who became a double agent, is identified by West, p. 218, as Gwilym Williams, a former Inspector of the Swansea Police.

[5] Farago, *The Game of the Foxes* (based on captured Abwehr records; without references), claims that there were 235 agents at some uncertain date in 1939; presumably he includes many German officials. There were some trials in 1939, as of Donald O. R. Adams (Oliver J., 25 September 1939, 7 years, Official Secrets Act, *The Times*, 26 September, CRIM 1/1120 (depositions)), and Joseph Kelly (19 May 1939, 10 years, stealing plans, *The Times*, 20 May). Hinsley and Simkins, 12, say 4 agents had been convicted and one deported, and at 41 that only 6 agents from the Hamburg Abwehr were known to be working in Britain in 1939.

[6] There were in April 61 German officials in London. *Daily Herald* and *The Times* for 2 May 1939 and CAB 23/98 CC 13 (39) and 14 (39) 4 and 30 (37) 7. West at 112 lists five other agents expelled about the same time; Hinsley and Simkins, 15, give a figure of 9.

[7] HO 45/25471. For the 5 journalists and German retaliation see PREM 1/226, referring to Cabinet Conclusions 30 (37) Conc. 7.

[8] HO 45/25758/863044/4 (memo of 22 September 1939).

for immediate detention to 524 (including 18Bs).[10] On 13 September only 124 had been arrested.[11] After four months 554 enemy aliens had been detained; the number of Germans and Austrians in Britain was then around 60,000 to 75,000, many of course being refugees.[12]

Most requests for 18B orders came from MI5, though the Police War Instructions laid down that Special Branch could originate requests in IRA cases. A memorandum by Norman Kendal, its head, notes: 'The Home Office view, and obviously the right one, is that this [the regulation] does not apply to a person who is a nuisance because of his criminal tendencies. In other words, 18B would never be used to intern a British subject who has a criminal record, however bad, and nothing else. There must be allied to the criminal record some political taint.'[13] MI5's requests for orders were very modest. On 16 January 1939 Harker submitted a list naming fifty men and two women.[14] Kell himself wrote to Holderness on 16 May: 'We have at present a small number of British subjects whom I consider it essential should be put under lock and key immediately on the outbreak of hostilities.' Kell wanted orders signed in advance, and held by MI5. But Maxwell resisted; with scrupulous respect for the ideal of legality, he thought it improper to ask the Home Secretary to sign orders 'under a power which does not at present exist'. And Maxwell, conceiving of his department as the watchdog for liberty, wanted to retain control.

On 2 June it was agreed that MI5 would submit requests to Maxwell, with short notes on the individuals concerned; these would go to the minister for approval, and orders would be prepared, but not signed, in advance. On 22 August twenty-three names were submitted.[15] Special Branch's IRA list contained eighteen names; some may have been covered by the Act of 1939. By 14 October IRA 18B orders had been made and eight individuals had 'voluntarily' returned to Ireland when offered this alternative to detention.[16] Prepared orders were signed on 1 September, when Code B passed into law.

[9] P. and L. Gillman, 'Collar the Lot!' How Britain Interned and Expelled its Wartime Refugees (London, 1980), 25, B. Wasserstein, Britain and the Jews of Europe 1939–1945 (London, 1979), 83–4, Hinsley and Simkins, ch. 2., HO 144/21258/700463/4, N. Stammers, Civil Liberties in Britain during the Second World War (London, 1983), ch. 2.
[10] Hinsley and Simkins, 29, record that MI5 was severely critical of the Home Office.
[11] HO 45/25114. 384 had left the country, 8 were in Ireland, one was in hospital, and 7 had become British subjects (possibly later held under 18B). Cf. Hinsley and Simkins, 31, referring to an earlier list.
[12] Parl. Deb. HC Vol. 356 cc. 1270–1 for February 1940.   [13] MEPO 2/6433.
[14] HO 45/25758/863044 (list not in the file).
[15] HO 45/25114/863686 (list not in the file). Hinsley and Simkins say that 19 were known or suspected spies, or 'of hostile origin', and 3 (one being Joyce) were simply 'pro-Nazi'.
[16] HO 45/25750/863014/1.

Two individuals on MI5's list were by then in Germany; one was William Joyce, later identified as the infamous but mythical 'Lord Haw-Haw'.[17] He and his wife Margaret escaped to Germany on 26 August on the advice of an MI5 officer, probably Maxwell-Knight. Joyce had been giving Maxwell-Knight information on the Communist Party; the hope, it is said somewhat implausibly, was that he would continue to do so from Germany. They may well have been friends.[18] At the trial of Joyce after the war it emerged that Joyce's passport had been renewed on 24 August, and the passport officer became distressed in answering simple questions about this remarkable action, for Joyce was on the arrest list. Once a very prominent member of the BUF, Joyce had broken with Mosley in 1937 and, with his friend Angus MacNab,[19] and John W. Beckett, also very prominent,[20] and Vincent Collier,[21] formed the National Socialist League, an extreme anti-Semitic fascist group.[22] The identity of the second individual who had left the country is not known.

Holderness evaluated recommendations from the papers; he did not check allegations independently. Conceivably at this stage in the war he may have had access to MI5's personal files.[23] He thought the case against two unidentified individuals was weak, and that action against one other—Commander E. H. Cole, a retired naval officer who was Chancellor of the anti-Semitic White Knights of Britain—should be

---

[17] See W. J. West, *Truth Betrayed* (London, 1987), ch. 8, and J. A. Cole, *Lord Haw Haw: The Full Story of William Joyce* (London, 1964), ch. 2. One broadcaster had a drawling Oxford accent, and Jonah Barrington of the *Daily Express* christened him 'Lord Haw-Haw'. He was probably Norman Baillie-Stewart, a former officer in the Seaforth Highlanders, convicted of espionage in 1933 and sentenced to 5 years (see West, *MI5*, 100–10), becoming 'the officer in the Tower'. He spent the war in Germany and was again convicted in 1946. Joyce did not have a drawling accent but came to be identified with 'Lord Haw-Haw'.

[18] Cole, *Lord Haw Haw*, 84–5. Maxwell-Knight interrogated William's brother Quentin in 1939 (HO 45/25690), which suggests that he was concerned with the Joyces. HO 45/25690 confirms that an order was signed but not served on William; presumably Maxwell-Knight falsely stated that Joyce had left by 24 August to give him time to leave. See C. E. Bechoffer Roberts, *The Trial of William Joyce* (London, 1946), 41–3, evidence of Harold Godwin.

[19] John Angus MacNab, known as Angus, born c.1907; educated Rugby and Christ Church, Oxford; the son of an ophthalmic surgeon who was killed on 1 November 1914 at Messines. Originally BUF Executive Officer of the Jewish Division; then with Margaret Collins Joint Director of the Press Bureau; prospective candidate for Leeds South. Worked with Joyce as a private tutor; detained on 23 May 1940, and remained in detention until 1943, probably being released in November or December. He remained a loyal friend to Joyce up to his execution for treason on 3 January 1946; he then was of the British People's Party. After the war he lived in Spain. R. West, *The New Meaning of Treason* (New York, 1964), gives some account of him.

[20] Detained on May 23 1940.

[21] Never detained and probably an informer.

[22] See Cole, *Lord Haw Haw*, ch. 7; R. Griffiths, *Fellow Travellers of the Right: British Enthusiasts for Nazi Germany 1933–9* (London, 1980), 278–9.

[23] For some there would be a Home Office aliens personal file.

deferred.[24] Cole, also Nordic League and Imperial Fascist League, seems never to have been detained.[25] The names of the remaining eighteen are in the file with a very brief statement of the case against each. Thus of S. A. Scott it is noted: 'Has received money from German sources.'[26]

At some point before 1 September three requests were dropped, the individuals having left the country.[27] A mere fourteen individuals were in detention on 14 September 1939. A fairly full picture emerges.[28] Six were British born and suspected of involvement in espionage. They were C. Burger, E. Quentin Joyce (one of William Joyce's brothers[29]), P. W. Rapp, S. A. Scott, T. Sharp, and W. L. Wishart.[30] Arthur Owens, also British born, was involved in espionage, and became the double agent SNOW.[31] Scott and Sharp were listed as double agents, but nothing more seems to be discoverable about them. H. E. E. S. Beurlen and R. W. Froebel were British born of German parents, and were also suspected of espionage, as was J. J. Kopp, a naturalized German, and Mrs Gallagher, Austrian but British by marriage. The other early detainees cannot all be identified with assurance. On the original list were William Muller (alias Knight) and his wife. He (and presumably his wife) was detained, but soon released under restriction.[32] Other early detainees, perhaps on the

[24] See R. Thurlow, *Fascism in Britain: A History, 1918–1985* (Oxford, 1987), esp. 78–83. Capt. A. H. M. ('Maule') Ramsay MP was a member. See Board of Deputies of British Jews (hereafter BDBJ) Intelligence Report C6/10/29 and HO 144/21381/250–1.
[25] HO 283/46. On the White Knights or Hooded Men see Thurlow, *Fascism in Britain*, 80–1, based on a BDBJ Intelligence Report, whose Defence Committee kept an eye on such organizations (BDBJ C6/10/9).
[26] HO 45/25114. William Lee Wishart, T. Sharp, Weger, Percy William Rapp, S. A. Scott, R. W. Froebel, G. E. Thomas, Edwin Quentin Joyce, Niepmann, Arthur (also George and Graham) Owens, C. Burger, H. E. E. S. Beurlen, Morath, J. J. Kopp, William Muller, alias Knight, Mrs Muller, Mrs Watson, and Mrs Gallagher. Hinsley and Simkins, 41, state 2 of 6 known agents were left at liberty: a Swedish woman, My Erikson, detained in December 1939 and a Welsh electrical engineer, obviously Owens. The 4 detained could be Wishart, Sharp, Scott, and Gallagher.
[27] Letter of 13 September from Kendal in HO 45/25114. They would be Niepmann, Morath, and Weger, all Nazi Party members.
[28] HO 45/25114 and HO 45/25758.
[29] William, himself a US citizen, had 3 brothers, Frank Martin, Edwin Quentin, and Robert Patrick, and a sister, dismissed from her job in the Ministry of Food in December 1939. Frank and Robert worked in the BBC, but lost their jobs in 1940. Frank was detained for 11 months and then joined the army, becoming an officer. Robert also served in the army as a non-commissioned officer in REME. In 1939 Quentin was employed by the Air Ministry in Bristol.
[30] All still detained when the new 18B came into force.
[31] Hinsley and Simkins, 41, describe him as a Welsh electrical engineer. See Andrew, 440–1, 481; West, *MI5*, 141–2 and ch. 7; Masterman, *The Double Cross System* generally. As Arthur Graham Owens he was in Stafford Prison on 15 September 1942 (HO 45/25752/863022/43). Hinsley and Simkins, 103, show him detained again under 18B on 21 April 1941. N. West, *MI5*, 272 has him in Camp 001, a wing of Dartmoor Prison.
[32] HO 45/25690, letter from G. St C. Pilcher of MI5 of 1 November to G. P. Churchill of the Advisory Committee recommends release subject to restriction; his wife may already have been released. See HO 45/25758/863044/19, 283/21.

first list, were a German born woman, Mrs Watson, suspected of being a paid spy, and Dr Otto B. Bode, who ran the German hospital in Dalston, and was soon released.[33]

The first detainees included two persons in Mosley's fascist party. William F. Craven, a late addition to the first list, was active in the Liverpool docks. He was soon released, detained again in June of 1940, and again released in April of 1941. In April 1943, by which time he belonged to the British National Party, he was sentenced to life imprisonment for attempting to communicate with the enemy.[34] G. Eric Thomas, arrested on 1 September, was a BU speaker and prospective Parliamentary candidate for Wood Green.[35] A suspected Gestapo agent he had foreign business interests and European contacts. The case against him was based on visits to Germany in 1934 and 1938, contacts with the German Chamber of Commerce in London, with the Auslands Organization, and with one Dr Keller. Mosley protested in *Action*, and Captain Maule Ramsay complained in the Commons about the conditions under which he had been detained.[36] He was released in October or early November; presumably the committee accepted that his contacts had been innocent. He was detained again on 24 May 1940; when he was eventually released is obscure, but he was not a very long-term detainee, which suggests that the case against him was not notably serious.[37] According to R. R. Bellamy, in his account of Mosley's party, Thomas was held in arduous conditions in an unlit cell for the first twenty-five days, and was refused access to both his wife and his lawyer; he was released rapidly after his second committee appearance.[38] This account, which comes from personal contact with Thomas, is plausible. Bellamy also less plausibly says his detention led the BU to collaborate with other groups opposing the war.[39]

Captain H. W. Luttman-Johnson, a Scottish landowner and retired Indian cavalry officer, who had served through the first war, was added to the first list, but was not in the event detained in 1939.[40] In Mosley's party for only a month in 1933 but strongly sympathetic to him, he was promi-

---

[33] *Parl. Deb.* HC Vol. 355 c.235–6. Detained 1 September to 6 November, and again in 1940.

[34] See *The Times*, 7 April, 8 June 1943; West, *MI5*, 163.

[35] See *It Might Have Happened to You!*, hereafter cited as *IMHHTY*, a pamphlet discussed in Ch. 10 below. See also *Parl. Deb.* HC Vol. 355 c.805–6.

[36] *Parl. Deb.* HC Vol. 353 c.1397–401.

[37] *Manchester Guardian* and *News Chronicle* for 25 May. The Beavan Diary (see Appendix II) has him as a house leader in the Isle of Man.

[38] Bellamy MS III 36–7. See Appendix II.

[39] 'This proved to be of great significance, for it led to the BUF's modest collaboration with other anti-war groups and provided the government with an excuse to silence all opposition a few months later.'

[40] His son has allowed me access to his diary and other papers.

nent in the Perth Unionist Association. In 1933 he became secretary and the organizer of the January Club, formed to attract important people to fascism. He was also involved in running the Windsor Club, which had premises at 23 Grosvenor Place in London, and appealed to well-connected right-wingers. The January Club functioned as a discussion group and dining club, and had close links with Mosley's party, which would recommend members for election. Its chairman was the poet and man of letters Sir John C. Squire, then editor of the *London Mercury*.[41] The club met in the Savoy and the Hotel Splendide, and its gatherings featured in *Tatler*; members included General Sir Hubert Gough, Captain Liddell Hart, Sir Philip Magnus Bt. MP, Sacheverell Sitwell, and Sir Charles Petrie. Luttman-Johnson shared Mosley's horror of another war, admired Hitler and Franco for their opposition to communism, favoured Anglo-German friendship, and had very right-wing friends, such as Francis Yeats-Brown[42] and Captain Maule Ramsay MP. He had visited Germany and had German friends. Thousands of persons must have been in like case, and why precisely MI5 wanted Luttman-Johnson detained in 1939, and why he was not, is unknown, though the probability is that his German contacts were thought to be sinister, rather than his work for the club.[43] As we shall see, he was to be detained in 1940.[44]

Clearly Home Office policy in the early part of the war was to detain members of Nazi organizations and persons suspected of acting as agents; mere 'hostile origin' was not enough. Sometimes suspicious individuals were left free for security purposes; thus Arthur Owens was released to become a double agent. Another example was My or May Erikson, not detained until December.[45] MI5 pressed unsuccessfully for more repressive action against enemy aliens, and no doubt had other suspects in addition to those mentioned.[46] No action was planned or taken against the Communist Party, the Peace Pledge Union, or Mosley's party, as

---

[41] 1884–1958.   [42] Best known as author of *The Bengal Lancer*.

[43] See Thurlow, *Fascism in Britain*, 100, and HO 144/20140/177 and 20141/300–6. In HO 45/25752 Luttman-Johnson is described as detained as Secretary of the Windsor Club. See Thurlow, *Fascism in Britain*, 100–1; Griffiths, *Fellow Travellers of the Right*, 49–56. The Club presumably had some connection with the Duke of Windsor who, with his wife, had fascist sympathies; Maj. 'Fruity' Metcalfe, the confidant of the Duke, was a member.

[44] See below p.221.

[45] Hinsley and Simkins, 41 and 324–5. Farago, *The Game of the Foxes*, 318, identifies her as May or Lady May, an associate of the supposed Duchess Montabelli di Condo, alias 'Duchess de Chateau Thierry' (there is no such Duke or Duchess). In HO 45/25752 Anna Sonia de Rois Bouillon turns up under this name in Aylesbury in 1943. My Erikson does not appear to be the same person as Vera Erikson (of numerous aliases), arrested in September 1940, and said to have been detained after her arrest. My Erikson does not turn up in lists of detainees; she could conceivably be Edeltrud Claudette Newirth alias the Countess von Constanza, in Holloway in 1942 (HO 45/25752), whose whereabouts was not to be revealed (HO 45/25752 sf. 40 May 1940).

[46] Cf. Hinsley and Simkins, 31–4.

organizations. Mosley anticipated action, and had made some contingency plans, and the decision to take no action against him was in line with Home Office liberal policy.[47] What little is known about individual detainees makes it impossible to say whether MI5's recommendations were generally reliable, and the official history is silent, content to use the evidence to celebrate MI5's successes rather than its failures. But the release of Thomas and the Mullers, and the rejection of other requests, suggests that its advice was not thought very reliable either by the Home Office or by its committee, and the detention of Quentin Joyce appears to have been quite unjustified, though this was not the view the committee took.[48] It is significant that none of the earliest detainees turn up in lists of very long-term detainees; this suggests that in the end they were thought fairly harmless. But if errors were made this did not involve any departure from the basic policy of restraint imposed by the Home Office.

Dingle Foot's Prayer

It was not therefore the use made of the regulation, but its potential for abuse, which generated opposition from liberals, who rejected as a matter of principle the civil service view that the executive should be trusted with arbitrary power. Code B was laid before Parliament on 5 September. Publication triggered a serious revolt in the Commons, led by the Liberal member for Dundee, the barrister Dingle Foot. It was he who on 27 January 1937 had moved, though with no success,[49] a modified version of John Dunning's motion: that the power of the executive had increased, was increasing, and ought to be diminished.[50] The protest at Code B in 1939 was an incident in a battle which began in the 1920s over the use of delegated legislation to bypass Parliament and reduce the powers both of parliamentarians and judges. To some protagonists what was principally involved was a conflict over *status* in the scheme of government between Civil Servants on the one hand, and judges on the other.[51] To others what was involved was the diminution in the significance of back-bench members of the Commons. Somewhat surprisingly complaints over bureaucratic secrecy hardly featured in the dispute. The principal academic critic was C. K. Allen, whose *Bureaucracy Triumphant*, published in 1931, took its title from a publication in the *Quarterly Review* in October 1923. The high point was reached in 1929, when Lord Chief Justice Hewart

---

[47] See below Ch. 9.   [48] HO 45/25690 and HO 283/43.
[49] *Parl. Deb.* HC Vol. 319 c.1026–36.
[50] On 6 April 1780 Dunning moved that 'the influence of the Crown has increased, is increasing, and ought to be diminished'. He won by 233 votes to 215.
[51] W. H. Greenleaf, *The British Political Tradition*, iii. *A Much Governed Nation* (London, 1987), Part 2, ch. 6.

wrote protesting articles in the *Daily Telegraph*, republished provocatively as *The New Despotism*.

His enemy Claud Schuster organized the classic riposte, a packed Committee on Ministers Powers, under the Lord Chancellor's Department which he ran.[52] He even contrived to be on it himself. Schuster's own conception of the problem was that

in recent years . . . it has been difficult for the State to obtain justice from the Judges of the High Court. It is not too much to say that in recent years the weight of prejudice against the State in the minds of many members of the High Court and the Court of Appeal has been such as seriously to affect the administration of justice. The prejudice arises largely from a feeling on the part of the Judges that they are bound to protect the individual against the State, which is laudable in itself.[53]

The report had to be acceptable, but to be credible there had to be an appearance of independence and balance in membership.[54] It was a bureaucratic triumph: it quieted public controversy without recommending any significant changes, and was essentially unanimous. According to P. A. Landon in his article in the *Dictionary of National Biography* it was largely written by Sir Leslie Scott, who received his reward from Schuster in the form of elevation directly to the Court of Appeal in 1935. I cannot but suspect that Schuster had his finger in the pie. There were reservations by Harold Laski and Ellen Wilkinson; they, being of the left, favoured executive power as a vehicle for collectivism, and preferred Civil Servants to judges.[55] Hence they had nothing to contribute of any significance.

Though the committee did not investigate the use of emergency powers, the report itself enthusiastically supported the need for them.[56] For cosmetic reasons something had to be said about limiting their use, and this was confined to platitudinous mandarin-talk:

In a modern state there are many occasions when there is a sudden need for legislative action . . . But emergency and urgency are a matter of degree; and the

---

[52] Also the 'Donoughmore' or 'Scott' Committee. The original chairman was the Earl of Donoughmore; he withdrew as chairman through illness and Sir Leslie Scott KC, later a judge, took over.

[53] See Greenleaf, *British Political Tradition*, 557ff., LCO 2/1133 and 1134. Schuster memorandum of March 1929 recommending an enquiry and analysing the problem as he saw it is in LCO 2/1133.

[54] The other members were: from the Civil Service Sir John Anderson and Sir Warren Fisher, from academia Professor Harold J. Laski and Sir William Holdsworth, from the law Sir W. Ellis Hume-Williams Bt., KC, and Gavin Simonds KC, from Parliament the Duchess of Atholl MP, the Revd James Barr MP, Viscount Bridgeman, Dr E. L. Burgin MP, the Earl of Clarendon, Robert Richards MP, Miss Ellen Wilkinson MP (described by Hume-Williams as a 'pert little shop girl'), and Sir John J. Withers MP. The Duchess of Atholl resigned and was replaced by the Countess of Iveagh MP.

[55] Cmd. 4060 of April 1932. Neither Hewart nor Allen gave oral evidence; Hewart was invited but declined. The Minutes of Evidence are incomplete.

[56] DORA was mentioned once in a submission from C. T. Carr. Minutes of Evidence at 208.

types of need may be of greater or less national importance. It may be not only prudent but vital for Parliament to arm the executive in advance with almost plenary power to meet occasions of emergency which affect the whole nation—as in the extreme case of the Defence of the Realm Acts . . . But the measure of the need should be the measure alike of the power and of its limitation. It is of the essence of constitutional government that the normal control of Parliament should not be suspended either to a greater degree, or for a longer period, than the exigency demands.

Thus was the public reassured through the leaden prose of Scott or Schuster, or some unholy combination between them.

Fear of the new despotism, unscathed by attacks upon it, was rekindled by Code B. It was not simply Regulation 18B which was alarming, but the general invasion of civil liberties, particularly the restrictions on expression of opinion embodied in Regulation 39A and 39B,[57] on industrial action by 2B,[58] and the extension of police powers of search and arrest by Regulations 88A, C, and D. Foot himself regarded the restriction on the expression of opinion as 'the most dangerous clause of all', but Regulation 18B attracted the most general criticism. On 31 October he and another barrister, K. Griffiths, Liberal member for Middlesborough South, moved to annul the Order in Council which had brought Code B into effect.[59] If they had succeeded the whole of Code B would have gone, and the Government would have been under pressure, though not a legal obligation, to release the twenty-four persons then in detention, whom MI5 thought particularly dangerous.[60] Earlier in the same year it had been Foot who had tried to limit the powers of the Home Secretary over IRA suspects by amending the Prevention of Violence (Temporary Provisions) Act to give them a right to appeal to a judge, a right to confront witnesses and cross-examine them, and a right not to be deported if the judge ruled against it. This had failed, but led to Sir Walter Monckton's appointment as a one-man advisory committee in IRA cases as a reassurance of fair treatment.[61]

---

[57] Thus 39B (1) made it an offence to 'endeavour to influence, orally or otherwise, public opinion in a manner likely to be prejudicial to the efficient prosecution of the war or the defence of the realm'. Other clauses gave a power of censorship which was virtually unlimited.

[58] In effect all industrial action was illegal if it affected essential services or enterprises engaged in war work of any kind.

[59] *Parl. Deb.* HC Vol. 352 c.1829–902. The NCCL had organized some protest. The material in its archives is discussed by Stammers, *Civil Liberties*, 18, citing NCCL 4, 'Wartime' s. 6 (Emergency Powers (Defence) Regulations) and NCCL 32/3 (Articles for the Press 1937–9). The NCCL at this time was closely associated with the CPGB, which feared the regulations.

[60] The committee had considered 24 cases, and made 19 recommendations, 13 being for continued detention and 6 for release. See *Parl. Deb.* HC 352: 1865–6.

[61] Ibid. 350: 1502 ff. for 17 July and 2167 for 1 August.

Anderson was now Home Secretary and Minister for Home Security; his speech was constantly interrupted, and he gave the impression of not having mastered his brief.[62] His somewhat patronizing and patrician manner, which earned him the nickname 'God's butler', did not help.[63] Dr Edith Summerskill asked with unconscious racialism: 'Is it in order for the Home Secretary to treat this as if we were natives of Bengal?' Anderson had indeed been Governor of Bengal from 1932 to 1937, and had come in for some criticism for his firm handling of the troubles there. He made much of the safeguard provided by the Advisory Committee, quoting Birkett, now appointed Chairman of the committee: 'Mr Norman Birkett has authorized me to say this: that it has been the earnest endeavour of himself and his colleagues to give every possible opportunity to the internee to state his case and answer any of the points which can be alleged against him.' He also argued, as Simon had in 1915, that 18B was a mere extension of alien control. When it was pointed out by Foot that the regulation, unlike the earlier 14B, did not include the words 'of hostile origin or associations' and could therefore be used to detain other categories of person, he argued that it was necessary to have a power to detain members of the IRA. The Labour Party supported Foot, and Herbert Morrison was particularly scathing; the regulation gave the executive 'really extraordinary sweeping powers under which, it seems to me, anybody whom the Home Secretary did not like could be hanged, drawn or quartered almost without any reasonable or proper means of defending himself'.[64] Sir Stafford Cripps also spoke powerfully against the regulations in their existing form.[65] So the government retreated rather than risk a division. The motion was withdrawn in return for a promise of informal all-party consultations, and the introduction of revised regulations.

The Consultations

The consultations involved meetings on Wednesday 9 November and 15 November.[66] Anderson himself attended with Osbert Peake, the junior

[62] HO 45/45503.

[63] Anderson is said by K. B. Plaice in *The Home Office 1782–1982* (London, 1981) to have been 'the greatest civil servant of all time' and 'God-like' in not possessing any sense of humour at all; see p. 41. The nickname is attributed to Brendan Bracken.

[64] *Parl. Deb.* HC 352: 1846.

[65] Ibid. 1895. David Kirkwood, who intervened in the debate, had, in the first war, been 'deported' from the Clyde to Edinburgh as a 'troublemaker' under DORA.

[66] CAB 75/3 HPC (39) 103 of 18 Nov. 1939 (Memo by Home Secretary) and HO 863004. Sf. 17 contains observations by the Attorney-General of 28 July 1941 arising out of the habeas corpus action by Ben Greene. Sf. 31A contains papers of December 1941 dealing with the genesis of the expression 'has reasonable cause to believe', reacting to protests over the Greene and Liversidge decisions; see Ch. 17 below.

minister, Maxwell, Holderness, Sir Granville Ram, chief Parliamentary draftsman, and Norman Brook, Anderson's private secretary. The Members of Parliament were, for the Conservatives, Commander Sir Archibald Southby Bt.[67] and Kenneth Pickthorn.[68] Sir William P. B. Spens, who was shortly to become Chairman of the 1922 Committee, later wrongly thought he had attended, and conceivably he was consulted.[69] For the Liberals there was Herbert Holdsworth[70] in addition to Foot and Griffith.[71] Labour provided Wedgwood Benn,[72] John Jaggar,[73] who missed the meetings because of influenza, and Sir William Jowitt KC.[74] Foot and Jowitt were most prominent in the discussions.

At the first meeting the possibility was raised that an order might be challenged in habeas corpus proceedings, though this is not specifically recorded in the minute. On 11 November Sir Oscar Dowson, the legal adviser to the Home Office, wrote a memorandum for Maxwell, responding to the questions which had been raised.[75] He said that the validity of the regulation—presumably whatever precise form it took—was assured. But there was concern about the secrecy involved in executive detention; members wanted to know whether an application for habeas corpus, though almost bound to fail, might nevertheless be used to secure publicity for a detainee. This worried Anderson and his officials. Dowson explained that a detained person certainly might apply for habeas corpus, and thus obtain some publicity: 'A certain amount of publicity is obtained if the application is made . . . since the applicant's affidavit would then be read in open court, and the facts on which he relied would become known.'[76] Members also wanted to know if an order made in bad faith might be successfully challenged in the courts. Maxwell asked the Attorney-General, Sir Donald Somervell, what he thought, and he replied on 14 November that in 'a case of clear excessive power' the court could order release. So far as 'bad faith' was concerned, he found it hard to see how it could in practice be established; nevertheless 'the court had power to go behind the order if it was shown to be practically a sham to

---

[67] Member for Epsom.

[68] Member for Cambridge and an academic; nominally a barrister.

[69] 1885–1973, later Baron Spens; a barrister, and 1943–47 Chief Justice of India. Together with Robert H. Turton, he attended later consultations on 1 and 2 May 1940. In a debate on 26 November 1941 (*Parl. Deb.* HC Vol. 367 c.815) he stated that he took part in the 1939 consultations.

[70] Member for Bradford South.   [71] Member for Middlesborough South.

[72] Member for Gorton, Manchester.   [73] Member for Clayton, Manchester.

[74] A prominent King's Counsel, member for Hartlepool; he became Solicitor-General in Churchill's administration and Lord Chancellor after the war.

[75] B. H. Bell (later Sir Humphrey) had submitted a memorandum to Dowson, mainly discussing the validity of the regulation.

[76] Habeas corpus proceedings are normally determined on the basis not of sworn oral evidence but of sworn written statements, affidavits, drafted by lawyers. In practice the court may also accept assurances by counsel, which function as a form of hearsay evidence.

cover up something which would be illegal. Short of some proved fraudulent misuse of power, the court could not look behind the Home Secretary's order.' Somervell's opinion looks suspiciously derivative of an opinion given in 1922 by Sir John Pedder, and the expression 'practically a sham' comes from Lord Justice Pickford's opinion in *ex parte Sacksteder* in 1918.[77] Given the Presumption of Executive Innocence, establishing bad faith was all but impossible. Probably the gist of this was conveyed to the Members of Parliament on 15 November, though with what emphasis it is quite impossible to say.[78] The Law Officers did not attend; their absence may have been contrived, lest they limited their future freedom of action by assurances given at the consultations. The fact that the minutes of the two meetings do not record the questions raised or the answers given must have been deliberate, and in any event assurances given would not bind a future court; it was safer no doubt to record nothing.

On 21 November, that is after the meetings were over, Maxwell wrote a memorandum, based on discussion with Anderson, Dowson, and Ram, and with the Attorney-General consulted on the telephone; this set out the official understanding of the relationship between the courts and the revised regulation with as much precision as was then possible. This was written before the new draft of 18B had been finally approved; it was presumably intended as a brief for Anderson if questions were raised in the Commons when the new regulation was published. 'The resultant general agreement was that whatever words are used in this regulation, whether they be "reasonable cause to believe" or "it appears to the Secretary of State" or "the Secretary of State is reasonably satisfied", the position as regards habeas corpus procedure will be much the same.' A court would only intervene if mistake as to identity could be proved, or it could be shown that 'there has been an entire misuse of the regulation and that the Secretary of State has not addressed himself to the considerations of which he is required to take account, or has in bad faith abused the powers given to him'. This document remained secret.

A draft of a new 18B had been prepared before the first meeting and was apparently circulated:

Where it appears to the Secretary of State with respect to any particular person as to whom the Secretary of State is satisfied (a) that he is a person of hostile origin or associations; or (b) that he is concerned in the preparation or instigation of acts prejudicial to the public safety or the defence of the realm that it is necessary, for the purpose of preventing him acting in any manner prejudicial to the public

---

[77] R. v. *Chiswick Police Station (Superintendent) ex parte Sacksteder* [1918] 1 KB 378. HO 45/19665 and 19666; see memorandum by Sir John Pedder of 11/8/22. See Ch. 2 n. 82 above.

[78] The War Legislation Subcommittee met on 13 November; CAB 75/30 WL (39) 7th meeting. Both Monckton and Holt-Wilson attended.

safety or the defence of the realm, so to do, the Secretary of State may make an order . . . [79]

This, like the old 14B, specified the categories of those who might be detained. At the first meeting it must have been suggested, though Holderness's minute does not say so, that the regulation should specify that the Home Secretary, before ordering detention, must be 'reasonably satisfied', or have 'reasonable cause to believe', that the detainee fell into one of the classes of persons who might lawfully be detained. Ram's recollection was that Foot made this suggestion, though Foot later denied this. The idea, wherever it originated, was supported by Jowitt.

In fact the expression 'is reasonably satisfied' was used at a meeting held after the debate, but before the consultations. This was attended by both Ram and the Attorney-General, and the suggestion may have come from the latter. Ram was initially nervous, as was Anderson, lest its use gave the courts a power to review a detention order on the merits. But further consideration led to the conclusion that it would not have this effect. So Ram—he, rather than Lindsay, seems to have drafted the regulation—in the end chose the second form of words, 'reasonable cause to believe', which was to become famous in legal circles in 1941. He thought the expression 'reasonably satisfied' was silly: how could you be *unreasonably* satisfied? Two drafts were circulated to the second meeting, both of which use the expression 'reasonable cause to believe', and one of which imposes the additional requirement that the Home Secretary had to think that it was necessary to exercise control over the individual concerned.[80]

Holderness's minute of the first meeting came before the War Legislation Subcommittee on 13 November. This was now a subcommittee of the Home Policy committee of the Cabinet, with Schuster as chairman. After the second meeting the proposals which emerged, together with a minute by Brook, went to the Home Policy Committee of the Cabinet, with an explanatory memorandum.[81] A number of regulations were modified but the only one discussed was 18B.[82] Anderson explained the wish 'that the classes of persons . . . should be defined as closely as possible', as in the earlier 14B. 'Hostile origin or associations' was intended to cover persons who 'are to all intents and purposes enemy aliens'. But there were other 'dangerous people', for example members of the IRA, who might need to be detained. They might not be 'of hostile origin or associations', or within the Prevention of Violence (Temporary Provisions) Act of July 1939, which excluded long-term Irish residents,

[79] Ram to Maxwell 20 November 1941.   [80] In HO 45/25503.
[81] CAB 75/3, Memo HPC (39) 103, CAB 75/1 (Minutes at 240). The Home Office paper on the revised draft is CAB 75/3 HPC (39) 103.
[82] Summary in Stammers, *Civil Liberties*, 20–1.

and did not permit long-term detention. Hence the new 18B, following in a modified form the Irish precedent of 1918, and using the language of the Prevention of Violence (Temporary Provisions) Act allowed the detention of persons recently engaged in 'acts prejudicial to the public safety or the defence of the realm'.

The basic text of 18B now read:

If the Secretary of State has reasonable cause to believe any person to be of hostile origin or associations or to have been recently concerned in acts prejudicial to the public safety or the defence of the realm or in the preparation or instigation of such acts and that by reason thereof it is necessary to exercise control over him, he may make an order against that person directing that he be detained.

The proposed changes to 18B and other regulations were all accepted by the Home Policy Committee.

Was Parliament Misled?

Home Office papers from 1941 emphasize that everyone involved in the consultations, especially the lawyers, realized that although the new regulation would limit the Home Secretary's powers, it was never intended that the judges might review detention orders on their merits, though they might be ready to interfere in extreme cases of abuse of power. The matter, as we shall see, became important late in that year in connection with the Liversidge and Greene cases, when it was suggested that the judicial interpretation of the regulation in these cases violated the understanding of Parliament in 1939. The Home Office and Law Officers were anxious to deny this. How widely it was the understanding in the Commons that there was no appeal to the courts under the new regulation is difficult to say. Southby later claimed that both he and the other Parliamentarians involved in the consultations thought that the inclusion of the words 'have reasonable cause to believe' was

to have this effect, namely that if the subject considers himself aggrieved by the action taken by a Minister of the Crown . . . he has the right to go to the High Court and challenge the Minister's action, and it is then incumbent on the Minister to prove to the court that he has indeed and in fact acted reasonably.

Sydney Silverman, a lawyer, stated in the Commons before the decision in *Liversidge* v. *Anderson* that it was the understanding that some sort of appeal to the judges had been introduced.[83] A letter from Kidd of the NCCL, which had protested against the regulations, to the *Manchester*

[83] *Parl. Deb.* HC Vol. 369 c.869 (4 March 1941), 376: 797, 823, 837–41, 26 November 1941. See also the Third Report from the Select Committee on Procedure . . . HCR 189–1 Session 1945–6 (1946) cited J. Eaves, *Emergency Powers and the Parliamentary Watchdog: Parliament and the Executive in Great Britain 1939–1951* (London, 1957), 45–6.

Guardian on 2 December assured the readers that there was now judicial review of detention orders; Kidd was advised by D. N. Pritt KC, a member of the Commons. Of course if the Members of Parliament were told, or the idea got around, that the courts would intervene in a bad case, the impression might well have been given that there was now an appeal to the courts. Spens, who was also a lawyer, dissented from Southby's understanding, but he was not at the meetings.[84] Perhaps the most significant evidence is, however, the fact that Jowitt, after he became Solicitor-General, assured the Divisional Court in 1940 in the *Lees* case, the first to arise under the regulation, that the courts were certainly entitled to investigate whether the Home Secretary had reasonable grounds for his belief that an individual was detainable. One can only assume that this was his understanding of the outcome of the consultations.[85]

What is perfectly clear is that any misunderstanding was entirely the fault of the Home Office. It would have been perfectly easy to have explained the official understanding, as set out in Maxwell's memorandum, in a ministerial statement. This was not done; of course if it had been there would have been further trouble with the Commons.[86]

Minor Safeguards in the New Regulation

At the consultations Jowitt pressed for legal representation before the committee, but this was resisted. As Anderson explained to the Home Policy Committee: 'it was most important not to appear to be importing any feature of a formal trial at law. It was of course the fact that in many cases persons detained were not fully capable of stating their own case.' The committee could allow representation, but 'An absolute right to be represented by counsel might be very embarrassing indeed in a case in which a substantial part of the evidence could not be disclosed.' Attorney-General Somervell, the head of the English bar, so dedicated we are told to the rule of law and the concept of the fair trial, agreed; if there was Parliamentary pressure an undertaking could be given that the committee would make rules under which legal representation could be arranged. This was simply hypocritical; representation was never permitted, and the policy had been settled at the committee's first meetings. The denial to detainees of a right to counsel is surely the most oppressive feature of the system established in 1939. But the idea of a legally managed 'day in

---

[84] *Parl. Deb.* HC Vol. 376 c.788–9, 26 November 1941.   [85] See below Ch. 14.

[86] See R. F. V. Heuston in '*Liversidge* v. *Anderson*: Two footnotes', *Law Quarterly Review*, 87 (1971), 171; his conclusion differs from mine, but when he wrote numerous papers were not available to him. His earlier article, '*Liversidge* v. *Anderson* in Retrospect', *Law Quarterly Review*, 86 (1970), 33 is, with C. K. Allen's *Law and Orders* (Oxford, 1945), App. I, the starting-point for any serious study of Regulation 18B.

court' in which witnesses could be confronted, and evidence openly challenged, was wholly incompatible with the world of MI5, where unchecked assertions and reports from agents and informers built up a file, where suspicion served as a substitute for proof of guilt, and where the object of suspicion was normally never even interviewed before the case against him was acted upon.

Some other changes were made. The original regulation authorized restrictions on conduct as an alternative to detention, and these might limit freedom of expression. The new 18B provided that the more severe restrictions could only be imposed after a detention order had been made, but suspended; this confined them to persons who fell within the new categories. The restrictions could prohibit or restrict 'the possession or use . . . of any specified articles', or they could be 'in respect of his employment or business, and in respect of his association or communication with other persons'. The power to restrict freedom of expression went entirely. A wider power to impose restrictions upon any individual was, however, retained by 18A, but orders under 18A could only impose restrictions on movement into particular places, or require notification of movement to the authorities. The practical effect of this may not have been great, but it was significant.

The second important change, made by 18B (6), required a monthly report to Parliament, stating the number of orders made and the number of cases, if any, in which the Home Secretary had not followed the advice of his committee.

The Members of Parliament also wanted detainees to be told the grounds of their detention, but failed to grasp that this might involve revealing very little; they did not press for a precise requirement. The new 18B (5) provided that

it shall be the duty of the chairman to inform the objector of the grounds on which the order had been made against him and to furnish him with such particulars as are in the opinion of the chairman sufficient to enable him to present his case'.

This made no practical difference, for the practice of giving detainees a written statement of 'grounds' and 'particulars', as in the earlier war, had already been adopted.

The form of 18B (5) is, however, very curious in making the chairman responsible, and was to cause problems. It emerged from the meeting of the War Legislation Subcommittee on 13 November.[87] Maxwell explained

that in point of fact the Advisory Committee do tell the appellant the general nature of the reason for his detention, but there were obvious difficulties in the

---

[87] CAB 75/30 WL (39) 7th meeting.

way of an obligation to tell detained persons the precise charges against them, as the information was sometimes of such a nature that it could not be disclosed.

So Anderson suggested placing on the committee, rather than the minister, a duty merely to give the detainee 'such particulars as may enable him to make representations showing why the order should not have been made'. Monckton agreed. Ram argued that in consequence the Home Secretary (who knew the reasons) must be required to give what information he had to the chairman, and legal proceedings could be taken to force the Home Secretary to reveal this information. Hence to avoid this, and preserve secrecy, the text of the new regulation carefully laid no obligation on the Home Secretary to reveal his reasons, either to the detainee or to the committee. As we shall see, he never did so, and this extraordinary arrangement was to cause some embarrassment. And only a detainee who appealed, or, technically, 'objected', was entitled to any explanation of why he was detained. Those who did not do so, sometimes on principle, need be told nothing.[88]

Members had also been concerned over the conditions of detention. They thought detainees should be better treated than remand prisoners awaiting trial. This was met not by explicit provisions of the regulation but by the publication, in January 1940, of a White Paper specifying the conditions under which detainees were, officially, to be held; an assurance was given during the consultations.[89] Again the point of this way of proceeding was to head off any enforceable legal right in detainees to special treatment, though it was later to be contended in litigation that the White Paper did give detainees enforceable rights.

The new regulation was strangely incomplete, since its form was dictated solely by political motives; it merely reacted to points raised. Thus it did not even give detainees a right to a copy of the order itself, nor did it require the order to be in writing. Numerous other obvious points were left open—for example the matter of periodic review—simply because they were not raised.

The Outcome of the Consultations

For the Home Office the consultations succeeded. The amended regulations were brought in on 23 November.[90] They provoked no opposition, and there was extensive favourable press comment, though the most perceptive statement was one that appeared in the *Scotsman* on 29

---

[88] It was provided by 18B (4) that a detainee could both make representations to the Home Secretary and object to the Advisory Committee, and that he must be informed of these rights; this was cosmetic only.
[89] See below Chs. 5 and 11.   [90] SRO 1939 No. 1681.

November: 'The alterations are in form rather than substance.'[91] The modification of other regulations probably helped to secure acceptance for the new 18B, which appeared significantly less oppressive. In reality Foot and his supporters had, so far as 18B was concerned, achieved virtually nothing. Anderson frankly told the Home Policy Committee that: 'the alterations now proposed to the regulation would help to remove criticism without making any serious inroad on any necessary future executive powers'. What had been fought off was any right to counsel, any explicit power of judicial review over detention orders, anything in the nature of a fair trial for detainees, any right to a full statement of the reasons for the order or the evidence supporting it, and any significant inroads into the secrecy of the processes involved. The only major consequence of the changes made in the original code, in particular that to Regulation 39B, was that it became improper, at least in the view of the Attorney-General, to intern an individual for 'acts prejudicial' for the mere expression of opinion, though in fact this was done in some instances.[92] But the protests over the original Code B may have reinforced the Home Office's reluctance to employ the power of detention freely, and during the period of the 'phoney war'—until the invasion of Denmark and Norway in April of 1940—it made very modest use indeed of its powers, much to the irritation of MI5.

[91] HO 45/25503 has press cuttings.
[92] See below Ch. 10 (case of the Marquess of Tavistock), Ch. 17 (release of Ben Greene).

5

Detention during the Phoney War

The November Review

The new regulation was analysed by L. S. Brass,[1] the assistant legal adviser to the Home Office, who identified five categories of potential detainees; logically there were really eight. But Home Office policy was to distinguish merely two basic categories—those of 'hostile associations (and/or origin)', and those involved in 'acts prejudicial'. Standard forms of order indicated which was involved, but gave no additional information.

There was a problem of transition. Thirty-five people had already been detained. The committee had heard twenty-four cases, recommending continued detention in only thirteen, and release in six, four subject to restrictions, figures which suggest that confidence in MI5 was already waning.[2] Anderson always accepted committee recommendations, following the practice in the earlier war. When the new 18B came into force Maxwell and Holderness thought that Anderson should review all existing orders: 'In order to comply with the spirit of [the new regulation] he ought now to direct his mind to the question whether as regards each person detained he has reasonable grounds to believe that such a person is of hostile origin or associations, or has recently been concerned in acts prejudicial . . .'[3] If not there should be release. So R. H. Rumbelow analysed the cases of the existing detainees.[4] A short memorandum setting out the case for continued detention was placed before Maxwell and Anderson, and initialled by them: thus was the formidable mind of Sir John Anderson, like some imposing piece of naval ordinance, directed to the question. The review was completed by 21 December, but T. W. Victor Rowe's case was sent back to the committee to decide whether he

---

[1] HO 45/25758.   [2] *Parl. Deb.* HC. Vol. 352 c.1865.
[3] At this time Holderness reported to Maxwell. By January or February of 1940 Newsam, who was senior to Holderness, became closely responsible for security matters.
[4] HO 45/25758/17. Some had been released without the advice of the committee. R. Plischke, a Czech, was at liberty pending consideration of his case by the committee; he was detained. He, Hildesheim, and Parmigiani, were the three 18B detainees who died on the *Arandora Star*, sunk by Gunther Prien on 2 July 1940. HO 45/25115 sf. 14, in ADM 199/2133 f. 196 and FO 916/2518 449.

was 'of hostile associations'; he was a regular British born citizen suspected of espionage. On 3 January the committee advised that he was, an
important decision on the interpretation of the new regulation, and so he
remained in detention.[5]

Of the twenty-four reviewed ten were suspected of involvement or
potential involvement in spying or related disloyal activity. Four had been
detained since the outbreak of the war, though not named on the original
list, and they included Rowe and one Oliver C. Gilbert.[6] Both were members of the small and extreme anti-Semitic Nordic League, and both also
belonged to the Right Club, founded by Captain A. H. M. Ramsay MP,
which we shall meet again in the summer of 1940. There existed in the
1930s a number of similar organizations.[7] They were watched both by
Special Branch and by agents run by the Defence Committee of the Board
of Deputies of the British Jews. They included the Pro-British
Association,[8] the National Citizens Union,[9] the Imperial Fascist
League,[10] the Liberty Restoration League,[11] the Militant Christian
Patriots,[12] the United Ratepayers Advisory Association, and the White
Knights of Britain (or the Hooded Men). Dedicated anti-Semites often
associated themselves with several of these organizations. The Nordic
League had been founded in 1937, originally as a secret society. In 1938 it
began to hold open meetings, which attracted up to 200 people, and to
establish satellite branches.[13] Special Branch had reports from an agent, a
former police inspector named Pavey, in the League, and regarded it as

---

[5] Material in the archives of the Britons and HO 144/21381/250.

[6] E. Fawcett (a BU member and formerly in the RFC, *Comrade*, 11), Gilbert, E. Loader,
and Rowe. The others were C. Burger, E. Q. Joyce, P. W. Rapp, S. A. Scott, J. Sharp, and
W. L. Wishart. Only 10 of those on the original list appear, so a number must have either
been released, had new orders made, or been dealt with under the prerogative. Those
released include Craven, Thomas, Mrs Muller, Mrs Watson, and Owens.

[7] Material in HO 144/21381, 21382 and 22454.

[8] Associated with Aubrey T. O. Lees, C. Featherstone-Hammond, and Dr Leigh
Vaughan-Henry, detained in 1940. The first two were Right Club.

[9] Associated with Capt. Ramsay, A. T. O Lees, Dr Leigh Vaughan-Henry, R. A. ('Jock')
Houston; Houston detained in 1940, was also Right Club.

[10] Dominated by Arnold S. Leese, detained in 1940, as was Harold H. Lockwood, its
political officer, on whom there are files, HO 45/25717 and HO 283/46. Leese's files may also
still exist.

[11] Not openly an anti-Semitic society. Sir William Holdsworth, the legal historian, was a
Vice-President. See below p.298.

[12] Officially closed in 1939. It published the *Free Press*.

[13] The Nordic League had premises at Druids Hall in Lamb's Conduit Street, and the
organizers of its meetings seem to have been the Revd G. Calverdale Sharpe, S. Vernon
Paske, J. C. Vanneck, and Capt. P. Elwyn Wright. Vanneck and Wright were Right Club
members. Individuals who attended its meetings included Capt. Ramsay, Prof. C. Serocold
Skeels, Maj.-Gen. J. F. C. ('Boney') Fuller, H. T. V. ('Bertie') Mills, R. A. ('Jock')
Houston, Victor Rowe, Brig. R. D. B. Blakeney, and William Joyce. Of these Wright,
Ramsay, Skeels, Mills, Houston, and Rowe were at various times detained.

pro-Nazi.[14] The Nordic League and the Right Club were the largest of these bodies in existence in 1939, but both officially closed down when war came. The League was primarily a talking-shop, where the faithful exchanged views on the evils of Jews and communists, watched films of the ritual slaughter of animals, and reflected upon the world conspiracy revealed in the ludicrous 'Protocols of the Learned Elders of Zion'[15] At some of its meetings Nazi propaganda was distributed, and cries of 'Heil Hitler' heard. It survived into the war as the Angles, the Holborn Public Speaking Society, and the Stonehenge Debating Society.

Rowe had served throughout the First World War in the Westminster Dragoons and Naval Air Service; he had been gassed on the Somme in 1918, and invalided out. A paid member of the BU staff until 1936, he then set up a business dealing in kitchen equipment and novelties, imported in part from Germany and Austria. He was arrested on 2 September. The reasons given him for his detention apparently included a claim that he had 'close association with prominent persons in the Nazi regime'; the flimsy basis was that he had been a founder member of the International Air Convention and had, back in about 1934, on his own admission, once sat next to Ribbentrop at a meeting in London. He was suspected of being a paid agent.[16] Rowe certainly had pro-German sympathies, and was extremely anti-Semitic, but was detained on what seems miserable evidence; MI5 thought he had contacts with German civil airline pilots at Croydon, and claimed he was 'a dangerous man in time of war if he should fall into hands which were capable of using him'. Since there was no evidence that he had ever actually done anything disloyal, his detention was maintained for his supposed 'hostile associations', rather than for 'acts prejudicial'. The committee thought him mentally unstable, and 'in no sense an intelligent, active schemer'.[17] Utterly insignificant, like so many detainees, he remained in detention throughout the war and he

[14] See R. Thurlow, *Fascism in Britain: A History 1918–1985* (Oxford, 1987), 79, relying on S. Salomon,'Now it Can be Told', BDBJ C6/9/21 C6/10/29 (which I have not consulted) and HO 144/21381/270–93.

[15] Derived from a work of fiction, M. Joly's *Dialogue aux enfers entre Montesquieu et Machiavel* (1864), and published as a sinister plan in 1905 in a book by S. Nilus, published in Russia. See *The Times*, 16 August 1985. They appeared in *The Times*, in London in 1920 (8 May) and were frequently thereafter published in a translation by a journalist, Victor E. Marsden, under the title 'The Jewish Peril: Protocols of the Learned Elders of Zion'. *The Times* reported that they were bogus in August 1920. Many reprints have appeared in numerous languages, sometimes under the title 'Protocols of the Wise Men of Zion'. See N. Cohn, *Warrant for Genocide: The Myth of the Jewish World Conspiracy and the 'Protocols of the Elders of Zion'* (London, 1967).

[16] Archives of the Britons, which include a statement by Rowe, not dated but after his release; HO 144/21381 of 1938–9.

[17] Report of 3 January 1940 HO 45/25758/145326.

claimed that he was not released until 25 August 1945.[18] Rowe belonged to a particular class of detainee, those who passionately held such eccentric political views, and who belonged to such bizarre organizations, as to be, in a popular sense at least, slightly mad.[19]

Gilbert, who ran a small electrical business, had belonged to the BU as well as the Nordic League and Right Club.[20] Like Rowe he was suspected of spying, though there was no actual evidence of 'acts prejudicial'; the evidence against him was weak, though stronger than against Rowe, and Holderness minuted: 'This is a clear case.' Maxwell and Anderson agreed. The 'Reasons for Order' given him stated that the order was made because: '(1) of his sympathy and close association with the Nazi regime both in this country and in Germany; (2) of his receipt of money from the Fichte Bund which is closely associated with the Auslands Organisation of the Nazi Party; (3) of his close association with a German espionage agent and also with a Japanese espionage agent . . .' His home had been visited, when he was away from it, by the supposed agent Ernst W. H. Kruse (also Kessler), and he was friendly with one Takuidi Egushi, associated with the Imperial Fascist League and Nordic League. Egushi, whose wife was English, had lived in England since 1914 and was the London correspondent of the Tokyo *Shimbun*.[21] He had been suspected of spying since 1927, but I have found no evidence that he was ever detained. Gilbert had visited Germany in May of 1939 in company with G. E. Thomas, who as we have seen was also detained. The committee, whilst conceding that nothing specific was proved, recommended continued detention in 1939, and again in 1941, but in 1942 recommended release.[22] This last recommendation has, for some reason, been weeded from the file. However, Gilbert was not released until 18 February 1944, so MI5 must have objected. He was, by then, a deeply embittered individual. As with Rowe, there was no evidence he had ever done anything disloyal, or he would have been detained for 'acts prejudicial'.

Three others were similarly suspected, but one had a German mother, one a father who was originally German but had been naturalized a Briton, and one was a mysterious character only thought to be British.[23]

---

[18] He was certainly still in detention on 19 April 1945 (letter in Britons' archives). All 18B detainees except one were released at the end of the war in Europe; if held after then it must have been on a criminal charge, or for mental illness.

[19] HO 144/21381/250-1, HO 45/25758.

[20] Gilbert's weeded files are HO 45/25692 and 283/37; and some subfiles are not available. Material in the archives of the Britons include a copy of an affidavit of 6 December 1943; he must have considered litigation.

[21] Letter from A. Gittens in Britons' archives. HO 144/22454 has him as Takyuki and correspondent for *Shin Aichi Daily News* and *Kokumin Daily News*.

[22] Reports of 18 October 1939, 27 November 1941, and 17 December 1942.

[23] E. F. Heath, T. C. H. Osborn, and C. H. Smith.

Some were, or had tried to be, double agents.[24] Four were British born of German parents and of these two were Nazi Party members, and the other two had lived in Germany and had strong associations with that country.[25] Of the remaining seven three were suspected of espionage. Mrs Gallagher was a suspected spy: originally Austrian, she had acquired British nationality by marriage. J. J. Kopp was a suspected spy of German origin but Haitian citizenship, and A. Schmidt was a Czech who had been reported by the French Secret Service. R. V. Kaufmann was of uncertain citizenship and a Nazi Party member, Mrs Kell (or Pfeffer) was British by a marriage of convenience, and had associations with the Nazi Party. Lydia Link was British by naturalization and an active Nazi Party member; her sister Maria was also to be detained. Anton Bernardi was probably a stateless person. He was of Austrian origin with a criminal record, and had been originally detained as an enemy alien.

Clearly in the early months of the war detention was still being used primarily to control suspected spies and active supporters of Nazism. Thus Adelbert H. Krogulski, who worked for the London Fire Brigade, was detained on the recommendation of MI5 in October of 1939. Though British by birth he had lived much of his life in Germany, and his mother had been German by birth, Austrian by marriage, and Polish after frontier revision. He was an honorary member of the Nazi Party and, during the 1930s, he had acted as leader of the Hitler Jugend in Britain for two periods. He turned out, in spite of his somewhat alarming record, to be an entirely harmless person, and was released in November, subject to restrictions, with the blessing of MI5.[26]

No members of the IRA appear on the December list; those who had been arrested were probably released on condition of returning to Ireland, or dealt with under the Act of 1939. By 23 May 1940 167 persons had been expelled under this Act.[27]

'Hostile Associations'

The expression 'of hostile associations' was originally supposed to embrace persons who were effectively, though not legally, enemy citizens. Thus the memorandum on Beurlen reads: 'H. E. E. S. Beurlen B 2314. British born of German parents; taken home to Germany at age of 12 in 1919: brought up and remained there until 1934. Has been working for German firm in England. Member of German Labour Front. A clear case of hostile origin or associations.' T. C. H. Osborn was another example; British born of a German father, who had been naturalized, he has been

---

[24] Heath, Scott, and Sharp fall into this category.
[25] H. E. E. S. Beurlen, R. W. Froebel, O. H. Meyer, and H. A. Schloss.
[26] HO 45/25693, 283/44.   [27] *Parl. Deb.* HC Vol. 361 c.290.

brought up in Germany and served in the First World War. He first came to England as an adult in 1939, and was arrested when trying to return to his homeland, Germany.

But with the blessing of Birkett's committee 'hostile associations' was extended to cover regular British citizens who had contacts which suggested a security risk, such as Rowe and Gilbert. Another example is W. L. Wishart: 'British born. Became friendly with German girl and through her went to Germany with an introduction apparently to a German agent. Received money in Germany, and was asked to supply information about motor cars, Army cars and big guns . . . A case of hostile associations.' This interpretation, based on practice in the earlier war, greatly enlarged the detention power, for it obviated the need to show actual wrongdoing—'recent acts prejudicial' or 'the preparation or instigation' of such acts. Indeed it entirely deprived the 'acts prejudicial' limb of the regulation of its point. Furthermore the *associations* might not have to be of a hostile character; perhaps any contacts with persons who were now enemies would suffice. Both the leading litigants over Regulation 18B, Ben Greene and Robert Liversidge, were detained under this extended interpretation of 'hostile associations'.[28] And even if there had been no contacts at all with enemy nationals, associations could be called hostile if they had been with other British citizens who were disloyal. Thus in Rowe's case the committee reported: 'There can be very little doubt that at these meetings [of the Nordic League] ROWE was associating closely with people who were hostile to the true interests of the country.' Except for Gilbert, the committee did not even know who they were.

All this was never explained to Parliament, and the practical effect was largely to destroy the protection of liberty which the Commons imagined it had achieved by tightening up the draftsmanship of the regulation.

18B and the Double-Cross System

An early detainee who does not precisely conform to the normal pattern was the *demi-mondaine* Annemarie Luise Frida Perry, born Wedekind in Berlin, the daughter of a surgeon and master printer specializing in fairy stories. Her case provides an illustration of a phenomenon we have already met—the detention of individuals who, if they had not ended up as detainees, might well have ended up as MI5 agents, and indeed may eventually have done so.[29] It is clear from Rumbelow's analysis that 18B was already being used in connection with the system of coerced double

---

[28] See below Ch. 16.
[29] See also the case of Vera Erikson or Eriksen, discussed in Hinsley and Simkins, 323–5; see Appendix III below.

agents.[30] This is described by J. C. Masterman in *The Double Cross System in the War of 1939 to 1945*.[31] The first was Arthur Owens.[32] Some were enemy aliens, and so could be held under the prerogative, but other aliens could be detained under 18B or held under the Aliens Order. Spies could be coerced by threat of trial and execution, and were; indeed some executions took place *pour encourager les autres*.[33]

Annemarie Perry was not at risk of death; there was no proof that she had ever done anything criminal at all. She had married a Savoy gigolo, Arthur Perry, in 1933, possibly to secure British citizenship; Diana Mosley has told me that there were both high-class and less high-class prostitutes detained with her in Holloway in 1940, some being refugees who had married English men to acquire citizenship. After being a dancer, Annemarie inherited money in 1924, and took to drifting around the world. She was maintained by a succession of wealthy admirers, and with the money acquired attempted to start a theatre in Berlin, but failed. For a time she was a hostess at Quaglino's in London. She offered her services to MI5 in 1938, and may have worked as an informant, perhaps for Maxwell-Knight, who seems to have specialized in recruiting women. She was arrested on 7 September; MI5 at first wanted her left at liberty so that she could supply them with pillow talk. But she was detained in December as 'of hostile origin'. The document given her said:

The said Annemarie Luise Frida Perry:—
  1. Was born in Germany of German parents.
  2. Married a British subject in February 1933 for the purpose of acquiring British nationality.
  3. Has admitted earning her living as a prostitute and is therefore in a position to obtain information of value to the enemy.
  4. Is of doubtful loyalty to this country.

---

[30] Rumbelow distinguishes agents and spies without explanation. Another spy detained early in the war was Mathilde C. M. Kraafte Andrew, 441, N. West, *MI5* (London 1983), 142, J. C. Masterman, *The Double Cross System in the War of 1939 to 1945* (New Haven, Conn., 1972), 41, but this must have been after the new form of 18B was introduced. She was a paymaster, and I imagine she was prevailed upon to reveal information. Hinsley and Simkins, 40, say, without naming her, that she was left at large for a time to provide leads, but provides no explanation of why she was never put on trial. She does not feature in lists of long-term detainees.

[31] See also his *On The Chariot Wheel* (London, 1975); Andrew, 439–1, 461, 480–2, 487–8; Hinsley and Simkins *passim*. West, *MI5*, chs. 7 and 8, esp. 307–8, gives extensive accounts of the system and a list which he claims, in my view incorrectly, is complete. An account from the German side by Maj. Gen. Erwin Lahousen was used as a basis for C. Wighton and G. Preis, *Hitler's Spies and Saboteurs* (New York, 1958), also published as *They Spied on England*. This was before Masterman disclosed the system.

[32] West's list, *MI5*, 307–8, includes two 'Britons of German descent' who operated as double agents from Sept. 1939 and April 1940 under the code names Charlie and Dragonfly. Hinsley and Simkins also date Dragonfly to April 1940, and mention Charlie as an early double agent; see pp. 40, 102, 103. Andrew has him as a photographer.

[33] See Appendix III.

On her own admission she had contacted Dr Unterberg in the German Embassy in Brussels just before she came to England, about working for Germany; her claim was that cultural propaganda was involved, not espionage, but MI5 suspected the worst. She denied ever agreeing to work for Germany. The committee decided that there was no evidence that she had in fact ever engaged in espionage, but concluded: 'there is in this case . . . an element of doubt which must be resolved in favour of national security'. Possibly MI5 wanted her detained *pour encourager les autres*.[34] Her case classically illustrates detention based not upon suspicion of espionage, but on suspicion of a mere potential for espionage. She was released in December 1943 with the approval of MI5. It is hard to believe that she ever posed any real threat to security, and if she did the threat was as great in 1943 as in 1939. Somewhere near forty prostitutes remained in detention as late as 1943 in the Isle of Man.

The German Espionage Ring

It is the business of security services in wartime to catch spies, and in the early part of the war MI5 gave the appearance of being very unsuccessful, since it had caught hardly any. We now know that there were hardly any to catch, but this was not obvious at the time, and the penetration of the fleet anchorage at Scapa Flow by Gunther Prien in October, though now thought to have had nothing to do with spies, must have suggested that MI5 had signally failed to perform its principal function. But late in 1939 MI5 contrived to discover the existence of a spy ring of devilish ingenuity,[35] for its members employed as cover perfectly regular businesses, which had legitimate access to government departments and, most critically of all, to naval bases, including Scapa. It comprised two groups of companies managed by persons of German ancestry. One, known as the Mercedes Group, which included a marketing firm, Block and Anderson, supplied typewriters, and duplicating and calculating machines to government departments. The other, principally involving Concrete Pumps Ltd., supplied pumps to defence installations, including those at Scapa. There was no evidence either of illicit collection of information, or of improper foreign contacts. But the beauty of the scheme was that in the nature of things there was unlikely to be any. At the point of collection the activities were perfectly legitimate, and illicit foreign contacts were easy to conceal in legitimate contacts, for example over the use of patents.

MI5 pressed for action, both the detention of individuals and defence blacklisting of the firms. The Home Office resisted since MI5 had no evidence whatever of misconduct. But in January Winston Churchill

[34] HO 45/25691.   [35] HO 45/25497.

intervened, strongly supporting MI5 over the detention of W. K. H. Markmann, the managing director and principal owner of Concrete Pumps Ltd.; given the disaster at Scapa he could hardly take chances with either the fleet or his own political future. Nor could he be resisted by the Home Office. Markmann, his wife, and his two daughters, were interned in late January.[36] But the Home Office continued to resist MI5's demands for further action, until the whole security situation altered in May of 1940; then, to its ultimate regret, it gave way.[37]

The Calm before the Storm

Until late May 1940 there were few orders made. So although the power of detention was effectively unconstrained, its use was severely restricted by Home Office respect for liberty and legality. The first report was submitted to Parliament on 13 December; by then forty-six orders had been made, and twenty-one persons released, eleven on returning to Ireland, eight subject to restrictions, and two, who were refugees, unconditionally. On 12 January 1940 it was reported that sixty-two orders had been made, but only forty-nine persons remained in detention. There had been four unconditional releases of persons of enemy origin arrested on entry pending enquiries; the Home Secretary did not, in the nature of things, have 'reasonable cause to believe' anything about them, and this was why they were detained. So their detention was technically illegal.[38] Twenty-nine orders related to regular British subjects, so five more such citizens had been detained; one was probably William Joyce's brother Frank.

In the next four months twenty-eight more orders, seven relating to regular citizens, were signed; releases kept the number in custody on 30 April down to a mere fifty-eight. Since the war began only thirty-six regular citizens had been detained. Very little can be discovered about them, though occasionally information was given, as on 14 December, when Anderson said that E. Loader was held for 'hostile associations'; he had visited Germany and was suspected of espionage.[39] A few other names are discoverable.[40] An intriguing case is that of E. C. P. (known as Peter)

[36] Markmann became camp leader at Ascot with the support of the BU (see HO 45/24893/840187 and the Beavan and Watts MS diaries); this suggests he had fascist sympathies.

[37] See below Ch. 9.

[38] This practice was legalized by SRO 1940 No. 681 of 9 May.

[39] *Parl. Deb.* HC Vol. 355 c.1236. Loader's order was revoked in August of 1942 (HO 45/25115, sf. for August 1942). Revocation implies that he was exonerated. Otherwise I know nothing about him.

[40] Charles Froman was detained in 1939; see HO 45/25758/86044/19. Schloss was detained by 30 November 1939 but was released before appearing before the committee. Other detainees in late 1939 and early 1940 were A. Bernardi, A. A. Froebel, Graf (or J. de Graaf), R. V. Kaufman (early November), Meyer, Rees (?), Jones, Hildesheim, R. Schmidt,

Whinfield, the son of Mrs Muriel Whinfield, herself later detained, and Lieutenant-Colonel H. C. Whinfield.[41] The family was friendly with the Mosleys and other right-wingers, such as Admiral Domvile and his wife. Mother and son were members of the BU, and Peter had been a prospective Parliamentary candidate; I am told that he had travelled extensively in Europe and was in Austria at the time of the Anschluss. He was arrested in late December or early January and, in a list supplied in the summer of 1940 to Churchill, he is described as one who 'tried to emulate Lord Haw-Haw'.[42] Apparently he had visited Switzerland and been in contact with German espionage agents, Peter and Lisa Kruger; perhaps he had intended to travel to Germany in order to broadcast there, or there could have been some other connection with enemy broadcasting.[43] In a camp report from the Isle of Man in 1941 he was described as 'A strictly pro-German man who was working directly for the Nazis before the war'. In July 1940 he was said to be in prison on a criminal charge, though no details are given.[44] He was probably released in 1943.

The Administration of the Regulation

Most requests for orders came from MI5, then based in Wormwood Scrubs Prison; Kell's diary describes himself as 'scrubbing' when working there. They were made on a standard form DR 8.[45] The Home Office would open a personal file, thus converting the human being involved into the object of bureaucratic action. As it progressed up the hierarchy of officials comments and recommendations would be written on the docket, and it would be passed from Holderness to Maxwell; after January of 1940 Newsam also was involved. If Maxwell approved, the file would arrive on Anderson's desk, with a summary, a recommendation (known in the Civil Service as a submission), and an order to sign. In 1943 in two conferences Anderson, whose capacity to get through paper was no doubt remarkable, described how he proceeded:

he took a broad general view of the information put before him . . . He did not hold an enquiry going meticulously into every detail. Having decided from his

Dorothea Knowles (aged 17, detained in December), Ost, H. H. Habla, E. H. B. Durrant, Hunger, Azevitch, Maria and Lydia Link, Rizza, Edeltrud C. L. Newirth alias von Costenza (see HO 45/25115 sf. 3 and HO 45/25752). Bernardi was released in April 1945, and de Graaf by 7 May. Froebel, Habla, Kauffman, and Osborne had their orders revoked at the same time; they had been shipped to Australia. Two IRA detainees were Margaret Nolan (December) and Margaret McDonnell (April).

[41] On 24 May 1940. She had been prospective candidate for Petersfield, and was a former member of the Conservative Party. See HO 45/25747 for the lists.

[42] The arrest is mentioned in Adm. Sir Barry Domvile's MS Diary (DOM 56 15 January 1940 and 20 Feb.1940).

[43] See HO 45/24895, also HO 283/1.   [44] HO 45/25758.

[45] e.g. see HO 45/25693 (October 1939, case of A. H. Krogulski). The recommendation came from Harker and was signed by John Maude on behalf of Vernon Kell.

knowledge of the case and his perusal of the dossier that detention was necessary, he ordered detention and then took no further part whatever until he received the report of the Advisory Committee.

Perusal of the dossier could mean reading the entire file, the entire docket, or just the summary and the recommendation. Probably most cases would occupy him for only a very few moments. Tricky points would be discussed with Maxwell and Holderness, and Anderson met Kell from time to time, and kept himself informed of the activities of the security service.[46]

The Conditions of Detention

At first males went to Wandsworth, the London remand prison, and females to Holloway.[47] In December 1939 a small number of males were moved to Walton Prison in Liverpool, and from March 1940 Walton came to be regularly used. In February Brixton, originally destined for closure, replaced Wandsworth.[48] On 7 May 1940 there were twelve men in Brixton, twenty-six in Liverpool, and fourteen women in Holloway.[49] On 18 November 1939, probably in response to Mosley's complaints about the treatment of G. E. Thomas, published in *Action* on 16 November, Kell wrote to the Home Office: 'I think the Secretary of State can rest assured that all interrogations undertaken by the department are conducted in a manner to which no possible exception can be taken.'[50] They took place in regular prisons. There are suggestions of harsh treatment in the cases of Thomas and Whinfield, notwithstanding Kell's assurance, which was no doubt sincere if ill informed. A wing of Dartmoor, Camp 001, may have been in use quite early in the war for potential double agents.

In January the Home Office published the promised White Paper on the conditions of detention. It stated: 'As persons detained in pursuance of Regulation 18B are so detained for custodial purposes only and not for any punitive purpose, the conditions of their confinement will be as little as possible oppressive, due regard being had to the necessity for ensuring safe custody and maintaining order and good behaviour.'[51] So they were to be separated from other prisoners, allowed their own clothes and association for meals, labour, and recreation, receive food and limited quantities of drink from outside, have at least one visit a week, have free access to counsel, and be able to write and receive letters, subject to censorship.

[46] TS 27/522 (Ben Greene), conference on 4 March 1943. TS 27/542 (John Beckett), conference on 9 March 1943.
[47] *Parl. Deb.* HC Vol. 355 c.1058.
[48] Memorandum of Assistant Prison Commissioner of 11 July 1940 and proof of evidence of W. H. Waddams (Secretary of the Prison Commission) in TS 27/512.
[49] W. H. Waddams in TS 27/512.   [50] HO 45/25758/863044/16.
[51] Cmd. 6162 of 1939–40.

As requested during the consultations, they were to be rather better treated than remand prisoners.

Unhappily the Home Office behaved badly over the White Paper, probably because of failures of communication with the Prison Commissioners, who have always tended to be a law unto themselves. It was not even sent to Governors until 11 March 1940. In reality the conditions of detention had been prescribed by secret Emergency Orders issued by the Prison Commissioners. The Crown even refused access to them in litigation in 1943, under the doctrine of Crown privilege, on the bogus ground that it would have been against the public interest to disclose them. The only interest involved was the wish of the officials to conceal their misconduct.[52] The first were issued on 1 September 1939; they imposed a ten-day period for making an appeal to the committee. The second, issued on 23 October 1939, no doubt with an eye to the debate, said detainees should generally be treated like remand prisoners, but be allowed no association, visits, or letters out at all without specific permission from the Prison Commissioners. The third, of 10 November, imposed solitary confinement until the decision of the committee, association thereafter only with other detainees whose cases had also been determined, no visits at all except from lawyers in the first ten days, and thereafter only one supervised visit a week except from lawyers. Lawyers' visits also were supervised, not the case with remand prisoners, and there was censorship of all letters. These secret orders were in force when the White Paper was issued, and thereafter. It was simply propaganda.

And at the best of times it could have had only a tenuous connection with reality. For in the real world the disgusting conditions of imprisonment were affected by factors like stinking sanitary arrangements and bedbugs; to be sure the bugs were not there as part of some oppressive policy, but they bit just the same. In the early months of the war, when numbers were small, decent arrangements could easily have been arranged, had the will existed.

Birkett was well aware that confinement in prison was necessarily penal, and wrote to Maxwell on 30 January 1940 saying that his committee would be happier if detainees who were not disloyal, such as those who were to all intents and purposes German and not British, were kept in camps.[53] Prison should be reserved for disloyal people like Loader and Gilbert; his suggestion entailed using detention improperly to punish them for crimes for which they had never been tried, but at least it did not involve humbug. Maxwell replied that he planned to put all detainees in a special wing of Liverpool Prison: 'The intention is that in the special

[52] Copies in TS 27/512; not in available Home Office papers. See below Ch 18 for the litigation.
[53] HO 45/25758/863044/20.

establishment the conditions shall be as little as possible oppressive.'
Birkett replied in his rather unctuous style: 'From my contact with the
Home Office since I have been here I have never doubted that humane
considerations would always have full weight with you and the Home
Secretary.' What conditions in the special wing were like between March
and June of 1940 I have not been able to discover.

The Advisory Committee[54]

The formal safeguard for detainees was their right to have their objections
to detention considered by the committee, as well as to make representations to the Home Secretary. Such representations, if made in time, were
simply passed to the committee. The committee was constituted in 1939
with two chairmen, Sir Walter Monckton[55] and Mr Norman Birkett
KC.[56] Monckton had interrogated IRA suspects under the 1939 Act, and
acted as Home Office adviser.[57]He soon became Deputy Director-
General of the Press and Censorship Bureau, and never presided over a
hearing. Until 7 June 1940 the principal work was with enemy aliens; the
number of cases heard was 288. Regulation 18B cases were less numerous;
between the outbreak of war and the end of April 1940 eighty-two (or perhaps sixty-nine) 18B cases were heard.[58]

The committee first met on 21 September under Monckton. Birkett
took over for the next meeting on 16 October.[59] He had been recommended by Schuster. Anderson had slight reservations, which were conveyed to Schuster:

The Home Secretary agrees that Birkett would do the job admirably. His only
doubt was whether some of the more conservatively minded people would think
(though I have no doubt mistakenly) that Birkett would be inclined to take too

[54] HO 283/21 and 22, and HO 45/25114 are the principal sources and include a history by
G. P. Churchill.
[55] Appointed by warrant on 13 October 1939. Walter T. Monckton, later Viscount
Monckton of Brenchley (1891–1965), after service in the First World War became a barrister;
excelled at delicate negotiations; advised the Duke of Windsor, King Edward VIII, during
the abdication crisis; knighted 1937. In 1940 moved to the Ministry of Information, as
Director-General. After the war he had a ministerial career and was thought at one time to
have been a future Lord Chief Justice, but instead went into the City. Life by Lord
Birkenhead and an entry in the *DNB* by David Karmel.
[56] 1883–1962. Appointed about the same time; began work on Monday 16 October; for two
short periods a Liberal MP; a highly successful advocate, though not a distinguished lawyer.
Appointed a High Court judge and knighted in 1941; Lord Justice of Appeal 1950; resigned
as soon as he had earned a pension; Baron Birkett 1958. *DNB* entry by Lord Devlin and an
excellent life by H. Montgomery Hyde, *Norman Birkett* (London, 1964).
[57] HO 45/25114/863086/2; *Parl. Deb.* HC. Vol. 350 c.2167 for 1 August 1939.
[58] The figures in reports differ trivially from those given by G. P. Churchill in HO
283/22.
[59] HO 45/25114/863086/2. The first case was that of William Muller.

liberal a view and give the aliens, rather than the country, the benefit of the doubt in cases where nothing very definite can be proved against the alien.[60]

No doubt the intention was that this anxiety would be communicated to Birkett, as it apparently was.

Birkett gave up his lucrative practice at the bar; he was nevertheless unpaid, as were the other members of the committee. They formed a distinguished group. Sir Arthur Hazlerigg, the thirteenth baronet, Eton and Trinity, was a Leicestershire landed gentleman who had, in a spirit of *noblesse oblige*, become engaged in public service. He had been a staff officer in the First World War from 1916 to 1919, and was thought, for some reason, to 'know the German mentality'.[61] His son tells me that he had come to know Birkett socially before the war, and presumably Birkett suggested his name; the contact may have been through cricket, for Hazlerigg had captained Cambridge University and Leicestershire, and Birkett was a devotee of the sport. W. E. Collinson, Professor of German at Liverpool University, was selected as 'a man of sound judgement'. He had worked as a Lektor in Cologne before the First World War, and during it served with Naval Intelligence; he was fluent in German.[62] Dr J. J. Mallon was Warden of Toynbee Hall in the East End of London; his familiarity with the alien immigrant population there may have suggested his selection.[63] Violet R. Markham (Mrs Carruthers) was a wealthy woman who devoted her life to politics and good works of one kind and another.[64] The Rt. Honourable Sir George R. Clerk, Eton and New College, was a recently retired diplomat, who had been Ambassador in Paris until 1937; he represented the Foreign Office interest.[65] The Secretary was G. P. Churchill, another retired diplomat, who was unpaid, as was his Assistant, one P. M. Churchill, possibly his son.[66]

The Committee's premises were at 6 Burlington Gardens, and it had a small staff—a superintendent of archives, and some shorthand and

---

[60] HO 45/25114/863686/2. Maxwell to Schuster, 6 October 1939.

[61] 1878–1949. He was created Baron in 1945. He had been Lord-Lieutenant and served on the County Council; he also became a Territorial Army Honorary Colonel. His family appears in *Burke's Peerage and Baronetage* 105th edn. (London, 1975), 1294.

[62] 1889–1969.   [63] 1875–1961. *DNB* entry by Asa Briggs.

[64] *DNB* entry by Susan Tweedsmuir and an entertaining autobiography, *Return Passage*. (Oxford, 1953).

[65] (1874–1951); *DNB* entry by Lancelot Oliphant and a *Times* obituary on 20 June 1951.

[66] George P. Churchill (1877–1973) had retired in 1937; his last recorded appointment was Consul-General in Algiers until 1927. The last 10 years of his service may have been with MI6. Peter Morland Churchill (1909–1972), not his son, was the well-known agent in France, and *Who's Who* has him, impossibly, with the French resistance from 1939. He had been an estate agent in France; conceivably he is the same person, obtaining temporary employment perhaps through contacts with Clerk. He ceased to act on 3 August 1940, by which time two other assistant secretaries had been appointed.

copy-typists. Churchill was Secretary until about 5 March 1941.[67] His appointment, and the choice of premises away from the Home Office, were intended to mark the committee's independence, and thus bolster confidence in its impartiality.

There was a second committee for Scotland, under the chairmanship of Lord Alness; the other original members were Sir Louis Gumley and Sir John Stirling Maxwell.[68]

There were also committees established in Colonial territories, for example in Gibraltar, where the committee, whose membership varied, consisted at one time of Colonel Lyon, Brigadier Parmentier, and Mr Cottrell, a local businessman. Persons detained in colonies could be moved to Britain, and the practice was then to obtain the report of the colonial committee from the Colonial Office; their cases were not considered by Birkett's committee, but the Home Office did not simply accept the Colonial Governor's decision, since under the Emergency Powers Act of 1939 there had to be a decision by the Home Secretary in person for detention to be lawful. The arrangements for transferring detainees to Britain were set up to *ad hominem* to deal with the curious case of Dr Branimir (or Brancko) Jelić, a Croatian nationalist, terrorist, and fascist. He was the right-hand man of Dr Pavelić, who was to become the Croatian fascist dictator, and was suspected of having been involved in the assassination of King Alexander in Marseilles in 1934 though he had in fact been in the USA at the time. Simply for political reasons, to please the Yugoslav government, the Foreign Office arranged for him to be removed by the Navy from the Italian *Conte di Savoia*, on which he was returning to Italy from the USA; he was landed at Gibraltar on 2 October 1939. He was detained there, and early in 1940 the Gibraltar committee under A. C. Carrara CMG, KC obligingly recommended his continued detention, though the evidence against him was very weak indeed.[69] He retaliated by going on hunger strike, and was forcibly fed. The Colonial Office was anxious to get him out of Gibraltar, but the Home Office was very hostile to having him in Britain; the Foreign Office supported the Colonial Office so long as there was no chance, if he was sent to Britain, that a British advisory committee might recommend his release, or the

[67] His assistant was replaced by Mrs M. Williamson on 17 June 1940.

[68] 1868–1955. A former MP he had been Secretary for Scotland 1916–1922 and Lord Justice Clerk 1922–1933. Scottish records should be in class HH 50, but are not. SH para. 173.

[69] HO 45/25147 and 148 (cases of Angelo and Biaggio D'Amato), FO 371/30224, 25029, 25030, 59516, 67444 (Jelić), SRO. No. 907 of 7 June. Later in 1941 by SRO. No. 1774 detention was authorized for persons compulsorily brought to Britain by the military. The bizarre case of *R.* v. *Governor of Brixton Prison ex parte Lannoy* (1942) 58 TLR 207, 350, upheld the detention of persons compulsorily brought to the UK as lawful under 3 (4) of the Aliens Order as persons who had been 'refused permission to land'; Lannoy had, like Jelić, been removed by the Navy from a neutral vessel, and of course had never asked to land in Britain.

Home Secretary decide to release him, a serious risk since there was little hard evidence. Eventually in June 1940 the Home Office gave way, and a new regulation was passed, 18BA, under which he could be moved to Britain, but have no right to a new committee hearing. He remained in detention throughout the war and, whilst on the Isle of Man, acted as doctor to some detainees. Jelić was long a survivor. At the end of the war he remained in detention under a deportation order, but in December 1945 he was released and given three months to leave the country. He retaliated by starting an action for false imprisonment against the Home Office as a delaying tactic; he also sued *Reynolds News* for libel in describing him as a member of the Ustasi in a piece published on 21 October 1945. The Yugoslav government wanted him back as a war criminal, but he had had no chance to become one, so the Foreign Office declined to act; extradition was out of the question since there was no real evidence of his complicity in Alexander's murder, though John Colville in the Foreign Office described him as a 'blackguard'. The Home Office let sleeping dogs lie. In 1947 he was still in England, suspected of helping Croatian fascists escape to the New World. On 28 January 1972 the *New York Times* reported that he was in West Germany as leader of the Croatian People's Association, suspected of complicity in the sabotage of a Yugoslav airliner. I am told, but cannot confirm, that he was thereafter assassinated by Tito's agents in about 1975.

The Procedures of the Committee

The first two meetings decided to allow no legal representation before the committee, though lawyers were allowed to assist detainees to prepare their case. Lawyers occasionally gave evidence to the committee, as in the case of Mosley in 1940. Morrison stated in December 1940 that lawyers were occasionally also heard on points of law, possibly when citizenship was in dispute, though I know of no example.[70] The Colonial committee in Gibraltar, and perhaps elsewhere, did allow legal representation, and G. O. Slade KC appeared for the brothers D'Amato there. Jelić was legally represented too.[71] Whether by committee or Home Office or Prison Commissioners' decision, appeals had to be lodged within ten days.[72]

On 10 January 1940 Birkett wrote a memorandum on the work, probably as a brief for Anderson if questions arose in the Commons.[73] If it were fair to judge from its tone Birkett would seem to have had a canine desire

---

[70] *Parl. Deb.* HC 367: 870 for 10 December 1940.
[71] HO 45/25148.   [72] *Parl. Deb.* HC Vol. 352 c.1592.
[73] HO 45/25754/863027. By this date the committee had heard 35 cases under 18B and made 30 recommendations; the figures for aliens were 126 and 98.

to please his master, the Home Secretary, but there is a better explanation; having devoted his life to ingratiating himself with juries, Birkett found it impossible to drop his court manner even when it became entirely inappropriate. His basic and superficially brutal principle of action was thus stated:

The paramount consideration at all times has been the national safety and national security. Every fact and every circumstance in each individual case has been examined in the light of that supreme necessity. When all the evidence had been heard and considered, if any doubt remained that doubt was resolved in favour of the country and against the individual, whoever he or she might be, whether one formerly in Hitler's entourage[74] or a humble domestic. Nothing has been permitted to obscure this vital matter.

This response to the slight misgivings over his appointment neatly reversed the basic principle of the English criminal law, laid down by the House of Lords in *DPP* v. *Woolmington* only five years earlier, as Birkett would well know.[75] A later passage adds that the committee was nervous of seeming too liberal, for public opinion, though currently quiet, might flare up, as it had done in 1915. The reference is to the wave of Germanophobia of that year, aggravated by official propaganda over the sinking on 7 May of the armed merchant cruiser *Lusitania*.

On the unimportance of legal representation Birkett, who had made his name as an advocate, and whose service on the committee was financed by the wealth he had thus acquired, had no doubts: 'The Committee were satisfied that the absence of legal assistance placed the appellant in no real disability, for they regarded it as a duty to assist the appellant to formulate and express the answers he or she desired to make.' He had made a similar profession of apostasy to Maxwell on the telephone in time for it to be used by Anderson in the debate of 23 October.

From Arrest to Hearing

The correct procedure on arrest was laid down in a circular drafted by Maxwell himself, and called the 'Maxwell letter'.[76] It was not a sentimental document. There was to be arrest without warning, and a search conducted. The detainee was immediately to be told of his right to make objections, and this was to be repeated by the Prison Governor in whose custody he was placed. He was also to be given a copy of the order; a second copy was for the Prison Governor and the third for return, endorsed,

[74] Probably Ernst (Putzi) Hanfstaengl, an early confidant of Hitler, who had come to England before the war. He was in detention in 1939; see G. Hirschfeld, *Exile in Great Britain: Refugees from Hitler's Germany* (Leamington Spa, 1984), 165, FO 371/23 089/C5615/18.
[75] [1935] AC 462.   [76] Text in TS 27/511.

to the Home Office. The order itself merely indicated the category involved, for example 'acts prejudicial'.[77] Hence, as the Secretary of the Scottish committee pointed out: 'When a person is made the subject of an order under 18B he is given no information as to the grounds on which the order has been made.'[78] Thus detainees might have no idea what had led to their arrest, though no doubt many could guess. Consequently any representations made by the detainee had to be written in ignorance ('save by intelligent anticipation') of the reasons for their detention.

The 'Maxwell letter' made no provision for informing relatives that a detention order had been made, nor where the detainee was being taken. An arrest was thus rather like a heart attack, or indeed a visit from the Gestapo, in its immediate social consequences. Many detained enemy aliens—often in fact refugees—were treated in the same appalling way, with even less justification, though the Home Office instructions were that they, unlike regular citizens, should be treated with consideration.[79]

The 'Grounds', 'Particulars', and 'Statement of the Case'

Detainees who objected, and not all did, were given more information. Regulation 18B (5) required that 'it shall be the duty of the chairman to inform the objector of the grounds on which the order has been made against him and to furnish him with such particulars as are, in the opinion of the chairman, sufficient to enable him to present his case'. To a detainee the 'grounds' and 'particulars' were critically important. Birkett acknowledged this: 'The Committee regarded it as most important, even in time of war, that each individual appearing before them should know what were the principal matters of enquiry in his or her case . . . Persons interned . . . were furnished beforehand with a concise summary of the grounds on which the order was made.' This summary, provided at least three clear days before appearance, was headed 'Reasons for Order'.

The 'grounds' rehearsed the relevant text of 18B, indicating that the detention was for 'hostile origin/ and or associations', or 'acts prejudicial,' and, so long as it conformed to the order, added nothing. For example Annemarie Perry received this statement of 'grounds': 'The Order for the detention of Annemarie Luise Frida Perry was made because the Secretary of State had reasonable cause to believe the said Annemarie Luise Frida Perry to be of hostile origin and that by reason thereof it was

[77] Under the new 18B the practice of giving no substantial information was established in a memorandum by Holderness of 15 December 1939; HO 45/25758. Earlier orders were even more laconic.

[78] Memorandum of November 1939 for the instruction of the Scottish committee by J Anderson (not the same person as Sir John, the Home Secretary); HO 283/21.

[79] Instructions by Newsam quoted in P. and L. Gillman, 'Collar the Lot!' 95 (London, 1980), (from FO 371/25244 and FO 916/2580).

necessary to exercise control over her.' Next came the more informative 'particulars' set out in numbered paragraphs; those given her have already been quoted. They could be extremely laconic, such as those given to Harry Sabini: 'Particulars. That the said Harry Sabini (1) is of Italian origin and associations; (2) is a violent and dangerous criminal of the gangster type, liable to lead internal insurrections against the country.' This example is typical in giving no indication of the source or nature of the evidence against Harry, whom we shall meet again as a litigant.

Home Office officials did not draft the 'Reasons for Order', except in police cases, nor was it practice to record on the file what precisely induced Anderson to sign an order; Anderson was disinclined to write comments on files. The job was done by MI5 officers, except in a few special cases when Birkett drafted the document. The Scottish secretary's memorandum sets out the practice, which was to provide:

a statement in general terms (*prepared by the Secret Service*) [my italics] of the nature of the grounds for making the order . . . It must be so drawn as to avoid any such particularity as might endanger the public interest. If the committee should feel that it gave the person detained less information than he ought to be and could safely be given to enable him to present his case, they should consult the secret service before amending it.

MI5, however, was never informed why an order had been made, and just had to guess, no doubt often correctly. Anderson claimed in 1943 that

His instructions were that the whole of the information known to the Home Office and to M.I.5 should be put before the Advisory Committee . . . It is admitted that there are cases, perhaps rare, when M.I.5 are not able to put the whole of their information before the Advisory Committee, that is when information comes from sources which cannot for security reasons be disclosed.[80]

But these instructions seem never to have been implemented; the committee did not, except very occasionally, have access to MI5 files, much less their agents;[81] nor for that matter did the Home Office; this was a consequence of MI5's independent position. In any event there was usually no record of precisely why an order had been made in the Home Office file.

Surprisingly Anderson only discovered precisely how the system worked after he ceased to be Home Secretary, but it was well understood by Maxwell, as appears from this note of a conference on 9 March 1943:

Sir Alexander Maxwell said that the Chairman of the Committee took the same view that he was responsible. He could not, however, undertake the work of drafting the particulars. The Home Office didn't take responsibility, but knew of the

---

[80] TS 27/522, draft minute of a conference 4 March 1943.
[81] See below Ch. 13 on access to MI5 over Mosley, and Ch. 17 over agents.

system which was carried out. Probably there was consultation as to how the work should be done, maybe between the Home Office, Churchill (Secretary of the Committee), and MI5. The Home Office hadn't any better suggestion than that MI5 should do the drafting, and Sir Alexander did not want a Home Office man drafting the Particulars.[82]

Thus MI5 largely controlled how much the detainee was told; Birkett could complain if the 'particulars' seemed inadequate, but had no authority over MI5 officers. Nor had the Home Office.

MI5 also produced a much fuller document, the 'Statement of the Case'. This set out in detail MI5's argument for detention as it stood just before the hearing. The 'Statement of the Case' had not been submitted when the order was requested; it did not then exist. Neither the 'Statement of the Case', nor the DR 8 form used to request detention, was ever shown to the detainee.

MI5 used some of its lawyers, not its investigative officers, to prepare both documents; they relied on MI5's personal files. Gonne St Clair Pilcher appears to have been in charge.[83] Birkett, or Churchill on his behalf, formally approved the 'Reasons for Order'. Birkett's MI5 information was normally confined to the 'Statement of the Case' unless, as in Mosley's case in 1940, MI5 was more forthcoming. The Home Office would also pass on relevant letters. Interaction became more difficult for by late 1940 the committee was at Ascot, MI5 at Blenheim Palace near Oxford, and the relevant department of the Home Office seems to have remained in London.[84] After 1941 however the Home Office took on the drafting of the 'Reasons for Order' in all new cases.

The Nature of Committee Hearings

The 'Statement of the Case' was a brief for the prosecution; from it Birkett conducted 'the interrogation from the Chair'.[85] Though often so called, hearings were in reality not appeals; the detainee could not appeal against a decision about which he was told so little. Nor were they trials; the evidence against the detainee was neither presented nor revealed on paper. Hearings were interrogations. So detainees had no warning of the

---

[82] TS 27/542.

[83] Pilcher (1890–1966) became a judge in 1942 and in *Who's Who* recorded his war service as 'Attached Officer War Office Sept. 1939–Oct. 1942'. Ironically his father, Maj.-Gen. T. D. Pilcher, had been a member of the British Fascisti Ltd. back in 1924 (C. Cross, *The Fascists in Britain* (London, 1961), 59). The others were A. A. Gordon-Clark (Cyril Hare, the novelist), James ('Jim') L. S. Hale, Sydney H. Noakes, E. Blanshard Stamp, John P. L. Redfern, and Thomas M. Shelford.

[84] Some administration connected with 18B was, however, conducted from Bournemouth.

[85] Markham, *Return Passage*, 224. Similarly the Birkett memorandum calls the hearing an 'enquiry'.

questions, and they had not been been interrogated by MI5 before the order was made. They had no chance to talk to others who had appeared before the committee, and often had no idea what the procedures were going to be. Indirectly, from Birkett's questions, a detainee might guess the nature of the case against him, and sometimes the evidence. Individuals of sharp intelligence and verbal facility could put up a fair showing. But most detainees were reduced to general denials, protests, or grovelling. Hence the more or less universal condemnation by detainees of the procedures followed as wholly unfair. In effect detainees were never able to defend *themselves*. Their protection was wholly in the hands of the committee.

Birkett fired questions, based on the MI5 brief, and on such letters as had been passed on by the Home Office; some detainees, for example Mosley in 1940, also submitted written objections to their detention. He and his colleagues, who might also ask questions, listened more or less patiently to the answers and explanations provided.[86] Then Birkett would formally give detainees a chance to make what points they wished. Hearings were brief; the committee sat for four hours a day and averaged five hearings. Birkett emphasized the importance of the detainee feeling that he had had 'a fair, courteous and considered hearing, in accordance with English traditions'. Violet Markham also extolled the decency of it all:

Periodically the House of Commons got excited over the presumed Star Chamber methods of the 18b Committee. It would have surprised some of the critics to have attended a meeting of the Committee and to have realized the patience, kindness, and essential fairness of the interrogation from the Chair. It was certainly a surprise to many of the suspects.[87]

But many 18B detainees took a different view.

Given the system, the committee could not adjudicate on evidence. The more important evidence was never presented to the committee at all, and only rarely were witnesses seen, in the absence of course of the detainee. Seeing witnesses regularly would have absorbed far too much time; there was no practice of even taking witness statements, and submitting these to the committee. Nor is there any reason to believe that MI5 investigative officers regularly saw witnesses; in any event they did not compose the 'Statement of the Case'. The material in it was commonly at third or fourth hand or worse. MI5 case officers did not appear.[88] Very rarely

---

[86] With some detainees the committee had a difficult time, as with the eccentric George H. L. H. F. Pitt-Rivers, whose loquaciousness Birkett was unable to control. See TS 27/514.

[87] *Return Passage*, 224.

[88] W. J. West in *Truth Betrayed* (London, 1987), 219 and 232 incorrectly claims that an MI5 officer always attended. The occasional presence of an MI5 officer has been confirmed to me by a private source. See below Ch. 13.

indeed MI5 agents were produced; the present Lord Birkett tells me that they were sometimes concealed behind a screen, to his father's intense irritation.[89] The committee thus worked principally from allegations summarized by lawyers and recorded in secret files, and from letters of support from the detainee's friends and acquaintances. The documents inevitably tended to be overshadowed by the impression of how the detainee performed under interrogation. Birkett was a barrister, and this is how barristers proceed in regular criminal cases. They rely on a written brief, and on what they can extract from witnesses by question and answer; they rarely, if ever, investigate anything at all. Birkett's committee was even more remote from the investigation of facts.

In effect it engaged in the assessment of character through the reaction to interrogation, and the less confidence there was in MI5's reliability, the more important this assessment became. There is something intensely and appallingly British about the real question at issue in so many of its hearings: is this detainee a sound, reliable chap? A good sound, reliable girl? I am reminded of an occasion when a pupil of mine was 'positively vetted' for a government job. After an agreeable pub lunch the investigating officer suddenly looked grave, fixed his gaze intently upon me, and enquired, 'Is she sound?' 'Yes,' I replied, fixing him with my glittering eye, since this seemed to be the appropriate way to react. General conversation then continued; the matter had been concluded. She could join the Foreign Office, or whatever.

Committee Decisions and Relations with MI5

Cases were usually heard within a month of arrest.[90] A shorthand transcript of the hearing had to be typed up, and there was a short delay whilst the committee prepared its report and recommendations, carefully distinguished from 'suggestions', which Anderson might not accept. The report and transcript were sent to the Home Office, so that the second decision—to maintain detention, to maintain detention but review in six months, to suspend the order conditionally, or to revoke the order— might then be taken.[91]

Anderson's invariable acceptance of recommendations was thought to promote confidence. In effect the Home Office took a moderately active role in the initial decision to detain, and delegated the second decision to the committee. Although the rationale of detention was *military* security, control was exercised by civilians, initially by the Home Office, and at the second stage by Birkett and his colleagues. This was an arrangement with

[89] See Ch. 17 below (case of Ben Greene).   [90] HO 45/25115/863834/3.
[91] HO 283/20 (Memo probably of November 1939 on procedure). For later review arrangements see Ch. 12. below.

an in-built potential for conflict. Furthermore committee decisions, based on face to face interrogation, could easily seem irrational to MI5 officers who had never met the detainee, and who relied on evidence never available to committee members. Birkett tried to keep relations with MI5 good. His practice was to inform MI5 of the provisional decision of the committee; by February 1940 the draft report was sent to MI5, which could then submit further information. 'In two cases MI5 produced fresh information of such a nature that the Committee reversed their previous decision; but where all the information has been placed before the Committee in the first instance, the Committee has adhered to their original decision, although in some cases MI5 have expressed their disagreement.' But friction was inescapable, and the entire system might have been designed to ensure unreliability.

It is plain from the account by Hinsley and Simkins that in the first year of the war MI5 was in an unhappy state, partly because of administrative problems, and partly because its officers thought that their efforts to foster security were being frustrated.[92] No doubt the fact that the organization was engaged in the pursuit of phantoms helped to create a sense of desperation. Some of the pre-war officers of MI5 were of little ability; the system of recruitment ensured general low quality, no doubt with important exceptions. Recruitment of new staff had begun late, and intelligence organizations attract peculiar and unreliable people.[93] The official history states that MI5 was 'near to breaking down completely by the spring of 1940'. This is blamed on volume of work, enhanced because of Home Office resistance to the mass internment of aliens; no doubt this was the story in MI5.[94] By early 1940 trouble developed over MI5's slowness in producing papers, and Holderness complained because it became difficult to make a satisfactory report to Parliament on the January figures.[95] Newsam grumbled that MI5 was improperly recommending detention first, and collecting evidence later.[96] Kell was put on the defensive, and on 10 February listed seven cases where the papers were lacking, and promised documents within a week.[97] In general delay would not exceed a month, an arrangement which the Home Office grudgingly accepted.

Since most detainees were in custody at MI5's request, there was also friction over recommendations for release, though in some instances MI5

[92] Hinsley and Simkins, ch. 2 *passim.*

[93] Personal information and some direct experience is here the only and inevitably unsatisfactory evidence.

[94] See Hinsley and Simkins, 32 and 39.   [95] HO 45/25115 sf. 3.

[96] HO 45/25115/863834/3 (Minute of 22 February).

[97] Cases of Durrant (order applied for 3 Dec.), Ost (9 Dec.), Hunger (11 Dec.), Azevitch (11 Dec.), Maria Link (5 Jan.), Rizza (26 Jan.), Markmann (30 Jan.). HO 45/25115 sf. 3. The worst case was that of Durrant.

may have been happy for the committee to decide. Trouble soon arose, and on Christmas Day of 1939 Birkett's diary reads: 'I resume my rather thankless task on January 2nd. I say thankless because M.I.5 of the Secret Service want everybody interned, whilst I cannot bring myself to send some simple German girl for years of detention, when I am quite satisfied that she has been in the country in some household for years and is not the slightest danger to anybody.' Birkett's philosophy was basically at odds with Kell and his officers, for he aimed, as he put it in his diary, to 'keep some small element of Justice alive in a world in which we are supposed to be fighting for it'.[98] Security, not justice, is the business of security services.

In his January memorandum Birkett expressly referred to the friction which had arisen. There were many cases—no doubt he had in mind principally aliens held under the prerogative—of persons in Britain who had joined the Nazi Party or German Labour Front under pressure, and membership might or might not be significant of a potential for disloyalty. Presumably MI5 was not convinced. The number of 18B detainees released on the recommendation of the committee, which claimed to lean in favour of security, suggest that its confidence in MI5 cannot have been high, for release had been granted in approximately 50 per cent of all cases.[99]

Massive weeding, wholesale destruction, and withholding of files makes it impossible to document the continued and probably growing friction with MI5 in the three months of 1940 before the fighting began. Much of the trouble no doubt concerned alien cases; Kell's diary records for 1 April 'Fiasco day at HO re aliens'. But there is direct evidence that the conflict extended to the use of 18B, as in the case of the supposed spy ring. In 1943 Anderson, speaking of 1940, said:

some time before the overrunning of Holland he considered in conjunction with Sir Vernon Kell what action would have to be taken in certain circumstances. *Kell had for months pressed him to deal with the fascists and with certain other parties such as the British People's Party and the British Council for Christian Settlement. Sir John had resisted this pressure* [my italics].[100]

This suggests conflict back in January or February. The official history suggests that it was in February of 1940 that MI5 came to think that Mosley's fascist party should be regarded as 'the English branch of the NSDAP and not merely a party advocating an anti-war and anti-government policy, but a movement whose aim is to assist the enemy in every

[98] Quoted Montgomery Hyde, *Norman Birkett*, 470.
[99] By the end of April 137 orders had been made, and 58 remained in detention; 15 had left the country.
[100] Conference on 9 March 1943 TS 27/542 (case of John Beckett).

way it can' possessing 'a core of fanatics who would be prepared to take active steps to this end if the opportunity occurred'.[101] Given this belief, a serious disagreement as to policy arose between Kell and Anderson. In March of 1940 Lord Hankey conducted an investigation into MI5; one reason was the bad relations then existing between MI5 and the Home Office, and between MI5 and the committee.[102]

Between January and the end of April only twenty-eight orders were signed and twenty-four executed.[103] Only seven of these orders related to regular British citizens. These figures represent a considerable rebuff for MI5, for even very selective action against the fascists and other extremists would have greatly increased them. It is not possible to tell how many cases of suspected espionage, unconnected with the supposed spy ring, were disputed.

Public Opinion and the Regulation

The liberal policy of the Home Office and its committee was, politically, always precarious. Birkett's attempts to develop confidence in the vigilance of his committee, as well as in its fairness, failed. But this was a consequence of the extraordinary military events of May and June of 1940, which neither he, nor anyone else, could have foreseen. The modification of 18B on 23 November, the White Paper of January, and Home Office practice effectively quietened critics of the system; secrecy ensured that little was known about it. Up to the formation of Churchill's government on 10 May 1940, little was said against executive detention either in Parliament or outside it.[104] But as the war progressed there was grumbling, not simply from MI5, at the failure of the government to act more ruthlessly, though more in the case of aliens than British subjects. Criticism became much more vigorous after the invasion of the Scandinavian countries in April. Until then the Home Office was not under severe pressure, from either opponents or devotees of Regulation 18B. And no detainee during this period sought to challenge the legality of detention in the regular courts.

From the viewpoint of the Home Office the system was working very satisfactorily indeed.

[101] At pp. 37–8; Hinsley and Simkins, maddeningly, do not either date this or quote extensively from the memorandum. The second quotation is from the history, not the memorandum.
[102] (1877–1963). Until retirement in 1938 Hankey was Secretary to the Cabinet and Committee for Imperial Defence and Clerk to the Privy Council. At this time he was Minister without Portfolio.
[103] Four persons, presumably IRA, were let leave the country.
[104] C. P. Cotter, 'Constitutional Democracy and Emergency' Harvard Univ. D.Phil. Thesis, 1953, 116, notes that between October 1939 and March 1940 only 24 parliamentary questions were asked about 18B.

The Defeat of Liberalism

A Negotiated Peace?

Support for a negotiated peace with Germany was widespread in late 1939 and early 1940; the most vocal groups campaigning for peace were the fascists, the communists, and the Peace Pledge Union (hereafter PPU). The Communist Party of Great Britain (CPGB) was considerably larger than Mosley's British Union (BU); in 1940 it had around 20,000 members.[1] The *Daily Worker*'s weekend circulation of over 100,000 copies was well ahead of *Action*'s 14,000 or so.[2] The PPU was not a political party, though it was associated with the left. Before the war almost 113,000 persons had signed the pledge, and in 1939 it had some 136,000 members; *Peace News* had a circulation of around 40,000 copies.[3] Of the three organizations the BU was far and away the smallest.

In wartime propaganda for peace can easily be interpreted as treachery, and the PPU, like the BU, feared government action, and took steps to protect itself by going 'underground'.[4] In September action against Mosley in particular was considered in the Home Office. Holderness took a hostile view of fascist propaganda: 'Mosley claims to be 100% patriotic. The object of the campaign is of course purely subversive, to win adherents to the British Union and to increase Mosley's prestige and power, in the hope that out of the misery and hardships of a long war he may eventually be able to establish a Fascist State with himself as Dictator.' But he advised against action, and Maxwell agreed. In October 1939 the Cabinet considered prosecution of the fascists and communists, which would have been easy under the original Regulation 39B, but concluded that it would

---

[1] CAB 98/18 (Memo of 17 January 1941), CAB 75/7 HPC (40) 92 (Paper by Ministry of Information, 27 April 1940).

[2] CAB 75/6 103 gives figures of 15,000 and 20,000 for *Action* and the *Daily Worker* mid-week figure as c.60,000–70,000. The BU also then published a bi-weekly *Action News Service* and the *BU Quarterly*.

[3] Hinsley and Simkins, 20; M. Ceadel, *Pacifism in Britain 1914–1945* (London, 1950); R. Barker, *Conscience, Government and War. Conscientious Objection in Britain 1939–1945* (London and Boston, 1982), ch. 7.

[4] S. Morison, *I Renounce War; The Story of the Peace Pledge Union* (London 1962), 39.

be difficult to exclude the respectable PPU from such a policy, which might backfire, and excite sympathy.[5]

Realistically worries about fringe political peace groups deflected attention from many in mainstream public life who also favoured a settlement, no doubt on condition that the terms furthered their view of British interests. Chamberlain and his Foreign Secretary, Lord Halifax, were of this persuasion. Support for appeasement did not suddenly die in September 1939; the problem facing Chamberlain and Halifax was that they thought Hitler too untrustworthy to deal with. There were also numerous private individuals of some status in society who either positively sympathized with Hitler and his attempts to reverse the humiliation of Germany in the Treaty of Versailles, or who viewed Russian communism, rather than German or Italian fascism, as by far the gravest threat, a view which was then by no means irrational.[6] Their activities, though more discreet, were potentially far more significant than those of the public campaigners. They included the Duke of Windsor, who dreamt of a possible return.[7] There is a revealing passage in the diaries of Alexander Cadogan, Permanent Under-Secretary at the Foreign Office, for 10 July 1940: 'Lunch to meet King and Queen. Gort,[8] Harold Nicolson, Monckton,[9] Ly. Nunburnholme[10] & P. Loraine[11] there. Sat between Lady N. & Monckton—facing the awful light. Talked often to King, who was amused at "C"'s[12] report of the Quisling activities of "my brother!"'.[13]

Nor was it necessary to be either an admirer of Hitler or of fascism, or a dedicated opponent of communism, much less any kind of traitor, to favour peace; the memories of the brutal war of 1914–18 had not faded in the Britain of 1940. Thus in February 1940 Richard Stokes, Labour MP for Ipswich, visited the German Ambassador in Ankara to discover what terms were on offer.[14] He reported to Lord Halifax:

[5] CAB 67/1 WP (G) (39) 36 of 14 October, CAB 65/1 WM (39) 49 of 16 October, HO 144/21429 (Holderness); Hinsley and Simkins, 35.

[6] R. Griffiths, *Fellow Travellers of the Right: British Enthusiasts for Nazi Germany 1933–9* (London, 1980).

[7] D. J. C. Irving, *Hitler's War* (New York, 1977), 144–5, 153–4, 158; M. Gilbert, *Winston S. Churchill*, vi. '*Finest Hour*' (New York, 1986), 613–14, 698–709. P. Ziegler in his sympathetic *King Edward VIII: The Official Biography* (London, 1990) discusses the evidence, particularly in chs. 21, 23, and 24.

[8] Lord Gort, formerly commanding the BEF.

[9] Monckton acted as the Duke of Windsor's personal legal adviser, and also may have acted as an informant to British intelligence on the Duke's activities. He certainly acted as an intermediary between Churchill and the Duke.

[10] Lady of the Bedchamber to the Queen 1937–47.

[11] Sir Percy Loraine, recently returned from Italy where he had been ambassador.

[12] Sir Stuart Menzies, head of the Foreign Office intelligence service, MI6.

[13] Not in the published edition; ACAD 1/8 in the Churchill College Archives.

[14] Stokes (1897–1957) was a wealthy businessman and a prominent Catholic. In the 1st World War he won the MC twice and the Croix de Guerre. He became a Minister after the war. The Stokes Papers (Bodleian Library) especially Box 16 and appointment diaries

I had proposed the interview to learn if there was in his opinion anything that could be done to put an end to the present war before the really bloody slaughter commences, having myself spent three of the best years of my life in the last war killing Germans, apparently to no avail, and having lost most of my friends in the process.[15]

Stokes was one of the Peace Aims group of MPs who continued to advocate negotiating peace long into the war.[16] During the 'phoney war' individuals of widely different political views discreetly investigated the possibility that a real war might still be avoided.

One approach, involving the Marquess of Tavistock and the British People's Party, attracted considerable prominence in right-wing circles. Tavistock, the twelfth Duke of Bedford from 12 August 1940, was an eccentric right-wing pacifist and political pamphleteer, as well as a writer on the care of parrots, parrot-like birds, and homing budgerigars. He believed in himself, Christianity, social credit, and the stupidity of the proletariat.[17] In January 1940 he obtained the 'Tavistock Peace Proposals' from Henning Thomson, Secretary to the German Legation in Dublin. These supposedly official terms included a free and independent Poland and Czechoslovakia, a plebiscite in Austria, a new League of Nations, general disarmament, the return of German colonies, and the finding of a national home for the Jews. At the time the going terms had been most recently stated by Hitler in a Reichstag speech on 7 October 1939.[18] Tavistock gave his terms to Lord Darnley,[19] who gave them to Halifax, with whom they had an interview on 24 January. Cadogan viewed them as 'absolute bilge'—fraudulent propaganda foisted on to Tavistock and Darnley, who were '(a) Pacifists and (b) Halfwits'.[20] On 9 February the

mention many meetings of the Peace Aims Group and note the meeting of the National Peace Council in Oxford in January 1942.

[15] Box 13, letter to Lord Halifax of 25 April 1940.

[16] Other members included P. J. Noel-Baker, MP for Derby, C. T. Culverwell, MP for Bristol West, Sir Ernest N. Bennett, investigator of haunted houses and once an academic, listed as Right Club, Lord Arundel of Wardour, a Count of the Holy Roman Empire, and Viscount Chaplin. Lords Darnley and Brocket were also active; Brocket was associated with the Nordic League.

[17] (1888–1953); published pamphlets on Regulation 18B, such as *Is This Justice? An Examination of Regulation 18B* (Glasgow, 1943) (HO 45/25729 contains a collection, such as *Why Have This War*, *The 'Can't Trust Hitler' Bogey*, and *This Concentration Camp Business*); financed the pamphlet *It Might Have Happened to You!* (1943); contributed to financing litigation against the Home Office in 1943; see below Chs. 10 and 18; wrote an autobiography, *The Years of Transition* (London, 1949).

[18] TS 27/522 has correspondence with Halifax; see also Tavistock's autobiography at 181–4. FO 371/26542 contains a summary of some other peace proposals from September 1939; 8 files are closed until 2017. In *Parl. Deb.* HC Vol. 358 c.2–3 (4 March) an unnamed assistant is mentioned; this was Capt. Robert C. Gordon-Canning, formerly BU, and in 1940 of the BPP, detained in 1940.   [19] The 9th Earl (1886–1955).

[20] Cadogan Diaries for January 22, names suppressed in the published edition. 'X' is Darnley and 'Y' is Tavistock. ACAD 1/9.

paper *Truth*, controlled by a confidant of Chamberlain, Sir Joseph Ball, published a letter from Tavistock claiming that peace on reasonable terms was negotiable.[21] On 14 February Halifax, no doubt influenced by Cadogan, expressed doubts as to their authenticity.[22] Tavistock then decided to go to Dublin to check; this involved deliberate contact with the enemy. He informed Halifax, who wrote a very curious letter saying that such a visit could only be unofficial, but that he could not prevent it. This can only be interpreted as an encouragement, but one designed to cover Halifax in case Cadogan's view proved correct.[23] Tavistock did visit Dublin; what then happened is obscure but the proposals, in breach of an understanding with Halifax, were published in the *Daily Telegraph* on 1 March and received wide publicity. The *Telegraph* was very hostile to the BPP, and called it a pro-Nazi organization; its Secretary, Ben Greene, was described as peddling German propaganda. Presumably the paper had been briefed by Cadogan. The BPP, under its wartime alias, the British Council for Christian Settlement in Europe, published 'Germany's Peace Terms. Official', and the correspondence with Halifax. The proposals were repudiated by the German Legation, and precisely how they originated, and for what purpose, remains one of the many minor mysteries of the period. In the Commons on 4 March R. A. Butler said that there was no evidence that the terms were genuine, and was evasive about Tavistock's visit to Dublin.[24] Butler, described by Cadogan in one of his diary explosions as a 'craven pacifist, a muddle headed appeaser and a nit wit', continued to be involved in approaches, but the subject to this day remains shrouded in secrecy.[25]

Anderson's views on peace negotiations are unknown. But under him the Home Office resisted pressure for more repressive action against peace propagandists and aliens.[26] The invasion of Scandinavia on 9–10 April, and the widespread belief that Norway's collapse was brought

[21] On *Truth* see below Ch. 9.

[22] Letter from Halifax of 14 February in TS 27/522.

[23] Similarly Halifax and indeed Cadogan had given discreet assistance to one Lonsdale Bryans who had set out to Italy and Switzerland. By February Cadogan viewed him as 'a washout and a crook' and he was disowned. See FO 371/26542.

[24] *Parl. Deb.* HC Vol. 358 c.3.

[25] R. Lamb in *The Ghosts of Peace 1935–45* (London, 1987) notes that Halifax and Chamberlain paid considerable attention to pro-Nazi right-wingers in the Conservative Party, naming Lord Brocket, the Duke of Buccleugh, the Marquess of Londonderry, Lord Ponsonby, and Lord Darnley. See also C. Ponting, *1940: Myth and Reality* (London, 1990), ch. 6; A. Roberts, 'The Holy Fox': A Biography of Lord Halifax (London, 1991), ch. 23; and J. Costello, *Ten Days that Saved the West* (London, 1991).

[26] The pressure to act existed outside MI5 before 9 April. See Hinsley and Simkins, 37, citing *Parl. Deb.* HC Vol. 357 c.1504–6 (23 Feb.) and 2245–6 (29 February), CAB 75/6 HPC (40) 45 of 2 March, CAB 73/2 CDC (40) 7th meeting of 28 Feb. CAB 73/3 CDC (40) 8 n.d., CAB 75/4 HPC (40) 11th meeting of 9 March. See also *Parl. Deb.* HC Vol. 357 c.980 (15 February, dealing with the Link).

about by 'Quislings', strengthened the pressure, and both within Parliament and outside there were demands for action.[27] Once fighting began in earnest, peace propaganda could more easily be equated with disloyalty, and with that all-embracing tool of repression, 'hindering the war effort'; even those who favoured negotiation by officials might also favour vigorous action against private propagandists until such negotiations were concluded.

On 22 April Anderson submitted a memorandum to the Home Policy Committee of the Cabinet which recognized the strong feeling that there should be more drastic action against those impeding the war effort; the impetus came from a meeting on 19 April of some seventy Conservative MPs to consider the Fifth Column.[28] He pointed out that 'It is, of course, extremely difficulty to interfere with these actions without contravening the traditional principle of allowing free speech and free association for political objects.' Hoping to appear to be doing something, he favoured introducing a power to detain aliens arriving from enemy territory who could not be deported, which he had been doing anyway, and a power to impose conditions as to residence upon persons under suspended 18B orders. On 23 April the committee invited him, with the Lord Chancellor and Secretary of State for Scotland, 'to consider as a matter of urgency in what directions the existing provisions of the law should be properly strengthened so as to enable action to be taken against organizations or individuals seeking to hinder the war effort of the country'.[29] The following day Anderson addressed the 1922 Committee, and 'appeared to have gone a long way towards satisfying those who heard his speech'.[30] On 25 April there were questions in the Commons; Anderson reminded the House that in the debate on 23 October there had been general sympathy with the idea that liberty to express minority views should be respected. But he added, with a note of menace: 'There is however a risk that the liberty allowed by our traditional principles may be abused by extremists of whom some are anxious to destroy that liberty.' He was reviewing the regulations, and there would again be informal consultations.[31]

On 27 April Anderson submitted another memorandum to the committee.[32] This included a horrific draft regulation creating an offence of 'Demoralizing the Population', punishable with up to ten years' penal

[27] Vidkun Quisling was leader of the Norwegian Nasjond Samling; for his minimal part in the invasion of Scandinavia see L. de Jong, *The German Fifth Column in the Second World War* (Chicago, 1956), 168ff.

[28] CAB 75/6 HPC (40) 87. CAB 75/4 HPC (40) 11th meeting of 9 March (Anderson's view of the fascists).

[29] CAB 75/7 HPC (40) 87 (Memo of 22 April), CAB 75/4 HPC (40) 13th meeting of 23 April.

[30] *The Times*, 25 April 1940. Presumably there was barracking.

[31] *Parl. Deb.* HC Vol. 360 cols. 353–6.   [32] CAB 75/7 HPC (40) 94.

servitude; it was surely designed to bring home the fact that an effective control over opinion would not be acceptable to the Commons. It would have become a crime 'to endeavour to hinder the efficient prosecution of the war . . . by discouraging the will of the people or any section of the people to achieve victory'.[33] The same day the Ministry of Information enhanced the pressure for action with a memorandum on the CPGB, BU, and Fifth Column; this hugely extended the latter concept to include not just an underground military organization, but 'all those elements in this country which oppose the national war effort'.

The New Regulations and the Treachery Act

The consultations were held on 1 and 2 May; Anderson also consulted Attlee for Labour, and Greenwood for the Liberals.[34] On 4 May Anderson made specific proposals which included amending Regulation 18B to allow persons to be directed where to live; otherwise it was to remain unaltered.[35] The committee agreed.[36] What emerged on 9 May was a power to control residence and travel when an order was suspended.[37] To control subversive propaganda there was a new Regulation 2C creating an offence of 'Corruption of Public Morale'. This enabled a warning to be given to anyone engaged in the 'systematic publication of matter calculated to foment opposition to the prosecution to a successful conclusion' of the war; if this was ignored then an offence, punishable by up to seven years' penal servitude, would be committed. Regulation 39A was also amended to strengthen the law against pacifist propaganda aimed at servicemen, and powers given by 94A to seize printing-presses used for propaganda.[38] The atmosphere in which these changes in the law were made was the converse of what existed in 1939, when Home Office powers were to be carefully constrained; in the consul-

[33] CAB 75/7 (HPC) (40) 87, 94. See CAB 98/18, CA (41) 5 (Committee on Communist Activities), cited N. Stammers, *Civil Liberties in Britain during the Second World War* (London, 1983), 23. Action was taken against the PPU on 2 May. See CAB 75/7 HPC (40) 87 and Morison, *I Renounce War*, 45–9.

[34] HO 144/21540 and HO 45/25504. Those who attended were Holdsworth, Pickthorn, Southby, Spens, Jaggar, Jowitt, Thurtle, Foot, and Griffiths.

[35] CAB 75/7 HPC (40) 102. Also proposed were amendments permitting the detention of aliens brought involuntarily to the UK (as after the Lofoten Raid), and permitting temporary detention of non-enemy aliens pending enquiries. See SRO 1940 Nos. 681 and 682.

[36] On 30 April and 7 May. CAB 75/4 HPC (40) 13th meeting, CAB 75/5 15th meeting.

[37] SRO 1940 No. 681 of 9 May. This amended the existing 18B (2) (b) by adding the words 'in respect of his residence' after the word 'business' and by adding to 18B (2) a new (c) ('requiring him to notify his movements in such manner, at such times, and to such authorities or persons as may be so specified') and a new (d) ('prohibiting him from travelling except in accordance with permission given to him by such authority or person as may be so specified').

[38] SRO 1940 No. 680.

tations it was now agreed that the right approach was that of 'entrusting the Home Secretary with wide powers and leaving it to his discretion to decide in what cases these powers should be exercised'.[39]

On 9 May Anderson explained the changes being made. The new power to regulate residence and travel reduced the need to keep persons in detention; the government now had adequate powers to deal with the *Daily Worker*, *Action*, and *Peace News*.[40] The principal targets of the new Regulation 2C were the CPGB, the BU, and the PPU.[41] Curiously enough the available papers make no reference to *Truth*, also engaged in propaganda against the war, but linked closely to the appeasement faction in the Conservative Party. There were other small organizations running their own campaigns; thus anti-Semitic members of the Nordic League had been employing 'sticky-backs' which could be affixed discretely inside telephone kiosks, and elsewhere, to oppose the war. This example is rather earlier, but gives the flavour: 'Last time it was KITCHENER WANTS YOU. This time it is the JEW HORE BELISHA WANTS YOU . . . ', and so on, surrounded with the initials PJ.[42]

At the same time the government also introduced a new Treachery Bill, which became law on 23 May.[43] This created an offence, punishable by death, for anyone who 'with intent to help the enemy . . . does or attempts or conspires with any other person to do any act which is designed or likely to give assistance to the naval, military or air operations of the enemy, to impede such operations of His Majesty's forces, or to endanger life . . . ' Ostensibly the purpose was to enable aliens entering Britain as agents to be tried for the new offence where, for technical reasons, it might not be possible to charge them with treason. To commit treason you have to owe allegiance, and it was said to be dubious whether a very recently arrived spy or saboteur, as opposed to a resident enemy alien,

---

[39] HO 144/21540.   [40] *Parl. Deb.* HC Vol. 360 cc. 1380–9.

[41] Thus in CAB 75/7 HPC (40) 103 there is a list of propaganda papers then (on 4 May) opposing the war, and this includes a list of right-wing papers: *Action, Action News Letter,* the *Patriot,* the *British Union Quarterly,* the *Free Press,* the *People's Post, Headline Newsletter* (connected with A. P. Laurie, H. St J. Philby, Adm. Domvile, and Ben Greene) and the *Angles* (published by Leese's IFL). Of the communist papers the *Daily Worker* and Claud Cockburn's *Week* were the most significant. 2C was never apparently enforced; the *Daily Worker* and *Week* were banned on 21 January 1941 under 2D of 29 May (SRO No. 828), which did not require a warning. HO 144/25580. The *Daily Mirror* was warned informally.

[42] Specimens in HO 144/22454; Hore-Belisha was dismissed from office on 2 January 1940. He was a favourite target for anti-Semitism; see e.g. *Truth* for 12 and 19 January. PJ is 'Perish Judah'.

[43] Originally The Assistance to the Enemy Bill in 1939. Defence Regulation 2A created an offence of doing acts likely to assist the enemy (etc.) with intent, with a possible life sentence. It was originally envisaged that serious cases would be prosecuted as treason. The Treachery Act was an alternative to attaching a possible death penalty to 2A. See CAB 75/3 HPC (39) 86, CAB 75/7 105, CAB 75/5 HPC (40) 11th meeting.

would owe allegiance; possibly the Law Officers had given an opinion on the point.[44] The legislation also enabled such aliens to be tried by courts martial, and accorded soldiers tried by civil courts the dubious privilege of being shot rather than hanged. The presentation of this legislation was somewhat disingenuous in not explaining that it bypassed the rule that two witnesses were required for an act of treason, a very important protection for the accused, eventually abolished in 1945.[45] During the war there were no treason trials; trials for treachery were simpler and led to the same result.[46]

The German Offensive in the West

The day after Anderson announced the changes in the regulations Chamberlain resigned, and Churchill took office. Anderson continued as Home Secretary and Minister of Home Security. The military situation rapidly grew worse. The Norwegian campaign dragged on until the capture of Narvik on 28 May, a belated and pointless success; the more terrifying and unnatural events took place on the Continent. On the very day Churchill took office the German armies launched their attack, principally through the Ardennes; by 13–14 May the river Meuse had been crossed, and, by the 15 May seven Panzer divisions had driven a massive breach between General Huntzinger's Second Army to the north and General Corap's Third Army to the south. The invincible French army was soon in a state of collapse; the Panzers were now free to go more or less where they wished. They turned north towards the sea. Coinciding with the attack through the Ardennes the German right-wing violated Dutch and Belgian neutrality and fell upon the northern forces, which included the nine divisions of the British Expeditionary Force. The rapidity of the German advance was almost incomprehensible. By 15 May the Low Countries had been entirely overrun. On 19 May the left-wing of the German forces reached the sea at Abbeville, cutting off both the BEF and large bodies of French troops; sixty divisions had been surrounded. The only hope lay in an attack to the south to stem the breach, cut the line of communication of the leading Panzers, and re-establish a line of defence. By 25 May this had clearly become impossible. Inevitably relations between the French and the British began to deteriorate.[47] On 27 May King Leopold of Belgium accepted unconditional surrender, and on

[44] Aliens owe 'local' allegiance if they are under the protection of the Crown.
[45] See *Parl. Deb.* HC Vol. 361 c.185. The Treachery Act lapsed in 1946 after the law of treason had been modified.
[46] See Appendix III.
[47] See E. M. Gates in *End of the Affair: The Collapse of the Anglo-French Alliance, 1939–40* (Berkeley, Calif., 1981).

the same day it was settled in London that Lord Gort, as Commander of the British Forces, had only one task: evacuation from the area around Dunkirk.

The evacuation, viewed by the British almost as a victory, and by the French as desertion, took place between 26 May and 4 June. The defeat destroyed the only effective army the British possessed, and gravely weakened Fighter Command of the RAF. Once it became clear that France was defeated Italy, on 10 June, declared war. This was followed on 16 June by the collapse of the French government of M. Paul Reynaud, and Marshal Pétain's government at once set about negotiating peace. An armistice was signed at 6.50 p.m. on 22 June, and one with Italy two days later. All that separated Britain from the German armies was the English Channel, so narrow indeed that heavy artillery could and did fire shells across it.

By 27 May the Chiefs of Staff were considering whether, if France fell, Britain could continue the war alone.[48] The situation greatly strengthened the hand of those, whether in or out of government, who thought that there should be a negotiated peace with Hitler, as he wanted, though whether a settlement would have long endured is necessarily uncertain. The matter was discussed at five Cabinet meetings between 26 and 28 May, well before France fell; Churchill initially wavered before committing himself to the view that Britain should, for the time being at least, fight on.[49] In public this necessarily was expressed as dogged opposition to any negotiation whatsoever.[50] When, by about 14 June, it became clear that France would ask for terms, the matter naturally became pressing. The Foreign Office, through Butler, engaged in an approach to Germany in mid-June.[51] The possibility was discussed at a Cabinet meeting on 18 June which, in the absence of Churchill, was presided over by Halifax.[52]

---

[48] CAB 80/11 COS (40) 168, CAB 66/7 WP (40) 168. The possibility of an invasion had been considered by the Joint Intelligence Committee on 23 May and 1 May (see Hinsley and Simkins, 48).

[49] Gilbert, 'Finest Hour', 410–13, discussing the War Cabinet meeting of 27 May 1940 (CAB 65/13 Confidential Annex) and the diaries of Halifax and Cadogan. What was principally considered was intervention by Mussolini. Fuller discussion is in Ponting, 1940 ch. 6; Costello, Ten Days, passim.

[50] The policy was announced to junior ministers on 3 June and in Churchill's speech to the Commons on 4 June, and again on 18 June in the 'finest hour' speech (Gilbert, 'Finest Hour', 463–8 and 569–70). It was apparently repeated in the Secret Session in the Commons on 20 June (see ibid. 577).

[51] See Ponting, 1940, 112–13 and Costello, Ten Days, App. 10 on this approach through Bjorn Prytz, the Swedish minister in London.

[52] See D. J. C. Irving, Churchill's War: The Struggle for Power (Bullsbrook, W. Australia, 1987), i. 334–5. Irving relies on an entry in Cadogan's diary relating to this meeting which ends 'No reply from the Germans', and on the fact that records for 17 and 18 June have not been fully released. See CAB 65/7 WM (40) 171st. Conclusions Item 5. See also Lamb, Ghosts of Peace and Roberts, 'Holy Fox'. For Butler see Gilbert 'Finest Hour',

Churchill's public pronouncements, particularly the 'finest hour' speech, which he was preparing as the Cabinet, in his diplomatic absence, wavered, was directed as much at some of his senior colleagues, as at the public generally.

By January 1941, with Halifax out of the way, Churchill was able to tell Eden, in connection with an approach through one Carl Bonde: 'Our attitude towards all such enquiries or suggestions should be absolute silence. It may well be that a new peace offensive will open upon us as an alternative to threats of invasion and poison gas.'[53] But in the summer of 1940, when he wanted to prevent Halifax from becoming involved in an approach through the Vatican, the embargo was significantly limited to peace terms from Hitler.[54]

There was, in 1940, not the least foreseeable prospect of Britain actually reinvading Europe, nor was this the rhetoric of Churchill's government; it was our beaches on which we were going to fight, not the beaches of Europe. In 1940 the only offensive weapon was economic blockade. As the war developed the apparent impossibility of reinvasion was to lend support to the evil and misguided notion that Germany could be defeated by area bombing, but in 1940 the RAF did not possess the equipment needed. Churchill's policy, initially apparently directed to securing peace, though not from Hitler, on acceptable terms, was dependent on the USA providing support, and even eventually entering the war, which seemed very improbable in May and June of 1940. The USA never did declare war on Germany; Germany declared war on the USA. Once committed to fighting on, however, Churchill's government, from which Halifax was removed in December 1940, succeeded in presenting its policy as absolutely necessary; otherwise Britain would be invaded and crushed, just as Belgium, Holland, Denmark, Norway and even France had been invaded and crushed. The policy was also presented in quasi-religious terms as a crusade against a devil, Hitler, and his evil faith, fascism.

Given such a policy, it inevitably followed that the most ruthless action should be taken to prevent any domestic weakening of the war effort, or any risk of a successful German invasion. And it hardly made sense to wage a crusade against organized fascism abroad, whilst tolerating fascist business as usual at home.

An additional and compelling reason for ruthlessly repressing the fascists was the belief in the existence, in Britain, of an organized military Fifth Column, of which the fascists might form a major part.

598–9. See FO 800/322 Churchill to Halifax on 25 June 1940 and Telegram 743 of 19 June, Mallet to FO.

[53] FO 371/26542.

[54] Halifax should say that 'we do not desire to make any enquiries as to terms of peace with Hitler . . . ' See Irving, *Hitler's War*, 341.

The Fifth Column

As we have seen, the idea of an 'enemy within' had long existed,[55] and in his memoirs Churchill recounts how he armed himself in 1939 for protection against the 20,000 Nazis supposedly then in Britain.[56] The concept could serve various functions; thus in April 1940 the *Jewish Chronicle* viewed it as an anti-Semitic myth, no doubt because it could be used to justify the exclusion of Jewish refugees from Britain; by June the paper favoured the idea, since it was now directed at the fascists.[57] Its basic function in 1940 was explanatory. The extraordinary military success of Germany in 1940 cried out for special explanation: the special explanation was the Fifth Column.

MI5 had long been clear on the matter; Kell, back in December of 1939, had sent out a letter stating that 'A number of well authenticated instances of illicit "light" signalling had been reported by the Observer Corps', and established a system for reporting this self-evidently mythical activity.[58] The press encouraged hysteria.[59] In 1940 the ubiquity of traitors, signalling to enemy aircraft with lights, became an established fact. The police and MI5 were of course inundated with reports.[60] Police circulars reveal other anxieties: suspicious cars visiting aerodromes, subversive groups wearing similar pullovers (presumably fascists), yellow paint markings on telegraph poles (in fact placed there in connection with a government-sponsored survey), possession of large coloured crayons, or copies of the *Fishing Gazette*.[61] Spying maidservants were a particular source of fear; a Mrs Margaret E. Newitt was detained from October 1940

[55] On the Fifth Column see FO 371/25193 (MI5 Security Bulletin No. 1 of 17 June 1940), INF 1/333 (includes memorandum on 'Fifth Column tricks'), INF 1/336 and 257 ('Defeatism and Fifth Column Activities'). The latter includes a memorandum of 1 June 1940 stating that the NBBS, a clandestine German radio station, was issuing instructions to the Fifth Column. Also WO 199/1981 (miscellaneous intelligence reports), 1982 (suspicious lights), MEPO 2/3442 (lights). S. Firmin, *They Came to Spy* (London, 1947), 11 and E. H. Cookridge, *Secrets of the British Secret Service* (London, 1948), 84 perpetuated this myth after the war; see de Jong, *German Fifth Column*, 208.
[56] *The Second World War*, ii. *Their Finest Hour* (London, 1949), 313.
[57] Issues for 26 April and 7 June.
[58] MEPO 2/3442, letter of 22 December from MI5 B3A. HH 55/864 (Scottish Police Circulars) for 25 June (4038) and 10 July (4074), the latter attempting to reduce the reporting of normal RAF lights.
[59] For examples see *The Times*, 23 April, the *Sunday Dispatch*, 31 March, 7 April, 14 April, the *Yorkshire Post* and *Daily Telegraph*, 16 April, *Daily Mail*, 19 April, discussed P. and L. Gillman, *'Collar the Lot!'* (London, 1980), 74–80.
[60] e.g. *The Times* for 23 April 1940. Hinsley and Simkins, 66, note that reports of signalling occupied the time of 5 officers, the files reaching a height of 5 ft. INF 1/336 (Home Press Summaries 17 Oct. 1940–9 Oct. 1941) contains press reports of supposed Fifth Column activities. Lord Lymington was reported for signalling by his neighbours no doubt suspicious of his political activities; see his *A Knot of Roots* (London, 1965), 197.
[61] HH 55/864, circulars of 25 March, 7 June, 11 June, 1 July.

until early 1945 because her domestic agency was suspected.[62] In March of 1940 MI5 and the GPO became anxious over a much less ludicrous threat—concealed radio beacons to guide enemy bombers; the Defence Regulations were amended to facilitate searches.[63] Naturally persons with German connections were under close popular scrutiny. Kurt Hahn's Gordonstoun School, for example, was obviously a spy centre, and five German teachers and eleven pupils were interned.[64]

Senior military officers shared these fears. General Ironside's diary for 31 May reads: 'Fifth column reports coming in from everywhere. A Man with an arm band on and a swastika pulled up near an important aerodrome in the Southern Command District. Important telegraph poles marked, suspicious men moving at night all over the country . . . Perhaps we shall catch some swine.' On July the General confessed to puzzlement: 'It is extraordinary how we . . . have never been able to get anything worth having. And yet there is signalling going on all over the place and we cannot get any evidence. A German wife of an R.A.F. man who has been in domestic service in the Admiral's house at Portsmouth, was run in for trying to get hold of some blueprints.'[65] The incident mentioned did happen; she was Mrs Marie L. A. Ingram, the German born wife of an RAF sergeant, convicted on 2 July with William Swift, a dockyard worker, and sentenced to ten years, though she was acquitted of stealing the blueprint. Swift got fourteen. Such proof of real misconduct became the tip of the iceberg of undiscovered treachery.[66]

The Fifth Column achieved official status even before the invasion of the Low Countries in a memorandum, 'Fifth Column Activities in the United Kingdom', adopted by the Joint Intelligence Committee on 2 May. Though still secret, its tone is caught by the following index entry: 'Fifth Column Activities in the United Kingdom. Activities in the United Kingdom. Organization probable. Precautions. Adequacy should be care-

---

[62] Presumably left at large at first under surveillance; from her file (HO 45/25739) there seems to have been no real evidence of misconduct against her.

[63] CAB 75/4 HPC 10th meeting of 12 March 1940. CAB 75/6 HPC 11 March. SRO 1940 No. 828. HH 55/871, police circular of 14 June.

[64] H. L. Brereton, *Gordonstoun: Ancient Estate and Modern School* (Edinburgh, 1968). Kurt Hahn (1886–1974) had in fact been imprisoned by Hitler in 1933; he was naturalized. There is a closed file (HH 55/649) in the Scottish Record Office; the description records the detentions. HO 215/14 has a plea by Hahn for the release of a number of people, some associated with Gordonstoun, including the scholar of Greek law, Professor Pringsheim.

[65] R. Macleod and D. Kelly (eds.), *The Ironside Diaries 1937–1940* (London, 1962).

[66] Archibald Watts, a BU D/L, was acquitted, but detained. She had obtained information from Swift with the intention of assisting the enemy, attempted to obtain information from a Corporal in the Tank Corps, and incited one Cecil Rashleigh to join the Local Defence Volunteers to obtain arms and ammunition. See *The Times*, 1 June, 3 July, 27 August 1940, *Daily Telegraph*, 1 June, *Daily Express*, 3 July, *News of the World*, 7 July, and N. West, *MI5* (London, 1983), 161–2.

fully considered. Action deferred till an emergency, too late.'[67] A slightly later report 'stressed in particular the completeness of the German plans for such an invasion, their effectiveness in sabotaging all attempts at resistance and the secrecy with which the German preparations were carried out.'[68] Whilst the Joint Intelligence Committee

did not feel *entitled* to recommend that the leading members of the British Union of Fascist and similar subversive organizations should be locked up forthwith, they felt that this should be done . . . we cannot rule out the possibility that 'Fifth Column' activities in this country, at present dormant, might well play a very active and dangerous part at the appropriate moment selected by the enemy. *Indeed the absence of sabotage up to date reinforces the view that such activities will only take place as part of a prearranged military plan* [my italics].[69]

The committee thought the IRA might be involved too.[70] The Ministry of Information waxed lyrical on the threat:

The Fifth Column may worm its way into the life of the country that is to be attacked in many ways. It may profess an invincible love of holy peace. It may profess detestation of Hitler while covertly influencing public opinion by slyly hinting at certain admirable aspects of his regime . . . Whatever its disguises, at the moment of action the Fifth Column acts as one man to perform its task.[71]

The classic official account, a memorandum by Sir Nevile Bland, British Ambassador to The Hague, dates from after the fall of the Low Countries.[72] Bland, like many who employ domestic servants, nourished a deep fear of their possible treachery: 'It is clear that the paltriest kitchen maid with such [i.e. German or Austrian] origins not only can be, but generally is, a menace to the safety of the country.' He was also suspicious of Jewish refugees, and certain that there was a German master plan, though he did not know what it was: 'I have not the least doubt that, when the signal is given, as it will scarcely fail to be when Hitler so decides, there will be satellites of the monster *all over the country* who will at once embark on widespread sabotage and attacks on civilians and the military indiscriminately.'[73] The same Foreign Office file contains a

[67] CAB 67/7 WP (40) 153 of 10 May. COS (40) 315 (JIC) 2 May 1940. The index entry is in CAB 75.

[68] Summarized in FO 371/25189.   [69] In FO 371/25189 420ff. dated 17 May.

[70] The IRA bombing campaign ended in March 1940. See T. P. Coogan, *The IRA* (London, 1990), 260–78; apparently the supposed German connection amounted to nothing.

[71] Memorandum of 24 May on Fifth Column Activities prepared by MI7 (b) in INF 1/333.

[72] FO 371/25189 at 420ff. (includes Home Office memorandum of 22 May on action taken to counter the invasion threat). With British official assistance a series of articles on the Fifth Column appeared in the *New York Times* for 20, 21, 22, and 23 August 1940, by Col. W. J. Donovan and E. Kowrar.

[73] Italics in the original. Bland was one of those appointed to look into Foreign Office security after the Burgess and Maclean affair, a fact which does not excite confidence in the result. See R. Cecil, *A Divided Life: A Personal Portrait of the Spy Donald Maclean* (New York, 1989), 157.

report on parachute troops. Many of these, the Foreign Office was assured, were servant girls of German or Austrian origin who had been recalled for training not long before the invasion. This is how they were dropped: 'I was told that the men and women sit tightly packed in a row. When the pilot pushes a button the bottom falls out of the plane, and they all fall out at once, in some cases thirty at a time.'

This and much other rubbish was taken seriously; the principal victims were aliens, but British subjects suffered as well. The folly of it all was recognized by some; thus the Home Morale Emergency Committee, a somewhat ludicrous offshoot of the Ministry of Information, recommended on 4 June 1940: 'The fifth column and aliens problem should be dealt with in a sedative manner. The Committee feel that a calm talk by Sir John Anderson on the subject might go far to check the almost hysterical wave of suspicion that is passing across the country'.[74] But this was exceptional. One product was a spate of ridiculous prosecutions under the Defence Regulations; another was the shooting of a number of persons at road blocks. Papers in the Scottish Records show that some citizens, held at the muzzle of a rifle wielded by an aged member of the Local Defence Volunteers (later the Home Guard) at road blocks, vomited through fear.

German success had nothing to do with the Fifth Column, in the sense of an organized military organization, and little to do with another bogey of the time—airborne landings, though these did play a small part.[75] But this is something we know through hindsight; it was not obvious in May and June of 1940. And those who believe in the enemy in our midst have minds insulated against evidence; its absence proves the extreme skill of the enemy.[76] Thus Bland on 30 May assured the public through the BBC: 'It is not the German or Austrian who is found out who is the danger. It is the one, whether man or woman, who is too clever to be found out.'[77] Harvey Klemmer's discussions of the threat with members of MI5 about this time produced estimates of the size of the Fifth Column which varied from 1,000 to 10,000.[78]

Thus Britain in the summer of 1940 came to resemble America in the time of Senator McCarthy, a society obsessed with the hunting down of witches. And the scheme of totalitarian government enshrined in the Defence Regulations, together with the professional witch-finders of Special Branch and the security service, lay ready to hand.

---

[74] INF 1/254. But the committee favoured interning the communist and fascist leaders.

[75] See de Jong, *German Fifth Column*.

[76] The MI5 officers principally concerned told Anderson on about 21 May that they had no actual evidence of agents posing as refugees.

[77] Quoted Gillman, '*Collar the Lot!*' at 110.   [78] See above Ch. 3.

The Home Office in Retreat

So it was that in May of 1940 Anderson was compelled to accept a policy, which he had previously resisted, of mass internment of enemy aliens, and to start to implement it.[79] Presumably this was the subject for discussion on 12 May when Kell took Maxwell and Scott of the Home Office out to lunch.[80] The first formal decision had been taken by the War Cabinet the day before, immediately after Churchill took office.[81] All male enemy aliens in a widely defined coastal zone were to be detained.[82] Five or six days later it was decided to intern all enemy alien males between the ages of 16 and 60 who had been placed in category 'B' by the Aliens Tribunals.[83] There were around 6,800 aliens in this category.[84] Those in category 'C', comprising above 64,000 individuals, were left for the moment unrestricted. The pressure came from the military, to whom the Home Office necessarily had to defer once a real or imagined threat of invasion became established. The Chiefs of Staff accepted the views of the Joint Intelligence Committee on 10 May.[85] Pressure to act against the Fifth Column also came from MI5, which on 11 May recommended the detention of 500 members of the BU, a recommendation which the Home Office officials resisted.[86]

On 15 May the War Cabinet itself discussed Bland's paper. Anderson said that there were a number of groups against whom action would need to be taken and, so far as citizens were concerned, mentioned those of Italian origin, and the British fascists and communists.[87] But he opposed premature action against the fascists and communists, which would enable them to rebuild their organization. On about 16 May MI5, with Home Office consent, circularized Chief Constables with a list of thirty-nine communists who were on a provisional detention list, but was

[79] Stammers, *Civil Liberties*, 37, Hinsley and Simkins, ch. 3 *passim*.

[80] Presumably Harold Scott as head of F division.

[81] Attended by Churchill, Halifax, and Chamberlain and by a number of military officers including the Deputy Chief of the Imperial General Staff, Sir John Dill.

[82] CAB 65/7, WM 119A. The history is set out by Stammers, *Civil Liberties*, ch. 2. See also J. W. Wheeler-Bennett, *John Anderson, Viscount Waverley* (London, 1962), 238–47, Gillman, '*Collar the Lot!*' and R. Stent, *A Bespattered Page? The Internment of His Majesty's 'Most Loyal Enemy Aliens'* (London, 1980).

[83] These tribunals existed to classify enemy aliens into three basic categories. Category 'A' aliens were to be interned. Category 'B' aliens, before the summer of 1940, had merely been subject to certain restrictions, for example as to their movements, and the ownership of cameras.

[84] Stammers, *Civil Liberties*, relying on *Parl. Deb.* HC Vol. 357 c.2410 of 1 March when the number in Category 'A' who had been interned was 569, the number restricted was 6,782, and the number left quite free was 64,244. The number of known refugees from the Nazis was 55,457.

[85] CAB 66/7, WP (40) 153 10 May.   [86] Hinsley and Simkins, 48.

[87] CAB 65/7 No. 123 of 1940. Amongst non-citizens he mentioned Czech refugees, and refugees from the Netherlands and Belgium.

informed that ministers were for the time-being against taking any action.[88] Anderson, with his record in Ireland and Bengal, was neither an inexperienced nor an unwilling user of detention against subversive groups if he thought it desirable. His point was ostensibly that of an administrator: it was not the right moment to act if action was to be effective. But he and his officials may also have been using the argument from unripe time to restrain unreasonable demands for infringements of civil liberty, which the evidence did not support as in any way necessary; action deferred may eventually become action never taken.

Another reason for delay may have been that MI5's information on the fascists was at least five months out of date, which indicates the administrative confusion which then existed in that organization. Three days earlier Cecil Liddell had written to Chief Constables:

We are anxious to know in the shortest possible time the leading officials of the Fascist movement in your area . . . the names on the attached list were the BU officials up to the end of last year . . . let me know if you can suggest any alterations in the list. If you think enquiries, which would take time, are needed to answer our enquiry fully would you be so good as to give me a provisional answer within the next few days.[89]

Anderson's fear that the BU might rebuild its organization may have also arisen because MI5, though suspecting the existence of an 'underground BU' and a conspiracy of the right, had as yet no hard information on the matter. And since MI5 had produced little evidence of 'hostile associations', or 'acts prejudicial', only a handful of fascists, and perhaps none of the leaders, could properly be interned under the existing Regulation 18B.

Churchill in the War Cabinet on 15 May supported action: 'a very large round-up of enemy aliens *and suspect persons* [my italics]'. His colleagues agreed, and it was at this meeting that the decision in principle was taken which led to the great incarceration of citizens during the summer of 1940. But precisely what action should be taken, and when, was left open and, given Home Office respect for legality, necessarily depended upon such evidence as MI5 could deliver. Anderson, Attlee, and Greenwood were asked to advise and report back. On the same day there was a conference between the Joint Intelligence Committee, Home Office officials, and representatives of MI5; what passed at it is not known. There was apparently some friction at this time between Maxwell and MI5 over MI5's

[88] The only source here is Hinsley and Simkins, 48–9, who give no reference. The list appears to have included some foreign communists as well as members of the CPGB. Britain had a sizeable resident Russian population.

[89] HO 45/25726. Cecil Liddell MC, brother of Guy Maynard Liddell, who also worked in MI5. There was a barrister, Cecil F. J. Liddell, probably the same person.

attempts to bypass the Home Office and put its views to the military direct.[90]

Kell, the following day, attended a meeting at Scotland Yard 'with P. Game & Knight & Sneath re BUF's etc.', presumably to make provisional plans for an operation against the fascists. Sir Philip Game was the Metropolitan Police Commissioner. Knight was Charles Maxwell Knight (he usually hyphenated his name), the bizarre MI5 officer made familiar through *The Man Who Was M* by Anthony Masters and Joan Miller's *One Girl's War*; he was in charge of MI5's B5 (b) section, which seems to have operated somewhat independently from the rest of MI5. Sneath was (Francis) Brian Aikin-Sneath, in charge of B7, the section concerned with the general surveillance of the BU and other right-wing groups. He was a somewhat intriguing individual. Born in 1905, he was the son of Francis Aikin-Sneath, who had been a cattle-farmer in Uruguay. He was educated at Harrow and Christ Church, Oxford; after reading chemistry he studied literature and then became an unsuccessful schoolmaster at Dulwich. He left to teach literature in Germany at the Universities of Kiel and Berlin. Originally agnostic, he was appalled by the rise of Nazism, and progressively adopted the view that Christianity was the riposte to it. Curiously enough, his aunt by marriage, Florence, had been active in the BUF in Chiswick until her death in 1935. He returned to England with his German wife, whom he had married in 1932, and joined MI5 on 1 May 1939, where his experience was naturally important. He retired from public service in 1965 and entered Wycliffe Hall theological college in Oxford. Both his grandfather Thomas and his uncle Donald had been clergymen. After ordination he became a curate at Hartley Wintney, where he is remembered as a thoughtful and deeply religious person. He died there on 22 April 1972. Until I contacted them his family was entirely unaware of his work with MI5; it is curious indeed that his part in the destruction of the BU has been so long concealed.[91]

On the day Kell was making his plans at Scotland Yard the Chiefs of Staff put forward proposals to the Cabinet, which included: 'vii. The control of known Communists, Nazis, members of the Link and the B.U.F. and similar parties, and any other British subjects suspected of subversive

---

[90] JIC (40) 29th meeting 15 May.

[91] He graduated in 1924. See FO 395/633 for an attempt by him to establish a British School in Berlin. Married Elizabeth Dudloff in 1932; OBE 1952. According to W. J. West, *Truth Betrayed* (London, 1987), 219–20 his job concerned German political exiles; some of his memoranda are quoted in A. Glees, *Exile Politics in Britain during the Second World War: The German Social Democrats in Britain* (Oxford 1982). In November 1952 he was appointed First Secretary (Information) at Helsinki, which I take to be an intelligence job. He was appointed Consul at Surabaya in 1954, and then moved to South America, becoming Consul (Commercial) at São Paulo in September, and holding consular posts there and at Santos.

activities should be tightened up.'[92] These vague proposals, and a paper by Anderson, were considered by the cabinet on 18 May.[93] Anderson described what had already been done; for example 100 members of the IRA had been convicted, and 167 expelled. His paper again argued that drastic action was premature. In the discussion, which seems to have focused on the fascists, Anderson is reported thus: 'In regard to the British Fascists the HS explained at length the difficulty of taking any *effective* action in the absence of evidence which indicated that the *organization as such* was engaged in disloyal activities [my italics].' Anderson respected legality, and under the existing law only a few individuals could be detained; their arrest would not cripple the organization as a whole. He thought it would be a mistake to act unless there was good reason to believe that the BU was about to assist the enemy, and at that point the leaders could of course be detained under the 'acts prejudicial' limb of 18B, which covered the preparation or instigation of such acts.

The mild conclusion reached, according to Churchill's summary, was that it would be desirable to 'stiffen up the measures already taken'.[94] On the same day Churchill made his personal views very clear in a memorandum to General Ismay: 'Action should also [i.e. in addition to action against aliens] be taken against Communists and Fascists, and very considerable numbers should be put in protective or preventive internment, including their leaders.'[95] Thus it came about that the cabinet, on 18 May, reaffirmed its policy of action of an unspecified kind against the Fifth Column, but left Anderson with freedom of action in implementing this policy.[96]

The Critical Decision

On 21 May there was a meeting between representatives of MI5, who almost certainly included Maxwell-Knight and Aikin-Sneath, and Anderson; the principal source is Hinsley and Simkins' official history, referring to an MI5 minute.[97] There was need to brief Anderson for the Cabinet because of the arrest on 20 May of Tyler Kent, a cipher clerk in the US Embassy, who had been abstracting secret documents; Captain A. H. M. ('Jock' or 'Maule') Ramsay MP was involved to some degree with Kent; a fuller account of this affair will be given in due course. MI5 again pressed for action against the fascists, although the BU had not been

[92] CAB 80/11 COS (40) 359 (JIC) 16 May, 364 18 May.
[93] The Home Office document was a paper on 'Invasion of Great Britain: possible co-operation of a 5th column'. CAB 67/6 WP (G) (40) 131.
[94] CAB 65/7, WM (40) 128 18 May.
[95] Churchill, *Their Finest Hour*, 49. See also CAB 65/7 WM 123 (40) 139.
[96] Stammers, *Civil Liberties*, 24–5, CAB 67/6 WP (G) (40) 131, and CAB 65/7 WM 128.
[97] Hinsley and Simkins, 50.

involved at all with Kent's activities. Anderson is quoted as saying that 'he needed to be reasonably convinced that the BU might assist the enemy and that unless he could get such evidence it would be a mistake to imprison Mosley and his supporters who would be extremely bitter after the war when democracy would be going through its severest trials'.

But the following day the cabinet decided to intern Sir Oswald Mosley and a number of his more prominent followers under a new addition to Regulation 18B, directed at the organization as a whole. This, 18B (1A), was passed by the Privy Council the same night.[98] Since surprise was essential there were no Parliamentary consultations. There is no evidence as to when the new regulation was drafted, or by whom; one file which may contain material is not available, and one that is appears to have the material removed.[99] The arrests began on 23 May. The same meeting approved in principle the arrest and either detention, or prosecution, of Ramsay. The Home Office in no way opposed or sought to delay this; clearly something had triggered action, and this was the Tyler Kent affair which, in conjunction with some other evidence, gave a new reality to the theory of the Fifth Column, and led to the great incarceration of the summer of 1940.[100]

For in the final days of May the restrained use of detention ended; seventy-three orders were implemented, and considerably over 400 signed, many on 30 May. Sixty-nine of those implemented related to British subjects, of whom fifty were ordinary native-born citizens.[101] These fifty detainees included the two very prominent individuals mentioned. Ramsay, the Conservative member for Peebles and Midlothian, had never been a member of the BU.[102] Thirty-four other individuals, including a number of BU officials, were detained by orders made on the same day, 22 May. They included two fairly well-known members of the BPP: John W. Beckett, a former Labour MP who had been a prominent member of

[98] CAB 65/7 WM 133. Churchill was absent but his views were known; the decision was taken by Chamberlain, Attlee, Halifax, and Greenwood.

[99] HO 45/25504, 25507.

[100] It has been suggested that a promise to cripple the BU was a condition of Labour Party support for Churchill. This idea was widely discussed at the Labour Party conference, in session when Chamberlain's government collapsed, but all sorts of foolish gossip circulates at such events. The documentary evidence—for example of Attlee and Greenwood acquiescing at first in Anderson's reluctance to take precipitate action—is quite incompatible with this theory.

[101] *Parliamentary Papers*, IV 203 (1 Sept. 1939–30 Sept. 1940).

[102] After a distinguished career in the 1st World War, in which he was badly wounded, he entered Parliament in 1931. In addition to the Right Club, founded in May 1939, and probably a development of the Co-ordinating Committee of the Nordic League, Ramsay had founded the United Christian Front in 1937. He explains his discovery, in about 1938, of the world Jewish conspiracy in his book *The Nameless War* (London, n.d. [1952]). See R. Griffiths, *Fellow Travellers of the Right: British Enthusiasts for Nazi Germany, 1933–9* (London, 1980), *passim* and esp. 354.

the BU and also of the National Socialist League, and Ben Greene, a former Labour Party activist and Quaker pacifist. Ramsay, Beckett, and Greene were detained under the pre-existing Regulation 18B, Ramsay and Beckett for 'acts prejudicial', and Greene for 'hostile associations'. But thirty-three of the orders made on 22 May were made under the new Regulation 18B (1A), explicitly designed to allow the government to cripple Mosley's fascist party. Eventually some 750 supposed fascists were interned. And on 28 May the Home Office accepted defeat in its long-running battle with MI5 over the supposed German spy ring; eight individuals were detained under 18B, including an unfortunate naturalized German lawyer, Frederick W. Braune, who had been solicitor to the German Embassy and had virtually no connection with the suspected companies at all; he had suffered the same fate in the First World War.[103] By 6 June 515 persons were in custody.[104] When Italy entered the war they were joined by another large group of around 600 Anglo-Italians, detained as 'of hostile origin or associations'. By the end of August the total was 1,428 [105]

It was the decision to proceed against the BU which initiated the mass detentions of the summer of 1940. We must now consider what it was about Mosley's party which led to this action, and what part the curious affair of Tyler Kent played in the matter.

---

[103] HO 45/25497. Those detained were H. H. Simon, G. N. Lange, E. Lange, K. Frowein, K. Wolff, and F. W. Braune ('hostile origins'); and W. E. Block and A. E. Block ('acts prejudicial'). Two other persons were detained under the prerogative. The MI5 officer concerned seems to have been J. C. Curry.

[104] *Parl. Deb.* HC Vol. 361 c.978.   [105] Figures in *Parliamentary Papers*, IV 203.

7

Fascism and the Fears of 1940

The Origins of Fascism in Britain

Why did the BU seem so threatening that it was singled out for suppression in May of 1940? Any answer requires some explanation of the history of fascism in Britain, more particularly because the terms 'fascist' and 'fascism' are so commonly used today as mere terms of abuse. Fascism defies any simple definition, and there are problems about its nature. For example Keegan has said that 'whether Hitler should be regarded as a fascist in the ideological sense is extremely doubtful'.[1] At first this seems perverse. If we identify fascists as people committed to certain political programmes, one such programme was the creation of a corporate state. This was central to Italian fascism; in Britain a principal exponent was Alexander Raven-Thomson.[2] Mosley adopted the idea, though he later partly repudiated it.[3] Corporatism appeared in the party constitution of 1938: 'The name of the Movement is the British Union and the faith of the Movement is the National Socialist and Fascist creed. The object of the British Union is to win power by votes and thereby to establish in Great Britain the Corporate State.'[4] But Keegan's point is that Hitler, to many a paradigm case of a fascist, had little interest in the matter.

Indeed many fascists, even prominent ones, had as little interest in policies as many devout Catholics have in theology. Policy, as Hector G. McKechnie, a leading British fascist, was to explain to Birkett in 1940, was absolutely none of his concern; it was a matter for the leader.[5] To McKechnie fascism was more a set of attitudes of mind, a movement to which you committed yourself, than a shopping list of policies with which you agreed. Nor is it easy to separate fascism from other established forces in European political life. Thus Lord Dacre has argued that General Franco was not a fascist; it is an error to confuse the old

[1] J. Keegan, *The Masks of Command* (London, 1988), 253.
[2] *The Coming Corporate State* (London, 1935). Also E. G. Mandeville Roe, *The Corporate State* (London, 1934).
[3] O. Mosley, *My Life* (London, 1968), 331–3, 361–2; R. Skidelsky, *Oswald Mosley* (London, 1975), 228, 308, 314–15.
[4] Saunders Papers, Sheffield University. The constitution of 1936 is similar.
[5] HO 283/48, hearing of 8 July 1940.

reactionary conservative tradition in European politics, to which Franco, like a number of British aristocrats, belonged, with an essentially radical and revolutionary bourgeois movement, with which he made common cause.[6] Again British fascism came to be associated with both anti-Semitism and nostalgic veteranism; both existed quite independently of fascism, as they still do.[7]

What follows is a short account of British fascism so far as this is relevant to the government's decision in 1940. The subject is still relatively unexplored, and official behaviour over records, especially those seized in 1940, has not helped.[8]

Organized British fascism originated in 1923, when, so the story goes, Miss Rotha Lintorn-Orman,[9] the wealthy granddaughter of Field Marshal Sir John Lintorn Arabin Simmons, whilst weeding her garden in Somerset, decided that Britain, like her vegetables, was being overrun by weeds—aliens such as socialists, communists, anarchists, Freemasons, and Jews; that the country was 'going to the dogs' became a persistent element in the movement. She formed the British Fascisti on 6 May 1923, which published *The British Fascist Bulletin*.[10] In so far as she had a model it was Mussolini's movement; there were, however, no organizational links. Her followers espoused patriotic loyalty to King and Country, unfocused opposition to the left, fear of bolshevism, and a belief that a crisis was coming. These were persistent themes in British fascism, as was political fervour and camaraderie. On 7 May 1924 her organization became the British Fascists Ltd. The first President was Lord Garvagh.[11] Brigadier R. B. D. Blakeney was prominent in the organization, which

[6] H. R. Trevor Roper, 'The Phenomenon of Fascism', in S. J. Woolf (ed.), *European Fascism* (New York and London, 1968).

[7] R. Griffiths, *Fellow Travellers of the Right: British Enthusiasts for Nazi Germany 1933–9* (London, 1980), 59–65; C. Holmes, *Anti-Semitism in British Society 1876–1939*, (London, 1979).

[8] In what follows I have relied partly on my own research into such collections of material as the Saunders Papers, MS accounts by and interviews with former BU members, and material in the PRO, in addition to published books, the most helpful being: C. Cross, *The Fascists in Britain* (London, 1961); R. C. Thurlow, *Fascism in Britain: A History, 1918–1985* (Oxford, 1987); and Skidelsky, *Oswald Mosley*. Also valuable are G. C. Webber, *The Ideology of the British Right 1918–1939* (London, 1986); Griffiths, *Fellow Travellers of the Right*; D. S. Lewis, *Illusions of Grandeur. Mosley, Fascism and British Society 1931–1981* (Manchester, 1987); and N. Mosley, *Beyond the Pale: Sir Oswald Mosley and his Family 1933–1980* (London, 1987). Fascist papers, such as *Blackshirt, Action*, the *British Fascisti Bulletin*, contain much information and photographs of individuals; the British Library at Colindale has a good but incomplete collection.

[9] 1895–March 1935; associated with the Girl Guide Movement from 1909 in Bournemouth; an ambulance driver in the war; decorated twice for bravery in the Salonika campaign; invalided home 1917; Commandant in charge of training drivers for the Red Cross.

[10] 1924–6. Also *British Lion* 1926–9.

[11] 1878–1956. Probably related to Robert C. Gordon-Canning, a prominent BU member.

was run on military lines, and resembled a veterans' society.[12] Many fascists were upper middle-class persons, often of military background; a number of individuals who were later to become prominent fascists, such as William Joyce, Arnold S. Leese, Dorothy Viscountess Downe, and Neil Francis-Hawkins were associated with the group. Its members stewarded Conservative meetings in the name of law and order to protect them from disruption, an activity we shall encounter again. There was a Grand Council whose members included the Rt. Hon. Sir Arthur Hardinge,[13] and Lieutenant-Colonel Sir Charles Burn.[14] A women's section was run by a Mrs A. M. Wroughton.

When, with the General Strike of 1926, a real crisis arrived, the party broke up into factions. Some were anti-Semitic; the longest lasting and noisiest was the Imperial Fascist League, though its maximum membership was only about 150. It was largely the creation of Arnold S. Leese, a fanatical anti-Semite whom we shall meet again.[15]

It or perhaps the National Fascisti of 1924 first used the blackshirt uniform, and by 1933 it was using the swastika as a badge in place of the *fasces*. The IFL alone of the many factions survived even the Second World War, during which Leese and a small number of his followers were interned.[16] The British Fascists Ltd. survived, though in a sickly state, only until Miss Lintorn-Orman's death in 1935.

The British Union of Fascists

Sir Oswald Mosley Bt., who came from the landed gentry, was educated at Winchester and Sandhurst, and had a distinguished record in the Royal Flying Corps in the First World War; he was invalided out in 1916, and worked in the Foreign Office and Ministry of Munitions. He became a Conservative MP in 1918 at the age of 23. He dissociated himself from the party in protest at the Black and Tans in Ireland. Re-elected for Harrow as an Independent in 1923, he joined the ILP in 1924. In the election of

[12] 1872–1952. After distinguished military career general manager of the Egyptian railways 1919–23; strongly anti-Semitic; left the movement in 1926, later involved in Leese's IFL. During the 2nd World War he served in the Home Guard, the ARP service and the National Fire Service. Another prominent member was Vice Adm. J. G. Armstrong (1870–1949).

[13] Ambassador to Spain up to 1919.   [14] 1880–1925.

[15] 1878–1956; ex-army veterinary surgeon; expert on the diseases of camels; influenced by the Britons, an anti-Semitic organization founded by Henry H. Beamish (1872–1948) in 1919; became a fanatical anti-Semite; in 1932 acquired control over the IFL (formed in 1928 by Brig. D. Erskine-Tulloch, Maj. J. Baillie, L. H. Sherrard, and Leese); an indifferent public speaker; eccentric if not unbalanced. See HO 45/24967 and 25386. Leese wrote an autobiography, *Out of Step: Events in the Two Lives of an Anti-Jewish Camel Doctor* (Guildford, 1951) and other polemical works, such as *My Irrelevant Defence: Being Meditations inside Gaol and out on Jewish Ritual Murder* (London, 1938).

[16] See Cross, *Fascists in Britain* esp. 62–5, 152–4. His paper was the *Fascist*, 1929–39, and after the war *Gothic Ripples*.

October 1924 he narrowly failed to defeat Neville Chamberlain at Ladywood, Birmingham, and in 1926 won Smethwick in a by-election. Brilliant in debate, bitter at the folly of the First World War, and determined to improve the social conditions which followed upon it, Mosley soon became a rising star; in 1927 he was elected to the National Executive, winning more votes, for example, than Herbert Morrison. In 1929 he became Chancellor of the Duchy of Lancaster, and fathered a radical plan for dealing with unemployment and industrial depression, 'the Mosley Memorandum'; it was rejected by the Cabinet in March 1930. Disillusioned, Mosley resigned on 20 May. In a dramatic speech in the Commons on 28 May,[17] and one to the Annual Conference of the Labour Party on 7 October, he established himself as a major political figure, the representative of the new against the old, and a possible future leader of the party. But the voting went against him, and Mosley was never prepared to bide his time; confronted with a major economic crisis, none of the three political parties were, in his view, capable of effective action. John Strachey recalled the spectacle of Mosley 'sitting silent and alone, brooding with an indescribable bitterness, as the old, portly Trade Union officials and nervous pacifist intellectuals filed out of a party meeting at which they had affirmed their undiminished confidence in Mr Ramsay MacDonald'.[18] So in February of 1931 Mosley broke with Labour, and formed his own New Party.[19] The old institutions had failed: new institutions must replace them. Such beliefs, widespread at the time, were central to the rise of fascism. In a modified version of the Memorandum ('the Mosley Manifesto') he espoused revolution, portraying the Parliamentary system of government as an obstacle to action. By now he had many enemies; individuals like Ernest Bevin, who sympathized with his ideas, distrusted him personally, and his ferocious oratorical skill did not endear him to his rivals.

The New Party was a fiasco. Under Mosley's direction it began to develop characteristics typical of fascist parties—for example it recruited a group of activists, 'the biff boys', to protect its meetings from disruption. Recognizing the failure of the New Party, Mosley turned to Continental models of 'the Modern Movement', and in 1931 he and Harold Nicolson went to Italy and Germany to study them. Like many others, Mosley was impressed by Mussolini, and adopted Italian fascist ideas, such as the vision of the cohesive corporate state: 'a society working

---

[17] *Parl. Deb.* HC Vol.239 c.1348–1372. His resignation statement on 21 May is at col. 404.

[18] *The Menace of Fascism* (London, 1934), 156.

[19] It published a paper, *Action*, from October to December 1931. See Harold Nicolson's *Diaries and Letters 1930–1939*, ed. N. Nicolson, i (London, 1966), 101 ff. Some members became founder members of the BUF, but it is difficult to establish who they all were; early members included Risdon, R. A. Plathen, Francis-Hawkins (?), I. H. Dundas, E. H. Piercey, Raven-Thomson, A. G. Findlay, F. M. Box, Col. H. W. Johnson, E. G. Mandeville Roe, P. M. Moir, W. J. Leaper, R. Forgan, Joyce, and Sutton.

with the precision and harmony of a human body. Every interest and every individual is subordinate to the overriding purpose of the nation.'[20] He decided that the recruits for his new movement should be sought initially in the fascist groups, whose members had become fascists because they were profoundly dissatisfied with existing political structures. Dr Robert Forgan, a former Labour MP who had joined the New Party, attempted on Mosley's behalf to unite the fascist factions, and a scheme to amalgamate the New Party with the British Fascists failed narrowly in May of 1932, as did other attempts.[21] Hence the British Union of Fascists, formed with thirty-two founder members on 1 October 1932, was misleadingly titled. But it picked up defectors and soon became far and away the largest fascist party in Britain. The timing of its launch helped; in 1932 unemployment nearly reached three million, and over the next two years the party attracted many adherents, much publicity, and extensive financial support. There was talk of it having achieved a membership of 40,000. In its early years the party was spending £100,000 or more annually, probably more even than the Conservative Party. But although it was, as new movements go, very successful, its membership, even if high estimates are accepted, was not large in national terms, and it flourished only in a limited number of areas. Forgan, who was in a position to know, estimated that in October 1934 its active membership was nearer 5,000 than 10,000; of course the number of more passive supporters would be much larger, and the party always suffered from a rapid turnover. It was never again as large as in 1934.[22]

Ideology and Policy

BUF policy was set out by Mosley in *The Greater Britain*, published in 1932 as a reaction to crisis. Since the existing constitution impeded action, it was to be radically changed. The primary function of Parliament would be to pass a General Powers Act—ironically rather like the Act under which Mosley was to be interned and his party destroyed in 1940—delegating power to the fascist government. Thereafter it would be answerable by plebiscite every five years. Parliament as a 'talking-shop' would cease; fascist members would not waste time at Westminster but operate locally to execute policy. For the future a Commons elected on an occupational franchise would play a limited role, offering constructive criticism only. Opposition members would have no function; government

---

[20] Quoted from *Action* by Cross, *Fascists in Britain*, 53.   [21] Ibid. 88.

[22] Ibid 131. Press reports at the time suggested much higher figures, one by the *News Chronicle* giving a figure of 17,000, presumably including passive subscribers; this is compatible with Forgan's statement.

must not be obstructed by minorities.[23] Society would be reorganized around twenty-four corporations in which government, management, and workers would be represented, and welded into a harmonious whole. These corporations would be co-ordinated through a National Council of Corporations, which would perform some of the functions of an upper house. The House of Lords would be replaced by a chamber of experts and notable citizens, and its function would be merely advisory. Unemployment would be tackled through public works; in the longer term protection would establish an economic system embracing the Empire which would be self-contained, based on what Mosley called 'autarchy'.[24] But there was no question of extending to 'backward nations' within the Empire a system of parliamentary democracy which had failed even in Britain. Control over banking and investment would ensure that money would be invested within this economy. A system of state-controlled education would ensure that merit would be rewarded, and that individuals, differing in their unequal capacities, would be channelled into appropriate work, some to lead, some to follow. In this brave new world the existing class system would disappear as an irrelevance. The policy set out in 1938 in Mosley's *Tomorrow We Live* did not differ substantially from the 1932 version, except in relation to the Jews, for by 1938 the party had become officially anti-Semitic.

To Mosley and his supporters fascism represented more than a mere political programme. It replaced religion. Thus W. E. D. Allen wrote of it as involving 'a political and spiritual transformation'.[25] It was, he claimed: 'the conscious revolt of a generation determined to escape its overhanging doom in the building of a new destiny'.[26] To Mosley, 'Fascism is a thing of the spirit. It is the acceptance of new values and of a new morality in a higher and nobler conception of the universe.'[27] Hence some of those attracted to the new movement did not simply believe that society was in a state of crisis, for which new ideas and institutions of the kind I have outlined were needed. They also had a mystical belief: with new and appropriate institutions, a new form of mankind would develop, a superman to inherit the new world which was to replace the old, which was responsible for the misery of the war and its aftermath. And although fascism cannot be viewed solely as a reaction to the war, it was certainly strongly influenced by the belief that those who had fought in it had been cruelly duped by the politicians as, I suppose, they had.

[23] O. E. Mosley, *The Greater Britain* (London, 1932), 28.   [24] Ibid. 131.

[25] 1901–1973; chairman of David Allen and Sons, an advertising agency 1925–70; Unionist MP but resigned 1931; in *Who's Who* described himself as a historian (he wrote numerous books) and deleted his fascist period; served in the Middle East, probably in overseas intelligence; appears in Army Lists during the war; OBE 1948.

[26] J. Drennan (an alias), *B.U.F.: Oswald Mosley and British Fascism* (London, 1934), 16–17.   [27] Ibid. Preface.

Two other beliefs derived from the war; they appear to be somewhat contradictory, but were nevertheless held simultaneously by fascists. One was that Britain should never again be dragged into another disastrous European conflict. That Britain should 'mind its own business' was a fascist slogan from the outset. The other belief was nostalgic and romantic: it had been the discipline, heroism, camaraderie, and patriotism which had brought victory in 1918. Surely, fascists argued, it must be possible to mobilize these same forces in peacetime to produce a community working harmoniously towards a regenerated society. Similar notions floated around after the 1939–45 war with talk of 'the Battle of Britain spirit'; the groundnut scheme in East Africa, and the egg production scheme in the Gambia were both based on the belief that military virtues could be harnessed to civilian ends. Both were fiascos.

It is possible that fascist attitudes to the use of force also derived from the wartime experience of violence unleashed on a previously unimaginable scale. In writing primarily of Italian fascists W. E. D. Allen makes this suggestion: 'Those who suffered violence, those who had *felt* violence, had in its excess lost all their horror of it. They had been taught violence for the ends of others, and they had learnt the effectiveness of force, and now they were prepared to use it for their own.'[28] All governments rely upon violence to coerce their citizens, but play this down; government stands for order, its enemies engage in violence. Fascists were not so coy; indeed some tended to glorify the use of coercive violence as itself noble, an attitude of mind necessarily inculcated in military organizations. Thus Mosley called for 'a morality of the Spartan pattern'.[29] Order and harmony in the new society could only be brought about by the determined use of coercion to rid society of the weeds which had so concerned Miss Lintorn-Orman. Mosley, in a curious passage on liberty under fascism, wrote that there would indeed be liberty in private life—he paraphrases J. S. Mill's principle—but obligation in public life, adding in a sinister aside that there would be no room under fascism 'for drones or decadents'.

This could refer to the Jews, but in *The Greater Britain*, even when the role of the City and the banks are under discussion, where one might expect to find it, there is no explicit anti-Semitism; the nearest we come is a contrast between 'genuine British and patriotic elements' in the City and those 'enmeshed in the trammels of foreign finance'.[30] Again in Allen's *Oswald Mosley and British Fascism*, although the supposed 'problem' of the Jews is mentioned, and an apologia for German anti-Semitism offered, the 'problem' is not presented as a special concern of the British fascists: 'The English, the French and the Italians are strong enough to

[28] Ibid. 211.   [29] *The Greater Britain*, 52.   [30] Ibid. ch.6.

ignore—or absorb—the Jews, but in Germany they remain a constant intellectual provocation to a people always sensitive to the newness of their nationhood.'[31] Anti-Semitism was not a necessary part of Mosley's fascist programme. Nor was there any organizational link between Mosley's party and foreign parties which would serve to create an international fascist orthodoxy.

The main factor in the relative success of the BUF was the intellectual brilliance, self-confidence, and oratorical skill of Mosley himself. He was, if ever there was one, an individual destined for great things and, like so many of those who dedicate themselves to politics, he had not the least doubts as to his own importance. By setting himself—nobody of course was asked—at the head of British fascism, he supplied the one ingredient it had previously conspicuously lacked, a leader. For quite central to fascist thought was the submission of the disciplined faithful to the will of the leader as a necessary principle of action, an idea again connected with the military world: 'The Leader must be prepared to shoulder absolute responsibility for decisions and must be surrounded by a team equally prepared to take responsibility for the functions clearly allocated to them. For the only effective instrument of revolutionary change is absolute authority.'[32] Mosley's character, often described as arrogant, fitted the role, and he combined his other talents with considerable personal courage. Eccentric individuals like Miss Lintorn-Orman, or the bizarre Arnold Leese, lacked the qualities required; the only British fascist who ever appears to have been the ghost of a threat to Mosley was William Joyce, an accomplished speaker and a person of high intelligence,[33] who achieved a powerful position in the party. But Joyce's own splinter group of 1937, the National Socialist League, was tiny. And no far left group in the 1930s produced a leader who remotely rivalled Mosley; the communists were indeed not in the business of having prominent national leaders at all. Although a number of persons of considerable ability were at one time or another associated with the party,[34] they tended to defect, or be excluded; Mosley's long-lasting lieutenants were in the main persons of little distinction, and it seems to have suited his vanity to be surrounded by such persons.

---

[31] J. Drennan [pseud. for W. E. D. Allen], *B.U.F.: Oswald Mosley and British Fascism* (London, 1934), 221.

[32] Mosley, *The Greater Britain*, 31

[33] At Birkbeck College (1923–7), where he obtained first class honours.

[34] For example Maj.-Gen. J. F. C. ('Boney') Fuller, Dr Robert Forgan, Capt. R. C. Gordon-Canning, W. E. D. Allen, and C. Wegg Prosser; the last left the party because of Mosley's anti-Semitism and vanity in surrounding himself with low-grade military men.

The BUF in the 1930s

From its first public gathering in Trafalgar Square on 15 October 1932 meetings (together with marches, rallies, and door-to-door canvassing) were the mechanism whereby it recruited, and advertised its policies; Rothermere supported Mosley with his *Daily Mail*, but ceased to do so in July 1934, and in the late 1930s the press largely ignored Mosley's politics, and the BBC excluded him. The appeal of the party is brought out in R. R. Bellamy's account of his own recruitment by a blackshirt in 1932: 'I asked him [a canvasser] what in short did Mosley stand for, and was told that he sought to combine in this new Movement of his, the discipline, good order and patriotism of the Right, with the reforms and social justice of the Left.'[35] Many of Mosley's ideas were indeed close to those held in the centre of orthodox politics; for example some of his economic ideas were taken from Keynes. Given the economic crisis of the period, and the widespread initial sympathy with both Mussolini and Hitler, his more radical proposals provided an attractive alternative to the governmental inertia of the period. High unemployment no doubt made it easier to attract young men and women, and his party was typically young.

Fascist policies were combined with intense patriotism and reverence for monarchy. Fascism was everywhere nationalistic; from the outset Mosley emphasized that his policies were 'English'.[36] Patriotism was expressed in the demand for strong air defences, in the slogan 'Britain First', and in the belief that the spread of European fascism would end the economic chaos which caused war, and was thus welcome.[37] Many ex-servicemen, some with distinguished war records, joined the party. Although from the very start anathema to the radical left, in competition for proletarian support, and violently disliked personally by many parliamentarians, for example by Herbert Morrison and Ernest Bevin, Mosley was not of course initially 'beyond the pale', any more than were Mussolini or even Hitler.[38] Much of what he stood for was in no way shocking.

Fairly soon, however, the party came to be viewed by many as a menace; hostility was in no way confined to the left. One factor was distrust of Mosley's character. Another was his contempt for Parliamentary democracy, and the association of the party with practices which seemed foreign, revolutionary, and violent. Reports of fascist excesses in Italy, Germany, and elsewhere helped to generate fear of British fascists; the BUF certainly had open association with Mussolini's party in its early

---

[35] Bellamy MS ii.42.   [36] Mosley, *The Greater Britain*, 20.
[37] Ibid. 156, 19, 152.
[38] The expression derives from an article in the *New Statesman* on 11 May 1979. See Mosley, *Beyond the Pale*, Foreword.

days; later such practices as the use of the tune of the 'Horst Wessel Lied' for the marching song of the party linked it to the Nazis. It is difficult to say what part fascist anti-Semitism played in generating fear of Mosley outside Jewish circles, but it certainly played some part, and no regular political party had ever attacked the Jews as Mosley did.[39] He himself had no previous history of anti-Semitism, but his party from the outset attracted anti-Semitic supporters, including extremists like Joyce, and Major-General J.H.C. ('Boney') Fuller.[40] Very soon the party itself became anti-Semitic. In late 1933 Jews were excluded from membership.[41] On 4 November 1933 Mosley published a stereotypical anti-Semitic article in *Action* under the title 'Shall Jews Drag Britain into War?' This typically claimed that Jews were not attacked on racial or religious grounds, but as a political organization within the state.[42] At disorderly meetings in Manchester and Plymouth in October 1934 he publicly attacked the Jews for disrupting the proceedings; it may well be that quite a number of his communist opponents at these meetings were indeed Jews. He formally declared an anti-Semitic policy on 28 October 1934; the Jews were his enemies because they had declared war on fascism. This was enormously popular with his supporters, as *Action* for 2 November reported: 'They Will It! They Will Have It!' Anti-Semitism, in particular the slum anti-Semitism which flourished in the East End of London, where the party achieved its greatest support, came thereafter to be a central feature of the movement. In Mosley's pamphlet *Tomorrow We Live* (1938) Jews were described as forming a state within the state; those who regarded themselves as Jews first, or who 'engaged in practices alien to the British character' must leave the country. The 'Final Solution'—this chilling expression was by then current—was a national home in some waste but potentially fertile area.[43] It remains uncertain whether Mosley used anti-Semitism cynically to generate solidarity, or became a convinced anti-Semite. Anti-Semitism, albeit in a mild form when compared with its expression elsewhere in Europe, was then widespread in the upper reaches of British society. Mosley's defence was that he never attacked Jews on racial grounds as inherently inferior or malign; his attack was on Jews only in so far as they operated as a political force.[44] However,

[39] See Skidelsky, *Oswald Mosley*, ch.20

[40] 1878–1966. Best known for his *Decisive Battles of the Western World* (London, 1954). Fuller was one of the more prominent supporters of Mosley. The *DNB* article by Michael Carver plays down Fuller's fascist and anti-Semitic past. See HO 144/22454/820861 and HO 45/24966/674112.

[41] Cross, *Fascists in Britain*, 123. Skidelsky puts the date of exclusion from membership as early 1934. Some few Jews remained as members, such as Lew Levishohn.

[42] 4 November 1934, discussed Skidelsky, *Oswald Mosley*, 384.

[43] p.109. Cf. *Action* for 21 January 1939: 'Let the Jews Beware, for the whispers may very well become a great shout for the complete removal of his race from our shores.'

[44] J. Guinness, *The House of Mitford* (London, 1984), ch. 27, accepts this.

in *Tomorrow We Live* he argued that they were inherently 'foreign': 'The simple answer is that he comes from the orient and physically, mentally, and spiritually, is more alien to us than any western nation.' *Blackshirt* called them 'sub-men'.[45] Even if Mosley did formally maintain a shaky distinction between racialism and politics in his speeches, many of his followers did not; in any event he lumped all Jews together. As Leader he was responsible, and the formal exclusion of all Jews from his party is quite incompatible with his defence. In his attack in 1934 he mimicked supposed Jewish accents in his speech, to tumults of applause. He succumbed to the temptation to play to the gutter.

The Party and Public Violence

The BUF had to contend with organized attempts to disrupt its meetings. In its early days it did not organize disruption of meetings of the left; instead it formed its own paramilitary Fascist Defence Force, known as the 'I' squad; E. Hamilton-Piercy, its commander, had earlier been a 'biff boy'. There is no doubt that the notorious Olympia meeting of 7 June 1934, and violent clashes at other meetings, made many believe, rightly or wrongly, that the party employed organized brutal violence to crush dissent at meetings, violence which could be used for other ends.[46] Violence continued to be associated with meetings, and the 'Battle of Cable Street' on 5 October 1936 passed into legend. In one sense all this represented a victory for the aggressive left-wing groups who undoubtedly set out to disrupt fascist meetings.[47] But they, unlike Mosley's blackshirts, did not look like a private army. Furthermore, in spite of Mosley's claims that his uniforms and accoutrements were purely British, and served innocent functions, for example enabling fascists to recognize each other in fights, one has only to look at photographs of the period to see that his blackshirts outwardly looked like Hitler's toughs. Indeed the flash in the circle, which replaced the *fasces* as the party symbol in 1935, looked sufficiently like the swastika at a distance to be suggestive of it.

The paramilitary character of the party went much deeper than mere legitimate self-defence. The BUF was revolutionary, and founded upon a belief in 'crisis' and 'the march to power'. Its military character was a response to this, and the blackshirts were the disciplined force whereby the will of the leader could bring order back out of chaos. Strachey, who

---

[45] Quoted Cross, *Fascists in Britain*, 125.

[46] *Parl. Deb.* HC Vol.290 c.1343 (Statement by the Home Secretary 11 June 1934) and cols. 1913–2041 (debate of 14 June). Police figures for London showed no injuries arising from meetings in 1932, 10 in 1933, and 45 up to this time in 1934. Parliamentary questions were asked about numerous other disorderly meetings. There is much material in HO 45/25462–3 (NCCL).

[47] There is a mass of material in the PRO on the subject in particular in MEPO 2 under 'Disturbances'.

was intimate with Mosley, stated that his enthusiasm for a youth section back in the days of the New Party was a self-conscious attempt to develop a private army to control the streets. MI5 seems always to have misunderstood the BUF, suspecting an underground organization would be employed to seize power. But the fascist belief was that the regular party, whose operations were mainly perfectly open, would itself be the instrument, as it had been in both Italy and Germany.[48] The battles with the communists demonstrated the power of the organization, and counted as victories, not disasters. As such they were welcome; there is evidence too that they encouraged recruiting. To this very day former members speak of the pride they felt in the courage and resolution with which the blackshirts, and in particular Mosley himself, confronted their opponents. They remain blind to the immense damage this did to the public perception of the party, which was to be critical in 1940.

The official reaction to disorders associated with the BUF's activities was the passage of the Public Order Act of 1936: 'An Act to prohibit the wearing of uniforms in connection with political objects and the maintenance by private persons of associations of a military or similar character; and to make further provision for the preservation of public order on the occasion of public processions and meetings and in public places'. This was directed primarily at the BUF and the particular forms of political expression which it had adopted; in particular the general practice of wearing political uniforms in public became illegal. The Act also greatly increased police powers—marches could be banned—and offences of using 'threatening, abusive or insulting words or behaviour', or possessing offensive weapons at meetings or processions, were created.[49] The Act also made the organization of 'quasi-military organizations' criminal; this part of the Act was never enforced in legal proceedings.

The tendency to view the BUF as the British Nazi Party was encouraged by the sympathy and indeed support for Hitler expressed from 1934 onwards, for example over the Roehm purge. In *Tomorrow We Live* (1938), in a passage dealing with Hitler's Germany, Mosley argued that Britain and Germany had a community of objectives—peace for Britain to develop the Empire, peace for Germany to incorporate all European Germans in the Reich.[50] There were also suspicions, which were baseless, of financial support from Hitler. Although the party had some members, probably not many, who were strongly pro-Nazi, and considerably more who were sympathetic to Germany, no evidence has come to light of organizational links with the NSDAP.[51] Since the war it has been suggested,

---

[48] Strachey, *Menace of Fascism*, 162.   [49] Sections 4 and 5.   [50] p. 115.
[51] There was suspicion in 1939 of links between the BU and the Anglo-German Information Service; HO 45/25741. All accounts of internment recognize the small pro-Nazi faction in the camps.

without proper documentation, that unsuccessful attempts were made by the Abwehr to use members of the party for disloyal activities.[52]

The Organization of the Party

BUF official policy had always been to seek power by winning an election.[53] Originally, however, it had no electoral organization, and it put up no candidates in 1935. One cannot but suspect that Mosley really thought that events would sweep him into power. No evidence has come to light of any plan for a *coup d'état*, and Mosley always denied any intention to organize one. But his denials miss the point: in crisis an assumption of power, however it came about, would not involve any challenge to institutions which effectively no longer existed, and his private army would be ready to do whatever had to be done when the moment came.

In 1936 the BUF became the British Union of Fascists and National Socialists, reflecting a shift in model from Italy to Germany. It came to be called simply British Union (hereafter BU). The same year the party organization changed, perhaps as a consequence of Neil Francis-Hawkins becoming Director-General of Organization.[54] In May a constitution was published under which local branches were to be reorganized into districts, corresponding to Parliamentary constituencies.[55] The original structure was based on branches, there being in 1935 some 600 branches and sub-branches.[56] In 1937 candidates stood in some local elections; from November names of prospective Parliamentary candidates began to be published in *Action*.[57] In the amended constitution of March 1938 the Deputy District Leader becomes the prospective Parliamentary agent. But because of the war the general election never came. The constitution of 1938, responding to the Public Order Act, also elaborately provided for

[52] L. Farago, *The Game of the Foxes* (London, 1971) 198. They were to assist four secret wireless stations in the UK. On the stations, set up in 1940, but not in the UK see below Ch. 8.

[53] Mosley, *The Greater Britain*, 39.

[54] Succeeding Ian Hope Dundas, who had succeeded Robert Forgan.

[55] Text (1936, also 1938) in the Saunders Papers. Fuller is said to have been involved in the drafting (Cross, *Fascists in Britain*, 140); his earlier report is quoted extensively by N. Mosley, *Beyond the Pale*, 87 ff. I have found no earlier constitution.

[56] Branches had a Branch Officer, Treasurer, and Sales Officer; L. Wise in a privately printed pamphlet, *Mosley's Blackshirts* (n:p., n.d.), 4. I am indebted also to Mr Robert Row.

[56] W. F. Mandle, 'The Leadership of the British Union of Fascists', *Australian Journal of Politics and History*, 12 (1966), 360, lists 103 candidates. There were at least 15 more candidates than appear in Mandle's article, but this does not affect his analysis. John Beckett, 'Bill' Risdon (both ex-ILP) and F. M. Box (ex-Conservative) prepared the party for elections.

[57] The BDBJ Archives contain lists of candidates. *Action* includes a number of photographs of candidates.

the strict legality of the actions of members. Indeed once uniforms became generally illegal, and the 'I' force disbanded, the paramilitary character of the BU was less prominent.

In 1940 members were primarily organized into somewhere between 180 and 200 districts.[58] About half were in London. Each had a male District Leader appointed by National Headquarters.[59] There had been a considerable fall from some 290 districts in January 1938.[60] Not all corresponded with constituencies.[61] Outside London the districts were organized into seven zones, each under an inspector.[62] London was organized into eleven areas, comprising ninety-four districts, and there were four unattached districts. [63] The size of districts varied—some had a mere handful of individual members. Thus in 1940 Lowestoft had three members, whilst Lincoln had eighteen.[64] There were three categories of member. Those of the First Division were committed to work two nights or days a week, of the Second one night per month. The Third Division had no obligation to work. Division I and II members were called 'Active Members'; earlier there had been simply two categories, 'active' and 'non-active'.[65] All had to pay dues and buy *Action*; membership in theory lapsed if two months were in arrears. Recruits signed a form of application to join Division II or III, and pledged to uphold the principles of the BU, be loyal to the leadership, obey the rules and standing orders, and (if in Division II) devote the appropriate time to the party. Entry to Division I was by promotion. There were also secret members: those who were nervous of the consequences of their membership becoming known.

Members were given a number and a card. This stated the 'objects of the British Union':

To win power for British Union by the vote of the people and thereby to establish in Great Britain the Corporate State, which shall ensure that

All shall serve the State and none the Faction.

[58] CAB 67/7 WP (40) 153 of 10 May 1940 (report of 2 May COS (40) 315 (JIC)) gives a figure of 188. A memorandum probably written by F. B. Aikin-Sneath, 14 April 1943 (CAB 66/35) gives a figure of between 180 and 200. In May 1940 MI5 acquired from Mosley's papers an out-of-date list of BU officers, agents, contacts, and speakers, 44 pages long, and updated to 25 January 1940. This seems to be the basis for figures quoted. See HO 45/25754/863027/3.

[59] Before 1937 called a District Officer. There could be Acting District Leaders, not yet confirmed by HQ.

[60] Special Branch report of 19 January 1938 HO 144/21281.

[61] Thus in 1939–40 Robert Saunders was District Leader of North, South, and West Dorset, which is not a constituency.

[62] CAB 66/35, Memorandum of 14 April 1943.

[63] HO 45/24895 sf. 3 (Special Branch report of 1 February). In January 1938 (Special Branch Report in HO 144/21281) U. A. Hick, a headquarters official, claimed there were then 84 London Districts.

[64] Information from A. S. Swan. Saunders in 1939 had 55 non-secret members.

[65] See *Mosley's Blackshirts*, 6 (Leonard Wise), 48 (Louise Irvine).

All shall work and thus enrich the Country and themselves.

Opportunity shall be open to all, but privilege to none.

Great positions shall be accorded only to great talent.

Reward shall be accorded only to service.

Poverty shall be abolished by the power of modern science released within the organized State.

The barriers of class shall be destroyed and the energies of every citizen devoted to the British nation, which by the efforts and sacrifices of our fathers has existed gloriously for centuries before this transient generation, and which by our own exertions shall be raised to its highest destiny—the Greater Britain that shall be born of the National Socialist Creed.[66]

There was no voting, so no lists of entitled voters were needed. Lists of members were held locally.[67] Names of all paid-up members were returned annually, primarily for auditing purposes.

Ideally at least, members were organized into teams. If a team contained at least six members the person organizing it became a team leader, and if it reached eighteen a senior team leader. Teams were supposed to be spontaneous groups, developed by a member who demonstrated his ability to recruit and organize.[68] A district also had a Deputy District Leader, who was the prospective parliamentary agent[69] and two Assistant District Leaders, one for Propaganda and one for Sales, primarily of *Action*.[70] In a large district there could also be a Sub-District Leader. There was also a District Treasurer. Women members, who occupied an important but subsidiary role in the organization, were separately organized (ideally into teams of eight) under a Women's District Leader. Overall control was maintained by a system of District Inspectors (responsible for a number of districts). Above the District Inspectors came in some, but not all areas, Regional Inspectors, and above them a small number of National Inspectors, attached to Headquarters. There were County Propaganda Officers, who might serve a number of smaller counties. Where the membership was large, such as London or Manchester, there were Regional Organizers; sometimes organizers were appointed as a temporary measure to build up membership and establish districts.

Members could also be organized by occupation, in accordance with corporate theory, into Industrial, Trade Union, or Business Groups;

[66] Card of Miss M. Morton, No.923, in BDBJ Archives.

[67] Examples in Saunders Papers.

[68] This account differs from Thurlow's, *Fascism in Britain*, 134–5. Before 1938 a different organization existed based on units of 6, each having their own unit leader. In theory at least 5 units formed a section and 3 a company, both sections and companies having their own leaders.

[69] He could be called DD/L (Canvass). But many districts had no DD/L.

[70] Also presumably *Fascist Quarterly*. In April 1940 the bi-weekly *Action News Service* was founded, and there were also local issues of *Blackshirt*, such as *Southern Blackshirt* and *East London Blackshirt*.

there were also Study Groups. In London Charles F. Watts ran a Cab Drivers Trade Group, implausibly said to have had as many as 1,000 members.[71] Somewhat similar, though called a district, was an organization run by Derek R. Stuckey, which had originated as the Federation of British University Fascist Associations; it operated in universities and schools.[72] There was also the British Traders Bureau, run by Peter Heyward.[73] This published *The British Trader* and opposed chain stores, price cutting, and monopoly. But the corporate form of organization was never much developed.

Devised largely by former servicemen, the organization of BU was readily adaptable to military ends, a fact which did not escape the notice of the security authorities.

The Size of the Party

There has been much uncertainty over the size of the BU.[74] MI5 obtained a list of paid-up members for 1939 in 1940; such lists were used to assess the capitation fee payable to National Headquarters.[75] There were about 9,000; support had increased considerably as the threat of war grew.[76] This was an end of the year figure based on financial returns and is likely to be below the true figure; it of course excludes 'secret' members, and is considerably larger than the figure for active members, which is not known. Probably the number of sympathizers or supporters—those who

---

[71] See 45/25702.

[72] HO 283/63, 45/25722. Stuckey was educated at Bradfield and became a law graduate of Oriel College, Oxford (BA, BCL). He joined in 1934, and in 1936 was Secretary of the Oxford University National Socialist Club; in 1934 this seems to have been called the OU Fascist Association, with the Revd E. C. Ratcliff of Queen's as Senior Treasurer and C. P. Chevenix-Trench of Magdalen as President. In January 1939 he became D/L of the Combined English Universities, and in June 1939 DI. He was interned.

[73] Real name Peter Perrins. The Secretary at one time was one D. M. Nommesen, an Anglo-German who was to teach Mosley German in Brixton.

[74] See Thurlow, *Fascism in Britain*, 122–32. See G. Webber, 'Patterns of Membership and Support for the British Union of Fascists', *Journal of Contemporary History*, 19 (1984), 575, is the fullest attempt to produce figures.

[75] Private information from a BU official. HO 283/13 at 64, HO 45/25754/863027/3, *Parl.Deb.* HC Vol. 363: 386–7 18 July 1940, CAB 66/35 WP (43) Memorandum by Morrison, 14 April 1943.

[76] Mr Row has confirmed this figure to me as 'about right'. A JIC report of 2 May 1940, cited above note 58, gives a figure of 8,700 *subscribing* members. HO 144/21281, containing Special Branch reports from January 1938, estimates 5,800 active members in January 1938, with about 3,000 in London. The print order for *Blackshirt* was then 12,000 and that of *Action* was 14,000, which is consistent. In February 1939 the paid-up members for 1938 were reported as 6,600, 3,600 being in London. Louise Irvine in *Mosley's Blackshirts*, 48, says that the list kept centrally was of 'currently active' members, but from conversation with her and from these and other sources it is clearly a list of paid-up members—in a loose sense the same thing as a list of currently active members. See also HO 45/25100 (brief for debate by Ross) which refers to between 8,000 and 10,000 'paying' members.

regularly bought *Action*, or were intermittent subscribers—was as many
again. Mosley at his committee hearing claimed that there were many
supporters who never paid subscriptions and were thus not counted; this
is what one would expect, but the number, which may have been considerable, is not discoverable. The circulation of *Action* in 1940 was estimated
as between 15,000 and 20,000.[77] If all districts had a full complement of
officers there would have been 1,100 or so local officials in early 1940, in
addition to something like forty senior and headquarters officials. The
actual numbers were certainly very considerably lower.

The members were typically young, many being liable to military service; for this reason, as well as through defections, the membership had
fallen dramatically by May 1940. Many District Leaders, perhaps the
majority, were in the services, and 'the organisational situation became
rather fluid'.[78] Women became increasingly important. A conference of
London officials on 15 April 1940 was attended by only about 210 individuals—there should have been over 500. If we guess, and it is no more, that
of the subscribing members only a third would be active, and that the war
halved the number, and assume the number of districts fell, then in May
1940 an average district would have around seven such members, and the
total would be about 1,200. My own impression is that the fall-off was
even more dramatic once the phoney war ended, and that the number of
persons visibly and actively supporting the movement in May, a haz-
ardous thing to do, may well have been close to the numbers interned,
just over 750. This was the view of Cross, who was very well informed on
the movement.[79] Indeed the small numbers of visible supporters encouraged the belief that the BU had 'gone underground'.[80]

The Headquarters Organization

The Special Branch had at least one informer in the party, P. G. Taylor,
the industrial adviser; he was known to Mosley.[81] One object of curiosity
was the source of funds, and at least in the later 1930s W. E. D. Allen may
have supplied information to MI5 on this subject. In its early days the
party had been affluent, in part because of a subsidy from Mussolini, paid

[77] CAB 75/7 HPC (40) 103.   [78] Letter from Mr Row of 4 September 1989.
[79] See Cross, *Fascists in Britain*, 195. Because of errors the 750 detainees would not corre-
spond with the active members. Some escaped, and some non-active members were
arrested.
[80] The Ministry of Information memorandum of 27 April 1940 adopts this view; see CAB
75/7 HPC (40) 92.
[81] Also McGurk or James Hughes. See *Mosley's Blackshirts*, 38. He appears by profession
to have been a private detective, but virtually nothing seems to be known about him.
Another MI5 agent, A. C. V. Bristol, was married to Lilian, sister of Neil Francis-Hawkins
(private information). See HO 144/21281, R. C. Thurlow, 'British Fascism and State
Surveillance, 1934–45', *Intelligence and National Security*, 3 (1986), 91–2.

between 1933 and 1936; there were also wealthy backers, such as Lord Rothermere.[82] It was possible to employ numerous officials.[83] But their number was drastically reduced by economies forced on Mosley in 1937; a circular in the Saunders Papers reports that 104 members of staff had been dismissed, whilst William Joyce and John Beckett, who had both been employed, left to found the National Socialist League. In February 1938 the paid staff was reduced to fifty-seven, fifty-two in National Headquarters.[84] The latter were organized into the Director-General's Department (under Neil L. M. Francis-Hawkins), District Administration (under Captain Brian D. E. Donovan), Reception and Premises, Research (under George F. Sutton with Ernest D. Hart), the Leader's Department (with Miss E. M. Monk, who acted as Mosley's secretary and also was incorrectly listed as secretary for Captain R. C. Gordon-Canning, at this time a sort of deputy for Mosley), and Policy (under Alexander Raven-Thomson). A. K. Chesterton, assisted by G. Dorman, edited publications, P. G. Taylor was industrial organizer and in-house MI5 spy, and there was also an accounts section and a secretarial pool. W. Risdon, formerly of the ILP and South Wales Miners Federation, was electoral adviser and propaganda administrator, Mrs. Anne Brock-Griggs was Chief Women's Officer, and Captain U. A. Hick (known as 'Hook' from his metal arm) was London Administrator. A. G. Findlay ran Public Relations and Accounts, Lieutenant-Colonel C. S. Sharpe Records and Personnel. There were four paid National Inspectors.[85]

By 1939 the costs of running the party were estimated at about £20,000 annually, and there were further economies; seven headquarters staff ceased to be paid.[86] Some junior employees were dismissed, and all National Inspectors apart from Hector G. McKechnie were taken off the payroll. By May 1940 there were only fifteen paid employees, and the organization relied principally upon voluntary workers.[87] When eventually proceedings were set in motion to confiscate the assets of the party,

---

[82] Thurlow, *Fascists in Britain*, 138–9, Cross, *Fascists in Britain*, 88–9. On Allen see Mosley, *Beyond the Pale*, 134, 174–5.

[83] HO 45/25386 (22 Jan. 1934) lists 20 HQ officers, excluding junior employees.

[84] List in HO 144/21281.

[85] W. H. Symes, R. Reynell Bellamy, R. A. Plathen, and J. W. I. Sant.

[86] William Risdon (electoral adviser and propaganda), Lt.-Col. C. S. Sharpe (records, personnel, premises), Capt. U. A. Hick (London Organizer), Olive Hawks (in research department), C. J. Garnett (receptions, enrolment, and transport), ED Hart (research), and Mrs A. Brock-Griggs (chief women's organizer); all but perhaps Risdon continued as volunteers. A report in HO 144/21429 shows that in September 1939 of those who had worked in HQ Ian Hope Dundas had gone to India, Gordon-Canning had left. Michael Goulding and J. R. Sutherland were in Eire, A. G. Findlay had left in August, John Sant was in the RE, H. K. Stevens had joined the Auxiliary Fire Service, Garnett the merchant navy.

[87] List in HO 45/24891.

the task was abandoned, there being nothing to confiscate; the organization had been kept going largely through Mosley's own contributions. As we shall see, he had plans to fund the party, but the war destroyed them.[88]

The BU and the War

As the likelihood of war increased, the leaders of the BU feared government action. MI5 obtained an account of a statement by Donovan, then Deputy-Director of Organization, at a senior officers' weekend meeting on 3–4 June 1939:

in the event of war the government would close down the movement's headquarters, arrest the high officials and attempt to seize the funds. Arrangements were being made whereby one key man would have charge of each area and would be responsible for transmitting messages to all under him. The funds would be scattered, so that the authorities could not obtain possession of them.[89]

Mosley anticipated arrest, and the idea of prosecuting him under the original Defence Regulations for his peace propaganda was considered, but opposed by the Home Office and Cabinet.[90] Funds were dispersed, and instructions were given to principal officers to appoint deputies as successors, and to use private addresses for mail; a 'hideout' was arranged for Hector McKechnie, who became Senior Administrator for London in September.[91]

On the outbreak of the war, Mosley, typically manifesting a public respect for law, issued a general instruction to his party, which included this passage:

To our members my message is plain and clear. Our country is involved in war. Therefore I ask you to do nothing to injure our country, or to help the other power. Our members should do what the law requires of them; and, if they are members of any of the Forces or Services of the Crown, they should obey their orders and, in every particular, obey the rules of the Service. *But I ask all members who are free to carry on our work to take every opportunity within your power to awaken the people and to demand peace.*

This passage, italicized in the original, refers to the campaign for peace and an accommodation with the fascist powers which had come to be the principal focus of Mosley's propaganda. Mosley explained: 'The war is no

[88] CAB 66/55 WP (44) 505 Memorandum by Home Secretary of 7 September 1944. TS 27/489 also contains relevant papers.

[89] Report of 12 June 1939 HO 144/21281.

[90] HO 144/21429, CAB 67/1 WP (G) (39) 36 14 Oct. 1939, 65/1 WM (39) 49, 16 October, Hinsley and Simkins, 35. See above, Ch. 6.

[91] HO 45/25700 (Francis-Hawkins at the Advisory Committee), HO 144/21429 (Special Branch Report of 12 September 1939).

quarrel of the British people; this war is a quarrel of Jewish Finance. So to our people I give myself for the winning of peace.'

The last major public meeting which Mosley had addressed took place in July of 1939 at Earls Court; it was attended by some 15,000 to 25,000 people (estimates vary considerably), and was entirely orderly, no doubt because the communists, under their own peace policy, made no attempt to disrupt it.[92] The theme was 'Mind Britain's Business'. The party continued to campaign for peace even after the phoney war ended in April of 1940; in May of 1940 police reports recorded 140 meetings in London. Britain, Mosley argued, had started the war in Scandinavia, and had no quarrel with Germany. The war was run by the 'Government of the Bankers for the Jews'. The party also gave some encouragement to members who conscientiously objected to the war.[93] Mosley's position was set out in *The British Peace and How to Get It* and in posters and pamphlets; one typically included this: 'WHO MASSED PROFITS IN THE LAST WAR AND WILL GAIN BY ANOTHER?' At an official level the campaign was pursued with strict legality, but the behaviour of members at the grass roots did not always conform. Thus J. W. Charnley, District Leader in Hull, records covert attacks on Jewish-owned shops there.[94] Police reports record a steady trickle of prosecutions under the Public Order Act. It is impossible to tell how widespread such activities were, or to what extent the leadership winked at them. And, like all political groups, as Mosley was the first to concede, the party certainly possessed its 'lunatic fringe'.

The By-Elections of 1940

In 1940 the party, for reasons which are obscure, for Mosley cannot have imagined that more than a handful of voters would support him, began to contest parliamentary by-elections. The first two, at Silvertown, adjacent to the East End of London, and in North-East Leeds, were fought during the phoney war, but the BU still fared very badly indeed. At Silvertown, where the Communist Harry Pollitt also campaigned for peace, T. P. Moran won a pathetic 151 votes to Pollitt's 966 and the winner's 14,000.[95] At Leeds, where no Communist stood, Sydney Allen did rather better,

[92] The hall held 30,000; the BU tradition is that it was full; some estimates are as low as 11,000.

[93] See CAB 75/7 HPC (40) 103, HO 144/21382, 21429.

[94] J. W. Charnley, *Blackshirts and Roses*, (London, 1990), 90, HO 144/21382 notes the prosecution in May of B. C. Perigoe, R. F. Stokes, and T. L. Pitt, of whom the first two were certainly detained.

[95] Former miner and Royal Navy cruiserweight champion; no mere pugilist; originally Labour Party; after Mosley's arrest assumed control of the BU; detained early June; classified as a 'troublemaker' in TS 27/533; became camp leader at Ascot; after release associated with Leese (HO 45/24968); post-war severely injured in a quarry explosion, and thereafter dropped out of politics.

but only obtained 722 votes to the Conservative winner's 23,000.[96]
Material in the Saunders Papers indicates that by the middle of May
members in his area were nervous of holding any meetings at all because
of the hostility they generated. Contesting the third by-election, at
Middleton and Prestwich, near Manchester, where the polling day was 22
May, was simply folly. The BU candidate, Captain F. Haslam, obtained a
derisory 418 votes against the Conservative winner's 32,000.[97] During the
campaign Mosley, now a hated individual, came near to being lynched.
For all practical purposes the BU was dead, and Mosley's career in
British politics dead too, unless of course the whole political landscape
were to change.

MI5 and the Party in 1940

Sources of information on the attitude of MI5 to the BU in 1940 are very
unsatisfactory. The official history is largely undocumented; the Home
Office file of Special Branch Reports for 1940 has been devastated.[98]
MI5's records, whatever they are, remain, absurdly, secret.

MI5 and Special Branch certainly used agents, and it cannot have been
difficult to discover information about the BU, which, unlike the security
service, had none of the characteristics of a secret society.[99] According to
Hinsley and Simkins, until the war MI5 did not regard the BU as a threat
to security in peacetime, and found no evidence of contacts with the Axis
powers 'of a kind that justified alarm'.[100] In 1940 its attitude changed, but
the official history does not say precisely when or why this happened,
though by early March it had come to believe 'that the BU should be
regarded as the English branch of the N.S.D.A.P.' It was 'not merely a
party advocating an anti-war and anti-government policy, but a movement whose aim it is to assist the enemy in every way it can'.[101] It had a
core of fanatics who would be prepared to take active steps to this end if

---

[96] Served throughout the 1st World War with the West Yorks Regiment; a large-scale
poultry farmer. Detained in 1940.

[97] Served in the 1st World War and won the Military Medal; detained in 1940.

[98] HO 45/24895, originally 830734, which apparently originally contained 151 or more
subfiles. Some of these have been moved to HO file reference 693036, which is not available;
the vast majority have been destroyed, for example—and I have not kept a complete list—
43–4, 46–56, 57A, 62–4, 66–70, 72–6, 78–93, 95–122, 124–9, 131–51.

[99] An agent known as 'Capt. Hawke' is mentioned in the BBDJ Archives (C6/9/3/ 1–2) in
a letter of 19 October 1936. He lost his BU job in March 1937 in staff reductions (private
information) and then attempted to penetrate Joyce's NSL. He can be fairly confidently
identified as Capt. Vincent Collier. Special Branch clearly had an informant, probably run
by Maxwell-Knight, for the 'secret meetings' discussed below.

[100] Hinsley and Simkins, 16. This is documented by reference to CAB 66/5 WP (43) 148 of
14 April 1943, but may also be based on MI5 records.

[101] This must be a quotation from an MI5 report of some kind, conceivably by Aikin-
Sneath.

the opportunity occurred. But it had still found no evidence that these extremist elements had been penetrated by the enemy for espionage or subversive purposes.[102] This view cannot have been based on evidence either of organizational links with the Nazi Party or of disloyal actions by members. Nothing has come to light since the war suggesting that any such links existed, and if any evidence existed in 1940 it would have been used in the interrogation of Mosley by Birkett, but none was. As for disloyal actions by members there had been very few. MI5's view—in effect that of Aikin-Sneath, Maxwell-Knight and their superiors, Liddell and Harker—must have rested on an impression of the general character of the movement and its membership, and beliefs as to what it might get up to in the future. It seems to me possible that it may have been Aikin-Sneath's experience as a horrified witness to the rise of the Nazis which led to the change in attitude in MI5, which had previously been principally anti-communist. But the extreme claim that the party was the British branch of the NSDAP was simply ridiculous; it is hardly surprising that no reference was made to it in Mosley's interrogation, or in any later source. That it was made indicates the level of incompetence which must have then characterized Kell's organization.

But in the Home Office file there are two items which perhaps explain MI5's attitude.[103] The first is an account of a visit to Mosley's headquarters on 24 January by Inspector Bridges and Sergeant Hughes of Special Branch, accompanied by an MI5 officer, who wrote the report; I assume he was Aikin-Sneath. The occasion was an affair involving Claude F. P. Duvivier, a naturalized Belgian farmer, and William A. Crowle, an ex-naval dockyard worker.[104] Duvivier was arrested on 8 January, and on 29 January was convicted by Exeter magistrates of offences under the Defence Regulations (there was no suggestion of espionage), and sentenced to six months' imprisonment. He had been the BU District Officer at Exmouth.[105] In a letter to Crowle he wrote, 'My heart goes out to those men on the *Graf Spee*[106]—heroes fighting for the cause, every one of them.' Crowle too was a BU member who supplied Duvivier with information about naval shipping which Duvivier planned to send to *Action* to show up the government's supposedly deceitful propaganda.[107] Presumably both were caught through intercepted mail. The point of the police visit was to secure a letter which Duvivier had sent to Captain Donovan.

---

[102] Hinsley and Simkins, 37–8.   [103] HO 45/24895.
[104] *The Times*, 17 and 31 January 1940, N. West, *MI5* (London, 1983), 160–1, Hinsley and Simkins, 38 n.
[105] C 6/9/3/1.   [106] The pocket battleship scuttled off Montevideo on 17 December.
[107] Some information concerned damage to HMS *Exeter*, but some dealt with shipping movements.

They met Mosley, who was obviously aware that MI5 was interested both in his possible contingency plans and in possible disloyal contacts. He thus assumed that they were investigating his transfer of BU funds to Mrs Norah Elam,[108] or the activities of E. C. P. Whinfield, a friend of the Elams, and well known to Mosley.[109] After the letter (which was of no significance) had been dealt with there was a conversation, in which Aikin-Sneath put some questions which clearly reveal his thinking at this time. He suggested to Mosley that some members had 'an almost unbalanced admiration of everything German. Did he approve of this?' Mosley agreed, and offered to produce a list of those expelled on this ground.[110] He added that he had forbidden his wife to contact her sister Unity to forestall possible criticism of pro-Nazi sympathies.[111] He was then asked whether the Germans might try to use pro-Nazi members of the BU 'for their own purposes' and Mosley, without agreeing, said—'I quite admit that an enemy agent would find the BU a good cover.' He was then asked about co-operation with other peace movements, and said he would co-operate with anyone except the communists. Behind this question lay knowledge of meetings which had been taking place between right-wing groups.[112] Mosley was specifically asked about the BPP. He gave his unflattering opinion of its principal members: Lord Tavistock—a 'good fellow' but 'woolly headed'; John Beckett—'a crook'; and Ben Greene—'a good fellow but not very intelligent'. The report concludes with an extremely hostile account of Mosley: 'immensely vain, a bad judge of men, extremely urbane and cunning. He is absolutely insincere. His chief handicap is probably his excessive vanity, which must make it difficult for him to take an objective view of any situation. It also makes it impossible for him to tolerate any other outstanding personality in his entourage.' Francis-Hawkins was called a nonentity, and Raven-Thomson described as rather dim, but less stupid. In effect this report encapsulates MI5's case against the party at this time, which was to be acted upon in May 1940.

The second item is a Special Branch report from an agent of a closed meeting of BU London District officials on 30 January. First there were

---

[108] A former suffragette who had been imprisoned, and been on hunger strike, she ran the London and Provincial Anti-Vivisection Society, a BU front organization, and her elderly husband Dudley acted as receptionist for the BU. Her flat was raided by the police about 18 December 1939; see DOM 56, 18 December. She was also called Mrs Dacre-Fox.

[109] See above pp. 78–9.

[110] Duvivier and Crowle were expelled. I suppose the list would have named Joyce and Beckett.

[111] Unity had been a close friend of Hitler and a fervent and exhibitionist fascist; on the outbreak of war she attempted to shoot herself, and returned to England with serious brain damage; she died without recovering in 1948. Diana Mosley also knew Hitler well and admired him; her fascist beliefs had not been as widely advertised as those of her sister.

[112] Discussed below.

speeches: by C. Featherstone-Hammond,[113] who (somewhat oddly) presided, on the peace campaign; by Donovan, stressing the fact that the party was a revolutionary party, and revolution was on its way; and by E. G. ('Mick') Clarke, in which the need for emergency arrangements in the form of a telephone link to all officials was mentioned. The Leader then entered, always a dramatic moment in the rituals of fascism. He told the officials that

our time is approaching . . . reward and victory are in sight. They [the fascists] knew what they wanted and knew what would happen but they must not talk—everyone present would know what he meant. They must bring in new members—not necessarily a large number but a moderate number of reliable men and women who would take their place in the ranks when the time came for the sweep forward, which the movement would make, as their brother parties in other countries had made when their hour of destiny struck.

The agent added that 'Underlying the whole of his speech there was a strong hint of a march to power by armed force.' Clearly if this was the tone in which Mosley addressed his officials in a closed meeting it is hardly surprising that MI5, even if there was no more concrete evidence to rely upon, began to take an unfavourable view, though more sceptical security officers would perhaps have viewed the speech as merely typical of Mosley's grandiloquent nonsense.

The BPP

MI5's primary concern was the BU, but Aikin-Sneath and Kell also showed concern over the BPP (alias the British Council for Christian Settlement in Europe—BCCSE).[114] The BPP had been formed in April 1939 by Lord Tavistock (President), Ben Greene (Treasurer), and John Beckett (Secretary), and ostensibly campaigned for peace, and other legitimate political ends. These included the right to security and social justice, the abolition of usury and adoption of social credit, and the abolition of land speculation; hints of fascism appear in article 12 of its programme, 'Safeguarding the employment and integrity of the British people against alien influences and infiltration', and elsewhere.[115] Its propaganda had a pro-German and fascist character, in particular *The Truth about the War*,

---

[113] Hammond, who turns up in the Domvile Diary (e.g. 31 March 1939) and in the 'secret meetings' of right-wingers, was associated with the National Citizens' Union, an anti-Semitic organization dating from the 1920s. He was also a member of the Right Club, and presumably a member of the BU, though not publicly associated with it. Possibly the report confused Charles H. Hammond with him.

[114] For what follows see TS 27/542 (especially an unsigned MI5 report on John Beckett, and a 'Statement of the Case' by A. A. Gordon Clark of MI5 of 2 June 1940).

[115] Greene Papers. Its 'People's Charter' does not contain any similar provision.

published in December 1939 and largely written by Ben Greene.[116] Of those involved we have already met the Marquess of Tavistock. John Beckett, who had been in the BU and NSL, had once been a Labour MP and achieved notoriety for an occasion on which he ran off with the mace; though unstable he was of considerable ability.[117] Ben Greene was a Quaker pacifist who, to put it no more strongly, kept strange company and lacked discretion.[118] On the outbreak of war the party became the BCCSE with Tavistock as Chairman, Captain R. C. Gordon-Canning of the BU as Treasurer,[119] and Beckett as Secretary. The foundation meeting took place at Admiral Domvile's flat on 15 September.[120] Ben Greene claimed to have severed all connection with it in November of 1939, but in fact continued to be connected informally with it.[121] In January of 1940 the party had, as we have seen, achieved some prominence over the 'Tavistock Peace Proposals'.[122]

The Secret Meetings

Aikin-Sneath's questions on co-operation with other groups were inspired by meetings held in 1939 and 1940 to co-ordinate the activities of a number of right-wing groups, all favouring a negotiated peace with

[116] Beckett wrote the preface. It was distributed in Afghanistan by the Germans as propaganda. See FO 371/25102.

[117] 14. *Parl. Deb.* HC Vol. 241 c.1466. He was suspended for 5 days. Wounded in the 1st World War; formed the National Union of Ex-Servicemen and acted as agent for C. R. Attlee; became MP for Gateshead and then Peckham until 1931; whip for the ILP group; became business manager, Strand Theatre; joined BUF 1934; Editor of *Action* and Director of Publicity; left or was expelled March 1937; founded NSL with Joyce 1937; in 1938 became Secretary of the BCAEC with Lord Lymington; then joined the BPP. He also ran the People's Campaign against War and Usury, and published his own *Headline News Letter*, writing as John Stone. See HO 283/26, TS 27/542, HO 45/25698, Cross, *Fascists in Britain*, 103–6, 171–2. There is a life of Beckett by C. Holmes in J. M. Bellamy and J. Savile, *Dictionary of Labour Biography*, vi (London, 1982), 24–9.

[118] Also involved was John Scanlon, who had been in the BU and earlier in the ILP.

[119] Gordon-Canning was wealthy; he had a distinguished war record (10th Hussars, MC) and an interest in politics; he had been a member of the BU from 1934; in 1938 he quarrelled with Mosley. In 1939 he married the film star Mary Maguire, and made a public statement distancing himself from politics, but he seems to have continued to be connected with the BU. See material in the Stokes Papers, Bodleian Library, Box 13. Mosley told Aikin-Sneath in January that he had not then left the party. But a Special Branch report of 27 March (HO 45/24895 sf. 42) claims that at that time Mosley was suing him for £9,000, for reasons not known. He was restricted in June 1940 and interned in 1940; see HO 45/25747 and *Parl. Deb.* HC Vol. 363 c.387 for 18 July.

[120] HO 144/22454; Richard F. Findlay of the Nordic League, Col. C. D. Roe, and C. E. Caroll of the Link were there.

[121] Other supporters in 1939 included noted right-wingers such as Dr Meyrick Booth, Lord Darnley, Prof. A. P. Laurie, the Earl of Mar, H. St John Philby, Henry Williamson, and Hugh Ross Williamson, and pacifists like Dr Soper as well as R. R. Stokes MP. (Pamphlet, undated, in Greene Papers.)

[122] See above 97–8.

Hitler. Mosley was certainly involved. Most of these groups were small and surely utterly unimportant; however, a general alliance of the far right would naturally cause concern in official circles.

The largest group whose leaders were involved in these meetings had officially closed down in 1939; it was the Link, formed in 1937 by Admiral Sir Barry Domvile.[123] By 1939 it had some 4,000 members, many being good-hearted people who wanted peaceful relations with Germany; it also attracted Nazi sympathizers and anti-Semites, as both members and speakers. It was covertly supported by the newssheet *Truth*, controlled by Sir Joseph Ball, a confidant of Neville Chamberlain. A few of its members, probably Germans, had been detained.[124] Admiral Domvile and Cola E. Caroll, its Secretary, attended some of the meetings; both were to be detained in 1940.

Of the other groups the most curious was the Right Club, an anti-Semitic and anti-bolshevist organization founded by Captain Ramsay MP.[125] Since he entered Parliament Ramsay had become increasingly eccentric. Up to 1935 he was primarily concerned over Russian bolshevism; from 1935 to 1938 he came to realize that the threat of bolshevism was international, and from 1938 he realized that the problem was the Jews and Masons.[126] In 1937 he became involved in pro-Franco propaganda, and opposition to godless communism, as Chairman of the United Christian Front. Hitler was to be admired for identifying the menace of organized world Jewry. Ramsay mixed in extreme anti-Semitic circles, and was a member of the Nordic League, in which MI5 had an agent. His object in forming the Right Club was to counter 'Organized Jewry' and oppose war, viewed principally as a Jewish plot. The means was the emancipation of the Conservative Party from Jewish control or influence.[127]

---

[123] See Griffiths, *Fellow Travellers of the Right*, esp. 307–17. Apart from Domvile himself prominent members were its Secretary, C. E. Caroll, editor of the *Anglo-German Review* for the Anglo-German Fellowship, and such pro-Nazis as Prof. A. P. Laurie and Prof. Sir Raymond Beazley, who was Vice-President. The Council included Lord Redesdale, Gordon Fathers, A. E. R. Dyer, and A. Crawford. Caroll was detained in 1940. There was also an Anglo-German Brotherhood, which in 1939 affiliated to the Link; see Griffiths, *Fellow Travellers of the Right*, 251–2, DOM 56 6 Feb. 1939.

[124] DOM, 21 August 1939. The diary for 2 and 5 September 1939 refers to four detainees— 'Old Pick and Co.' Pick may have been J. J. Pickmere, described in HO 45/25752 in September 1941, when detained on the Isle of Man, as having lived in Germany and as being a rabid pro-Nazi.

[125] Earlier involved in an organization known as the Co-ordinating Committee of the Nordic League, which had the end of securing unity on the right. See Griffiths, *Fellow Travellers of the Right*, 354.

[126] See A. H. M. Ramsay, *The Nameless War* (London, [1952]). There is much on Ramsay in Griffiths, *Fellow Travellers of the Right*, esp. 353–5.

[127] The file on Ramsay in the BDBJ Archives (in C6/9/3/2) associates Ramsay with the Militant Christian Patriots, an emanation of the Nordic League. HO 144/22454 also has much on Ramsay, noting his attendance at a meeting of National Citizens' Union in com-

The red ledger of the Right Club has recently come to light, and appears to date from May to August 1939.[128] It records in Ramsay's writing the names of 141 men and 100 women; it seems not to have been kept up since other evidence suggests a membership of about 350. It is unclear on what basis names were entered; inclusion of a name suggests but does not prove membership. Some individuals may have joined what they took to be purely an anti-bolshevik organization rather than an anti-Semitic organization, and others may have had little idea of what they were joining. Members came at some point to be organized in three grades—an outer circle, a second circle, and an inner or 'pioneer' circle.[129] There were membership cards, a subscription of 10 shillings, and the club employed the symbol of an eagle and snake.[130] The ledger names eleven members of the Commons, not all being Conservatives.[131] Some, such as Sir Harold P. Mitchell, who became Vice-Chairman of the Conservative Party, and A. F. Edmonson, who was a Conservative whip and later Chairman of the Carlton Club, were of some prominence. Some may have merely been sympathetic to Ramsay's support of Franco. Peers included the fifth Duke of Wellington, the nineteenth Lord Sempill and the fourth Baron Redesdale, who sat in the Lords, and the twelfth Earl of Galloway, who did not. There were a number of other wealthy and well-connected persons, but most were not people of any prominence.[132] The ledger indicates that many members also belonged to such groups as the Nordic

pany with Henry Newnham, the Editor of *Truth*, Aubrey Lees (see below p. 298 *et seq.*), J. C. Vanneck of the Right Club, and Leigh Vaughan-Henry, formerly BU (see below p. 174 n. 9).

[128] I am grateful to Dr Richard Griffiths for a chance to inspect it. In HO 144/22454, heavily weeded, is material on Parliamentary questions in 1944 by Messrs G. L. M. Mander MP and T. Driberg MP asking for the list to be released. A minute by S. Hoare reads: 'It would be quite wrong to publicise the names of the members, many of them no doubt simple minded people who did not know the nature of the activities of the leaders of the organisation. The names include Mr Stokes, MP [this is an error, a different Stokes being a member], Sir Ernest Bennett, the Dukes of Wellington and Montrose, and some other fairly well known people . . . most of the leaders of the Club, the so called "Inner Circle" are detained under 18B, and some (Anna Wolkoff and Mrs Hiscox) are in prison.' Maxwell suggested illegally destroying the list rather than risking its disclosure. See also *Parl. Deb.* for 12 October 1944, col. 1926.

[129] These categories do not feature in the ledger.

[130] Some information about the Right Club came out in the case of *Ramsay v. New York Times Co. Ltd.* on 17 July 1941 and following days; see *The Times* for 18, 19, 23, 24, 25 July and 1 August. Various membership figures were mentioned. There were said to be 181 'stewards' and 187 'speakers', about 368 members in all, a membership of 270 (or 275) men and 200 (or 100) women. All this seems very overblown.

[131] They were Commander Sir Peter Agnew (Cranborne), Sir Ernest N. Bennett (Cardiff Central), Col. Sir Harold P. Mitchell (Chiswick), Thomas Hunter (Perth and Kinross), Sir Samuel Chapman (South Edinburgh), Albert J. Edmondson, first Baron Sandford (Banbury), J. H. McKie (Galloway), Lt.-Col. Charles I. Kerr MC, DSO, first Baron Teviot (Montrose), Maj. the Hon. J. Staunton (Salford South), Mrs Mavis C. Tate (Frome), and Lord Colum E. Crichton-Stuart (Chester).

[132] Names include William Joyce, A. K. Chesterton, A. F. Loveday, author of books on Spain, and Francis Yeats-Brown, author of *The Bengal Lancer*.

League, the National Socialist League, or the Militant Christian Patriots; there were a few from the IFL, the Link, and the BU. It is not clear that the 1939 Right Club as such ever did more than hold a few meetings, at some of which the Duke of Wellington presided. According to an MI5 report of October 1939 there were plans to acquire premises, run a library, and infiltrate the Armed Services; it all sounds like hot air, and the same report notes that Ramsay was quite unbalanced on Jewish matters.[133] It would be ridiculous to suppose that all those named in the ledger formed a cohesive active political group, much less that they were all disloyal people. But many were certainly anti-Semitic and very right-wing.

Some 'inner circle' members were recruited after the war began, and do seem to have formed an active group, of whom a few became involved in 1940 both in anti-war propaganda and in disloyal activities connected with the Tyler Kent affair, which I discuss in the next chapter. The ledger was not kept up to date, and does not therefore contain the names of all these individuals. Ramsay, who was involved in the meetings, was to be detained in 1940 in this connection, and almost all of the few members of the Right Club who were also detained were involved either in the meetings or with Tyler Kent.

Domvile recorded the meetings in his diary, which escaped MI5.[134] On 10 July 1939 he wrote: 'We are thinking up a plan to amalgamate all the parties who think the same on foreign policy.' In that year regular fortnightly meetings were held, attended by Mosley, prominent members of the BU, and persons associated with such other groups as the Right Club, the BPP, the Nordic League, and the Information and Policy group, as well as by maverick figures such as Captain George H. Lane-Fox Pitt-Rivers. The first took place at Gordon-Canning's flat on 19 September; neither Mosley nor Ramsay attended. Gordon-Canning had been prominent in the BU and was also associated with the BPP.[135] That of 26

[133] HO 144/22454. See also *Jewish Chronicle*, 8 August 1941. The ledger contains no information on the club's meetings or activities.

[134] DOM 56 (National Maritime Museum) covers the early part of the war. Information also in HO 45/25728 (Lees), and HO 144/21933 and HO 45/24895 (Allen). Material in TS 27/496A refers to meetings on 13 and 17 February, 17 April and 24 and 29 May. The meetings are discussed by Thurlow, *Fascism in Britain*, 178–87. Except in some points of detail my account conforms to his. Those who attended at one time or another included, in addition to Mosley, Ramsay, and Domvile, R. C. Gordon-Canning (one-time BU and BCCSE), 'Commandant' Mary Allen (BU), Neil Francis-Hawkins (BU), George Lane-Fox Pitt-Rivers, Aubrey T. O. Lees (RC), The Earl of Mar, Norman Hay (RC and *IP*), Viscount Lymington (later the Earl of Portsmouth), H. T. ('Bertie') Mills (RC, involved with The People's Campaign against War and Usury and the magazine *New Pioneer*), C. G. Grey (Editor of the *Aeroplane*), Maj.-Gen. J. F. C. ('Boney') Fuller (BU), Francis Yeats-Brown (RC), Professor A. P. Laurie, R. F. Findlay (RC), Lt.-Col. C. D. Roe (RC and Link), Launcelot Lawton (RC and *IP*) Lady Pearson (BU), Lady Dunn, and Lord Tavistock (BCCSE).

[135] Attended by Beckett, Greene, A. C. Streatfield (Link), Colonel Roe, Richard F. Findlay (RC), Caroll (Link), F. B. H. Drummond (RC), Domvile, and his wife,

October was planned at a smaller meeting on 13 October, attended by Mosley, Domvile, Norman Hay, and Neil Francis-Hawkins; Ramsay, though expected, failed to turn up. The group now included Lords Tavistock and Lymington.[136] Domvile called it Oswald Mosley's meeting. The third meeting, on 8 November, featured Ramsay as well as Mosley. Lords Tavistock and Lymington were there, and Herbert T. V. ('Bertie') Mills, C. Featherstone Hammond of the National Citizens' Union (also apparently BU). Aubrey T. O. Lees attended for the first time.[137] The last two meetings of 1939 were of a different character, being simply discussion groups; the subject for 22 November was 'Menace to Freedom'.[138]

Further meetings took place in 1940. On 17 January a small group of seven met at Francis-Hawkins's flat: Mosley, Laurie, Lancelot Lawton, Hay, and Mills, as well as Domvile. This looks more like a serious negotiating meeting. It may be significant that six days later Domvile was admitted into the 'inner circle' of the BU, whatever that was.[139] There were larger discussion-group meetings on 7, 13, and 29 February.[140] On the last two occasions the subject was the Tavistock Peace Proposals.[141] Further meetings took place at A. Huth-Jackson's home on 13 March[142] and 17 April, the last attended by Mosley; these again do not give the impression of planning or negotiating meetings, but rather of discussion groups.[143] Other encounters may have been more significant; for example on 6 May Domvile records that 'Maddocks came to dinner. I have a high opinion of his ability and loyalty—one of Mosley's best men.' Maddocks was Hubert Maddocks, a former Link speaker, who must have been a

[136] Nine attended—Mosley, Laurie, Ramsay, Tavistock, Lymington, Lawton, Hay, Francis-Hawkins, and Domvile.

[137] A Colonial Civil Servant; see below p. 298 et seq.

[138] On 22 November and 6 December. Domvile lists in addition to himself and his wife ('Pudd') and daughter Miranda 15 persons at the first meeting, and over 30 at the next. Domvile does not say that Mosley attended the second. Raven-Thomson and Francis-Hawkins of the BU were present, as well as Norah Elam and her husband. The Fullers attended on 6 December.

[139] Domvile wrote for Action under the pseudonym Canute or Naval Expert (see e.g. 18 January 1940). Mosley in My Life untruthfully says that Domvile had no connection with the BU.

[140] See DOM 56 and HO 45/24895/16.

[141] Those attending included Lymington, Lord Mar, Fuller, Gordon-Canning, Beckett, Ben Greene, Stuart Morris, and Lord Arnold.

[142] This was attended by a considerable number of people, including Mrs Whinfield, Norah Elam, Mrs Duff, Lady Pearson, Col. Elliott, Mills, Tavistock, Miss Laurie, and Francis-Hawkins. There was large public occasion in the Criterion on 5 March 1940; in addition to Mosley those who attended included the Domviles, Countess Downe, Fuller, Greene, Henry Williamson, Pitt-Rivers and MI5's P. G. Taylor. See HO 45/25895. The owner of the flat appears to have been Annabel Huth-Jackson, née Grant Duff, author of A Victorian Childhood (London, 1932).

[143] See a Special Branch report of 2 June in HO 45/25728. TS 27/496A refers to a meeting on 24 May.

secret member of the BU. We can have no idea what was discussed and what the significance of the reference to loyalty was. After the first arrests further meetings may have taken place on 24 and 29 May; Thurlow doubts whether the meeting of 24 May took place at all, but meetings to discuss the arrests would be natural enough.[144] It is clear from *Action* that these meetings produced some little co-operation; for example Mills wrote for the paper on 14 October 1939, and Lawton on 4 January and 29 February 1940, but beyond that the evidence is lacking. But if anything very sinister was discovered about them we should know from the transcript of Mosley's advisory committee hearing.

MI5 and Special Branch certainly knew in early 1940 of some of these meetings; thus a Special Branch report of 20 February reports meetings on 9 November and 7 February.[145] Inevitably a conspiracy theory evolved, explicit in a Special Branch report of 24 May 1940. Arguing that Aubrey T. O. Lees be detained, it said he attended a private meeting convened by Mosley:

for the purpose of discussing with the leaders of various pro-fascist and anti-Semitic groups the formation of a vast secret revolutionary organisation, in which all would collaborate. Amongst those present at this meeting were Mosley, N. L. M. Francis-Hawkins, Lord Lymington, Captain G. H. L.-F. Pitt-Rivers, Admiral Sir Barry Domvile, the Earl of Mar, Captain A. H. Ramsay, Featherstone Hammond and Norman Hay.

The meeting in question presumably took place in April.[146] We can be reasonably confident that this theory of a sinister underground organization had begun to develop some time earlier; the source could be Maxwell-Knight, whose somewhat independent division of MI5 seems to have been very much hand in glove with Special Branch. The Home Office file on Mary Allen refers to meetings at 48 Ladbroke Grove in March, April, and May, the purpose being, it was said, to plan collaboration and a *coup*.[147]

How convinced the more sensible Home Office officials were of the significance of the secret meetings is another matter. Maxwell was certainly very sceptical, and on 5 June he responded to Kendal's 'vast secret revolutionary organisation' with a request for more information. Kendal toned down his claim; there had been secret meetings 'for the purpose of setting up a co-ordinating organisation of all the various fascist groups which would carry on open and undercover activities with the aim of

[144] Domvile does not record them; the evidence is a Special Branch report of 22 June in HO 45/25728 and TS/496A.
[145] HO 45/25895.   [146] HO 45/25728, also HO 45/25700 (Francis-Hawkins).
[147] A Special Branch report of 25 June 1940 in HO 144/21933/330. This was the home of Norah Elam, and Mrs M. Bothamley, who had gone to Germany and was tried after the war for involvement in German broadcasting, had lived there.

establishing a fascist government in Britain'. The report, based on 'a very reliable informant', went on to concede 'that a certain amount of collaboration resulted from the meetings but no concrete plans were made, principally because those present could not agree on a leader. All were convinced that sooner or later an opportunity would arise for a "march to power" and that the closest co-operation between all the fascist bodies was an urgent need.'

The belief that in the crisis fascism would triumph was of course standard form; given some common sense this picture of the secret meetings deprives them of any real significance. The fascists gathered to dream dreams; something more like 'plotting' may have taken place at more intimate gatherings, but there is no real evidence of this, and Maxwell was surely right to be sceptical. The idea that those who attended the secret meetings, many being eccentrics, actually mattered was silly.

As for Mosley himself, he was surely enough of a realist to appreciate that in 1940 his disintegrated party, whether or not allied to a few groups of cranks, had no immediate further significance in regular politics, and it is conceivable that he toyed with the idea, as Cowling has suggested, though of course without any evidence, that 'his only hope was a German occupation'.[148] The only concrete evidence of his views was that he thought fascism would flourish again in the aftermath of a long war.[149] Diana Mosley has told me that he never imagined that the French army could collapse; consequently he did not expect an occupation of Britain, but rather a drawn-out struggle. But there is no way of being absolutely sure what Mosley imagined would eventually become of himself or his country in May 1940, except that he was on record as doubting the possibility of a German invasion and, to be fair, had consistently appeared and behaved as a patriot, however misguided. But the history and public character of his party, its opposition to the war and sympathy with Germany, his private pronouncements and public commitment to the idea of revolutionary fascism, and the paramilitary organization of his followers, many intensely loyal to him as Leader, all combined with the belief in the Fifth Column to make the BU the obvious target for repressive action in May of 1940. If there was a Fifth Column in Britain, it must surely be associated with the nearest the British had to a Führer and a Nazi Party.[150]

[148] M. Cowling, *The Impact of Hitler: British Politics and British Policy 1933–1940*, (Cambridge, 1975), 194.

[149] Report in HO 45/24895.

[150] For speculation as to Mosley's significance in May 1940, see N. Longmate, *If Britain Had Fallen* (New York, 1974), ch. 8, and J. Lukacs, *The Duel, 10 May–31 July 1940: The Eighty-Day Struggle between Churchill and Hitler* (New York, 1974), 78–80. Writing after the war, Mosley naturally repudiated suggestions that he was a traitor, as he did at the time. He assumed, probably correctly, that he would have been shot if an invasion had occurred in 1940.

8

The British Fifth Column

The Raid on May 20

On May 20 at about 11 a.m. Charles Maxwell-Knight, Inspectors Keeble and Pearson, and Franklin C. Gowen, Second Secretary at the US Embassy, raided the flat of Tyler G. Kent, a code and cipher clerk in the US Embassy.[1] Captain Guy Liddell had rung Herschel V. Johnson, the Counsellor, at 12.30 p.m. on 18 May, and Maxwell-Knight explained the background at 3 p.m. that day.[2] At the Foreign Office on 19 May Johnson saw Cadogan, the Permanent Under-Secretary, who evasively told him that he 'knew in a general way through a report from the British police of what had happened, though he was not familiar with the details'.[3] Johnson agreed to waiving of Kent's diplomatic immunity, being assured that any proceedings would be in camera. Waiver was confirmed by Ambassador Joseph Kennedy and, after the arrest, by the State Department.[4] Cordell Hull explained in a telegram of 22 May:[5] 'The purpose of waiving immunity was that the British authorities might proceed

---

[1] The principal sources are Joan Miller, later Joanna Phipps, *One Girl's War: Personal Exploits in MI5's Most Secret Station* (Dingle, Eire, 1986), a collection by Charles Parsons in the Library of the University of Yale (MS Group 310 Tyler Kent Collection), a collection of documents in the US Archives in RG 59 (esp. Boxes 481 and 554) and RG 84, Kent's much blacked-out FBI file (including documents released in 1991), and W. A. (Earl) Jowitt, *Some Were Spies* (London, 1954). The best analysis is W. F. Kimball and B. Bartlett, 'Roosevelt and Prewar Commitments to Churchill: The Tyler Kent Affair', *Diplomatic History*, 5 (1981), 291. See also A. Masters, *The Man Who Was M: The Life of Maxwell Knight* (Oxford, 1984), ch. 6; and R. Thurlow, *Fascism in Britain: A History, 1918–1985* (Oxford, 1987), ch. 9; R. Harris, *The Times*, 4 December 1982; R. J. Whalen, *The Founding Father: The Story of Joseph P. Kennedy* (New York, 1964), 310–20. W. J. West's analysis in *Truth Betrayed* (London, 1987), esp. 235–7, seems to me to go beyond the evidence, as in part does J. Costello, *Ten Days that Saved the West* (London, 1981), also published as *Ten Days to Destiny: The Secret Story of the Hess Peace Initiative and British Efforts to Strike a Deal with Hitler* (New York, 1991). In the compressed account which follows, written before the publication of R. Bearse and A. Read, *Conspirator: The Untold Story of Churchill, Roosevelt and Tyler Kent, Spy* (London, 1991), I have used all available sources. Bearse and Read contains some minor errors but in general seems to me to be reliable; the book adds much detail from interviews and US sources.

[2] Memo of 28 May by Gowen, US Archives RG 59 Box 481 123.

[3] Memo of 28 May 1940 by Johnson, RG 59 Box 481.

[4] Telegrams 1276 (7 p. m.) and 913 (8 p.m.) of 20 May.

[5] Cordell Hull to Kennedy, Telegram 944 of 22 May.

against Kent. There is no objection to formally charging the offender with violations of British law. Publicity in connection with such charges might not be helpful under the circumstances.'[6] The alternative would have been Kent's deportation, and he could have been charged with offences in the USA.[7] Earlier the same day Maxwell-Knight had raided the flat of Kent's friend Anna Wolkoff, or Volkoff.

Kent was in bed with a Mrs Irene Danischewsky, who was of Russian origin, and had been Kent's mistress since January. Gowen was, somewhat oddly, given her address and telephone number, but told her phone was tapped; he supposed her to be an MI5 agent who knew the raid was coming. He was assured that she knew nothing, and she was allowed to leave as soon as she had dressed.

Kent was found to be in possession of numerous documents or copies of documents purloined from the US Embassy, together with the locked ledger of the Right Club. He was arrested and later, with Anna Wolkoff, put on trial; an account of the aftermath of the affair, which is not directly relevant to this book, is given in Appendix IV.

Kent's Antecedents

Kent had previously worked in the US Legation in Moscow, where he was regarded as idle and incompetent. Born on 24 March 1911 at Newchwang in Manchuria, he was the son of a US Consular official. The Kents left China in 1913 and moved to Leipzig, where he first attended school; they then moved to Berne, and later to Belfast. They returned to America in 1919, but left after a short time for Bermuda. Kent became an excellent linguist, fluent in German, Italian, French, and Russian, and had attended Princeton, the Sorbonne, the University of Madrid, Campbell College in Belfast, and George Washington University. Both in Moscow and in London, where he had free access to the files, he abstracted documents on a large and uncertain scale. In Moscow, as an FBI report of 13 January 1951 put it, he led a 'boisterous life', smuggling furs and jewellery with a Miss A. J. Barrett, a Legation clerk.[8] One of his Russian mistresses was Tanya or Tatiana Alexandrovna Ilovaiskaya, clearly an agent of the NKVD, who subsequently moved to Paris and New York. He owned three photographs of her, two in the nude. Whilst on post in Moscow Kent travelled widely in Europe; he gave medical and dental treatment as a reason, and in 1951 told the FBI that he acted as an official courier, but this does not seem to have been true.

---

[6] Ibid.   [7] Kent was originally held under a deportation order.

[8] Telegram from Ambassador Kennedy to State Department on 24 May 1940, RG 59 Box 481.

Kent was moved to London in October 1939, and came into contact with Anna, then aged about 38, the fanatically anti-Semitic and anti-communist daughter of Admiral Nicholas Wolkoff, a Russian who had, at the time of the revolution, been Naval Attaché in London. The Wolkoffs settled in Britain in 1919, and in 1935 Anna had been naturalized. She became a high-class dressmaker, and worked for such well-connected clients as Wallis Simpson and Pamela Jackson (formerly Mitford). The Wolkoffs ran the Russian Tea Rooms near South Kensington underground station, a centre of anti-bolshevik intrigue, and they became involved with Ramsay's Right Club; its 'inner circle' members continued to meet after the war began, with Anna acting as organizing secretary.[9] He was friendly too with Enid Riddell, who was also in the club and the Nordic League, and with Catherine Ridley and Patricia Dalgleish, whose names are not in the ledger. Enid Riddell's flat was raided on 21 May. His Russian contacts included E. Sabline, former Chargé d'Affaires, and then President of the Russian Refugee Council. A curious feature of the wartime Right Club is its foreign contacts; thus Guy Niermans was described as its principal agent in Belgium,[10] and Jean Nieuwenhus, Second Secretary at the Belgian Embassy, appears to have had connections with it. In 1940 some members were using 'sticky-back' labels to disseminate anti-war propaganda: 'A Bayonet is a weapon with a worker at each end' and 'War destroys workers, not Hitlers'.[11] Some were anti-Semitic. According to Joan Miller Anna and her friends were compiling a list of persons opposed to the Nazis of whom an example would be made once the country was in German hands.[12]

Kent joined the club, probably in January of 1940, and at his trial was evasive as to the reason for this, though he admitted to being anti-Semitic.[13] He said that the club was principally engaged in disseminating propaganda on 'semitic questions, freemasonry and labour topics'.[14] There were many who believed that the Russian Revolution was the product of a conspiracy of Jews and Freemasons, and Anna and her friends were no doubt of this persuasion. Kent seems to have tried to infiltrate White Russian circles at the behest of Russian paymasters. His FBI file significantly reveals that when he was arrested he possessed a British fifty pound note.[15] Fifty pound notes were rarities, and Kent had no explanation; US officials were not paid in British currency.

---

[9] The pre-war secretary had been John Carlton Cross (*Jewish Chronicle*, 8 August 1941), who was apparently not detained.

[10] Trial transcript at 93.   [11] Trial transcript.

[12] Miller, *One Girl's War*, 33.

[13] In 1940 he said May, but in September 1951 he said January. He described the club as 'an anti-semitic organization of approximately five hundred members whose purpose it was to counteract pro-Soviet influence in England'.

[14] Transcript 134.   [15] Interrogation on 7 September 1951.

Presumably he was illicitly receiving large sums of money. At the time Ambassador Kennedy thought Kent was 'associated with a gang of spies working in the interests of Germany and Russia'.[16] Material in the very heavily blanked-out FBI file also suggests that Kent was supplying documents to the Russians; for example a memorandum of 4 April 1944 has this: 'The Bureau files fail to disclose the identity of the foreign power Kent was furnishing information to. At that time [i.e. in 1940] the general tenor of newspaper releases indicated that he was working for the German government. At the present time it would appear that Kent was actively engaged in espionage for the Russian government.'[17] There is no certain evidence as to what he was up to, but common sense suggests he was simply a dishonest individual who liked high living and knew that purloined documents could command a considerable price. My own belief is that Kent was open to offers generally.

Kent and MI5 Surveillance

Since his arrival on 5 October 1939 Kent had been strongly suspected of espionage; the Stockholm police had reported to MI5 on Ludwig Mathias, a naturalized Swede of German extraction thought to be a Gestapo agent. Mathias visited Kent on 8 October at the Cumberland Hotel, and was seen leaving with a bulky package.[18] The obvious conclusion was that Kent had delivered documents to him.[19] Although MI5 soon discovered who Kent was, the American Embassy was told nothing about the matter until 18 May. Johnson in his account of the affair wrote:

I immediately told Captain Knight that in my opinion it was most regrettable that Scotland Yard had not informed us of these circumstances at the time, as regardless of whether anything of an incriminating nature had been discovered about either Mathias or Kent, we would never have kept the man in the Code Room if there had been the slightest ground for suspicion against him.

Ambassador Kennedy also protested.[20] Liddell of MI5 had in fact warned Johnson on 7 February 1940 that Kennedy's communications with the President were being obtained by the Germans, the agent being called 'Doctor', and possibly operating from Berlin.[21] US officials should have

[16] Telegram 1276, 20 May 1940, Kennedy to State Department. Breckenridge Long took the same view.
[17] It must be emphasized that this statement refers to suspicion, not knowledge. I have been informed that his name featured in decrypts of German communications.
[18] Memo by Johnson.
[19] At his FBI interrogation Kent said he met Mathias on a boat from Bergen *en route* to England and had no idea then that he was an agent. He admitted to carrying a box of cigars through customs in England for Mathias, a box he accidentally left in a taxi cab; he denied giving Mathias anything.
[20] See also Whalen, *Founding Father*, 212.   [21] See now Costello, *Ten Days*, ch. 6.

had some suspicions about the security of communications from London, and apparently did.[22] Possibly Liddell's aim was to exonerate MI5 from blame when Kent was eventually unmasked; the Embassy had, as it were, been warned, but in the papers this excuse does not appear.

Kent's activities compromised all the American diplomatic codes and ciphers.[23] At first sight the failure to tell the Embassy about Kent seems extraordinary. One suggested explanation[24] is that the intelligence services were also interested in Kennedy, who was viewed with extreme hostility by the Foreign Office, though quite why leaving Kent alone would assist the surveillance of Kennedy is not clear.[25] The Foreign Office must have been told about Kent in 1939, but it has destroyed or withheld all papers connected with the Kent affair dating from 1939 and 1940; it must have something to hide. Somewhat oddly it was only on 18 March 1940 that Cadogan issued a circular in the Foreign Office saying that reports of conversations in the US Embassy might be available to the enemy;[26] it may be, however, that there had been an earlier circular on the matter. Cadogan was no stranger to dishonest cipher clerks, and owed the US authorities something for a warning provided after the defection of Walter Krivitsky; investigations had begun in September 1939 into the Foreign Office communications department, from which there had been leaks for years. There were two principal suspects, of whom one, Captain John Herbert King, who worked for the Russians, was secretly tried on 18 October 1939. Cadogan's diary recorded that the security service was 'on the track of others'.[27] Conceivably Kent was left alone in the hope of fur-

---

[22] See now Costello, *Ten Days*, ch. 6, 137.

[23] The Johnson memo states at 10 that 'among the papers were the true readings of telegrams to the Department in the Embassy's most confidential codes . . . ' Kennedy telegraphed the State Department on 25 May to the effect that no codes were now secure. The most secure cipher was the 'Strip Cipher'. See also F. L. Israel (ed.), *The War Diaries of Breckenridge Long* (Lincoln, 1966) for 22 May and 22 June, quoted J. P. Lash, *Roosevelt and Churchill: The Partnership that Saved the West* (London, 1977), 137, and Costello, *Ten Days*, esp. App. 5.

[24] By Masters, *The Man Who Was M*, 112.

[25] FO 371/24251 f. 54ff. discussed D. E. Koskoff, *Joseph P. Kennedy: A Life and Times* (Englewood Cliffs, NJ, 1974), 238 and FO 371/28217.

[26] FO 371/44628/406 (20 May–23 November 1945). Cadogan's circular is mentioned in FO 371/24251.

[27] See N. West, *MI5* (London, 1983), 90; Cadogan MS Diary ACAD 1/8 entries for 4, 9, 10, 11, 26 September; CRIM 1/1129; D. Cameron Watt, 'Francis Herbert King: A Soviet Source in the Foreign Office', *Intelligence and National Security*, 3 (1988), 62–82. The trial led to a sentence of 10 years; its occurrence remained secret until 1956. The other suspect was R. C. Oake (see Cadogan Diary for 25 September). He had been appointed a cipher officer on 1 February 1920, and he was dismissed from the Foreign Office on 1 January 1940. King had been recruited in 1935 by Henry Pieck, a Dutchman, to whom he had been introduced by Oake; in 1936 Pieck left London and his contact thereafter was one Petersen. Pieck had made a number of other contacts in the Foreign Office. In all King received £2,500; he claimed to believe that these were a share in stock-dealing profits assisted by his leaked copies of Foreign Office cables. When some of this money was found in a safe deposit at his

ther discoveries of a London 'ring', but allowing him to remain active for
so prolonged a period still seems bizarre.

J. Costello in his *Ten Days that Saved the West* has recently suggested
an explanation which seems just possible.[28] If British intelligence agents
were able, by burgling Kent's flat from time to time, to obtain copies of
the purloined documents—not yet encoded—this would be of great assistance in breaking the US ciphers, especially the difficult 'strip cipher'. It
is notorious that the Foreign Office did engage in this type of spying on
its supposed friends. According to this theory the more Kent stole the
better pleased the British would be—but then why kill the goose? In any
event the breaking of US ciphers cannot at this time have been high in the
priorities at Bletchley.

Whatever the explanation for the inaction since 1939, there is also therefore a need to explain why the decision to raid Wolkoff's and Kent's flats
was taken at this particular moment; they had after all been left alone for a
considerable period. The simplest explanation is that in May 1940 MI5
was in conflict with the Home Office over the danger from the Fifth
Column; clearly if the Kent raid produced evidence of an active British
Fifth Column, MI5's case would be strengthened, and although MI5
must have known in general what would be found in the raid there may
have been hope of a better haul. A different explanation was given to
Johnson before the raid by Maxwell-Knight:

During the first week in May 1940 a search warrant was executed on the premises
of another member of the Right Club who was known to be in communication
with a British subject engaged in assisting the enemy in Germany. As a result of
this search Anna Wolkoff took alarm, and she told another member of the Right
Club that her 'most incriminating papers' had been handed to Tyler Kent, who
had locked them up in a safe at the United States Embassy.

If this story was true it could explain why MI5 decided to act, assuming the
decision was taken by MI5, though no papers were in fact found in the
Embassy. But there were obvious disadvantages in arresting Kent; in particular the whole story might have been very harmful to relations with the
USA, though in the event it does not seem to have caused any serious trouble. One obvious consequence of the arrest of Kent was a general interrup-
tion in American diplomatic traffic for some weeks; one can only speculate
as to whether the Foreign Office had some reason to wish for this.

Costello has recently set out a much more elaborate theory in the book
to which I have referred. According to this the Kent raid was initiated by

lady friend's place of work he claimed in a statement on 25 Sept. that it represented gam-
bling winnings. On 28 Sept. he confessed, and it rather appears as if he did so to exonerate
his friend, a Miss Helen Wilkie. He denied having handed over the cipher.

[28] Costello, *Ten Days*, 129.

Churchill himself as an elaborate 'sting' operation. It had three functions. The first was to discredit the defeatist Ambassador Kennedy. It is wholly obscure why the raids would have this effect. To be sure Maxwell-Knight's conversation with Johnson may have indicated the degree to which the Embassy was kept under surveillance, and Costello sometimes seems to be saying that the aim of the operation was simply to frighten Kennedy (not the same thing as discrediting him) by indicating that MI5 had been keeping an eye on him and his dubious activities. This cannot have come as news to either Kennedy or Johnson, nor would the operation discredit Kennedy with Roosevelt, who cordially hated him anyway. At the most it would reflect badly on Johnson and his staff for lax security. The second purpose was to produce proof of a dangerous Fifth Column plot, against which action could be taken (as it was) to menace those of Churchill's political enemies who favoured a negotiated peace; presumably they would fear being locked up next. There is not a shred of direct evidence that Churchill was directly involved in so bizarre and politically dangerous a scheme. Nor is it easy to see why locking up Kent, the eccentric Ramsay, and the fascist Mosley and his lieutenants would cause a moment's anxiety to individuals in mainstream politics—for example Halifax, Butler, Lloyd George—who favoured negotiations with Germany. There could be no question of locking them up! The third purpose was to enable Kent, once arrested, to be employed as a hostage to blackmail Roosevelt into falling in with Churchill's wishes. He would function as such because of the knowledge he had of Roosevelt's exchanges with Churchill; Roosevelt would know that his chance of re-election would be damaged if Kent told all in public, and so would be to some extent in Churchill's power. Again there is no direct evidence at all of this, and Roosevelt could not possibly have been worried about any Churchillian threat to hinder his re-election; Churchill had not the least interest in his losing the election. There is to be sure evidence that Kent was kept incommunicado so as not to cause embarrassment to Roosevelt in the election, but that is a different point. I find Costello's theory utterly unconvincing; if there was something in the nature of a 'sting', its source is more probably MI5 than Churchill. Costello's argument is also unhappy on detail; for example he says that Churchill ordered the scheme to be implemented on Sunday 19 May; his footnote is irrelevant, and in any event the decision had been announced to Johnson the previous day. His understanding of the technicalities of 18B is shaky, and his theories seem to me to go well beyond the evidence.[29]

---

[29] Costello's account is based in part on documents which he says have been removed from the US National Archives. These documents are again in the US Archives, being declassified on 13 April 1989.

Maxwell-Knight and the Right Club

Maxwell-Knight had been running agents in Ramsay's Right Club, in particular Joan Miller, Marjorie Nora Mackie (known both as Mrs Amos and, incredible though it seems, Miss Amor), and Hélène Louise de Munck.[30] Two other possible agents appear in the ledger, Philip Brocklehurst[31] and Vincent Collier. Maxwell-Knight took a grave view of the club: 'This is a definitely "Fifth Column" organization which under the cloak of anti-Jewish propaganda conducts pro-German activities, has contacts in British government offices and also in foreign Legations. These Legation contacts are used to communicate with countries abroad and even with Germany by means of the diplomatic bags.'[32] As a general account of the Right Club this seems grossly misleading, but Maxwell-Knight was presumably writing of the few members still active in 1940; had his view been accepted as generally true many more members of the club would have been detained than were. MI5 was, at this time, desperate to deliver something dramatic to the Home Office.

Kent's Contacts

The number of documents found was about 1,500, filed in part under classifications such as 'Germany', 'Turkey', 'Czechoslovakia', 'British Cabinet', 'Churchill', 'Halifax'; there were numerous empty folders, with headings such as Ireland, Spain, Sweden.[33] Many were neither confidential, nor of any particular importance.[34] They went back to January of 1938. The largest collections related to Germany, Italy, and Poland, and very few related to Russia. One must assume that those found were merely those not passed on. Other purloined documents were found at 1 Edwardes Square, then unoccupied.[35] Kent soon admitted showing some telegrams to Anna Wolkoff and Ramsay, and Ramsay had visited Kent's apartment on a number of occasions, and been alone there with a typewriter.[36] He lent Anna two telegrams from Churchill to Roosevelt; she

---

[30] Kent's personal file reference was PF 49074/B5B, the B5B referring to the section run by Maxwell-Knight.

[31] Identified by A. Masters as a former journalist; not presumably the baronet of that name.

[32] Memorandum in US National Archives RG 84. This memorandum appears to have been that mentioned in the Cabinet on 22 May.

[33] Transcript 132 gives a figure of around 500; in Kent's appeal the figure given was 466. A later State Department Press release of 2 September 1944 gave a correct figure of 1,500. An inventory is in RG 59 File 123 Kent Tyler G. The documents were of course taken away by the American officials. See now Bearse and Read, *Conspirator*, 293–7.

[34] Johnson Memo 10.

[35] *Post Office Directories* give the previous resident as Arthur Rowlatt.

[36] Johnson Memo 14.

had these photographed by a Russian photographer, Nicholas E. Smirnoff, and the prints were never found.[37] He also showed Anna a telegram from Roosevelt to Churchill.[38] Smirnoff was, as one would expect, suspected of complicity, and, after giving evidence at Kent's trial, was detained under Regulation 18B.[39] Kent had also apparently given documents to Mathias, and to Mrs (Dr) Christobel Nicholson, wife of Admiral Wilmot Nicholson, both members of the Right Club.[40] Other material had been passed by Anna through Lieutenant-Colonel Don Francisco Maringliani, Duke del Monte, Assistant Military Attaché at the Italian Embassy in London, whom she called Mr Macaroni, to Hans Mackensen, the German Ambassador in Rome, and thus to the German government.

Less is known about Anna Wolkoff than about Kent, since no transcript of her trial is available.[41] She was charged with three offences. One related to obtaining the two telegrams which were photographed by Smirnoff. The third was formally a more serious charge—that with intent to assist the enemy she attempted to send a coded letter to William Joyce containing advice on radio propaganda.[42] The use of code of course indicated previous contacts with Germany. This was to be transmitted via the Romanian Legation, since her contact in the Italian Embassy was ill at the time; she handed this letter to Maxwell-Knight's agent Hélène, who of course handed it over to him. Hélène then returned it to Anna, who wanted to add to it, and Anna then handed it over to an unidentified MI5 agent, 'X'. According to Joan Miller's account of the matter the letter, somewhat modified, was indeed sent to Joyce.[43] The point of sending it was presumably to pave the way for further contact. The decoded text of this letter, which Anna apparently did not write herself but which was handed to her by an unidentified third party early in April, included the following passages:

Talks effects splendid news bulletins less so. Palestine good but IRA defeats

[37] He had been in the financial division of the pre-revolution Russian Embassy. He was presented at the trial as an innocent agent.
[38] This was No. 872 of 16 May 1940. It was not used in the trial because the US government was unwilling to have the text proved in court.
[39] One would like to know what became of him—did he become a coerced double agent? He does not appear in Nigel West's supposedly comprehensive list in *MI5* at 307–8, nor in any sources I have seen.
[40] 1872–9 June 1947. His name is not, however, in the ledger.
[41] The trial transcript has some information. Jowitt, who prosecuted, gives an account in *Some Were Spies*, ch. 6.
[42] Part of the text, decoded, is given in the trial transcript at 185.
[43] *One Girl's War*, ch. 2. The intermediary was Mrs Amos's (or Amor's) son, a naval officer. Her real name is said to have been Marjorie Mackie; see Masters, *The Man Who Was M*, 80 n. 4.
[44] Here followed information on quality of reception and wavelengths.

object. Stick to plutocracy avoid King . . . [44] Workers fed up, wives more so. Troops not keen. Anti-Semitism spreading like flame everywhere all classes. Note refujews in so-called Pioneer Corps guaranteed in writing to be sent into firing line. Churchill not popular. Keep on at him as Baruch[45] tool and war-theatre-extender sacrificer Gallipoli etc. Stress his conceit and repeated failures with ex-proselites and prestige. Altmark[46] atrocities debunked by Truth.[47] This is only free paper, circulation bounding. Big man behind paper, no fear ruin. Nearly all your friends still sound, e.g. pay gay oo hundred percent [sic], though Lewis wants murder you.[48] All league sound.[49] Family not persecuted by public but only by Anderson who keep Q.[50] imprisoned and gets F. and R. sacked BBC.[51] Still family not in distress, master teaching school again.[52] Baphomet [or BAP home T] very friendly, wife also.[53] Ironside[54] believed very anti-Jewish, not so anti-German, possibly British France if things reach that stage here.[55]

The text ended by arranging an acknowledgment by code on the German 'New British Broadcasting Station', and it was acknowledged.[56]

Anna's defence was that the message had been planted to incriminate her, and that she had in turn given it to Hélène to incriminate her. As a defence this was implausible, though it is quite possible that it was indeed

[45] Bernard Baruch, a friend of Churchill, and thought by anti-Semites to be a major figure in the world Jewish conspiracy.

[46] The *Altmark*, a vessel on which British prisoners taken from merchant vessels had been held by the Germans. On 16 February the vessel was boarded in Norwegian waters and the prisoners rescued.

[47] This paper was under the control of Sir Joseph Ball; see below p. 186.

[48] The boxer T. ('Kid') Lewis. He was a Jew, one of the few who had been associated with the BU.

[49] The NSL, Joyce's breakaway party.

[50] Quentin, William's brother, detained under Regulation 18B.

[51] Frank Joyce and Rosemary Joyce, both of whom had worked for the BBC, lost their jobs. See p. 55 n. 29.

[52] Probably Angus MacNab.

[53] The passage in brackets is presumably an alternative decoded version. The reference is obscure.

[54] General Ironside, according to his diaries, was thought by some to be unreliable. The suggestion of anti-Semitism relates to conflicts with Hore-Belisha; his diaries refer to Hore-Belisha as 'the Jew'. He wanted Maj.-Gen. Fuller as Deputy CIGS; Fuller was a fascist and strongly anti-Semitic. (Fuller Diaries in the Liddell Hart Centre for Military Archives, entry for 27 September 1939; reference provided by Mr Richard Thurlow). Suspicions of Ironside connected with his visits to a house in Holland Park are recorded by M. Muggeridge, *Chronicles of Wasted Time: An Autobiography* (Washington, DC, 1973), 373-7. Muggeridge worked for MI6. Conceivably the reference is to 17 Stanley Gardens, where Dr Leigh Vaughan-Henry lived; see below p. 174 n. 9.

[55] Other passages are given by Jowitt, *Some Were Spies*, 71-2. These include 'Butter ration doubled because poor can't buy—admitted by Telegraph—bacon same. Cost living steeply mounting. Shopkeepers suffer. Suits PEP. Regret must state Meg's Tuesday talk unpopular with women. Advise alter radically or drop. God bless to all leaguers and CB [Concordia Bureau].'

[56] A curious feature of the coded message is that it had on it the words 'Schlüsselwort—Weissreich—Spitzname'; the second word was taken to refer to Whitelands, which had been the BU HQ under the name the Black House. The first word means 'code word' and the last 'nickname'.

initially planted on her.[57] There is no indication who wrote it; the text suggests it was a former member of the NSL, and if it originated with MI5, which seems unlikely, this could have been Collier. Conceivably it was Admiral Domvile, who, as we shall see, was detained for some sort of misconduct involving German broadcasting, but this is merely speculative. Jowitt's account of the trial says that the letter, after it had been retrieved from Hélène, was handed to an agent, X, and that a naval officer who was present when this was done could not be traced.[58] This was not true; Joan Miller identifies the naval officer, and presumably MI5 did not tell Jowitt the truth, a fact which suggests some dishonest conduct by Maxwell-Knight. Probably it was suspected that Anna had communicated with the enemy on other occasions.

Ramsay and the Churchill–Roosevelt Cables

The documents Ramsay saw included a very few cables between Churchill and Roosevelt. Two, those copied by Smirnoff, were used at Kent's trial. These revealed that Churchill had arranged for the British Navy to give American shipping preferential treatment over the blockade, which was generally known.[59] Some of the documents not produced at the trial were considered more 'sensitive', and both governments were uneasy about any revelation of the correspondence. In particular the State Department refused permission to use Telegram 872 (Roosevelt to Churchill) of 16 May, a pencilled copy of which had been found in a sealed envelope in the possession of Christobel Nicholson.[60] This refusal led to her acquittal when she was eventually brought to trial on 14 February 1941, over eight months after her detention under 18B on 26 May 1940. On acquittal she was kept in detention; she was eventually released in 1943.[61] The telegram in question would have revealed that Roosevelt, though sympathetic to lending Britain some fifty old destroyers, was unwilling to raise the matter at the moment, and would have in any event to secure the consent of Congress.[62] It contained other passages

---

[57] Miller, *One Girl's War*, 35.   [58] *Some Were Spies*, ch. 6.

[59] W. F. Kimball, *Churchill and Roosevelt: The Complete Correspondence*, i. *Alliance Emerging* (Princeton, NJ, 1984), Doc. C-5x, 29 Jan. 1940, p. 33, Doc. C-7x, 28 Feb., p. 34; Bearse and Read, *Conspirator*, 285. When interviewed by the FBI in 1951 Kent claimed, quite falsely, that he had only seen these two items in the Roosevelt–Churchill correspondence.

[60] Kimball, *Churchill and Roosevelt*, Doc. R-4x, 16 May, p. 38. The text is in Lash, *Roosevelt and Churchill*, 131–2; Bearse and Read, *Conspirator*, 288.

[61] See Griffiths, *Fellow Travellers of the Right*, 354–5; Thurlow, *Fascism in Britain*, 197, citing HO 45/25748 (memo on Ramsay); C. K. Allen, *Law and Orders* (Oxford, 1945), 249; CAB 65/40 156th conclusion Minute 4 (Confidential Annexe 14, November 1943). A. C. B. Eyre, her brother, wrote to *The Times* on 12 August 1942 in protest, arguing that the committee must have recommended her release.

[62] Churchill had asked for these in his cable 1216 of 15 May.

showing that Roosevelt was being helpful to Britain over the acquisition of war materials in the USA. What may have been particularly sensitive was a passage in which Roosevelt showed that he was considering the possibility of a naval squadron visiting Ireland; Churchill had asked for this because of rumours of threatened German landings there. Though the cable was in no way improper, the guarded sympathy it showed to Churchill's requests might have caused some political embarrassment in an America where isolationism was a strong force. Permission was refused until after the results of the US Presidential election, and long after the sale of the destroyers to Britain in return for bases was public knowledge; this suggests it was the Irish question which was critical.[63]

Ramsay knew of Kent's activities in early May, yet did not at once inform the authorities; his excuses for this make no sense. But little else is known about his involvement in the whole affair, nor why he gave Kent the out-of-date Right Club ledger.[64] His own defence, set out on 23 August in Brixton Prison, was absurd: Churchill's correspondence with Roosevelt was improper, and Chamberlain needed to be told. He failed to inform Chamberlain because he went on holiday on 9 or 10 May before he had time to see all the documents.[65] Mosley, in Brixton with Ramsay, must have known a lot about the affair. In *My Life* he states Ramsay's defence, but could see nothing improper in Churchill's actions.[66] The correspondence was indeed perfectly proper, but extremely strange, for it involved using a mode of communication known to be quite insecure; the code used for the cables had been broken years before. Furthermore transmission through the Embassy placed the documents in the hands of Kennedy, who opposed American involvement in the war. Conceivably Churchill actually intended there to be leakages.[67]

What else if anything Ramsay had done which was thought to justify his detention for 'acts prejudicial' remains somewhat obscure. He was never tried, and says little in his book *The Nameless War*, except to admit distributing leaflets, his anti-Semitic poem 'Land of Dope and Jewry',

[63] Permission was withheld by a telegram of 19 November 1940 No. 3781, State Department to Kennedy.

[64] There was nothing obviously incriminating about the ledger. Two files on Ramsay, HO 45/25696 and 25742, are closed. HO 45/25748, dealing primarily with Parliamentary privilege, is open.

[65] A. H. M. Ramsay, *The Nameless War* (London, [1952]), 103. Roosevelt up to 20 May 1940 sent cables on 11 September 1939, 1 February, 5 March, and 16 May 1940. Only the last was found with Kent. Churchill sent cables on 5 and 16 October and 25 December 1939 and 7, 29, and 30 January, 28 February, 7, 15, 18, and 20 May. Those of 30 January, 28 February, and 20 May were found with Kent. The idea of a sinister correspondence was raised in the House of Commons by J. McGovern in a question to Morrison on 11 November 1941.

[66] O. Mosley, *My Life* (London, 1968), 405–6; this caused repercussions in the USA.

[67] Since I wrote this Costello has made the same suggestion.

and some anti-Semitic sticky-backs.[68] On 25 August 1940 the *New York Times* published an article, based on a cable from their London correspondent, Raymond Daniell, which accused Ramsay of having sent material obtained from Kent to the German Legation in Dublin. Ramsay, who denied this, successfully sued the paper for damages, but obtained only a derisory farthing. Valentine Holmes represented the newspaper, no doubt with Home Office approval, and presented Ramsay as a traitor. The Home Office informally assured the *New York Times* that no evidence existed to support the story about the Legation, but refused to give the reasons for detention. The story appeared in the New York edition of the *New York Times* in an article on the Fifth Column by Colonel William J. Donovan and E. Kowrar on 22 August 1940; this was based in part on information provided by officials in Britain.[69] He was slightly mad, and given his fear of bolshevism, itself an emanation of a world Judaeo-Masonic conspiracy centred in New York, he was no doubt capable of more or less anything.

Some little light is cast on the matter by a speech by Richard Stokes 16 June 1944. Ramsay had told him, absurdly, that he was detained because he believed in the 'Protocols of the Learned Elders of Zion', and knew of the Churchill–Roosevelt correspondence. More significantly Ramsay denied that he had anything to do with 'the Loch Lomond Wireless'.[70] This is a reference to one of the German clandestine stations broadcasting at this time, and suggests that he was thought to have given the station some assistance; conceivably he was thought to have written the message to Joyce. Ramsay had given the wavelength of the station in a question in the Commons on 20 March.[71] Stokes goes on to say (the story must have come from Ramsay) that the detained Prince Henry of Pless had been offered release if he was prepared to say that Ramsay had revealed what had been said in a secret session of the House of Commons. There was a secret session on 13 December 1939, and the published *Goebbels Diaries* for 19 December say this: 'Long Report on the secret session of the English Parliament. I shall have this broadcast by the clandestine radio

---

[68] *Do You Know?* and *Have You Noticed?* Papers in the archives of the Britons shed no light, but indicate that Ramsay thought his interrogation by Birkett was oppressive. The offensive poem (text in the ledger) goes: Land of Dope and Jewry, | Land that once was free, | All the Jew boys praise thee, | Whilst they plunder thee, | Poorer still and poorer, | Grow thy true born sons, | Faster still and faster, | They're sent to feed the guns.

[69] Apart from HO 45/25748, which deals only with privilege. Bearse and Read in *Conspirator*, 228, quote a Home Office memorandum dated 24 June setting out accusations against Ramsay which they think was written by Maxwell-Knight, and which they say is either in HO 144/21995 or HO 144/22454. There must be some mistake. For the action see *The Times* for 18, 19, 23, 24, 25 July, and 1 Aug. 1941. See SH para. 65.

[70] See *Daily Express*, 26 February 1940. A BBC spokesman said the Loch Lomond station was probably foreign but its location was then uncertain.

[71] *Parl. Deb.* HC Vol. 358 c.1940.

stations.'[72] Whatever is made of the supposed diary, one can guess that Ramsay was also suspected of passing information from the secret session to the enemy. To do so would have constituted treason, and this was how his conduct was described to the War Cabinet on 22 May.

The Cabinet Decision of 22 May

The raid was, as we have seen, discussed in the Home Office on Tuesday 21 May, when much of the information I have set out would have been available.[73] The BU was also discussed with two MI5 officers—surely Maxwell-Knight and Aikin-Sneath—who said that around 25 to 30 per cent of its members would go to any length if ordered by Mosley. But they lacked evidence of 'acts prejudicial', or 'hostile associations', to justify arresting Mosley or his lieutenants. MI5 suggested there was some sort of sinister conspiracy between Mosley and Ramsay; the report mentioned in the Cabinet papers claimed that Ramsay was 'in relations' with Mosley; this expression can only refer to the 'secret meetings'.

Hinsley and Simkins, with access to MI5's records, give no clear account of MI5's case against the BU as it stood on 21 May. However, in January of 1941 Anderson reported what it was:

The essence of the case against the Fascists was that their preparations were being made in secret, that there was no evidence which would justify their prosecution, and that there was an urgent need for rapid action. *There had been reason to believe that they were preparing in secret plans which would enable them, in the event of an invasion of the country, either to range their members on the side of the enemy or by a coup d'état to seize power and make terms with the enemy* [my italics].[74]

At the time the idea that Mosley might achieve power as head of a puppet government was widespread. On 28 May 1940, as the evacuation from Dunkirk was getting under way, Churchill met his full Cabinet to plead the case for continuing the fight. If peace was made, he argued, Britain would become 'a slave state, though a British government which would be Hitler's puppet would be set up—"under Mosley or some such person"'.[75] And William C. Bullitt, the US Ambassador in Paris, informed Roosevelt

[72] F. Taylor (ed.), *The Goebbels Diaries 1939–1941* (London, 1982), 69 for 19 December. On 10 February, however, he says the information has not come from a spy. Pless was a wealthy landowner in eastern Europe; he was detained in 1940.

[73] Kell in his diary notes 'Long sitting at HO'.

[74] CAB 98/18 (Committee on Communist Activities). Meeting of 20 January 1941. The committee comprised Anderson, Bevin, Alexander, Duff Cooper, and Somervell, with Norman Brook as Secretary.

[75] See M. Gilbert, *Winston S. Churchill*, vi. *'Finest Hour'* (New York, 1986), 419–20, for a full account; the quotation is from the diary of Hugh Dalton, and see H. Dalton, *The Fateful Years: Memoirs 1939–45* (London, 1953), 35–6. See also Gilbert, *'Finest Hour'*, 486. In a message to Roosevelt on 15 June, with Mosley safely locked up, Churchill spoke of a possible pro-German government without mentioning Mosley at its head.

on 16 May 'that, in order to escape from the ultimate consequences of absolute defeat, the British may install a government of Oswald Mosley and the Union of British Fascists which would co-operate fully with Hitler. That would mean the British navy would be against us.'[76] Many people at this period must have had similar thoughts.

There is no reason to think that even in 1940 Anderson ever believed in MI5's alarmist theory of the secret plans. According to Hinsley and Simkins's curiously brief account, which appears to be based on an MI5 minute, he remained sceptical, rightly as it transpired.[77] We know that Maxwell was not impressed either by Kendal's overblown accounts of the 'secret meetings'. One file contains the nearest we have to Anderson's account of his own attitude in late May of 1940.[78] After mentioning Kell's pressure to act earlier he goes on:

When the emergency arose, and Holland was overrun, Sir John looked at the matter again. He decided that *if* any action was to be taken to put out of the way people who might be potential rallying points for the enemy he must make a job of it. He would not begin until he felt he could see it through. Also he could not deal with the fascists as the regulation then stood as their particular cases rested more on their general position and outlook.

This does not say that Anderson thought action was necessary, merely that if this was thought necessary, that is by the War Cabinet, of which he was not then a member, his task was to implement the decision effectively. This, given respect for legality, required a change in the law.

When the War Cabinet met at 10.30 a.m. on 22 May he seems to have acquiesced in the view that the moment for action had now come; in effect he deferred to MI5 and the military. He told the Cabinet that the leader of 'a certain organization [the Right Club, not the BU] had been concerned in subversive activity'.[79] Thus what he specified was 'subversive activity', also called in the papers 'treasonable activities', and not mere propaganda, which had previously been the source of anxiety. Chamberlain had raised the matter at the request of Churchill, who had left for France, and told Chamberlain that over aliens and the fascists 'I

[76] O. H. Bullitt (ed.), *For the President—Personal and Secret: Correspondence between Franklin D. Roosevelt and William C. Bullitt* (Boston, 1972), 190–1. In P. Turnbull, *Dunkirk: Anatomy of a Disaster* (New York, 1978), he is quoted as saying on 4 June that the British planned 'to conserve their fleet and air force and their army, and either before a German attack on England or shortly afterwards, to install eight fascists trained under Oswald Mosley and accept vassalage to Hitler'. A similar passage is printed in Bullitt, *For the President*, 450.
[77] See pp. 50–1. They quote *esprit d'escalier*: 'MI5's representatives "longed to say that if somebody didn't get a move on there would be no democracy, no England, no Empire, and that this was almost a matter of days"'. The passage brings out the sheer silliness of MI5 at this period.
[78] TS 27/542.   [79] Particulars in CAB 65/7 WM 133 (40).

will agree to whatever the Cabinet thinks best'.[80] Chamberlain referred to a report: 'the general effect of which was that Captain Maule Ramsay MP who was the principal organizer of an organization known as the "Right Club", had been engaged in treasonable practices in conjunction with an employee (a United States citizen by name Tyler Kent) of the US Embassy'.[81] Anderson then explained: 'a woman named Anna Wolkoff who had been interned some two or three days previously,[82] had been in relations with an employee at the United States Embassy . . . It appears also that Captain Ramsay was in relations with this woman and also with Sir Oswald Mosley, though, as regards the latter, not in connection with this woman.' Had Mosley been involved with Anna he could have been detained for 'acts prejudicial' without any change in the law. Anderson explained that the Right Club 'had hitherto been regarded as a semi-secret society, mainly anti-Semitic in its objects, and pro-Nazi only in a secondary degree'. Chamberlain, apparently relying on Maxwell-Knight's report, spoke of the Club as 'carrying on pro-German activities, and secret subversive work, with the object of disorganizing the Home Front and hindering the prosecution of the war. Furthermore . . . the report discloses that Anna Wolkoff has means of communicating with the enemy.' Anderson and the Law Officers were instructed to consider whether Ramsay should be interned, in which case he could be interrogated, or prosecuted, in which case he could not.

The decision was to intern him. One reason was that when the matter was looked into more calmly by the Law Officers it was by no means clear that any offence under section 1 of the Official Secrets Act 1911 could actually be proved, and this, rather than treason, which entailed a death penalty, appears to have been the only charge seriously considered.[83] Further action against the Right Club was left to Anderson's discretion, and in the event only twenty of its members, as best I can judge, were ever detained.[84] There is indeed no direct evidence that anyone was detained simply because they were members.

At the same time Anderson pointed out that MI5 had failed to produce any evidence that the BU was involved in Fifth Column activities, and reported the view of the two MI5 officers. Action was impossible under

---

[80] Gilbert, 'Finest Hour', 378. Churchill Papers: 20/13.
[81] CAB 65/13 WM (40) Minute 9, Confidential Annexe.   [82] In fact two.
[83] HO 45/25748, Thurlow 197.
[84] O. C. Gilbert and T. V. Rowe remained in detention from 1939. The others were A. E. Baker, Mrs Ruth Beckett, C. Featherstone-Hammond, Richard F. Findlay, Norman Hay, Thomas Hosey, R. A. 'Jock' Houston, Lancelot Lawton, A. T. O. Lees, H. W. Luttman-Johnson, H. T. V. Mills, Mrs Mary Newnham, Mrs C. Nicholson, Capt. Ramsay, Miss Enid Riddell, Prof. C. S. Skeels, Miss Molly Stanford, and Miss Fay Taylour. Adm. Wolkoff may have been a member; he was interned. Iris Ryder, a first cousin of the Duke of Hamilton, may also have been a member.

the existing regulation, and Anderson did not favour reintroducing the original form of 18B, no doubt fearing political protest. If, in spite of the lack of hard evidence, the War Cabinet thought that no risks should be taken, what was needed was a new power to intern persons who belonged to organizations having hostile associations, or subject to foreign control, so that he no longer had to be satisfied 'in each particular case . . . that the individual had been concerned in prejudicial acts'. He did not want the party, in reaction to a few arrests, to be able to rebuild itself as an underground organization, which would be far more dangerous: 'It was necessary to arrest all the Fascist leaders under Defence Regulation 18B at the same time, since otherwise the leaders of the Fascist movement might have gone underground.'[85] Anderson envisaged initially arresting between twenty-five and thirty individuals—'It would be seen whether this was sufficient to cripple the organization, or whether it would be necessary to proceed further.' The War Cabinet authorized whatever was needed 'to cripple the organization'. The decision was taken by Chamberlain, Attlee, Halifax, and Greenwood; also present for this item, however, were Cadogan, Caldecote, Pound, Eden, Duff Cooper, Newall, and Ironside. Of these persons we can be confident that Cadogan, Pound, Eden, Newall, and Ironside would strongly favour action.[86]

Once it was decided to arrest Ramsay—he was after all a sitting member of Parliament—Mosley would certainly realize that he too risked imminent detention. He would therefore implement any plans he might have either to 'go underground', or to activate the existing underground organization, whose existence MI5 suspected. Hence it must have seemed good sense to delay no further in acting against Mosley and his party, especially when the military situation was growing worse with every moment, although neither Kent, Wolkoff, nor indeed Ramsay had any direct connection with the BU.

The Detention of the Aliens

The intensity of the fear of the Fifth Column at this time is dramatically illustrated by the decision, two days later, to detain all enemy aliens whatsoever. MI5 pressed for this, securing the support of Eden, the Secretary of State for War, who is quoted as saying that 'he did not want to have a lecture from John Anderson on the liberty of the subject'.[87] The adminis-

[85] Memo of November 1942, drafted by Dowson in conjunction with Maxwell. In TS 27/512.
[86] Eden was Minister for War, Pound was First Sea Lord, Newall was Chief of the Air Staff, and Ironside was CIGS.
[87] Hinsley and Simkins, 50. The remark was made on 20 May at a meeting between Eden, Kell, and the Director of Military Intelligence. For Churchill's support see PREM 4/39/4A, letter to Anderson of 15 June 1940.

trative problems were daunting, for there were now over 70,000 enemy aliens in the country.[88] When Italy entered the war Anglo-Italians fell within the new policy, which was mercifully never fully implemented, though by October around 28,000 enemy aliens were in custody; in March the total had been just under 2,000.[89] The figure of 28,000 may be contrasted with the daily average prison population at this period, between 8,000 and 9,000 people. The arrest of the aliens caused terrible distress. The worst single incident was the torpedoing of the *Arandora Star* on 2 July 1940 carrying aliens to Canada, when 486 Italians and 175 Germans died.[90] Detainees sent to Australia on the *Dunera* suffered deliberate ill-treatment.[91] It was all a dreadful business, though the policy was soon reversed in response to pressure from both inside and outside the government machine. MI5 did not come out of the affair of the *Arandora Star* well; those selected to be sent abroad were supposed to be the most dangerous, but the choice of Italians had been quite incompetent. They included, for example, a Signor Anzani, for twenty years resident in Britain, and Secretary of the League of the Rights of Man. Some were British subjects. In the Foreign Office, where the policy produced fury, R. E. T. Latham minuted on 27 June: 'The Home Office has finally yielded to military pressure and has adopted the pathetic policy of interning all male aliens.'[92]

But the sheer brutality of the government's action against both aliens and fascists served the need to demonstrate the government's utter ruthlessness. The most dramatic expression of this ideological need was to be 'Operation Catapult', which culminated in naval action at Mers el-Kebir against French battleships, with heavy loss of life and a legacy of bitterness, but demonstrating to the world that Britain really was determined to fight on.[93] Churchill's own view of the matter at the time was made clear on 4 June:

There is, however, another class, for which I feel not the slightest sympathy. Parliament has given us the power to put down Fifth Column activities with a strong hand, and we shall use those powers, subject to the supervision and correction of the House, without the slightest hesitation until we are satisfied and more

[88] CAB 65/7, WM 137. Newsam on 17 June thought the figure was about 77,000; PREM 4/39/4A.

[89] *Parl. Deb.* HC Vol. 358 c.2107. N. Stammers, *Civil Liberties in Britain during the Second World War: A Political Study* (London, 1983), 60 n. 28, explains the difficulty in accurately stating the total number interned.

[90] List in FO 371/25210.

[91] B. Patkin, *The Dunera Detainees* (Stanmore, NSW, Australia, 1979).

[92] FO 371/25257/135. A report on the *Arandora Star* by Lord Snell WP (40) 432 is in FO 371/25210, also CAB 66/13 WP (40) 432, and see HO 215/169.

[93] For justification see W. S. Churchill, *The Second World War*, ii. *The Gathering Storm* (London, 1968), 201; and for a balanced account E. M. Gates, *End of the Affair: The Collapse of the Anglo–French Alliance, 1939–40* (Berkeley, Calif., 1981), 329–73.

than satisfied that this malignancy in our midst has been effectively stamped out.[94]

No doubt the Kent affair acted as a trigger, but action against Mosley's party and other supposed Fifth Columnists was surely only a matter of time; it is quite inconceivable that the fascists would have been left alone once the Battle of Britain began, though mass detention was not the only form that repression could have taken, nor was it what Anderson initially envisaged.

Rationalizing Repression

Once the BU detentions began MI5 would naturally seek evidence of a conspiracy of the right, both to justify what had been done and to build upon it; there is abundant evidence that they did this, but came up with nothing. Hence when Acting Director Harker submitted a memorandum on the matter in September 1940, after the party had been crippled, and after it was known that no significant underground BU had ever existed, he was on the defensive. He reported that after eight years of investigation MI5 had accumulated 'a vast mass of evidence . . . On the basis of this evidence we had come to certain conclusions with regard to the nature of the British Union movement.' The case against it was not that it was under German control; Mosley wanted power for himself, but only a complete military collapse would put him in office in Number 10: 'Doubtless a situation was envisaged in which the country would be forced to ask for terms of peace, and should this situation arise Hitler would only make peace with an England led by MOSLEY. It was therefore MOSLEY's aim to make it difficult for the government to carry on the war.' This placed a sinister interpretation upon Mosley's peace movement. The BU as an organization was a danger because it collected together people who were likely—presumably in crisis conditions—to assist the enemy, though of course by no means all of its members fell into this category. The memorandum makes no point of a planned *coup d'état*, or of the underground BU. Harker's argument is wholly conjectural; it assumes that Mosley was a more significant figure in German eyes than he probably was. No evidence has come to light of any plan of Hitler's which involved Mosley as the head of a British government. Very abbreviated notes of two conversations in which Hitler talked about Mosley have been published; one took place on 14 June 1940, and the second on 15 June. This was well before any scheme for the invasion of Britain had been decided upon. Hitler appears to have viewed Mosley more as a thinker than as a man of action or popular leader; though regarded as defective as

[94] *Parl. Deb.* HC Vol. 378 c.787–96.

a personality, he was given credit for understanding 'the German-European idea' (*germanisch-europäische Idee*). He might have been the intellectual leader of an understanding between Germany and Britain; he might have been able to avoid the war. Hitler did not regard Mosley as finished or played out, but the whole tone of the conversation, in so far as one can judge from cryptic notes, entirely lacks any suggestion that Hitler envisaged placing reliance upon Mosley in future plans. Common sense suggests that had Britain sued for peace in 1940 or 1941 there were numerous other more plausible candidates for the role of Pétain. Indeed Mosley signally lacked the docility desirable in a puppet ruler.[95]

A second lengthy rationalization is to be found in the Cabinet papers for 1943.[96] It reads more like propaganda than does the earlier memorandum, and probably originated as a draft white paper, the `Black Book of British Fascism', written by Aikin-Sneath, intended for publication as a warning against fascism.[97] It set out an account of the history of the BU, and the suspicion (though no proof) that it had been funded from abroad both from Italy and, though the evidence was thought less conclusive, from Germany. The organization was thought to be pro-German, and indeed pro-Nazi. The evidence produced for this was less than impressive: Mosley's marriage in Germany, the visit of some members to Germany in 1937, and their welcome by Julius Streicher, the supposed singing at some meetings of the 'Horst Wessel Song',[98] and Mosley's negotiation with Germany over the establishment of a commercial radio station.[99] However, it was conceded that 'no evidence has been obtained showing that the British Union was at the time it was banned engaged in the organization of sabotage or espionage on behalf of the enemy'. The memorandum goes on to say:

Although amongst the members of the BU there were persons who had joined without any realization that its policy involved disloyalty, most of them were imbued with the leadership conception and were prepared to follow the leader blindly.[100] It was feared that the Leader might welcome the Germans as the fore-

---

[95] HO 45/25754/863027/3. This memo, dated 1 September, ends with a reference 'B7', this being the division to which Aikin-Sneath belonged; he may well have written it. D. Engel, *Heeresadjutant bei Hitler, 1938–1943 Aufzeichnungen des Majors Engel. Schriftenreihe der Vierteljahrshefte für Zeitgeschichte* No. 29 (Stuttgart, 1974), at 82 and 85 (Engel was one of Hitler's adjutants).

[96] See on what follows CAB 65/34 WM (43) WC 60 (43) 1 and 2, 66/35 WP(43) 148 of 14 April 1943.

[97] See HO 454/25754 memo of 4 September 1940.

[98] See *The Times* 29 July 1937. The BU used the tune of the 'Horst Wessel Lied' for their own marching song: 'Comrades: the voice of the dead battalions . . . '.

[99] Discussed below p. 278.

[100] The memo lists a number of cases of misconduct BU members: Duvivier, Ingram and Swift, R. F. Stokes, one-time Right Club, a former BU in the British Nationalist Party run by Edward Godfrey, convicted of evading national service and sentenced to 12 months. Some

runner of that 'advance of Universal Fascism throughout the World'...that, in fact, the BU was the counterpart in this country of Major Quisling's Nasjonal Samling,[101] or the Dutch National Socialist party under the leadership of that Mussert who was publicly thanked by Hitler after the successful invasion of the Low Countries.[102]

The reference to the advance of fascism was in fact taken from an article in *Blackshirt* in 1933, referring to Italian, not German fascism; it will be noted that the blind followers are no longer a mere 25—30 per cent. When this document was written it was not known that German military success had owed virtually nothing to a military Fifth Column either in Scandinavia or the Low Countries.[103]

The Cabinet decided against publishing this indictment of the BU. The main anxiety was that Mosley, in common fairness—and the Cabinet was not prepared to abandon fairness even in Mosley's case—would have to be given a right of reply, and the Cabinet had before it his protest at the continued detention of his followers; to the points it made, with considerable power, the 'Black Book' had no reply, and indeed it conceded Mosley's principal point, which was that there was no proof of disloyal conduct either by the BU or by him.[104] It was safer not to try to justify the action taken against the party publicly, a prudent though hardly a courageous decision. There was no public demand for any such justification; in general the British were perfectly happy with the crippling of the fascist party.

In November 1943 the Duke of Bedford gave notice of his intention to initiate a debate in the House of Lords on 18B; this took place on 25 January 1944, and the Home Office in the person of Ross, under Newsam's supervision, produced a lengthy brief for Simon who, as Lord Chancellor, was persuaded to state the government case. This provided a Home Office rather than an MI5 rationalization. It explained that the fall of Denmark, Norway, and the Low Countries had been 'hastened by treachery, and by the corruption of morale from within by individuals or organisations which were under enemy influence or control . . . The times were too serious to allow any avoidable risk to be taken.' The brief then went on to give a balanced account of the policies advocated by the BU and argued that 'the pro-British isolationist policy skilfully attracted a number of otherwise loyal persons and blinded them to the insidious pro-

BU members released from detention promised to join up but failed to do so (S. H. E Martin, G. E. Parry, and C. C. Hoar). See below pp. 167–71.

[101] Vidkun Quisling's national socialist party.

[102] Anton A. Mussert was leader of the National-Socialistische Beweging der Nederlanden, the largest Dutch fascist party.

[103] See L. de Jong, *The German Fifth Column in the Second World War* (Chicago, 1956), *passim* and esp. chs. 10, 11, 15.

[104] CAB 65/34 60(43) of 28 April. CAB 66/36 WP (43) 67 (Mosley's protest).

Axis propaganda carried on by the organisation'. It went on to claim in effect that the BU denunciation of the war corrupted morale, and argued that the 8,000 to 10,000 paying members of the party, being organized on military lines, were 'capable of considerable mischief'. The brief has nothing on the underground BU or the threat of a *coup*; this probably reflects the fact that officials like Maxwell and Newsam never at any time thought there was anything in MI5's more alarming suspicions. The basic case was that the party was pro-German and undermined morale, and might get up to mischief. It is a remarkably honest document in not attempting to overstate the case.[105]

The Miniature Fifth Column

In retrospect Home Office scepticism was vindicated. There never was an organized British Fifth Column of any military significance; in this sense the Fifth Column was a myth. Only a tiny number of disloyal persons—for example Klaus Fuchs—were to be found amongst the aliens. Hinsley and Simkins say that by mid-July even MI5 was 'in private', 'very much inclined to doubt' whether an organized Fifth Column existed.[106] By the autumn, when a vast amount of information had been obtained through interrogations and searches, it was quite clear that the whole idea was misconceived. But in May of 1940 matters looked rather different. For example it was widely believed that German broadcasts showed up-to-the-minute knowledge of conditions in Britain, which could come from the British Fifth Column. Hence in May it did not seem implausible that the misconduct of Kent, Wolkoff, and Ramsay was the tip of an iceberg, and had some connection with these broadcasts.[107]

During 1940 four and sometimes five radio stations, ostensibly located in Britain and operated by groups opposed to the war, were operating.[108] Their broadcasts were quite distinct from those associated with 'Lord Haw-Haw of Zeesen'. The most prominent was the short-wave New British Broadcasting Station. It was reported on 28 February in the *Daily Express*, when a BBC spokesman said it was probably a foreign station.

---

[105] HO 45/25100. [106] At p. 59.

[107] In the first interview with Kent Maxwell-Knight said that on 16 April Anna had told her friends (that is MI5's agents) about a report of a conversation between US Ambassador Joseph Kennedy and Lord Halifax which dealt with the Norwegian campaign, and that on 21 April she had obtained information about negotiations, involving an MI5 officer, to purchase certain radio equipment in the USA. The officer involved was the Earl of Cottenham (1903–43), an extreme right-winger, who from 1939 to 1940 worked for MI5 as transport officer.

[108] See W. A. Boelcke (ed.), *The Secret Conferences of Dr Goebbels: The Propaganda War 1939–1943* (New York, 1970), 69; W. A. Balfour, *Propaganda in War 1939–1945* (New York, 1970). PREM 7/2 (Desmond Morton's memos to Churchill) notes anxiety in May 1940 over a station broadcasting from near Bremen which might be confused with the BBC.

The *Sunday Dispatch* published its wavelength of 50.63 on 3 March, and said it was German; on 11 April *Action* repeated this and said it claimed to be British. On 20 March, when Ramsay asked Sir John Reith, Minister of Information, about nightly talks on this station, which used the signature tune 'Loch Lomond', Reith replied that he knew about it, and it was thought to be located some hundred miles from Berlin. The NBBS purported to issue instructions to the British Fifth Column.[109] The other stations were the Workers Challenge Station, the Christian Peace Movement, Radio Caledonia, and a supposedly Welsh Nationalist Station.[110] W. J. West suggests that the authorities were so nervous of these broadcasts that all public reference to them was suppressed,[111] but this is incorrect. Thus on 8 May Reith referred to warnings given to the public about them, which would be repeated; they began on 25 April and were repeated on 24 and 25 May and 7 June. The authorities were, however, concerned; a police circular of 1 July mentioned 'gummed labels referring to the New British Broadcasting Station' as something to be sought in police searches.[112]

A British Fifth Column could help by supplying information or advice about the broadcasts, or by advertising them in Britain, for example by 'sticky-backs'. Both forms of help were criminal. On 8 May Reith said that he was aware of the fact that posters advertising the enemy broadcasts were being put up in Britain, adding: 'the posters advertising the enemy stations are, of course, themselves of enemy origin'.[113] The police had some success in identifying the culprits, and although dates of arrest are not known, some would be in May. Thus on 4 July 1940 *The Times* reported the trial of William Saxon Steer for committing acts likely to assist the enemy in fixing 'Here is the new wavelength of the BBS' 'sticky-backs' in telephone kiosks. At the trial Mr M. A. Frost of the BBC overseas intelligence unit explained that it was a German station, and Steer was sent to prison for seven years; he belonged to the BU[114] On 6 July the press reported the conviction of Rex (or Wilfred) Freeman and his mother, Mrs Violet L. Freeman, for printing and distributing 'sticky-backs' advertising the NBBS. He was a member and propaganda officer of the BU in Stoke Newington; he received five years and his mother

---

[109] *Parl. Deb.* HC Vol. 358 c.1970, also 359: 151, 3 April, 360: 376–7, 25 April. INF 1/257 Memorandum of 1 June 1940, INF 1/848 5 Sept. 1940.

[110] The four stations were listed in *The Times* on 24 August 1940 under the title 'Billingsgate on the Air'.

[111] *Truth Betrayed*, 207.

[112] *Parl. Deb.* HC Vol. 360 c.1249. The police circular 4056 is in HH 55/864. CRIM 1/1203, 1208 note warnings.

[113] *Parl. Deb.* HC Vol. 360 c.1249.

[114] See also the *Daily Mirror*, 4 July. Steer was a violinist. He was committed for trial on 3 June; see *The Times* for 4 June; CRIM 1/1203 (depositions).

one.[115] On 20 June *The Times* reported the committal for trial of William Bruce Tomkins, a 27-year-old fascist who possessed advertisements for the NBBS. He said, possibly truthfully, that he thought it was a British station run by the British People's Party. He had obtained the leaflets from the office of the Kingston BU.[116] Outside the capital on 21 May Mrs Olive Baker, a 39-year-old nurse who had joined the BU in 1939, was committed for trial on 12 June; she distributed postcards advertising the NBBS. Formerly a schoolteacher in Germany, she had returned to England in 1939, and was in contact with Admiral Sir Barry Domvile, soon to be detained. A search revealed 400 'sticky-backs' saying `Mosley for Peace', and eight photographs of Hitler; there was also a pass signed by Goebbels and a letter from Unity Mitford. Whilst awaiting trial she cut her wrist and wrote 'Hail Mosley' and 'Heil Hitler' in blood in her cell. She was convicted at Bristol Assizes on 5 July, and sentenced to five years' imprisonment.[117]

Clearly anyone who actively assisted the clandestine stations was engaged in Fifth Column activity, and anxiety over British traitors was strengthened by the knowledge that Joyce, and other renegades, were in Germany assisting Goebbels in his work.[118] The distribution of 'sticky-backs' gave reality to the conception of an *organized* Fifth Column: some organization had to be involved, though to this day it is obscure what it was. Those involved might well do worse things if an invasion occurred.

There were other suggestive cases about this time.[119] That of Mrs Marie L. A. Ingram came to trial in early July, but must have started from arrests sometime in May. This was a classic 'Fifth Column' case

[115] *Manchester Guardian* and *Daily Express*.

[116] CRIM 1/1203 (Freemans), 1208 (Tomkins). He was tried on 25 July 1940.

[117] Information from a memorandum in the BDBJ Archives on General Fuller (C 9/3/1), *The Times*, 21 May, 11 June, *News Chronicle*, 11 June, *Daily Mirror*, 5 and 6 July, *Daily Express*, 11 June, *Bath Weekly Chronicle*, 15 June and 6 July, and from the Domvile Diary for 1939 and 1940. There is a reference in PREM 4/39/4A.

[118] After the war a number of renegades were tried: F. McLardy and T. H. Cooper, former BU (HO 45/25805), Mrs Atherton-Smith, former Link and Anglo-German Friendship Society (HO 45/25809), Marietti Smart, former BU (HO 45/25828), E. S. Bowlby, former BU (HO 45/25828), Margaret F. Bothamley, former RC (HO 45/25794), J. G. Lingshaw (HO 45/25792), R. W. Purdy, former BU (45/25798 PCOM 9/2124, HO 336/8), Mrs F. D. Eckersley, RC (see *Parl. Deb.* HL Vol. 148 c.462.). See also C. E. Bechoffer Roberts, *The Trial of William Joyce* (London, 1946), 18 ff.

[119] Donald O'Byrne, another BU member, was given 3 months for pushing *Action* at soldiers and for having a revolver and ammunition (*Manchester Guardian*, 4 June 1940). Frederick Roesch, British born of German descent, was sent to prison for 10 years in July (*The Times*, 4 July) for obtaining information likely to assist the enemy. Peter Farmer, a BU D/L from Northampton, was sent to prison for distributing leaflets to soldiers (*News Chronicle*, 24 June 1940). Lilian R. Yates, a domestic servant, was tried in camera at Bristol Assizes on 3 July 1940 and sent to prison for 2 years for possession of materials likely to assist the enemy; the case may have involved the NBBS (*Daily Telegraph*, 13 June, *Bath Weekly Chronicle*, 15 June and 6 July).

which, as we have seen, disturbed General Ironside (present at the Cabinet on 22 May), for Mrs Ingram was a domestic servant of German origin working in the home of an admiral in Portsmouth.[120] This incident lent reality to MI5's view that there were members of the BU, wild men and women, who were indeed prepared 'to go to any lengths'.[121]

A few prosecutions later in 1940 and in 1941 continued to give some reality to the fear of the Fifth Column.[122] Four Leeds BU members were jailed for trying to keep the party going after it was proscribed, and then interned; one, Reg Windsor, was subjected to interrogation in MI5's special centre, Latchmere House.[123] Roy L. T. Day of the BU was imprisoned for eighteen months in October; he published a pamphlet *Uncensored British News Bulletin* with two other former BU members; it gave information about the NBBS and purported to describe a secret session of Parliament.[124] In November Thomas H. Beckett, formerly BU, was sent to prison for three years for possessing a list of aerodromes compiled from Air Ministry records. He was later interned.[125] In December Mrs Dorothy P. O'Grady was sentenced to death under the Treachery Act for making plans to assist the enemy and cutting telephone cables on the Isle of Wight; on appeal her sentence was reduced to fourteen years' imprisonment.[126] At some point in 1941 Professor Serocold Skeels of the IFL was imprisoned for attempting to communicate with the enemy, and later interned.[127] Elsie S. C. Orrin, a schoolteacher and member of the BU, was sent to prison for five years by Mr Justice Humphreys in June 1941 for inciting servicemen to disaffection. She had said that Hitler was a good ruler, and a better man than Churchill; Churchill himself recorded his disapproval of this savage sentence for a mere expression of opinion.[128] On 16 June Norah C. L. Briscoe, a typist in the Ministry of Supply, and Gertrude B. ('Mollie') Hiscox, former member of the Right Club, the Link, and the BU, and the mistress of 'Jock' Houston, were

---

[120] *Daily Telegraph, Daily Herald, The Times* for 3 July 1940. *Express and Star* for 9 March 1956 (divorce proceedings). CRIM 1/1197.

[121] William A. Guthridge, BU Willesden, sent to prison for 7 years in July for cutting cables to telephone kiosks on 23 May (*The Times*, 25 July 1940); this was a protest at the arrest of Mosley. See CRIM 1/1211. The 62-year-old Lt.-Col. J. P. Cherry of the BU was convicted of painting anti-Semitic slogans at Lord's Cricket Ground (*Daily Telegraph*, 15 June); he was thereafter interned.

[122] Hinsley and Simkins in App. 5 lists some which were extremely trivial.

[123] Information from J. Warburton. Another, W. Longfellow, died soon after release from detention. SH para. 188 has it that they were suspected of conspiracy to commit arson, but given immunity from prosecution.

[124] *The Times*, 22 October 1940.

[125] Hinsley and Simkins, App. 5, p. 319. *Jewish Chronicle*, 15 November 1940.

[126] *The Times*, 18 December 1940 (trial before Atkinson J.), 11 February 1942. An account by N. West, *MI5*, has it that MI5 reached the conclusion that she had engaged in a fantasy.

[127] HO 45/24967

[128] *Manchester Guardian*, 26 June 1941, Gilbert, *'Finest Hour'*, 895 n. 3.

tried before Asquith J. at the Old Bailey and pleaded guilty to a number of charges under the Defence Regulations; charges carrying the death penalty were withdrawn. They were sent to prison for five years. They had communicated secret information to an individual they believed to be a German agent, or so it was said; he was in fact a disreputable MI5 agent Harald or Harold Kurtz, whom we shall meet again.[129] And in October of 1941 William G. Snape and Joseph A. Thomwood, who were apparently BU members, were convicted after a trial, partly in camera, for offences connected with advertising the NBBS. It was said that they had heard of the impending action against the BU; certain chosen members went underground to continue the peace campaign.[130]

With hindsight a handful of cranks distributing sticky-backs or engaging in other disloyal conduct falls far short of the Organized-Fifth-Column-Poised-Ready-to-Strike-as-One-Man dreamt up by Bland and others in 1940. But the point remains: a British Fifth Column, that is a number of individuals who were, with some element of organization, clandestinely assisting the enemy, actually existed.[131] So far as the BU was concerned the number of their members involved was tiny. Informants have told me, however, that amongst those detained, some for membership or support of the BU, there was a small disloyal pro-Nazi faction, whose views may have become more extreme in detention; the party naturally attracted admirers of Hitler. In May 1940 it was perhaps inevitable that the significance of occasional acts of disloyalty would seem greater than it does in retrospect. No doubt had MI5 been better officered it would have been better able to judge their significance at the time.

---

[129] Richard A. Houston, an extreme and unbalanced anti-Semite, one-time BU and Right Club, Nordic League, and other similar bodies. Detained under Regulation 18B in December 1940 after having evaded arrest since May. Norah Briscoe had originally been detained under Regulation 18B but released. See below Chs. 16 and 17. See HO 45/25741.

[130] *Manchester Guardian* and *Daily Telegraph*, 17 October 1941.

[131] HO 45/25728 contains a report of a meeting on 10 November 1940 at Molly Stanford's flat at which Aubrey Lees suggested advertising the NBBS, but Molly Stanford opposed this as risking a sentence of 5 years.

9

The Great Incarceration Begins

The New 18B (1A)

On 22 May Parliament passed the Emergency Powers (Defence) Act, which formally conferred on the executive the powers appropriate to a totalitarian state at war; it could now, by regulation, 'make provision for requiring persons to place themselves, their services, and their property at the disposal of His Majesty as appears to him to be necessary or expedient'. That evening the Privy Council passed the new 18B (1A), to be enforced on 23 May as a secret law, for it had not then been published.[1] Its text formed a concise 'Statement of the Case' against the BU; though Anderson in the Commons on 23 May referred to organizations in the plural, the party was to be its only victim; it was not used against the Right Club, the Communist Party of Great Britain (CPGB), or any other group.

It covered those who were, or had been, either members of a certain sort of organization or active in the furtherance of the objects of such an organization—one with respect to which the Secretary of State was 'satisfied' that either: '(a) the organization is subject to foreign influence or control, or, (b) the persons in control of the organization have or have had associations with persons concerned in the government of, or sympathies with the system of government of, any power with which His Majesty is at war'. This loose draftsmanship reflected MI5's lack of hard information against the BU. MI5 had no proof even of foreign funding; unless searches produced new evidence it would be impossible to show that the BU was under foreign control. Hence influence was included.[2] The required influence (or control) did not have to be from an enemy power; this would be deliberate, for Italy had not entered the war, nor was Russia at war with Britain. The new regulation allowed the detention of persons who had never been members of the offending organization, or who had long since given up membership; it was indeed to be used against

---

[1] SRO 1940 No. 770. HO 45/25507 may contain papers, but is closed; HO 45/25504 should but does not.

[2] MI5 reported in 1935 that no funds were coming from Germany (HO 45/25385, and see 45/25393, report of 6 July 1940).

such persons. As to membership (or support) there had to be 'reasonable cause to believe'.

There was a further condition; the Home Secretary had to be satisfied 'that there is a danger of the utilization of the organization for purposes prejudicial to the public safety, the defence of the realm, the maintenance of public order, the efficient prosecution of any war in which His Majesty may be engaged, or the maintenance of supplies or services essential to the life of the community'. This encapsulates the theory of the work of the organized Fifth Column, not yet unleashed. It was not the *prior* record of the organization which was critical, *but the use to which it might be put in the future.*

So much was explained by Anderson to the Commons on the 23 May. Action had not been taken against the BU because of the opinions expressed by its leaders, or their propaganda, but 'because of the danger that the organization of which the persons concerned were leading members might be used in the execution of acts prejudicial to the security of the State'.[3] And in December 1940 Morrison, by then Home Secretary, said: 'This was a case where there was an organization which we had reason to believe, and I think the House generally believed, was actually or potentially dangerous to the State. We apprehended that in the case of invasion by Nazi Germany these people might actively assist the enemy.'[4] But many members of the BU thought that it was the peace campaign which led to their detention. Hence they resented the fact that the party had never been formally warned, as it could have been under Regulation 2C, in force from 9 May, to cease its propaganda against the war; failure to heed such a warning could incur seven years' imprisonment. From 29 May a newspaper could also be banned without warning, and it had been Anderson's intention to use this power against *Action*.[5] Furthermore they argued—and here nobody could deny that they had a point—that in May of 1940 the BU was a perfectly legitimate political party; indeed it actually had a candidate standing in a by-election in which polling day was fixed for 23 May. Indeed the logic of the government's position was that any electors who voted for the BU in this by-election rendered themselves liable to detention.

The party did not long remain legal. On 26 June, by a new regulation, 18AA, the executive assumed a power to proscribe and wind up organizations of the character set out in 18B (1A). The BU and related orgnisations were not in fact proscribed until 10 July.[6] Although difficult to believe, were it not documented, this delay was not an oversight:

If immediate steps had been taken to make it illegal to carry on the work of the British Union, it would have made it more difficult to ascertain who were the

[3] *Parl. Deb.* HC Vol.361 c.290–1.   [4] Ibid. 367: 877 for 10 December 1940.
[5] SRO 1940 No. 680 (2C), SRO No. 828 (2D).
[6] SRO No. 1078 and SRO No. 1273. See below Ch. 13.

individuals comprising the 'second line' and prepared to continue the activities of the Union after more prominent members had been interned.[7]

Hence BU members, many soon to be arrested, were deliberately encouraged to believe that they were free to continue party activities:

The Police moved into British Union's offices for a complete investigation of all files and correspondence. On enquiry at Scotland Yard and the Home Office the answer was given that the organization was free to continue its normal existence and that no restrictions were placed upon its newspaper 'Action' and that the office would be available once more when the police had finished their 'audit'.[8]

Passage of the new regulation on the evening of 22 May was a formality; I am told that a party of more junior Home Office officials went out for a celebratory meal. No doubt in MI5 too there were rejoicings; the great incarceration could now begin, and the country be saved, in the nick of time, from the Fifth Column.

The Initial Detentions

Earlier on 22 May Kell had delivered his list of thirty-six candidates for detention.[9] After discussion with Maxwell it was presented to Anderson, who accepted it.[10] One order was for Mosley himself. His name was one of thirty-three, set out in a schedule to a single detention order, an 'omnibus order', signed that evening. The number thirty-three must have been a macabre joke, for there had been thirty-two founder members of the party with Mosley back in 1932. At the same time three individual orders were signed under the normal Regulation 18B. One was Ramsay's, for 'acts prejudicial'; his arrest was at once notified to the Speaker of the Commons.[11] The other two were for Ben Greene ('hostile associations')

[7] CAB 75/8 HPC 40 (174) Home Office Memorandum of 22 June 1940.
[8] See *IMHHTY* Cf. C. Cross, *The Fascists in Britain* (London, 1961), 194.
[9] Dr Leigh Vaughan-Henry's name was removed; Maxwell-Knight anticipated a meeting between him, an agent, and a Prof. Samuel F. Darwin-Fox (letter of 14 June 1940 in TS 27/533). Vaughan-Henry was a Doctor of Music and Philosophy, a conductor, and (as Leigh Henry) writer on music; prisoner of war in the First World War; BBC before the war; married to a German wife; left BUF in 1935; mixed in anti-Semitic and pro-Nazi circles; attended meetings of the Empire Loyalty League, the National Association, the National Citizens' Union, the Nordic League, Information and Policy, and the Imperial Socialist League; not in the Right Club ledger; arrested on 10 June under 18D after a raid on his home led by Maxwell-Knight; suspected of having musical codes for use to contact Germany; from 17 June held under 18B (1A) as was Darwin-Fox, at one time a Prof. of English Literature at the University of Fribourg; later also under a 'hostile associations' order; interrogated Ham Common. Also raided in the same operation was Miss Daisy B. Evelyn of 66 Lansdowne Road; she does not seem to have been detained.
[10] Letters of Jenifer Hart of 23 October 1942 in TS 27/522, and of Holderness of 22 August 1942.
[11] HO 45/25748/863003.

and John W. Beckett ('acts prejudicial'). Greene had never been a member of the BU.[12] Beckett, once a prominent member, had left it with Joyce in 1937.[13] In May 1940 both were connected with the BPP. Kell's idea was that it too should be crippled by using 18B (1A). However, Maxwell thought there was enough against both to use the ordinary regulation, so their names came off the schedule.

Mosley himself was arrested on 23 May. Ironically *Action* appeared on the same day with an item headed 'Mosley States His Position':

The question has been put to me why I do not cease all political activity in an hour of danger to the country. The answer is I intend to do my best to provide the people with an alternative to the present government, if, and when, they desire to make peace 'with British Empire intact and our people safe' . . . The charge sometimes implied, rather than openly stated, that I desire to assist the enemy has been met with my contempt. Such a charge cannot lie against a man or a movement who for years before the war warned the country to be armed and prepared against any attack, and in particular to achieve parity in the air with the strongest other nation, while the drivelling treachery of Labour and Conservatism was betraying our defences in a manner which has now been admitted.[14]

The article went on to state the official BU position—members should obey the law—and invading parachutists, if any arrived, should be treated for what they were, enemy soldiers. Mosley emphasized that he personally would fight an invader, but doubted whether Britain could be successfully invaded.

Events had overtaken this, his final public pronouncement as Leader.

Most arrests took place on 23 May. Since the fascists were thought dangerous there was a show of military force; C. F. ('Charlie') Watts, one of those detained, saw four tanks in Albemarle Street where he worked.[15] Anderson promised a list of those arrested, but only the names of those in this first round-up were released, apparently in two press statements.

All can be identified. Three, though detained under Regulation 18B (1A), were not members of the BU at all. Angus MacNab, a close friend of Joyce, had once been, but had left in 1937 with him to found the NSL. He then associated with the BPP.[16] Herbert T. V. ('Bertie') Mills was associated with the Nordic League, the IFL, and earlier with Lord Lymington's British Council against European Commitments. He was a

---

[12] See Ch. 16 below.   [13] See above p. 139 n. 117.
[14] Issue 220.   [15] Watts MS, 3.
[16] A devout Catholic; son of an ophthalmic surgeon killed on 1 November 1914 at Messines; educated Rugby and Christ Church, Oxford; with Joyce ran a coaching establishment in London; joint director of the BU Press Bureau with Margaret Collins; prospective Parliamentary candidate for Leeds South; remained in detention until at least February 1943; after the war lived in Spain; remained a faithful friend to Joyce during his trial and up to his execution; assisted J. A. Cole in writing his biography. See Watts MS, 34, HO 45/25690, 25713, HO 283/23, J. W. Charnley, *Blackshirts and Roses* (London, 1990), 159–60.

member of the Right Club, and involved in the 'secret meetings' in 1939 and 1940.[17] Geoffrey Wright may at one time have been in the BU but, like MacNab, had joined Joyce's NSL as a council member, treasurer, and local leader in Sutton.[18]

The remaining twenty-nine (in addition to Mosley) were in the BU, but only eight were Mosley's lieutenants. In the first rank were Neil L. M. Francis-Hawkins, Director-General of Organization,[19] Alexander Raven-Thomson, the Editor of *Action* and Director of Policy,[20] Captain Brian D. E. Donovan, Assistant Director-General (G) and the official who organized the districts,[21] and E. G. ('Mick') Clarke, Propaganda Administrator and a mob orator prominent in the East End.[22] Mosley was later to tell Birkett that these four were leading people in the movement, though the developed MI5 view was that there were six 'leaders'.[23] The additional 'leader' (apart from Mosley) was Hector G. McKechnie, National Meetings Organizer and Senior London Administrator.[24] These five lieutenants were to remain in detention until the autumn of 1944.

Next in importance came such individuals as George F. Sutton, Mosley's secretary and Director of Research,[25] the one-armed Captain U. A. Hick ('Captain Hook'), who had been Senior Organizer for the London District,[26] and Olive Burdett, who had succeeded Anne Brock-

---

[17] On Mills see R. Thurlow, *Fascism in Britain: A History, 1918–1985* (Oxford, 1987), at 170, 172 and 241–2; involved in the National Front after Victory, a neo-fascist group formed in 1944, which merged with the BPP.

[18] HO 283/23, also information from J. Wallder.

[19] A doctor's son; former communist; in the British Fascisti from May 1923, joined Mosley in 1932 or 1933; adjutant of the Fascist Defence Force; Director-General 1936. Files on him, severely vandalized, are HO 45/25700 and (largely retained) 283/40.

[20] The movement's intellectual; had a private income; studied politics in Germany and America; wrote *Civilization as Divine Superman*. (London, 1932). Home Office material on him has not been released.

[21] Irish; aged 43 in 1940; joined the army in August 1914 when 16; commissioned 1917; served in France, was wounded; MC; in the army of occupation in Turkey and on the North-West Frontier in the Indian cavalry; in 1939 volunteered for war service but was not accepted; at one time a schoolmaster. His files are HO 45/25705 (devastated by weeding) and HO 283/55. Donovan's father-in-law was also interned, conceivably for association with the IRA (private information not confirmed by any documentary evidence).

[22] Saunders Papers, HO 283/48.

[23] HO 283/13. Birkett had asked if there was an 'inner council'. The theory of the 6 leaders is to be found in HO 45/25699.

[24] His files, much weeded and some retained, are HO 45/25699 and HO 283/48. A former pilot in the RAF; Vice-Consul in La Ceiba, Honduras, 1922–30; appointment 'terminated'; joined BUF in 1933; succeeded R. A. Plathen as organizer of meetings; became a salaried National Inspector March 1939, and in August Senior Administrator for London; by repute of considerable ability, and so viewed by MI5.

[25] Formerly in the Royal Field Artillery and wounded 4 times in the 1st World War; founder member of the BUF Bellamy MS iii 61; *Fascist Week*, 15 March. 1934.

[26] He lost an arm in the 1st World War, and had also served in the Boer War. Bellamy MS iii. 66. HO 144/21429 says he had left NHQ by 1940.

Griggs in 1940 as Chief Women's Organizer.[27] Next came eight minor functionaries or helpers. A. E. Baker was the BU printer.[28] Major Harold H. A. de Laessoe and his wife Diana S. E. de Laessoe were voluntary helpers; Major de Laessoe was the BU 'expert' on Africa, where he had spent a considerable part of his life.[29] Maurice T. Pacey worked in a junior role as an accountant.[30] The elderly husband of Mrs Norah Elam, one E. Dudley Elam, a retired Civil Servant from the Ministry of Health, was the unpaid receptionist.[31] F. E. Burdett, Olive Burdett's husband, is a dubious case; he was or had been District Leader in Peckham, but there is some evidence of a connection in some uncertain capacity with National Headquarters (NHQ), though he was not a paid official.[32] James L. Shepherd was a former communist who became District Leader in Islington; he was circulation manager for *Action*, and signed a collection of BU autographs recorded during detention as 'Business Manager BU, Circulation Manager *Action* and Hon. Sec. British Traders'.[33] Charles H. Hammond, formerly Royal Navy, had served under Shackleton; he was an assistant national inspector and had been prospective candidate for Norwich. He had held a paid position.[34] Two others had at one time been headquarters officials, and may have still helped on a voluntary basis. One was William Risdon, who had been paid Chief or Assistant Chief Election Agent, but had been dismissed from this post two months before the war, and by 1940 was inactive.[35] Mrs Anne Brock-Griggs had been Chief

---

[27] Her maiden name, which she used after the war as a writer, was Hawks; she had been on the editorial staff of the Wellington Press and Amalgamated Press, and joined the BU in 1933, working as a speaker and in the Research Department. She was a Parliamentary candidate.

[28] Name in the Right Club ledger. Baker suffered from leprosy; see O. Mosley, *My Life* (London, 1968), 407–8.

[29] On the de Laessoes see below p. 308 and HO 144/21992, 45/25109, TS 27/511.

[30] HO 45/25704 and HO 283/55. Formerly D/I for London South, and before that D/T and D/L of Norwood District.

[31] He suffered from ill health in detention; see *Comrade*, 16. He seems to have been released by about 1 August. He had attended some of the 'secret meetings', which perhaps explains his detention. He died in December 1948. See also Watts MS, 33

[32] Watts MS, 5.

[33] See Rowe MS. Prospective candidate for Islington. See also HO 45/2893 and HO 283/9 (file on Mosley).

[34] Once Conservative, then ILP; joined BUF in 1934. He appears in HO 45/25752 as a permanent resident in Brixton Prison, categorized as a leader. Charnley notes his removal from the Isle of Man after the riot there, and Charnley his association with the Union movement after the war. His service with Shackleton was with the North Russian Expeditionary Force in 1918–19.

[35] HO 283/13 (statement of Mosley). HO 45/21429 (Special Branch report). Apparently not detained for long. Appears as chief agent in the Bellamy MS iii. and named as assistant by J. W. Charnley in *Mosley's Blackshirts*, 34. In the Saunders Papers he is also called Propaganda Administrator. See also HO 283/13. He had been a miner (associated with Aneurin Bevan) and member of the ILP; he was a Parliamentary candidate for South Dorset for the New Party in 1931. He was probably a founder member of the BUF.

Women's Officer until 1940, when she had been dismissed for inefficiency.[36]

Of the remaining eleven Andrew Burn was a Civil Servant in the Ministry of Health and a secret member of the party.[37] Guy Bruning was a national speaker of no great prominence; in 1938 he had looked after printing. His brother Clement, who in 1936 was an Administrative Officer concerned with propaganda, had gone to Germany, and been employed in Goebbels's propaganda service. By 1940 Clement, for obscure reasons, had been sent to a concentration camp, where, apparently, he died.[38] Mrs Norah Elam, also known as Mrs Dacre-Fox,[39] was a former suffragette and member of the Womens' Social and Political Union; she ran the London and Provincial Anti-Vivisection Society, a cover organization for the party. Its premises were raided on 23 May, or perhaps a day or so later, and there had been an earlier raid.[40] About James Elison nothing is known to me except that he held no post at NHQ.[41] Robert Ling too had no connection with NHQ; he was a member of the Ealing District. E. Stennett (or Stennell) Sandall was an ordinary member in Birmingham, who had a brother who worked in a hotel in Germany; he had been visited by Germans. Apparently at the time of his arrest he possessed a revolver, which he had taken from another member, one Rounds, to keep him out of trouble. This all explains both his selection and the fact that he was specially interrogated.[42] Ernest Saunders was a team leader in the Westminster Abbey District, which probably operated from Sanctuary Building.[43] G. W. Scott was District Leader of Richmond on Thames.[44] G. E. Thomas, who had been detained in 1939 on suspicion of espionage, as we have seen, held no office in the party. 'Charlie' F. Watts, the brother of Captain O. M. Watts, the fashionable yacht chandler of

[36] HO 283/13; described in HO 45/25747 as a prominent fascist; the wife of an architect.
[37] Daily Telegraph, 24 May. Burn was RFC in the 1914–18 war; joined the party in 1933. In 1939 he was a Clerk, High Grade. He regained his Civil Service job after 1945, becoming a Higher Executive Officer in the Ministry of Health 1948–50; he then moved to Housing and Local Government and appears to have retired in 1952 or 1953. Active in the Union movement from 1948 until his death on 31 October 1976. There is a tradition in fascist circles that he was involved in the preparation of the Beveridge Report.
[38] HO 144/21281, 21429, HO 283/13 at 33, Saunders Papers. A prospective Parliamentary candidate. Guy signed the BU collection of autographs in Peel Camp on 24 July 1941 at the time of his release: 'I am leaving this prison for a bigger one—Britain under Democracy.' See also Comrade, 14. Three other brothers were BU.
[39] Some doubt surrounded her second marriage to E. Dudley Elam. See HO 45/25747. There is some confusion between Dacre-Fox and Darwin-Fox.
[40] Prospective candidate for Northampton. The raid is mentioned in Parl. Deb. HC Vol. 361 c.652–3 for 30 May, where it was stated that the premises of the society were being used for BU business.
[41] Name in Action for 30 May as Euson.
[42] In Latchmere House. Watts MS, 5, 34, information from S. L. Irvine.
[43] Information from J. Warburton and Watts MS, 5.
[44] Signed autograph book on 18 June 1941 prior to release.

Albemarle Street, was either the District Inspector or Leader of Westminster, and was based at NHQ; he ran the London Cab Drivers Group, said to have 1,000 members.[45] Mrs Muriel G. Whinfield held no position; she had been a prospective candidate and her son was, as we have seen, already in detention. She had attended some of the 'secret meetings'. Of those arrested in the first sweep fourteen had at one time or another been nominated as Parliamentary candidates.[46]

The first arrests did not include all the paid officials. By May 1940 there were only fifteen, or sixteen if one includes Sutton, paid by Mosley himself; all were in due course detained.[47] The list of 22 May includes no National Inspectors at all,[48] but three were later detained: John W. I. Sant, who had been one until 1939 and was serving in the Royal Engineers,[49] Richard R. Bellamy, and 'Tommy' P. Moran, who assumed control of the party after Mosley's arrest. Other officials or voluntary helpers who were later detained were Ernest D. Hart of the Research Department, McNeil Sloane, H. K. Stevens (who had been secretary to Neil Francis-Hawkins and had joined the Auxiliary Fire Service), and W. C. Luckin, a journalist. Some who escaped came to be suspected by party members of being MI5 agents; an example is Lieutenant-Colonel C. S. Sharpe, who had in fact resigned from the party in 1939 and tried, without success, to rejoin his regiment. He had grown tired of having to hide from his friends.[50] The only clear case is that of P. G. Taylor, the in-house MI5 spy. A number of individuals earlier associated with NHQ escaped detention, probably because they were no longer involved in 1940.[51]

---

[45] The Watts MS notes that he held the BU gold award. Cross, *Fascists in Britain*, 179, claims that only Ralph Gladwyn Jebb held the 'gold distinction', but this seems incorrect. Capt. Watts was BU Branch leader in Mayfair.

[46] Beckett, Brock-Griggs, Burdett, Clarke, Donovan, Norah Elam, Hammond, MacNab, McKecknie, Raven-Thomson, Shepherd, Sutton, Thomas, and Whinfield.

[47] List in HO 45/24891 compiled so as to allow them to be paid; they were Francis-Hawkins, Donovan, McKecknie, Raven-Thomson, Shepherd, Clarke, Hammond, Pacey, K. Bisney, E. D. Hart, M. O'Connell, H. Hibbert, Mrs Olive Burdett (formerly Hawkes), Mrs E. M. Steele, and Miss K. M. Marston.

[48] An order of march of 1 May 1938 in the Saunders Papers lists four National Inspectors: Symes, Sant, Garnett, and Bellamy. One for the last May Day rally of 7 May 1939 lists McKecknie, Bellamy, Garnett, and Moran, but not Symes. Symes and Garnett were not detained.

[49] HO 144/21429. The son of a consular official in Turkey; Civil Servant in the East; joined BU 1933; involved in Northern administration with Hone.

[50] HO 283/13 65–6, HO 144/21429. He had been Assistant Director-General (G) in charge of records, personnel, and premises. He later served in the Home Guard.

[51] For example A. G. Findlay, once Director of Public Relations and supervisor of accounting, C. J. Garnett, and P. Syme, former National Inspectors, and C. V. S. Hillman, former electoral instructor and inspector. There is a mistaken tradition in BU circles that Richard Findlay was arrested in error for A. G. Findlay of the BU. On R. Findlay, a Right Club member, see HO 214/67; he is listed in HO 45/2893; he became Camp Leader at Peveril Camp in the Isle of Man. See HO 283/13 65–6.

The explanation for some oddities in the list could be MI5's incompetence. At Mosley's committee hearing Birkett, briefed by Aikin-Sneath, questioned Mosley about leading members and officials of the party.[52] He was obviously working from a list which was quite out of date. Thus he asked him about A. K. Chesterton, who had resigned in 1938—Mosley typically claimed he had been expelled—and Geoffrey Dorman, editor of *Action* until 1937, who had resigned well before the war and was in the RAF. But some omissions may be explained because individuals were left at large in the hope that this would make it easier to discover the plans for going underground. Thus Miss E. M. Monk, who was a personal secretary to Mosley, was never detained, though E. B. Stamp of MI5 told the Home Office on 30 October that MI5 were keeping an eye on her.[53] The inclusion of individuals who were not major figures in the BU, or not members at all, may also have not been irrational; sometimes we can guess at an explanation. Mosley had transferred funds to Norah Elam; MacNab was an associate of Joyce and might be in contact with him; Mrs Whinfield's son was suspected of disloyal attempts to contact the enemy and contact with German espionage agents.[54] She had attended the 'secret meetings'. G. E. Thomas had already been suspected of espionage. Andrew Burn, the Civil Servant, was a friend of 'Charlie' Watts, the organizer of the London Cab Drivers Trade Group, and might know of cells in the Civil Service. Of Watts MI5 said: 'Although he was never influential in the hierarchy of the organization, he is to be considered as one of its most efficient and revolutionary members.'[55] Burn, Watts, and one Howard Hall, a butler—secretary to Sir James Hamet Dunn Bt., a Canadian lawyer and banker, were suspected of organizing an undercover organization known as the Home Defence Movement, which distributed pamphlets and 'sticky-backs'. Watts' cab drivers were alarming as giving the Fifth Column mobility, and Watts was suspected of possessing explosives and publicizing the NBBS. Pacey as an accountant was someone who could be interrogated, as he was in Stafford Prison, to discover information about party funds and Mosley's travels, for he he had been Mosley's driver; he had NBBS sticky-backs. Sandell was in possession of a weapon and was subjected to special interrogation; armed fascists would be particularly dangerous. The evidence does not explain all cases, but there is little of it to be had.

A principal function of the first arrests and searches, and the special interrogation of such persons as Donovan, Watts, Pacey, and Sandell, was

---

[52] HO 283/13 65–6.

[53] HO 45/24891. Miss Monk assisted Oswald Hickson to tidy up some of Sir Oswald's affairs. She later married C. J. Garnett.

[54] HO 283/1.

[55] 'Statement of the Case' by A. A. Gordon-Clark, 28 June 1940, HO 283/74; also HO 45/25702.

to discover if MI5's graver suspicions had any foundation. When Mosley himself was arrested by Inspector F. W. Jones, he cheerfully assured him that 'ever since the outbreak of war, he had been expecting arrest and that naturally he had made some precautions for the safe custody of such of the British Union of Fascists records as he did not wish to fall into the hands of the authorities'. But much remained to be seized, and amongst documents found in his custody was a forty-four-page typed list of officers, agents, contacts, and speakers, corrected up to 25 January 1940.[56] A search of Donovan's home produced several lists, a card index of women members, and a loose-leaf book with reports of womens' meetings, which showed that his wife Heather, soon to be detained, 'held an executive post in the British Union'. There was also a list of sympathizers in Sussex. In McKechnie's home was a notebook of Essex members, and a sketch-map of regions.[57] Some officials had hidden their records; thus in October of 1939 Robert Saunders concealed his list of his members in an encyclopedia.[58] But senior officials do not appear to have paid much attention to security, and the hundreds of searches in June and July must have deluged MI5 with material.

Mosley's Contingency Plans

The BU had indeed made contingency plans; a scheme had been explained by Donovan at a meeting of officials in June 1939, and initiated by a circular from Francis-Hawkins on 4 September; deputies for all officials should be appointed and their names sent to NHQ. As we have seen, MI5 knew that such plans existed, and knew about the dispersal of funds.[59]

Amongst papers belonging to Norah Elam was found a suspicious list of eight names.[60] The BU did not have a governing body; policy was the will of the Leader. But the constitution did provide for the succession if the Leader died without having nominated his successor. A council would choose, its members being nominated by Mosley in a document held by his solicitors (normally Messrs Randolph and Dean or Iliffe Sweet and Co.). I suspect the eight merely constituted this council; they were McKechnie, Donovan, Francis-Hawkins, E. Dudley Elam, J. H. Hone,[61]

[56] HO 45/24891. I have found no confirmation of the existence of any significant secret archive, though collections of such documents as *Action* do exist.
[57] HO 45/25704.   [58] Saunders Papers.
[59] Report of 12 June 1939 HO 144/21281. Report of 18 September 1939 in HO 144/21429. The contingency scheme was set up by a circular of 23 Oct. 1939, copy in CRIM 1/1197.
[60] See HO 283/48.
[61] Hone had a distinguished record with the Gordon Highlanders and held the Mons Star. A prospective candidate; became a National Inspector with responsibility for the north of England. See *Mosley's Blackshirts*, 34 (Ch. 7 n. 55 above) and Rowe MS. Hone was detained in 1940, but probably an early release. *Comrade*, 7.

Commander C. E. Hudson,[62] K. E. Marsden,[63] and R. Temple-Cotton.[64] These could not conceivably have been leaders of an underground organization; their association with the BU was public knowledge. MI5 must have accepted this; otherwise all would have been long-term 'leader' detainees, but only Donovan, McKechnie, and Francis-Hawkins were so categorized.

Also discovered was a document, signed by Mosley, which read: 'Mr Hector G. McKechnie has my complete confidence and is entitled to do what he thinks fit in the interests of the Movement of his own responsibility.' The name had been inserted, and MI5 suspected correctly that others had been authorized too; before the advisory committee Mosley volunteered that they had been distributed on 1 September 1939 to more or less all area leaders.[65] It was understandable in 1940 for MI5 to place a sinister interpretation on this at first, and it did. Watts, recording his impressions of his special interrogation by MI5, wrote: 'My impression was during this cross-examination that the Government were not worried so much about the propaganda, but were looking for an underground organization which they thought existed to take the place of the detained and banned British Union.'[66] Similar suspicions were put by Birkett to Mosley, who said that when war came he feared arrest on some trumped-up charge, and consequently made contingency plans. Birkett blundered by asking him: 'But why should the law permit the Movement to be continued and you as Leader of the Movement to be arrested?' Mosley saw his chance and replied: 'That is precisely what has happened.' It was game, set, and match to Mosley, for at the time of this exchange the party had indeed not been proscribed.

It may well be that other suggestive evidence came to light in June of 1940. Thus Charnley was interrogated about a possible police group in London; perhaps one did exist.[67] But one document found in a raid intended to accomplish the arrest of the eccentric R. A. ('Jock') Houston

---

[62] OBE and RNR, D/L in Bognor Regis and a prospective Parliamentary candidate. He was a founder member of the Anglo-German Friendship organization and active in the Anglo-French Friendship organization. Sometimes thought to have been the BU holder of the VC, but this confuses him with a Lt.-Col. C. E. Hudson.

[63] County Propaganda Officer in the north of England. Possibly related to Victor E. Marsden who publicized the 'Protocols of the Learned Elders of Zion'.

[64] A horticulturalist from Branscombe in Devon, and regional inspector; also prospective Parliamentary candidate for Exeter.

[65] Presumably regional inspectors and area organizers. One known recipient was Charles H. Hammond; see HO 45/25752/sf. 30, list of 25 September 1941. Ralph Gladwyn Jebb was another (HO 283/13 101). Jebb was a Regional Inspector for Wessex and had been candidate for West Dorset and earlier D/L in Salisbury. He lived at Downton Manor, and was the son of a Victorian explorer, Jack Jebb. He was a member of the family which produced the diplomat Lord Gladwyn Jebb, and was a distant relative of the Queen Mother. He wrote under the name Andrew Andrews. He died in 1977.

[66] Watts MS, 43.   [67] Charnley MS, 119; a few police officers were detained.

produced a bizarre example of an underground organization dreamt up by a crank. Houston, a house painter and street bookmaker, with a considerable criminal record, had been in the BU as an official and speaker until October of 1936, when he had been expelled. Aggressive and violently anti-Semitic, he formed the Nationalist Association, and joined the Nordic League, which found him too extreme to be tolerable. He also belonged to the Right Club.[68] The document included this:

With the internment of Mosley the scheme designed by Donovan to meet such an emergency has been put into operation. Deputies have taken over the job of leading Fascist 'officials' and carry on the work of the 'movement' secretly . . . Lord Lymington[69] is 'Deputy Leader' and the only people I know to be associated with him at the moment are Bailey,[70] Sharpe,[71] Marion Sullivan[72] and Dr McNair Wilson.[73] Lymington expects that he will soon be called upon to form a cabinet.

The basis for this rubbish was, however, real enough—Donovan's scheme. A similarly fantastic underground organization was the brainchild of the eccentric Dr Leigh Vaughan-Henry, originally due for arrest on 23 May. This was initially taken seriously by Special Branch and MI5.[74] He had been making plans for a provisional government, said he had an organization divided into cells of twenty-five members prepared to come on to the streets and take control, possessed numerous codes, and had investigated arms purchases. Common sense would suggest that all this was fantasy, but the summer of 1940 was a bad time for common sense, and Vaughan-Henry was interned in June.

[68] See HO 283/41 and HO 45/25713. His detention order was the omnibus order of 30 May, but he evaded arrest until 14 December.

[69] 1898–1984, in 1943 the 9th Earl of Portsmouth; much involved in campaigning for a negotiated peace; a fellow traveller of the right, but never in the BU. Author of *The Tory Path* (1931), *Famine in England* (1938) and an autobiography, *A Knot of Roots* (1965). Also in the English Array, formed in 1936 and the English Mistery, romantic back to the land and merry old England groups. In 1938 he formed the British Council against European Commitments. See generally R. Griffiths, *Fellow Travellers of the Right* (London, 1980), 317 ff.

[70] Probably A. J. A. ('Bill') Bailey, a former artilleryman, who had been a candidate for Shoreditch in the municipal elections fought by the BU and a prospective Parliamentary candidate. An informant tells me he left or was expelled with Joyce in 1937. A James A. Bailey appears in a Special Branch report on the Nationalist Association in 1939 (HO 144/22454) and a John Bailey was a Steward in the Right Club.

[71] Presumably the Revd Calverdale Sharpe, a Unitarian Minister.

[72] Misses M. Sullivan and F. Sullivan, both of the Nordic League, were in the Right Club.

[73] Medical correspondent to *The Times* 1914–42 and a prolific author both under his own name and as Anthony Wynne; a right-wing Catholic.

[74] 'Statement of the Case' in TS 27/533 dated 28 November 1940.

Keeping the Party Alive

In the event T. P. ('Tommy') Moran[75] took over quite openly as Leader, an announcement appearing in the last issue of *Action*, and a fairly junior member of the staff of NHQ, one K. Bisney, attempted to keep the administration operating. On 27 May 1940 Bisney issued the first of two 'Emergency Instructions', referring explicitly to the contingency plan of 1939: 'CARRY ON as usual. Deputies have been appointed and the following instructions are to take effect immediately . . . [here followed financial instructions] TAKE NO PANIC MEASURES AND AWAIT FURTHER INSTRUCTIONS FROM NHQ ON ALL MATTERS.'[76] His second and last instruction says that meetings may still be held, and Area Officers were to arrange them, adding: 'it must be remembered by all officials that we have nothing to hide . . . Speakers should not concern themselves only with Mosley's arrest, but should stress the essential and consistent patriotic nature of the movement. In reply to 5th. column accusations, point out that our policy for the last seven years is a direct denial.' There were no more instructions; the unfortunate Bisney and Moran had joined the Leader in detention. Indeed Bisney's memoranda suggest that, whatever might have been reasonably suspected, the Donovan scheme was not intended to establish a clandestine organization at all. After Mosley's detention *Action* appeared publicly on 30 May, and stated that 'unless and until *Action* is proscribed as illegal, we shall carry on, subject to the censorship'. It repeated part of Mosley's 1939 message:

To our members my message is plain and clear. Our country is involved in war. Therefore I ask you to do nothing to injure our country, or to help any other Power. Our members should do what the law requires of them, and if they are members of any of the Forces or Services of the Crown, they should obey their orders and, in every particular, obey their Service.

'Mosley's Message' was also littered down Fleet Street by defiant fascists. The issue carried the slogan 'Free Mosley—Save Britain'; the headline was 'We Carry On'. The same slogan appeared in the final issue of 6 June, which also exhorted women to keep the party going.[77] Though *Action* did not become illegal until 10 July, no further issue appeared. E. D. Hart, editor of its last issue, had been detained by an order of 30 May. In the absence of working contingency plans some members engaged in local initiatives; *British Freedom* had a brief circulation in Hull, Leeds, Lincoln, and York.[78] There may have been other such ventures, but they amounted to little.

[75] See above p. 179.   [76] Saunders Papers.

[77] Issue 221. *Action News Service* appeared on 4 June for the last time so far as I know.

[78] Charnley MS, 91; this was produced by Charnley, Vic King, and Harry Townend. See pp. 203–4 for the supposed underground BU in the north.

Had there really existed any clandestine fascist organization, it is quite inconceivable that MI5 would not have discovered it; there never was such an organization. But well before this was realized the great incarceration had developed a momentum of its own, and an aggressive new expediting committee had become involved in the attack on the Fifth Column.

The Swinton Committee

On 22 May Anderson had only committed himself to arresting a small number of fascist leaders, and on 25 May he told the Home Policy Committee that he was planning to warn both *Action* and the *Daily Worker* under Regulation 2C. But the procedure was slow, and he wanted a power to ban without warning; this was introduced on 29 May by Regulation 2D. But there must have been continuous pressure for more detentions; on 25 May MI5 was informed that Churchill wanted 'all fifth columnists' interned; Anderson was told this.[79] On 27 May the War Cabinet considered a grim paper from the Chiefs of Staff discussing whether Britain could continue the war alone if France fell. The conclusion was that so long as British morale held this was possible; a consequential recommendation was ruthless action against the Fifth Column, and the proscribing of subversive organizations.[80] The Cabinet accepted this paper, and one outcome was the establishment of a new expediting committee, the Home Defence (Security) Executive, under the chairmanship of Lord Swinton, 'the object of which is principally to consider questions relating to defence against the 5th. Column *and to ensure action*' (my italics). It was an offshoot of the Home Defence Executive, intended to ensure that military needs were promptly fulfilled. A report by Lord Hankey on MI5, circulated about the same time, wholeheartedly accepted the belief in the Fifth Column, and urged that 'the fullest possible weight' be given to any of MI5's recommendations to counter it. Presumably this report also helped to wear down Anderson's reluctance to extend the use of detention.[81]

The committee was established under the Lord President of the Council, Chamberlain.[82] Its papers are, ridiculously, closed, but some

[79] HO 144/21540. The source for Churchill's view is Hinsley and Simkins, 52.

[80] Chiefs of Staff Paper No. 168 CAB 80/11, discussed at the meeting at 11 a.m. on 27 May CAB 65/7 WM (40) 141, CAB 65/13 ff. 165–73 Minute 9 Confidential Annexe.

[81] Though signed on 11 May not circulated at once; possibly it went to the War Cabinet for the meeting of 27 May. No documentation is available, but a paper by Eric Seal in PREM 4/97/11 of 25 July 1940 states that the only recommendations were of a 'trifling character'. See also Hinsley and Simkins, 40. Quotation from HH 50/68, probably written by Churchill or Swinton.

[82] CAB 65/7 WM (40) 144 of 28 May, Andrew, 478–9; J. A. Cross, *Lord Swinton*, (Oxford, 1982), 225–9; N. Stammers, *Civil Liberties in Britain during the Second World War: A Political Study* (London, 1983), 38; P. and L. Gillman, *'Collar the Lot!'* (London, 1980), 141–3. See CAB 66/7, WP (40) 168/COS (40) 390, Paper from Chiefs of Staff dated 25 May

have leaked into other files without any apparent harm to the national interest.[83] It was not an executive body; formally it could only make recommendations on 18B to the Home Office, and Swinton was not a minister. But it could in effect appeal through the Lord President to the War Cabinet, and until Anderson succeeded Chamberlain as Lord President in October 1940 this reduced the independence of the Home Office. The very existence of the committee, which was attended by representatives of MI5, the War Office, and MI6, as well as the Home Office, inevitably encouraged more repressive action.

Its composition was very curious. In addition to Swinton it had two 'independent' members, and representatives of Churchill and Chamberlain. Sir Joseph Ball was a member as Chamberlain's nominee, acting as Swinton's deputy.[84] A somewhat mysterious figure, he had been in MI5 as Major Ball, from 1914 to 1927. From 1930 to 1939 he ran the Conservative Party Research Department, in which capacity he engaged in forms of espionage; from 1934 to 1939 he was deputy head of the National Publicity Bureau, originally established in 1931 to campaign for the national government. It became a Conservative front organization. Ball was intimate with Chamberlain and a strong supporter of his policies. In about 1936 he secretly obtained control of the weekly news-sheet *Truth*; it was used to support Chamberlain and attack his opponents.[85] Chamberlain seems to have been privy to this, and after the war began *Truth* 'became stridently anti-Churchill, anti-Semitic, anti-American and pacifist: and as such accurately reflected the real state of Ball's and Chamberlain's minds from 1939 onwards'.[86] The editor of *Truth* in 1940 was Henry Newnham, who had far-right contacts.[87] His wife, who was in the BU, was detained in early July.[88] The contradiction involved in Ball's

and CAB 65/13 Confidential Annexe. Hinsley and Simkins, 52–3 describe the establishment, referring to CAB 66/8 WP (40) 172 of 27 May, which is closed. Also closed are CAB 93/2–7, PREM 3/4181/ 1–3, and a file in the Swinton Papers 270/6/33. There is also closed material in CAB 114.

[83] An example is in FO 371/25248 f. 416 (Meeting of 22 July 1940). See also CAB 98/18 CA (41) cited Stammers, *Civil Liberties*, 130 nn. 78–9 (Communist Activities Committee).

[84] *DNB* entry by Lord Blake. See also R. Cockett, *Twilight of Truth: Chamberlain, Appeasement and the Manipulation of the Press* (London, 1989), 10–12, 114–15, 175, 161–5, 183–4. Cockett's account is based in part on the Vansittart Papers in Churchill College, Cambridge, memo on 'The Control of the Newspaper Truth' and 'Report on Truth and the Truth Publishing Company Ltd.' Vansittart Papers 11 2/31 and 32.

[85] A memo in the US Archives (RG 84 Confidential file, US Embassy 1941 124–820.02, A. N. Steyne to Herschel Johnson, claimed that the management of *Truth* was pro-German and controlled by Sir Kingsley Wood, Lord Essenden, Lord De La Warr, Malcolm Macdonald, and Geoffrey Shakespeare, with editorial control in the hands of Ball and Crocker. All were members of the National Publicity Council; it seems unlikely that the 5 named were closely involved.

[86] Cockett, *Twilight of Truth*, 11.

[87] See HO 144/22454 for his attendance at the National Citizens' Union.

[88] *Daily Express*, 6 July.

membership of the committee is very strange. *Truth* campaigned on behalf of 18B detainees, in particular Admiral Domvile, but it did so from a hawkish position. The line it adopted was that detainees should be put on trial and, if convicted, shot; there should be martial law under General Ironside.[89] This in effect meant that most detainees would be released.[90] The link between the Swinton Committee and *Truth* was strengthened by the appointment to the staff of the committee of William C. Crocker, a solicitor who had established a reputation through exposing insurance frauds. Crocker too was involved in the running of *Truth*. In the summer of 1940 Crocker was appointed to reorganize MI5, but failed in this enterprise, apparently from hostility within the institution.[91] Ball also secured the appointment of Reginald Duthie or Duthy, a business associate, and Kenneth Diplock, a barrister and later a House of Lords judge much involved in security issues, to the staff of the committee. Alfred M. Wall, General Secretary of the London Society of Compositors and a former communist was, somewhat oddly, the second independent member. The Secretary was William Armstrong, later the Head of the Civil Service; Ronald Wells of the Home Office also joined its staff. Isaac Foot, a Liberal MP, joined it in August 1940, apparently as a third independent member. Major Desmond Morton, one of Churchill's personal advisers, was his representative.[92]

The Swinton Committee caused misgivings in the Commons; in July Churchill refused to give any information about it and it was described by Richard Stokes as 'this rather odd secret Gestapo, which had been formed under Lord Swinton with a couple of toughs named Crocker and Ball'.[93] Why Churchill encouraged this strange Chamberlainite body is a

---

[89] Issue of 14 June.

[90] Issues of 24 May, 20 August 1940 and 27 December 1940, 10 January, 17 January, 7 February, 2 May 1941. On 17 May 1940 it argued there was no Fifth Column in Britain. On 9 August 1940 it attacked the *Daily Worker* for championing the cause of the detained communist John Mason and pointed out that the paper never protested at the detention of Ramsay, Domvile, and Gordon-Canning.

[91] Crocker (1886–1973) was a solicitor with Wood Lord, Lord and Co.; became President of the Law Society; knighted 1953. Hinsley and Simkins, 68, do not name him and say he joined the Security Intelligence Centre (i.e. the staff), but resigned in September 1940. Obituary in *The Times* 1 October 1973; autobiography, *Far from Humdrum: A Lawyer's Life* (London, 1967). See also H. Dearden, *The Fire Raisers: The Story of Leopold Harris and his Gang* (London, 1934). Dearden turns up as the psychiatrist who devised MI5's interrogation techniques.

[92] At a meeting in July the Home Office representatives were Newsam, A. S. Hutchinson, and E. N. Cooper, the War Office's Col. R. C. Reynolds and Maj.-Gen. Sir Alan Hunter, MI6's Lt.-Col. Valentine P. T. Vivian, MI5's Harker, Capt. Guy M. Liddell, then head of B Division, J. C. Curry, and T. F. Turner. Also attending were Ball and Wall. Wall, who died aged 67 in October 1957, had been a Communist Parliamentary candidate in the 1924 election, and from 1926 to 1938 was secretary of the London Trades Council. During the war he also served on the National Arbitration Union.

[93] *Parl. Deb.* HC 363 c.603 and 731. See also ibid. 374: 1108 and 1454–64.

mystery, though he may not have known of Ball's connection with *Truth*, or even of the paper's connection with the Conservative Party, the details of which are obscure. Desmond Morton's fall from grace may have been a consequence of revelations about the committee.[94] Conceivably Ball was anxious to protect 'fellow travellers of the right' from detention.[95]

The atmosphere in which the Swinton Committee was born is illustrated by its first meeting on 28 May, when it was told by the Lincolnshire police, through MI5, that BU officials were preparing to assist German parachutists.[96] The source may have been an informant by the name of Parker, described later by the committee as 'a man of poor intelligence . . . who had notions of sinister Fifth Column activity on the brain'.[97] At its second meeting, also on 28 May, it was informed that the Home Office had decided to detain BU officials on a list supplied by MI5; it would also be told of the decision, taken that same day, to give way to MI5 over the supposed German spy ring. Both decisions would be reluctantly taken.

The Second and Third Rounds of Arrests

The next round of arrests took place early in June, and the War Cabinet was informed on 4 June that 'the 350 local officials of the British Union of Fascists were being arrested'.[98] This was under an omnibus order with a schedule which eventually, through amendments, comprised about 345 names, signed on 30 May.[99] Maxwell informed Anderson: 'This list which contains three hundred men and thirty five women has been compiled as regards London by Scotland Yard in collaboration with M.I.5 and as to other places by M.I.5 largely as a result of information supplied by Chief Constables to whom the individuals are known as prominent or active members of the British Union.'[100] Discrepancies over the numbers suggest that names were added to the schedule after the order had been signed, and obviously Anderson could not have considered each case individually.

The schedule of thirty-seven women is available but not the men; neither were published, though the press named many of them.[101] Thus *The*

---

[94] Maj. Sir Desmond Morton (1891–1971) had been ADC to Haig; between the wars he ran the Industrial Intelligence Centre, and fed Churchill with information. According to Sir John Colville, *The Fringes of Power: 10 Downing Street Diaries 1939–1955* (London, 1985), 759, his influence with Churchill declined during the war. See also the same author's *Footprints in Time* (London, 1976), 94–5. PREM 7 contains Morton's memos to Churchill.
[95] For the later history see below Ch. 12.   [96] Hinsley and Simkins, 53.
[97] See TS 27/513 and HO 45/23679/840412 (case of Fane). The Lincolnshire police organized the detention of virtually all members of the BU in the area.
[98] CAB 65/7 WM (40) 154 at 371.
[99] Accounts differ slightly. See TS 27/512 (Arbon), TS 27/513 (Fane), TS 27/493 (Smeaton-Stuart), TS 27/522 (Greene).
[100] Copy in TS 27/493.   [101] HO 45/25714. It is possible to identify most of the men.

Evening Standard on 3 June reported the arrest of the former British heavyweight boxing champion, Joe Beckett; others mentioned included Frank Joyce, the 23-year-old brother of William.[102] In Bristol C. H. Hewitt, a quarry proprietor, and M. P. J. Mountjoy were arrested; Hewitt, a wounded veteran of the war, was a District Leader, also active in the Link, and Mountjoy had resigned a District Leadership in January for domestic reasons.[103] In Canterbury it was Richard R. Bellamy and Arthur Smith, described as leaders of the local branch, which had its headquarters there at 6 St Alphege Lane, and Harold Elvey, an ordinary member.[104] Smith was publican of the King William IV and a veteran of the First World War, with three medals; Bellamy was in fact a National Inspector and Director of Propaganda, in Canterbury as election agent for Lady Pearson. Action against branches in Bournemouth, Hastings and St Leonards, Manchester, Leeds, Lowestoft, Worthing, Bury St Edmunds, Bognor Regis, and Tunbridge Wells was reported. Press reports made it clear that action against the Fifth Column extended beyond the BU by reporting, for example, the arrest of Norman Hay, who with Lancelot Lawton ran *Information and Policy*, a fortnightly periodical started in July 1939.[105] Both were Right Club, and had attended the 'secret meetings'. On 24 May *The Times* also reported 167 expulsion orders against IRA sympathizers, and on 25 May it reported 76 further arrests in Ulster, under the Civil Authorities Special Powers Act. There was also evidence of co-ordination with the Canadian government in *The Times* on 31 May: on 29 May five leaders of the Canadian fascist National Unity Party had been arrested, including the Führer, Adrien Arcand.[106]

Detentions were not the only manifestations of the ruthlessness of Churchill's government at this period. In addition to the Emergency Powers (Defence) Act of 22 May, there was the new draconian Treachery Act of the same date. Power to ban publications 'calculated to foment opposition to the prosecution to a successful issue of any war in which His Majesty is engaged' was acquired seven days later.[107] On 11 June it even became a criminal offence to 'publish any report or statement relating to matters connected with the war which is likely to cause alarm or despondency'; by 25 July there had been seventy-four convictions for this

---

[102] *The Times, Daily Telegraph*, 4 June; *Evening Standard* 3 June as 22 (ages differing).
[103] HO 45/25754.
[104] *Evening News*, 4 June, *Evening Standard*, 5 June.
[105] *Daily Telegraph*, 6 June 1940.
[106] Also Dr Noel Lecarie (named as Decario). See L.-R. Betcherman, *The Swastika and the Maple Leaf: Fascist Movements in Canada in the Thirties* (Toronto, 1975), 145–7 giving the total as 11, and generally. Arcand and his lieutenants were held in detention until July 1945. There were also detentions in Australia, on which see B. Muirden, *Puzzled Patriots* (Melbourne, 1968), and in New Zealand.
[107] By Regulation 2D (SRO 1940 No. 828). See CAB 65/7 WM (40) 144 of 28 May.

grotesque offence.[108] The police acquired extended powers of arrest and search on 31 May[109] and 11 June,[110] and the Home Secretary a general control over all police forces on 31 May.[111]

By late June it was even being suggested that local declarations of martial law by the military might become necessary. This Maxwell contrived to resist; he preferred a more draconian set of regulations, a power in Regional Commissioners to make regulations at the request of the military, and reliance on the common law defence of necessity.[112] So in July the Emergency Powers (Defence) Act No. 2 gave the executive power to set up special war zone courts, run by judges without juries. The loosely drafted bill gave virtually no indication of what was in mind, though it was explained that the courts would be civil, and would administer real law—not military or martial law. In fact the Home Office was resisting excessive demands for military rule. But there was considerable Parliamentary criticism of the blank cheque which was to be signed.[113] Britain had, within a very few weeks, become, in the name of liberty, a totalitarian state. Though there were always those who protested, in the desperate conditions which then existed totalitarianism seems to have been more or less what most people wanted. Thus Cadogan in his diary for Thursday 23 May 1940 greeted the initial arrests thus: 'Maule Ramsay and Mosley arrested! Quite right. But there are 1,000's of others who ought to be. First in order Van's friend Puttlitz.'[114] The entry precisely catches the mood of the time. Mass Observation conducted a survey on 24 May, and found that the government's action was quite extraordinarily popular.[115]

A further spate of arrests, principally during June, involved around 370 more persons; the eventual total of 18B (1A) orders was 753.[116] No avail-

---

[108] Regulation 39BA (SRO 1940 No. 938). For figures see *Parl.Deb*. HC Vol. 363 c.965.
[109] SRO 1940 No. 843, Regulation 18D.
[110] SRO 1940 No. 926 Regulations 14A and 88.
[111] SRO 1940 No. 846.   [112] HO 45/20245.
[113] See *Parl. Deb*. HC Vol. 363 c.65–146, 702–58, HL Vol. 117 c.3–40, 55–77.
[114] The reference (cut in the published version) is to Wolfgang Gans, Edler Herr zu Putlitz, who provided Sir Robert Vansittart with information about Germany, and apparently was in England in 1940. See A. Glees, *Secrets of the Service. British Intelligence and Communist Subversion* (London, 1986), 84, 148, 220–8. Cf. *Daily Herald* for 17 May on the internment of aliens: 'Country Saved from Fifth Column Stab', or even the liberal *Manchester Guardian* for 13 May. The press had clamoured for tougher measures even before the end of the phoney war. See L. de Jong, *The German Fifth Column in the Second World War* (Chicago, 1956), 100ff.
[115] Wartime Report No. 135, quoted by Skidelsky, *Oswald Mosley* (London, 1975), 462. Halifax recorded his delight in his diary: 'I am glad to say we succeeded in getting a good deal done about fascists, aliens, and other doubtfuls, Tom Mosley being amongst those picked up.' Quoted A. Roberts, '*The Holy Fox*': *A Biography of Lord Halifax* (London, 1991), 269, Mosley was called 'Tom' by friends and 'Kit' by Diana Mosley.
[116] CAB 65/10 WM (40) 293 of 21 November. Memo by Home Secretary WP (G) 40 308.

able papers explain this escalation; presumably it became impossible to check the recommendations of Chief Constables.[117] Figures later released showed that 216 requests came from MI5, between 20 and 30 from Special Branch in conjunction with MI5, and the remaining 500 or so from Chief Constables. Whether MI5's Regional Security Liaison Officers or Regional Commissioners vetted Chief Constables' requests is uncertain.[118] In one case, that of John Ellis, it is clear that the Regional Commissioner, Lord Harlech, was involved, and Lord Denning in his memoirs claimed that he had detained 'the Nazi parson' and others; in reality he was merely legal adviser and as such presumably gave advice.[119]

The Home Office and Civil Liberty

Even at this period the Home Office attempted to encourage restraint through a circular to Chief Constables of 14 June.[120] Searches should be confined to those who are 'active leaders', or those about whom 'special information' has been received; detention under 18B (1A) was only the policy for 'active leaders' or 'individual members who may be engaged in specially mischievous activities'—'there is no intention of ordering the general detention of members of the organization'. The circular adopted a similar tone in relation to detention for 'hostile origin or associations' and for 'acts prejudicial'. In the former case information had to be supplied showing the necessity for detention. In the case of 'acts prejudicial',

specific information must be given showing the nature of the activities which are regarded as prejudicial. While the Secretary of State is anxious that full use shall be made of this power he cannot base an order on a mere statement that a Chief Constable regards the individual with suspicion. Sufficiently specific information must be given . . . to enable the Secretary of State to apply his own judgement to the case.

---

[117] Thurlow, *Fascism in Britain*, 211–12, citing Nigel West and S. Saloman, 'Now it Can Be Told' BDBJ C 6/9/2/1, says the Board of Deputies through their 'mole' Capt. X obtained a list of all members of the BU and gave this to the authorities. This is incorrect; the agent left the BU in 1937, and no such list existed.

[118] From mid-June 1940 MI5 began to decentralize, and established Regional Security Liaison Officers, first in the most threatened Civil Defence Regions, whose headquarters were at Tunbridge Wells and Cambridge. There were also Regional Commissioners appointed under the Regional Commissioners Act 1939 to co-ordinate civil defence, and on 2 July by SRO No. 1135 of 1940 the Home Secretary was empowered by 18BB to delegate detention powers under 18B, but not 18B (1A), to such commissioners. On 27 September a power to detain temporarily was delegated to commissioners outside London, but they never acquired any power of long-term detention under 18B (1A). SRO No. 1774 of 1940.

[119] *The Family Story*, 130. For Ellis see HO 45/25726 and 283/33.

[120] MEPO 21/6433. Hinsley and Simkins, 66 n. giving no date quote a Home Office instruction encouraging vigilance against the Fifth Column. Conceivably the quotation is from a minute of a verbal instruction given at a meeting.

Probably Maxwell did succeed in reducing the number of requests for orders; there could have been many more. But the number of detainees continued to rise, reaching a peak at the end of August of 1,428.[121] And a mere three days after the Home Office had tried to reduce the temperature MI5's first Security Bulletin was issued, listing 'the principal groups from which Fifth Column activities may be suspected in the country'— the IRA, the BU, and other right-wing organizations, the Communist Party, enemy aliens, Czech refugees of the far left, other aliens, traitorous British subjects, and 'concealed' enemy aliens—persons who are by naturalization, marriage, or accident of birth British subjects. The bulletin also drew attention to the NBBS. If MI5 had been trying to initiate a witch-hunt, it could hardly have done better.[122] Later, in April 1941, after the full scale of the witch-hunt had become obvious through the work of the committee, the Home Office issued a circular; the gist was that informers should be told that unless they were prepared to sign witness statements they might not be taken very seriously. But this came too late to make any significant difference and was soon weakened by a circular of 15 November allowing the use of police interview reports and reports from unidentified known police informants.[123]

Throughout the summer the Home Office continued to fight a rearguard action to protect civil liberty against MI5 and the military. Thus when the War Zone Courts regulations were published they were designed to exclude the military from adjudication, and maintain a civil system of government, providing a fair system of trial, though without juries, with appeals in serious cases.[124] The War Office continued to argue that in the event of invasion commanders might still need to rely on martial law, shooting offenders out of hand, perhaps after summary military trial; after lengthy arguments the Home Office and Law Officers contrived to persuade the War Office to tone down its instructions on the matter to military commanders, which were not settled until March 1941.[125] The military were also placated by the invention of the invasion list.[126] In August the Home Policy Committee settled a draft of a new 18B (1B) which permitted the detention, in a zone of military operations, of persons whose 'recent conduct . . . or any words recently written or spoken by such a person expressing sympathy with the enemy, indicates or

[121] The reports to Parliament are in the published *Parliamentary Papers*, the references being IV 203 (1 September 1939–30 September), IV 247 (1 October 1940–30 September 1941), IV 221 (1 October 1941–31 August 1942), IV 345 (1 September 1942–30 September 1943), III 227 (1 October 1943–31 October 1944), V 75 (1 November 1944–9 May 1945).
[122] Copy in FO 371/25193.   [123] MEPO 2/6433 of 28 April 1941. SH paras. 179–81.
[124] They became law on 7 August; SRO 1940 No. 1444, amended for Scotland by No. 1445 on 19 December. See HO 45/19078 and for Scotland HH 50/70–77.
[125] HH 50/70 and 71.
[126] HO 45/25506 and 25141; SRO No. 1682 of 19 September.

indicate that person is likely to assist the enemy'; this modified a more draconian earlier draft, and the committee insisted that the Home Secretary should retain ultimate control, rather than Regional Commissioners or military commanders. Between 800 and 1,000 persons were initially listed; by April 1944 the number of women had risen to 320, and the number of men was 830 though figures in the sources seem inconsistent. This scheme was never implemented and all orders were destroyed in September 1944.

Home Office dedication to regular civil government and legality even in the event of an invasion reached its high point in July 1940 over the deeply British issue of dogs. Animal posts were to be set up to cope with stray dogs (and other creatures), but the officials were concerned to ensure their return, if possible, to their owners, a policy respected in the Dogs Act of 1906. A mere invasion ought not to affect property rights. So the posts were to maintain registers, facilitating thereby searches by distraught dog owners. But the draftsman of the regulation, in deference to the battles which would presumably be raging around the posts, provided that all that had to be entered in the registers was 'a brief description of the dog'.[127]

The Italian Orders

But events moved against the Home Office, and over the Anglo-Italians Anderson made the mistake of trusting MI5, with embarrassing consequences. Italy declared war on 10 June; the press had fuelled fear of an Italian Fifth Column.[128] Regular Italian citizens could be detained under the prerogative. Eventually about four thousand were.[129] There were also many Anglo-Italians who were dual citizens. Some were fascists, and many more belonged to the Fascio.[130] MI5 gave the impression, which was quite false, that it was well informed on the Italian communities, and knew who had joined the Fascio. It listed 1,500 dangerous persons, of whom 300 were citizens. Harker thought a thousand of them were professing *fascisti* and 'desperate characters', who might be used 'for attacks on key individuals and key points in the country by gangster methods'. All

---

[127] SRO No. 11134 of 2 July.

[128] e.g. John Boswell in the *Daily Mirror* on 27 April. FO 371/24932 has a protest by the Italian Counsellor on 4 May.

[129] Hinsley and Simkins, 55, quoting CAB 93/2 HD (S) 8th meeting of 26 June. This is not available. At p. 15 they give a figure of 19,000 for Italians resident in Britain; this is a pre-war figure. See C. Holmes, *John Bull's Island: Immigration and British Society, 1871–1971* (Basingstoke, 1988), 192–4.

[130] On what follows see HO 144/21254/700450/21 (draft press notice), FO 371/25192 (letter of 11 June from Halifax), FO 371/25193 f. 87 (letter giving Harker's views on 27 May), CAB 67/6 WP (G) (40) 131 (Anderson's memo), FO 371/25193 f. 101 (memo by Nigel Ronald), FO 371/25192 ff. 95, 221, and 25210 f. 81 (information on arrests), CAB 65/7 WM 128 (40), CAB 65/13 f.419 (churchill's report of 11 June), and CAB 65/7 161 of 11 June 1940.

members of the Fascio should be arrested.[131] The Home Office perforce accepted this; Anderson wanted all those on the dangerous list to be dealt with simultaneously. The Home Office plan, once the decision to act was taken, was to intern the 'desperate characters', whether citizens or not, first, and then males of Italian origin between the ages of 18 and 60 of less than ten years' residence in Britain. On 18 May the Cabinet altered this to twenty years, and lowered the age to 16, and also ordered the detention of 'such British Italians as were members of the Fascist Party'. The timing of action was left to Anderson and Halifax, since premature action might trigger Italy's entry into the war, and there were hopes of Mussolini helping to negotiate a peace.[132]

Between 8 and 11 May MI5 listed some 300 Anglo-Italians for detention under 18B.[133] Their names were placed on a schedule to an omnibus order; Anderson formally approved this, and signed an undated order, probably on 14 May. By then the list had been reduced to 275. By 10 June, when the order was dated, three further schedules had been added, bringing the total to 369. It is not clear that Anderson ever even saw these schedules.[134] Anderson reported the arrest of the 'desperate characters' to the Cabinet on 11 June.[135] Further orders in June, July, and August added another fifty-eight, and eventually, by steps which are obscure, some 600 persons, many of whom did not belong to the Fascio, were detained by these 'Italian Orders', which thus involved nearly as many individuals as the BU orders. A considerable number, about 200, were detained in Scotland. It has proved difficult to secure information about the Anglo-Italian detainees. Whereas continuity in the British fascist movement has tended to preserve information, the Anglo-Italian detainees were not linked by political enthusiasm, and seem to have wished to forget the whole awful affair. I have failed to locate organizations or individuals with information.[136]

Arrests, beginning on 11 June, were extensively reported, such as those of the Quaglino brothers, Armando Ferraro of the Mayfair Hotel, Luigi Bianchi, the Head Chef of the Café Royal, Italo Sangliaconi, Manager of the Piccadilly Hotel since 1927, and even Rene and Burni Manetti, clowns

[131] Letter of 27 May in FO 371/25193. Members swore an oath of allegiance to Mussolini
[132] CAB 65/7 WM 126 (40), FO 371/25193, CAB 65/7 WC Conclusions 146 (40).
[133] CAB 65/7 WM 148 (40) for 30 May and WM 149 (40) for May 31.
[134] TS 27/509. The three schedules were added on about 28 May, 3 June, and 10 June. HO 45/25758/863044/59 gives the figure and has lists of names with dates of orders of 10 June, 14 June, 3 August, and 9 August. In all there are 372 names.
[135] CAB 65/7 WM (40) (Conclusions).
[136] There is a novel, The Count of Torrigia (Joseph Syndica Drummond), Difficult to Hold, published in 1954 by Anglo-Italian Publications. I am indebted to Mr M Caesar for this reference and for a loan of a copy.

in Bertram Mills Circus for some fifteen years.[137] *The Times* for 11 June reported anti-Italian demonstrations in Soho, and a raid on an Italian Club carried out by a hundred police officers. It is not clear which MI5 officer was directly responsible under Harker for the whole fiasco; it may have been J. C. Curry. C. H. N. Adams, a solicitor and Oxford graduate, and H. Everett (probably a barrister, Henry Everett) were concerned with Italians in the summer of 1940, but their job may have been to clear up the mess.[138]

Within the Foreign Office, where officials were anxious not to burn all bridges with Italy, there was growing scepticism over MI5's competence. A memorandum by Cadogan includes these passages:

As the discussions with MI5 proceeded there grew up a strong suspicion that in actual fact they had little or no information, let alone evidence, in regard to more than a fraction of the persons they had led the Home Secretary to describe to the Cabinet as 'desperate characters' . . . They arrested as particularly dangerous the two brothers Quaglino, and Sovrani, the well-known restaurateurs on the ground that they were members of the Fascio and contributed to party funds . . . I confess to some misgiving myself: without for one moment suggesting that the Home Office are tainted with Fifth Column, I cannot rid myself of the conviction that many of their methods and habits are singularly adapted to forward all forms of disaffection.[139]

In fact MI5 had no complete lists of members of the Fascio, and knew little about fascism in Britain; this accounted for the 'atmosphere of sullen and superstitious ignorance behind which MI5 invariably takes refuge in their dealings with other departments'.

But Cadogan's outburst came too late to protect the Anglo-Italians. Such Home Office files as the weeders have spared give no hint of how bad it all was; here there has surely been some covering of tracks. In particular no reports from the special committee for the Italians, chaired by Sir Percy Loraine, Italian Ambassador until June, has been allowed to see the light of day in Home Office papers. However, many of his personal papers have survived, with the odd result that the Public Record Office now preserves in the Loraine Papers many copies of documents which the Home Office has destroyed as being unfit for preservation. No doubt Loraine protested strongly in his reports.[140] Apart from the Foreign

---

[137] *Daily Telegraph* for 12 and 13 June. In Australia many Italian immigrants were detained. See G. Cresciani, *Fascism, Anti-Fascism and Italians in Australia 1922–1945* (Canberra, 1980), esp. chs, 8 and 9; the total reached was 3,651, of whom around 711 were naturalized citizens. By September 1944 a 'hard core' of 135 fascists remained in detention. Whether there was co-ordination with MI5's operation is unknown.

[138] HO 45/25754.

[139] FO 371/25210. Similar views are expressed by H L. Farquhar of the Foreign Office in a letter of 27 Aug. to Loraine in FO 1011/215.

[140] FO 1011/215 and 216.

Office files the one other document which attests to the administrative confusion over the Italians is available in the Treasury Solicitor's papers.[141]

The Communists and Pacifists

The CPGB was certainly under foreign influence and control, but its members escaped detention. Only one known party member, John Mason, was interned.[142] The CPGB was much larger than the BU; it too had secret members, and plans to operate clandestinely; some members were certainly willing to engage in espionage. By May it had 20,000 members, and was well organized.[143] Little was known in 1940 about communist 'moles', but Hinsley and Simkins say that in May of 1940 there were good grounds for thinking that the party had a 'well placed' informant, prepared to warn the party of impending action. They neither identify a suspect nor indicate what, if any, action was taken.[144] At the Cabinet on 15 May it was thought that action might have to be taken against it, and the Joint Intelligence Committee thought it dangerous.[145] On 17 May a Home Office Cabinet memorandum, presumably from MI5, said there was no evidence that the party had been instructed to work for a German victory.[146] Pressure for action continued; on 18 May the Chiefs of Staff named communists along with others as persons over whom control should be tightened up, without specifying detention.[147] MI5 at this time prepared contingency plans for arresting its leading members.[148]

The CPGB was next raised at the request of the Home Office at the Swinton Committee on 28 May.[149] The committee recognized 'the delicacy of the whole question', and after consulting Ernest Bevin, the Minister of Labour, who detested the communists, it concluded, on 29 May, that apart from taking powers to ban the *Daily Worker* (or other publications) without warning under Regulation 2D, agreed by the Cabinet on 28 May, no further action should be taken.[150] Over the summer MI5's view seems to have changed; by July it opposed action against

---

[141] TS 27/509. Available papers are HO 45/25088 (Orazio M. R. Bottachi), HO 45/25759 (Gilda Camillo), HO 45/25761 and 283/52 (Lorenzo Ogni), HO 45/25720 (Harry Sabini), HO 45/25760 and 283/72 (Nicodemo Vanucci). Holmes in *John Bull's Island* discusses the Italian arrests and trouble in Soho. Trouble in Dundee is noted in police reports in HH 55/21 and 22.

[142] Hinsley and Simkins, 19–20, 35, 320.

[143] CAB 67/7 WP (40) 153 of 10 May COS (40) 315 (JIC) 2 May.

[144] See generally Glees, *Secrets of the Service; Secret Service*, Andrew, 408, 460.

[145] CAB 65/7 WM (40).   [146] CAB 67/6 WP (G) 131 of 17 May.

[147] CAB 80/11 Report of Chiefs of Staff Committee 18 May 1940 (40) 366.

[148] Hinsley and Simkins, 48 and 57.   [149] Ibid. 53.

[150] CAB 67/7 WM (40) 144 of 28 May. The new regulation was brought in on 29 May by SRO 1940 No. 828.

the party, and a circular drafted by MI5 advised Regional Commissioners to treat party members, unlike fascists, like any other member of the public.[151] It is possible, though there is absolutely no evidence, that this was the result of communist penetration of MI5. Roger Hollis was the officer concerned with the party.[152] If he was not a communist, and the case against him remains entirely unproven, there were others of left-wing views in MI5 at the time. Churchill's own view was stated with some bitterness to Stafford Cripps in 1941: 'We were left alone for a whole year whilst every Communist in England, under orders from Moscow, did his best to hamper our war effort.'[153] There was, however, a principled argument for the communists; its members had no love of fascism, and in any event the country was not at war with Russia.[154] The predominant reason for leaving the communists alone was surely that the party was too powerful; Bevin feared industrial unrest, and there might be trouble from the left-wing of the Labour Party.

In the event the *Daily Worker* was not suppressed until 21 January 1941, when Claud Cockburn's *Week* suffered the same fate. The decision was made after long consideration of communist activities, one option being the detention of a considerable number of the leaders of the party, and its proscription. Swinton favoured a new regulation under which any organization impeding the war effort would be declared illegal.[155] Maxwell opposed drastic action as likely to be ineffective, and a committee under Anderson agreed.[156] Some hints of incredulity in the papers over the ease with which prominent communists secured employment in aircraft factories suggest either innefficiency in MI5 or communist sympathy. Bevin now claimed that the party's influence in industry was overstated. Apart from making arrangements to exclude leading communists from ports and keeping them out of aircraft factories, the Cabinet agreed to taking no further action. In January 1941 Churchill wrote bitterly to Morrison

---

[151] Hinsley and Simkins, 48 and 57.

[152] Hollis joined MI5 in 1938. See Glees, *Secrets of the Service*, 392 (the division is incorrectly stated). Documents connected with Mason and the release of Mosley confirm that he was dealing with the communists between 1940 and 1943. See Andrew, 460, B. Penrose and S. Freeman, *Conspiracy of Silence* (London, 1987), ch. 11.

[153] Memo of 28 October 1941 quoted M. Gilbert, *Winston S. Churchill*, vi. '*Finest Hour*' (New York, 1986), 1228.

[154] See also CAB 98/18, Committee on Communist Activities 1st Meeting of 20 Jan. 1941, where the difference in treatment between the BU and CPGB is explained in a similar way.

[155] CAB 98/18 for 27 January 1941.

[156] See Hinsley and Simkins, 79–82, based largely on available papers, but including a reference to CAB 93/2 HD (S) E 22 meeting of 9 January, which is closed. CAB 65/20 refers to WP (41) 244, a Security Executive paper on Communist Shop Stewards of about October 1941, which is closed. See CAB 65/10 WM (40) 295 and 296 and 310 of 25, 27 November and 27 December, CAB 66/10 WP (40) 482 of 23 December, CAB 66/14 WP (41) 7 of 10 February, 27 of 10 January, CAB 65/17 WM (41) 5 of 13 January, 18 of 17 February, CAB 98/18 CA (41) 3rd meeting of 5 February.

grousing at the immunity of the communists, especially D. N. Pritt; Mosley being now locked up, which surely 'Sauce of the goose is sauce for the gander!' Once Germany attacked Russia and became, grotesquely, an ally, the party was safe; thus 'those filthy Communists', whom Churchill thought 'were really more dangerous than the fascists', escaped.[157]

As for the pure pacifists, the idea that the supporters of the PPU might form a Fifth Column can never have seemed plausible, though activists might encourage conscientious objection. In May of 1940 the four principal officers, and two group leaders, were charged and tried for incitement to disaffection in publishing a poster: 'WAR WILL CEASE WHEN MEN REFUSE TO FIGHT. WHAT ARE YOU GOING TO DO ABOUT IT?'[158] This was a symbolic warning; undertakings were given, the poster was withdrawn, and the defendants bound over to be of good behaviour. There were other isolated prosecutions of pacifists,[159] and a few pacifists were detained, most notably Ben Greene, but in his case not for pacifist activities.

There were also an uncertain number of cases in which propaganda against the war was a central factor in detention. One involved a Liverpool solicitor, George H. Stock, who was detained under an 'acts prejudicial' order of 16 September 1940.[160] He had formed his own Peace Front to oppose the war. The 'Reasons for Order' included the allegation that he had: 'since the war attempted to influence public opinion against the prosecution of the war by inciting persons to join the "Peace Front" and by other methods'. It also alleged association with disloyal persons now detained, attempts to communicate with Italian officials before the war with Italy began, encouraging conscientious objection, possession of pacifist literature, and interruptions to public meetings, sometimes by giving the fascist salute. The committee concluded that he was 'a capable man with strong streaks of crankiness and vanity, but they do not find anything subversive or disloyal about him'. His Peace Front had ceased to operate in April and he had not given the fascist salute; he was wrongly thought to be connected with the BU. He was released under conditions on 23 April 1941. Although he should never have been detained in the first place, his detention was not solely based on pacifist propaganda. Another marginal case is that of F. H. U. Bowman; he was detained because of suspicions of disloyal actions, but his continued detention was

---

[157] Colville, *Fringes of Power*, 263 (12 October 1940), PREM 4/39/4A.

[158] Alex Wood (Chairman), Stuart Morris (General Secretary), Maurice Rowntree (Treasurer), John Barclay (National Groups Organizer), Ronald Smith, and Sidney Todd. Wood was a physicist and Fellow of Emmanuel College, Cambridge. See S Morison, *I Renounce War: The Story of the Peace Pledge Union* (London, 1962), 45–9.

[159] For example Donald P. O'Byrne of the Croydon BU was prosecuted for distributing *Action* to soldiers (*Manchester Guardian*, 4 June 1940). The charge was for insulting behaviour; he also had a revolver and ammunition.

[160] HO 283/67. This does not include the Statement of the Case.

in fact recommended and maintained for his pacifist activities.[161] There were apparently other cases, and John Beckett's continued detention rested solely on his activities as a propagandist. As we shall see, the official theory came to be that it was legally improper to detain individuals merely for propaganda against the war, but this did not lead to the release of those who had been so detained.[162] Given the arsenal of offences for which propagandists could be put on trial, and the public nature of their activities, it is impossible to justify the use of 18B against such persons.

[161] HO 45/25729 and LCO 2/2712.
[162] See below, Ch. 17.

$\Longrightarrow$ 10 $\Longleftarrow$

It Might Have Happened to You!

The Crippling of the BU

In 1943, with finance from the Duke of Bedford, G. A. Aldred, a Glasgow anarchist, published a pamphlet under the title used for this chapter attacking 18B; it records the experience of detainees, and was mainly compiled by John Wynn, himself detained under 18B (1A) from June 1940 to January 1943.[1] Wynn, a schoolfriend of Richard Stokes MP, the principal critic of the regulation, had been an army officer and RFC pilot. He was managing director of Gyrotones Ltd. He was a friend of the anti-Semitic Harold Lockwood of Leese's IFL.[2] His pamphlet is the fullest contemporary account of 18B, and the claims made in it appear, so far as they can now be checked, to be reliable; I have used material from it as well as its title.

Olive Burdett, Norah Elam, Muriel Whinfield, and Diana de Laessoe had already been detained when thirty-seven more women were scheduled on the order of 30 May.[3] Mrs Beaumont of Freckenham was probably an error. A masseuse working for Elizabeth Arden, she was released after two months without coming before the committee.[4] Of the remainder two had been Parliamentary candidates,[5] three were Women's District Leaders,[6] and one was a temporary District Leader at Normanton.[7] Two were officials of some kind in Bournemouth.[8] Iris Ryder, active in the peace campaign, had been convicted in 1939 of defacing an air raid shelter notice.[9] Mrs Winifred Greenfield, wife of the

---

[1] One contributor was 'A Distinguished University Professor, Philosopher and BA (Oxon.)—himself still in detention', possibly S. F. Darwin-Fox. Detainees appear under initials, and I have used a key made by L. Grundy, a former BU detainee.

[2] HO 45/25717/840692.

[3] By 17 October a further 30 women had been detained.   [4] DOM 56, 3 August 1943.

[5] Mrs Alma V. Hudson, wife of Commander C. E. Hudson, the D/L at Bognor Regis, and Miss Louise A. King of Ipswich for Ilford. Mrs Hudson had three teenage children. HO 45/25754.

[6] Miss Florence E. Hayes of Bournemouth, Mrs Heather Donovan of Westminster District, and Miss C. E. M. Cornes of Leeds.   [7] Mrs Lister.

[8] Miss Elizabeth J. W. Griffin and Mrs Norah Pearson, the former probably being Treasurer; *Daily Telegraph*, 4 June.

[9] *Daily Herald*, 24 October 1939. Miss Griffin organized an appeal to pay her fine. She became housekeeper to the elderly Maj. and Mrs de Laessoe, after their release in 1943.

Headmaster of Poole Grammar School, also seems to have been an activist.[10] Mrs L. Temple Cotton was the mother of a prominent BU member, Rafe, a Parliamentary candidate and regional inspector for Devon, also detained.[11] Constance and Marjorie Clare were probably officials in Hove. Ruth Beckett was the wife of the detained boxer; she had a three-week-old baby, presumably detained with her.[12] Ann Good became Mosley's secretary after the war. The others were probably active members; by 1940 women had come to play an important part in keeping the party alive.

For the men the picture is much the same. Under the letter 'A' in my card index there are eleven names of BU detainees. The Revd Montague Yates-Allen is probably 'the Nazi parson' of Lord Denning's *Family Story*: 'Most of my work in Leeds was to detain people under Regulation 18B . . . As an instance I would tell of the "Nazi parson" in a village in Yorkshire. He often spent his holidays in Germany . . . Although there was no case against him, no proof at all, I detained him under 18B. The Bishop of Ripon protested, but we took no notice.'[13] Of Moss Vicarage in Doncaster, Yates-Allen was a prominent fascist, who joined Mosley in 1935; he also founded the Doncaster Branch of the Link.[14] Captain William F. Avery was a candidate and county propaganda officer for South Hants and Southampton.[15] Four appear to have been local officials.[16] The remaining five seem to have been ordinary members, presumably selected as active, though some may have well have been officials.[17] Those under letter 'B', forty-six in all, present much the same picture. Four were prominent fascists—Beckett the boxer,[18] Bellamy, Captain R. Gordon Berry,[19] and Captain C. H. Bentinck Budd, once very prominent in the movement but in 1940 an adjutant with the Royal

[10] *The Times*, 4 June.   [11] HO 45/25754, *Comrade*, 7, 19.

[12] *The Times*, 4 June and *Evening Standard*, 3 June.

[13] 130. Allen, however, did not live in a village and his Bishop was the Bishop of Sheffield, not Ripon. Denning was the legal adviser to the Regional Commissioner. HO 45/25114. HO 333/4 Home Office Circular 60/40 has a list of August 1940.

[14] A graduate of St Edmund Hall, Oxford; secretary of the Yorkshire Beekeepers Association; author of *European Bee Plants and their Pollen* (1938) and *Honey of Different Countries*. His daughter Betty was also detained (*News Chronicle*, 14 September).

[15] Of the Portsmouth BU; a drummer boy in the South African war; in the 1914–18 war promoted on the field of battle to commissioned rank for bravery; ended his days as a Chelsea Pensioner, dying in the 1970s.

[16] F. W. Antley (precise office not known), Frank Arbon, D/L Lincoln and later a litigant, Jack Austin, probably D/L East Bristol (he was an accountant who later became a Buddhist monk), and John R. Auther, D/L Barnet.

[17] W. Allen (of Manchester), Desmond Ambrose, John Archer, G. C. Arnold, and T. J. Ashworth Jones (of Tottenham).

[18] Beckett was no intellectual, and no doubt entirely patriotic; he was notably distressed in prison. He and his wife were released on 18 December 1940.

[19] Described as prominent in HO 45/25747; an error for R. Gordon-Canning. See below p. 215 n. 106.

Engineers at Colchester; we shall meet him as a litigant.[20] Also on active service was Pilot Officer Bates and H. T. Brock-Griggs,[21] with the RAF in Singapore when detained; their connection with the BU in 1940 is obscure. Twelve were officials.[22] One, Bisney, we have met.[23] W. E. Birch was a schoolmaster who had left the BU in 1936; his wife was of German origin and was detained as 'of hostile origin'. His detention was an error.[24] George Burrows[25] of Shrewsbury was serving with the RAF; his wife was pregnant and was arrested too, lodged in a police cell, began to haemorrhage, and lost her baby, being provided with inadequate medical attention.[26] It is hard to see how either could have been active members in June 1940. The remaining twenty-six, so far as available evidence goes, were ordinary members, but some were surely officials of one kind or another.

By the summer of 1940 the war had much reduced both the number of officials and the districts actually operating.[27] Mosley in *My Life* claimed that three out of four District Leaders, typically young, had joined up;[28] this may not be much overstated. For example in Croydon in 1938–9 there had been four districts, built up by one Leonard ('Jack') Capleton.[29] Three of the District Leaders were in the services in 1940, leaving Capleton, detained in June, to run all of Croydon.[30] Many ordinary members were also on war work. J. R. Auther, the 19-year-old District Leader of the Barnet District, had in 1940 only four members, Surtees in Lowestoft two.[31] My own list of districts which lost their district leaders

---

[20] Ch. 15 below.

[21] Before the war a Civil Servant and ordinary member of the Chelsea BU; presumably related to Anne Brock-Griggs. See *Comrade*, 7, HO 283/46 and Watts MS, 73.

[22] Eric Ball, Assistant D/L and speaker, J. L. Battersby, D/L Stockport, A. Beavan, D/L West Ham, Beer, D/L Folkestone, Clifford Beet, NHQ speaker, K. Bisney, Deputy Administrator NHQ, Birtwhistle, D/L (see memo in HO 45/25714 by Smeaton-Stuart), W. N. Bray, D/L or perhaps D/T Handsworth, George H. Brooksbank, AD/L, Charles Brown, D/L Wavertree, William C. Brown, D/L York, and A. F. Bull, D/L Brixton.

[23] See above p. 184.

[24] Smeaton-Stuart memorandum, HO 45/25714. After release he wrote the pamphlet *Suffer the Little Children*, published by the 18B Publicity Council.

[25] Or Borrows.

[26] *IMHHTY*, at 5 (Case of G. B.), arrested 22 June.

[27] I rely in part here on information from former members.

[28] O. Mosley, *My Life* (London, 1968), 402.

[29] *Comrade*, 17 as L. Capleton, also HO 45/25754. Employed in the Air Ministry, and aged 34 in 1940.

[30] Information from a former member.

[31] HO 45/25754 memo by Maxwell 30 September 1940. Information from Arthur W. Swan.

[32] Barnsley (Frith), Bethnal Green NE (Plaskett), Bethnal Green SW (Foley), Birmingham Handsworth (Bray), Blackpool (Howe), Bognor Regis (Hudson?), Bridgenorth (Instone), Brighton (Jeeves), Bristol? (Hewitt), Bristol? (Mountjoy), Bristol E. (Austin), Brixton (Bull), Bromley (Fowler), Camberwell (Hempel), Canterbury (Bellamy),

by detention totals sixty-nine.[32] It is certainly incomplete. But the arrest of even this number of local leaders would have had a serious effect on a party already in difficulty; the arrest of 750 officials, active members, and other supposed sympathizers was bound to be devastating. C. Cross, well-informed on the BU, thought as we have seen that the detainees 'represented almost the entire active membership', adding that those detained included 'some very small fry'.[33] In 1946 Lord Swinton put the same point more brutally in the House of Lords: 'As to the scum, quite rightly, we put lots of them inside at the critical time, but a good many of them did not matter very much.'[34] The detentions, and the fear they generated, effectively destroyed what was left of the party; its activities ceased, and it never revived. Anderson's brief had been to cripple the BU, and that is precisely what he had done.[35]

One documentable case illustrates both the fear caused by the initial detentions and the witch-hunting atmosphere of the times.[36] John Ellis was a considerable businessman in Leeds. He had joined the BU as a non-active member in 1935 or 1936, and had entertained Mosley during a speaking tour; he had attended two meetings since the war began, and disassociated himself when Holland was invaded. Being attracted by fascism, he possessed a quantity of BU literature, and texts of some of Hitler's speeches. Alarmed by the arrests in early June, and by police enquiries, he dumped this in a wood near Heversham, where it was found by the police. Ellis was also fascinated by weapons; he owned a number of sporting firearms—three .22 rifles, five shotguns, and three air powered weapons, and a .32 automatic. At this time control over firearms was far less strict than today; in particular .22 rifles were in no way special. He dumped some weapons and ammunition in another wood. The Chief Constable of Yorkshire believed that people like Ellis 'will do all in

Cheltenham (D'Alessio), Croydon (Capleton), Derby (Antley), Doncaster (Walter), Doncaster (Drury or Denton), Dorchester (Fitzgerald), Dorset W. (Saunders), Dorset N. (Wonfor), Dumfries? (Moffatt), East Ham (Osborne), Edinburgh (Thompson), Epping (Pelling), Exeter (Forward), Eye (Creasy), Folkestone (Beer), Gloucester (George), Halifax (Russell), Harrogate (Lister), Horsham (Nightingale), Huddersfield (Grundy), Hull E. (Danby), Hull (Charnley), Islington (Shepherd), Kidderminster (Jermy), King's Lynn (Ilett), Kingston on Thames (Danby or more probably Nickolls), Lancaster (Eaton), Leeds Branch unknown (Wood), Leeds Silvertown (West), Limehouse (Mason), Liverpool (Gill), Lincoln (Wilkinson), Liverpool Wavertree (Brown), Lowestoft (Surtees), Luton (Jessup), Manchester Prestwich (Ferris), Manchester (Burns?), Northampton (Farmer), Ossett (Teale), Reigate (Clifford), Richmond on Thames (Scott), Rotherham (Day), Shoreditch (Flockhart), Sheffield (Hamley), Slough (Elliott), Southport (Jones), Stockport (Battersby), Tottenham (Steele), Uxbridge (Dye), West Ham (Beavan), Westminster Abbey (Saunders), Willesden (Keller), York (Brown), Yorkshire somewhere (Downing).

[33] *The Fascists in Britain* (London, 1961), 132 and 195. But see p. 131 n. 79 above.
[34] *Parl. Deb.* HL Vol. 140 c. 55.
[35] Hinsley and Simkins, 61–2 and 79.
[36] HO 45/25726, HO 283/33. Ellis was released on a list of 28 September.

their power to further the cause of the British Union, in an endeavour to establish Mosley as Dictator' and procured his detention, but failed to have his wife, not a BU member, detained as well. The police case, set out by E. B. Stamp of MI5, put a grave interpretation on the matter. Thus his company had been engaged in cleaning military uniforms: 'it is strongly suspected that he is doing this for an ulterior purpose, because in the event of an invasion, he would have a considerable quantity of British uniforms in his possession.' The fact that his business included motor transport could also be given a sinister interpretation. The committee, chaired by J. W. Morris (later Lord Morris of Borth-y-Gest), recommended release: though he had indeed been an enthusiastic fascist, he was entirely loyal. Morris stuck to this decision in spite of opposition from MI5; the Home Office agreed. Lord Harlech, the Regional Commissioner, expressed alarm and bewilderment: 'There is, as you are perhaps aware, an underground fascist organization in this region.' Ellis, Lord Harlech claimed, had possessed sinister marked maps of the coast—in fact even the police report found nothing sinister about them. Maxwell minuted on the file: 'This is an illustration of how exaggerated and inaccurate statements are prompted by the natural instinct for discovering "spies".' He wrote to Harlech pointing out that members of the BU could be perfectly loyal, and that legitimate anxieties over Ellis had been set at rest; it was not the policy to detain such people. But the arrest of people like Ellis no doubt increased fear and effectiveness of the operation.

Another documentable case involved a medical student, Henry A. Steidelman, detained in late July not so much as a BU supporter but as a pro-Nazi and potential spy.[37] Here the grounds for suspicion were stronger. He had been active in the London University National Socialist Society, and became a District Leader. He was a friend of Norman Baillie-Stewart (alias James Hope), convicted of espionage in 1933, and from 1937 in Germany.[38] Steidelman visited him and had been in contact with Marianne Emig, secretary to Herman Goertz, convicted of espionage in Britain in March 1936.[39] MI5 thought Steidelman acted as a courier, and two fellow medical students gave evidence which initially seemed to confirm the case against him. In February 1941 the committee recommended release, and after a second hearing his order was suspended in May 1941, though his name remained on the invasion list until 18 March 1944. Had he been warned and left at liberty he would surely have kept clear of politics, though it is conceivable that MI5 was right in their suspicions of his loyalty.

[37] HO 45/25735, 283/66.
[38] References in the file to 'unrestrained indulgence' suggest sexual misconduct. On Baillie-Stewart see also N. West, *MI5* (London, 1983), 100–10.
[39] West, *MI5*, 114, CRIM 1/813.

Errors, Mistakes, and Inconsistencies

Steidelman's case did not involve a crude mistake. Nor did that of Ellis; there were grounds for suspicion. That crude mistakes were made, so that persons who had nothing or virtually nothing to do with the BU were arrested, cannot be doubted. How many such cases there were it is quite impossible to say. One indicator is the number of those released without appearing before the committee at all. Up to the end of 1940 there were ninety-eight such releases. But sixty-seven were Anglo-Italians who were set free when the minimum age for detention was raised to 18. The remaining thirty-one were cases where, in the words of the file, release was ordered on the basis of 'suspicions explained to S. of S.'[40] Some would be blunders, sometimes brought to light by letters of protest to the Home Office.[41] Such letters, of which there must have been many thousands, have been almost wholly weeded from surviving files.

J. R. Smeaton-Stuart, himself detained by the order of 30 May, and released on 16 November 1940, wrote a 'Report on the Functioning of Regulation 18.B of the Defence Regulations (1939)'. He sent it to the maverick Earl Winterton MP for use in the Commons debate of 10 December.[42] In January Winterton sent it to the Home Office: 'I am very concerned at the allegations made in this document, as if they are only half true they constitute, in my opinion, a serious state of maladministration.'[43]

Born in Singapore, Smeaton-Stuart served in the Army in the First World War, and then farmed in Kenya for ten years, where he lost all his money; he drifted about the Empire and in 1934 joined the party in a spirit of disillusion typical of the period. The country was going to the dogs. He became a paid area organizer and election agent for East Anglia, and a candidate for Southend. In 1937 he quarrelled with Mosley and left the BU to join the Norfolk Conservative Party. On release he was excluded from Norfolk, where his home was; he was no doubt outraged at the way he had been treated.

He complained that simple errors had been made. Thus he mentions N. Headley, a schoolmaster; and George Wilkins of Middleton, neither of whom were or ever had been members; and one Sawyer of Wrentham in Suffolk, who happened to be a friend of Surtees, the District Leader in Lowestoft;[44] P. Love DFC, a works manager and former RFC 'ace' in

[40] HO 45/25115 sf. 14.
[41] e.g. *Parl. Deb.* HC. Vol. 367 c.845 (woman detained on 5 July and thought to be in the Right Club, released on 23 August without an appearance).
[42] Ibid. 367: 836ff.
[43] In HO 45/25714/840452; see also HO 283/64 and TS 27/493 (he later litigated).
[44] Arthur W. Swan, Treasurer at Lowestoft, has confirmed that Sawyer was entirely unconnected with the party.

No. 1 Squadron, who had never been a member, though he shared a house with someone who was, and had an academic interest in fascism; and Gore, released without appearing before the committee at all, whose brother was a member.

As well as mistakes, some revealed in litigation,[45] there were some quite absurd arrests. One incident has passed into detainees' folklore as symbolizing fascist patriotism. It involved Eric Hamilton-Piercy and Colin P. Dick. Hamilton-Piercy had been with the 'biff boys' in the New Party, and then became a founder member of the BU and commander of the tough 'I' squad. He left the party in 1936 when it was disbanded. Dick, a wealthy businessman supporter, appears to have still been a member in 1940; he had worked with NHQ before the war. They were on the Thames in the motor launch *Advance* when the call came for the little boats to sail to Dunkirk. On their return from the beaches, with the vessel damaged by machine-gun fire, both were detained. They were released immediately after appearing before the committee in August of 1940.[46]

Smeaton-Stuart and others also complained of inconsistencies. Of eighteen members in Lincoln all were detained, whereas, according to Smeaton-Stuart, of the 153 members of the King's Lynn District the police arrested a mere five men and one woman, in addition to two men who were not members at all.[47] In Lowestoft there were in May 1940 two members, Surtees and Arthur W. Swan.[48] Both were arrested, along with the unfortunate Sawyer.[49] But of the fifty-six members of Robert Saunders's district only he and three other individuals seem to have been detained. In Lancaster, where relations with the police were good, only two members were detained, and no great effort was made to identify others.[50] In Birmingham, where the BU ran five districts, only two members were detained in early June, though an uncertain number of other individuals were later arrested there.[51] In Manchester there were several districts 'but the odd position was that some D.L.s and active members were not arrested at all (we always assumed that this was due to the local police attitude)'.[52] Some districts, such as Battersea, appear to have escaped

[45] See below Ch. 14.
[46] Accounts in *IMHHTY*, 7; Cross, *Fascists in Britain*, 195, *Comrade*, 13, Bellamy MS iii., the Duke of Bedford's *Is This Justice? An Examination of Regulation 18B* (Glasgow, 1943), 17, HO 45/25714, Rowe MS, 3. They are said to have ferried some 450 soldiers.
[47] HO 45/25714; the police obtained a list. In the Stokes Papers, Box 13 there is a memo by Oswald Hickson citing King's Lynn as an example of inconsistency. Stannard, a working man, Wilkin, a postman, and Potter, a lorry driver, were detained, whereas Viscountess Downe, the Parliamentary candidate, was not.
[48] The peak membership had been 17.
[49] Letter of 18 December from Arthur Swan.
[50] Robert Row and William Eaton. Information from Mr Row.
[51] They were S. L. Irvine and T. P. Moran. Irvine's fiancée, Miss C. L. Fisher, who was a W D/L, was not detained until November. Information from Mr and Mrs Irvine.
[52] Letter from Robert Row of 5 November 1989.

completely.[53] Police intelligence could be quite out of date. Thus J. A. Williams's father, who had ceased to be an active member, was detained with his son on Tyneside, where the police officer concerned, though very correct in his behaviour, was strongly opposed to the BU. Of two sisters, Dorothy and Margaret, the former as an active member 'was all prepared to "pack a small bag"—but no, it was Margaret they took away'. She had been active in the south of England, but on moving to Tyneside had become non-active for business reasons.[54]

Allegations of Discrimination

Smeaton-Stuart also made graver allegations:

it is remarkable that several very important officials were never arrested. Among these the following were not arrested:—Messrs Hillman, Garnet and Symes all of whom held high posts and Colonel Sharpe and Mr Hughes (alias Captain P. G. Taylor of MI5) voluntary or unpaid members of the headquarters staff of the B.U. Prospective candidates whose names had been published in the Press: Viscountess Downe, Commandant Mary Allen, Lady Pearson, Sir Lionel Berkley Hore Haworth,[55] Admiral Powell (who was also a District Leader)[56] and Major General Fuller who was a member of the Directorate of Policy. Also if Ex-members were to be included why was Major Sir Jocelyn Lucas, Bart., MP excused?[57]

He also claimed that 'Detainees of means and influence receive priority of interrogation and or release', naming Lady Pearson, Mrs Sherston,[58] and Basil Miller,[59] contrasting them with the less important people who remained in prison.

There is little direct evidence, but some initially suspicious cases have an innocent explanation. Thus 'Mr Hughes' (P. G. Taylor) was an MI5 agent; Sharpe and Hillman were not involved with the BU in 1940, the aged Adm. Powell had resigned as District Leader in Portsmouth in 1939 since he was on the Royal Navy Reserve of Officers.[60] Symes, who had

---

[53] Information from J. Warburton.   [54] Information from J. A. Williams.

[55] Sir Lionel, formerly Indian Civil Service, was candidate for Chelsea; he was inactive.

[56] 1871–1952. Vice-Adm. G. B. Powell CMG had a distinguished naval record; he was candidate at Portsmouth Central.

[57] Portsmouth S. 1939–66; he had worked as assistant to Sir Henry Page Croft MP. *Who's Who* records he had 'hunted several packs of hounds'; his main interest was pedigree dog breeding. A Special Branch report in HO 144/21281 shows him involved with the NSL and the BCAEC.

[58] Presumably the wife of 2nd Lt. W. E. Sherston, also detained. Both brought *habeas corpus* proceedings in 1940. She appears to have been released by October 1940; he remained in detention until 1943 (Saunders Papers). He was a wealthy Old Etonian; he farmed from Otley Hall, Ipswich. An admirer of Nazi Germany, but revelations of Nazi atrocities led him to reject fascism; he became interested in wildlife conservation, and was a friend of the late Peter Scott.

[59] An acting Pilot Officer in the RAF (HO 45/25727).   [60] Mosley in HO 283/13.

had been a pilot in the First World War and involved in the fascist flying club movement, had been a National Inspector in 1939, but he ceased to be active on the outbreak of war; he may have co-operated with MI5 in its attempts to discover the source of BU funds.

The escape of the bizarre and conceited busybody 'Commandant' Mary Allen OBE is, however, documented.[61] A former suffragette, and erroneously supposed to be a police officer, she had run her own uniformed voluntary organization, the Women's Auxiliaries Service, defunct in 1940.[62] She mixed in right-wing circles, and had joined the BU in 1939; an article of hers attacking 'the modern undisciplined female' appeared in *Action* on 23 May. She attended some of the 'secret meetings', and had been a friend of Margaret Bothamley, who was working for the Germans in 1940. There was considerable public demand for her arrest.[63] In 1940 she had holed up with her companion Miss Helen B. Tagart and miscellaneous dogs, in an isolated cottage in the Red River valley near Nancledra in Cornwall; local rumours inevitably suggested she was up to no good. The Chief Constable of Cornwall and Special Branch wanted her detained. Newsam minuted: 'Whether or not Miss A. is really dangerous, her detention would allay a great deal of uneasiness which is felt in many quarters.' But Aikin-Sneath opposed this, since there was no evidence of activity since Mosley's arrest. Anderson's minute reads: 'The woman is good at self advertisement and I dislike her and all her works, but I have never yet felt convinced that she is really dangerous.' By way of compromise an order was made but suspended on condition that she went into a sort of village arrest, without car, telephone, or wireless set. There was nothing at all sinister about her escape; the Home Office can only be faulted for supposing that anyone so silly required to be controlled at all.[64]

The immunity of Dorothy, Viscountess Downe, former Lady-in-Waiting to Queen Mary, and her friend,[65] and of Lady Pearson[66] raise suspicions. Both were prominent fascists. Pearson was the sister of Brig. Sir Henry Page Croft MP, Parliamentary Under-Secretary for War in 1940. She was the BU candidate for Canterbury, and was indeed arrested under Regulation 18D but released under a restriction order. It is said that her brother angrily approached Anderson directly. Her agent,

[61] HO 144/21933.

[62] In 1914 she had formed a voluntary women's police force, and after the war had operated in Ireland and the Rhineland. She masqueraded as a police officer when abroad.

[63] For example the *Daily Mirror* on 28 April 1940.

[64] Some documents remain closed; perhaps they contain informants' reports.

[65] Candidate for North Norfolk. On 10 December Stokes referred to her as a notorious fascist and friend of Queen Mary. *Parl. Deb.* HC. Vol. 367 c.845.

[66] Lady (Susanna) Grace Pearson was the widow of the contractor, Sir Edward Pearson (d. 1925). See HO 45/25747.

Bellamy, was detained, as was her secretary, Mrs de Grey Whitham, as well as other minor Canterbury fascists.[67]

The most puzzling case mentioned by Smeaton-Stuart is that of Major-General J. H. C. ('Boney') Fuller: his immunity must have been the result of a deliberate decision, but no papers are available.[68] His relationship with Mosley in 1940 is obscure, but he had been prominent in the constitutional reorganization of the BU before the war.[69] He had attended Hitler's birthday celebrations as recently as May of 1939. An associate of extreme right-wingers, and in the Nordic League, he was violently anti-Semitic, and admired the Nazis.[70] He attended some of the 'secret meetings' in 1939 and 1940; he continued during the war to publicize his desire for a negotiated peace with impunity. Diana Mosley records his wife as saying at the time: 'They'll never arrest Boney. He knows too much.'[71] The reference could be to knowledge about right-wing connections, in particular those associated with the paper *Truth* and the Swinton Committee. Perhaps he was suspected of being the military organizer of the underground BU; it would then have been wiser to leave him at large under surveillance than to detain him. Fuller undoubtedly had supporters in military circles, including General Ironside, which may have helped.

There were others whose immunity caused comment, such as Air Commodore Sir J. A. Chamier, who was a known BU supporter; he became Commandant of the Air Training Corps.[72] There had been 118 nominated Parliamentary candidates.[73] Forty-four only were detained.[74]

---

[67] See *Parl. Deb.* HC. Vol. 362 c.1011, when Anderson denied discrimination. Her brother in his autobiographical *My Life of Strife* [London, 1946], makes no reference to the incident or to his sister's politics.

[68] His biographer can give no reason; A. J. Trythall, *'Boney' Fuller: The Intellectual General 1878–1966* (London, 1977), 215. On the invasion list. Home Office file destroyed.

[69] Cross, *Fascists in Britain*, 140.

[70] He wrote 'The Cancer of Europe' in the *Fascist Quarterly* for 1935 (65). See Thurlow, *Fascism in Britain: A History, 1918–1985* (Oxford, 1987), 80, 131, 158, 181; and R. Griffiths, *Fellow Travellers of the Right: British Enthusiasts for Nazi Germany 1933–9* (London, 1980), esp. 314 and 324. He published in *Truth* in November 1939 a piece denying allegations about German concentration camps.

[71] *A Life of Contrasts: The Autobiography of Diana Mosley* (London, 1977), 172.

[72] L. Wise in *Mosley's Blackshirts*, 6 (see above, Ch. 7 n. 55).

[73] W. F. Mandle lists 102 in 'The Leadership of the British Union of Fascists', *Australian Journal of Politics and History*, 12 (1966) 360. There were also Mary Allen, Doreen Bell, M. G. Clarke, Lady Pearson, Olive Hawks (Burdett), Miss M. Barrington, Miss Sylvia Morris, Miss L. A. King, L. E. Cameron-Walker, Mrs Anne Brock-Griggs, Norah Elam, L. M. Reeve, Dorothy Countess Downe, Mrs Muriel Whinfield, F. C. Fane, and R. N. Creasy.

[74] In addition to those detained on 23 May they were Sidney Allen, Capt. W. F. Avery, A. A. Beavan, C. H. Bentinck-Budd, J. W. Charnley, R. Temple Cotton, J. Dowty, W. G. Eaton, F. C. Fane, R. N. Creasy, Capt. R. C. Gordon-Canning, Capt. F. Haslam, C. H. W. Hewitt, J. H. Hone. Commander C. E. Hudson, A. E. Ilett, R. Gladwyn Jebb, F. Jorian Jenks, R. Jones, B. F. Lister, T. P. Moran, J. N. P. Mountjoy, R. R. Bellamy, J. Sant, W. E. Sherston, J. R. Smeaton-Stuart, and E. P. C. Whinfield (detained in January 1940). Mosley in

But many had ceased to be active or had resigned.[75] Joyce and Bruning were in Germany in 1940, and the Earl of Erroll was about to be murdered in Kenya.[76]

It is noticeable, however, that lists of 'prominent persons' detained, supplied to Churchill, include hardly any top people.[77] Only the Mosleys, Ramsay, the Domviles, George Henry Lane-Fox Pitt-Rivers, and Prince Henry of Pless really count as such.[78] There were numerous people in the upper echelons of British society who had very right-wing sympathies, or thought the real enemy was Russia; some found a home in the Conservative Party, and thus were identified with legitimate politics; an example is Lord Brockett. Many others would have no formal association with the BU or indeed any other political group. There were also wealthy backers of the BU who were either secret members, or not members at all. By discretion once the war came, or by involvement in patriotic activities, such as joining the Home Guard,[79] they did not attract the attention of MI5, which was in any event swamped by work; deference to the upper classes may have had some influence. Some may have been discreetly moved from responsible positions; thus the *New York Times* on 21 August 1940 reported that the 8th Duke of Buccleugh had been removed from the post of Steward of the Royal Household on 10 May because of his far-right sympathies. And the public message was that status was no protection. Thus the *Evening Standard* reported on 8 August the arrest of Miss Joyce Tregear, a society lady, the daughter of Lieutenant-Colonel and Mrs F. C. Tregear of Forres, who had filmed as Lilian Bell, and the *Mirror* on 6 June that of another society lady, Mrs Douglas Duff of Folkestone. This formidable widow of an officer of the 9th Lancers—she had left him because of his drunken habits—had explored in Tibet, acquired an air pilot's licence, and is said to have qualified as Able Seaman in one of Gustav Erikson's sailing barques.[80] No doubt conditions in Holloway would have seemed luxurious in comparison to those which obtained on the futtock shrouds of *Moshulu* or *Pamir*.

My Life claims that the BU holder of the VC was never detained; I have not identified him. A. C. E. Hudson, a former army officer, held the VC, DSO, and MC but the Hudson in the BU was a former naval officer.

[75] For example the Catholic C. F. Wegg Prosser, who became a member of the Labour Party (see Cross, *Fascists in Britain*, 173–4). F. H. Lawton, a barrister and later a High Court judge, had joined the armed services and apparently distanced himself from the party before this. W. J. Leaper, a journalist, left the party in 1936. W. H. Symes was no longer active; A. K. Chesterton resigned active membership in 1938.

[76] See J. Fox, *White Mischief* (London, 1982).   [77] See below p. 214.

[78] HO 45/25747. On Pless see Note to the Paperback Edition above.

[79] As did Lord Redesdale, who had joined the Right Club in 1939.

[80] Bellamy MS iii. at 34. Mr Eric Newby thinks it more probable that she was a passenger who worked with the crew. In detention she was represented by Oswald Hickson; see HO 45/25758; she had joined the BU after the war began.

The Duke of Bedford

The only peer considered for arrest, so far as we know, was the Duke of Bedford; he was never connected with the BU, though he sympathized with its foreign policy and attitude to the war.[81] Hugely self-important, he went out of his way to seek publicity for his views. In June 1940 his name arose in connection with that of Frederick H. U. Bowman, an eccentric militant pacifist, who claimed to be an actor. Bowman had become friendly with Enrico Tona, the Italian Consul in Liverpool, and also had contacts with Bedford over the Tavistock Peace Proposals. His home was raided, and a plan, thought relevant to the defences of the Mersey Tunnel, was found. He was charged with improper possession of this document.[82] The Director of Public Prosecutions wanted Tavistock questioned, presumably as his involvement was suspected.[83] MI5 had no objection; Newsam agreed, but Maxwell was nervous. After he had talked to the Director—what was said went unrecorded—the charges were dropped and Bowman was detained.[84] Conceivably Maxwell feared some form of scandalous exposure, perhaps of others in high places, or political trouble in the House of Lords.

The Duke's own internment was considered in December 1940, and again from June 1941.[85] He had corresponded with Morrison, the Home Secretary, over propaganda he had published, distinguishing those who were disloyal, who would help the enemy in the event of an invasion, and those who, like himself, would simply try to obtain better terms from the invader; this he thought patriotic. A paper by Morrison of 14 November pointed out that previously those detained for 'acts prejudicial' were thought guilty of criminal offences, but could not be tried because the evidence was either inadequate, or could not be revealed in public.[86] Could it also be used against those who had merely made statements 'highly prejudicial to the defence of the realm', such as the Duke:

He advocates a negotiated peace with Hitler, and in his propaganda combines pacifist opinions with defeatism and pro-Nazi opinions. He blames the government for the policy which led to war; he finds excuses for Hitler and refrains from any disapproval of Nazi acts, he suggests that an Allied victory is unlikely, and that a negotiated peace is the only way of saving the country from ruin.

---

[81] He succeeded on 12 August 1940.   [82] Regulation 3 (3) (c).
[83] Under Regulation 80A.
[84] HO 45/25729. Tavistock's Home Office file, which could still exist, is 840773.
[85] See HO 45/25747, CAB 65/19 WP (41) 267, 14 November, CAB 65/20 WM (41) 115, 17 November, and Hinsley and Simkins, 62 n.
[86] It instances members of the IRA, those who had tried to obtain secret information, had contacted the enemy, been involved in sabotage, or tried to slow production.

Morrison thought he could be detained for 'acts prejudicial'; to Maxwell his case was indistinguishable from that of Beckett, who had been detained. The fact that he could easily have been prosecuted after a warning receives no mention in the papers.

But Somervell, the Attorney-General, advised that 'great difficulties might arise if we were to intern the Duke of Bedford merely because of his propaganda activities'.[87] His argument was that back in 1939, under Parliamentary pressure, the original Regulation 39B had been withdrawn; it had made it an offence to endeavour, whether orally or otherwise, to influence public opinion in a manner likely to be prejudicial to the defence of the realm or the efficient prosecution of the war. Hence peace propaganda became legal, unless covered by the modified 39B—which, it was conceded, did not catch the Duke—or unless covered by Regulation 2C, which required a warning prior to prosecution. It would be improper, and indeed illegal, to detain the Duke under 18B for acts which had been made lawful in 1939. A court, he argued somewhat implausibly as we shall see, might even release such a person in habeas corpus proceedings. In the event the Duke was not detained, nor was he proceeded against under Regulation 2C; it is said he was warned but this is not likely.

Somervell was a somewhat devious lawyer; his opinion may merely have served to excuse action thought imprudent on some other ground. Deference may have played a part, and the Duke was a member of the Lords. Roberts in his life of Lord Halifax records that letters sent to him from the lower orders expressing anti-war or pro-Nazi sentiments were sent to Special Branch; more exalted correspondents received courteous consideration.[88] Certainly some less exalted individuals were detained for propaganda activities without exciting Somervell's sympathies.[89]

Fascists in the Armed Services

A small number of those arrested were on active service; given belief in the Fifth Column, they were a particularly grave threat, though ironically most BU servicemen were left alone, since joining up could alternatively count as evidence of loyalty. The selection appears to have been largely random. Thus D. A. Gourdon, who had joined the BU in 1937 at the age of 17, enlisted in the Royal Artillery in May of 1938. He was posted to the BEF in France in 1939; he retained contact with members when on leave. He was evacuated from Dunkirk. On 22 July, now safe in England, he was detained by an order of 12 June, which had eventually caught up with

[87] The memo by Maxwell (6 January 1941) is in HO 45/25698.
[88] A. Roberts, 'The Holy Fox': A Biography of Lord Halifax (London, 1991), 152.
[89] See above pp. 198–9 and below p.370.

him.[90] We may contrast the case of W. A. Clarke.[91] About the time of
Dunkirk he was marched before his Colonel and Adjutant for 'a hell of a
grilling'. He was asked if he was a fascist:

I replied 'No, but I'm a member of British Union'. They wanted to know the difference. I replied that British Union was a British movement. They said 'But
you've dropped that now?' My reply was that I no more dropped my political
ideas than any Tory, Labour man, or Liberal in the Forces. However they let me
go'.[92]

There may have been quite a number of others less fortunate, but names
are hard to come by.[93] It is possible to be more certain about serving
officers arrested: Captain C. H. Bentinck Budd, Lieutenant Howard V.
Crisp,[94] and Second Lieutenant Dudley M. Evans, formerly District
Leader of Worthing, all of the Royal Engineers, Lieutenant Richard J. A.
Hamer of the South Wales Borderers, Lieutenant V. G. Tofts of the East
Surrey Regiment, Second Lieutenant William E. Sherston, Pilot Officer
Bates,[95] Acting Pilot Officer Basil Miller, and Squadron Leader Wallace
Thompson.[96] Robert Liversidge, whose case is more fully discussed later,
was also a serving officer in the RAF when arrested.

The Fascist Parsons

Another curious group consisted of parsons, of whom five were detained.
In addition to Denning's 'Nazi parson' there was the 67-year-old Revd H.
E. B. Nye, Rector of Scampton in Lincolnshire since 1935, and an enthusiastic fascist writer in *Action*. He was detained on 1 July, and all his
parishioners signed a petition for his release, which occurred, with the
blessing of MI5, on 25 August. He accepted his fate with Christian submission: 'I have no complaint against the government for their actions.
Although I am well known as a fascist there is not one single person in the
village of Scampton who knows what fascism means; I have never intro-

[90] Denis A. Gourdon MS given me by Mr J. Warburton. Gourdon remained in detention
until 12 April 1943. Joseph Gough of the Birmingham BU was also detained after Dunkirk;
see *Comrade*, 19.
[91] Letter of 6 October 1946, Saunders Papers.
[92] Another example is W. A. Clarke, who ran a fascist cell in the army; references in
Saunders Papers.
[93] Examples are J. Sant, E. T. Instone (BU autographs on 1 April 1941), Joseph Gouch
(after return from Dunkirk; *Comrade*, 19), Ernest Forge, a Corporal in the Welsh Regiment,
Penne of the East Yorks Regiment.
[94] Crisp had never been in the BU. After release he was prevented from rejoining the
army. *Parl. Deb.* HC Vol. 373 c.1778–9.
[95] Miller signed the BU autograph book on 5 October 1941. On Sherston see below, Ch.
14.
[96] Thompson or Thomson is listed in the week ending 27 July. Bellamy MS iii. 158 has
him as of the Barnet BU and as released at Huyton before the move to the Isle of Man.

duced politics from the pulpit.' Later, in 1948, he took a less kindly view: 'in 1940 the iniquitous 18B caused every known fascist to be rounded up . . . Some pitiful tragedies resulted from this indiscriminate severity, and I know of at least one clergyman who died shortly after release.' In fact Nye, who was chaplain to the well-known RAF base, had abandoned his activities in 1939 and, as he put it, regarded the war as 'just and inevitable'.[97] His arrest may have been connected with that of Squadron Leader Thompson, who was at Scampton in 1940 and was detained. The parson who died, in 1941, was the Revd H. S. Tibbs of Teigh Rectory near Oakham. Also detained were the Revd John V. Thomas, Vicar of Langton-by-Wragby, Lincoln BU,[98] the Revd G. H. Dymock, Vicar of St Bede's, Bristol,[99] and the Revd K. P. Scwabcher, Curate of St Marks, Plumstead.[100] A government even prepared to detain parsons was clearly likely to stop at absolutely nothing.

Churchill's Prominent Persons

Churchill took a lively interest in the great incarceration and received weekly lists of 'Prominent Persons' detained until 14 September 1940.[101] Names include Fay Taylour, who could have come straight from *Vile Bodies*, a racing driver and member of the Right Club,[102] and Christobel Nicholson, who had been involved with Tyler Kent.[103] Churchill was also informed of the detention of the former Brighton policeman, E. P. Jeeves,[104] and of some of the serving officers. Listed too was Mrs Bertha

---

[97] *Yorkshire Post* 28 August 1940, HO 283/45, BBDJ Archives 'Rogues Gallery'. After the war Nye went over to Rome and resigned his living. He wrote an account of his abandonment of fascism in the *Catholic Herald* for 7 May 1948, from which I have quoted.

[98] Noted in *Reynolds News* for 30 June. After the war he became a service chaplain.

[99] See *Comrade*, 19. He died in 1956.

[100] On the latter, who may have been detained as being of enemy origin, see the *Daily Herald* for 31 July 1940. R. Griffiths, *Fellow Travellers of the Right: British Enthusiasts for Nazi Germany 1933–9* (London, 1980), 175 n. 1, lists a number of parsons who supported BU—The Revds A. Palmer, E. C. Opie, M. Yate—Allen, and Ellis Roberts, and the eccentric Geoffrey H. Dymock. Palmer (of Brendon, Milverton), Opie (an Australian who worked with the Diocese of London), and Roberts (who was elderly) seem not to have been detained. The Revd Calverdale Sharpe, a Unitarian Minister associated with the far right, also escaped.

[101] HO 45/25747. See J. Colville, *The Fringes of Power: 10 Downing Street Diaries 1939–1955* (London, 1985), 177 (29 June 1940). PREM 4/39/1 has these lists but is closed.

[102] She may be seen winning the Ladies' Race at Brooklands at 98 mph in a video of 1931 currently available. She joined the BU during the war because of her opposition to it; see *Action*, 26 October 1939 (with photograph). She died in 1983.

[103] See above p. 154.

[104] He had been dismissed in December 1939; see *Action* for 21 December; after arrest on 4 June he was interrogated in Latchmere House. An informant tells me that another police officer, Bill Simons, of the Brixton BU, was detained; he belonged either to the City or Metropolitan Police. Jeeves was suspected of being an MI5 agent; after release he died by falling or being pushed off a train.

Colvin-Graham, described as an active fascist, the wife of a parson fined for innocently ringing his church bells, in ignorance of the ban on this activity,[105] and Captain Robert Gordon-Canning, misdescribed as Gordon Berry, who had been a close associate of Mosley but by 1940 was connected with the BPP.[106] Some names are intriguing: Mr D. M. K. Marendaz was noted as owning two aerodromes in Bedfordshire.[107] Formerly in the RFC, he ran a flying school and some weeks before his arrest had been fined for photographing an RAF training plane, no doubt entirely innocently. A friend of Mosley, he was known as the designer of the Marendaz Special sports car.[108] Then there was the mysterious Dr Jelic, the Croatian fascist, thought, as we have seen, to have been implicated in the assassination of King Alexander of Yugoslavia in Marseilles.[109] Giovanni Celeste Sperni was the former Mayor of St Pancras who had 'risen to his present position by a career of fraud and corrupt practice', and Prince Henry of Pless, described unfairly as a pro-Nazi, and a vast landowner in Poland.[109a] The lists also name Friedrich W. Braune, by birth German, who had practised law in England since 1912 and had been detained in the First World War; he was now suspected of involvement in the German spy ring. Soon released, he represented his fellow detainee Liversidge in the leading case on 18B.[110] Other prominent Anglo-Germans listed were Dr Otto B. Bode of the German Hospital in Dalston, earlier detained and released, and his wife Maria; he was to act as medical officer for detainees on the Isle of Man.

Two prominent names which do not appear in these lists are those of the author Henry Williamson, and the Arabist and explorer Harry St John B. Philby. Williamson, best known today outside literary circles for *Tarka the Otter*, was permanently affected by the horror of the First World War, in particular by the absurdity of the resumption of fighting after the Christmas truce of 1914. He attended the Nuremberg rally in

[105] By SRO 1940 No. 1042 of 19 June 1940.

[106] See Stokes Papers. Arrested on 12 July 1940 on a BU order; informed that he was detained as a prominent member of the BU and pro-Nazi; precise connection with the BU in 1940 uncertain; appeared before the committee on 28 August and again during November; informed of the decision to maintain detention on 29 January 1941; appeared again in May 1941 and undertook to abandon all political activity; he gained the impression that the committee would recommend release, but was told on 24 November that he would remain in detention. Gordon-Canning, who appears in *Who's Who* before the war as living at Sandwich Bay, appears in the 1942 edition married to Hélène Teresa Maguire of Melbourne; his child was born when he was in detention and he was allowed out to see it; this child died whilst he was in detention.

[107] One was at Barton.

[108] *Sunday Express*, 18 August 1940, *Comrade*, 27, *Classic Sportscar*, February 1989, *The Times*, 9 November 1989.

[109] See above Ch. 5 n. 69, J. W. Charnley, *Blackshirts and Roses* (London, 1990), 134–5. He is noted as a 'troublemaker' in TS 27/533.

[109a] On his exoneration see App. VI.   [110] See below, Ch. 17.

1935 and became an admirer of Hitler.[111] He joined Mosley as a potential saviour of society, and was a frequent contributor to *Action*. His autobiographical *The Phoenix Generation* (1965) presents Mosley as Sir Hereward Birkin. His *Solitary War* (1966) is again autobiographical, and is dedicated to the Mosleys.[112] It tells of his arrest and release by the police, as 'Phillip Maddison', in June 1940, under Regulation 18B (1A).[113] At this time Williamson was farming at Stiffkey in Norfolk.[114] It is more or less certain that Williamson was never detained, though he gave the impression that he had been; he was questioned because of local rumours that he was engaged in disloyal activities.[115] Afterwards he remained in Norfolk and may have suffered some local unpleasantness as a 'Nazi'.

Philby was a maverick individual, with left-wing political views; he certainly was detained, but Churchill's lists had by then been discontinued. Like Williamson, he had a horror of war, and as the European situation deteriorated made his views known; in consequence he was considered as a peace candidate for the PPU. Nothing came of this but, through Lord Tavistock, he contested the Hythe by-election as candidate for the BPP in July 1939, winning a mere 578 votes. He was supported by the BU, by the BPP, by the Domviles, and by the pro-Nazi Dr Meyrick Booth. John Beckett acted as his agent.[116] He returned to Arabia as adviser to Ibn Sa'ud, and made himself unpopular in British official circles by encouraging Arabs to keep out of the conflict. Having, with some difficulty, obtained permission from the British Minister in Jedda, he set out for the USA. Because he was suspected of planning to engage in anti-war propaganda there, and no doubt also because of the company he had kept at Hythe, he was arrested in India on 11 August, brought back to England, and detained, presumably for 'acts prejudicial'. After a four-hour appearance before the committee be was released unconditionally in late 1940 or early 1941.[117]

---

[111] In *The Flax of Dream* (London, 1936) he says 'I salute the great man over the Rhine, whose life symbol is the happy child', and in *The Phoenix Generation* (London, 1965) he is presented sympathetically. See Griffiths, *Fellow Travellers of the Right*, 134–7.

[112] Thus Lady Breckland is Lady Downe.   [113] Ch. 24.

[114] Obituary in *The Times*, 15 August 1977; Brocard Sewell, *Henry Williamson: The Man, the Writings. A symposium* (Padstow, Cornwall, 1980); L. Lamplugh, *A Shadowed Man: Henry Williamson 1895–1977* (Barnstaple, Devon, 1990); and an article in the *DNB* by R. Frere. Williamson's *Story of a Norfolk Farm* (London, 1941) carries the story to 13 June 1940, perhaps the date of arrest.

[115] See D. Farson, *Henry: An Appreciation of Henry Williamson* (London, 1982), 108–12.

[116] DOM 56, entries for 11 to 21 July.

[117] H. St J. B. Philby, *Arabian Days: An Autobiography* (London, 1948), ch. 9, gives an account. The 'particulars' included allegations that he had told the French minister in January 1940 that France would lose the war, that Ibn Sa'ud had expelled him, and that he aimed to raise money for peace propaganda. His claim was that he was going to the USA to be reunited with his family there. He wrote a fuller account of his experiences, which may survive. There is a *DNB* article by R. Wingate.

Churchill's Cousins

The first list included two cousins by marriage of Churchill. One was Diana Mosley, arrested on 29 June; given the option of taking her ten-week-old son with her into detention, she declined. Her arrest was welcomed in Beaverbrook's *Sunday Express*: 'Lady Mosley Arrested at Last'. The paper drew attention to her own and her sister Unity's friendship with Hitler, and referred to her marriage to Sir Oswald—'one of the most mysterious episodes in the life of the British Fascist leader'—in Hitler's private office in 1936 or 1937, and his being 'best man'.[118] It claimed that she was so fervent a Nazi that she taught her two sons by her former marriage to give the fascist salute. She had been kept under surveillance, her letters and telephone calls intercepted, in the hope, apparently vain, that information might be obtained about the underground BU. Lord Moyne, relying on his grandson's governess, reported that she held dangerous opinions; she was certainly a committed fascist and idolized her husband, but she played no part in the running of his party. MI5 requested her detention to prevent her acting as a go-between in attempts to keep the party going. There was apparently little substance in this, though she did try to ensure that BU staff were paid.[119] In any event all interviews were recorded. Essentially she was detained for being Mosley's loyal wife.

The other cousin was George Henry Lane-Fox Pitt-Rivers, a wealthy Dorset landowner. He was an appalling bore, with academic pretensions, who mixed in far-right circles, held racialist views, and was, understandably, thought to be pro-Nazi.[120] In *Who's Who* he gave his recreations as 'historical research and refuting politicians', and he claimed to have 'established the methodology of the science of eugenics, interactions of race, population and culture'; he was somewhere between eccentric and dotty. He knew Mosley, Joyce, and other right-wingers, and sympathized with their ideas; he had attended some 'secret meetings'. Though detained under an 18B (1A) order, he had never been a member of the BU, nor was it suggested he had been; he had run his own Wessex Agricultural Defence Association, which opposed tithes, and espoused corporatism. The committee before which he appeared in November 1940 pointed out that the grounds given for his detention could not be maintained, but recommended his continued detention, essentially because of the intense antagonism which his views were likely to cause if he had been released;

---

[118] In fact October 1936.

[119] HO 144/21995 sf. 2. There is an account of her detention in *A Life of Contrasts*, ch. 17, and *Loved Ones: Pen Portraits by Diana Mosley* (London, 1985), Appendix.

[120] 1890–1966. A grandson of General Pitt-Rivers; educated Eton and Worcester College, Oxford; served in the Dragoon Guards and was severely wounded.; for a while ADC to the Governor-General of Australia.

after patiently tolerating his ramblings for two days, Birkett and his colleagues thought that 'Captain Pitt-Rivers could not be described as normal'. In January 1941 release was recommended on the basis of
undertakings of good behaviour, but he was not in fact set free until 1942.
He was one of those who litigated.[121]

The appearance of these two cousins in the Home Office lists may have
brought home to Churchill the reality of the action he had supported—
the detention of the beautiful and charming Diana Mosley, whom he
knew well, and her separation from husband and children, and that of the
bizarre Pitt-Rivers, whom Clementine at least would know was both
harmless and dotty.[122]

Admiral Sir Barry Domvile

Apart from the Mosleys and Ramsay, the most notable name supplied to
Churchill was that of Admiral Sir Barry E. Domvile.[123] Born in 1878, the
son of Admiral Sir Compton Domvile, he had spent forty-four years in
the Royal Navy. Assistant Secretary to the Committee of Imperial
Defence before the First World War, he then commanded destroyers and
cruisers in the Harwich force. After the war he became Director of Plans,
and from 1922 to 1925 Chief of Staff to the Commander of the
Mediterranean Fleet. After commanding the battleship *Royal Sovereign*
he became Director of Naval Intelligence, and then commanded the
Third Cruiser Squadron. Appropriately loaded with decorations and
orders he retired as Admiral in 1936. In 1937 he founded the Link.[124] The
Link, disbanded in 1939, had around 4,000 members, some being fascists
and admirers of Hitler.[125] The national council included pro-Nazis such
as Professor A. P. Laurie and Professor Sir Raymond Beazley. Domvile
mixed in anti-Semitic and pro-German circles, and was himself an
admirer of Hitler.[126] He had visited Germany in 1935 and been feted; he
liked Himmler.[127] He was an invited guest at the Nuremberg Nazi Party

---

[121] TS 27/514.

[122] Colville, *Fringes of Power*, 29 June, describes Churchill as being 'piqued', and incorrectly says that Pitt-Rivers was Mosley's second in command.

[123] His Home Office file, which exists, was 840680, and his Special Branch reference was
320/EPA/4977. See also TS 27/491, and his *From Admiral to Cabin Boy* (London, 1947 but
completed 1943), with an introduction by Capt. Cuthbert Reavely, former BU and a 'steward' of the Right Club.

[124] Domvile, *From Admiral to Cabin Boy*, 64. Domvile had been on the Council of the
Anglo-German Fellowship.

[125] See Griffiths, *Fellow Travellers of the Right*, esp. 179–82, 277–9, 306–17.

[126] Many entries in his diary confirm this, and indicate his close association with representatives of the German government and Nazi Party in London and Germany. For example on 1 September 1938, the birthday of the Link: 'Have a very nice letter from Himmler.'

[127] He describes his visit in ch. 10 of his autobiography *By and Large* (1936).

rally in September of 1936. In 1939 he visited Salzburg from 10 July to 7 August, a visit attracting criticism.[128] In the same year he and his wife were prominent in support of Philby at Hythe; she joined the BPP but soon deserted it and rejoined the BU. Domvile attended some of the 'secret meetings' in 1939 and 1940, and was admitted on 23 January to the 'inner circle' of the BU of which he was probably already a secret member.[129] To judge, however, from his rather strange diaries his principal interest was walking his three dogs, over whom he had virtually no control.

Domvile was detained on 7 July for 'acts prejudicial'; his wife Alexandrina,[130] and one of his sons, Compton, were also detained,[131] as was Caroll, Secretary of the Link. Admiral Nicholas Wolkoff, Anna's father, was detained about the same time, perhaps because of involvement with Domvile.[132] Domvile remained in detention in Brixton Prison as a 'Leader' until 29 July 1943. Given his naval record, it is hard to think of him as a disloyal person, but he had come to develop aberrant political views. According to his own account, it was during the First World War when he was working in the Admiralty under Churchill that he began to have 'a strong suspicion that there was some mysterious Power at work behind the scenes controlling the actions of the figures visibly taking part in the government of the country'.[133] Anyone who has worked in a large organization will know the feeling, which normally passes. Domvile, however, came to the conclusion that this was 'Judmas'—'the Judaeo-Masonic combination, which has wielded such a baneful influence in world history'. It is likely that Domvile only fully adopted this theory whilst in detention, when he spent long periods in solitary confinement.[134] He even came to believe that Regulation 18B had been 'clearly outlined' in the Protocols of the Learned Elders of Zion'.[135] A letter to Ramsay in 1948 says that he had learnt from Arcand, the Canadian fascist, that it was indeed Roosevelt who had ordered the detentions under 18B; this fitted everything Domvile knew.[136] Before the war, though an admirer of Hitler, he seems merely to have shared the sort of

---

[128] *The Times*, 8 August 1939. He attributed adverse publicity to the work of Lt.-Col. Hinchley-Cooke of MI5, who was part-German. See DOM 56, 8 August.

[129] DOM 56.

[130] He called her 'Pudd'. She was born in 1895, the daughter of Baron Eduard Van de Heydt.

[131] There were two other children, of whom one was killed on active service. Compton had apparently been a merchant navy officer.

[132] The report of Domvile's arrest, dated 11 July, is in TS 27/491.

[133] *From Admiral to Cabin Boy*, 14.

[134] At 81 he says he decided this 'only in recent years', that is in the 1940s.

[135] *From Admiral to Cabin Boy*, 64.

[136] Letter of 20 October 1948 in Britons' Archives.

anti-Semitic views no doubt then common in the officer class of the Navy; it is, however, possible that his paranoia had already begun to develop.

When Domvile was arrested by Inspector Keeble many papers were seized, including diaries going back to 1916, the most recent from 8 November 1938 to 2 January 1939; Keeble correctly suspected that he had hidden his current diary.[137] Special Branch had obviously been told to search 'in regard to wireless and broadcasting matters' but found nothing apart from two slips of paper bearing a short rhyme which was thought suspicious, of which I can make nothing.[138]

The basis for Domvile's 'acts prejudicial' order is not certainly known.[139] He had long been of interest to MI5. His diary for 6 January 1939 records that 'A nice young man called Coart brought me a book from Pitt-Rivers'; 'Coart' would be Harald Kurtz, who used, but presumably could not pronounce the name 'Court', and was one of Maxwell-Knight's agents, whom we shall meet again. The timing of Domvile's arrest is significant. On 5 July, as we have seen, Olive Baker was sentenced to five years at Bristol Assizes. She features a great deal in his diary, and it is significant that Domvile knew at once of her arrest, which he recorded. An informant tells me that Domvile had a 'pro-Nazi' mistress, and she is the most likely candidate; his married life was such that he recorded on 22 November 1939: 'Slept with Pudd for the first time for a long time. She felt lonely.'[140] On Olive's arrest he called her a 'silly little ass', and on her conviction 'poor little fool', perhaps for being caught. At her trial a letter from Domvile was read out, the gist of which was that Ramsay's Parliamentary question on the NBBS in March 1940 was a clever ruse to advertise the wavelength of the station. The police report of his arrest indicates that the authorities were principally interested in illicit broadcasting; a Mr A. M. Abrams from the BBC was in attendance. Indeed one

[137] These and other papers suggested associations with the Mosleys, the Ramsays, Norman Hay, Commandant Mary Allen, Mrs Whinfield, Mrs Huth Jackson, Gen. J. F. C. Fuller, Capt. G. L.-F. Pitt-Rivers (with whom he had been staying at the time of Pitt-Rivers's arrest) and Capt. R. Gordon-Canning, as well as numerous German officials. There was also a draft book (perhaps this draft developed into *From Admiral to Cabin Boy*) and peace literature.

[138] Inspector Keeble's haul was inspected later by one A. M. Abrams of the BBC—apparently connected with MI5. The rhyme was thus described: 'the same cyclostyled rhyme of eight lines about "the hidden Bare Paw's Lair" and a lost ball, "Just as simple as BC"'. Messrs Sanders and Foyer were also involved; they were connected with the Swinton Committee.

[139] His book is uninformative; presumably because he was embarrassed to say. A libel case, Domvile v. *Associated Newspapers Ltd.* (*The Times*, 27 February 1942) was based on a false statement that he was held under the defence regulations on charges of sabotage, attempts to get secret information, or seeking to make contact with the enemy. This statement derived from a misleading Commons statement by Morrison on 26 November 1941.

[140] After her release he records Olive living near Bath (DOM 56, 2 October 1943), and on 15 August 1944 she is in the company of Capt. Budd, by then a former detainee, on whom see below Ch. 15.

cannot but suspect that Domvile himself was a distributor of NBBS 'sticky-backs'. His diary for 5 February 1940 contains this curious entry on a visit to London: 'I took district from Sloane Square to Temple'. It seems likely that Domvile was suspected of co-operating with German clandestine broadcasting in some way or other; conceivably he had been involved with Anna Wolkoff in this connection.

The Statistical Picture

Most detention orders were made in a period of three months. June saw the peak of 826, 370 being for regular British citizens; most would be for BU supporters or Anglo-Italians.[141] Many names were mentioned in the press; there was no censorship.[142] Restriction orders were also reported— such as that on Major Davidson Houston on 8 June; he was later detained. Churchill was told he was 'possibly crank only, but he has excited much public comment by his pro-Nazi remarks, and has been interned for that reason'.[143] Press reports made it clear that organizations other than the BU were under attack. Thus H. W. Luttman-Johnson, known as Secretary of the January and Windsor Clubs, was arrested.[144] Action was also taken against the IFL by the detention of Arnold S. Leese, Harold H. Lockwood, and C. J. Dobbin; Lockwood was thought more dangerous than Leese by MI5, and remained in detention until April 1945.[145] The names of many other detainees would be known through the local press or gossip; the public were fully aware of what was happening. There was no general protest. By the time Herbert Morrison succeeded Anderson on 4 October 1940 the mass detention of new suspects was over; in that month only thirty-three orders were made, and thereafter the figure never rose above twenty a month. Little information is obtainable about those

---

[141] 339 were for persons of enemy origin (most would be Anglo-Italians) and 13 for persons of alien but not enemy alien origin.

[142] There is a collection of press cuttings in the NCCL archives in the University of Hull (NCCL 22/4); my own searches have not been comprehensive.

[143] See HO 45/25747.

[144] The Windsor Club had premises at 23 Grosvenor Place, and existed by 1935; membership, kept confidential, was by invitation. The January Club had an address at 104a Gower Street. In the Anglo-German Fellowship and Link; a vocal supporter of Franco, with a horror of communism; detained on the BU order of 30 May; had only formally been BU for a month in 1933; had visited Germany and had German friends; in 1937 wrote to H. R. Hoffmann, German propagandist, saying he would help Germany to put things right in certain circumstances, referring to a communist revolution. Though the committee seems to have favoured his release and must have pointed out that the basis for his detention could not be supported, his detention was maintained in September 1940, the ground being changed to 'hostile associations' (Luttman-Johnson Papers). See also G. C. Webber, *The Ideology of the British Right 1918–1939* (London, 1986), 153.

[145] *Daily Telegraph*, 7 June 1940. See Griffiths, *Fellow Travellers of the Right*, 96–101 and HO 45/25747, 283/46.

detained by Morrison; Margaret Newitt, arrested in October 1940 on suspicion that the domestic agency she ran was a cover for espionage, is an
exception.[146] Some cases must have caused problems for the new Home
Secretary, such as that of the French Vice-Adm. E. H. Muselier, arrested
on 2 January 1941 in possession of £50,000 in cash, and in bed with a
Piccadilly *cocotte*, on suspicion of treasonable associations with the Vichy
regime; this proved to have been an error and he was soon released. Mr
Justice Singleton investigated the affair.[147] But Morrison's task was
mainly to decide who might be released, rather than who should be
detained.

In the course of the European war a total of 1,847 orders were executed,
and an uncertain higher number made. All but thirty-six related to
British subjects.[148] In addition some people were detained abroad in
British dependencies under local versions of the regulations, and moved
to Britain under Regulation 18A; they do not feature in the British statistics.[149] In December 1940 over a thousand detainees were in custody. At
the end of 1941 there were 627; of 1942, 486; of 1943, 266; of 1944, 65. By the
end of April 1945 a mere eleven remained. The figures I have given represent interference with civil liberty on a massive scale.

The reports to Parliament do not indicate into which of the three basic
categories ('BU', 'hostile origin or associations', 'acts prejudicial')
detainees fell. They do give the number who were either aliens, of enemy
or alien origin, or of doubtful nationality.[150] A little under half (the figure
is 876) fell into this category, the majority being of 'enemy origin'; a con-

---

[146] HO 45/25739. By birth German; married a British man who died 1931; detained as of
hostile origin; remained in detention until 1945. Since her agency could have been closed
down, and the case against her rested solely on suspicion, her detention seems to have been
wholly unnecessary. Her attempt to claim compensation failed.

[147] West, *MI5* 172 has it that Kenneth Younger of MI5 was responsible. J. Lacouture, *De
Gaulle: The Rebel, 1890–1944* (London and New York, 1990), ch. 5 has the story, blaming one
Maj. Meffrie (also known as Howard); Meffre was detained. See also K. Young, *The Diaries
of Sir Robert Bruce Lockhart, 1939–1965* (London, 1980), 556, F. Kersaudy, *Churchill and De
Gaulle* (1981) 12, FO 954/8, Cadogan's Diary.

[148] 22 related to non-enemy aliens, 8 to enemy aliens and 6 to persons of dubious nationality. In 9 cases the 18B order was revoked and the individual detained under the prerogative;
Leopold and Olga Hirsch, detained as spies, would be an example; see TS 27/555. Others
were Agostini and Bernardino.

[149] HO 45/25111 lists a number of such persons who were at one time held in Latchmere
House. Others, like Maj. H. H. Beamish of the Imperial Fascist League, were interned
abroad, in his case in Southern Rhodesia. See HO 45/24968. E. Jeffrey Hamm, who had been
in the BU as a non-active member, was detained in the Falkland Islands, where he was a
schoolteacher, and then illegally moved to a camp in South Africa. On his being returned to
England in 1941 he was released but restricted; he then joined the army, but was discharged
and again restricted in 1944. He became active after the war in the Union movement. See
HO 45/25740 and his *Action Replay: An Autobiography* (London, 1987), chs. 8–10.

[150] HO 45/25758 relates to the statistics; the subfiles covering the summer of 1940 have
been destroyed. See SH para. 285.

siderable number would be Anglo-Italians, and the others nearly all Anglo-Germans.

The remaining 971 victims of the great incarceration were straightforwardly British citizens. In the first and second round-up of fascists the numbers detained under BU orders totalled about 370, and over the whole course of the war there were 753 such orders.[151] By July 1941 approximately 800 'hostile origin and/or associations' orders had been made; by 26 November the figure was 902, and in the whole course of the war would be a little above this.[152] As for 'acts prejudicial', 114 orders had been made by November 1941; again the total over the course of the war would be a little higher to make up the total of 1,847.

Figures were also given on 26 November 1941 which broke down those still in detention into the three categories: of the 663 persons still in custody 217 (32 per cent) were 'BU', 375 (56 per cent) 'of hostile origin or associations', and 71 (10 per cent) 'acts prejudicial'. Later, on 21 July 1942, another breakdown was given of the 529 remaining detainees. Of these 141 (26 per cent) were 'BU', 332 (60 per cent) 'of hostile origin or associations', and 66 (12 per cent) 'acts prejudicial'.[153] Unfortunately these breakdowns were misleading, as Home Office officials well knew, since the category 'of hostile origin or associations' included two entirely different types of detainee. One comprised persons of alien blood or connection, the other normal citizens suspected of espionage or disloyalty on evidence too weak to justify an 'acts prejudicial' order. No attempt was ever made to explain this to the Commons.

The breakdowns do, however, bring out the fact that the principal use made of Regulation 18B was the crippling of the BU. Its second most significant use was against the Anglo-Italian community; there were about 600 Anglo-Italian orders. It was also used against a much smaller class of persons of other alien blood or connection, mainly Anglo-Germans. One can only guess at the total number in this category; the figure is concealed in those held for 'hostile origin or associations' after the Anglo-Italians and 'dangerous' British citizens have been subtracted. Somewhere about 250 people would be a reasonable estimate. The regulation was also used, though only to a very limited extent, against those supporters of the IRA who could not be expelled under the Act of 1939 and were not allowed to return to Ireland, or refused to do so; the number would be very small.[154]

---

[151] HO 45/25115, *Parl. Deb.* Vol. 376 HC c.849–52 'about seven hundred'; *Parl. Deb.* HC. Vol. 373 c.944 'just under eight hundred'.

[152] *Parl. Deb.* HC 373: 944, *Parl. Deb.* HC. Vol. 376 c.849–52 (26 November).

[153] *Parl. Deb.* HC. Vol. 381 c.1516. By then 1,817 persons had been detained.

[154] Figures in HO 45/25115 show that at least 22 IRA detainees were released on condition of returning to Ireland.

The Dangerous Citizens

Lurking within these figures is the category of regular citizens, not associated with the BU, who were thought to be in some way 'dangerous'; they were interned either for 'acts prejudicial' if there was some sort of evidence of wrongdoing, or for 'hostile associations' if there was none. One can only guess, but perhaps as many as 150 persons had been detained as falling into this mixed class by 1942. An example of a 'hostile associations' detainee of this type was the mysterious Ronald Gordon. He had long lived in Germany, and taught English to the German police; whilst in Berlin he had come into contact with a Special Branch officer, and on his return to England in 1939 he set up a school teaching German to members of Special Branch. Conceivably he was some sort of spy, but MI5 knew nothing about him, and it was uncertain who he was; he claimed, falsely, to have been born in Inverness in 1879. If it was the same person he had been arrested in Australia in the First World War and sent back to Germany in 1918; he was not forthcoming about his early life, and it was suspected that he was possibly a criminal who needed to conceal his true identity. He was detained from 1940 to February 1944.[155]

But who most of the supposedly 'dangerous' regular citizens were, and why they were detained, is largely unknown, and unless MI5 records have been preserved—itself an idiotic state secret—it will remain unknown. Those detained for 'acts prejudicial' included, in addition to Ramsay and Domvile (and presumably his wife and son), a few individuals about whom there is definite information—Thomas G. St B. Baker,[156] Alfred E. Block and W. E. Block,[157] F. H. U. Bowman,[158] W. A. Crowle,[159] Erland Echlin,[160] Arnold S. Leese, and Harold H. Lockwood of the IFL,[161] C. G. F. Salinger,[162] George H. Stock,[163] Anna Wolkoff,[164] and A. G. L. Thornton;[165] and we can be fairly sure of some others—Admiral Nicholas Wolkoff and Eugene Smirnoff, Mrs Christobel Nicholson, Mrs Mathilde Kraafte, Professor Serocold Skeels, and E. C. P Whinfield, for example. Salinger's case illustrates the way in which suspicions could understandably arise in 1940. A solicitor in Brussels, he had been convicted and imprisoned for forgery and fraud. He was released early on 16 May, and on return to England suspected of being set free to become a spy. His

---

[155] HO 45/25734, 283/39.
[156] HO 283/28, see also HO 214/45, HO 45/25732. He belonged to the Nordic League and joined the Maida Vale BU in 1939 (private information).
[157] HO 45/25707 and 25497.   [158] HO 45/25729 and LCO 2/2712.
[159] HO 45/25115. Crowle was probably released in 1943.
[160] Reference in HO 45/25115. See below, Ch. 18 n. 5.
[161] The Leese 'Reasons for Order' are in the Bleach Papers. HO 45/25717 and 283/46.
[162] HO 45/25709 and 283/62.   [163] HO 283/67.
[164] HO 45/25115. She was later tried.   [165] HO 45/25115. Nothing known.

staying at the Royal Automobile Club in London was thought very suspicious; it was much frequented by service officers, including de Gaulle. These suspicions proved baseless, and Salinger was released in late 1940; there may well have been quite a number of similar detentions at this period, when spies were everywhere.

Captain T. G. St Barbe Baker's case illustrates the detention of eccentrics of no conceivable significance.[166] The brother of the founder of the Men of the Trees, he associated with various anti-Semitic right-wing organizations; I have been told that he had acted as an MI5 informant. In the First World War he had won the MC, been wounded, gassed, and twice buried alive, and he appears to have been unbalanced. He used the alias Colonel Moore Hope, and claimed knowledge of Hitler's secret weapon—flooding France to within fifteen miles of Paris by opening the floodgates of the Rhine; he was accused of 'the systematic dissemination of subversive views and of false information calculated to hinder the successful prosecution of the war'. There is much rubbish in his files; only a security organization, or a political fringe group, could take someone like Baker seriously.

Orders for 'acts prejudicial' may have been employed against a few individuals detained for hindering war production. One known case is that of John Mason, the communist, who was to litigate. The NCCL, being under communist influence, took up his case; initially it opposed 18B; by 1942 it had come round to favouring detention without trial, but only of course for fascists.[167] In 1940 it was also concerned over Miss Kota Rink, Mohan Lalli[168], and Walpole, a Ministry of Supply draftsman, released after four months' detention in October 1940 without ever needing to come before the committee, possibly an 'acts prejudicial' case. Some of these may have been communists.[169] It also supported T. E. Nicholas, a Welsh bard, communist, and dentist, and his son T. Islwyn Nicholas, who must have been 'acts prejudicial' cases. The Nicholases— father and son—were categorized by the police as 'reds', but were probably not party members. On arresting the son a police officer is said to have remarked: 'Nicholas, I've got you where I want you at last . . . I've got you and I'm going to keep you.' D. N. Pritt took up their cases, and

---

[166] His files are HO 283/28 and 45/25732.

[167] See generally HO 45/25463. Speakers' notes for 1939 (NCCL 76/1) oppose 18B, and a memo of 29 January 1940 presented to Attlee was strongly opposed. HO 45/25463 sf. 93 has protest against the change in the regulations on 9 May 1940. But memos of 14 January 1942 (77/2), 17 July 1942 become schizophrenic.

[168] See NCCL 76/2A, memorandum of 14 August 1940 for Lord Privy Seal.

[169] Miss Kota Rink, detained on 17 May 1940, had been an active anti-fascist and was Secretary of the Holborn and City Trades Council. She was released in mid-October after appearing before the committee in September. Lalli was a British Indian subject, detained in June.

claims that the committee allowed him to appear informally for them; probably he merely gave some evidence.[170] The detention of the Nicholases seems to have been the result of personal animosity from the Chief Constable of Cardiganshire, J. J. Lloyd Williams. Orders for 'acts prejudicial' may also have been used in supposed cases of sabotage, as in a case mentioned by Hinsley and Simkins involving former BU members in the Leeds area.[171] A factory making military clothing was involved. Apparently the orders in this case were signed by Morrison in blank, and by mistake left in a pub during the drive north, but happily recovered in time; conceivably authority was given by telephone.[172] 'Acts prejudicial' orders may also have been used against spies who were not of enemy nationality, such as Sjoerd Pons, acquitted at his trial.[173] Such persons may have been held as being 'of hostile associations', or under the Aliens Order. I have heard rumours, which I cannot confirm, that in addition to members of the IRA a few Welsh Nationalists were detained for 'acts prejudicial'. The reference could merely be to father and son Nicholas; there is evidence that Vaughan-Henry was suspected of contact with nationalists.[174] In Scotland at least two Scottish Nationalists, Arthur Donaldson and Matthew Hamilton, were detained for 'acts prejudicial', though what they were thought to have done is not known.[175]

As for regular citizens detained as 'of hostile associations' the most notable were Robert Liversidge and Ben Greene, who achieved legal immortality in the leading cases on 18B. Both were entirely loyal. Others were Arthur C. H. Campbell,[176] Edward L. Diamond,[177] H. W. Luttman-Johnson,[178] Hamilton S. L. Knight, Borough Surveyor of Guildford and later Squadron Leader,[179] Professor S. F. Darwin-Fox, originally detained as being of the BU, recalled by detainees as both eru-

---

[170] *The Autobiography of D. N. Pritt* (London, 1965–6), Part I, 231–2; he says a swastika had been found on a bridge. They appeared before the committee under Morris on 10 October, and were released on 23 October. T. E. Nicholas wrote sonnets in prison on toilet paper, which were smuggled out; they were published in translation (by Daniel Hughes) as *The Prison Sonnets of T. E. Nicholas* in London in 1948. See *Baner ac Amserau Cymru*, 17: 24 July, 14 August, 25 September, 9, 16, and 23 October 1940. I am indebted to Prof. Daffydd Evans for information.   [171] Appendix V.

[172] Private information. See 170 n. 123 same case.   [173] Hinsley and Simkins, 321–2.

[174] TS 27/533 (Ham Common interrogation). L. Mosley in *The Druid* (London, 1982), 58, wrongly claims that the Welsh Nationalist Party had been proscribed, and that many of its members 'put in jail under . . . Regulation 18B'.

[175] *Parl. Deb.* HC. Vol. 371 c.1098, 372: 353, 373: 2110. There are closed files in the Scottish Records. Donaldson was only temporarily detained by the Regional Commissioner.

[176] TS 27/509 and HO 144/21635. His case involved considerable confusion, and is discussed below. Though his order was for 'hostile associations', the ground given him was membership of the BU, and he should really have been detained for 'acts prejudicial'.

[177] HO 45/25721.

[178] Ref. in HO 45/25115; I have kindly been allowed access to his surviving papers.

[179] HO 45/25695.

dite and averse to washing,[180] and former Squadron Commander
Frederick J. Rutland DSC, AM.[181]

Given the atmosphere of the times, identifying 'dangerous' individuals
must have been a very unreliable business; we can be sure that mistakes
were made, and harmless if sometimes eccentric or troublesome people
detained on the basis of gossip, informers' reports, and the like; Baker is
an example.[182] In some instances this can be documented; indeed the two
principal litigants, Ben Greene and Robert Liversidge, illustrate the
point. We only know so much about them because they litigated, which
was not possible for most detainees, because the Treasury Solicitor's files
on them have not been withheld or destroyed, and because their side of
the story can be to some degree recovered from private papers or personal
contact. So far as Greene is concerned, both the Home Office and Lord
Chancellor's Department, and of course MI5, are still withholding
records; the Home Office allowed me privileged access to their file on
Liversidge, which I can see no reason whatsoever for keeping out of the
public records. We can assume that there were other cases quite as bad
and some much worse.

One case of error which is documentable received considerable publicity; it involved Hamilton S. L. Knight.[183] Knight, who was British by
birth, was the Borough Surveyor of Guildford. He was detained on 28
May as 'of hostile associations'; he was held in Brixton until 28 October,
spending up to twenty-three hours a day in solitary, including times when
there were air raids. The background was that 'his colleagues have
informed against him and the local populace are demanding his internment'. He was

strongly pro-Nazi and his special knowledge renders him a potential danger. His
wife is said to be of German extraction and he has visited Germany frequently and
speaks the language fluently; he is said to have given information to the captains of
German ships; his intimate relations with a German girl have aroused the suspicions of the police; and he has lost no opportunity of associating with enemy aliens
and refugees.[184]

Pilcher, who composed the 'Statement of the Case', amplified these allegations.[185] Apparently what touched off his arrest was an occasion on 21
May when he told his ARP staff that they could join up if they wished,
and he 'advised his female staff to learn German as this would enable

---

[180] See HO 45/25115. I am told he was a member in 1936.   [181] See below Ch. 18.
[182] Other clear cases amongst those mentioned are those of Diamond, Block, Knight, and
Salinger, and in common sense there was no reason to detain the eccentric Bowman, or
Stock. Rutland also, though very foolish, may well have been entirely loyal.
[183] HO 45/25695.   [184] Minute of 24 May by Rumbelow.
[185] G. E. Wakefield, a Gray's Inn barrister working for MI5, was also involved in the
case.

them to get good jobs when the Germans took control of England. When asked whether the Germans really would invade this country he replied:– "certainly they will, and I have got two swastika flags to put on the municipal buildings when they arrive".' The 'Reasons for Order' instanced visits to Germany on at least two occasions, association with enemy aliens before and since the war, and 'public expression to his pro-German and pro-Nazi sympathies'. The committee, under J. W. Morris KC, saw witnesses and recommended his release as an entirely loyal person who had made some foolish remarks. It found that his wife (from whom he was separated) was Welsh, not German, that his association with aliens and visits to Germany were entirely innocent, and that he was in no sense pro-German, though he had thought that Germany would be hard to beat in war. He did indeed have an Austrian girlfriend whom he wished to marry. The incident on 21 May, as alleged, had not taken place, though it was true that Knight at the time was very pessimistic as to the outcome of the war, and did advise his shorthand typist to learn German, a remark the committee regarded as 'very indiscreet'. Ten days before his detention he had volunteered to join the Royal Engineers. It is clear that, typically, MI5 had never troubled to interview Knight before he was detained.

He was released on 2 December, the order being suspended on condition of reporting his place of residence to the police; he was enraged since the letter sent to him suggested that he had been associated with the BU. His case was publicized; thus the *Sunday Express* on 9 December 1940 carried an article entitled 'A Victim of 18B'. He appealed against the suspension, at first without success, and with difficulty secured its revocation in March 1941 on his joining the RAF. He continually corresponded with the Home Office, and was particularly furious when his girlfriend was detained.[186]

On 28 May 1942 he sent the Home Office a card:

Per Ardua ad Astra

Lest we Forget . . .
This is to remind you that on this day, 2 years ago, your predecessor, the despotic ANDERSON, committed the crime of putting an innocent man in prison without trial—just one of the black crimes committed under the infamous 18B. H. S. L. Knight. On Active Service.

He sued the Borough of Guildford for wrongful dismissal and arrears of salary; the case was heard before Mr Justice Hilbery in July 1942, and the evidence of misconduct against him collapsed, though as a matter of law his claim failed, his contract having become unenforceable through

---

[186] She was Bertha Lais, released in July 1941.

change of circumstances. Knight became a Squadron Leader; after the war he sought compensation or some other form of rehabilitation for the period he had spent in prison. As in all other cases this was refused, though he did eventually secure employment.

I suspect there were numerous such cases involving persons less persistent than Knight; *glasnost* over surviving records, especially those of MI5, might help to clear the point up. Hinsley and Simkins, though conceding that MI5, in particular B division, was in a seriously disorganized condition in 1940, discuss not a single case of unjustified detention in their history, written with full access to records and, presumably, to surviving MI5 officers. This is supposedly the result of a policy of not mentioning individuals in the official history; in fact numerous individuals are mentioned in the history, but never the victims of MI5's incompetence. It is as if it really does not matter what happened to people, so long as we won the war.

$\Longrightarrow$ 11 $\Longleftarrow$

The Experience of Detention

Arrest without Warning

Detention normally began with arrest without warning. Thus Lieutenant Richard J. A. Hamer was arrested on parade.[1] So was Gunner/Surveyor D. A. Gourdon of the 1st Survey Regiment RA at Brandon on 22 July, after his return from Dunkirk.[2] George R. Merriman, a journalist, never got there; he was about to set off in the motor yacht *Dorbetta* when the police arrived.[3] C. F. Watts had just reached his office: 'Just as I was settling down to sort over the incoming morning mail I was called downstairs . . . On the stairs I met four big men in lounge suits, big boots and bowler hats; obviously policemen, disguised as gentlemen.' These officers conformed strictly to their instructions, and advised Watts of his rights.[4] Captain Budd had a final drink with his colonel, who protested at his arrest. Frederick Hooper, a Devonshire farmer, was half-way through shearing his sheep; those next in line were spared the indignity.[5] Ronald N. Creasy was refused a phone call to his wife, children, or foreman, but allowed to collect some tobacco. Some few received advance warning from sympathetic officers.[6]

There were ugly incidents. R. R. Reynolds of Tottenham was slapped; another officer told him: 'If I had my way I would let these men put you against the wall and shoot you.'[7] Andrew Burn was struck in the face by an officer wearing a ring.[8] Violence was not one-sided; Watts's wife hit Detective Sergeant Smith: 'I'm not having my husband arrested by a Jew anyhow.' The victim of this attack 'took it all in good part and afterwards admitted that although he looked like a Jew, he probably hated them more than we did.'[9] Some resisted arrest.[10] Leese, no stranger to prison, hid up from late June until 9 November in the countryside. Armed with a stout stick and assisted by his wife, he attacked the 'morons' who came to arrest him. In Guildford Police Station: 'I smashed everything breakable and tore the noisome blankets into strips and stuffed them down the WC.'

---

[1] Bellamy MS iii. 137.   [2] Gourdon MS.   [3] Bellamy MS iii. 128.
[4] Watts MS, 1.   [5] Bellamy MS iii. 118.
[6] Charnley MS, 93. *IMHHTY* 6 (D. J. Ibberson).   [7] *IMHHTY* 6.
[8] Bellamy MS iii. 76.   [9] Watts MS, 3.   [10] e.g. Rowe MS, 1.

For this he was later imprisoned for a month; his wife was fined twenty pounds.[11] R. A. ('Jock') Houston evaded arrest for over five months, living with his girlfriend Molly Hiscox in Windsor.[12] On a visit to his home he saw a policeman riffling through his belongings, and planted a vigorous kick on his backside. The officer arrested him.[13] Domvile felt the need for whisky as his home was searched; in due course he collapsed. His wife thought he was having a fit, but the police surgeon diagnosed alcohol, and he spent the night at a police station; more fortunate than most, he took with him a complete Shakespeare and a copy of *Good Bye to Life* by D. Hulme.

Amongst the Anglo-Italian communities the 600 18B detentions coincided with 4,000 or so arrests under the prerogative, and produced terror. The scenes in Newcastle were thus described:

When Italy entered the war the local Italians—men only—were rounded up and brought into our jail . . . After a few days their female relatives were allowed a final visit before the men were transported elsewhere. The Italians are a volatile and voluble people and when time was up all pandemonium broke loose with weeping, wailing and shrieking. Most of the women had to be forcibly hustled out by the police (as I could see by squinting through my Judas window). In the event, this was indeed a final parting because some of the men, I believe, were lost on the 'Arandora Star'.[14]

The distress was aggravated by the youth, and age, of some detainees:

In Edinburgh a boy of 15 was locked up in jail, eight others were only a year older; twenty in all below the age of 18. They were released a few months later when the authorities had recovered some of their mental balance and a little of their decency . . . Two old men of 80, many years naturalized, and both with sons in the British Army, remained in detention eight months. Two other men, invalids, were only released in time to die out of internment.[15]

Charnley recalled a 15-year-old Italian boy, named Di Campi, possibly arrested in error for his father, crying at night in the same room as his in Ascot Camp.[16] There were at least sixty-seven Anglo-Italian detainees under the age of 18.[17] The arrest of the very young and the very old was not confined to the Anglo-Italians.[18] There was 'Old Buggery', an outspoken 66-year-old veteran of the Boer War, the North-West Frontier,

[11] A. S. Leese, *Out of Step: Events in the Two Lives of an Anti-Jewish Camel-Doctor* (Guildford, 1951), 63. In 1936 he served 6 months for public mischief (an article in the *Fascist*).
[12] HO 283/41, HO 45/25713. This story is also told of Leese.
[13] Camp leader on the Isle of Man; released late 1944. See also HO 45/25713 and DOM 56 for 23 May 1944. A. R. Beavan also evaded arrest (see HO 45/25752).
[14] J. A. Williams MS.   [15] *IMHHTY* 9.
[16] J. W. Charnley, *Blackshirts and Roses* (London, 1990), 119.   [17] HO 45/25115.
[18] e.g. Dudley Elam, arrested on 23 May, and soon released, Lt.-Col. Cherry, the 63-year-old former CO of the Durham Light Infantry. See Watts MS, 33, 81, *IMHHTY* 8.

and the First World War.[19] Walter W. Johnson, Chairman of an engineering company in Leeds, spent his seventieth birthday in Ascot.[20] G. Palmer Thompson, aged 74 or so, and terminally ill with cancer, was carried off the train at Lime Street on his way to Walton Prison, where he died.[21] A number of others died soon after release; it was and still is Home Office policy to release those likely to die.[22] Three 18B detainees died on the *Arandora Star*, though what they were doing on the vessel is obscure.[23]

Arrests separating parents, particularly mothers, from young children, seem peculiarly harsh: 'Mr G.[24] of Liverpool . . . His wife was away tending a sick relative, and his two children were expected home from school in a few hours time . . . Permission to telegraph his wife, or arrange for anybody to look after his children was refused.'[25] Diana Mosley, more fortunate than most, chose to leave her baby with a nanny: 'One poor woman had a little boy aged eighteen months who was dragged away from her to a "Home" by the police. I was lucky.'[26] Mrs Josephine Birch was detained on 31 May; she took her fifteen-month-old child in with her, but in conformity with the brutal policy of the Prison Commissioners forbidding children over a year old in prison, he was taken from her and placed in an institution, and returned to her a year later. She gave birth to a girl on 27 January 1941. This child died of whooping cough in the Isle of Man on 15 November 1941. Three 18B babies were born in Holloway to detainees.[27] Since there were only a handful of women detainees it is impossible to understand, let alone justify, Home Office practices over their detention in London during the blitz. Even in 1940 arrangements

---

[19] Really T. W. Buttery. Bellamy MS iii. 114.   [20] Information from J. Warburton.

[21] Bellamy MS iii. 116, giving his age as 76; *IMHHTY* 6; Case number 8 in the 'Tragedies' in the pamphlet by Henry St George, *In Search of Justice*. See also HO 45/25115.

[22] Bellamy MS iii. 152. Albert Potter of Swaffham, a Boer War veteran, whose business premises were vandalized, did; also Col. Kiddell-Monroe of the York BU, who was very elderly, possibly case 2 ('CM') in *Search of Justice*, a 69-year-old Boer War veteran; also 'RR' (*In Search of Justice*, Case number 6, 'RR'), R. Rix of the 17/21 Lancers a shell-shocked war veteran, detained 1940, released 1941; also Case number 9 (Mr W.—not identified), who died 3 months after unconditional release leaving a blind widow and 3 young children. Bellamy MS iii. 118 notes Maurice Fitzgerald, a former D/L Dorchester, released just before he died; also Clement Hill (private information).

[23] F. Hildesheim, R. Pliscke, and G. Parmigiani (HO 45/25115). The same file notes the deaths in detention of G. Palmer Thomson and C. Barnick. FO 371/25210 notes that Hildesheim was British. Pliscke was a Czech.

[24] A. Giulianotti.

[25] *IMHHTY* 9, recording that the police were apologetic.

[26] *A Life of Contrasts: The Autobiography of Diana Mosley* (London, 1977), ch. 17. She also had a 19-month-old child, Alexander. She was unwilling to take the child to Brixton because of the risk of bombing. TS 27/491.

[27] The 18B Publicity Council published *Persecuted Women in Britain Today* and *Suffer the Little Children*. The Birch case is also number 11 in the pamphlet *In Search of Justice*. The mother of one baby was a detainee of Polish origin identified in the pamphlet as Francis. There was one Edna Francis Munn in Holloway under 18B in 1943.

could surely have been made to treat them and their infant children with more humanity.

Families and Dependants

No special arrangements were made for the care of families and dependants; they could apply like anyone else to the Local Assistance Board.[28] Nor were they informed of detentions. Restrictions on visits and letters made contact between families and detainees difficult, and the war disrupted travel. When Watts moved to Stafford Prison he did not see his wife again for six months.[29] The move to the Isle of Man made matters worse. Most of the inhumanity was not of course the product of some wanton desire to inflict suffering; it simply mirrored what normally happened when someone was imprisoned, and the officials concerned had become inured to this.

Ostracism aggravated the plight of families; to have been detained was to be identified as a traitor. Bellamy records some particularly bad cases, for example:

Edith Charnley, wife of the District Leader of Hull, was left wholly without means . . . She was compelled to give up her home, sell most of her possessions in order to defray the cost of removal of the remainder of her furniture to her native Southport, where she made application to the Public Assistance Board for relief for herself and her two children, a tiny tot of a girl and a baby boy of five months. She was told by the officer who examined her case: Your husband is a bloody traitor, and should be shot. You will get nothing from us, neither you nor your children. As far as I am concerned you can either go to work or starve.[30]

The story is entirely plausible; the fascists were widely hated, and even those not detained could be ostracized.[31] Mrs Cunningham, whose husband was on the order of 30 May, was roughed up; Mrs Elliott, whose husband Charles W. Elliott had been District Leader at Slough, had her windows broken, and was grateful for police protection.[32] I have myself spoken to an individual of some prominence in public life whose father was detained and soon released. His sister can still recall the tauntings at school, and to this day the detention hangs like a cloud over the family. Family anxieties persist; numerous relatives have attempted over the years to discover from the Home Office information about detainees; they have had virtually no success.

[28] *Parl. Deb.* HC Vol. 377 c.1256.   [29] Watts MS, 31.

[30] Bellamy MS iii. ch. 9 catalogues this and other cases. Charnley, *Blackshirts and Roses*, 156–7 is similar.

[31] Bellamy records the story of a close acquaintance, a Miss L. M. Reeve, active in East Anglia, and prospective candidate for SW Norfolk; she was ostracized and her smallholding became part of a battle training area; she was twice evicted. She hanged herself.

[32] Bellamy MS iii. 139–40.

The Conditions of Imprisonment

Detainees might first be lodged in police cells. Bellamy was held in Canterbury Police Station: 'Sleep was impossible, because the neighbouring cells contained poor unfortunate women, refugees and the wives of refugees who had fled to England from Middle European countries to escape Hitler.'[33] J. A. Williams reacted badly: 'the experience of being pushed into a darkened cell (blackout in force) and the door locked was fairly unnerving. It is then that the awful thought begins to gnaw at the political prisoner—"THEY have locked me up without any reason, therefore THEY have no reason to let me out ever . . . ever . . . ever".'[34] Diana Mosley independently puts the same point: 'It is probably difficult for someone who has not experienced it to imagine how demoralizing it is to be imprisoned without trial. It is like being kidnapped—you cannot see the end.'[35] For those arrested in error the sense of hopelessness was particularly acute: 'Leo Mortell was sunk in silent introspection. He could not understand why he had been arrested, a sense of bewilderment I shared. Frank Danby and I had at least been active in our opposition to the war, but Mortell had expressed no political interest for years.'[36] It might be many months before a detainee received any explanation of why he had been arrested. If, like Royston Knott, a detainee by way of protest refused to appeal, it might be years; detained on 12 June 1940, Knott was not given the 'Reasons for Order' until March 1943.[37]

Detainees *en route* to prison, or from one place of detention to another, could have humiliating experiences. Bellamy met up with a group of detainees from Sussex who had been shackled together to form a lengthy chain gang, which excited much interest.[38] Private Hopkins, detained on active service, had the buttons and badges of his uniform cut off in Liverpool by his officer escort.[39] But the vast majority of detainees were treated correctly. On arrival at prison there were the pseudo-sanitary rituals of degradation—the bath and the baring of the privy parts; some at Walton Prison were simply made to step in and out of an empty bath to

[33] Bellamy MS iii. 108. He noted the entirely correct behaviour of the police officers.
[34] Williams MS, 4.
[35] *Loved Ones: Pen Portraits by Diana Mosley* (London, 1985), 178. L. Grundy in a MS account makes the identical point.
[36] Charnley, *Blackshirts and Roses*, 97, 99, 109. Mortell was released after a few weeks in detention.
[37] Information on Knott from the Britons' Archives.
[38] Bellamy MS iii. 112. The gang included a County Councillor (J. Sidney Crosland), a retired officer of the Colonial Service, an accountant, a retired army officer, a shopkeeper, a commercial traveller, an estate agent's clerk, a house painter, a shoemaker, and some farm workers.
[39] *Is This Justice?*, 19 The Watts MS at 81 gives a similar account. L. Grundy has a variant of the story.

keep the record straight. Thus cleansed the detainees were ready for the bugs which inhabited the prison.

Until May of 1940 there was no shortage of prison accommodation. The Prison Commissioners realized that the action against the BU would cause problems, and warned Governors on 27 May, but the scale of the detentions in the summer of 1940 exceeded their expectations. The prisons selected were Brixton and Liverpool for men, and Holloway for women.[40] The crisis was aggravated by shortages of staff, and by heavy demands on accommodation from the armed services.

For women there was ample space in Holloway, though some cells had long been unoccupied.[41] Most British women were held in 'F' wing, but Anglo-Germans and Italians were placed in 'E' wing, which also contained the condemned cell. The prison, notwithstanding the denials of the Governor, Dr Mathieson, was extremely dirty, with very inadequate lavatory accommodation; it was largely unheated. Blankets, made of canvas, were disgusting. It must be emphasized that these conditions were normal in Holloway; in general the prison staff behaved entirely correctly.[42] Brixton had spare accommodation for men, and 'F' wing, which contained about 200 eleven by seven foot cells, was used to hold detainees before their appeals. It was decided to hold 'leaders' and 'troublemakers' in London after their appearance, rather than send them to Liverpool or elsewhere.[43] They were segregated in 'C' wing, which was not infested with bedbugs.[44] The maximum held there was around 300, and conditions were always better than in other prisons;[45] the Governor at the time was the much-wounded C. F. Clayton, a humane and efficient man.[46] Prison officers were often former servicemen, and so too were many detainees, including Mosley himself.

In Liverpool cells in the old womens' prison, derelict for nine years, were brought into use in the first week of June.[48] Numbers rose from 74 on 4 June to 649 by 3 July. All sources confirm the dreadful conditions in

---

[40] TS 27/512 (W. H. Waddams to all local prison governors).

[41] The best description is by Diana Mosley in *A Life of Contrasts*. The 'Mrs D' who appears is Mrs Duff.

[42] Diana Mosley wrote warmly of three prison officers but not of the male Governor, a Dr Mathieson. He later became Governor at Brixton and wrote the medical report on Derek Bentley, not a sympathetic document. See C. Berry-Dee and R. Odell, *'Dad Help Me Please'* (London, 1990), App. 2.

[43] The date and reason for this decision is uncertain; some leaders spent time in Stafford Prison. In addition to Mosley and his lieutenants (Francis-Hawkins, Raven-Thomson, Donovan, Clarke, and McKechnie) Beckett, Domvile, Gordon-Canning, C. H. Hammond, Leese, Ramsay, and Vaughan-Henry were at one time or another classified as leaders. Rolf List was kept in Brixton for his own protection; he had acted as a camp informer.

[44] Watts MS, chs. 3 and 4.   [45] On 23 June 1940. Memo by Waddams in TS 27/512.

[46] Watts MS, 11.

[47] Mosley in *My Life* (London, 1968), 406 also speaks well of Chief Warder Watson.

[48] Apart from two wings used for young prisoners.

this decrepit unheated accommodation, previously occupied by pigeons.[49] The Prison Commissioners claimed that 'In the short time available everything possible was done to make it habitable before it was taken into use and it was at least hygienically clean before the detainees arrived.' But this was not really true; in addition to livestock, chamber pots were chipped and encrusted, and washing facilities minimal. For many there was no cutlery, no toilet paper, and no newspapers to use as a substitute. When shaving became possible after some ten days a dozen or more shared a single blade; some went three weeks without a bath of any kind.[50] Later weekly baths were organized. Mr Thomas Hunter, MP for Perth and Kinross, with an assistant Prison Commissioner,[51] confirmed that 'during the initial stages [the detainees] suffered considerable discomfort', which is strong stuff indeed from a Prison Commissioner.[52]

Matters were probably not helped by the attitude of Governor J. Holt to the detainees, whose arrival caused him many headaches. He made much of the problems caused by the 'privileged' status of the detainees:

The special privileges allowed . . . mean much additional work for the Staff from items like the purchase and distribution of food, newspapers and cigarettes, to the constant enquiries and correspondence necessitated from letters from importunate or aggrieved relatives and the business and legal affairs of the detained men.[53]

In prisons the attitude of the Governor tends to influence the whole character of the institution.

Initially BU detainees—the Fifth Column—were treated as very dangerous. Battersby records: 'Apparently they had expected gangs of real desperadoes, for the warders, who looked apprehensive, were all heavily armed as we exercised.'[54] And Charnley records how a prison officer from Hull—officers were moved to Walton to cope with the influx—shouted into his cell: 'Now we've got you, you Fascist bastard, we'll put you against a wall and shoot you any day now. All bloody traitors should be shot. We are only waiting for our orders. It might even be tomorrow.'[55] The threat may have been made to seem more real by the execution which took place about this time in Walton, marked, as was traditional, by the

---

[49] Charnley, *Blackshirts and Roses*, 102. Smeaton-Stuart memo in HO 45/25714.

[50] Bellamy MS iii. 123. J. L. Battersby in *The Bishop Said Amen* (Poynton, Cheshire, 1947), 4–5, is similar.

[51] C.R., presumably C. Ross.

[52] Memo of 11 July. He says that matters had improved, but that it was impracticable to conform to the White Paper of January 1940, Cmd. 6162.

[53] Memo to Prison Commissioners of 9 July 1940.

[54] Battersby, *Bishop*, 4, also Bellamy MS iii. 123.

[55] Charnley, *Blackshirts and Roses*, 103. Bellamy records how one warder would call out to the inmates: 'It won't be long now before we get our orders to shoot you. Probably tomorrow. Have a good night's sleep. It might be your last.'

hammering of all cell doors in the prison at the moment of death.[56] But in general prison officers appear to have behaved very correctly once their initial patriotic hostility had waned.[57] Conditions improved, but remained poor. Work became available, and detainees could earn about 3 shillings a week; letters, at first not allowed, began to be received, and visits, though not from children, were permitted. Detainees came to acquire convict skills—for example the ability to pass messages between cell windows, using thread from mailbags.[58]

In the last week of July a wing of Stafford Prison, unoccupied for over twenty years, was brought into use:

we were taken to a great big queer shaped building named 'The Crescent'. Inside this building was a cold dank atmosphere, smelly with mildew and gas. Apparently it had been condemned and disused since the last war when it had been used as a military prison . . . there was iron everywhere and in far greater quantities than at Brixton. Big iron staircases, bare, and railings everywhere . . . No two cells seemed the same shape or size, in fact I think it must have warped from the damp and age.[59]

Conditions in Liverpool and Stafford were always worse than those in Brixton, although long periods of solitary confinement—and associated labour was not always available—was oppressive.[60] In London and Liverpool there were air raids. Detainees were not moved to shelters; lights normally went out at 9 p.m. but were turned off in raids.[61] Some prisoners, for example those shell-shocked during the First World War,[62] were acutely distressed by being locked in their cells.[63] In Holloway the practice was to unlock the cells, but turn off all lights, leaving detainees loose in the darkness. None of the prisons were directly hit, though bombs fell near Holloway, Brixton, and Walton. Even those who, like Mosley, could pay for extra food, suffered in health.

We have seen how the conditions of detention did not conform to the White Paper of January 1940, but were governed by secret Emergency Orders. In response to the crisis further orders were issued on 27 May and 24 July. No visits were allowed for the first ten days without express permission from the Commissioners, except by lawyers; reports of what

---

[56] Charnley, *Blackshirts and Roses*, 107. See also 108; detainees were shown the wall before which they might be shot.

[57] Watts MS, 28 refers to one Corbell in Brixton as 'a very efficient but human screw'.

[58] Charnley ch. 3 gives an account of the conditions which conforms to accounts from informants.

[59] Description by Watts.

[60] B. Domvile, *From Admiral to Cabin Boy* (London, 1947), 104–10.

[61] Ibid. 106; Smeaton-Stuart memo.   [62] Smeaton-Stuart memorandum.

[63] *Parl. Deb.* HC Vol. 365 c.838. H. S. L. Knight in particular complained of this to the Home Office in August 1945 (HO 45/25695); Mr Liversidge is another example (personal information).

was said were to be sent to Gonne St Clair Pilcher of MI5. By being refused unsupervised meetings with lawyers detainees were treated worse than remand prisoners. Letters to MPs were to be submitted to the Commissioners for approval before transmission, and, if MI5 directed, all correspondence was passed to MI5.[64] After ten days visits from friends or relatives were to be strictly limited to one a week, and Governors had no discretion to allow more. Letters were limited to not more than two a week, 'and replies thereto', and their length restricted to 'a length not exceeding an ordinary sheet of prison notepaper'. This included letters to lawyers, and letters concerning business matters. In July letters to MPs, except personal friends, were entirely forbidden; this disgraceful embargo ended on 23 October, in response to pressure from Isaac Foot MP of the Swinton Committee, but even after the rule changed a certain amount of covert censorship continued.[65] Another small concession had come in on 24 July; detainees were not to be handcuffed during transfer or production without special permission from the Commissioners. No doubt some of the responsibility for the rules belonged to MI5, which must have put its wishes to the Commissioners.

In the early summer of 1940 even the Commissioners' repressive instructions were not observed. At a conference on 29 June 1942, concerned with actions against Anderson and others, the Attorney-General

asked what steps had been taken to adapt the accommodation so as to provide conditions of detention in accordance with the White Paper. Mr Hoare explained that prior to May and June 1940 only a handful of 18Bs had been detained and the . . . instructions had been complied with, but the prisons could not cope with the big influx of detainees and until the internment camps were started—about the end of 1940—conditions of detention were little different from those of ordinary prisoners. There were no facilities for association for meals or games and those detainees who did not choose to take part in associated labour spent 23 hours a day in their cells. The Attorney-General then picked on Article 6 of the White Paper as to communications. He pointed out that this said nothing about limiting the number of letters a detainee might write. Mr Hoare explained that the practice had been to allow detainees to write the 2 letters allowed to ordinary prisoners plus extra ones at the Governor's discretion, but to allow unlimited correspondence would have thrown too great a burden on the prison authorities in censoring.[66]

If weekly visits had been allowed in Liverpool there would have been a hundred a day, and it would have been impossible to supervise them. Hence the number was reduced and their duration shortened.[67]

Prisoners, however, find ways around rules; it is clear from the papers

[64] These instructions, only partly reproduced here, are in TS 27/512.
[65] See Smeaton-Stuart memo. Detained aliens were still prevented from writing to MPs. See *Parl. Deb*. HC Vol. 365 c.835.
[66] TS 27/512.   [67] Memo by C. Ross in TS 27/512.

of Luttman-Johnson that in Stafford letters were being smuggled out and that more than the regulation number were allowed in.[68] But visits by his wife involved travel down from Perth, in one case for a half-hour meeting and a second one of fifteen minutes; a permit was at first needed each time, and his letters continually reflect the depressing conditions. But they were better than Brixton, where he had written, when asking for books and solitaire: 'Remember I have got *nothing* to do in my cell for 20 out of 24 hours, except when I sleep.'[69] The idea that incarceration in a British prison at this time could be anything else but oppressive, even if the White Paper had been observed, was always ridiculous;[70] no attempt was made to inform Parliament of the realities, and the officials actively prevented detainees communicating with their members. Official behaviour was essentially fraudulent. Thus on 6 June 1940 a dishonest Home Office reply to a question stated that the instructions in the White Paper were being observed 'as far as practicable', dishonest because the qualification deprives the statement of all significance.[71] The Emergency Orders and other relevant documents have fortunately escaped permanent suppression, though in litigation, as we shall see, the Crown lawyers resisted their discovery.

Latchmere House

Bad treatment of detainees mainly arose from administrative failure, not deliberate decision. There is some evidence however of intentionally severe treatment by MI5 officers and prison staff in 1939. Thus a report in *It Might Have Happened to You!* claims that:

A detainee brought into Wandsworth Prison early in December 1939 was completely isolated from his fellow detainees: was subjected to continuous third-degree questioning: was refused permission to acquaint his parents of his whereabouts, was not allowed to see his solicitors, and was told the most damnable untruths concerning his parents' attitude to him: all in an attempt to persuade him to lay false evidence against an organization to which he belonged.[72]

The individual was probably E. C. P. Whinfield, a suspected agent.[73] The same pamphlet also claims that detainees in September and October of 1939 were housed in windowless cells, made to observe total silence, and

---

[68] Letter of 12 October 1940.
[69] In Stafford the regime was 6.30 slop out, 7.0 breakfast shut in cells, 9.30 cells unlocked, mailbag sewing and other duties, 10.45 to about 11.45 exercise, lunch shut in cells until 2.0, 2.0–3.0 mailbags or other work, 3.0–3.45 exercise, 4.0–5.30 tea in cells, 5.30–7.30 association, then locked up until next day.
[70] The principle stated in instruction 1 of the White Paper may have been modelled on s. 39 of the Prison Act 1877.
[71] *Parl. Deb.* H. C. Vol. 361 c.978.   [72] *IMHHTY* 17.

kept in solitary confinement apart from a half-hour's exercise and slopping out; no visits were allowed. These accounts could well be true.[74] Many of the early detainees were suspected spies; this is the sort of treatment they might expect. Although never an 18B detainee (though he might have been) John H. King, a spy detected in the Foreign Office, was, according to Cadogan, who knew, subjected in September 1939 to 'the third degree', though it is not clear precisely what this meant.[75]

Institutionalized bad treatment only began when Latchmere House (Camp 002) on Ham Common was opened in June 1940 as MI5's interrogation centre, principally for aliens and captured agents.[76] It was a country house formerly used as a mental hospital for officers.[77] A military officer of MI5 was in charge, Colonel R. W. G. ('Tin-eye') Stephens, formerly Indian Army, and said to have been half-German, though this is also said of Lieutenant-Colonel W. E. Hinchley Cooke. It is said he was extremely unpleasant, and war legitimizes sadism. Officially it was under Home Office control, though the military provided the commandant and guards.[78] 'Control' here is somewhat ambiguous; Home Office officials or civilian prison officers were never directly engaged.[79]

Latchmere House was not formally approved as a prison for 18B detainees until 15 March 1943, but it was verbally authorized by Anderson in a phone call to Swinton in 1940, in response to pressure from his committee and MI5.[80] It was for short-term detention only. Maxwell directed

---

[73] The Domvile Diary for 15 January 1940 notes a meeting with Whinfield's mother, who mentioned the ill-treatment of her son, whom she supposed to be 'in for the duration'. The organization would be the BU.

[74] For complaints about the treatment of G. E. Thomas see above p. 56.

[75] A. Cadogan, *Diaries*, entries for 4, 21, 25, 26, 27, 29 September, discussed Andrew, 606. N. West, *MI5* (London, 1983), 90 has it that King was plied with drink and confessed. His informant would not be likely to mention ill-treatment.

[76] The first inmate of whom I know was Dr Leigh Vaughan-Henry, arrested on 10 June and placed there until 18 June. TS 27/533. Camp 001 was a part of Dartmoor Prison.

[77] Latchmere House is discussed in the official history, Hinsley and Simkins, 67, 70–1, 175, 179, 184–5, 341–2. Accounts are in *IMHHTY* 20, 21; Watts MS, chs. 6 and 7; Smeaton-Stuart memo (HO 45/25714); Battersby, *Bishop*, 17–34; A. Raven-Thomson, 'Ham Common', *Union*, 19 June 1948; L. Vaughan-Henry, committee transcript in TS 27/533; Bellamy MS iii. 165–8; Stokes Papers Box 13 (Statement by Capt. B. D. E. Donovan), *Comrade*, 24 and 25. There is also said to be an article by Philip Shelmerdine in the *Catholic Herald* but I have not located it. There is also an undocumented account by Nigel West in *MI5*, in particular 179–87.

[78] Correspondence between Ramsay and Somervell (Letter of 29 October in Britons' Archives) and answers to questions in the Commons in September and October; *Parl. Deb.* HC Vol. 365 c.103, 236, 375–6; 367: 841 have references to it.

[79] See *Parl. Deb.* HC 365: 103, 375–6, for 17 Sept., 8 and 9 October 1940, and 367: 837 for 10 December. West claims that as a result of an incident of violence Morrison thought the centre should be placed under civilian control, presumably meaning that it should be staffed by prison officers, but relented.

[80] HO 45/25111, with references to Home Office file 700516.

that weekly lists should be provided of who was there.[81] MI5 did not provide lists, but a nominal roll was kept in the Home Office by Maxwell's
private secretary, Miss Jenifer Fischer Williams, one of the few officials
allowed to know anything about the place. Hinsley and Simkins say that
twenty-seven British subjects, who are not named, were interrogated
there between July and October, when MI5 (not according to their
account the Home Office) decided to use it only exceptionally for British
subjects, as in the case of Duncan Scott-Ford in 1942; in fact its use began
earlier, in mid-June.[82] From November 1940 special Home Office permission was required for its use for British subjects, its general authorization
for them being withdrawn, and monthly reports were to be supplied to
the Home Office.[83] Most of its inmates would be held under the prerogative or the Aliens Order.

The names of nineteen and perhaps twenty-one of those sent there are
discoverable, one not being originally 18B.[84] The choice of some is easy to
explain; having persuaded the government of the risk from the Fifth
Column MI5 was now desperately trying to find some evidence that it
really had existed. Thus Donovan, Raven-Thomson, and McKecknie
were prominent BU officials, and Stevens was secretary to another prominent official, Francis-Hawkins. Compton Domvile was presumably interrogated in the hope of extracting information against his father. Jorian
Jenks was also a prominent BU member, and one of those authorized to
carry on if Mosley was arrested. Dr Leigh Vaughan-Henry claimed to run
a secret organization and Maxwell-Knight thought he had developed a
system of transmitting messages to Germany in musical broadcasts; he
was also thought to have information about Welsh Nationalists. C. F.
Watts was feared as organizer of the London cab drivers and as involved
with an organization known as the Home Defence Movement. Windsor

---

[81] HO 45/25111 sf. 4. Memorandum by C. P. Hill of 29 May 1943.

[82] See n. 76 above.

[83] The evidence suggests that this arrangement was not properly operated.

[84] J. L. Battersby (D/L Stockport), Compton Domvile, Capt. B. D. E. Donovan,
Downing (a D/L in Yorkshire), Basil Gill (BU), F. Paul Jeeves (Brighton police officer and
BU), G. Jorian Jenks (BU Agricultural Adviser and journalist—probably holder of one of
Mosley's letters of authority), Vic King of the Hull BU. See above p. 184 n. 78 and 181–184
generally. Hector McKecknie, Peters (nothing known), Alexander Raven-Thomson, E.
Stennell Sandell (original detainee, ordinary BU member), P. Shelmerdine (BU agent for
the election at Middleton and Prestwick), J. V. Shields (BU, thought to be from the North-
East), H. K. Stevens (BU, Secretary to Francis-Hawkins), Dr Leigh Vaughan-Henry, C. F.
Watts (BU D/I), and Reg Windsor (BU NE Leeds, Treasurer). Also possibly to be included
are Eddie Gore, BU, a cinema owner, and a former journalist whose name may have been
Crisp, conceivably Lt. H. V. Crisp of the RE, not, I am told, a BU member. Also Duncan
Scott-Ford. Stokes in *Parl. Deb.* HC Vol. 367 c.844 refers to a person detained on 3 June,
sent to Latchmere House 29 September, kept there for 10 days, returned to Brixton and his
order revoked on 4 November.

had been involved in trying to keep the BU alive after it had been proscribed, and it was believed by the Regional Commissioner for Yorkshire
that an underground BU existed there. Jeeves was a police officer, and
presumably the authorities were fearful of a cell in the police service;
alternatively he may have been a stool-pigeon.[85] Scott-Ford was a different case. He was interrogated in 1942 in the hope of obtaining the names
of others giving Germany information on convoy sailings. The choice of
the others is mysterious.[86] One noticeable fact is that the authorities did
not subject the Mosleys to Latchmere House; they were socially elevated
enough for there to be fear of repercussions if they had gone there.

The techniques adopted at Latchmere House are clinically described
by Hinsley and Simkins in an appendix, so drafted as to impose responsibility on the Home Office for what went on.[87] According to Nigel West
the techniques employed were devised by a psychiatrist, one Dr Harold
Dearden.[88] He was a prolific popularizing author, and connected with the
solicitor Crocker of the Swinton Committee, having written a book about
his work, *The Fire Raisers*.[89] Latchmere House must indeed have been
the brainchild of Swinton, Ball, and Crocker. An account by Compton
Domvile states:

It was not long before my memory began to deteriorate. Certain periods of my life
completely disappeared from my mind. Others who shared my experiences at
Ham Common have since remarked on similar symptoms in themselves. I . . . was
able to consult the resident doctor. He stated to me plainly that the treatment was
intended to produce a state of 'mental atrophy and unreserved loquacity'.[90]

The system used did not involve outright physical torture. Detainees
were placed on starvation rations, kept in long periods of isolation (punc-
tuated with occasional association with others, no doubt in bugged
rooms).[91] They were moved about from one cell or room to another for
no apparent reason, and told of impending moves or release which never

---

[85] Private information.

[86] Battersby records the presence of a man who had been expelled from Austria by the
National Socialists and was in a disturbed condition. The reference could be to Leopold
Hirsch.

[87] Hinsley and Simkins, 341.

[88] West, *MI5*, 183. HO 45/25111 confirms he was the medical officer.

[89] Dearden wrote two autobiographical works, *The Wind of Circumstance* published
before the war, and *Time and Chance* (1940). He was a member of the Bath Club, which
appears to have had members connected with British intelligence in the 1930s.

[90] Compton Domvile had been a merchant navy officer; he had contracted sleeping sick-
ness, and at this time was unwell.

[91] Hinsley and Simkins say, 342, that under Home Office regulations solitary confinement
was allowed for up to 28 days. No date is given for these regulations, nor have I found any
reference in Home Office papers. Their existence, if they applied to 18B detainees, would
have involved deliberate deception of Parliament. The reference may, however, be to the
normal rule governing solitary confinement as a punishment.

took place, so as to induce feelings of insecurity. They were also kept locked in during air raids. They were thus reduced to a state of anxiety in which they had little idea what was going to become of them. There was mention of firing-parties and hanging, and a great deal of sinister silence. Suitably weakened, they were interrogated from time to time, with the usual 'good guy–bad guy' techniques, bright lights, and so on. Access to the outside world was cut off. Fellow detainees disappeared without explanation. Detainees stayed for varying periods; Donovan for example stayed for three weeks and four days.[92] A dishonest reply to a Parliamentary question by Osbert Peake, the junior Home Office minister, said: 'Persons are not detained there for any length of time, but are brought there for a few days for the purpose of such inquiries as cannot conveniently be made in camps or prison establishments up and down the country.'[93] According to Raven-Thomson, Mosley, hearing about Latchmere House, threatened legal proceedings. Vaughan-Henry protested to the advisory committee, which strongly recommended a Home Office enquiry in its report. We can guess that there were other protests and recommendations.[94] Possibly it was Mosley's protest which explains why its regular use for British subjects was soon ended.

There was fear in MI5 that information about Latchmere House, and the double agents, might leak. So a Camp WX was established first in Stafford Prison, and later in the Isle of Man, for former inmates. By 1945 there was also a Camp MX on the island, about which nothing is known. Some individuals were held incommunicado in Dartmoor too, where a wing was known as 001. MI5 also established Camp 020R at Huntercombe Place, in theory a mere adjunct to Latchmere House, for short-term detention. By 1943 its staff had swollen to 574, guarding 104 inmates. It came to be MI5's private long-term prison, established without proper authority.[95] This, together with suspicions of conditions there, and the general attitude of MI5 officers to the idea that prisoners had any rights at all, caused considerable anxiety in the Home Office in 1943: 'here we are now faced with a fait accompli; and the Security Service have established a private internment camp of their own staffed by DPW for which the S of S will presumably have to answer to Parliament if necessary . . . ' The camp was not normally used for British subjects, but some alien inmates may have originally been held under Regulation 18B; later they seem to have been held under the Aliens Order, and were thus excluded from normal statistics. In 1943 there was a Canadian and a South African in

[92] Richard Stokes knew of one case where a detainee was there for 30 days. See *Parl. Deb.* HC Vol. 367 c.831 ff.

[93] On 17 September 1940. Peake (1897–1966), later Viscount Ingleby, was junior minister 1939–44.

[94] TS 27/533; report of 14 February 1941. See below Ch. 18.

[95] See HO 45/25111 sf. 4, HO 215/42 (reference to Camp MX).

Latchmere House under 18B, and seven aliens held under 18BA. According to P. Knightley in his book *The Second Oldest Profession* another secret prison was established by the Special Operations Executive at Inverlain Lodge in Invernesshire.[96] If this is so, they too were probably held under the Aliens Order rather than 18B. There is something particularly repulsive about the establishment of these secret prisons in Britain, and the fact that to this day virtually no documentation about them is in the public domain.

The Move to the Camps

As early as 11 June it had been suggested that detainees should be held in camps.[97] The original plan, which was abandoned, was for a single camp at Bury. The first opened on 31 July 1940, when 617 detainees from Liverpool were moved to the winter quarters of Bertram Mills's Circus at Ascot racecourse.[98] York racecourse camp was opened at the beginning of November for between 400 and 500.[99] A third camp was opened at Huyton, Liverpool, in March 1941, comprising four streets of semi-derelict council houses, and some four acres of open space, surrounded by barbed wire.[100] Huyton took detainees from York and Ascot, which were closed, and Stafford Prison ceased to be generally used from mid-November. Detainees naturally called the camps concentration camps.[101]

For security—for detainees were the Fifth Column—the Army provided the guards, but the Home Office was in charge. There were officers from MI5, who reported on detainees for Birkett's committee.[102] Camps had perimeter security—towers with machine-guns, electric boundary lights, barbed wire, and patrols.[103] This reduced fear of a breakout, but

---

[96] P. Knightley, *The Second Oldest Profession*, (London, 1986), 398, citing PRO 32 10611/MA/08233. This reference does not work, but PRO may be an error for WO; if so the file is closed and he may have seen it under privileged access. G. Markstein's novel *The Cooler* (London, 1974) describes it. HO 215/196 mentions a camp Knapdale at Lochgilphead, Argyll, and HO 45/25111 Woodhouse Camp at Glencorse. A list of 9 July 1940 in HO 45/25758/863044/40 contains the names of individuals whose whereabouts MI5 wished for some reason to be concealed; they include E. C. P. Whinfield, said at this date to be in prison on a criminal charge, also Lydia Link, Frank Rees Jones, Margaret Titford, Rose Falkner, Edeltrud Costenzo, and Herta Weinfildeve. Perhaps they became double agents.

[97] HO 45/25752.   [98] Camp POW 7.

[99] Most of the detainees in York came from Ascot, and some particularly 'tough' Canadian soldiers acted as escorts for the move, during which shots were fired in the air. See *IMHHTY*

[100] There is a grim description of Huyton in P. and L. Gillman's *Collar the Lot! How Britain Interned and Expelled its Wartime Refugees* (London, 1980), 97–9.

[101] Except when other references are given what follows is based on *IMHHTY* 19 ff.

[102] Typically a note by A. S. Leese in the Britons' Archives names military officers and claims they were all Jews and part of the conspiracy. See *Parl. Deb.* HC Vol. 387 c.679 for 10 March 1943 (similar accusation by Ramsay).

officialdom continued to worry about enemy parachutists linking up with the dangerous fascists.[104] The Ascot Camp was close to the Berystede Hotel, from which Birkett's committee operated after its London premises had been bombed.

Detainees were free to do more or less as they liked under an elected camp leader:

Tommy Moran had been elected . . . and had set up an organization based on the leadership principle . . . and the smooth way the camp was running when I arrived showed the capabilities of Moran and his assistants . . . it was not as if they had only British Union men to organize. There was a mixture of all sorts. A little over 50% were members or ex members . . . The remainder were made up of Italians, Germans, Croats, Hungarians, Jews—all claiming British Nationality by birth or naturalization. Then there were quite a few English, Irish, Scots and Welsh, non-British Union, and a smattering of communists and I.R.A. . . . Each room had its separate room leader, elected by vote.[105]

No attempt was made to segregate different categories—Anglo-Germans, Anglo-Italians, BU. One consequence of this was bullying. Charnley notes how there were a number of Jews in detention—one Sellman and his son, Bobby Rietti, and two diamond merchants, Lipshitz and Kuchinsky, who although not ill-treated were, as he puts it, 'to some degree ostracised'; this would of course be by anti-Semitic fascists.[106] Detainees performed all the work of the camp themselves. Thus the position of chef was held for a time by Rudi Rottensheimer, naturalized under the name Rothwell.[107] At some point one Santarelli, who is described as *maître d'hôtel* at the Savoy, took over, assisted by a man who had been head chef at Reece's restaurant in Liverpool.[108] After some time local working parties were established, which reduced the boredom.[109]

At first the camps were in bad condition. In Ascot the kitchen had for a while to stretch rations for 400 or fewer to over 700. A Home Office memorandum conceded that 'the conditions in these camps were not, however, entirely satisfactory' and this was, as one might expect, an understatement.[110] Huyton, previously used for the aliens, many of them elderly and infirm, was in a dreadful state when the detainees moved in, and is

[103] Watts MS, 49.

[104] HO 45/25752/863022/4, WO 32/10671 and 10672.

[105] Charnley (MS at 17) notes that the only communist detained was John Mason; the reference may be to others who were not party members. See also 51–2.

[106] Robert Rietti, detained on 10 June, was an Anglo-Italian who later developed a career as an actor. See Charnley, *Blackshirts and Roses*, 121 and generally ch. 6.

[107] Originally Austrian and detained with his son, a university student.

[108] Bellamy MS iii. 156, noting that master baker John Charnley was senior assistant cook.

[109] Battersby, *Bishop*, 15.

[110] See also Knott MS and memo. of 18 November 1942 in TS 27/512.

said to have contained a decomposing corpse.[111] But the camps were cleaned up, canteens established, and at York and Huyton modestly paid work was established. At Huyton too there were working parties helping to clear up bomb damage.

Detainees could also organize concerts, boxing matches, and lectures.[112] Conditions for visits improved, though they were limited to thirty minutes; in Brixton somewhat longer visits were permitted.[113] As Bellamy put it: 'life in a prison camp did offer one welcome amelioration. Prisoners had the opportunity to mingle with their fellows, and to have hours of unrestricted conversation; at last they could swop stories of recent incidents and of the events leading up to their arrest'.[114] And to put the treatment of the detainees in perspective many in the armed services in Britain in 1940 must have endured conditions quite as bad as those of the detainees; the catch-phrase of the period was 'Don't you know there's a war on?'

The idea of moving detainees either to a Dominion or Colony, such as St Helena, developed out of concern over security in the event of an invasion.[115] But moving detainees out of the jurisdiction required legislation, and there was nervousness of political opposition.[116] The Isle of Man was in due course chosen, but it too had its own legal system; hence the passage of the Isle of Man (Detention) Act in 1941. On Monday 12 May 550 men arrived; at this time there were about 780 detainees in all. The men went to Peveril Camp at Peel, 'M' Camp, comprising a number of large boarding-houses by the sea wall, and terraces of smaller houses, all surrounded by barbed wire.[117] Rushen Camp at Port Erin was used for women, who shared it with aliens. Detainees enjoyed considerable freedom: 'The morning is taken up with one or other of the many activities we have organized. In the educational sphere a man may study French, German, Italian, Spanish, Russian and several other languages. We can play tennis and bowls if we are so inclined.'[118] Beavan's diary records on 24 May 1941: 'Formed a House school for studying Political Economy and for remainder of detention intend to do a lot of quiet study, organization

---

[111] Watts MS, 22. Bellamy MS iii. at 167 and Arthur Mason in *Comrade*, 13, have variants of the same story, which improved in the telling, but Bellamy was himself in Huyton.
[112] Charnley, *Blackshirts and Roses*, 112.   [113] Leese, *Out of Step*, 64.
[114] Bellamy MS iii. 157.
[115] Letter of Lord Swinton of 15 July 1940 in HO 45/25752; Hinsley and Simkins, 54, citing a paper from the CIGS of 9 June; CAB 80/12 COS (40) 438 of 8 June, CAB 66/10 WP (G) (40) 273 of 20 July (Anderson's report to the Cabinet).
[116] See *ex parte O'Brien* [1923] 2 KB 361. Some 18B alien detainees were sent to Australia, and 3 died on the way to Canada. See HO 45/25115, noting 5 18B detainees in Australia in 1945 (G. H. Alesden, A. A. Froebel, R. Habla, R. V. Kauffman, and T. C. H. Osborne). *IMMHTY* at 9 claims that 9 18Bs were sent abroad, 7 on the *Arandora Star*.
[117] See C. Chappell, *Island of Barbed Wire* (London, 1985).
[118] Battersby, *Bishop*, 37.

if possible to get books.' Detainees could share houses with whom they wished, but moves required official permission, and something was done to separate Jews from fascists; some persons of dual nationality were let live in alien camps.[119] There was outside work on farms with modest earnings, visits to the cinema, football, amateur dramatics, gardening, and rabbit hunts. Women were allowed out to go shopping locally. Food was never plentiful, particularly for the young and active; domestic rabbits were raised, and seagulls trapped and eaten. But in Huyton Camp even cats had not been safe.[120]

Some few detainees still remained in prisons, principally Brixton, Holloway and Walton, though Dartmoor, Stafford, and Aylesbury were also used.[121] A list of 15 September 1942 shows sixty-five detainees in Brixton, twenty-six of them for legal consultation or appearance before the committee. One of 7 April 1943 lists sixteen permanent residents, eleven being 'Leaders'. Two were unsuited to camp life, one was a camp informer in for protection, one was to be interrogated by MI5, and one was in Brixton to facilitate visits to his sister, who was in Holloway.[122] Conditions there were good: 'I had a bed complete with springs, and quite a large portion of the window opened to admit fresh air. The floor was tiled. Altogether a very Ritzy affair.'[123] Many restrictions went; detainees were allowed long periods of association, and lights were left on until 10 p.m. Cricket and rounders were played in the exercise yard. Bizarre arguments went on in 1942 over a gas ring for evening drinks; the Governor wanted its use limited to one hour, but Newsam minuted on 17 June: 'I am afraid that I don't agree with the Governor. If we allow the use of a gas ring at all it seems to me merely arbitrary to say that 50—60 detainees shall use it only for one hour at a time.' So they got four hours and escaped 'night starvation'.[124] Holloway kept most women not moved to the Isle of Man. On 15 September 1942 it contained twenty-five 18B women, the best-known being Diana Mosley.[125] Only one, Olive Burdett,

[119] HO 215/169.
[120] Bellamy MS iii. 183. HO 214/ 67 lists detainees in poor health in 1944, who included A. J. V. Hepburn-Ruston (father of Audrey Hepburn, appears as J. V. A. Ruston as Consul at Samarang, Java, 1923–4), S. F. Darwin-Fox, and 'Rutland of Jutland' (see below p. 381).
[121] Arthur Graham Owens (presumably the agent SNOW, also George Arthur and Arthur George) is in Stafford on 15 February 1942 and in Dartmoor on 2 February 1943. On 2 February 1943 Anne Bouillon or Anne S. de Rois, supposed Duchesse de Château Thierry, Mathilde C. M. Kraafte, and Stella E. Lonsdale were in Aylesbury, moved there as troublesome, and Gilda Cammillo and Yolande Coppola were in Edinburgh. There is no Duchess of Château Thierry; the place is associated with the battle of the Marne in the 1st World War. Detainees were also in a number of internment camps; see HO 45/25111.
[122] Lists in HO 45/25752. Wolkoff (probably in his 70s) and Cecil Serocold Skeels (aged 70 in June 1943) were unsuited to camp life.
[123] Domvile, From Admiral to Cabin Boy, 116.
[124] HO 45/25753.

was a BU 'Leader', though she was never treated as an important lieutenant.[126] The prison also contained a number of members of the Right
Club, including Mrs Nicholson. An intriguing inmate was the Australian
Clara Marguerita Shorland, who later established a reputation as a
poet.[127]

In 1941 husbands in Brixton were allowed fortnightly visits to wives in
Holloway. The suggestion originated with Birkett and Richard Stokes
MP, and was at first resisted by Home Office officials with a perverse
ingenuity which it would be difficult to rival even in academia. By
January 1941 Morrison had come to favour the idea, eventually adopted so
long as there was equality of treatment in all cases, no lengthy travelling,
and no serious cost to public funds. And, as Newsam the realist pointed
out, the risk of pregnancies simply had to be accepted.[128]

Churchill's Intervention

Churchill had long been a romanticizer over habeas corpus, and although
initially a strong advocate for detention he soon began to have doubts.[129]
In 1941 he became increasingly concerned; being privy to the 'ultra'
decrypts, which Morrison was not, he would have advance notice of any
threat of invasion.[130] He must have long realized that the Fifth Column
was a myth and on 5 November 1940 made his 'increasing scepticism'
clear to the House of Commons.[131] And if an invasion did occur the
authorities were well armed with powers to deal with any internal threat.
Those on the invasion list could be arrested; Regional Commissioners
could order the temporary arrest of others, subversives could be tried by
the War Zone courts, and the army could also shoot individuals out of

[125] See HO 45/25753 sf. 25 for Holloway in July 1941; it contained 863 women; 682 were
either 18Bs or aliens held under Art. 12 (5) A and the prerogative.

[126] Olive Burdett was sent to the Isle of Man in August of 1941, but returned to London
to enable her parents to visit her. As Olive Hawks she published a novel written in deten-
tion, *What Hope for Green Street?* (1945), which gives some account of fascism in the East
End; her other books included *These Frail Vessels* (1948), *Time is My Debtor* (1947), *A
Sparrow for a Farthing* (1950), and, with Eustace Chesser (illustrations by Quentin Crisp),
Life Lies Ahead (1951).

[127] Christobel S. Nicholson, Enid M. Riddell, Iris Ryder, Mary ('Molly') A. G. Stanford,
and Fay Taylour. A list of 2 February 1943 has 16 permanent residents; by now Ryder and
Taylour had left.

[128] See HO 144/21995 (Diana Mosley).

[129] See J. Colville, *The Fringes of Power: 10 Downing Street Diaries 1939–1955* (London,
1985), 178 (29 June) 263 (28 October). P. Stansky, *Churchill. A Profile* (New York, 1973)
quotes a memo of his from his time at the Colonial Office (1905–8) in which he waxed elo-
quent on the evils of detention without trial.

[130] CAB 120/744 cited M. Gilbert, *Winston S. Churchill*, vi. *'Finest Hour'* (New York,
1986), 896 n. 2, list of 8 November 1940. Anderson was given decrypts.

[131] *Parl. Deb.* HC 365: 1248. He indicated that the matter had been 'exaggerated' on 15
August 1940. See *Parl. Deb.* HC Vol. 354 col.957.

hand if it became necessary to do so, as even the legalistic Home Office conceded.[132] Holding hundreds of citizens in detention had become an unnecessary extravagance, and assorted ill with Churchill's self image as the champion of European liberty.

He did not at first suggest ending detention, but merely improving the lot of detainees; in January 1941 he was asking 'whether we could keep them in more humane conditions'.[133] Allowing married couples to live together was under consideration in the Home Office in August, on his initiative.[134] Detainees should be 'interned rather than imprisoned'.[135] The Home Office made incredibly heavy weather of the matter, and on 22 October Maxwell minuted that it was thought unwise to take any action at this time.[136] No doubt the reason was fear of the illiberalism of the left-wing of the Labour party. The court decisions in the Liversidge (and Greene) cases in early November[137] led to strong attacks on 18B, and on 10 November the Cabinet considered Churchill's proposed reply to a Parliamentary question by Commander Bowers asking if, in the light of the grave constitutional issues raised, the law might be modified so as to introduce judicial review of decisions. This spurred Morrison, under fire over married couples, to promise a paper on the subject.[138]

On 15 November 1941, in anticipation of the forthcoming debate on the regulation, Churchill wrote menacingly to him:

Feeling against 18B is very strong, and I should not be prepared to support the regulation indefinitely if it is administered in such an onerous manner. Internment rather than imprisonment is what was contemplated. Sir Oswald Mosley's wife has now been 18 months in prison without the slightest vestige of any charge against her, separated from her husband.

He again asked why married couples should not be interned together. Churchill had in fact been approached through Clementine on behalf of Diana Mosley, whom he knew and apparently liked.[139] The numbers involved were small—the Mosleys, the Domviles, the de Laessoes, and the Burdetts were the only persons of any prominence, and there were eleven other couples.[140] Morrison proposed to release Lady Domvile and transfer the others, except the Mosleys, to married accommodation on the

[132] See above p. 192   [133] HO 45/25752.

[134] HO 45/25753. Monckton, who, somewhat oddly, visited and reported on the Mosleys, had raised the matter, as had Stokes. HO 45/25753. Monckton may have been acting for Churchill.

[135] CAB 65/20 WM (41) 115 of 17 November. See also W. S. Churchill, *The Second World War*, ii. *The Gathering Storm* (London, 1968), 627.

[136] See HO 45/24891, 25117 and 25753, HO 215/360.

[137] Discussed below Chs. 16 and 17.

[138] CAB 65/20 WM 110 (41) of 10 November, minute 5.

[139] J. Guinness, *The House of Mitford* (London, 1984), 506.

[140] There is a list in the file. The unfortunate 'Mr and Mrs' Battersby turned out not to be married.

Isle of Man. He was, however, extremely reluctant to do anything for the Mosleys 'both on security and political grounds'.[141] Before the matter came to the Cabinet the idea of housing the Mosleys and the de Laessoes in Holloway had been put forward; the Cabinet agreed on 24 November, and this was announced on 11 December.[142] They were given flats in the preventive detention wing, and two other couples lived there for a short time before release.[143] Visiting rules were relaxed, and in 1943 Alexander (4) and Max (3) stayed for two nights, with predictable results when they had to leave.

Reactions to Detention

Whatever the conditions some detainees reacted badly. Thus Iris Ryder spent her time in Holloway engaged in compulsively cleaning and re-cleaning her cell.[144] Domvile, brooding over his lot in Brixton, became paranoid: writing of the advisory committee he says: 'The Home Secretary is not bound by the findings of the Committee, and admits to consulting all sorts of outside authorities with a finger in the pie; this is all part of the general hocus pocus, *but I have little doubt that Judmas was the real arbiter of one's fate as an 18B* [my italics].'[145] A particularly striking case is that of James Larratt Battersby, known in fascist circles as 'the mad hatter'. He was a director of Battersby's Hats, and had been a District Leader at Stockport. Detained in June 1940, he went to Latchmere House, where 'everything possible was done to agitate, frustrate and torment us'.[146] On the Isle of Man he became a close friend of the unbalanced Captain Thomas G. St Barbe Baker MC, who came to identify Hitler with Christ, conducting bizarre religious ceremonies. Amongst others who attended with Battersby were C. L. G. de Guerin, said to have become insane in detention, and W. G. Barlow, who was a wealthy BU supporter and at one time a racing driver.[147] The transcript of Baker's committee hearing is a pathetic record of a very sick person. He told the Commandant at Peel 'that these are the last days of the Mammon world in which God will overthrow the old order and establish his Kingdom on earth. Much will be written about Thomas Baker before

---

[141] CAB 66/17, CAB 65/20 WM (41) 115th meeting concl. 5, 116th meeting concl. 6.
[142] CAB 65/20 WM (41) meeting of 24 Nov. The Cabinet had before it Morrison's paper, WP (41) 279
[143] Mosley, *A Life of Contrasts*, 192. One comprised Thomas and Marta Swan; he had been District Treasurer of the Epping BU and Marta Swan was of enemy origin. I have not identified the other couple.
[144] Information from Diana Mosley. She was a cousin of the Duke of Hamilton.
[145] *From Admiral to Cabin Boy*, 105.
[146] Battersby, *Bishop*, 23. This strange book, though published in 1947, appears in part to consist of a diary written in detention.
[147] See above p. 225.

many months have passed . . . '[148] Battersby too developed religious mania and was treated for depression.[149] Released after three years in June of 1943 'through the will of God', he then appeared before a conscientious objectors tribunal, explaining his willingness to 'broadcast my witness to the nation'. After the war he and others set up a religious centre, Kingdom House, in the hamlet of River, near Petworth, Sussex, to continue the worship of Hitler, believed to be Christ returned.[150] Battersby achieved notoriety for disrupting the two-minute silence at the Cenotaph in 1952,[151] and committed suicide in 1955, jumping into the paddles of the Mersey ferry, which decapitated him. His suicide note ended: 'Through the sacrifice of the Aryan martyr the world victory is assured. Heil Hitler.' Cause and effect are hard in these areas to prove, but detention does not seem to have been good for Battersby.

Another pathetic case was that of Daniel Delargez. The son of a Scots miner and a German mother—they had quarrelled and separated—he had been brought up in Germany until he was 8 or 9, and had been continuously unhappy in England. His mother had been detained—he was then 17—and in a desperate attempt to return to his childhood he had set out in a rowing boat in August 1941 across the Channel. He was caught, and sentenced to three months in prison. Detained in Brixton, he suffered from claustrophobia, screaming to be let out; the myth, universal in such establishments, that the food is drugged with bromide, preyed on his mind. He was befriended by another detainee, Frederick C. Wiseman, who described him as being 'like a recently beaten dog looking for a master'.[152] Moved to Peveril Camp, where it is clear that he was humanely treated, his condition became worse, and in 1942 he was moved to the County Mental Hospital at Whittingham in Lancashire. Again it is hard to see that his detention did him or anyone else any good. Reports from Peveril Camp show that at least six detainees were transferred to the mental hospital, and that the health of a significant number of the long-term detainees was poor.[153]

---

[148] HO 214/45 lists Duvivier, Rowe, and Echlin also as attending.

[149] Charnley, *Blackshirts and Roses*, 175–6.

[150] Information from R. Row, who tells me that it was raided by some army officers; there was a fight and it closed down. Those attending were Baker, A. J. Schneider, Battersby, and Barlow; the latter financed it.

[151] He was charged with insulting behaviour. See *Daily Telegraph*, 10 and 18 November 1952, 5 October 1955.

[152] Wiseman Papers, Imperial War Museum. F. C. Wiseman, a preparatory school teacher, had been the BU District Treasurer in Worcester. The pamphlet *In Search of Justice* notes this case as Case number 4 in its list of 'Tragedies'.

[153] HO 215/36. Darwin-Fox is said to have become insane in detention. J. L. Lockhart, detained at the age of 19, was a voluntary patient in a mental hospital at the time of his detention, but was officially viewed as neither mad nor certifiable. See HO 45/25752. Joe Beckett, the boxer, became melancholic and tearful (Grundy MS).

A more common reaction was resentment and outrage. Thus W. K. J. Stevenson, whose clothes had worn out in detention, refused to replace them; let the Home Office pay: 'I did not ask to be put in a British Concentration Camp and then be robbed of my living.'[154] The Home Office gave way. Jon Sigidur Oddson is another example. A trawler skipper and owner, detained as a BU supporter, he was of Icelandic origin, long resident in Britain, and naturalized. He opposed the war, and resented the occupation of Iceland; there were suspicions of his loyalty, though Birkett's committee in December of 1940 stated that 'the committee has not the slightest doubt of Oddson's loyalty, and recommend his immediate release'. He remained in detention from August 1940 to July 1943. The committee before whom he appeared in 1942 reported: 'It is difficult to interview ODDSON. He is greatly hurt and crushed by his detention and obviously seems to be suffering from a sort of weariness of spirit.'[155] In some cases outrage became obsessive; Ben Greene brooded continuously on the injustice of his detention.[156] Robert Liversidge, as I can attest, strongly resents his experiences over forty years later. Both were entirely innocent of disloyal wrongdoing. In a more general sense the vast majority of 18B detainees were innocent; they had done nothing illegal. It is in the nature of preventive detention to detain the innocent, and detainees naturally, and quite correctly, regarded detention as unjust. As the Labour Lord Chancellor Jowitt said in the House of Lords in 1946: 'After all, let us be fair to those people who were imprisoned under Order 18B, and let us remember that they have never been accused of any crime; not only have they not been convicted of a crime, but they have not been accused of a crime. This should be remembered in all fairness to them.'[157] In making this statement Jowitt was not of course saying that they should not have been detained, a quite separate question.

The sense of injustice was aggravated by the stigma of disloyalty. This particularly outraged those members of the BU, the great majority, who conceived themselves to be intensely patriotic; patriotism was central to the ideology of fascism. Hence much was made of the military distinction—the medals and wounds—of detainees.[158] On 30 November 1940 120 ex-servicemen in York Camp wrote a letter of protest.[159] The pamphlet *It Might Have Happened to You!* has a special section on the ex-service detainees, quoting a speech by Sir Irvine Albery on 10 December 1940:

---

[154] HO 215/39, letters of 18 July 1941 and (Domvile) 20 July 1942.
[155] HO 45/25738, partly retained, HO 283/51. In detention he seems to have become associated with the far right, but this may have been a consequence of his detention.
[156] Private information.   [157] *Parl. Deb.* HL Vol. 144 c.848.
[158] The current newssheet *Comrade* is much concerned to making this argument by recording the war service of former BU members.
[159] See HO 144/21992/840194 (file on Major H. H. A. de Laessoe DSO, MC) seen on privileged access.

A great many of the men under Reg. 18B served this country loyally and faithfully in the last war and many of them are decorated. Is anybody . . . justified without the most definite evidence in suspecting men who served this country in the last war . . . and women too, merely because they happen to have had some association with principles which perhaps are not approved?[160]

It also refers specifically to the 63-year-old Lieutenant-Colonel Cherry and to 'J. W. and E. C. D., both officers and Pilots of the Great War' who headed the ex-service section at Peel Camp.[161] It is impossible to give figures, but my general impression is that the number of 18B detainees who were straightforwardly pro-Nazi, and favoured a German victory, or who engaged in disloyal and criminal conduct, was very small indeed, though as we have seen there were some such.

Active Resistance to Authority

In spite of the nervousness of the authorities there was little active or even passive resistance to authority. Some few detainees, for example Leese and Knott, refused to co-operate at all.[162] Pitt-Rivers had to be forcibly dragged to his committee hearing.[163] Leese went on hunger strike and induced the Brixton authorities to forcibly feed him to secure publicity when Stokes was due to ask a question about his case.[164] But Frederick H. U. Bowman, or 'Sir Frederick' as he later called himself, was the most persistently non-co-operative detainee whose case is documented.[165] In Brixton he founded the Frederick Bowman Freedom League, for which he obtained headed paper. In July 1942 he attempted to escape from Brixton disguised as a cleric; he was punished by being put on 'No. 1 Diet' for nine days.[166] He began a hunger strike but, on being moved to hospital, said he was willing to take liquid voluntarily, and did so. He was again punished in October for his intransigence in refusing to accept his punishment by fifteen further days 'No. 1 Diet'. He again went on hunger strike, but said he was willing to swallow voluntarily the sustenance which Dr Grierson proposed to feed him forcibly by tube, an inherently danger-ous and very unpleasant procedure. Bowman thought he had thus beaten the system, but the authorities refused his offer, and forcibly fed him on 2 November; plainly this was not medically necessary, and was simply a

[160] *Parl. Deb.* HC Vol. 367 c.792, 835.

[161] J. W. is John Wynn, and E. C. D. is E. C. Dunn, also formerly RFC.

[162] HO 214/45 has a list of detainees who refused to co-operate with the review of 1943 —P. E. Wright, W. G. Eaton, V. R. Pepler, S. E. (or E. C.) Dunn, and W. E. Sherston.

[163] Charnley, *Blackshirts and Roses*, 117.   [164] Leese, *Out of Step*, 65–7.

[165] HO 45/25729 and 25753. On 7 December Stokes took up his case with Morrison with-out success; a copy of Morrison's letter of 15 January 1943 is in the Britons' Archives.

[166] Bread and water for 3 days, prison diet for 3 days, bread and water for 3 days.

punishment. In desperation it was decided to release him conditionally; he refused to accept the conditions, and eventually the Home Office thought it was simpler to release him unconditionally. It was even suggested that he be forcibly expelled from prison. After release he sued for assault—the penal forced feeding: Valentine Holmes advised settling the action, but Morrison refused to agree, although it seems quite clear that Grierson's action was illegal. In the event Bowman, who conducted his own case before the irascible Mr Justice Charles, whom he annoyed, lost in what was surely not one of British justice's golden moments.[167] Bowman continued to be a thorn in the flesh of the authorities after the war, bitterly complaining at having been excluded from the Royal Enclosure at Ascot.[168]

These were isolated acts, but rumours that detainees were to be sent abroad caused talk in Walton Gaol of a mass breakout, but nothing was done.[169] In the Isle of Man there were demonstrations, and one minor but much publicized riot.[170] On 17 September 1941 six detainees had tunnelled a way out of the camp.[171] One of them, Arthur L. Mason, had been District Leader at Limehouse, and had previously escaped from Huyton with Alexander J. Markl.[172] Three of them, Mason and two IRA men, John Barry and Joseph Walker, acquired a boat, Sunbeam, in which they set out to row to Ireland. They were picked up by HMS Radiant and returned to Peveril, where it got about that the unpopular acting Commandant, a Captain Ryan, had refused them food.[173] This provoked the riot, which lasted all night, and which the authorities were unable to control. There were two minor injuries. Eventually peace was restored by negotiations between Osbert Peake from the Home Office and 'Mick' Clarke (or possibly Richard Findlay) for the detainees; Peake had flown over in connection with the escapes, and it is said he was pelted.[174]

[167] See DOM 56 for 22–4 March 1944.
[168] See LCO 2/2712. He claimed to have been presented at a levee in 1934.
[169] Bellamy MS iii. 130.
[170] The Beavan Diary notes a demonstration on 2 June 1941. There is a highly coloured account in Chappell, Island of Barbed Wire, ch. 15. I have relied principally on HO 215/492 and 493, Charnley, Blackshirts and Roses, 136–45, and accounts by Arthur Mason in Comrade, 15 and 18.
[171] Arthur L. Mason (former D/L Limehouse, Joseph Barry (IRA), Joseph Fleming alias Walker (IRA), Christopher Schirmer (apparently an Anglo-German born in Ireland and holding an Irish passport), and two others. They may have been C. W. Barnick, D. M. Egan, or J. C. Preen; see HO 45/25752.
[172] Comrade, 13. Mason reached London and was arrested in the home of John and Ada Wilson, who were imprisoned for 6 weeks for harbouring him. Markl was a BU detainee from south London.
[173] The Commandant was a Maj. Dunne, who may not have taken up his appointment when the riot occurred. In June the Commandant was a Capt. Petrie; there was a petition for his removal (Beavan Diary, 16 June 1941). His assistants, Lts. Grant and Neville, seem to have been well liked.
[174] See his DNB entry.

Churchill, hearing of this on the BBC news, was alarmed lest it seem that the government was showing weakness to fascists. He suggested arming the guards with buckshot to encourage them to fire on detainees without hesitation, a repulsive suggestion naturally rejected by the Home Office.[175] Instead the camp was placed under a metropolitan police officer, Superintendent S. M. Ogden, assisted by fifty constables, who took over on 13 October.[176] Some eighteen individuals on a hurriedly compiled and inaccurate list of 'troublemakers' were moved to Brixton and Walton.[177] There were other escapes; thus one individual escaped from the military hospital at Rainhill in order to visit his fiancée, and remained at large for some three weeks, and in 1943 there were eight incidents involving seventeen detainees.[178] But the vast majority of detainees accepted their lot with resignation, as prisoners, in general, everywhere do.

The Defence Regulations made no provision for enforcing discipline on detainees, and Dowson initially thought that a set of disciplinary regulations ought to be authorized by Order in Council. Maxwell, no doubt concerned to head off political trouble by secrecy, opposed this, and his scheme, accepted with some misgivings over its legality, was to justify punishments by calling them withdrawal of privileges conferred under 18B (8); thus a detainee in solitary was simply being denied the privilege of association, rather than being punished illegally. In the event no special disciplinary code for 18Bs was ever introduced; the Home Office applied a code devised for aliens detained under the prerogative.[179] Troublesome detainees were also moved from camps to prisons as a punishment. The legality of these practices was never canvassed in litigation.

[175] CAB 65/20 WM (41) 4, PREM 4/39/4A, personal minute of 23 Sept. 1941.
[176] HO 215/490.
[177] Two were IRA—W. H. Barrie and J. Carberry; 14 were BU—E. G. ('Mick') Clarke, D. J. Beet (a Leeds D/L), J. W. Charnley, L. Flockhart, C. H. Hammond (who held a letter of authority from Mosley), C. Hill (D/L), T. K. King (AD/L Westminster), J. Lloyd (Acting D/L), J. L. Lockhart, R. M. Lomax (who had been discharged from the army for fascist activities), K. E. Marsden (Regional Inspector), M. J. Ryan (D/L Wandsworth), G. S. Surtees (D/L Lowestoft), C. Taylor (ordinary member). M. A. Reale was Anglo-Italian, and so was Pasquale di Mascio, apparently an epileptic. Charnley adds one T. J. Ashworth Jones, a Welshman, and says that one 'Jimmy' had been in the army. Perhaps this was Lloyd. Supt. Ogden suggested in December of 1941 that 6 of them, Beet, Hill, King, Lockhart, Ryan, and Surtees, might be allowed to return as 'they were roped in rather hurriedly to make up the number'. A Home Office minute acidly points out that the military authorities were never asked to make up any number. See HO 45/25752. Of the BU detainees Clarke and Lloyd were moved to Brixton, and Flockhart and Hammond ended up there after a spell in Walton. Barrie of the IRA went there and was released in June 1942, but Carberry was deported to Eire. By the end of May 1942 only Charnley, Lomax, and di Mascio remained in Walton. Beet, Marsden, Reale, Ryan, and Taylor had by then been released.
[178] Charnley, *Blackshirts and Roses*, 127–8, HO 215/36.
[179] HO 215/186, 196, HO 45/25104.

Hail Mosley and 'F' 'Em All

Of all reactions to detention the most curious was that of the fascists in Ascot Camp.[180] At first they were demoralized and quarrelsome:

Some men were blaming the Leader and the Movement for their arrest and detention, and were beginning to feel bitter and wished to God they had never joined. Some were blaming the British Public and were openly saying that they hoped Germany would give them a good hiding. Some said they would only see British Union put into power by Hitler; could only visualize being ultimately released by the men in grey green uniforms . . . Others, (thank God the majority) said that they would resist such a step with their lives.

The author of this passage, Watts, responded by forming the 'HAIL MOSLEY AND "F" 'EM ALL ASSOCIATION'. Many signed his membership book and the letters HMFEA began to be chalked on walls in the camp.

In September Watts was approached by Battersby, Flockhart, and Reynolds[181] over a plan to commemorate the foundation of the party. This event took place with the Camp Commandant's permission in the hall formerly used for training the circus animals. There were speeches by Watts, by the elected camp leader J. Duckworth, and by representatives of London and of the north, south, east, and west counties. Notes were kept by Basil Gill.[182] There were fascist hymns—'Hymn to Britain' by Ralph Dawson of Canterbury, 'British Battle Song' by F. C. Wiseman and 'Britain Awake', the fascist marching song. There was even a reading from Oswald Mosley's *Comrades in Struggle* by Arthur W. Swan of Lowestoft. But the high point of the evening was the ghostly entry of the Leader himself as his health was drunk:

This was the signal for the curtains of the stage to be drawn aside to reveal a life-size portrait of the Leader. It was a remarkable likeness, and the effect it had on the assembled Blackshirts was terrific. The whole audience sprang to their feet, their pent up emotions and fervour rushed to the surface and burst forth with as passionate a cry of salutation—Hail Mosley!—as I have ever heard. I shall never forget that moment.[183]

As a result of this the party was reconstituted under Watts's leadership with the aim of keeping alive 'the Spirit of BRITAIN FIRST', with a Social Leader, R. R. Bellamy, a Policy Leader, J. L. Battersby, and a Physical Leader, C. Dickinson; a paper, *Unity*, was started, the first of its two issues including the text of the 'Holloway 18B Song', somehow smuggled to Ascot. The next event organized was an Armistice Day Parade for the ex-servicemen:

---

[180] See Watts MS, chs. 9–13 and the Wiseman Papers.
[181] D/L Shoreditch and AD/L Wood Green.
[182] Later in the RAF and killed in a flying accident.   [183] Watts MS, 62.

More than a third of the British population of Ascot were on the parade. They included Admirals, Commanders, Colonels, Majors, Captains, Squadron Leaders and many junior officers and N.C.O's, both of this war and the last. The medal ribbons were a sight and included a D.S.O., D.F.C. and many D.C.M.s and M.C.s . . . There were a number of 1914/1915 Stars, many with the Mons Rosetta. At least two Long Service Medals and last but by no means least, a grand old gentleman from Gillingham, Kent, with the two medals of the South African War. Old 'Pop' Williams was a very proud man indeed to be an 18B in the company of his three sons.[184]

On Mosley's birthday some 230 BU detainees gathered to celebrate, and the ritual of the portrait was repeated, with the additional symbolism of the empty chair. The scene was described by Clement Hill:

with our tin cans held aloft we toasted our Leader. As the cans were raised, a rustle of curtains turned our gaze in the direction of the stage and a portrait of the Leader came into view, a portrait executed with lifelike clarity upon a blackout board, with a cut out of the Flash and Circle beneath it. No picture, sketch or photograph has ever brought a more spontaneous burst of cheering than that which echoed and re-echoed throughout the building that night . . . We saw no lifeless portrait, but a living thing becoming more animated and vibrant with emotion as wave after wave of cheering, banging and stamping of feet broke around us.[185]

So it was that the more dedicated of the BU detainees regained their *esprit de corps* by this ritual reinforcement of their fascist beliefs, and by submission to their absent yet present Leader. Arthur Beavan's diary of his time in the Isle of Man indicates that a disciplined organization survived there too.[186] It comes as no surprise that many who were to be active in trying to revive forms of fascism after the war had remained loyal to the Movement in detention. There is absolutely nothing to equal persecution for consolidating ideological belief.

[184] Ibid. 79–80.
[185] Ibid. 85–6; the description is also quoted in the Wiseman Papers.
[186] I have a copy of the menu for the BU Agricultural Dinner held there on 16 April 1941.

12

The Bureaucracy under Stress

The Home Office Loses Control

The massive increase in the use of detention between May and September of 1940 placed great strains upon the bureaucracy. In addition to 18B detainees there were around 28,000 enemy aliens, detained under the prerogative, and a substantial number of non-enemy aliens, of whom, by November, 895 had been made subject to orders.[1] There were also IRA expulsion orders to be made.[2] In terms of paper alone this meant over 30,000 Home Office files, not to mention those of the committee and MI5.

Regulation 18B orders remained in theory under Anderson's direct control, but their judicial and individual character could not survive the imposition by the War Cabinet of political and military policy. Legally the Home Secretary personally made the orders; although the point never arose in litigation, the making of such orders involves in legal theory a 'quasi-judicial' decision, the performance of which cannot be delegated. But the idea of Anderson applying his own judgement to each case was now fanciful; Home Office officials took the decisions, perforce accepting most of MI5's recommendations which they had no way of checking, and relying on Birkett and his colleagues to check them *after* detention had occurred. Crudely, it was lock up first, and worry about it later. In June of 1940 Anderson made 826 18B orders alone, and at ten minutes an order 137 man hours would have been involved. In July the total was 436. Later, in litigation over prison conditions in 1940, even Lord Justice Goddard, never one to cause trouble to the authorities, hinted at some duplicity in affidavits put in by the Home Office in litigation:

---

[1] *Parl. Deb.* H. C. Vol. 365 for 20 November gives the figure. All orders were revoked at the end of the war. Orders were made under Article 12 (5A) of the Aliens Order and DR 20A, on which see HO 213/240. Appeals went to a committee chaired by Sir Francis O. Lindley, a retired diplomat, originally only for cases where foreign governments protested; it was secret and comprised Lindley, A. F. Aveling of the Foreign Office, and Newsam of the Home Office. It evolved into an advisory committee; members included C. R. Havers KC (later a High Court judge 1951–67), and the Secretary was Inspector J. Holmes of Special Branch. The committee heard some 500 cases; all its papers have apparently been destroyed. See FO 371/25254, HO 213/1069.

[2] Whether Monckton still advised on IRA orders is obscure.

What—500 people, every one of whose cases are to be personally considered by the Secretary of State? . . . it must take a very considerable time for consideration to be given to 500 separate cases . . . But individual cases have to be considered; and in other cases which are reported and which I have in mind, the Home Secretary swore that he had considered each case.[3]

The Attorney-General, seeking to excuse the Home Office, had unwisely emphasized how many people had been detained in a very short period. No doubt even during the summer of 1940 checking by senior officials sometimes took place, for example in the case of Aubrey Lees, who was a Colonial Office official.[4] This would be true of other important people such as Diana Mosley, Domvile, Captain Pitt-Rivers, or Prince Henry of Pless.[5] Some requests for orders which were rejected may also have been considered personally by Anderson and his senior officials, as we know happened in the case of the Duke of Bedford; 'Boney' Fuller's file must surely have come before Newsam, Maxwell, and Anderson too.[6]

But most decisions to detain were now illegally delegated.[7] Hence the language of the regulation could only be reconciled with reality by a degree of fiction or mendacity, as no doubt Lord Justice Goddard well knew. Indeed in the case of 18B (1A) orders, and the Italian orders—and probably others—the initial decision as to whom to detain in reality passed out of the Home Office entirely to MI5, Special Branch, and Chief Constables, whose recommendations could not be checked even by junior officials. MI5 was also in a state of very considerable administrative confusion at this period;[8] although DR 8 forms were approved on behalf of MI5 it had to rely upon Chief Constables for information as to whom to detain, they being guided, it was hoped, by exhortations embodied in the circular to Chief Constables of 14 June. The part played by MI5's Regional Security Liaison Officers is obscure, but in the early summer of 1940 they only existed in some regions.[9] Special Branch also initiated some orders, the number by October 1944 being 224; its unreliability is illustrated by the case of Aubrey Lees and that of Harry Sabini, who both became litigants.[10] Precisely what documentation accompanied a request

[3] Transcript in TS 27/512; for discussion see below p. 348.
[4] See above p.142 et seq and below p. 298 et seq. [5] Detained in mid-August 1940.
[6] See above p. 209.
[7] Apart from the power to delegate authority for interim detention orders to Regional Commissioners by SRO 1940 No. 135.
[8] Hinsley and Simkins, 67–70.
[9] Ibid. 66, noting the appointment of such officers in Civil Defence Regions 4 (Cambridge) and 12 (Tunbridge Wells). A Home Office circular of 1 July (in HO 45/25758/115456) instructed Chief Constables to send copies of requests to such officers; by the end of September the whole country had been covered by this system. N. West gives a list of 12 such officers. Some, like Alan S. MacIver (probably), John C. Maude, John C. Phipps, and Geoffrey P. Wethered were barristers; one, Gerald A. Glover, was a solicitor.
[10] TS 27/496A. See also HO 45/25720. See below Ch. 14.

for a detention order at this time is unclear; it may well have been confined to the laconic DR 8 form alone in the case of an individual order. With omnibus orders even DR 8 forms may not have been provided.

In the Home Office attention thus came to focus upon whether to maintain detention, or release the detainee, conditionally or unconditionally, once more information became available. Normally this would be after the detainee had been before the committee, and its report had been received. Under Anderson this secondary decision was simply delegated to Birkett's committee, whose recommendations were automatically accepted. Morrison, Home Secretary from October 1940 until the end of the war, did not follow this practice. In November 1940 three recommendations were rejected. In December there were eighteen rejections, and in January 1941 fifty-five. Morrison did make a fair number of new orders, 168 in all; his latest order was made in August of 1944. But he was principally responsible for releasing, or delaying the release, of his fellow citizens, rather than detaining them. Naturally disagreements between the Home Office and MI5 now tended to arise at this secondary stage.

Unlike the primary decision to intern, this secondary decision was, under Morrison, actively taken by the Home Office, whose officials were able to consider each case, using information derived from the committee report, the associated documents, and MI5's observations. Some individual cases were given serious attention by Morrison in person, but many must have been settled by his officials, particularly in late 1940 and early 1941. As we shall see, some questions of general policy also became the concern of the Swinton Committee, and even the Cabinet; Morrison was no doubt kept informed and made his contribution to the outcome. The precise mechanics of decision-taking during the war are not easy to establish from the available papers. A complicating factor is that at some point in late 1940 A. S. Hutchinson and the more junior officials involved with 18B, principally E. N. Cooper and H. H. C. Prestige, appear to have been based in Bournemouth; presumably liaison over individual cases with Newsam, Maxwell, and Morrison must have suffered.[11]

Shifting the point of decision to the secondary stage in no way reduced the burden on Home Office officials; it probably made matters worse. Committee hearings generated a mass of paper—the original documents were now afforced by letters from friends of the detainee, and sometimes from Members of Parliament, the 'Reasons for Order', the 'Statement of the Case' (not available when the original decision to detain was made), the transcript, sometimes very lengthy, of the hearing, the report itself, and MI5's observations. I know of not a single surviving file which is complete. It is hardly surprising that handling all this paper began to pre-

[11] Luttman-Johnson Papers.

sent serious problems, even though the staff of the Home Office increased greatly during the war. One consequence was formal errors of one kind and another; these, as we shall see, attracted particular attention in the courts, where the judges derived some malign satisfaction from criticizing the Civil Servants.

The officials reacted by initiating a secret review of the Italian orders, which appear to have been in a particularly bad state; this was carried out by lawyers in the Treasury Solicitor's Department.[12] It revealed an alarming number of mistakes. The 'grounds' of the order provided to the detainee might differ from the order, or the 'particulars' might not conform to the 'grounds', or the 'copy' of the order might not conform to the order actually signed.[13] We can be certain that there were other internal investigations which have not been allowed to survive, as one which led to the release of a number of detainees after the case of Captain Budd was before the courts.[14] Other paperwork also fell into arrears; on 27 June 1940 there were 230 cases where orders had been issued, but the Home Office did not know whether they had been served or not.[15] Since it became impossible to keep check on the bulky individual files a system of cards was introduced for statistical purposes, but even this was defective.[16] The reports for October, November, and December omit the number of cases disposed of by the committee, either because no accurate figures were available or because the situation was too embarrassing.

The Advisory Committee

Birkett's committee could not handle the increased work. On 7 June 1940 he was relieved of appeals from enemy aliens, until then his main concern; he had heard 288 alien appeals, and only sixty-nine appeals under 18B.[17] On 17 June John W. Morris KC, MC, who held the office of Judge of Appeal in the Isle of Man, was appointed Deputy Chairman, and the committee began to sit in two panels, Birkett retaining overall responsibility.[18] In July,[19] Hubert J. Wallington KC[20] and Alexander T. Miller KC[21] were also appointed as deputies to create four panels. Another

---

[12] In TS 27/509.   [13] There were 46 instances of this.   [14] See below Ch. 15.

[15] HO 45/25758. A circular on 1 July exhorted Chief Constables to report back promptly.

[16] See HO 45/25115 especially sf. 14 for December 1940.

[17] See HO 283/22 (memo of 5 March 1941 by G. P. Churchill) and HO 45/25114.

[18] Morris (1896–1979) became a judge of the High Court in 1945, served on the Court of Appeal 1945–51, and became a Law Lord as Lord Morris of Borth-y-Gest, 1960–75.

[19] On 11 July and 22 July.

[20] Died 1962. Originally a solicitor; called to the bar in 1910; chairman of one of the committees which classified aliens; 1940–2 chaired the Aliens Advisory Committee for the Midland Civil Defence Region 9; judge in the Probate, Admiralty, and Divorce Division 1944–60.

[21] 1875–1942, called to the bar in 1908.

deputy, Archibald W. Cockburn KC[22] was added on 19 August; additional ordinary members were appointed, so that by mid-August there were fourteen members in addition to Birkett himself. A further deputy, E. Paul Bennett VC, MC, Metropolitan Police Magistrate, was appointed on 30 December.[23] Mr Geoffrey W. Russell, a solicitor from Garrett and Co., joined the committee on 3 October, and in November became a deputy chairman allowed to preside over a division when Birkett, Morris, and Cockburn were all not available.[24]

Matters were not improved by the bombing of 6 Burlington Gardens, the premises used in London. In September the committee moved to the Berystede Hotel at Ascot. This was inconvenient for the lawyers, and after the move only Birkett's, Morris's, and Cockburn's panels normally sat.[25] They acquired six additional assistant secretaries.[26]

On 26 August responsibility for the Anglo-Italians was transferred to a new committee under Sir Percy Loraine. A wealthy landowner and baronet, he had been a somewhat unsuccessful Ambassador to Italy from 1939 until Italy entered the war. Having favoured the Munich agreement he was left by Churchill without employment.[27] The decision to set up a special Italian Committee was announced in Parliament on 15 August.[28] A conference was held at the Home Office on 26 August to organize its work.[29] The principal Secretary, A. E. Watkins, had been in the Consulate General in Naples, and the legal member was Richard

[22] 1887–1969. Called in 1913 he had been Recorder of Oxford 1936–8, and was at the time Deputy Chairman of London Sessions. He was an Oxford graduate. He never rose to become a High Court judge.

[23] 1892–1970. Called to the bar in 1923.

[24] HO 213/563 has list of members of the committee.

[25] Those who regularly sat after the committee moved to Ascot were Sir George R. Clerk (1874–1951), Sir Arthur Hazlerigg, Mrs Jacqueline T. Cockburn JP and wife of A. W. Cockburn, Mr G. H. Stuart-Bunning OBE, JP, Mr Geoffrey M. Russell, Prof. William E. Collinson, Prof. J. L. Brierley OBE, JP (1881–1955), Chichele Prof. of International Law in Oxford, Violet R. Markham, and Mrs Madeleine Robinson, formerly Miss Symons (a London JP). Other members included J. J. Mallon JP (Warden of Toynbee Hall), C. C. Walkinshaw, Mrs Evelyn Lowe, Sir Harry Pritchard, formerly President of the Law Society, Mr J. P. Crump, formerly Lord Mayor of Birmingham and a trade union official, and F. J. Mansfield, formerly President of the National Union of Journalists. Pritchard did not sit after August, and from September Wallington, Miller, Lowe, Walkinshaw, and Crump did not sit. Although the Home Office denied, no doubt technically correctly, any 'resignations', Wallington may in reality have dropped out intentionally. See *Parl. Deb.* HC Vol. 371 c.33 for 22 April 1941. An attempt to recruit the writer J. A. Spender failed.

[26] Miss M. Williamson (17 June), Mr F. H. Bygott (18 June), Mr E. L. Philip (5 August), Mr W. R. Parkin (5 September), Miss C. V. Williams (29 August, but only served for two weeks), and Miss Redmayne (3 October).

[27] 1880–1961. See the entry in the *DNB*. Many of his papers are in FO 1011, including papers on the Advisory Committee for 1940 (FO 1011/215) and for 1941–3 (FO 1011/216).

[28] *Parl. Deb.* HC Vol. 364 c.942.

[29] In addition to the Home Office and Prison Commissioners H. L. Farquhar represented the Foreign Office and C. H. N. Adams represented MI5.

O'Sullivan KC; later George Worth, who had been an honorary civil assistant to the military attaché in Rome, and long lived in Italy, became Secretary to the second panel. H. L. Oates, of the Special Branch, succeeded him in January 1941.[30] Two diplomats, C. H. Bateman[31] and O. A. Scott,[32] were drafted in to help, together with Professor Harold C. Gutteridge KC, an academic lawyer and linguist of some ability, later Professor of Comparative Law in Cambridge.[33] The Italian Committee at first had premises at Romney House in Marsham Street and soon moved to Mylor House, Ascot. In late September a second panel was set up under Sir Rollo F. Graham-Campbell, Chief Metropolitan Police Magistrate.[34] The second panel moved to the Isle of Man.[35] The committees—there may have been more than two—were responsible for around 600 18B detainees, apparently mostly of dual nationality,[36] and supposed to be members of the Fascio, and around 3,000 Italian nationals. But many detainees were released by administrative action without appearing before the committee; of the dual nationals ninety-seven had been released by 17 September 1940. The committees, or perhaps that presided over by Loraine, heard in all 2,994 appeals.[37] The special Italian committees were partly a response to protests over delay in hearing appeals—apparently virtually none had been heard when the first was set up. On 24 August J. Anderson, the secretary of the Scottish committee, wrote to the Home Office saying that until the Italian committee started work 'I suppose I have no alternative but to continue to pour forth a stream of soothing commonplaces to the Solicitors who are writing to me (in a state of gradually increasing fury) about the delay in disposing of their clients' cases'. Partly it was a response to pressure from the Foreign Office for more sympathetic and informed treatment of Anglo-Italians and Italian residents.[38]

The Scottish committee, whose original chairman was Lord Alness, later replaced by Lord Jamieson, did not sit at all between May 1940 and the end of August.[39] There were close to 200 detainees in prison in Scotland though releases by administrative action had reduced them to

[30] Recommended by the Master of the Rolls.
[31] CMG, seconded 27 August 1940 to 18 December. Later Ambassador in Mexico.
[32] Seconded 1 October 1940 to February 1942. Later knighted and Ambassador to Peru.
[33] (1876–1953). Gutteridge soon resigned to care for his ill daughter.
[34] 1868–1946.
[35] See HO 45/25758, TS 27/496A, and HO 45/25720/840793, HO 213/1068.
[36] Home Office memo of guidance for the new committee in HO 45/25758/11546. On 17 Sept. 601 dual nationals had been detained.
[37] HO 213/1068. 4,100 had been detained, but some 1,100 had been sent out of the country. Invalids and the infirm were supposed to be exempt.
[38] For Italians there were Foreign Office 'assessors'. New members were Sir John L. Macleod and William Elgar, a trade unionist.
[39] Papers are in HO 45/25755.

150 by mid-September.[40] On 15 August the Lord Advocate wrote to Anderson protesting at the delay: 'I am deeply concerned at the continued failure of the authorities to give these people the right conferred under the Defence Regulations . . . it is certain that release would be recommended in at least some of the cases.' At the end of August he complained again; by then 171 appeals were outstanding. The largest group comprised 137 Anglo-Italians, whose cases, it was decided, were to be transferred to Loraine's committee; in the event a special Scottish Italian committee was set up, but virtually nothing seems to be discoverable about it. No records exist in Edinburgh. Its members were J. L. Clyde KC, Lieutenant-Colonel the Hon. Anthony Murray CMG, DSO, and Miss Marion M. Martin. Six BU cases went to Birkett; the BU hardly existed in Scotland. This left twenty-eight cases, but at the end of August MI5 had only produced papers for three of them. When in September Pilcher of MI5 did find time to deal with the paperwork he found that three detainees, Louis Meotti, Charles Frenz, and Elly Jooster (or Robertson), were entirely harmless people whose detention he could not support, and Maxwell arranged for their release in October without appearance before the committee. Although MI5 had approved detention on the standard DR 8 form—in the case of Frenz this was in fact submitted some weeks *after* his order was signed—the villain of the story was the Chief Constable of Dundee, J. Neilans, who had imagined for no good reason that they were spies.

In spite of these and other changes,[41] it took a very considerable time for the backlog of cases to be cleared. So disorganized was the bureaucracy that in July only thirty-one cases were disposed of; at the end of that month there were 1,373 detainees. The figure for August for cases disposed of rose to 111, but in September actually fell to ninety-three; in the course of the first full month at Ascot only 200 cases were heard. These figures reveal something approaching a collapse of the system. From October no figures were published, though it was between October 1940 and late February 1941 that most hearings took place. But by the time Birkett and his colleagues moved back to London on 22 February 1941 1,100 cases had been heard, 704 of them at Ascot.[42] At the end of that month the number in detention had fallen by 499 from its peak figure. On 3 March 1941, when G. P. Churchill, no doubt exhausted, retired as Secretary, only twenty-two appeals were outstanding.[43] In April the

[40] Some in Barlinnie and some in Saughton, Edinburgh.

[41] The Italian Committee did not produce transcripts of all hearings. At a meeting of the Home Defence (Security) Executive on 6 November (HO 45/25754/863027/6) Birkett raised other problems, such as a shortage of typists; he wanted more chairmen to be appointed, and suggested reducing the size of each panel.

[42] HO 283/22.

[43] HO 283/22. Birkett's panel heard 190, Morris's 183, Cockburn's 264, and Bennett's 67.

English committee, its major work now over, was reconstituted with Birkett, Morris, and Cockburn as chairmen, and six other members.[44]

Obviously many detainees waited very long periods before they appeared before the committee; as we shall see this was made the basis for habeas corpus proceedings. On 24 October Morrison conceded that on 3 October approximately 400 detainees had not appeared after three months' detention.[45] Even after appearance there were further delays before the committee report was prepared, and eventually the secondary decision taken as to what was to become of the detainee.

Birkett himself suffered from overwork, and in 1941, after the backlog had been cleared, agreed to visit the USA as a British propagandist; no doubt the reason was Lord Halifax's disastrous early period as Ambassador to Washington. He asked to be relieved of the chairmanship. Various replacements were considered. Maxwell, after consulting Schuster and Lord Swinton, thought that no mere barrister would suffice, though there was some support for A. T. Denning KC; a real judge would be needed to reassure the public, and head off trouble in Parliament. The first choice was Mr Justice Asquith, whom Swinton thought 'had shown a wise appreciation of the security point of view'. The reference must be to something dubious he did in conducting the trial of Karl Drucke and Werner Walti under the Treachery Act, the day before Swinton wrote this. A third spy, Vera Erikson, was not put on trial, and possibly Asquith was 'understanding' about this. The little that is known about this case raises suspicions, and an understanding judge may have been much appreciated.[46] Other judges suggested were Mr Justice Lawrence, who was thought to be potentially 'awkward', and Mr Justice Lewis. After other suggestions had been canvassed it was decided to retain Birkett, and have Morris stand in for him for the time being.[47] Soon after his return Birkett was made a judge, the appointment being offered, surely not accidentally, on 3 November, the day the Liversidge and Greene cases were decided. The committee was chaired at last by a real judge, and one with whom the civil servants could live; he retained his position until the war ended.

[44] Stuart-Bunning, Clerk, Mrs Cockburn, Miss Markham, Russell, and Stott. Clerk resigned on 9 May 1941, writing that 'we have been sustained by the knowledge that we were striving in a reeling world, perhaps not altogether ineffectually, for the maintenance of trust in British justice and by the hope that the Home Office, and even MI5, appreciated our sincerity, even when they rejected our recommendations'. He was reappointed in October 1942.

[45] *Parl. Deb.* HC Vol. 365 c.1122.

[46] See Hinsley and Simkins, 323–5, N. West, *MI5* (London, 1983), 317–21, 342–3; West claims that Erikson (who had various names) had been one of Maxwell-Knight's agents. West gives her real name as Vera de Cottani-Chalbur.

[47] John Morris KC, Lord Samuel, and N. L. C. Macaskie KC, the Recorder of York, who had been chairman of the Regional Advisory Committees on aliens.

The Problem of Multiple Appeals

A new anxiety now developed.[48] Mrs Heather Donovan, wife of Captain Donovan, had been released in November 1940 on condition that she resided with her parents, reported weekly to the police, and did not engage in any BU activities.[49] On 2 January she asked for the first two restrictions to be lifted, and on 9 February said she wanted to live with Mrs Stuckey, and work on her farm in Berkshire; her husband, Derek R. Stuckey, was in detention. A law graduate of Oriel College, Oxford, involved in the Universities National Socialist Club, he became in 1939 District Inspector of University Districts, his concern being fascists in universities and schools; he was, however, primarily a farmer.[50] Birkett was agreeable and permission was given. But, alarmed at the volume of work which might be produced by repeated appeals, he thought detainees only had a *right* to appeal once; he conceded that the text of 18B (3) was not very clear.

L. S. Brass, deputy legal adviser to the Home Office, disagreed. He thought that a detainee could appeal against the original order, against a refusal to suspend the order, against a condition attached to suspension, and against a revocation of a suspension. In effect a detainee could appeal as often as he wished until the order was revoked. Sir Oscar Dowson agreed. Brass did not think that 'a person would behave vexatiously in this way'; if one did then the Home Office could simply delay taking any decision, leaving the detainee with nothing to appeal against.[51] S. Hoare suggested there was no right to more than one appearance; unless there was new information the committee could simply repeat its former recommendation. Apparently Gordon-Canning had just put in a second appeal, though there had been no change in circumstances.[52] Birkett at this time was confronted by a protest by the solicitor, Oswald Hickson, against the refusal of a hearing in the case of J. R. Smeaton-Stuart, who had been released in November 1940, but excluded from Norfolk, where his home and work were.[53] Birkett thought that in cases where the com-

---

[48] HO 45/25754/112162.

[49] MI5 had resisted her release, recommended by Morris's committee somewhere about September. She had joined when 19 in 1934, and was WD/L in Westminster Abbey District. She married Donovan in January 1940 (HO 45/25754/863027/3; memo of C. M. Liddell, 19 September 1940).

[50] HO 144/21429 (with photo) 45/25722, 283/63. Stuckey held a BA and BCL degree, and had joined in 1934; detained on the order of 30 May. The committee (J. W. Morris) had recommended release on 9 September; MI5 objected, and his order was not suspended until 24 September 1941.

[51] Opinion of 29 March 1941.   [52] Memo of 1 April.

[53] HO 283/64, 45/25714, TS 27/493. The 18B order had been revoked and the restriction order was under 18A, but Birkett seemed to think that the 18B order had been suspended on condition.

mittee recommended complete revocation of an order, but the Home Office suspended the order and imposed conditions, there should be a right to a second appearance, but before a differently constituted committee.[54] Otherwise he was against what he called cumulative appeals.

Eventually, on 15 May, the Law Officers gave a formal opinion on the matter. There was no limit to the number of times a detainee could appeal, but there was no obligation on the committee to reinvestigate matters which they had already investigated in the past, or provide a new hearing every time an appeal (technically an 'objection') was submitted. They thought, however, that: 'if . . . the Committee in the exercise of their discretion come to the conclusion that there are new facts to investigate or that the circumstances which have intervened require or may appear at first sight to require an investigation of new facts or of old facts in a new light they should again hear the objector in person'. They thought that if the matter ever came to court—in the event it never did— 'any Court would construe safeguards for the liberty of the subject in the way most favourable to liberty'. The problem of repeated vexatious appeals never arose. One reason was that this opinion was never communicated to detainees, who had no idea of their rights in the matter; such are the benefits of keeping legal rights secret.

The Home Office in Disgrace

The delay in deciding cases, and the treatment of detainees in general, came in for much criticism. In the Commons Richard Stokes was the most persistent critic; consequently he was often approached on behalf of detainees, particularly by Oswald Hickson, the lawyer principally involved in representing them.[55] Stokes' papers include for example material dealing with Captain Donovan's experience in Latchmere House, apparently supplied through Hickson.[56] Material was also supplied to him by Withers and Co., who represented Robert Gordon-Canning.[57] Another persistent questioner was the Conservative Sir Irving J. Albery.[58] Other Conservative critics were Rear-Admiral Tufton P. Beamish,[59] Earl Winterton,[60] Captain William T. Shaw,[61] Captain Pierse

---

[54] Memo of 21 April.

[55] The Stokes Papers (Bodleian Library), esp. Box 26, 18B file, correspondence of August 1949 with E. A. Prince (working on a thesis on 18B). Most of Stokes's papers on 18B have not survived.

[56] Ibid. Box 13 Folder 47. Statements by Domvile (presumably Compton), Raven-Thomson, and Vaughan-Henry relating to Latchmere House are missing.

[57] Ibid. Folder 7.

[58] Member for Gravesend. 1874–1967. It is perhaps worth saying that he was not of the far right in his political views.

[59] Member for Lewes. 1874–1951.   [60] Member for Horsham. 1883–1968.

[61] Member for Forfar County. 1879–1965.

C. Loftus,[62] and Commander Sir Archibald Southby.[63] Those Conservatives of the far right, such as the members of the Right Club, adopted a prudent silence, apart from Ramsay himself, who continually sent in questions from his cell in Brixton. From Labour there was the maverick John McGovern,[64] Rhys J. Davies,[65] Geoffrey L. M. Mander,[66] and Sydney Silverman.[67]

Stokes was relentless in his questions. Many complained of delays before appearance. Thus on 8 October he asked when the committee was going to hear the case of E. L. Diamond,[68] and on 17 October he asked about Mrs Kathleen Bidie, detained on 6 June; he was told that she had appeared on 9 October. On 17 October he raised the case of women detainees, claiming that of the sixty-seven who had been arrested since the beginning of June only fifteen had been before the committee; Morrison was able to reply that the correct figure was forty, but evaded the point of the question by not saying how long the delays had been. He specifically mentioned Mrs Rita K. Shelmerdine, and was told that since she had applied for habeas corpus her case was *sub judice* and could not therefore come before the committee, which does not seem to have been legally correct.[69] On 19 December he elicited the information that 1,238 appeals had by then been heard, 315 persons released, and 341 detainees were still awaiting a hearing—many must have been waiting for four months or even more.[70] As the committee dealt with the backlog the focus of questions shifted to the delays in the Home Office in deciding what was to be done after the committee had reported.[71]

On 10 December 1940, and again on 4 March 1941, there were debates in the Commons.[72] From what was there said, questions put to Ministers, and correspondence, it is clear that delay was only one source of complaint. The procedures followed by the committee were attacked—the absence of legal representation,[73] the inadequate information provided to

[62] Member for Lowestoft. 1879–1956.   [63] Member for Epsom. 1886–1969.
[64] ILP Member for Shettleton, Glasgow. 1887–1968.
[65] Member for Westhoughton, Lancs. 1877–1954.
[66] Member for East Wolverhampton. 1882–1962.
[67] Member for Nelson and Colne. 1895–1968.
[68] HO 45/25721; detained as 'of hostile associations', 13 June; order was revoked on 18 October after a hearing probably early in October. See below p. 284.
[69] See below p. 288.
[70] These figures do not precisely tally with other papers.
[71] For example his questions on 19 December (*Parl. Deb*. HC Vol. 367 c.1367–8) relating to D. S. Lawley (detained 3 June, committee 13 August), A. W. Scott (detained 19 June, committee 27 August), and J. C. Preen (detained 1 June, committee about 1 August). Morrison had by 19 December decided to release Lawley and continue the detention of Scott and Preen. See also 6 February (*Parl. Deb*. HC 368: 1059).
[72] *Parl. Deb*. HC Vol. 367 c.886–884 and 369: 864ff.
[73] Stokes on 19 December (*Parl. Deb*. HC Vol. 367 c.1342–6, Rhys Davies on 23 January, 368: 281, Stokes, Winterton, and Loftus on 10 December, 367: 844, 849, 863.

detainees,[74] the detainee's ignorance of the evidence against him and inability to confront witnesses.[75] And if detention was to be continued, ought not detainees be told why?[76] Other criticisms related to the punitive conditions of detention. Could not husbands and wives be detained together?[77] Why was the Home Office using stool-pigeons in Holloway, in particular Miss Amor?[78] What was going on in Latchmere House?[79] Were detainees kept locked in their cells during air raids?[80] Then there was the suggestion that wholly unjustified detentions had taken place through the incompetence of MI5. In the debate in December Stokes mentioned the case 'of a lady, with two small children, who was locked up for five months'. When her house was searched a diary was found for 1938 with the entry 'M.49 Destroy British Queen. Instal Italian Queen.' It took MI5 six weeks to find out that 'this lady kept bees, and that this entry referred to a method of improving the breed of bees . . . '[81] The reference is again to the case of Rita Shelmerdine and her husband Philip, who had even been interrogated in Latchmere House.[82] When detainees were released without even having to appear before the committee could they not be compensated?[83] The surviving documentation on these and other complaints, many of which would have been raised in correspondence, must be the tip of the iceberg. But in spite of them there was a general acceptance amongst members of the Commons that the power of detention without trial was necessary in the conditions of the time; what was attacked was the administration. There were, however, those who thought that detainees should either be tried, or released. The *News Chronicle* put the point succinctly on 27 July: 'Sir Oswald Mosley and his fellow Fascists should be tried. If they are found guilty the British public will be able to stomach whatever penalty the State may inflict. If they are innocent they should be set free.' From the right *Truth* took the same line,[84]

---

[74] Lyons on 10 December (*Parl. Deb*. HC 367: 860), correspondence between Stokes and Maxwell in January 1941 (Stokes Papers, Box 13 Folder 47).

[75] Stokes on 10 December (*Parl. Deb*. HC 367: 872), Silverman on 4 March (369: 870–1).

[76] 19 November (365: 1825).

[77] Beamish on 19 December (367: 1342), Davies on 24 April (371: 241).

[78] Stokes to Maxwell, 27 January 1941 (Stokes Papers). See above p. 153.

[79] Stokes Papers, Box 13 Folder 47. Stokes asked questions on 17 September and 9 October (*Parl. Deb*. HC 365: 103, 236, 375–6). Latchmere House was also raised in the debate on 10 December (367: 841–2). No doubt Stokes corresponded with the Home Office.

[80] D. N. Pritt on 17 October (365: 838). At this period the fellow traveller Pritt was opposed to 18B, no doubt fearing its use against communists.

[81] *Parl. Deb*. HC 367: 846.

[82] O. Mosley, *My Life* (London, 1968), 404, has the story, adding that Philip Shelmerdine later gave services to medicine and the Church: he entered a religious order after the war and became a medical missionary and possibly a priest. His tombstone at Gunnersbury has a Latin inscription: 'Who, when other priests were turned into savage wolves alone remained faithful'. Died 1987.

[83] Stokes on 19 March (*Parl. Deb*. HC 370: 158–9).

as of course did numerous detainees.[85] But in spite of complaints and protests the government was never under any real threat.

The Administration of MI5

The Home Office took most of the blame, though MI5's responsibility was occasionally mentioned, as by Eleanor Rathbone, who was active on behalf of the detained aliens, in the debate on 10 December.[86] The committee depended upon MI5 both for the 'Statement of the Case', and the 'Reasons for Order'. In the summer and autumn of 1940, under the acting directorship of Harker, MI5 was, as we have seen, in a poor administrative state. Lord Hankey's investigation, begun in March, was partly concerned with MI5's constitutional position, MI5 wishing to establish itself as an originator of policy independent from the Home Office, a proposal opposed by Home Office officials. But Hinsley and Simkins report that Hankey also investigated allegations from the Home Office and Birkett that MI5 was both over-suspicious and incompetent. Hankey reserved his opinion on the efficiency of MI5 in a report considered late in May 1940. No changes were made to MI5's constitutional position, and nothing of importance came out of the report.[87] But both Kell and his deputy, Holt-Wilson, were retired early in June, and Harker took over as acting director.[88] Harker was not a success, or perhaps one should say a disaster, and the Swinton Committee's attempt to use the solicitor Crocker to reorganize the institution failed. Matters were not improved by bombing; on the night of 24 September some of MI5's records were damaged in Wormwood Scrubs; the reconstruction of the index and other records took until June 1941. MI5 then moved to Blenheim Palace, using some of the Oxford colleges to house its staff, with further disorganization. Matters grew worse, and, according to Hinsley and Simkins,[89] Churchill was informed by 'a close political associate'—perhaps Duff Cooper—that the institution was in a very poor state; by December Desmond Morton informed him that Swinton was now in control of MI5, which was in danger of collapse. What it needed was a civilian head who would be responsible not to Swinton, but to a Minister.

The account in the official history, which I have summarized, suggests to me that what had come to light through the unidentified 'close political associate' may well have included the weird indirect connection between Swinton's committee and the management of *Truth*; Morton's proposal

[84] 9 August 1940.   [85] See above p. 1.   [86] *Parl. Deb.* HC Vol. 367 c.854.
[87] Hinsley and Simkins, 39–40, PREM 4/97/11, memo of Eric Seal, 25 July 1940.
[88] Andrew, 668, relying on Kell's Diary and Cadogan's MS diary in the Churchill College Archives; Kell's retirement, which he viewed as dismissal, was on 10 June.
[89] pp. 67–9.

was perhaps intended to prevent MI5 falling under the control of a Chamberlainite far-right group hostile to Churchill. Be that as it may, Morton fell out of favour with Churchill. Crocker resigned in the autumn of 1940; the Liberal Isaac Foot MP joined the committee in August 1940. Duthy seems to have ceased to work for the committee in 1940 or early 1941. Ball, however, lasted until about February 1942. Swinton was disposed of by being appointed resident minister in West Africa in June 1942. On his departure Duff Cooper, later Lord Norwich, became head of the Security Executive and *in loco parentis* to MI5.[90] A retired Civil Servant, Sir Herbert Creedy, formerly official head of the War Office, took over the administration and he apparently became the chairman of the Security Executive (as it came to be called) from 1943 until the end of the war.[91] From October of 1940 Anderson, as Lord President, became the Minister ultimately in charge of MI5, and he was no doubt behind the changes made. Until he became Chancellor of the Exchequer in September 1943 he was in control of all domestic policy in Britain.

After Crocker's failure a former Indian Police Officer, Sir David Petrie, was appointed to investigate MI5 and make recommendations; in March of 1941 he became its Director. This appointment was no doubt instigated by Anderson, and not Swinton; Anderson would have known him as Governor of Bengal. It proved successful.[92] But in the period between May 1940 and March 1941, the period critical for 18B, MI5 was unreformed. It must be emphasized that published material on MI5 during the war conveys a distorted picture of an organization principally concerned with catching and using spies, in which it was very successful. But MI5's main achievement in the early part of the war was to secure the detention, at huge cost, of somewhere over 30,000 people, amongst whom there were virtually no spies at all. Its positive achievements were modest in the extreme.

So far as 18B was concerned, the work of drafting the necessary documents fell badly into arrears. A fragment of a letter of 5 August by G. P. Churchill[93] shows him protesting at the delays, referring to Domvile,

[90] The expression is used by Anthony Simkins in his *DNB* article on Sir David Petrie. In his autobiography, *Old Men Forget*, (London, 1953), 311, Duff Cooper implies, wrongly, that he took decisions as to who should be interned and released.

[91] This is stated in his *DNB* entry. See also HH 50/68.

[92] Petrie (1879–1972), who was a graduate of Aberdeen, joined the Indian Police in 1900 and became the Director of its Intelligence Bureau 1924–1931. He was Assistant Director of Criminal Intelligence 1911–12, and had served on Special duties from 1915 to 1919, no doubt dealing with communist and nationalist movements. He wrote *Communism in India 1924–1927* (Calcutta, 1972) and *Developments in Sikh Politics 1900–1911: A Report* (Amritsar, 1972). After retirement in 1936 from the Indian Public Service Commission he gave advice on intelligence in Palestine (1937–8) and emerged from retirement to become a 2nd Lt. in the Intelligence Corps in Cairo.

[93] In HO 283/45 (A. T. O. Lees). HO 144/21995 includes a letter of 8 August from E. B. Stamp of MI5 to G. P. Churchill saying that MI5 is doing its best; it is clear that Churchill

Pitt-Rivers, one R. Rollo,[94] and Lady Mosley.[95] Domvile's was a bad but not exceptional case. He was detained on 7 July; his case was not actually dealt with by the committee until four months after his arrest, some time, as we shall see, after he began habeas corpus proceedings. Pitt-Rivers's case was similar: arrested 27 June, 'Reasons for Order' 12 October, a sham hearing to support the claim that action was taking place on 25 October, a resumed hearing 8 November, a report dated 21 November.[96] The de Laessoe case was worse; detained on 23 May, he and his wife were not heard until 17 October. Robert Gordon-Canning was arrested on 12 July; he appeared before the committee on 28 August and again in November. The decision to continue detention was not taken until the end of January 1941.[97]

These were very prominent individuals; less important people were Cecil G. F. Salinger, Leigh Vaughan-Henry,[98] and Darby Sabini. Salinger was detained by an 'acts prejudicial' order of 31 May. The 'Reasons for Order' were not settled until 1 October. Over a month later, on 6 November, the committee recommended release; this was accepted on 11 December, almost seven months after his arrest. He was apparently a perfectly loyal individual. Vaughan-Henry was arrested on 10 June 1940 under 18D; on 17 June an 18B (1A) order was made and, since he had long left the BU, an additional 'hostile associations' order was served on 30 December. He received the 'Reasons for Order' under this on 3 January 1941, and those under the earlier order on about 26 November. He appeared before the committee in January. Darby Sabini's was another very bad case. He was no model citizen to be sure, being a member of the Sabini racecourse gang; he was detained in June.[99] He had still not appeared on 5 December.[100] The pamphlet *It Might Have Happened to You!* refers to a case in which there was a delay of seven months between arrest and hearing; this would be Vaughan-Henry's case.[101] Oddson's file[102] has a note of protest by Birkett to E. B. Stamp of MI5:

P. S. I really must ask that this matter [i.e. producing papers] be dealt with at once. We have had no reply whatever to the letters of Sept. 4th. and Oct. 12th. and

was anxious over delays in the case of prominent people, such as Domvile, Lady Mosley, and Capt. R. C. Gordon-Canning.

[94] R. Rollo, a BU detainee, signed the autograph book in York Camp on 1 February 1941 with a drawing of 'lights out', and presumably was then released.

[95] HO 144/21995, her heavily weeded file.

[96] See TS 27/514.

[97] Stokes Papers, Box 26.

[98] HO 283/62 (Salinger). TS 27/533 (Vaughan-Henry).

[99] Stokes gave 6 June as the date; his brother was detained by an order of 14 June (HO 45/25720). Darby's detention was reported in the *Daily Express* for 8 July.

[100] *Parl. Deb.* HC Vol. 367 c.644–5. See also the case of F. W. O. White (col. 1367), detained 3 June, who waited four months before his appearance; his order was then revoked.

[101] *IMHHTY* 30.   [102] The pages on Oddson are very incomplete.

a very ugly situation is arising. The solicitor takes the view that this is a case where the man should not have been detained at all. These delays are most grievous to the committee who feel most deeply about it.[103]

Oddson had been arrested on 27 July and an 18B (1A) order made on 5 August. He did not appear before the committee until 10 December. Some of the delays may have arisen because MI5 was still seeking evidence to support detention long after arrest, and Naval Intelligence may have been concerned over Oddson.

To maintain good relations Birkett's committee sent its draft reports to MI5 for comment; tardy replies caused further delay. On 28 October an exasperated Birkett discontinued this practice.[104] But more prompt committee reports were now held up in the Home Office. Oddson's case is one extreme example. The committee recommended immediate release in December 1940; the Home Office decision to reject the recommendation was not taken until May of 1941.[105] A less extreme example is the case of Diana Mosley. She was arrested on 29 June and, because MI5 did not produce the 'Reasons for Order' until 5 September, and presumably the 'Statement of the Case', which has been weeded from the file, later than this, she did not appear before the committee until 2 October. The report, recommending continued detention, was submitted shortly after this.[106] The decision to maintain detention was not taken by the Home Office until 6 January 1941.[107] Why there was so long a delay in her particular case is obscure, though the grounds for detaining her, except as punishment for her marriage and intransigent fascism, seem very weak indeed. Conceivably there were internal disputes over her internment.

But one factor which became increasingly important was a serious conflict which developed in late 1940 between the committee and MI5. Until this was resolved many committee recommendations acquired a controversial character, and decisions were in consequence held up. In the course of this conflict the independence and integrity of the committee was seriously threatened. So too was the traditional role of the Home Office as protector of civil liberty, a role which had of course been gravely weakened by the crisis of the summer of 1940.

---

[103] HO 283/51.   [104] HO 283/22.   [105] HO 45/25738.
[106] Only part of a draft has escaped the Home Office weeders.
[107] HO 144/21995.

13

The Integrity of the Advisory Committee

The Interrogation of Mosley

The threat to the integrity of Birkett's committee stemmed from the War Cabinet decision of 22 May. Until then the committee evaluated the threat to security posed by individuals; there had to be a case against each person, and each recommendation was independent of what was recommended for other detainees. And every decision reviewed had been taken, at least formally, and often in reality, by the Home Secretary in person, acting as a sort of judge. Political considerations only entered into the work in so far as Birkett wanted the public to retain confidence in his committee as being both fair, and vigilant. After May 22 all this changed; the War Cabinet had decided that the fascists were potentially dangerous, and the BU was to be crippled. There could be no question of the committee going against this, and recommending the release of Mosley and his principal followers, quite irrespective of what emerged in hearings. Nor was the release of Ramsay conceivable. The detention of the lesser BU activists also implemented a general policy decision, as did the arrest of the Anglo-Italian members of the Fascio. Where, after May, individuals were detained simply on the basis of their own actions or sympathies, the committee could proceed much as before; such cases, however, now formed a minority.

The threat to the integrity of the committee was acute in the case of Mosley himself.[1] He exercised his right of appeal, but Birkett must have known that his appearance was a charade.[2] Hence the records reveal the unfortunate Birkett torn between two wholly incompatible undertakings. One was to try to investigate a question, 'Is Mosley covered by

---

[1] Also Ramsay and perhaps Domvile, but documentation is not available.

[2] The committee files are HO 283/1 (memo on the case by Birkett), 2 (copy of same), 3 (closed, probably MI5's comments on Birkett's memo), 4 (memo by Birkett after his visit to MI5), 5 (closed, probably notes from MI5), 6 (material relating to BU companies), 7 (documents submitted by Oswald Hickson on behalf of Mosley), 8 (closed), 9 (brief for committee), 10 (report on secret bank account for resumed hearing of 15 July), 11 (miscellaneous correspondence), 12 ('Reasons for Order'), 13 (transcript of hearing 2 July), 14 (transcript 3 July), 15 (transcript 15 July), 16 (transcript 22 July), 17 (recommendations), 18 (draft report). The Home Office papers are HO 45/24891–4; 24891 has the report, and details of Mosley's arrest. PREM 4/39/5 is closed.

Regulation 18B (1A)?', which was quite absurd, since 18B (1A) had been carefully drafted to ensure that it did cover him. The other was to embark on the political task of constructing as good a case as possible against Mosley and hope, at the hearings, to demonstrate to his colleagues, or to Mosley, or to posterity, or I suppose to Birkett's own conscience, that it had been right to lock him up. Birkett's predicament was made worse by fear that Mosley, who had won their last encounter, might make him and his committee look both dishonest and ridiculous.[3] This nervousness surely increased when, in early July, Mosley sent his written defence to the committee. Viewed dispassionately it was a powerful reply to the 'Reasons for Order' supplied to him. In its opening paragraph it made a telling point:

The main suggestion is that I and my colleagues are prepared to help the enemy of my country . . . I ask what shred of evidence can be produced to support it? . . . The police have raided my flat, my wife's flat, the London house we used to occupy, my children's house in the country. They have also raided the offices of British Union. At the end of this process what shred of evidence can they produce to support the allegation that I would play the traitor to my country?[4]

No doubt MI5 had hoped to find such evidence; it is quite clear that they had no success. Nor did MI5 have agents with anything to offer; if there had been, Birkett's brief, and the questions asked of Mosley at the hearings, would reveal this.

Birkett set out the position in a memorandum analysing the evidence in the Home Office files.[5] The evidence that the BU was under foreign influence (much less control) he described as 'somewhat scanty'; no doubt there was some copying of foreign fascist models, but beyond this there was only suspicion of foreign funding. Evidence that leaders of the party had associations with the enemy was very scanty indeed. There were individual fascists who had improper associations, but none were leaders of the BU[6] What was needed was evidence that those in control had been co-operating with the Germans, either directly or through agents, or, he added desperately, 'through organizations such as "The Link". If "The

---

[3] In 1934 Mosley sued the *Star* for libel; Birkett lost, appearing foolish during cross-examination. See R. Skidelsky, *Oswald Mosley* (London, 1975), 322, O. Mosley, *My Life* (London, 1968), 351–5.

[4] 'Sir Oswald Mosley in reply to the Reasons for his detention says:–', dated 1 July, is in the committee papers.

[5] Dated 4 June.

[6] He mentions E. P. C. Whinfield (above, p. 78), Clement Bruning (above p. 178), Joyce, and William Spranklin. William, more properly Philip, Spranklin had by 1939 joined Goebbels' Foreign Press Office in Munich; he had previously been a BU speaker. See R. Griffiths, *Fellow Travellers of the Right: British Enthusiasts for Nazi Germany 1933–9* (London, 1980), 314. He escaped from Germany, was detained and released, and killed by a flying bomb in 1944. D. Pryce Jones, *Unity Mitford. A Quest* (1979) 192–3.

Link" can be connected directly with Germany, and the BU can be connected directly with "The Link", that would be some kind of evidence which at the moment is absent from these papers'.

Birkett was reasonably convinced that the BU was run by persons in sympathy with German and Italian fascism, which was obviously true. He also thought that 'There is abundant evidence . . . that there is danger of the organization being used for purposes prejudicial to the public safety, the maintenance of order, and the efficient prosecution of the war.' In the nature of things it is hard to see why he was so sure of this; in reality the only hard evidence was the BU peace campaign, not the official reason for the government's action. Birkett's memorandum concluded: 'But throughout the files, although there is abundant evidence of fierce criticism of British policy, there is nowhere any evidence that the leaders of the BU desire a German victory, or have any other concern than to take the fullest advantage of the present situation in order to bring BU, to power with Mosley as its leader.'

This memorandum went to the committee, and must also have been sent to Maxwell, where it would cause some consternation. So on 11 June Maxwell arranged for Birkett to visit MI5, and discuss the matter with Aikin-Sneath, who would make available all MI5's evidence.[7] The outcome was a 'Reasons for Order', dated 19 June, drafted by Birkett himself. It set out the best case Birkett could make.[8] It said nothing about the 'underground' BU, or plans for a *coup d'état*, or about Mosley being 'in relations' with Ramsay.[9] Birkett also produced a brief for the hearing; MI5, somewhat oddly, did not provide their usual 'Statement of the Case', unless it is in one of the closed files. So the prosecution case was compiled by the chairman of the supposedly independent reviewing committee, a situation unlikely to make Birkett feel comfortable.

The main points were the BU's commitment to fascism, its opposition to the war, the belief that it had until 1937 been financed by Italy, its distribution of German propaganda, and Mosley's involvement in a plan to set up a radio station in Germany. Again there was no mention of any secret underground organization, planned *coup d'état*, conspiracy of the right, or foreign control over the party.

Birkett had obviously become very sceptical of MI5's claims. Thus an MI5 report of 21 January 1939 had said that until 1936 Mosley was being financed by Mussolini, and hinted at German funding thereafter. Birkett noted that the Chairman of the BU Trust had, on 25 January, offered to provide evidence that the party had no improper source of funds, and in the event an auditors' report, dated 18 April, had been submitted. MI5's

---

[7] HO 283/4.   [8] Appendix V.   [9] See above p. 161.
[10] From 1 September 1938 to 31 January 1940 the BU received £34,000, of which £30,000 came from two individuals, one being Mosley with £24,000, and the other being unnamed.

information on finance was, he said, 'vague and sketchy'.[10] Again on 18 May MI5 had said: 'We know that up to the outbreak of war British Union leaders were in the closest touch with the German Nazi leaders. Mosley, Raven-Thomson, W. E. D. Allen,[11] Major General Fuller, Gordon-Canning[12] and other leaders were frequently in Germany.' But Birkett pointed out that there was no proof of contact since the war began, which was what really mattered. In his written defence Mosley added, apparently truthfully, that neither Francis-Hawkins nor Donovan, both important officers, had ever visited either Germany or Italy.

The first hearing took place on 2 and 3 July; given the weakness of the case provided by MI5, it was, predictably, little short of a disaster.[13] Mosley, who was far and away sharper in debate than Birkett, adopted a style of breezy candour, and had an answer, though not always an entirely plausible one, to everything put to him. Over the anti-Semitic policy he admitted that since October 1934 he had attacked the Jews, since they attacked him; he had violent arguments with Mussolini over this, who had said 'I was all wrong'.[14] When Birkett argued that the emblem of the party—the flash in the circle—and such practices as the use of banners—were copied from the Nazis, Mosley replied that the emblem had in fact been invented by Piercey ('who was on the fighting side of our movement'), and that the use of spectacle was suggested by the Durham Miners' Gala. He simply denied any Italian funding, covering himself by saying he did not enquire into the source of funds. Of course Birkett and his colleagues must have known that it was perfectly normal for British political parties to receive money from dubious secret sources, as they still do. Birkett put to Mosley MI5's theory that his party contained members who would go to any lengths. Mosley conceded that the movement had indeed attracted a lunatic fringe, which included pro-Nazis—individuals mentioned included Claude Duvivier,[15] H. W. Luttman-Johnson,[16] Richard F. Findlay,[17] H. P. Puller,[18] and Joyce—but that was a problem

[11] See above p. 120.
[12] Gordon-Canning had quarrelled with Mosley for reasons which are obscure; in 1940 he was with the BPP. What formal link, if any, Fuller had with the party in 1940 is obscure.
[13] The committee comprised, in addition to Birkett, Clerk, Hazlerigg, Mallon, Markham, and Morris. At the resumed hearing on 15 July Miller and Mrs Cockburn attended; on 22 July the panel was Birkett, Morris, Wallington, Collinson, Hazlerigg, and Markham.
[14] Transcript 37. In his written defence he claimed: 'Our anti-semitic policy is profoundly different from that of Germany, e.g. in broad definition, the Germans are against the Jews for what they are; we are against the Jews for what they do. This has been publicly defined. To suggest that we have learned anti-semitism from the Italians is purely absurd as the Italians did not adopt anti-semitism until several years after we did.'
[15] See above p. 136.   [16] See above p. 221.
[17] Birkett had been told that Findlay and Luttman-Johnson had in 1937 written pro-Nazi letters. Findlay was an associate of Luttman-Johnson and in the January Club. He had been a candidate in the Norwood by-election, put up by Randolph Churchill.
[18] Not identified.

in all political organizations.[19] Birkett tried to suggest that some such members had been involved in publicizing the New British Broadcasting Station; badly briefed, he imagined that its existence and wavelength could only be discovered from the 'sticky-backs'. Mosley pointed out that information about it had been published in the *Daily Dispatch*—in fact in the *Sunday Dispatch* for 3 March, repeated in *Action* on 11 April. Anyway there was no official involvement of the BU in the matter.[20] Birkett had from MI5 no evidence to the contrary, though the repetition of the wavelength in *Action* was a form of advertising. Birkett also probed into the BU's contingency plans.[21] Mosley conceded that he had issued a number of letters of authority to carry on the movement.[22] He feared that although his organization was perfectly legal, he might be arrested, and in these circumstances it was perfectly legitimate for him to make such arrangements. As we have seen, Mosley won the argument over this quite decisively, leaving Birkett looking silly.[23]

At first sight the most alarming information at Birkett's disposal was the plan to establish a broadcasting station in Germany.[24] Commercial broadcasting, funded by advertisers, was illegal in Britain; it was highly profitable, and the two principal stations transmitting to Britain before the war were Radio Luxembourg[25] and Radio Normandie.[26] Mosley planned to fund his political activities by setting up stations to the west, south, and east of Britain. In 1937, through Dudley Evans,[27] he met F. W. L. C. ('Buster') Beaumont,[28] heir to the seignory of Sark, with whom he entered an agreement to establish a station on the island. As Mosley knew, this arrangement needed the consent of the Privy Council, but his hope was that if he obtained a number of concessions in countries outside British control it would bow to a *fait accompli*.[29] MI5 discovered about the Sark agreement through searches arising out of Mosley's arrest.[30]

---

[19] Other individuals mentioned were E. P. C. Whinfield, C. F. Watts and H. Hall.

[20] Reference not traced.   [21] 2 July transcript at 77 ff.

[22] See above p. 181.   [23] See above p. 182.

[24] Transcript of 2 July at 103 and for 3 July at 19 ff.

[25] Run by the Havas Agency, with Gerald Keith as their agent in Britain.

[26] Run by Capt. Leonard F. Plugge, Conservative MP for Chatham.

[27] See below p. 385. Detained under 18B on active service as a 2nd Lt. in the Royal Engineers. See HO 283/34 and 45/25727. See also *Is This Justice?*, 25 and *Comrade*, 7.

[28] Son of Sybil Hathaway by her first marriage. In 1940 in the RAF; Lady Mosley tells me that he had at one time been BU. He was killed in 1941.

[29] Sark is not governed by the United Kingdom Parliament.

[30] See note of a telephone call from Aikin-Sneath in HO 283/11. The report of Mosley's arrest lists amongst the property seized correspondence with Beaumont in January 1940, with references to Dudley Evans, an agreement of 4 June 1937, and other documents relating to a radio station on Sark, and an agreement of 18 July 1938 between W. E. D. Allen and J. E. F. Bernhart, Director of Berlin-Grunewald, relating to the German station. The scheme and the fascist involvement had been mentioned by 'William Hickey' (the communist and informer Tom Driberg) in the *Daily Express* on 13 Jan. 1938. I am indebted to C. G. P. Lakeman for this reference.

Negotiations were also begun to establish stations in Germany, Denmark, Belgium, and Ireland; with Germany there was success, an agreement being reached in 1938 for a station on Nordyk. MI5 already knew about this, probably through W. E. D. Allen. German interest was purely financial; in order not to discourage advertisers, it was critical that Mosley's interest be kept secret, and for the programmes to exclude political propaganda. There was no sinister connection with the German propaganda broadcasting of 1940, and neither of the stations had ever come on the air.[31]

The Adjournment of the Hearing

After two discouraging days Birkett adjourned the hearing, which was not resumed until 15 July; by then the party had been proscribed.[32] Birkett must have reported to Maxwell, and the point of the adjournment was obviously to give MI5 a chance to come up with a better case, and give time to interrogate other prominent fascists; no documentary evidence however is available. McKechnie appeared on 8 July,[33] Donovan sometime earlier,[34] and Watts on 9 July.[35] Ramsay too appeared sometime in early July; he said that in a conversation with Mosley he had been invited to take over Scotland 'in certain circumstances'. But, surprisingly, most interrogations at Latchmere House—notably those of Watts, Donovan, and Raven-Thomson—began in August; the only interrogation in June seems to have been that of Vaughan-Henry, who had long left the BU.[36] Mosley's lieutenants who went there were interrogated after the signing of the report on Mosley on 29 July.[37] Given Birkett's character, it is unlikely that he would have been happy about using evidence obtained by third-degree methods; probably these interrogations were undertaken by MI5 in a desperate effort to redeem a reputation which must have been severely tarnished by inability to come up with a good case against Mosley and the BU. The arrest of Domvile on 8 July may, however, have

[31] Diana Mosley acted as agent in the German negotiations, assisted on legal matters by F. H. Lawton. See *Loved Ones: Pen Portraits by Diana Mosley* (London, 1985), 171–4. For the Sark agreement, which gave Mosley 75% of the profits, the UK Company was the New Museum Investment Company, related to David Allen and Son. This was also involved in the German agreement, which gave Mosley 45%. The UK Company was Air Time Ltd., a subsidiary of Radio Variety Ltd. R. P. Eckersley, former Chief Engineer for the BBC, a member of the Right Club, and a member of Mosley's New Party, and presumably BU, was involved in the planning. Robert Boothby was also involved; see R. R. James, *Robert Boothby: A Portrait of Churchill's Ally* (London, 1992), 197–8.
[32] HO 283/15.   [33] HO 283/48.   [34] HO 45/25705.   [35] HO 283/74.
[36] TS 27/533 (Vaughan-Henry). Donovan was moved to Latchmere House on 9 August. (Stokes Papers, Box 13 Folder 47) and J. L. Battersby in *The Bishop Said Amen* (Poynton, Cheshire, 1947), 17, says he went there in mid-August.
[37] HO 283/17.

been a response to Birkett's suggestion that an association with Germany through the Link might further the case against the BU, and it is certain that an MI5 agent, probably the disreputable Harold Kurtz, was involved in the Domvile case.[38]

Between the hearings the only fruitful investigations were into the BU funds. A bank account had been operated between 1933 and May 1937 in the names of W. E. D. Allen, Ian H. Dundas,[39] and Major G. J. H. Tabor.[40] Considerable sums in foreign exchange had been paid into it. But there was no evidence as to the source of this money.[41] In addition Aikin-Sneath, through some underhand trick or other, secured 'from a very secret and delicate source' accurate details of the defence which Mosley proposed to present at the adjourned hearing.[42] These were supplied to Birkett to assist him to win the battle of words with Mosley, and it is not a little astonishing that Birkett was sufficiently nervous to accept this aid. Mosley was allowed to visit his flat in Eaton Square on 11 July and have access to papers for his defence, but little came of this visit. The hearing was resumed on 15 July, and Aikin-Sneath was present on the final day, 22 July. Mosley was pressed on the matter of finance, and made to look evasive; otherwise the hearing achieved nothing of value.

At the end of the hearings it is claimed by Mosley that he said to Birkett: 'There appear to be two grounds for detaining us—(1) a suggestion that we are traitors who would take up arms and fight with the Germans if they landed and, (2) that our propaganda campaign undermines the civilian morale.' Birkett, so it is claimed, replied: 'Speaking for myself, you can entirely dismiss the first suggestion.' It is also said that Birkett told Mosley that he was detained because of his propaganda campaign.[43] This is in fact a garbled account of the exchange. Mosley, referring to his service in the Foreign Office in 1918, said: 'Anyhow I did spend those four months in a position where, if I had been a traitor, I could have done heavens knows what damage.' Birkett replied: 'I do not think that anybody in their wildest statements said that you were anything

---

[38] HO 45/25754/863027/6 (Meeting of Home Defence (Security) Executive 6 November). Kurtz had approached Domvile, as appears from his diary for 6 January 1939 (DOM 55).

[39] The original general secretary of the party.

[40] Tabor was secretary to Dundas.

[41] HO 283/5 presumably relates to all this; also HO 45/25393 (interview on 6 July with Tabor). Tabor, who had been private secretary to W. E. D. Allen, was interviewed by Aikin-Sneath (letter of 25 July in HO 283/6) but claimed to know nothing of the source of the money.

[42] Letter from Aikin-Sneath of 27 June in HO 283/6.

[43] Quoted by Richard Stokes, *Parl. Deb.* HC Vol. 367 c.839 (10 December 1940). The source was presumably Oswald Hickson. The story has been repeated elsewhere, as by Mosley himself in *My Life*. See also N. Mosley, *Beyond the Pale: Sir Oswald Mosley and his Family 1933–1980* (London, 1987), 172, suggesting that the committee recommended release. This was written before the files became available.

approaching a traitor in those days at any rate.' Mosley replied: 'Thank you very much.' Birkett then went on to say that a person could be detained who was not a traitor, and in consequence a detention order did not necessarily imply that the detainee was one. Mosley, without access to the transcript, might well have concluded from his recollection of this exchange that Birkett had withdrawn any allegation of treachery.

Birkett's report, inevitably recommending detention, perforce made bricks with little straw; it could not be very convincing.[44] On 10 July, under Regulation 18AA of 26 June, the BU had been proscribed, significantly only on the limited ground that 'the persons in control of that organization have had sympathies with the system of government of a power with which his Majesty is at war and there is a danger of the utilization of the organization for purposes prejudicial to the efficient prosecution of the war'.[45] Birkett had, as we have seen, always thought there was evidence on these two matters. The task of the committee was simplified by the order of 10 July; it only needed to decide two questions—'was Mosley a member?', which he obviously was, and 'was it necessary to exercise control over him?', which the War Cabinet had decided affirmatively. Nevertheless Birkett reviewed the case against Mosley generally, and rejected some allegations—there had been no official support for distributing German propaganda, nor encouragement of visits to Germany. The business of the radio stations 'does not assume the importance which at first sight it appeared to have'. But the BU was, according to Birkett, under German influence, and Mosley did have sympathies with the German system, and associations with German leaders.[46] Mosley himself claimed, apparently correctly, to have only met Hitler twice, once for lunch in 1935, and once on 6 October 1936 at the time of his marriage. On the need for control, critical to the case, Birkett relied in part on the fact that some members of the BU had been convicted of offences, and in part on the BU's anti-war propaganda, which was 'highly prejudicial to the efficient prosecution of the war'. As we have seen, very few members had been convicted, though it was undisputed that the party did have its wild men and women. He also turned on its head Mosley's statement to his followers when the war began: '. . . I ask you to do nothing to injure our country or to help any other power . . .'[47] He argued that it was 'the strangest message to give the supporters of an intensely patriotic

[44] In HO 283/18 (draft) and HO 45/24891.

[45] SRO 1940 No. 1078. The Order was No. 1273.

[46] See J. Guinness, *The House of Mitford* (London, 1984), 375 and 383–4. Diana Mosley, as was conceded at the time, and has been confirmed to me personally by her, knew Hitler well, and met him on a considerable number of occasions. A full account is given in chs. 30, 31 and 33. Diana had visited him at Bayreuth as recently as 1939.

[47] Quoted in the final issue of *Action* of 30 May. In the issue of 23 May Mosley had defended his continued peace programme.

organization'; the need to make it showed that in reality the BU was not patriotic at all. Furthermore Mosley was devious and evasive, for example over foreign funding and over respect for the law. But the report made no claim whatever for the existence of the organized Fifth Column; it was never mentioned. The justification for detention was ultimately made to depend not on concrete evidence of misconduct or planned misconduct but, as was typically the case, on a hostile assessment of Mosley's character: 'he was of inordinate ambition, and aspired to the possession of undisputed and even autocratic power. This temper of mind and outlook must be considered when dealing with the evidence given over four days relating to the matters in question.' So Mosley the fascist was dangerous, and not to be trusted. In the nature of things it is quite impossible to say whether Birkett and his colleagues were right or wrong in this judgement.

About Ramsay's appearance in early July virtually nothing is known except that continued detention was recommended.[48] The report remains secret to this day. His detention was arguably a breach of the privilege of Members of Parliament against arrest, and was referred to the Committee of Privileges.[49] Under the chairmanship of Attlee, Deputy Prime Minister and a member of the War Cabinet which had decided to act against him it predictably decided that no breach was involved; this was accepted, though not without controversy.[50] There had been previous cases in which Irish members had been detained without this being treated as a breach of privilege, such as John Dillon and others in 1881, and De Valera, Plunkett, Cosgrave, and McGuinness in 1918.[51] There had never been a clear decision one way or the other, but the committee argued against extending members' immunity from the ordinary law; if a safeguard was needed it relied on Parliamentary scrutiny of the executive, and the general support for 18B. The committee brushed aside the argument that its recommendation made it possible in principle for the executive to lock up its opponents indefinitely without either trial or public disclosure of what they were supposed to have done. A later attempt in 1944 to reopen the question, and at least require the government to justify its action in secret session, failed by 135 votes to 31.[52] The acceptance by the Commons of the detention of one of its own members in conditions of complete secrecy seems quite bizarre in a liberal democracy, but we must recognize that during the war Britain was not, in any real sense, a democratic state, and the times were desperate; furthermore Ramsay excited no

[48] *Parl. Deb.* HC Vol. 361 c.1370 (MI5 is investigating); 363: 611 for 23 July (report has been received).

[49] *Parl. Deb.* HC Vol. 363 c.1165, 1513.

[50] The report, dated 9 October, is in *Parliamentary Papers* 1939–1940 as (164) III 623. It was accepted by the Commons on 11 December: *Parl. Deb.* HC Vol. 367 c.933–991.

[51] There had also been 6 detentions in 1715 under habeas corpus suspension legislation.

[52] *Parl. Deb.* HC Vol. 400 c.2317 ff. (16 June).

sympathy. Far stranger is the tolerance of secrecy over the affair fifty years later.

Diana Mosley

Once Mosley and Ramsay had been disposed of, deciding that the other prominent fascists and right-wingers should remain in detention was a mere formality, as Birkett and his colleagues must have been very well aware.[53] Diana Mosley, though a dedicated fascist, and an admirer and indeed something of a friend of Hitler and the Goebbels family, presented a slight problem, since she had played no active part in the BU at all. She did not appear before the committee until 2 October, and MI5's 'Statement of the Case' has been weeded from the file. The ostensible reasons for her detention were that she had acted as an intermediary between her husband and the German government and Hitler, had transmitted instructions after her husband's detention for carrying on the BU, had supported her husband, and had expressed fascist views. Harker of MI5 described her as 'this extremely dangerous and sinister young woman'.[54] The first charge related to the radio station negotiations before the war, and the second to her attempts to ensure that junior members of the staff were paid their wages; there was nothing either illegal or improper in these activities, and in any event all visits were monitored and a record supplied to MI5.[55] The expression of fascist views depended in part upon a report by her former father-in-law, Lord Moyne, based on gossip from his grandchildren's governess, who clearly detested her.

Any problems Birkett might have had were solved when Diana Mosley appeared in a belligerent and unrepentant mood before the committee. She made no secret of her support of the BU, of her strong fascist sympathies, of her friendship with Hitler and liking for Himmler, and of her utter contempt for the committee. She herself has written: 'Birkett was very hostile towards me, and I was very hostile towards him.'[56] She thought that if Birkett had behaved honourably he could only have recommended the release of her husband, a view which, as we have seen, was not simply absurd, given the weakness of the evidence against him. She

---

[53] Donovan must have appeared early in July or in late June; the report recommending his detention was dated 8 July (HO 45/25705). Francis-Hawkins appeared on 4 July (HO 283/40). McKechnie appeared on 8 July, and the report was dated 24 July (HO 283/48). We may guess that all the more prominent 'leaders' would be seen during July except Gordon-Canning, who appeared, for obscure reasons, on 28 August and again in November. Of other right-wingers John W. Beckett appeared on 10 July. Aubrey T. O. Lees on 29 July and again on 1 August (HO 283/45).

[54] See HO 144/21995 and Guinness, *House of Mitford*, 492–4.

[55] See Guinness, *House of Mitford*, 382–3 and 499 for an account of the negotiations.

[56] *Loved Ones*, 211.

could think of no occasion, public or private, on which she had ever condemned any of Hitler's actions. She deeply regretted the war, and had little use for Churchill, of whom she remarked, not without perception: 'I
have known Winston Churchill since I was a small child. He is more
interested in war than anything else in the world.' The committee was
thus encouraged by her to reach the politically necessary conclusion: 'It
would be quite impossible, having regard to her expressed attitude and
her past activities with the leaders of Nazi Germany, to allow her to
remain at liberty in these critical days . . . Lady Mosley would be
extremely dangerous if she were at large.' The final claim, viewed dispassionately, is surely utterly absurd; in October 1940—that is during the
Battle of Britain—the only dangers involved in her release would have
been public outrage against the government, and a risk, had she been so
foolish as to preach fascism, of violence against her. She was in reality
detained for being Mosley's wife, and the committee was happy to recommend her continued detention to punish her for intransigent fascism.

The Conflict with MI5

Once the committee turned to less prominent people it began to reassert
its independent role. This soon brought it into serious conflict with MI5.
Friction between MI5 and the Home Office and its committee had long
existed. An aggravating factor may have been the tendency of higher Civil
Servants to view the officers of MI5, not recruited, as they were, on a
competitive intellectual basis, but on social contacts, with some disdain.
As more of MI5's crude errors came to light in the later months of 1940
this disdain was heightened. One fiasco which may have particularly irritated the Home Office was the affair of the German spy ring, over which
the Home Office had reluctantly deferred to MI5 in late May. A minute
by Maxwell, dealing with the cases of Alfred and Walter Block, Edward
Diamond, and Fare Prescott, all detained in consequence, reads:

In view of the strong and very definite advice from MI5 that the internment of
these people was required on security grounds the Home Office at last in May 1940
felt it was no longer justifiable for the Home Secretary to refuse to act on this
advice. The examination of the four cases by the Advisory Committee shows con-
clusively that the suspicions of MI5 were entirely unfounded and that we have
detained these four gentlemen quite unjustifiably.[57]

Some few scandalous cases are documented.[58] Others are mentioned in
pamphlets, or in questions in the Commons; for example Albery on 26

[57] HO 45/25707 and 25721. See above p. 77.
[58] In addition to these four, Simon, Wolff, and Klinghardt (HO 45/25721), Hamilton
S. L. Knight, later Squadron Leader Knight (HO 45/25695), and Harry Sabini (HO 45/25720
and TS 27/496A).

November 1941 referred to a man of 67 with a wife of 63 detained as supporters of the BU; the husband was dying and had been released whilst the wife remained in detention.[59] Up to 31 December 1940 at least thirty-one detainees (apart from under-age Italians) had been released before appearance because suspicions were 'explained to the Secretary of State'. Some, but not all, would be cases reflecting badly on MI5; but about most of them nothing is known.[60] It is significant, however, that the available records do not fully document a single case of mistaken identity, nor a single case of extreme inhumanity, though there certainly were such cases.[61]

The cumulative effect of MI5's mistakes and unfounded suspicions was to confirm Birkett and his colleagues in the belief, formed before May of 1940, that MI5 was illiberal, disorganized, and incompetent. Even before the great incarceration Birkett had written of 'gross mistakes and pathological stupidities'.[62] Now MI5 had even failed to come up with a convincing case against Mosley himself, thereby forcing Birkett and his colleagues into agreeing a report which at the least came close to compromising their integrity. Any residual confidence in MI5 must have vanished when Birkett and his colleagues realized, as they must have done by October of 1940, if not much earlier, that the organized Fifth Column, in the name of which the number of 18B detainees had risen from just over 100 to around 1,500, and the aliens to 28,000 or so, was, and always had been, a baseless myth.

The 'Desperate Characters'

Probably MI5's incompetence reached its peak over the Anglo-Italians.[63] The documentary evidence dealing with the release of Anglo-Italians is minimal but many of Sir Percy Loraine's own papers survive and there is a Foreign Office file.[64] Loraine's committee was set up when there were thought to be 390 Anglo-Italians in detention, but by late September the figure was 514, ninety-seven having been already released. The Foreign Office was much concerned and had no confidence in MI5. There was

[59] *Parl. Deb.* HC Vol. 376 c.783.

[60] HO 45/25115. The number may be higher; the figure quoted may refer only to Anglo-Italians.

[61] For example G. Palmer Thompson, detained when terminally ill with cancer of the throat; see above p. 232.

[62] Hinsley and Simkins, 39.

[63] See above p. 193 et seq. There is some reason to believe that the police took the opportunity to lock up Italian criminals against whom no evidence existed which would justify normal arrest: 'petty gangsters, pimps, racecourse razor slashers and the like'; see L. V. Thompson, *1940: Year of Legend, Year of History* (London, 1960), 136–7. This fits only one documentable case, that of Harry Sabini and his brother Darby; see Ch. 14 below.

[64] FO 1011/215, 216, FO 371/25210.

consequent friction between the Foreign Office and MI5, supported by Swinton, over the guidance to be given to Loraine's committee; the MI5 view was that membership of the Fascio should be treated as more or less conclusive proof that the detainee was dangerous. The Foreign Office successfully disagreed, and thought MI5 to be over-suspicious, and ill informed.[65] Once the work was under way there was further trouble, focused on Romelo Antonelli, whom Loraine wanted to release, though it was conceded he had belonged to the Fascio. A letter of 16 October from Harker to A. E. Watkins shows Harker objecting to the recommendation, and in general to the release of members of the Fascio, and Loraine, vigorously embattled, replying: 'You say that the case of Romelo Antonelli is the case against the Italian Fascist Party. We must reply that we are not sitting to try the Italian Fascist Party, but to hear the appeals of persons who, in the capacity of British subjects, have the right to make such appeals.' A note by a Home Office official reads: 'The atmosphere seems a bit tense between the Italian Advisory Committee and MI5; but perhaps they will be able to resolve their differences without recourse to "higher quarters".'[66] MI5's view was that if persons like Antonelli were released something like 70 per cent of the Fascio members would be set free. They, MI5 argued, represented 'a serious danger so long as there is a possibility of invasion of the country'. On 29 October Loraine suggested that if Harker would not agree the matter should be aired 'in higher quarters'; apparently it never was, and MI5 eventually gave way.

By November Loraine, a somewhat prickly individual, was discussing with Newsam whether he ought to have a 'full blooded row' with MI5; in December he wrote to Newsam in connection with the case of one di Mambro expressing his lack of confidence in MI5, who had relied on flimsy evidence. MI5 in its turn resented the fact that the Italian Committee was prepared to make its own independent enquiries. By December Loraine was suggesting an entirely new form of committee to sort out the differences, with representatives of the Home Office, the Foreign Office, the War Office, MI5, the police, the Special Operations Executive, the Learned Societies, and his committee. But in the end what drove him to tender his resignation, on 2 December, was a row over George Worth, secretary to the Isle of Man panel. It turned out that Worth, who was married to an Italian and had lived in Italy before the war, had regularly spent vacations in the village of Pofi between 1929 and 1935, where he and his wife had contributed to local charities. In 1932 the local fascists had made him an honorary member of the Fascio, and he had thought it churlish to object. Morrison and his officials thought it

---

[65] The Foreign Office relied on a memo by Prof. Bruno Foa, once legal adviser to the Consulate General in Naples; MI5's memo is not in the file.

[66] The correspondence is partly in HO 45/25754/863027 and partly in FO 371/25210.

inevitable that Worth, whom Loraine had recommended, and who had worked for British intelligence in Italy before the war, must cease to act as secretary. Loraine thought this outrageous. He was also annoyed that one Cetralango, whose detention his committee had recommended, had been released, and he was exasperated by the lack of co-operation from MI5, and the general lack of co-ordination between those concerned with the Italian detainees. But at a long meeting with Morrison, Maxwell, and Newsam his resignation was not accepted, and peace was restored; Worth was found another job in the Ministry of Home Security, and on 13 December a Home Office conference set up arrangements to encourage the release of more dual nationals who were willing to join the Auxiliary Military Pioneer Corps. But Morrison did not give way either over Cetralango or over Antonelli, whom he refused to release.

Some few Anglo-Italian files have been allowed to survive; none concern scandalous cases. An example is that on Ogni Lorenzo, who was unwilling to fight against his co-patriots; called up in 1942, he deserted and eventually made a pathetic attempt to row to France in the hope of being reunited with his family.[67] His detention was understandable enough. Another case is Orazio M. R. Bottachio, who ran a restaurant in Southampton, detained on 10 June; he was a member of the Fascio in the city, founded in 1934, and active in the Associazioni Nazionale Combattenti Italiani, a veterans' club, having himself fought in the First World War. He had also joined the Partito Nazionale Fascisti. No doubt he seemed to MI5 to be an enthusiastic fascist, though in reality he was nothing of the sort; enthusiasm for fascism amongst the Italian community in Southampton had faded after one D'Anneo, Italian Vice-Consul, had left in about 1937, if indeed it had ever amounted to much. Bottachio was released in December 1940.[68] Negative evidence suggests that many of the 'desperate fellows' whom Harker wished interned under 18B, of whom Bottachio must have been one, were fairly soon released, as he was, some by administrative action.[69] Names of Anglo-Italians do not appear at all commonly in such records as are available after 1941. Probably after December 1940 MI5 did not oppose the release of many of the Anglo-Italians. On 24 August the Home Defence (Security) Executive took a

[67] HO 45/25761, HO 283/52. Gilda Camillo, a member of the Fascio Femministi, was detained in 1942 in Glasgow; her sympathies were wholly with Italy, and she was thought to have discouraged Anglo-Italians from war service (HO 45/25759). She appeared before the Scottish committee.

[68] HO 45/25088. Two similar cases, Victor Marricotti and Pietro Malvisi, are documented in a memo by Scott in FO 1011/215.

[69] Hinsley and Simkins add virtually nothing, but mention Lord Snell's report on the *Arandora Star* disaster (CAB 66/13, WP (40) 432, 463 of 24 October, 25 November), which concluded that some of the Italians on MI5's dangerous list were nominal members of the Fascio and entirely loyal.

policy decision to release without a hearing all dual nationals aged under 18, of whom there were sixty-seven.[70] Probably this too was a response to an explosion from Loraine.[71] Possibly MI5's acquiescence was encouraged by a change in the officer directly involved.[72] But in November 1941 there were still between 150 and 200 dual nationals in detention. The Italian Committee ceased to operate after February 1942: later cases came before Birkett's committee, with O'Sullivan and Scott also sitting with him.

The Issue of Principle

The dispute with MI5 over the Anglo-Italians centred not upon cases of crude error but on cases of admitted Fascio members, whose detention seemed entirely unnecessary to the committee, but whose release was opposed as a matter of principle by MI5. The same problem arose more acutely over the BU, and the dispute could be very acrimonious, as in the case of Rita Shelmerdine.[73] She was a married woman with two small children, aged 5 and 2, detained on 11 July as 'an ardent supporter of fascism'. Her husband Philip, also detained, was a BU official. In her representations she said: 'I joined the British Union in August 1938 after having very carefully read the policy in various publications and it seemed to me that the ideals of the British Union were entirely patriotic and pro-British.' She had indeed helped at meetings, and sold *Action*, but the main case against her was based upon statements she was supposed to have made which demonstrated her ardour. She started habeas corpus in October 1940, primarily on the basis of the delay in hearing her appeal; she obtained her hearing.[74] The report of Birkett's committee is a blistering document:

The Committee entertain no doubt in this case that Mrs Shelmerdine should be released at once . . . The Committee feel bound to record their regret that Mrs Shelmerdine, the mother of two young children, should have been detained since the 11 July upon evidence which they are bound to say does not merit detention at all. They hope . . . that immediate effect will be given to their recommendation and that Mrs Shelmerdine may go back to her two young children at once . . . The

[70] Paper in FO 371/25210. Hutchinson and Newsam represented the Home Office, Farquhar the Foreign Office, Pilcher, J. C. Currie, Miss Weeks, and C. H. N. Adams MI5; the other member was Reginald Duthie or Duthy.

[71] HO 45/25115/863834. Some detainees were as young as 15.

[72] See above p. 195. Adams represented MI5 at a conference on the Italian Committee on 26 August 1940 (HO 45/25758/145326). H. Deedes and H. Emmett of E6 were concerned with Italians in 1942–4 (HO 45/25759), as was A. W. Roskill, a barrister (HO 45/25761).

[73] HO 45/23736/860393, TS 27/491. See above p. 288.

[74] Along with Maj. Harold de Laessoe, Mrs Emily D. V. Durell, and William E. Sherston. The first hearing was on 7 October, when the case was adjourned. See below Ch. 14.

Committee felt so strongly about this case that they communicated with MI5 by telephone in order to obtain their concurrence which they hoped from the facts of the case would be immediately forthcoming. After immense difficulty, which lasted the whole day, they were able finally to speak with Mr Stamp of MI5,[75] although the Statement of the Case was signed by Mr Redfern. Mr Stamp said he had read the papers, and, in view of the reports from the police, they were quite unable to agree . . . To detain Mrs Shelmerdine any longer would be to perpetrate an injustice and they recommend in the strongest possible terms that Mrs Shelmerdine should be immediately released.

MI5, not to be put off, formally objected, and in the Home Office A. S. Hutchinson minuted that no doubt she was an active fascist, but also no doubt there was no need to detain her. Maxwell noted on the file on 5 November: 'S. of S. discussed this case with me. He decided to sign a revocation order, and to have a talk with Birkett later about the Report and about the general attitude of the Committee to these Fascist cases.' The Order was revoked on 8 November, and she was released five days later.

But the conflict between the committee and MI5 did not principally depend upon differing assessments of individual cases. It arose over a matter of principle, and was an almost inevitable result of the policy of crippling the BU by detaining, as a class, its active members. This policy was quite at odds with the approach of the committee: that cases should be treated individually, and harmless and patriotic people released even if they had been active supporters of what had been, after all, a legal politi-cal party. The Shelmerdine case is an example. The MI5 view was that it was not the business of the committee to investigate whether a recently active member was harmless and patriotic. This would lead to the release of so many detainees that the Cabinet policy of crippling the party would be frustrated. The committee, particularly Chairmen Wallington and Morris, emphatically disagreed.[76]

What is remarkable about MI5's attitude is that, as we have seen, it had come to the conclusion 'in private' that the threat from the supposed organized Fifth Column had been a myth. I take it that Hinsley and Simkins are, in using this expression, delicately indicating that MI5 did not advertise this change of view, in the name of which some 30,000 or so persons had been needlessly imprisoned.[77] Yet if MI5 was right then the very basis for the crippling of the BU was now gone. But this point seems never to have been raised. The assumption seems to have been that the BU, an evil organization, having been crushed and proscribed, it ought not to be allowed to revive, and further that it was legitimate to use deten-tion and not simply criminal prosecution, a far cheaper not to mention fairer mechanism, as the means to this end.

[75] E. Blanshard Stamp.   [76] The dispute is most fully covered in HO 45/25754.

The character of the dispute can be illustrated from a less emotive case than Shelmerdine's, in which Morrison himself favoured MI5's view. It involved Derek R. Stuckey, a farmer and organizer of fascists in universities and schools, whom we have already met.[78] He appeared on 23 August before J. W. Morris's panel; on 9 September it recommended release: 'The Committee did not feel there was any harm in Stuckey, though they deplored the kind of activity to which he has lent himself *since the outbreak of war* [my italics].' The time he spent on BU work was 'inconsiderable', and he had the conventional attitude of BU detainees to the war: 'He affirmed himself as being resolute in his determination not to tolerate the defeat of Britain.' MI5 had objected to the draft report: 'Stuckey was a man of education who could have no illusions as to the objects of the BU. He had sought to gain adherents for that organization among schoolteachers and even schoolboys. In view of his enthusiasm for the cause we cannot place the hope in his future behaviour which is expressed by the committee.'[79] Maxwell sent the case back for reconsideration since Morrison had grave doubts about releasing him; on 14 December Morris replied that the committee saw no reason to change their view. Stuckey remained in detention until 24 September 1941. In November MI5 raised no objection to his being allowed to join the armed services; by 1944 he rose to the rank of Captain[80]

The Management of the Dispute

Before May detention solely concerned the Home Office, but now Swinton's committee was involved; it could take questions to the War Cabinet through the Lord President, Chamberlain, or, from 3 October, Anderson.[81] On 13 July Swinton wrote to Maxwell, after discussions with Pilcher of MI5 and with Birkett, urging him to persuade Anderson to instruct the Committee 'that the scope of the enquiry in these cases should be directed to whether the internee had or had not been active in the furtherance of the organization and not as to whether it was necessary to detain him or her as an individual'. This was MI5's position.[82] Maxwell arranged a compromise; as a general rule cases would be handled in this way, but not when there had been a significant change of heart by a detainee; an example given by Birkett was P. F. C. Chalker, who had left the BU in April of 1939. But trouble continued. On 22 August E. B.

---

[77] Hinsley and Simkins, 59, referring also to a statement by Churchill in Parliament on 22 August (*Parl. Deb.* HC Vol. 354 c.957). See above p. 164.

[78] HO 283/63, 45/25722. See above pp. 130, 266.

[79] Letter of 4 September by S. H. Noakes.

[80] Nigel Watson, the MI5 officer involved, was a Russian linguist who became a partisan in Yugoslavia. N. West *MI5* (London, 1983), 351.

[81] See Hinsley and Simkins, 52–3.   [82] HO 45/25754/863027/2

Stamp of MI5 claimed that Birkett's committee was not operating Maxwell's compromise, which, he argued, entailed always continuing the detention of anyone active since the war began. Stamp argued that if the committee did not mend its ways the consequence would be the release of 70–75 per cent of the detainees, and the BU, which was since 10 July an illegal organization, would revive; he did not explain why, if this were to happen, it could not be countered by the use of regular prosecutions. Presumably what he feared was 'the underground BU' in some new form.

In late August Aikin-Sneath wrote a lengthy memorandum setting out MI5's view of the BU; this was after the interrogations in Latchmere House, in which he must have been involved. MI5 no longer believed that the BU or part of it formed an organized Fifth Column; the idea is never mentioned. Yet it remained potentially dangerous, not because it was under German control, but because it collected together individuals some of whom were likely to assist the enemy. Like other troublesome organizations, such as the IFL, it had been destroyed; MI5 did not want it to revive.[83]

This memorandum was considered at a tense meeting with Birkett and his deputy chairmen in early September.[84] By then about twenty cases were in dispute.[85] 'Mr Wallington emphatically repudiated the idea that a man should be interned merely on the ground of being an active official of British Union. He contended that if this principle were accepted the work of the Committee would be a farce. The only task would be to confirm automatically decisions arrived at by MI5.' Aikin-Sneath asked him what principle he would apply? He replied in typical common law style: 'I have no principle. It is not possible to lay down a general principle.' In fact, however, he did have one; he argued that as a man of wide experience he could tell on all the facts 'whether the person before him was likely to be a danger to the country or not'. Like Birkett he was commited to the assessment of character through interrogation. The releases which would follow from this approach were precisely what alarmed MI5, since Aikin-Sneath realized that most BU detainees, whatever might be said of the long-term implications of their politics, were patriotic and loyal. The meeting achieved nothing.

On 4 September Aikin-Sneath suggested a new compromise—any detainee who had been an active official *until May* should remain in detention; each case would then be reviewed after six months. If no danger, presumably of an invasion, then existed, they could be released.

---

[83] A letter from Liddell of MI5 to Maxwell on 19 September stated that internment had brought about a complete cessation of pro-Nazi activity.

[84] Probably on 3 or 4 September.

[85] The chairmen involved were Morris (9 cases), Wallington (8 cases), Birkett (2 cases), and Miller (1 case).

Meanwhile Aikin-Sneath, who seems to have had a sense of missionary zeal in his hatred of fascism, should be given two weeks to compile a *Black Book of British Fascism*, which could be published as a government paper.[86] This would warn people away from sympathy with the movement, and thus discourage any revival; Aikin-Sneath must have imagined that the general public read such documents. His scheme was never taken any further and, as we have seen, his Black Book was never published.

On 18 September, by when there were thirty-five to forty cases in issue, Maxwell, Newsam, and Hutchinson met the chairmen, and did a little leaning: 'The Committee was of course entirely independent; it was not for the Home Office to advise the Committee but vice versa. It might happen in some cases, however, that the Home Secretary did not feel able to accept the Committee's recommendation, but the Home Secretary wanted to reduce such cases to a minimum.'[87] Birkett said that they had been assisted by hearing the Home Office view, and added 'that they would in future keep the preventive aspect of the question well to the fore in their minds'.[88] On 1 October Birkett wrote a note of advice for his colleagues.[89] This set out the factors which needed to be investigated—was the detainee a person of influence, what was his present attitude to the BU, had it changed since the outbreak of war, does he sympathize with Germany, or is his support of Britain lukewarm? Birkett laid particular emphasis on character: 'The personality and character of the appellant should be regarded as very important. If he is honest and sincere, and convinces the Committee that he is no danger to the state, this fact should be clearly recorded.' Whether intentionally or not this ensured that the dispute would continue.

It next went before Swinton's committee on 15 October,[90] on 31 October,[91] and again on 6 November.[92] The committee now came close to becoming a court of appeal in disputed 18B cases. It had, as we have seen, decided that Anglo-Italians under 18 be released, and ruled that an Anglo-Italian who refused military service should always be kept in detention.[93] At the first meeting the opposing views were presented.[94] It was explained that the Home Office had originally thought that mere

---

[86] See the memo of 14 April 1943 (CAB 66/35), discussed above p. 165.

[87] HO 45/25754/863027.

[88] One case mentioned was that of Lees, interned under 18B (1A), who had never been in the BU at all; Maxwell agreed he could be released, which he was on 27 September 1940. His case is discussed below p. 298 *et seq.*

[89] In HO 283/64 (case of Smeaton-Stuart).   [90] HO 45/25754.

[91] HO 45/25754/863027/5A; also CAB 93/2 HD (S) E 17th meeting, cited Hinsley and Simkins, 64, but not available.

[92] HO 45/25754/863027/6.

[93] FO 371/25210. This ruling was before 24 October.

[94] Attended by Swinton, Foot, Wall, Maxwell, A. S. Hutchinson (of the Home Office), and Pilcher of MI5.

membership of the BU justified detention: 'The Home Office had adopted the principle in the first place in order to catch all the rogues and fanatics; it appeared that they had caught a great number of harmless people as well.'[95] Pilcher, for MI5, resisted any change. A compromise was suggested by Swinton; some detainees could be released with MI5's agreement, some reconsidered with MI5 offering new evidence, some could be released with grudging acquiescence from MI5 under restrictions, or on condition of joining the army. Any remaining cases could be referred informally to his committee for an impartial opinion as to what should be done. The meeting then decided two specific cases, those of Rafe Temple-Cotton and his mother; he had been a Regional Inspector of the BU and one of the eight persons entitled to nominate a successor to Mosley, so one can understand MI5's anxieties. It was, however, settled that they could be released; both must undertake to give up political activities, and he was to join the army. This meant that the Swinton Committee was usurping the position both of Birkett's committee and of the Home Secretary himself.

But matters grew worse. By the end of October the committee had heard 317 cases, recommending release in 199; MI5 disagreed in 111.[96] But the next meeting saw the defeat of MI5.[97] It was agreed that when the chief ground for detention was being an officer or active member of the BU the Home Secretary should rubber-stamp recommendations for release, and release unconditionally. But 'where the Security Service established that there were exceptional reasons for detention over and above office or membership' the Home Secretary would consider whether the reasons were sufficient to justify continued detention or restrictions.

Birkett and Harker both attended the third meeting.[98] Of the 111 cases in dispute 96 simply involved officials or active members, and on these MI5 now accepted it had lost.[99] Examples would be Charles H. W. Hewitt, District Leader in Bristol; Ralph N. Clarke, temporary District Leader, whose phone had been tapped by MI5; Mrs A. V. D. Hudson, Women's District Leader and wife of Commander Hudson, one of the eight authorized to choose a new leader; I. F. Carlile, Assistant District Leader in King's Lynn, who possessed 'sticky-backs', but was believed by the committee when he said he had not used them; F. S. Clifford, 'who

---

[95] Quoted Hinsley and Simkins, 61.

[96] HO 45/25754/863027/6 (meeting of 6 November). Sf. 5A (meeting of 31 October) has Harker objecting to about 100 recommendations.

[97] This was attended by Harker and Brig. H. I. Allen, Lt.-Col. J. H. Adam, and Messrs D. C. H. Abbott and T. F. Turner of MI5 and Lt.-Col. V. P. T. Vivian and Capt. J. F. Cowgill of MI6. Turner was another barrister recruited by MI5.

[98] The others were Swinton, Foot, Maxwell, Hutchinson, Pilcher, and W. Armstrong (the Secretary).

[99] HO 45/25754/ 863027/3, Memorandum by Stamp of 22 August.

294   THE INTEGRITY OF THE ADVISORY COMMITTEE

was a District Leader who wrote a letter to Oswald Mosley (to which the Committee did not attach much importance) on 25 May 1940 wishing him best wishes for his speedy release'. Only fifteen involved special additional factors, enabling MI5 to maintain opposition to release.[100] At this meeting other sources of friction were ventilated—for example MI5's slowness in producing papers, and Birkett's insistence that MI5 should not in effect have a veto over committee recommendations for release. The production of MI5's agents before the committee was also raised, and Birkett, no doubt in an attempt to lower the temperature, said he did not wish to see the agent involved in Admiral Domvile's case, who may have been Harold Kurtz; his committee would accept the assurance of MI5 as to the reliability of information from agents. It was a concession he would come to regret.

The Swinton Committee compromise was, in substance, accepted by the War Cabinet on Thursday 21 November. About 60 per cent of the 750 BU detainees would be released, either unconditionally with a warning not to engage in BU activities under pain of re-detention or prosecution, or conditionally with the order suspended with conditions of residence and reporting to the police as well.[101] On 28 November Morrison made a statement to the Commons to the effect that although it had been right and necessary to detain the fascists, it was now safe to release a considerable number of the less important members.[102] This coincided with a Cabinet decision to release a considerable number of the 19,500 aliens then detained. So far as the Anglo-Italians are concerned, there was no public statement, but around 400 were free by November 1941.

The Persistence of Friction

This restored Home Office control, and the independence of Birkett's committee, though its power had been permanently reduced. Morrison, no pillar of liberalism, seems to have sympathized with MI5 in thinking the committee too soft, and continued to reject some recommendations; he seems to have succumbed to the temptation to use 18B to punish fascists. In December of 1940 he disagreed with the committee over fifteen

---

[100] HO 45/25115/863834/14 has a list of 18 cases where Morrison disagreed with the committee in December, 14 being BU cases (G. C. Arnold, Jack Austin, J. S. Crosland, G. Drake, Marjorie Clare, D. M. Evans, F. Haslam, Wm. Hunt, John Mountjoy, J. Preen, C. P. Radford, Jack Steele, George Thomson, and Richard Wynn). These may be the cases mentioned in early November. J. N. P. Mountjoy had been in the British Fascists Ltd. and joined the BU in 1932, and was a D/L from 1937 to 1940, resigning for domestic reasons. Marjorie Clare was active in Brighton.

[101] CAB 65/10, WM (40) 293 of 21 Nov. Minute 10, considering the Home Office memo (WP (G) (40) 308). See Hinsley and Simkins, 61–2.

[102] *Parl. Deb.* HC Vol. 367 c.310.

18B (1A) cases and four hostile origin or association cases.[103] In January 1941, when decisions were taken by the Home Office over the principal cases then in dispute, he rejected fifty-five recommendations.[104] Morrison's practice allowed MI5 to reopen cases after the committee had reported. Birkett and his colleagues

viewed the procedure which has been followed in these cases with much disquiet, and havè frequently set that disquiet on record. The principal ground for this disquiet has been that the decisions of the Advisory Committee, given after full and careful consideration of all the facts, and with national security as the all important consideration, have been made the subject of acute contention and have lost the character the Advisory Committee intended them to bear, of dispassionate reviews of all contentious matters.

Birkett did not mind Morrison rejecting a recommendation; he did object to MI5, after its case had been rejected by the committee, being able to present it a second time behind the back of the committee to the Home Office.[105]

Trouble with MI5 persisted throughout the life of the regulation, and reached its peak in late 1941, as we shall see, over the case of Ben Greene; it must have been aggravated by the fact that Birkett, an old-fashioned gentleman, was out of sympathy with the repulsive activities taken for granted in the security service—spying on neighbours, opening private letters, employing lying agents and stool-pigeons, and all the disagreeable practices of the trade.[106] Disagreement with the Home Office also persisted. The reports to Parliament recorded new cases of disagreement—thus there were eighteen in March 1941 and twenty-five in April, but thereafter the numbers were never higher than five in one month, as in April 1943; these disagreements could arise on a first hearing or on a review of the case. Running totals were given from February 1941, and by the end of 1941 of the 627 remaining detainees seventy were persons whose release had been recommended.[107] The figure for the end of 1942 was seventy-seven out of 586, for 1943 twenty-eight out of 266.[108] The passage of time reduced the area of conflict, and by the end of 1944 a mere three out of sixty-five detainees were persons whom the committee would have released.[109] Sometimes the Home Office released a detainee when the committee had recommended continued detention, and from June 1941 special attention was drawn to this as if it was proof of Morrison's liberalism.

---

[103] There is a list of names in HO 45/21515.

[104] Figures for rejections for following months of 1941 were: February, 8, March, 18, April, 25, May, 5, June, 2, July, 2, August, 3, September, 1, October, 2, November, 1, December, nil.

[105] Memo of 21 April 1941 in HO 45/25754.   [106] See below p. 369.

[107] Of whom 45 were hostile origin or association cases.

[108] 22 were hostile origin or association cases.   [109] There were 19 such cases in all.

And even after the Cabinet decision of November 1940 the number of detainees remained considerable. At the end of 1941 there were still 627 in custody, and 486 at the end of 1942.

The scale of release recommended by the committee, and largely accepted, entailed the view that the power of detention had been grossly over-used; this, for political reasons, had to be denied.[110] Thus in the debate on 10 December 1940 Morrison, without indicating that any error had been made, referred to the BU as 'an organization we had reason to believe, and I think the house generally believed, was actually or potentially dangerous to the State. We apprehended that in case of invasion by Nazi Germany these people might actively assist the enemy.'[111] On 16 January 1941 Morrison addressed the assembled Chief Constables and concluded 'by thanking Chief Constables for their good work in May, June and July of 1940, as a result of which the government had been able to cope with the "Fifth Column" menace without anxiety and without internment on too large a scale'.[112] In reality much of the fault must have rested on their unreliable recommendations, which MI5 had been unable to verify. It was convenient, if not very honest, to keep alive the myth of the Fifth Column as a justification, and Home Secretaries are wise to avoid criticizing their Chief Constables. To this day many who lived through this period continue to believe in the Fifth Column, as they believe in other myths which came to be established in those grim times, myths which may have served a useful function in consolidating support for the policy of fighting on alone.

[110] As it was by Morrison on 28 November (*Parl. Deb*. HC Vol. 367 c.310).
[111] *Parl. Deb*. HC Vol. 367 c.876.
[112] MEPO 2/1643 (Extract from the Minutes of the 39th Meeting of the Central Conference of Chief Constables).

— 14 —

The Early Challenges in the Courts

The Text of the Regulation

The original Regulation 18B was designed to give the Home Secretary an arbitrary power of detention; neither its scope nor its validity were ever raised in the courts. The amended 18B was undeniably legally valid, but its more specific text appeared to set limits to the powers of the Home Secretary; potentially the courts had a role in ensuring that these limits were observed. Furthermore on some important questions it was silent. Thus it did not specify the form of a detention order—for example would an oral instruction suffice? Did a written order have to be signed by the Home Secretary? Or would Maxwell's signature be enough? Must a detainee be told why he was being arrested? How much had he to be told? These and other gaps again made it possible for the judges, if they wished, to hold detention illegal if it did not satisfy whatever requirements they regarded as the tolerable minimum—for example perhaps a written order, with a copy for the detainee, was essential. So, as is always the case, there were choices for the judges to make. They could play an active part by setting firm limits to the discretionary power conferred on the executive, and by spelling out more precisely the rights of a detainee. Alternatively they could be passive, accepting more or less anything which emanated from the Home Office. And there was nothing in the text which ruled out applications to the courts for habeas corpus, or other legal remedies.

All this was appreciated in the Home Office and, as we have seen, there was some anxiety lest the use of words such as 'have reasonable cause to believe' in the new 18B might give the courts a power of review.[1] The consensus was, however, that a court would only intervene if mistake as to identity could be proved, or it could be shown that there was 'a case of clear excessive power' or 'bad faith', or 'a sham'.[2] Of course a detainee would, somehow or other, have to show that the regulation had been abused, and given the secrecy of British government it was difficult to see how this could be done. Until there were legal decisions on the matter the role of the courts in 18B cases necessarily remained rather uncertain.

[1] See above p. 63.   [2] See above p. 62.

The Case of Aubrey T. O. Lees

The first case to come before the courts involved the colonial Civil Servant, Aubrey T. O. Lees.[3] The litigation was funded by the Liberty Restoration League, founded 'To Oppose State Despotism. To Defend the Natural and Constitutional Rights of the Citizens', under its Chairman, the Duke of Wellington. It was the intention to take the case, if need be, to the House of Lords, but this was never done; who precisely put up the money is uncertain, but I like to think that Sir William Holdsworth contributed.[4] Lees had been a regular army officer; after joining the colonial service he had worked in Palestine as Assistant District Commissioner for the Jaffa District under the mandate. He disagreed with British policy there over Zionist immigration, and was very anti-Semitic. He returned to England in 1939 and lived at 10 Courtfield Gardens in London with Ella Durant, a governess who was in the BU; he subsequently married her. His next employment would have been in the Gold Coast, untroubled by conflicts between Arabs and Zionists and, because of the climate, not a popular posting. He was detained on 21 June 1940 on an 18B (1A) order, which had earlier been cleared with the Colonial Office.[5]

The initiative for Lees's detention came from Kendal of Special Branch, who described him as 'a traitor of the worst type'. According to Kendal Lees had been active in support of the BU, the BPP, the British Constitutional Union (another alias for the Nordic League), and the Right Club, of which he was indeed a member. He had, as we have seen, attended some of the 'secret meetings' to which Kendal ascribed an exaggerated importance.[6] He also had associated with Lieutenant-Colonel James P. Cherry,[7] Dr Leigh Vaughan-Henry,[8] Stanley Stone,[9] and Lord Tavistock, and had expressed sympathy with Hitler's policy of oppressing the Jews. The police also held against him the fact that he had given evidence in favour of one John A. Webster, who had been prosecuted in London, presumably under the Public Order Act, in connection with fascist activities. After receiving a Special Branch report which, amongst other allegations, stated that Lees had joined the BU, Maxwell, though not impressed by Kendal's overblown account, recommended an order, and Lees was arrested. The order was under 18B (1A), and was not for 'acts prejudicial', which Maxwell had originally thought was the appro-

---

[3] Born 1890.

[4] Letter of 4 January 1941 in Saunders Papers. The League existed by 1935; its Chairman was Capt. Bernard Ackworth DSO, RN (Luttman-Johnson Papers). See above p. 71.

[5] HO 283/45 and HO 45/25728, also TS 27/496A (Sabini). The habeas corpus action was before the Divisional Court on 12 July, 22 August, and 9 September; reported [1941] 1 KB 72 and 57 TLR 26 and 68.

[6] See above p. 144.   [7] Detained in June 1940.   [8] Later detained.

[9] Not identified; there seems to have been no detainee of that name.

priate category. The text simply rehearsed the language of 18B (1A): 'Whereas I have reasonable cause to believe Aubrey Trevor Lees to have been or to be a member of or to have been active in the furtherance of the objects of an organization' etc. The order thus did not say whether Lees was thought to be a member of the BU, or not.

A search disclosed papers relating to other 'secret meetings' held at 48 Ladbroke Grove in February and May.[10] Lees admitted attending one of these meetings, at which Mosley and 'Commandant' Allen were present.[11] There can be no doubt that Lees had indeed been in touch with a number of individuals opposed to the war, most being of right-wing and fascist sympathies.[12] He also possessed a number of the 'sticky-backs' used to disseminate propaganda against the war.

Lees appealed, and the 'Reasons for Order' and 'Statement of the Case' were prepared by Stamp of MI5. He was lent the Home Office file; there was no adequate MI5 file.[13] This was the first 18B (1A) case initiated by the police to be processed, and Stamp had agreed to handle such cases. The 'Reasons for Order' were supplied on 25 July, and, as was normal, Stamp simply deduced why Lees had been detained from the papers. The basic ground given was membership of the BU: '1. The Secretary of State has reasonable cause to believe that you have been a member of the organization now known as the "British Union"; and to have been active in the furtherance of its objects; and that it is necessary to exercise control over you'. Since this was an 18B (1A) order the 'grounds' also had to say why the BU was covered by the regulation, so Stamp set out the case against Mosley and his organization in four further standard form paragraphs. The 'particulars', in so far as they related to Lees, went on:

(a) You, Aubrey Trevor Lees, have been active in the furtherance of the said organization by expressing pro-Fascist views, by furnishing the said organization with material for propaganda, by attending meetings at which Oswald Ernald Mosley, hereinafter referred to, was present, such meetings being held for the purpose of co-ordinating Fascist and anti-Semitic activities in the country, and for negotiating a peace with the leader of the German Reich.

(b) You have been propagating anti-British views and endeavouring to hinder the war effort in this country with a view to a Fascist revolution.

But Stamp's 'Statement of the Case' made curiously little of the meetings, and did not state that Lees had been a member of the BU, possibly

[10] Inspector Jansby and Constable Fennell also found papers dealing with supposed British atrocities in Palestine, right-wing propaganda material, and correspondence with Lord Tavistock.
[11] On 13 and 17 February and 29 May.
[12] He apparently had the cards of Greene and Gordon-Canning and a note of Gen. J. H. C. Fuller's address.
[13] Lees was on file with MI5 as attending a Nordic League meeting in April 1939, and a meeting of the 'Friends of Spain'.

because his supposed membership was made clear in the 'Reasons for Order'.

On 12 July, before Stamp had prepared the papers, Lees applied to the Divisional Court for habeas corpus. His solicitor was Oswald Hickson. Hickson, who was not a fascist, but simply a lawyer of liberal views, was senior partner in the London firm of Oswald Hickson and Collier. This firm also represented Captain Ramsay, and on 29 June *The Times* published a letter from Hickson protesting, on behalf of his client, at a statement made in the House of Lords on 13 June by Lord Marley, to the effect that Ramsay had been nominated as gauleiter for Scotland; the letter also denied that Ramsay had been in communication with the enemy, or was an enemy agent. Lees was thus the second of numerous detainees represented by Hickson. Presumably it was because he acted for Ramsay that Hickson became involved in other 18B cases.

In habeas corpus proceedings if a plausible case was made out in the applicant's sworn affidavit, the court's practice was to adjourn the hearing; notice could then be given to the Governor of the prison, and to the Home Office. The proceedings were thus adjourned on 12 July, and this provided an opportunity for Lees to come before the committee.[14] Lees appeared at 6 Burlington Gardens on 29 July, and again on 1 August.[15] The BU had by then been proscribed, so all that was in issue was whether he had been a member or supporter, and, as the committee maintained (against the view of MI5), whether he also was someone who needed to be detained.

The committee decided that Lees had never been a member or supporter of the party, and recommended release. Although, for reasons to be explained, its draft report was not actually sent to MI5 until 25 August, the conclusion was passed to MI5 before this; Stamp was unable to come back with proof of membership, but thought there was ample evidence that Lees had been a supporter. The committee's report was not signed until 5 September. It was never the practice to reveal the contents of such reports to detainees or their advisers, so neither Lees nor Hickson, who tried to find out from the secretary, knew the recommendation. Irritated that his client was still detained on an erroneous ground, he pressed on with the habeas corpus proceedings; he also wrote to the committee on 31 July pointing out that Lees was not and never had been a member, and demanded his immediate release.

---

[14] In some instances the Crown lawyers took the view that an application to the court made it improper for the committee to hear the case, it being now *sub judice*. I can see no legal justification for this view.

[15] Birkett, Clerk, and Hazlerigg. Rumbelow suggested that since the case had been put up by the police they might wish to attend; they were, however, never told the date of the hearing.

The Attorney-General, Somervell, must have been told of the findings of Birkett's committee. It would be embarrassing for the Crown to resist an application for habeas corpus if the judges knew that the Home Secretary had been formally advised that an error had been made, and that Lees ought to be released. But counsel have an obligation not to mislead the court, and for Somervell to argue the case, and say nothing about the error, would come close to professional misconduct. It was a situation in which official ignorance represented bliss, and this perhaps was why Somervell did not himself appear in the case; the Crown was represented by the Solicitor-General, Sir William Jowitt. But behind the scenes Somervell prevailed on the compliant Birkett to delay sending out either draft or final report until the legal proceedings were finished. Hence it could truthfully be said, if there were judicial questions, that the committee had not yet reported. This conduct, it must be confessed, reflects little credit on either Somervell or Birkett.

Lees's case came up again on 12 August and was argued on 22 August; the judges were Humphreys, Oliver, and Croom-Johnson, three senior judges of the division, and as grim a trio as could be exhibited by the judiciary of the period.[16] Lees was represented by Gerald Gardiner and J. W. Williamson, and Jowitt was assisted by Valentine Holmes, who was Senior Treasury Counsel, and who handled all actions by detainees during the war. Two other counsel, G. D. Roberts KC and H. K. Sadler, held watching briefs; possibly they were retained by the Association of Civil Servants or by the Liberty Restoration League.[17]

Habeas corpus proceedings are normally determined on affidavits filed by the parties, not on oral evidence. Lees's affidavit said that he did not know whether the allegations made against Mosley and the BU were true or not, that he was not, and never had been, a member of any political group, nor a subscriber to the funds of any such organization, and that he had not supplied information to the BU. He conceded that his political views were radical, and that he had attended some meetings at which Mosley was present, but the meetings did not have the purpose suggested. He denied propagating anti-British views, and said that as a Crown servant for the past twenty-three years he would not welcome a fascist revolution. He had offered to join the army, and had only withdrawn this offer at the request of the Colonial Secretary. He conceded that he did not like Jews, or Lord Halifax.

The Crown lawyers naturally did not wish to reply in detail to the points raised by Lees; that would invite the Court to review the detention order on the merits. They could have simply relied on the order itself as a

---

[16] The first hearing on 12 August is noted in *The Times* for 13 August, the second on 23 August.
[17] Or possibly the Colonial Office was separately represented.

complete answer, and argued that, given an order valid on its face, the court had no power to investigate the legality of the detention further. This bold course was probably rejected because it might have caused trouble in the Commons, where at least some members thought that the courts had acquired a right of review when 18B was amended; Jowitt had taken part in the consultations and this may indeed have been his own understanding.

The strategy adopted by Jowitt and Holmes was to concede that the court was indeed entitled to review the legality of the order, and decide whether the Home Secretary had reasonable cause for the beliefs which led to his signing it; there is no documentary evidence as to whether this was agreed with the Attorney-General, though it very probably was. Consequently an affidavit had to be filed by Anderson. But the lawyers settled for a laconic document, which simply asserted that the Home Secretary had investigated the matter, acted in good faith, and decided that Lees was detainable. The affidavit was of course drafted by Holmes, a lawyer of very considerable competence, and the central passage, whose text came to be used in subsequent cases, read thus:

Before I made the said order I received reports and information from persons in responsible positions who are experienced in investigating matters of this kind and whose duty it is to make such investigations and to report the same to me confidentially. I carefully studied the reports and considered the information and I came to the conclusion that there were clear grounds for believing and I did in fact believe that Mr. Aubrey Trevor Oswald Lees was a member and was and had been active in the furtherance of the objects of an organization as respects which I was satisfied . . . [the text then went on to rehearse the text of Regulation 18B 1A].

The affidavit, by mistake, failed to say that Anderson was satisfied that it was necessary to detain Lees, so a second affidavit was put in which said this—in later litigation one standardized affidavit sufficed.

The central issue presented to the judges placed them in a dilemma.[18] Lees had been detained, according to the 'Reasons for Order', as a member of the BU; he swore he neither was, nor ever had been, a member. Anderson's affidavit significantly did not contradict this; the implication was plainly that Lees was telling the truth. Anderson merely said that when he made the order he *thought* that Lees was a member, and had grounds for this belief. If Lees was detained as a member, and in fact was not a member, surely the judges, charged with the protection of liberty, should order his release. Yet, equally surely, the judges, before ordering release, should determine the facts of the matter, and settle the question of membership. Yet how could they do so without delving into secret

---

[18] It was also argued that the order was defective in failing to specify whether Lees was thought to be a member, or merely active in the support of the BU; this was rejected.

intelligence matters, and indeed opening a door to the courts through which every 18B detainee would shortly pass? And if the judges did investigate the facts they would be assuming the functions of both the advisory committee and the Home Secretary, appointing themselves as the final arbiters of detention orders. So if ever a case presented a dilemma, Lees's application did, so long of course as the court accepted the strategy of the Crown lawyers.

Jowitt's Theory

Jowitt, however, offered the judges a way out of the dilemma, presenting a theory as to the functions of the courts which explained the strategy followed by the Crown over the affidavits, was unlikely to cause trouble in the Commons and flattered the judges:

he [that is Jowitt] disclaimed at once the view that the Court was bound to accept the evidence of the Home Secretary, and he accepted the view that the power of the Home Secretary to make the order was dependent on whether he had reasonable cause to believe the information he received. It followed therefore that he agreed that, if the applicant could establish that at the material time[19] the Home Secretary had no reasonable cause for his belief, the applicant would be entitled to his release.[20]

But, he argued, the court had Anderson's affidavit, which there was no reason to doubt, and that was the end of the matter, unless the court inspected the reports which were mentioned in it. This they could not do.

It was impossible for the Court to embark on a consideration of what the reports received by the Home Secretary were, and he [counsel] would take the responsibility of informing the Court that it would be quite impossible for the reports and the names of the persons making them to be disclosed. It would obviously be against public policy that should be done.

Why, however secret, they could not be shown to the judges, he did not explain, and the statement was essentially rubbish. However, the judges would know that if they did ask to see the reports the Crown would probably refuse to permit this under the doctrine of Crown privilege, which allowed the Crown, supposedly in the public interest, to refuse disclosure of documents. At this period the courts always accepted assertions of privilege, though it was not settled that as a matter of law they had to do this.

Jowitt's (or perhaps Holmes') Alice in Wonderland theory, according to which the court, though entitled to investigate the matter, must in effect not do so, but simply accept the laconic Crown affidavits, was

---

[19] Presumably the date of the order.   [20] Transcript in TS 27/496A.

gratefully accepted by the judges. It was, as we shall see, entirely at odds
with the revised theory which the Crown lawyers adopted the following
year in the Liversidge and Greene cases, and claimed to have always been
the understanding when the amended 18B came in—that the courts had
no jurisdiction to investigate whether the Home Secretary had reasonable
grounds or not.

At the end of argument Lees's application was refused. An agreed written opinion was delivered on 9 September. Its author, Sir Travers
Humphreys, had been a skilful advocate, but he was not possessed of any
great talents as a lawyer, and his colleagues were no more generously
endowed. His opinion simply regurgitated Jowitt's theory. It started from
a proposition rooted in the rhetoric of the rule of law: 'Now the Court
entertains no doubt that upon an application for a writ of habeas corpus
the Court has power to inquire into the validity of the order of detention,
*and for that purpose to ascertain whether the Home Secretary had reasonable
cause for the belief expressed in the order* [my italics].' This, so Humphreys
said, had been conceded by the Solicitor-General, as indeed it had. But
the courts were not there to act as courts of appeal from the Home
Secretary, and it was quite out of the question for the courts to see the
material upon which the Home Secretary based his decision. He then
stated a second principle: 'It is not for us to determine whether, in our
opinion, the applicant *ought* to be interned; we are concerned only to
inquire into the *legality* of his detention [my italics].' But if there was no
reasonable basis for Anderson's belief, detention would be illegal—so the
basis for the belief had to be investigated, somehow or other, without the
court having access to the relevant material. At this point, boxed in by
Jowitt's theory, he tried, in a desperate passage, to explain how one could
investigate something, whilst not investigating it: 'How then is a court to
decide the question whether the Secretary of State had reasonable suspicion for his belief?' His solution was a device traditionally used by common law judges when confronted by problems which intellectually defeat
them. 'In our opinion no general rule can be laid down and each case
must be decided upon its own facts.' And, 'on the facts', Anderson said he
had reasonable grounds, and the judges believed him: 'We accept those
statements made upon oath by Sir John Anderson . . . ' Lewis Carroll
could hardly have done better.

Lees decided to appeal to the Court of Appeal.

The Aftermath of the Decision

On 24 August Birkett sent the draft report to MI5 for comment. Lees's
case was the first in which a conflict between MI5 and the committee is
clearly documented: the views of MI5 and the committee were quite

irreconcilable. MI5 thought that even if Lees had never been a member, he had been an active supporter, and now attached more significance to the secret meetings; the committee had been gullible, and too ready to accept Lees's version of the events. But the committee, unable to interrogate MI5 agents because of MI5 objections to their appearance, had perforce to do its best with such evidence as it could evaluate, and this usually meant only the evidence of the detainee. On 5 September the signed report, unchanged, was sent to the Home Office. Whilst concluding that Lees was neither a member nor a supporter, it noted that Anderson, when he signed the order, might well have had reasonable cause to believe the contrary, a statement obviously included to support the affidavit put in by the Crown in the court hearing.

Maxwell backed the committee against MI5, and on 19 September recommended release.[21] The following day Anderson wrote: 'I agree that we must let him out but I shall not be at all surprised if we have to lock him up again very soon.' The order was suspended subject to restrictions; Lees had to notify his address or any proposed absence from his address for more than twenty-four hours. He was also placed on the 'invasion list'.[22] He actually left prison on 1 October. The following day his appeal came before the Court of Appeal.

Gerald Gardiner, his client having been released, asked for costs; the Crown opposed this, Jowitt arguing that the fact that the Home Secretary had decided, on the advice of the committee, to release Lees in no way showed that the initial decision to detain him had been wrong. What he did not explain, perhaps because he was kept in ignorance, was that this advice had been in reality available at the time the case was argued in the lower court. Gardiner persisted in his appeal. His basic contention, which pinpointed the absurdity of the Jowitt theory, was neatly set out in this passage:

If it were considered sufficient, in order to detain a person under those regulations, merely to make an affidavit of the kind made by the Home Secretary, then it was virtually useless for any person to make application by way of habeas corpus. Were such a person as innocent as the day or a true patriot, however wrongfully he was in prison, the Home Secretary had only to make an affidavit saying that, at the time, he reasonably believed certain allegations to be true to prevent the person being released.[23]

It is clear that Lord Justice Du Parcq took this point, but nevertheless thought that in the case of 'an obvious blunder' or where there was 'strong evidence' an applicant might still succeed. In the event the court

---

[21] The case was mentioned at the meeting in the Home Office on 18 September. See above p. 292.
[22] See above p. 192.   [23] 57 TLR at 69.

rejected the appeal and expressly approved the opinion delivered by Humphreys, which thus became an authority treated as binding both on the Divisional Court and the Court of Appeal in future cases, though this, as we shall see, was later denied by the Court of Appeal in Greene's case in 1941.[24] The decision indeed entailed the view that a court could, in a proper case—one perhaps involving 'an obvious blunder'—order release because the Home Secretary had no reasonable basis for his belief. But Lees did not obtain his costs, and the Treasury Solicitor pursued him for Crown costs of £176, which were presumably paid by the Liberty Restoration League.

Lees was in fact due to sail to West Africa to take up his new appointment on 24 October; he wrote pointing out that it was curious that the Janus-faced government wanted him to take up this appointment and yet subjected him to a restriction order. It was an unwise move. The Colonial Office asked for the order to be revoked, and after much correspondence Lees was retired on pension in December of 1940. Retirement did not protect him from Kendal, who in November of 1940 returned to the attack, relying on an undercover agent run by Maxwell-Knight.[25] This agent reported on a meeting on Sunday 10 November at the flat of 'Molly' Stanford.[26] This was attended by Lees, Ella Durant, Molly herself, and the agent, who may have been Harold Kurtz.[27] At this meeting plans to assist detainees were discussed.[28] Another topic was propaganda in favour of a negotiated peace, as advocated by the New British Broadcasting Station. Maxwell wrote a long memorandum on the matter for Morrison, recommending no action against Stanford, but detention for Lees. He was

---

[24] Lord Justices MacKinnon and Goddard sat in the Court of Appeal in both Lees's and Greene's cases. MacKinnon did not then view it as not binding.

[25] Details in HO 45/25728/860060/4

[26] 45 Queen's Gate Gardens. Mary Stanford (on whom see R. Thurlow, *Fascism in Britain: A History, 1918–1985* (Oxford, 1987), 202, 203, 205–6, 215), was an associate of Anna Wolkoff and had been a member of the Right Club. She was interned in 1940 but released in September of 1940 as harmless on the initiative of MI5, perhaps as an MI5 agent. She was interned again in 1941 for involvement in the activities of Norah C. L. Briscoe and Gertrude G. Hiscox, tried on 16 June 1941 before Asquith J. on charges under the Defence Regulations connected with the abstraction of documents from the Ministry of Supply. Charges of conspiracy under s. 1 of the Treachery Act 1940 were withdrawn, and both were sentenced to 5 years' penal servitude; the offence under 2A, which required intent to assist the enemy, carried a maximum of life. On their release on 12 September 1944 from Aylesbury Prison they were subjected to restriction orders under DR 18A. Relevant material is in HO 45/25741.

[27] Information in HO 45/25728 reveals that in the Briscoe/Hiscox case in 1941 Maxwell-Knight was using two agents. One, referred to as X, was Harold Kurtz, on whom see below, pp. 366–370. The other, known as Q, was a married man of British birth and parentage. He had associated with fascist or pro-Nazi groups such as the British Union, the Imperial Fascist League, and the Link.

[28] It was said that Mrs Maule Ramsay, two Members of Parliament, Messrs Shaw and Pickthorn, and General Fuller might help.

nervous; the agent was unidentified, and would not be produced to the committee, who might well reject the story; Lees might litigate, and awkward questions might be asked. But Maxwell thought that if Lees had advocated assisting the NBBS by circulating a chain letter this was 'not a legitimate peace proposal but a proposal to assist the enemy by giving currency to the enemy's propaganda'. Morrison decided to take no action 'on the very meagre statement from an informant'. So Lees remained at liberty, but continued to excite the interest of MI5 for his right-wing associations as late as 1944.[29]

His case defined the role of the courts over Regulation 18B until Greene's case reached the Court of Appeal in 1941, when the Crown lawyers abandoned the theory they had sold to the Divisional Court and Court of Appeal in 1940, as we shall see. Although Lees lost, Humphreys' opinion offered hope to detainees, and so encouraged others to litigate, and since Lees was released, it seemed that his suit had brought some pressure on the Home Office.

Hickson's Proposal to Release the Fascists

The Lees case induced in Hickson a sense of outrage at the behaviour of the Home Office officials. During August he acquired Mosley as a client, and thereafter he became the lawyer principally involved in such cases.[30] On 21 August he had an interview with Maxwell, and in a letter summarized his feelings: 'I feel it is very dangerous to the community that a large number of men and women should be held in prison under the conditions under which they are detained under Regulation 18B. They are not treated as well as prisoners on remand, and a great many of them feel very greatly their position. It is intolerable that men, who are not charged with any crime, and have committed no crime, should be taken about from prison to prison handcuffed, and left in solitary confinement for most of the 24 hours, and not permitted to see their friends and relatives except for limited periods in the company of an officer of the prison.'[31] He eventually secured an interview with Osbert Peake, the Junior Minister, and made various suggestions about the treatment of detainees—for example that committee reports should be made public—and he also suggested that the BU detainees should be released so long as they gave undertakings to conform to restrictions on their conduct, which could be imposed

---

[29] The restriction order remained in force; he had been associating with Frank Clifford, one-time BU D/L of the Reigate Branch, detained from June to November 1940, and had been in touch with the Duke of Bedford, Ramsay, and Domvile. The MI5 officer then concerned was the lawyer T. M. Shelford.

[30] Mosley's regular solicitors seem to have been Iliffe Sweet and Co. or Randolph and Dean.

[31] HO 45/25758 Letter of Hickson to Maxwell of 21 August.

under Regulation 18A. All his suggestions were rejected, and in consequence his campaign against the regulation was thereafter principally conducted through litigation. Increasingly he came to be viewed by the authorities as a troublesome and somewhat fanatical nuisance. For their part officials in the Home Office, and the Crown lawyers in particular, reacted to court proceedings by fighting them quite ruthlessly, and sometimes indeed with a certain lack of scruple, except there was political danger in doing so. Their basic motive seems to have been that of protecting the department from outside criticism or interference; defending the interests of the department appears to be central to the ethos of Civil Servants. The behaviour of Somervell over the report, and the opposition to the award of costs in the Lees case illustrate this. To the Home Office the French proverb certainly applies: *c'est un animal méchant. Quand on l'attaque, il se défend.*

The Domvile Case and its Companions

The next applications for habeas corpus were made to the court on 7 October 1940, after the final outcome of Lees's case was known.[32] There were five applicants; the most prominent was Domvile, detained on 8 July for 'acts prejudicial'. Applications were also made on behalf of the elderly Major Harold H. A. de Laessoe DSO, MC, Rita K. Shelmerdine,[33] Miss or Mrs Emily D. V. Durell, and Second Lieutenant William E. Sherston, all except Sherston being clients of Hickson. Gerald Gardiner appeared for the first four detainees, and Frederick Wallace for Sherston. The applications were adjourned until 22 October.

Because of the involvement of Domvile these applications attracted considerable notice. The other litigants were less publicly known. Major Harold H. A. de Laessoe, together with his wife Diana, had been detained under an 18B (1A) order somewhat earlier, on 24 May 1940, in the first BU arrests.[34] Born in Tehran, the son of a Captain A. F. de Laessoe CMG, of the Indian Civil Service and Foreign Service, he was over 60 at the time of his arrest. He had served in the Matabele War (1896–7), and then in the Rhodesian Civil Service (1899–1909). Immediately before the First World War he had been the Manager of the Liebig company's estates in Rhodesia. He then served with the Rifle Brigade in France (1914–18), winning the DSO and MC and becoming a staff officer. After the war he obtained land concessions in Africa for Bovril Ltd., and acquired a large concession in Angola on his own account; this was expropriated by the Portuguese authorities in 1938, and he lost his entire fortune. He and his wife, who was Bavarian in origin, returned to England, and he became a

---

[32] Hawke and Macnaghton JJ.   [33] See above pp. 269, 288.
[34] See TS 27/511 and HO 144/21992 (seen on privileged access). One subfile, number 28, was withheld, being closed until the year 2045. The family was Danish in origin.

BU District Inspector. Mrs Rita Shelmerdine we have already met.[35] Miss or Mrs E. D. V. Durell, aged 56, had been in Holloway since 19 July, apparently on an 18B (1A) order.[36] Second Lieutenant William E. Sherston (and his wife) had been detained a little earlier, on 16 July, on an 18B (1A) order.[37]

Lord Chief Justice Caldecote, who had been present at the Cabinet meeting which approved the crippling of the BU, presided at the hearing on 22 October; Churchill had disposed of him in a reshuffle earlier that month by making him Chief Justice.[38] The gist of the applications was that the delay in telling the detainees why they were detained, and in giving them hearings before the committee, was so serious as to make their detention wholly unlawful. On 7 October none of the five had even been given the 'Reasons for Order'.[39] By 22 October Domvile had received the reasons, and on that day he was driven from Brixton to the Berystede Hotel, Ascot, to appear before the committee. Birkett had arranged for his wife, whom he had not seen since his arrest, to join him for lunch, and the occasion passed off very pleasantly, lasting only an hour. He was also allowed to see his son Compton, who was in the camp at Ascot.[40] His application for habeas corpus was adjourned, and eventually withdrawn on 28 November 1941 after the Lords' decisions in the Liversidge and Greene cases; consequently no affidavit from the Home Secretary was ever put in.

The appearance of Domvile before the committee on 22 October was simply a charade, designed to suggest that delay in dealing with his case was over. On 5 November, after the judges had decided the other four cases, Domvile again appeared; by then Birkett must have received MI5's 'Statement of the Case', making it possible for him to conduct a hostile interrogation at a genuine hearing. Domvile himself realized that something must have happened between the hearings; he did not know the procedures involved, which were then secret.[41] This incident, involving

---

[35] HO 45/23736/860393. See above p. 288.

[36] Apparently also known as Dorothea. She was the daughter of a parson, and was an anti-vivisectionist; there are letters from her in the Wiseman Papers (86/1/1) in the Imperial War Museum of 22 July 1943 (from The Old Vicarage, West Wickham, Cambs.) and 2 October (from Long Meadows, Risely, Berks.), showing her active in the 18B Publicity Council.

[37] See counsel's application in TS 27/491.

[38] The Times, 23 October. As Sir Thomas W. H. Inskip he had been Minister for the Co-ordination of Defence in Chamberlain's administration, and Lord Chancellor from late September 1939 to May 1940. He was Secretary of State for Dominion Affairs under Churchill.

[39] Domvile had also alleged that he did not even have a copy of the order as it had been taken away, and made complaints about the conditions of his imprisonment. Shelmerdine additionally complained that the copy she had been given was a form with her name filled in; she had no way of telling if an order had in fact been made.

[40] B. Domvile, From Admiral to Cabin Boy (London, 1946), 11ff.

[41] On the following day Birkett told the Home Defence (Security) Executive that he did

as it does special treatment of the most prominent litigant, and a some-what cynical manipulation of the procedures, reflects little credit on the Crown lawyers or on Birkett, Clerk, and Hazlerigg. No documentary evi-dence explains their compliance, but presumably they were anxious to protect the Home Office, whose committee they were, from criticism.

The other four applicants had also not received their 'Reasons for Order' when they commenced proceedings, though they apparently had by 22 October.[42] Counsel suggested that the court should fix a date by which they must come before Birkett's committee, or be released. The Crown lawyers put in affidavits from both Anderson and Morrison saying that the delay had been caused by the sheer number of cases, and that everything that could be done to speed matters up was being done.[43] The court did not set a date, expressed itself satisfied with the situation, and dutifully ruled that although it could and would intervene in a case of excessive delay, on the facts it 'did not accept the contention that there had been greater delay than there ought to have been'. Lord Caldecote, however, continued:

> I think it convenient to take the opportunity of once more putting on record the view, which I hope and believe the court will always take, that when powers of this sort are used they will be used with due regard to the fact that the liberty of the subject is involved, and, therefore, scrupulous care must be taken to give the subject his full rights under the regulations which confer the power on the Home Secretary.[44]

As reported in the *Solicitors' Journal* he mentioned the need for 'all possi-ble expedition'.[45] But this was mere empty humbug. Of the other litigants Rita Shelmerdine, as we have seen, appeared before the committee imme-diately after the hearing, which took the view that she should never have been detained in the first place; she was released in mid-November. Durell may also have been released fairly soon, but Domvile, de Laessoe, and Sherston were not. As we have seen, there were many other cases of very serious delay indeed, but it was plainly idle to expect the judges to do anything about it in habeas corpus proceedings.

Lord Caldecote's Proposal

In truth Lord Caldecote was not satisfied, and on 1 November, clearly well-informed—though his letter does seem to conflate the cases of the

not wish to see the MI5 agent involved, who was probably Harold Kurtz. (HO 45/25754/863027/6).

[42] De Laessoe received them on 9 October, ie after over 4 months in prison.

[43] The notes for counsel in TS 27/491 also mention the damage done to the London premises of the committee in two air raids in September.

[44] Text from TS 27/511.   [45] *Solicitors' Journal* (1941), 11.

aliens with that of the 18B detainees—he wrote personally to express his concern to Morrison 'as a friend':

I am told that the Birkett Committee is working regularly but that they cannot do more than two or three cases a day . . . I am told that at present there are a large number of cases where there is reason to believe that the Committee have reported months ago and upon which no decision has been given by the Home Office . . . Other information I have received is that the conditions under which the internees are held is rather distressing. The accommodation may be perfectly proper for persons who have been found guilty of offences . . . but not at all suitable for persons who are simply detained *pending enquiry* [my italics].

His conception of what was going on—detention pending enquiry—is perceptive, and I imagine he had been talking to Birkett. He said it had been the understanding that the committee should be a substitute for the courts in reviewing cases, and noted his own knowledge of cases where

I am satisfied that if the machinery had done its work quickly a great deal of suffering and anxiety would have been saved . . . I shall be very sorry indeed and I am sure you would be if hereafter it was thought that we had been a little callous about the conditions in which these persons have been interned. A great many of them richly deserve internment but a great many also of them are wholly innocent and known to have the most friendly feelings towards this country.[46]

Lord Caldecote did not confine himself to exhortation—he offered the loan of some judges, possibly Lord Justices of Appeal, to speed up the process.

The Home Office discussed this sensible proposal with Schuster of the Lord Chancellor's Department and rejected it.[47] Ingenious Civil Service reasons were devised: it would be difficult to reconcile the independence of a judge with an advisory role, embarrassing to reject judicial advice, a judge might hear a habeas corpus case involving a detainee whose case he had reviewed on the committee, a judge could not be in charge of one division of the committee and a mere King's Counsel of another. That these arguments were a little contrived is clear, for Birkett, though appointed to the bench in November 1941 to provide reassurance after the Liversidge and Greene decisions, continued as chairman.[48] The truth was that the Civil Servants were nervous of strong-minded judges; they knew Birkett, and could live with him, though it is clear that his experience with MI5 and the Home Office must have made it very difficult for him to live with them.

---

[46] His letter is in HO 45/25114/863686.

[47] Minute by Maxwell of 8 November 1940; the Lord Chancellor agreed on 11 November.

[48] The Lord Chancellor, Lord Simon, wrote to Birkett offering a judicial appointment on 3 November 1941 (see H. Montgomery Hyde, *Norman Birkett* (London, 1964), 474).

Mathilde Randall and Harry Sabini

Although the five habeas corpus applicants had failed, their lawyers may have nevertheless been rather encouraged. The proceedings seemed to have influenced the Home Office. Like Lees, Shelmerdine was soon set free, and possibly Durell too; Domvile at least was told why he was detained, and had his hearing. Although the judges were obviously very reluctant to rock the boat, they might yet do so if a case was bad enough. The next two cases brought to court must have seemed to be just the sort in which success might well be achieved.

One involved Mathilde Randall, and the complaint was again delay, not in giving her a hearing, but in taking the Home Office decision after the committee report was received.[49] She was the German born wife of a Brighton butcher, George H. Randall. He had served in Germany after the armistice, where presumably they met. He had been an active BU member, detained on 3 June. She had never been a member, and was detained on 3 July as 'of hostile origins'. The initiative came from the Brighton police, after local demonstrations against the Randalls and their shop. Mrs Randall did not receive her 'Reasons for Order' until early November. The 'grounds' simply rehearsed the allegation that she was of hostile origins and that it was necessary to exercise control over her, and the 'particulars' were disgracefully laconic, though probably typical of the period: 'The said Mathilde Randall, (1) was born in Germany of German parents, (2) has expressed sympathy with the German cause and the Nazi regime.' She and her husband appeared on 18 November; on 25 November Birkett's committee recommended the immediate release of both:

After a close examination of both Mr and Mrs Randall the committee came to the conclusion that in the case of Mrs Randall there was nothing against her at all. She seemed to be a thoroughly decent woman, devoted to her husband and the business and divorced from any political ideas at all, her one wish being that the country should win the war and her home and business life be resumed normally.

MI5 objected to both recommendations: 'As regards Mrs Randall, although she has obviously given great offence in the past, we have not such strong objections to her release, and would concur in it provided that she left Brighton and reported her movements to the police.' Her solicitor somehow discovered that the committee had recommended release, and since nothing happened, applied for habeas corpus and mandamus, the latter being an order a court could make to compel a legal duty to be performed. Her counsel was the aged Walter H. Moresby, once MI5's legal officer. The case came before the court on 20 December, which gave leave

[49] See TS 27/495. I am informed that her Home Office file no longer exists.

to apply for a writ of mandamus, presumably ordering the Home Secretary to determine whether she should be released or not. She was released on 4 January 1941. Her application was therefore withdrawn, but must have seemed successful. She had, after all, obtained her liberty, albeit after six months' entirely unjustified detention; the wall of secrecy surrounding the executive meant that there was no way of telling what part the legal proceedings had played. Her husband was probably released about the same time.

Sabini's case seemed, at first sight, even stronger.[50] Harry Sabini (alias Henry Sabini, Harry Handley, Harry S., Harry Roy, and Henry Handley) had been detained under a 'hostile origin' order of 14 June 1941 at the request of the Metropolitan Police. He had been born in Clerkenwell, the centre of the Italian community in London, on 20 August 1900 to an Italian father and English mother, whose maiden name was Handley. His father died when he was nineteen months old, and he had never visited Italy, or learnt to speak Italian. He was one of six brothers, of whom one, Darby Sabini, had also been detained about the same time.[51] Rumour amongst detainees was that one 'Papa' Marsh, also detained, was, with the Sabinis, suspected of complicity in the Croydon bullion raid.[52] The police described Harry as

one of the leading lights of a gang of bullies known as the Sabini gang who under the cover of various rackets have by their blackmailing methods levied toll on bookmakers . . . He is a dangerous man of most violent temperament and has a heavy following and strong command of a gang of bullies of Italian origin in London.

But the report conceded:

We have no knowledge that he has previously engaged in any political activities but . . . he can at best be described as a dangerous gangster and racketeer of the worst type and appears to be a most likely person who would be chosen by enemy agents to create and be a leader of violent internal action against the country.

Harry Sabini's actual convictions were very modest. He had been fined £3 for an assault in 1922, and in the same year he had been required to find sureties for his good behaviour for twelve months, with six months' imprisonment in default. There had been a fracas at an Italian club in Clerkenwell; he had threatened someone with a revolver, and been shot. He also had minor convictions for obstruction and drunkenness. The most serious conviction was that of his brother Joseph, who had been sen-

---

[50] TS 27/496A and HO 45/25720/840793. His court cases are reported in *The Times* for 21 January and 17 May 1941.

[51] *Daily Express*, 8 July 1940. The other brothers were Frederick alias Bob Wilson, Charles, Joseph alias Henry Lake, and George.

[52] Information from A. S. Swan. I have not identified this incident.

tenced to three years' penal servitude in 1922 for shooting with intent to cause grievous bodily harm. But Regulation 18B gave Kendal a golden opportunity to break up the Sabini gang.

Harry appealed, and was given the 'Reasons for Order', dated 27 November, after five months in detention. The document described him as Harry Sabini, alias Harry Handley, and incorrectly stated that his order was for 'hostile associations'. The particulars continued: 'That the said Harry Sabini, (1) is of Italian origin and associations, (2) is a violent and dangerous criminal of the gangster type, liable to lead internal insurrections against the country.' His case came before a division of the Italian Committee on 3 December.[53] The file, which is incomplete, does not include the report, but the error must have been noticed, and we may assume that release was recommended, there being no coneivable justification for using 18B against the Sabini gang. Indeed the fact that an order had ever been made reveals how the Home Office had lost control over the system in 1940.

Harry however, became impatient,[54] and applied for habeas corpus, his application being heard on 20 December immediately after that of Mathilde Randall. The initial basis was mistaken identity; his affidavit denied that he had ever used the name Harry Handley. Humphreys, sitting with Atkinson, said: 'We both think in this case that the applicant has made out grounds for the relief asked. The main point appears to be that it may well be that this person has been confused with someone else of the same name. If that be so, of course there is no ground at all for detaining him. The matter ought to be cleared up.' So the case was adjourned until 20 January.

The case posed technical problems for Valentine Holmes. It had always been assumed that a court would order release for mistaken identity. But this was not a simple case, where Smith had been confused with Jones; the detainee was indeed Harry Sabini; he argued that he could not possibly be the 'Harry Sabini' against whom the order was directed. Possibly there was another 'Harry Sabini' who did use the alias 'Harry Handley'. So the Crown lawyers were compelled to submit evidence to demonstrate that this Harry Sabini was indeed known as 'Harry Handley', and that his record fitted the description given of him in the 'Reasons for Order'. Only thus could it be shown that the right person had been detained. In addition to a standard affidavit from Anderson they put in affidavits from

---

[53] Comprising Sir Rollo F. Graham-Campbell, C. H. Bateman CMG, MC, and O. A. Scott DSO.

[54] His case, and presumably that of Darby, had been taken up by Victor Cazalet MP. Cazalet was a strong opponent of government policy over aliens, and coined the phrase 'this bespattered page in our history' in a debate on 22 August 1940. See *Parl. Deb.* HC Vol. 364 c.1538 and R. R. James, *Victor Cazalet: A Portrait* (London, 1976).

police officers that he accepted the name 'Harry Handley', that he had been known under this and other aliases for many years, and that he had a criminal record which conformed to the description given in the particulars. They even went to the remarkable length of putting in an affidavit from a member of the committee, Oswald A. Scott, stating that Harry had made nothing of mistaken identity at his hearing. The case classically illustrates the readiness of the executive to place material normally treated as confidential before the court if this was needed to win the case and protect the department. No doubt sometimes confidentiality was in the public interest; often the interest involved was that of the department in protecting its activities from public scrutiny and criticism.

This strategy succeeded; it was clear that Harry had perjured himself. His counsel, G. O. Slade, had to concentrate his argument on the error in the 'Reasons for Order', and the much better point that someone who had lived all his life in Britain, and was a British subject by birth, could not rationally be described as being 'of hostile origin' simply because his father, whom he had never known, was an Italian who had died many years before any conflict between Britain and Italy existed. Even this was resisted by the Crown lawyers, and Jowitt persuaded the court to agree, in defiance of all common sense, that Harry could be so described. This absurd and indeed disgraceful ruling was indeed the only judicial interpretation of a category used in Regulation 18B ever given by the courts. Perhaps if Harry had never lied over his identity the point might have secured his release.

Harry, who surely should have never been detained in the first place, was set free on 18 March 1941, after nine months in detention. He was promptly charged with perjury and on 8 July 1941 sentenced to a further nine months *pour encourager les autres*. His case did have two consequences. It established judicial review in cases of mistaken identity, though no such case ever subsequently came to court. In addition his case, and that of Mrs Randall, alerted the judges both to the risk of formal errors by the officials, and to the meagre nature of the particulars supplied to detainees. And even the Divisional Court judges, after their wrath against the perjurer Sabini had cooled, must have realized that his detention had been a clear case of misuse of the regulation.

Indeed in the incestuous little world in which the King's Bench judges lived there must, by early 1941, have been general knowledge that all was not well with the administration of Regulation 18B.

$$\Longrightarrow 15 \Longleftarrow$$

The Courts in Confusion

The Case of John Mason

In 1941 a number of detainees had recourse to the courts: Captain Charles H. Bentinck Budd, Arthur C. H. Campbell, Lieutenant Francis C. Fane, Ben Greene, Robert W. Liversidge, Granville Norman Lange and Eric Norman Lange, H. W. Luttman-Johnson, John Mason, and Captain George H. L.-F. Pitt-Rivers. There were possibly others; some actions were formally begun, as by Mosley and Ramsay, but were never actually pursued.[1] In addition J. R. Smeaton-Stuart after his release tried to collect damages for false imprisonment. Of these litigants Greene and Liversidge went to the House of Lords, and I shall defer consideration of their cases to later chapters.

Of the others Mason's arrest was of some political significance, since he was a communist shop steward.[2] He was detained on 15 July 1940 as being 'involved in attempts to slow down war production' and therefore guilty of 'acts prejudicial'.[3] In court, where he was represented by D. N. Pritt KC, it was said that all he was told was that 'he had systematically tried to impede the production of arms and ammunition in the factory in which he was employed'; this is from the 'Reasons for Order'. Hinsley and Simkins attribute his detention to 'secret sources', presumably agents or intercepts.[4] Since many other communist shop stewards must have behaved in the same way, it is puzzling why he alone was selected. Hinsley and Simkins say he was the only communist, meaning known

---

[1] HO 144/21992/840194/5 mentions actions in late 1940 by 2nd. Lt. Richard Hamer, the Mosleys, and Ramsay. The Mosleys and Ramsay according to HO 144/21995 commenced proceedings for false imprisonment and breach of statutory duty in June 1941. HO 45/25714 notes the Lange brothers' suit for false imprisonment in late 1940 or early 1941; the action seems to have lapsed. A list of 30 June 1941 mentions the Mosleys, Ramsay, Luttman-Johnson, and Lange, and the Beavan Diary mentions a suit by Hepburn-Ruston.

[2] No papers are available; the case is in *The Times* and *Daily Herald* for 4 February 1941, *Evening News*, 3 February. See R. Croucher, *Engineers at War* (London, 1982), 92–3, noting protests in the *Daily Worker* for 3 August 1940 and following issues, and in the *New Propellor* (cartoon of 15 February 1941). See also NCCL archives 76/1 and 2.

[3] *Parl. Deb.* HC. Vol. 369 c.273–4, questions by Messrs Thurtle and Gallagher. Also HO 45/25114. Versions in the newspapers differ trivially; the *Evening News* has 'systematic attempts to hamper and impede production of arms and munitions'.

[4] Hinsley and Simkins, 320.

party member, ever detained.[5] There is no reason to doubt this. It was consistently said that no individuals were ever detained simply for being communists.[6] Mason was a member of the Amalgamated Engineering Union, and Secretary of the Mexborough Trades Council; his union protested, but was convinced by the Home Office that he had not been detained for union activities.[7] The available papers do not indicate in detail what he was supposed to have done.[8] He appeared in September before the committee, which recommended continued detention.

Mason took legal proceedings of a particularly interesting form, which makes it unfortunate, and perhaps sinister, that the available material is so scanty. He sought a declaration that his hearing before the committee was irregular and contrary to 'natural justice', a remedy called *certiorari* (to quash the committee report), and one called mandamus (to order a proper hearing). The order sought would have required the Chairman of the advisory committee to give him the 'grounds on which [the] order was made suffcent to enable him to present his case before them'.[9] 'Natural justice' is a technical expression used to describe whatever minimum standards of fairness the judges are prepared to insist upon in hearings of a judicial nature before administrative bodies or officers. Any successful attack on the committees procedures would have been very damaging politically, as the Crown lawyers would appreciate. The brief report in *The Times* indicates that in addition to complaining at the meagre particulars provided to him, he also said he had no real opportunity to prepare his case before appearance.[10]

Mason's application thus gave the judges an opportunity to insist upon less oppressive procedures by Birkett's committee; it is possible that Birkett and his deputies might even have welcomed such a move, which would have strengthened them in conflicts with MI5. But Lord Caldecote and his colleagues, Humphreys and Singleton, did nothing, and no subsequent litigation offered the judges a second chance. The refusal of the application on 2 February was not covered in the law reports; one cannot but suspect censorship. Presumably the court held that the Chairman had complete discretion over the grounds. Negotiations between William Gallagher MP and Maxwell led to a new hearing in May 1941, and Mason

---

[5] Ibid. See above p.196. [6] *Parl. Deb.* HC. Vol. 361 c.671, 374: 1478.

[7] Statement in the *Amalgamated Engineering Union Journal* quoted ibid. 369: 273, Hinsley and Simkins, 320. HO 45/25114 notes a meeting between Wall of the Swinton Committee, Legatt of the Ministry of Labour, and Hollis of MI5 on his case.

[8] Croucher says that action of one kind or another was taken against a number of shop stewards at this period.

[9] NCCL archives 76/2A. The case came up on 2 February 1941 before the Lord Chief Justice, Humphreys, and Singleton JJ.

[10] Mason's solicitors were Silverman and Livermore.

was released in June on the recommendation of the committee.[11] I have not been allowed to see papers which survive.

The Budd Boys

Captain Budd had been prominent in Mosley's party.[12] Born on 16 August 1897, he joined the 5th Dragoon Guards at the age of 16; he served in France and rose to the rank of Captain. He was severely wounded in 1915 at Loos, losing a leg and suffering head injuries. He became a seaman, eventually enlisting for a short time in the US army. After an attempt to join the White Russians he rejoined the British army, and was discharged in 1919 with a 70 per cent disability pension. He served in Ireland during the troubles as a member of the auxiliaries, whose reputation was bad.[13] On returning to England he became a Conservative member both of the Worthing Borough Council and the Sussex County Council.[14] He joined the BUF in 1933, becoming the first fascist councillor. He was a paid official up to 1937, first as Area Organizer for West Sussex and Hampshire, and then as National Inspector for the Midlands and North Wales. He was also nominated as Parliamentary candidate for Birmingham Ladywood. In March 1937, when lack of finance forced Mosley to retrench, he lost his paid post. He may have worked as a volunteer at headquarters during 1938; he himself denied being active for the party after that year. He became somewhat notorious for wearing his black shirt at Council meetings, and because in 1935 he stood trial along with Mosley, Joyce, and Bernard Mullens at Lewes Assizes for riotous assembly at a meeting in Worthing on 9 October 1934. All were acquitted.[15] In 1939 he resigned from the party and, on 4 August, reported for duty with the Royal Engineers.

Budd's name was scheduled in an 'omnibus order' under 18B (1A) of 11

---

[11] Hinsley and Simkins, 320.

[12] The main source is TS 27/506 and Bellamy MS ii. 74 ff. His Home Office file is withheld. Subfile references to 840641/3 and 824541/101A suggest that a considerable body of material survives. See also C. Cross, *The Fascists in Britain* (London, 1961), 142 and 179; J. D. Brewer, *Mosley's Men: The British Union of Fascists in the West Midlands* (Aldershot, 1984), 43. *Budd No. 1* (argued 26 and 27 May) is in *The Times*, 28 May 1941, 9. *Budd No. 2* (as *ex parte Budd*) is in [1941] 2 All ER 749 (Divisional Court), and [1942] 1 All ER 373 (Court of Appeal), also 58 TLR 212, and *The Times*, 11 June 1941, 6, 25 June, 3 July. The reports of *Budd No. 2* add information about *Budd No. 1*. Leave to appeal to the House of Lords was given by the Court of Appeal; see *The Times*, 26 Feb. 1942. Budd was released about 25 May 1943. *Budd No. 3* (as *Budd v. Anderson, Morrison and Williamson*) is in [1943] 2 All ER 452, and contains information about the original arrest and action.

[13] Ex-officers working with the Royal Irish Constabulary.

[14] He had also been President of the British Legion and a member of the League of Frontiersmen.

[15] Cross, *Fascists in Britain*, 142; O. Mosley, *My Life* (London, 1968), 355; R. Skidelsky, *Oswald Mosley* (London, 1975), 354.

June with about twenty-four or twenty-five others.[16] The original order remained in the Home Office, and failed to state that the Home Secretary found it necessary to exercise control over the persons listed. When Budd was arrested on 15 June 1940 he was serving as adjutant; before being removed in handcuffs, he was given a supposed copy of the order.[17] Three of these 'copies' were prepared, as was done with individual orders. These documents, not of course signed by Anderson, but by Maxwell, had been prepared by a Principal in the Home Office, Thomas B. Williamson, and all wrongly stated that the order had been made for 'hostile associations', whilst correctly referring to Regulation 18B (1A).[18] The error was discovered in August, but no action was taken; in addition to Budd, twelve others remained in detention.[19]

Budd received the 'Reasons for Order', dated 25 July, which correctly stated the basis for the order. He appeared before the committee about 1 August. In view of his prominence before the war it is possible, though not certain, that the committee recommended continued detention.[20] It is unclear how the error was discovered or by whom; the committee or MI5 officer would only spot it if attention was somehow drawn to the copy. In 1943 in his analysis of the history of the case in Budd's third action Mr Justice Asquith claimed that Budd was always well aware that his detention was connected with his membership of the BU, whilst conceding that he also thought that he was supposed to have had contacts with Germany, which he had not. Presumably such contacts, which would constitute 'hostile associations', featured in the 'Reasons for Order'.

Budd was represented by Hickson as agent for Marsh and Ferriman of Worthing, who did notice the error; Budd would give them the copy he had received. They briefed J. Scott Henderson, and applied for habeas corpus. The application first came before the court sometime early in May 1941, probably about 7 May.[21] It was then adjourned and, on the

---

[16] The sources vary. All were in the forces.

[17] He was in Churchill's 'Prominent Persons' list. See HO 45/25747.

[18] The text read as follows: 'whereas I have reasonable cause to believe the persons mentioned in the schedule to this order to be persons of hostile associations and that by reason thereof it is necessary to exercise control over them: Now, therefore, I, in pursuance of the power conferred on me by the Defence (General) Regulations, Reg. 18B (1A), hereby make the following order: I direct that the persons mentioned in the schedule to this order be detained'. Each copy apparently listed all the names.

[19] Statement of Morrison on 10 June 1941. *Parl. Deb.* HC. Vol. 372 c. 23–4. They were Jack Austin (an accountant, and later a Buddhist monk), Tom Barneveld (signatory to the autograph book, and apparently RAF), Andrew Burn (the Civil Servant), Donald S. Chambers (of Epping BU, trumpeter, RAF at time of detention, signed autograph, later served in the army and d. 18 June 1943), Ralph M. Dawson (antique dealer in Canterbury, signed autograph), Dye, Foster, Clement Hill (of Hendon BU, mentioned in Watts and Charnley MSS), Perks, A. Schneider (signed autograph), Seabrook, and Steward. Burn's inclusion is mystifying since he was arrested on an order of 22 May. See HO 45/25115.

[20] Otherwise his case would appear in the dispute between MI5 and the committee.

[21] The Crown was represented by Jowitt and Holmes.

advice of the Law Officers, affidavits were filed by Anderson and Morrison. No doubt these mainly followed the standard form settled for Lees's case, but Anderson's went further; it admitted the error, whilst submitting that Budd had not been prejudiced.[22]

Ben Greene, whose case is more fully discussed later, had already applied for habeas corpus, and his application had been argued before the court on 2 May. He had been detained for 'hostile associations', but in error been told it was for 'acts prejudicial'. When Budd's application came up for argument on 27 May: 'two of the three previous applications, namely Sabini and Greene,[23] had disclosed mistakes by the Department and the Advisory Committee, and to use a colloquialism "the temperature of the Court was rising"'. Two of the judges—the odd man out was apparently Tucker J.—made severe comments on the failure of the Home Office to provide any explanation as to how the mistake had come about. Late in the day Jowitt decided to appease them by the ritual sacrifice of the unfortunate Williamson; this broke all normal conventions under which the anonymity of individual Civil Servants was sacrosanct. An affidavit admitting his error, and pleading pressure of work, was hastily sworn and presented. But this was after the opinion of the court had been delivered and the damage done.[24] The judges unanimously ordered the release of Captain Budd.

There being no transcript, it is not entirely clear how this decision was justified technically. But from what was said and quoted in later cases, and from the report in *The Times*, it is apparent that the senior judge, Humphreys, expressed himself fairly strongly in criticizing the Home Office: 'Looking at the document given to Captain Budd, it was found that it was not a copy of anything which the Home Secretary had ordered. It was not a question of it being a technical mistake. It was a totally different document.' He went so far as to say that 'the Court was the traditional guardian of the liberty of the subject and it was entitled to demand that every safeguard conferred on the subject by the regulation should be observed . . . In particular, a person who was detained was entitled to know at the outset the precise grounds of his detention'. But he did not base his decision on the error, but on the form of the original order. In the first place it was an omnibus order—'necessarily of the most vague and general terms possible'. In the second place it did not state that the Home Secretary had been satisfied that it was necessary to exercise control over

[22] The documents are not available, but an account on which I have relied is in an undated memo, probably of October 1941, in TS 27/506, probably written by an official in the Home Office, perhaps Newsam. There is an account in SH paras. 110-16.

[23] Ben Greene's case was argued before the Divisional Court (Humphreys, Singleton, and Tucker) on 2 May.

[24] In the report in *The Times* Humphreys J. makes it clear that when he gave his opinion he did not know how the error occurred.

Captain Budd. The application should succeed because 'no sufficient care and attention were paid to Captain Budd's individual case by the Home Secretary. He was quite unable to say on the evidence that the Secretary of State had had reasonable cause to believe that it was necessary to exercise control over Captain Budd.' He did not rule that the Home Secretary had not had reasonable grounds.

This is from the report in *The Times*; a quotation from a transcript in Budd's second application confirms its substance:

this is just the case which was in the minds of the members of the court who were responsible for the judgement in Lees' case when they observed that, not only had this court power to inquire into the validity of the order for detention, but, for that purpose, it will ascertain whether the Home Secretary had reasonable cause for the belief expressed in the order.[25]

Singleton J. agreed, and apparently was not satisfied that reasonable cause existed, but did not base his decision solely on this point, he expressed serious concern over Home Office errors and omnibus orders; he formally agreed with the third judge, Tucker, who based his opinion on the failure to conform to Regulation 18B (4)—because of the error Budd had been deprived of his right to make representations to the Secretary of State, since anything he said would be misdirected to showing that he was not 'of hostile associations'.

The decision was extremely embarrassing for the Home Office. Budd was of course released, as were the twelve other detainees, who came to be known in fascist circles as 'the Budd Boys'.[26] The remarks made by Humphreys, and the reasoning adopted by Tucker, also suggested a greater readiness to review cases, and Humphreys had, alarmingly, cast doubt upon the validity of omnibus orders, under which hundreds of arrests had been made. Clearly the judges had become irritated with the Home Office and its cavalier attitude to the court, and that did not bode well for the future. Home Office officials may also have known or suspected that errors had taken place in numerous other cases; there must surely have been an investigation, as in the case of the Italian orders, but no documentation is available. On 7 June, in a letter to Sir John Moylan, Maxwell wrote: 'We are likely to have considerable difficulty in the future owing to the comments of the High Court in the Budd case.'[27]

---

[25] In *ex parte Budd (No. 2)* Stable J. quotes from what is presumably a transcript of Humphreys' opinion, which is in substance the same. See [1941] 2 All ER 760. See also 751.

[26] The date of signing the autograph book suggests that the releases took place on 1 June 1941.

[27] HO 215/196. The letter concerned the camp regulations; Maxwell did not want rules enforced which would enable a detainee to complain that the provisions of 18B were not being followed.

The Case of Arthur Campbell

The officials also knew that a further embarrassing case was in the pipeline, that of Arthur C. H. Campbell. He had been in the BU until 1937; he remained known in Derby as an enthusiastic fascist, was somewhat unbalanced, and, according to the authorities, was a vocal supporter of Hitler.[28] His arrest on 22 June 1940 was instigated by the police.[29] The order, for 'hostile associations', was signed by Anderson on 19 June. According to a Home Office minute, when Anderson signed all he had before him was the DR 8 form 'on which, by reason of a visit to Germany and presumably residence there for some six months [allegations which Campbell denied at the hearing], it was decided that the order on the grounds of hostile associations be made'. The DR 8 form referred to this visit, and to defeatist talk by Campbell, but did not mention the BU, though it did refer to Campbell as having once deputized for Mosley. A minute of 14 May 1941, perhaps by Newsam, remarked:

I think it would have been better on the facts shown on the DR 8 submitted by MI5 to have made the order on the ground of 'acts prejudicial'. On the meagre information which the form contained relating to BU activities it would have been impossible to use DR 18B (1A). The 'acts prejudicial' could either have been the systematic undermining of the patriotism of men of military age or the aggressive pro-German and anti-British views.

These points were merely formal. No reasonable person would have detained an individual without trial or term set on the basis of the miserable contents of the form, and before the summer of 1940 this would never have happened. But the case illustrates the fact that at this period the normal practice, adopted because the officials were overwhelmed by work, was to detain without any serious consideration of the matter at all, and see if there was reasonable cause to detain only after the committee report was available. On any basis this was a shocking use of 18B, since the conduct alleged against Campbell, in no sense an organizer of fascists, could perfectly well have been made the subject of a formal warning and, if necessary, a criminal charge.[30]

---

[28] TS 27/507, HO 283/64, and HO 144/21635/840921 (three subfiles destroyed). He was described as a 'fanatical agitator' by the Commandant of the Ascot Camp; during detention he was at first in Walton Prison, Liverpool, then in the Ascot Camp, and he was removed from it to Brixton as a punishment.

[29] On the standard form DR 8: 'This man is thought to be intentionally injuring the country by systematically undermining the patriotism of men of military age.' The DR 8 was approved by Harker.

[30] Under Regulation 2C (Corruption of Public Morale), or Regulation 39A (Seducing Persons from Duty or Causing Disaffection). By waiting a day or so Campbell, if he had persisted in his activities, might also have been charged under Regulation 39BA (Disturbing Reports), which came into force on 11 June 1940.

On 26 June Campbell sent in his appeal: 'I beg to submit that I am not, and never have been, a person of hostile associations, though I freely admit that for a year ending July 1937, I was a member of the British Union in London.' This letter went on to draw attention to his service in the Royal Marines Light Infantry from October 1914 to September 1919, and to that of other family members.

On 2 September the 'Reasons for Order' were sent to him; they and the 'Statement of the Case', which is not in the file, had been prepared by John P. L. Redfern of MI5. Redfern wrongly assumed he had been detained under 18B (1A). The 'Reasons for Order' rehearsed its text, said that Campbell had been a member of the BU, and added that he had been active in its support 'in expressing anti-British and pro-Fascist views'. On 4 October Campbell appeared before the committee,[31] which recommended continued detention, as he was still a keen fascist. The committee, which would have no copy of the order, would have no obvious way of discovering Redfern's error. It came to light in December, when R. E. W. Willcox was going through the papers. Willcox thought it did not matter:

Although this is a technical error no actual injustice has been suffered by Campbell as the evidence shows he was a member of the British Union and he admits he gave up half a window in his premises in Finsbury for a Fascist Book Shop and used his shop in Finsbury as a meeting place for the Finsbury Branch.

In fact Campbell had left London in July of 1937. But Hutchinson and Newsam, remarkably, agreed, so Campbell remained in detention.

By late December 1940, possibly as a consequence of his being moved to Brixton, Campbell had come into contact with Hickson, who spotted the error.[32] On 13 May 1941 he informed the Home Office of his intention to apply for habeas corpus, though he would await the outcome of Budd's case. At about this time the officials realized that the whole story, if revealed in court, might prove very embarrassing indeed. Quite apart from the error, an internal Home Office memorandum of 14 May 1941 described the 'Reasons for Order' as being:

of the most meagre character and deserves all the criticism which has lately been received that a detainee is put before the Advisory Committee without any proper knowledge of what is alleged against him. All the statement in fact informs him is that he has been guilty of anti-British and pro-German views. There is no reason why a much fuller statement of his actions should not have been brought to his notice on the lines of the statement of the case.[33]

The more that came out in court, the worse it would be for the reputation of the Home Office.

[31] A. W. Cockburn KC and Prof. W. E. Collinson.
[32] Campbell was also held at one time in Leicester.   [33] Almost certainly by Newsam.

So behind the scenes there was considerable alarm. Newsam, writing on 20 May to the Treasury Solicitor, Sir Thomas Barnes, had described it as a case 'of extreme difficulty'; the difficulty lay in winning the case without damage to the reputation of the department. Barnes, like the other lawyers in his department, seems to have thought his only duty was to win cases for the executive, and suggested Campbell be offered a new hearing. If the committee found that Campbell was not 'of hostile associations' the order could be revoked, and he could always be detained under a new order for 'acts prejudicial', or under 18B (1A). The advantage claimed for proceeding in this way was not to do justice to Campbell; it was to protect the Home Secretary from a possible action for false imprisonment. Fairness to Campbell did not secure a mention in Barnes's letter.

But all attempts to placate Hickson and buy off the application failed; he wrote: 'We may say we are getting rather tired of the continual apologies on your part for the gross errors of which your department is guilty and which you make no endeavour to put right.'[34] He refused the offer of a rehearing.

On 27 May Budd's release was ordered, and on 28 May Campbell's application was made to the court, which as usual adjourned to give the Home Office a chance to reply. That same day Birkett contributed to the official anxiety; in a letter to Hoare at the Home Office he conveyed the judicial view:

I deeply regret the necessity for this [the offer of a new committee], for repeated cases of this kind bring the administration of the Advisory Committee into great disrepute with the Judges. I know from private conversations with the Judges how strongly they feel upon this matter, and I think you must be ready to hear some rather scathing comments from the Bench.

Nevertheless preparations were made to fight the case. The delicate question was how much of the truth to reveal in public by affidavit. It never seems to have occurred to anyone to tell the whole truth. The draft affidavit prepared for Anderson, but never sworn, bordered on the outright mendacious.[35] By para. 2 it denied any responsibility for the 'Reasons for Order': 'I had no knowledge of and was not consulted as to the grounds which were stated in the document, given to Campbell in pursuance of paragraph 5 of Defence Regulation 18B, to be the grounds on which the Order had been made against him.' Even this let the cat out of the bag; detainees were not being given Anderson's reasons for their detention at all. But para. 4 tried to suggest that the Home Office did have a hand in the matter, whilst playing down the fact that in virtually every

---

[34] This was a reply to Home Office letter of 24 May admitting the mistake and saying that Campbell would have an early opportunity to put his objections anew to the committee.

[35] Full text in TS 27/507.

case, including this one, the 'Reasons for Order' were drafted by MI5: 'It is the practice of the Home Office (and of the Security Services) to assist the Advisory Committee in drafting the statement of the grounds to be given to an objector . . . ' Para. 5 added:

It is the duty of the officers responsible for assisting the Committee in drafting a statement of the grounds to consider the whole of the material, and I am informed that when they were preparing the statement in this case the outstanding feature appeared to them to be that Campbell had been a member of the British Union and had been active in the furtherance of the objects of that Organization.

The affidavit ended by admitting that an unfortunate mistake had been made, whilst giving no explanation as to how this happened, as if this was some sort of mystery. Devious though this document was, it could hardly have failed to reveal the extraordinary practice under which MI5's lawyers simply guessed the grounds for detention orders, and their guesses were given to detainees as the 'Reasons for Order'.

On 30 May a conference took place about the case. The minute reads: 'When Mr Holmes learned the facts as to the mistake he thought Campbell ought to be let out at once to avoid exposing the Home Office to further strictures from the court.' No doubt he was also alarmed at the possible judicial reactions to the affidavit, presumably drafted by officials in the Treasury Solicitor's department; conceivably he had only recently been told how the system actually worked. After rapid consultations with Barnes, Maxwell, Newsam, and Hoare the decision was taken to release Campbell. Hickson refused to withdraw his application, and went to the court for costs, which unlike Lees he obtained, with consent, given no doubt not out of any sense of decency to Campbell but to ensure there was no opportunity for awkward questions to be asked. The hearing was confined to a mere ten minutes.[36] But Campbell enjoyed only a brief spell of liberty, being detained again by an 18B (1A) order signed by Morrison and dated 5 June. The same fate befell the unfortunate Captain Budd. The twelve 'Budd Boys' were the only beneficiaries. Apparently, though the evidence is not clear, new orders were signed for them too, but at once suspended, no doubt on conditions. I have been told they were required to drop any legal proceedings as the price of freedom; I have no confirmation of this, but it is notable that the two who had litigated—Budd and Campbell—remained in detention. I have been refused access to Budd's file. It looks as if the Home Office and the lawyers were anxious to discourage other litigants. At the time many detainees in the Isle of Man, encouraged by the doubts cast by Humphreys on the validity of omnibus orders, had begun to take steps preliminary to litigation, as by swearing

---

[36] Humphreys, Tucker, and Stable.

affidavits.[37] The message they were given was clear: even if they won they would at once be detained again.

Campbell subsequently appeared before the committee, with J. W. Morris KC in the chair, on 7 August 1941.[38] Its report was severely critical of the procedures under which it had to operate:

> The committee feel that the enquiry which they were conducting was beset with many difficulties. The statements alleged to have been made by Campbell were about fifteen months ago. Campbell said that he would very much like to be confronted with his accusers . . . No procedure can satisfactorily take the place of that whereby witnesses are heard in the presence of the persons affected by their evidence, and whereby such person may himself have the opportunity of testing and probing and perhaps exposing the testimony which is given.

The recommendation was release; Campbell was no longer 'dangerous'. This must have been opposed by MI5, and on 1 October 1941 Morrison rejected it. There was a further review of the case and on 25 November it was decided to suspend the order, and he was released. In July 1941 he began an action against Anderson, Morrison, and Williamson for false imprisonment from 22 June 1940 to 1 July 1941,[39] and for libel, Williamson being sued as the official who had sent the detention order to the Chief Constable of Derby, and thus published a defamatory document. On 21 November 1941 the claim for libel was struck out as legally impossible; such a communication is privileged and cannot be sued upon. On 30 January 1942 Holmes advised that in the light of the Liversidge and Greene decisions of 3 November 1941 the action must fail; all that the Crown had to do was to tender the detention orders. It appears to have been withdrawn as hopeless, as indeed it surely was.

Budd's Second Action

Budd, like Campbell, was persistent, and after his redetention he again applied for habeas corpus.[40] The new order was under Regulation 18B (1A); the 'Reasons for Order' simply rehearsed the text of the regulation and stated the need to detain him. His application came before Lord

[37] On the new orders for the Budd Boys see Morrison, *Parl. Deb.* HC Vol. 381 c.1513. On preparations for litigation see Beavan Diary for 27 June 1941; also private information. The barrister J. W. Williamson visited the detainees there. See also SH para. 115.

[38] With G. H. Stuart Bunning, Mrs E. Lowe, and Mr W. Stott.

[39] Presumably the date the writ was issued.

[40] According to the Beavan Diary for 27 July 1941 some £600 to pay for the case had been raised by detainees in Brixton—presumably wealthy individuals like Mosley and Gordon-Canning, though no names are given.

Caldecote, sitting with Macnaghten and Stable, on 23 and 24 July.[41] Budd's case for release was based upon four distinct contentions.[42]

The first was that the Home Secretary had no reasonable cause to believe that it was necessary to exercise control over him. This was supported in a number of different ways. One was that none of Budd's commanding officers had any complaint to make of him since he enlisted in 1939. Another, perhaps more powerful, was that the BU had been proscribed and its property seized—how could the necessity for control over a former supporter now exist? Another was that since his release from detention he had done nothing to justify re-arrest; in fact he had been unwell and recuperating in his home in Worthing. All this worried the Crown lawyers, whose affidavits consequently did not follow the standardized form used in Lees's case, in which the existence, but not the contents, of secret reports was mentioned. Something had to be leaked to help to win the case. Morrison's added:

I had and have information as to the said Budd's membership of the organization and as to his collaboration with those in control of it; *also as to acts in furtherance of and in sympathy with its objects after he had become an officer in His Majesty's Forces and during the war*. Reviewing all the information I came to the conclusion and had reasonable cause to believe and did in fact believe that which is set out . . . [my italics].[43]

Otherwise no information was given, the Crown lawyers being prepared as usual to reveal as little as they thought they could get away with. Here the revelation was designed simply to prejudice the court against viewing Budd's military service as furthering his case.

The second, based on remarks by Tucker J. in the first action, was that the failure, on his arrest, to provide him with an explanation of why he was being detained deprived him of his right to make representations to the Home Secretary, as opposed to objections to the committee. How could he make such representations if he had no idea why the Home Secretary thought it necessary to detain him? Again the point was a powerful one, and could have been advanced by all detainees. It was also argued that a fuller statement must, at the least, be before the court when it adjudicated in an application for habeas corpus. Without one, on what conceivable basis could it adjudicate?

The third was that there was no reasonable ground for thinking that the

---

[41] The Beavan Diary has it that J. H. V. Hepburn-Ruston's case was due to be heard about this time. I have found no confirmation of this.

[42] These have to be gleaned from the opinions in the report in [1941] 2 All ER 749 and *The Times*, 25 June 1941, 6.

[43] The text is from the law report at 754. The full text is not available, but a paraphrase on 754 makes it clear that otherwise it was in standard form.

BU was an organization which fell within the terms of Regulation 18B (1A); it appears that this was not much pressed in argument before the court.

The fourth was that since his release had been ordered it was illegal to redetain him on the same grounds as before. The passage quoted from Morrison's affidavit was perhaps also intended to counter this argument, suggesting that the matter had been reconsidered by Morrison on the basis of new information; it is impossible to say whether this was actually true.

Lord Caldecote delivered the majority opinion of himself and Macnaghten J. on 2 July. So far as the 'reasonable cause' points were concerned he conceded that in Budd's first application two of the judges ordered release because they were not satisfied that reasonable cause existed.[44] But there were then procedural irregularities (and an omnibus order); here everything was formally in order. To investigate the matter would, he thought, involve the court in an operation which was not its business. He did not explicitly reject the doctrine settled in Lees's case, but again deprived it of all practical significance by accepting the Home Office affidavit as conclusive so long as no formal irregularities appeared. As for the second argument, he relied on the provision in Regulation 18B (5) requiring the Chairman of the committee to give the grounds and particulars; this implied that these did not have to be given at the time of arrest. The third argument he rejected because the BU had been lawfully proscribed. The fourth argument he rejected for two reasons. One was that the second detention was not for the same cause as the first, a rather ridiculous reason, since the court had no idea what the cause was. The second was that since the second detention was not open to the formal objections which could be raised to the first, it was not unlawful.

This opinion was a miserably undistinguished essay in technical legal reasoning, but its message was clear: the court would accept whatever the Home Office decided, and make no attempt to secure to detainees fair treatment even over the few rights they had been given in the regulation, so long as there was bare respect for form. Only one formal point was left open—the validity of omnibus orders.

The third judge, Sir Wintringham Stable, dissented; in a memorable phrase, not of course to be found in his opinion in the case, he did not believe that judges should be 'mice squeaking under a chair in the Home Office'.[45] Even if we did not know that he later used this expression, the text of his opinion shows that he thought the Home Office had adopted a

---

[44] Humphreys and Singleton; Lord Caldecote wrote as if he had spoken to Singleton to clarify his view.

[45] Letter from Stable to Lord Atkin of 5 November 1941 quoted by R. F. V. Heuston, 'Liversidge v. Anderson in Retrospect', Law Quarterly Review, 86 (1970), 33 at 49.

disrespectful attitude, and his concern was not so much with civil liberty as with judicial status. Given that the court could investigate the existence of reasonable cause, as had been ruled in *Lees*, here was an applicant, an army officer with a distinguished record of service, who had recently been released by the judges, two of whom had doubts as to whether a reasonable cause for his detention existed. The Home Office had him re-arrested within a few days, and now gave the judges hardly any more information than had been provided for the earlier case, and this in an affidavit which was largely in common form. Stable concluded that on the material before the court he could not be satisfied that reasonable cause existed. Furthermore, since an issue in the case was whether it was lawful to redetain Budd for the same cause as he had originally been detained, the court was entitled to know what that cause was, and the Home Office had failed to inform it. Stable would have been prepared to adjourn the proceedings in order to enable the Home Office to present to the court 'the fullest material possible, so far as is consistent with the public interest and the public safety'. But clearly his colleagues, to whom he would put this suggestion, were unwilling to accept this offer of compromise.

Budd's case reached the Court of Appeal in February 1942, that is after the Liversidge and Greene decisions; he predictably lost.[46] So Budd was not released, and no serious inroads were made upon the secrecy surrounding Home Office decisions. The refusal of access to the Home Office papers on the case, presumably as being 'sensitive',[47] raises the suspicion that the full story of the case involves disreputable official behaviour, though it may be simply irrational. Possibly Birkett's committee wanted him released, and he may have been kept in detention by Morrison for political reasons after it was known that he constituted no possible threat to security. He was eventually set free in late May of 1943.

About some of the other cases begun in 1941, such as Luttman-Johnson's, little is known; proceedings in his case appear to have been deferred to await the outcome of the Liversidge and Greene cases.[48] Smeaton-Stuart's suit for damages for false imprisonment was the first such action to come to trial, being decided by Tucker J. on 26 June 1941.[49] I shall deal with it later in connection with the Liversidge case. Potentially the most important was Lieutenant Francis C. Fane's application for

---

[46] The case was heard on 13, 16 and 25 February and is reported in 58 TLR 212 and [1942] 1 All ER 373, the Court consisting of Greene MR, MacKinnon and Goddard LJJ. Budd's later action for false imprisonment before Asquith J. is reported [1943] 2 ALL ER 452.

[47] Letter from the Home Office of 22 April 1988, giving no reason and not even using this expression.

[48] See above n. 1.

[49] Reported as *Stuart* v. *Anderson and Morrison* [1941] 2 All ER 665.

habeas corpus.[50] A former naval officer, he hoped to rejoin the navy. But he had been a BU official, and was scheduled under the omnibus order of 30 May 1940. On his arrest he was given a document under Maxwell's signature saying that an order had been made; this was not a copy of the order, nor did it say that Anderson had been satisfied that it was necessary to exercise control over him.[51] The basis for his application was that so far as Fane could tell there was no valid order by Anderson at all.[52] However, Fane was released on 18 July, and his application was withdrawn; Home Office practice over omnibus orders, and their validity, were never adjudicated upon. Maxwell noted on his file with reference to his approval of release: 'I have, of course, in no way been influenced by possible proceedings; that must not happen in other cases.' Fane's detention had been under review for some time, the committee favouring release, viewing Fane as entirely patriotic, and MI5 opposing this. After release he apparently served in the merchant navy.

The Hypocritical State of the Law

The legal situation after *Budd No. 2* was essentially hypocritical. In theory the courts could investigate whether the Home Secretary had reasonable grounds for the belief that the individual concerned fell into a category of persons whom it was lawful to detain, or indeed investigate any other matter which related to the legality of detention. Yet it was also settled that the courts should not seek access to secret or highly confidential information, and in any event the Crown could refuse to produce documents under the doctrine of Crown privilege; at this date the courts always in practice accepted the assertion by the Crown that the production of a document would be against the public interest, though there had been suggestions that the judges could check whether refusal was justified.[53] The courts also took the position that it was not the job of the courts to substitute their decision as to the merits of detaining a particular individual for that of the Home Secretary, the assumption being that such questions were for the committee. In some situations the application of the received doctrine set out in Lees's case was not problematic—for example detention would be unlawful if no order had ever been made, or

---

[50] TS 27/513 and HO 45/23679/840412. Fane, who came from a country landowning family, was detained in part because of information from informers. His file once contained correspondence, now destroyed, with Lord Justice Scott about his detention.

[51] Not, I think, an actual signature, but a typed copy.

[52] The Beavan Diary for 21 June indicates that a number of detainees were considering taking the same point.

[53] See C. K. Allen, *Law and Orders* (Oxford, 1945), 330ff. In *Duncan* v. *Cammell Laird & Co.* [1942] AC 624 the Lords ruled that courts had to accept Crown claims to withhold documents on the ground of public interest. Previously this is what had happened in practice.

if the person arrested was not the person named in the order. But beyond such simple cases it was hard to be sure of anything except that the judges were easily satisfied, for example by laconic assurances in affidavits that all was as it ought to be; they applied the Reading Presumption of Executive Innocence. As they gained experience in handling 18B cases, and presumably picked up information about the system through informal channels, they became uneasy with the settled doctrine. The decision in *Lees* portrayed the judges as vigilant guardians of the liberty of the subject; in consequence they were in some sense responsible for protecting the rights of detainees. But the reality emerging in practice was that so long as minimal formalities were observed, the Home Office could win virtually any case by putting in affidavits of standard form; if it lost it could always issue a new order. The judges must have realized that they were simply upholding Home Office decisions about which they knew virtually nothing, except that some of them seemed pretty odd. Nor can they have been taken in by the fiction that Anderson in person took detention decisions, brooding as it were over each case.

Even over matters of mere form the courts had provided very limited guidance; thus doubt had been cast on the validity of 'omnibus' orders, but there was no decision one way or the other as to their validity. Again as to the rights of the detainee, the presiding judge in *Budd No. 1* had said that a detainee was 'entitled to know at the outset the precise grounds of his detention', but eight weeks later *Budd No. 2* ruled that a formal rehearsal of the text of the regulation, which gave him no idea why he had been detained, sufficed. In the cases back in October of 1940 it had been said that excessive delay in operating the system might be a ground for relief; this was pure humbug, since months of detention without any hearing would be tolerated. As to the mechanics of the system, the judges seemed to prefer ignorance to understanding. They could have pressed the Crown lawyers for an account; they never did so, accepting instead the miserably uninformative standard form affidavits. It is therefore hardly surprising that they failed to develop a rational body of doctrine which spelt out the boundary between the legal requirements for valid detention on the one hand, and the area of discretion within which the Home Secretary was sovereign on the other.

The only circumstance capable of galvanizing the judges into action was blatant lack of respect for their status, as in Budd's first application. The judges were prepared to behave like mice, so long as they were treated like lions. But they must have been sensitive to the hypocrisy involved, and one way out of the uneasy position into which they had been placed by Humphreys' opinion in the Lees case was for them to wash their hands entirely of responsibility in the matter, blame this on 'the law', and announce that through no fault of theirs the courts had no role in the matter. Given the doctrine of precedent and the Court of Appeal's approval of Humphreys' opinion in *Lees*, this solution was only clearly open to the House of Lords, which was certainly not bound to follow that decision. It was therefore essential that one or more appeals should be taken to that tribunal to which was ascribed, at this time, legal infallibility.

$$\Longrightarrow 16 \Longrightarrow$$

The Web of Suspicion

Robert W. Liversidge

The detainees who did take appeals to the Lords were Robert Liversidge and Ben Greene. Both lost, the judicial opinions being delivered on 3 November 1941; the resulting legal position seemed, from a technical point of view, exactly what the Home Office wanted. But success had its price, for the two cases brought the Home Office, the security service, and the courts, into very considerable disrepute. The detention of both Liversidge and Greene was entirely understandable, but they were in fact loyal citizens who, in an absolute sense, ought never to have been detained.

The first to be arrested was Liversidge.[1] He was born on 11 June 1904 at Haringey, the son of Asher and Sarah Perlsweig, Jewish immigrants from Russia; Asher was a rabbi. He was named Jacob, but called Jack. He had four brothers.[2] One, Maurice, became a distinguished rabbi and Zionist, a founding member of the World Jewish Congress, and head of the World Jewish Congress Department of International Affairs in New York, and its representative at the United Nations.[3] Of his three sisters the eldest acquired the name Liversidge by her first marriage.[4] Jack left school at 14, and in about 1926, after working in uninspiring jobs, became associated with persons dealing in shares. In July 1928 two of them, David and Dore Baumgart, were tried at the Old Bailey for conspiracy to defraud a Mrs Heath of £16,000; David was acquitted but Dore was convicted and gaoled, and it was alleged that Jack had sold the shares. In 1940 he conceded that he had, when he was very young, got into bad company, but denied any knowledge of the fraud, and there is no reason to doubt the

---

[1] TS 27/501, Home Office files 863004 and 840/66 (also references to L 8573 and MI5 PF 49333) seen on privileged access, and information derived from Mr Liversidge, some by me, and some by Prof. De Lloyd Guth, correspondence with individuals who knew him, such as Lord Selkirk, and standard histories of the RAF.

[2] One became an artist, apparently using the name Pearl, another a manager for Marks and Spencer under the name Pearce, and one an accountant.

[3] He died in New York on 14 January 1985; *Jewish Chronicle*, 25 January 1985. Maurice was educated at Owen's School, Islington, University College, London, Christ's College, Cambridge, and the LSE.

[4] The youngest became by marriage Mrs Caute.

truth of this. A warrant was issued for his arrest, but was never executed. About this time he left England and travelled to Australia, South Africa, America, and Canada. The result of this incident was that he acquired a police file, and anyone who is so unfortunate cannot correct or question what is in it. In 1931 he acquired a Canadian passport under the name Liversidge, which he was then using, and stated that he had been born under this name in Toronto on 28 May 1901.[5] The warrant was withdrawn on 22 August 1933, before his return to England. For four years he ran a sound recording studio in Hollywood, and met a Warner Brothers starlet, Wanda Stevenson, whom he married in 1936.

On his return to England he engaged in various successful business enterprises. In 1936 he became general manager of the London Amalgamated Trust, a firm dealing in house property and scrap metal, and in 1937 he became managing director of the Carbonite Diamond Company, concerned with industrial diamonds. By 1938 he controlled a company dealing in the wholesale brokerage of oil royalties. There were other business schemes, including an attempt to secure the rights in the first practicable helicopter, the Focke Achgelis FW 161. He became a wealthy man, and in September 1937 formally changed his name to Robert William Liversidge. His return to London came to the attention of the police through a spiteful informer, and they decided that Liversidge and Perlsweig were the same person. In July 1938 his Canadian passport was impounded, but no proceedings were started against him.

During this period Liversidge became associated in business with individuals, some very right-wing, who had been connected with British intelligence. His co-directors in the oil business included the fourth Earl of Verulam (also a director of British Thomson Houston), Lieutenant-Colonel Cudbert Thornhill, and Lieutenant-Colonel Norman G. Thwaites. The Earl, something of a personal friend, had interests in communications; he was an electrical engineer and ran Enfield Cables, and MI6 apparently ran a unit in a number of country houses on his estate near St Albans.[6] Thornhill had been engaged in intelligence in Russia as military attaché in Petrograd from 1916 to 1918; he worked in the political intelligence department of the Foreign Office from 1940 to 1946.[7] Thwaites was our man in New York in the First World War; he recruited the spy Sydney Reilly. He edited Air and became interested in fascism,

---

[5] Son of Robert William Liversidge of Haddon Hall, Sherborne Street, Montreal and Sarah Goodson of London, Ontario.

[6] See N. West, GCHQ: The Secret Wireless War 1900–1986 (London, 1986) 215. On the Earl (1880–1949) see Who Was Who, iv.

[7] 1883–1952. Who Was Who, v.

acting as chairman at meetings of the January Club run by Luttman-Johnson.[8] Liversidge knew Compton Mackenzie, and was a friend of William Stephenson. Stephenson became known as *A Man Called Intrepid*, or *The Quiet Canadian*, these being the titles of books about him by another Stephenson and by Montgomery Hyde, which give somewhat overblown accounts of his work during the Second World War.[9] Liversidge had also obtained specifications for a secret method of transmitting radio messages, which he supplied to the War Office through Major-General John Hay Beith, better known as the writer Ian Hay. On 10 December 1940 Richard Stokes MP, who was well informed about detainees, stated in the Commons that detainees fell into certain categories: 'Then there is another category, which might apply to anybody. They are members of a military intelligence department, one of whom seems to be held because he knew too much about the irregular dealings in oil in a particular part of Europe.'[10] This obscure remark could refer to Liversidge, though it has been suggested to me that the reference is to one Thomas Wilson, a detainee said to have been at one time an agent involved in sabotage of oil wells in Romania.[11] It seems possible that Liversidge had some sort of connection with British intelligence in the 1930s. The nature of his business activities naturally involved contact with foreigners, and no doubt some were dubious people.

As a Jew Liversidge had no reason to be anything but opposed to the Nazis, and at the time of Munich he volunteered, without success, for service in the army. On 12 September 1939 he applied for a commission in the RAF Volunteer Reserve. Having for some reason misstated his date and place of birth in his Canadian passport application, he repeated the same story in this application. No doubt his motive was simply to ensure that he could join up and serve his country; there must have been many technically improper applications by patriotic people at this period. As he himself said: 'My reason for joining the RAF was to serve my country and satisfy myself and my family.'[12] His sister, Mrs Caute, and perhaps other members of the family, may have viewed some of his activities, and indeed some of his friends, with disfavour. He was commissioned Pilot Officer on 26 November. In the RAF he served as an intelligence officer with Bomber Command at Wyton and Wattisham, initially in

[8] 1872–1956. *Who Was Who*, v. He wrote *Velvet and Vinegar* (1932) and *The World Mine Oyster*; I have not traced a copy of the latter. See Andrew, 299–301, 316; R. Griffiths, *Fellow Travellers of the Right: British Enthusiasts for Nazi Germany, 1933–9* (London, 1980), 49–53, 137. See above p.221.
[9] See Andrew, 507, 650–3, 661.   [10] *Parl. Deb.* HC Vol. 367 c.839.
[11] Wilson litigated; see *R.* v. *Anderson ex parte Wilson* reported in *The Times*, 8 October 1943. The source is ultimately a detainee Arthur Mason, whose account I have from J. Warburton. See below pp. 375–6.
[12] Statement to the police of 30 April 1940.

photographic intelligence. He then moved to Fighter Command at Biggin Hill, and from there to Fighter Command Headquarters at Bentley Priory. He served with outstanding success.

Early in 1940 MI5 came to suspect that a racket was being run in Seaton internment camp, in which 'three notorious German Jew swindlers, in consideration of a payment of £500 per head, were offering to effect the release of internees through improper pressures brought to bear in high places'.[13] The possible contact, it was suspected, was none other than Norman Thwaites—said by Captain Stevens of MI5 to be 'notorious as a nominee for share pushers'.[14] As an associate Liversidge was therefore investigated, the RAF's newly formed security service being involved. Liversidge's incorrect application came to light, and his business contacts with suspicious foreigners, especially a Dutchman, one Van Lighten, who had tried to join MI5. So Liversidge was arrested on 26 April, and charged under the Air Force Act with making a false statement in his application.[15] His flat was searched, and the web of suspicion was extended when the police found the addresses of André Ply, a Frenchman refused admission to Britain, and of one Weinbloom, suspected of currency offences. Liversidge himself believes that suspicion arose in some way because Special Branch had been in touch with him after he joined up in connection with his archive of material on oil royalties, which he made available to the authorities.

Liversidge was interviewed and admitted that he was Jack Perlsweig. This admission made it possible to proceed against him either under the Air Force Act, or under a provision of the Defence Regulations.[16] But his patriotic motive would have meant that no serious penalty would have been imposed, though his commission could have been terminated.

Given the hostile police reports on him, and the somewhat curious life he had led, it is hardly surprising that the Air Ministry viewed his presence at Fighter Command Headquarters with alarm, though he had never been convicted, or indeed tried, for any offence. He had access there, as the papers put it, to 'very secret information'. This probably refers simply to normal operational information. But Liversidge himself came to believe that his detention was somehow connected to the fact that he, together with another officer, McCarthy, had set up a section which had been able to forecast, by means which remain somewhat obscure, enemy action in the air, and had successfully anticipated a raid on Scapa Flow.[17]

[13] 'Statement of the Case.'

[14] Possibly a barrister, Robert William Stevens, in civilian life.   [15] S. 25 (1).

[16] DR 1 (1) (e) which made it an offence to 'make any statement, having reasonable cause to believe that the . . . statement is likely to mislead any person in the discharge of any lawful functions in connection with the defence of the realm or the securing of the public safety'.

[17] Liversidge's system had nothing to do with the navigational beams investigated by R. V. Jones.

At the time most aircraft navigation was by dead reckoning, map-reading, and star or sun shots. Aircraft could, however, obtain radio fixes by taking bearings on ground beacons, or by requesting bearings to be taken on their own transmissions. Since the beacons were turned on before a raid, some warning that a raid was coming was possible, but this did not give information as to the direction in which the aircraft were flying. Liversidge's system, which did give such information, depended upon interception at Cheadle of transmissions from reconnaissance or other aircraft requesting such bearings from satellite beacons, and interception of the request, which had to be decoded. Approximately two hours' notice of raids over the North Sea was possible. This had excited agitated curiosity from Air Marshal Dowding.

Independent evidence shows that there was indeed a raid on Scapa Flow at the appropriate time, which was intercepted.[18] Liversidge identifies McCarthy as having been a colonial magistrate in West Africa. This is baffling; there was such a person, but he seems never to have been in the RAF.[19] It is conceivable that the real anxiety over Liversidge was fear that he knew something about the breaking of the German Enigma codes; it was in early April that some Luftwaffe traffic was being read for the first time, and this would be known both to Dowding, and to the Director of Air Intelligence, Charles Medhurst.[20] If the same raid was already anticipated by Dowding through Enigma decrypts this would explain his astonishment when Liversidge also predicted it independently.

Liversidge's Detention Order

A month elapsed between Liversidge's arrest, on 26 April, and the signing of his detention order on 26 May. Captain Stevens suggested detention under 18B, but after discussion with J. L. S. Hale of MI5 and the police it was agreed that neither 'hostile associations' nor 'acts prejudicial' could be proved, which left only a charge under the Defence Regulations or Air Force Act. On 3 May Kendal of Special Branch wrote to Lewis Evans, Deputy Director of Public Prosecutions:

---

[18] On 10 April a raid was intercepted by Hurricanes, and 4 German aircraft were shot down. D. Richards, *The Royal Air Force 1939–1945* (London, 1974–5), i. 68.

[19] Sir Leslie E. V. McCarthy (22 Dec 1885–20 June 1967) was Crown Counsel and Solicitor-General (1934–40) in the Gold Coast, and a judge there 1941–8. He was also described by Liversidge as having worked at the interception station at Cheadle, to have been involved in deciphering German codes, and to have been in the signals in the 1st World War. According to Liversidge McCarthy was disposed of by being posted to India or Egypt. Possibly Liversidge has confused a nephew of the lawyer, possibly Andrew Joseph McCarthy, also like Liversidge in the Administrative and Special Duties Branch.

[20] J. Garlinski, *Intercept: The Enigma War* (London, 1979), 53.

I am told this evening that you have been approached about the Liversidge
Perlsweig case. I may be wrong, but I am certain there is danger ahead here. The
case is one in which, if MI5 have any real reason, they ought to apply for internment under 18B. This they will not do and tried their best to bounce me into
charging him under 1 (1) (e).

Kendal went on to argue that such a charge would be ridiculous; an Air
Force offence was involved, and the Air Force should deal with it.

On 15 May the Air Minister, Archibald Sinclair, wrote to the Home
Office: 'I am certain you will agree that it is most undesirable that a man
with the unsavoury and indeed dangerous associations of Perlsweig, who
during recent months has had access to information of a most secret character, should be left at large either in the Service or in the Country.' The
letter suggests that detention was the only satisfactory solution.

The Home Office officials thereupon set about the task of justifying
making an order. Rumbelow persuaded Pilcher of MI5, against his better
judgement, to put up a case. Rumbelow then constructed a justification:

The grounds for an order under 18B are admittedly flimsy but I do not think they
are entirely non existent. Liversidge has apparently associated with certain enemy
aliens who are now interned . . . and this is strictly 'hostile associations'. Moreover
Liversidge obtained access to secret information by false representations and as
his history makes it clear that he might be tempted by the offer of money to perform hostile acts, there could be 'reasonable cause to believe' that he has 'been
recently concerned in the preparation of "acts prejudicial . . ."'.

Harold Scott was so impressed that he minuted: 'I fail to see why MI5 felt
so shy of this case. It seems clear that he must be detained, and his association with enemies who have been interned condemns him.'[21] Newsam
agreed, as did Maxwell, who conceded that 'it is clearly a case where the
Home Secretary is being asked to pull chestnuts out of the fire for the Air
Minister'. And when the file reached Anderson he honestly admitted that
'though the grounds for making an order under Reg. 18B may seem somewhat flimsy there are I think sufficient technical grounds to justify action
in the present grave situation'. So the order was signed. Liversidge was
lodged in Brixton Prison, and his commission terminated on 28 May.

The 'Statement of the Case' was drafted by Pilcher, who sent it the
committee after extraordinary delay on 12 September, adding:
'Presumably the grounds were hostile associations or acts prejudicial or
both. The case is rather an unusual one and I think in the circumstances
the Chairman of the Committee before whom he appears should draft the
"Reasons for Order".' This was done, and they were settled on 2 October,
over five months after the initial arrest. Again MI5's reluctance to accept
responsibility for the case is curious, though Stamp of MI5 had, back in

[21]   1887–1969. Later Sir Harold and Metropolitan Police Commissioner 1945–53.

July, telephoned the Home Office, obscurely 'to say that his is a very bad case, and he sees no reason why his appeal should have special authority'. Possibly 'special authority' meant an accelerated hearing; something peculiar was going on.

The particulars read as follows:

1. The said Liversidge was born of Russian parentage. His father's name was Asher Perlsweig, a Jewish Rabbi.

2. The said Liversidge adopted the name of Watkins, and in the year 1927 was associated with one Baumgart in a conspiracy to defraud.

3. In the year 1935 the said Liversidge was using a Canadian passport containing false particulars.

4. At or about this time Liversidge adopted the name of Stone and was associated with a notorious sharepusher, Shapiro, in attempting to defraud.

5. On 12 September, 1939, the said Liversidge applied for a commission in the R.A.F. Volunteer Reserve and supported his application by false particulars. By the false particulars so supplied he was successful in being appointed a Pilot Officer and was performing the duties of Intelligence Officer at a Fighter Command in the country and had access to information of a very secret character.

6. The said Liversidge was an associate of swindlers and international crooks.

7. The said Liversidge was associated from time to time with Germans and with those associated with the German Secret Service.

8. On or about 26 April 1940 the said Liversidge supplied further false particulars on an official form, and was put under close arrest in respect of this offence.

Of course only paragraph seven of this offensive document was in any way relevant to 'hostile associations'.

Liversidge was represented by his lawyers, Silkin and Silkin, who pointed this out and asked: 'Will you please let us have particulars, giving names, dates, places and circumstances'. These were refused.

The 'Statement of the Case' was a much fuller document, devoted to making bricks with very little straw. It conceded that Liversidge had never been charged, let alone convicted, of any offence, but nevertheless claimed he 'has a very bad record'. It then stated the facts of the Baumgart conviction in 1928, and went on to report the receipt of an anonymous letter in 1935, as a result of which Liversidge was located in London in 1937, living with his wife Wanda Stevenson in possession of the Canadian passport. It then set out the belief of Scotland Yard, based solely upon an anonymous informant, that Liversidge, under the name of John Stone, had been involved with Albert and Julius Shapiro in defrauding a Miss Ida R. Mussoon of $86,000 in New York; the New York police, informed of this, declined to seek extradition. Again no evidence of Liversidge's involvement in the offence, if indeed it ever occurred, existed. There was no suggestion that Liversidge was involved in the conspiracy in Seaton Camp, but it was claimed that Liversidge was an 'associate' of Van Lighten, a suspected German agent, and was implicated with Leon Nussbaum and Richard Markus, a German now interned, in dealings in industrial diamonds which were probably fraudulent.[22] On this insecure basis Liversidge was 'an associate of swindlers and international crooks'. It concluded:

Liversidge is not of hostile origin. He has however been associated with Germans and also apparently with a Dutchman who was in touch with the German Secret Service. Liversidge's record shows that he is completely unscrupulous and it may well be that he has been recently concerned in acts prejudicial to the public safety, although we have no direct evidence of this. In no circumstances are the R.A.F. prepared to take Liversidge back into the R.A.F., and we submit that in view of the valuable information which he possesses it is essential in the interests of security that his detention should be continued.

This document was no doubt produced after discussions with a representative of the RAF security service.

Liversidge appeared before the committee on 10 October. Birkett put the allegations in the 'Statement of the Case' to him, and though he admitted having the false passport, and having used the alias John Stone, he denied all allegations of fraud and any improper association with Van Lighten.[23] Many testimonials to his good character were received, and the committee also saw, at her request, a Miss Clare McCririck,[24] an actress whose stage name was Miss Gwynn, and who was at this time planning to marry him. She, in company with Aneurin Bevan, who seems to have been a friend of Liversidge, visited the Home Office to protest at the delay in bringing him before the committee.

The report, dated 15 October, stated that the case 'caused considerable anxiety to the committee', and that 'The nature of the case plainly is one of a very peculiar character.' There was no proof that Liversidge had been involved in frauds, and no evidence at all of disloyalty. The ground for detention—'hostile associations'—'is really difficult to substantiate'. The only real reason for detaining him was his possession of secret information, which in any event he denied, and doubt as to his reliability. It was hardly a moment for risking any weakening of Fighter Command, for the Battle of Britain was under way. Birkett's committee concluded:

At the same time, following the principle which they have consistently followed in these cases, they entertained doubts as to the propriety of releasing him in view of the attitude of the Air Force authorities and are compelled, therefore, to the conclusion that the proper recommendation should be that he should remain in detention.

[22] The accusation of diamond swindles appear to have arisen because of quarrels between Liversidge and business associates over a scheme to produce usable diamonds by fusing bort.

[23] Transcript in HO L8573, not in the PRO.

[24] Daughter of a Maj. D. H. G. McCririck of the Somerset Light Infantry.

But the passage of time might change the situation, so the case should be reviewed at a later date, as it was to be on 4 December 1941. This recommendation was accepted by Morrison, after a long and unexplained delay, on 11 December. One may guess that Morrison was approached by Bevan about the case. Liversidge's case was one of the worst examples of delay which can be fully documented.

Strict proof is lacking, but the attitude of those in authority to Liversidge seems to have been coloured, at least in part, by anti-Semitic stereotyping. I suspect too that some sort of conflict between MI5 and MI6, who may have found Liversidge's knowledge of the oil business useful, may underlie the case, but there is no direct evidence. It is clear that the papers I have seen do not tell the whole story.

Ben Greene the Pacifist.[25]

Ben Greene was born in Brazil on 28 December 1901. His mother was born a German national.[26] In 1908 he and the family came to England, where he attended a local preparatory school, and then Berkhamsted Grammar School, where his uncle, Charles Greene, was Headmaster. His cousins, the author Graham Greene and Hugh Carleton Greene, later Director-General of the BBC, also attended this school. Ben went up to Wadham College, Oxford, in 1919, where he associated with the Labour Party and Society of Friends, becoming a full member of the latter in 1922. He went through some sort of religious crisis whilst at Wadham, and left without taking a degree. He then spent three and a half years doing relief work, principally in Germany, Poland, and Russia, but also in Czechoslovakia and Austria. In late 1923 he returned from Russia, where he had worked on famine relief with the Quakers, the Save the Children Fund, and the American Relief Administration. He then worked for C. R. Attlee in the Limehouse election; in this context he would have come to know John Beckett. He joined the Independent Labour Party in 1924, and was employed by it as a research worker. In the same year he became a secretary to Ramsay MacDonald, handling relations with ILP members. He unsuccessfully contested Basingstoke in 1924.

[25] TS 27/522, and 542 (file on John Beckett), LCO 2/1454, and papers in the possession of his son Edward P. C. Greene, who has kindly given me full access. What follows is largely based on a 'Statement by Ben Greene' and 'Representations to H. M. Secretary of State by Ben Greene' in the Greene Papers, B/6 and 'Personal Notes', Greene Papers, not listed. I have also relied on the account he gave to the committee on 23 July, in TS 27/522. His case is discussed by A. Masters in *The Man Who Was M: The Life of Maxwell Knight* (Oxford, 1984), ch. 8. The Home Office possesses material on his case but has refused me access to such of it as is of any interest, in spite of support from the Greene family. There is also closed material in LCO.

[26] Greene had 2 brothers and 3 sisters, one of whom, Barbara, was in Germany during the war.

Although for many years an active member of the labour movement, Greene's principal motivation was pacifism. As he explained in 1941:

As a member of the Society of Friends I am opposed to war and believe that everything should be done to obviate the causes of war. I have throughout the period between the two Great Wars expressed and propagated my convictions that the unrevised Treaty of Versailles carried in it the potentialities of future wars and I worked continuously to get this fact recognized.

He consequently disagreed with Ramsay MacDonald's policy of guaranteeing existing frontiers, and thus despaired of finding a place in Labour politics; for a while he became a supporter of Lloyd George.

Greene married in 1925, and joined his father's coffee business, working for a time in New Orleans. He returned to England, and in 1927 became managing director of his own small company, Kepston Ltd., in Berkhamsted. It made mechanical power transmissions for mills. Compulsively attracted to politics, he served for six years on Berkhamsted Urban District Council, and for two on Hertfordshire County Council. In 1937 be became a Justice of the Peace. He also re-entered national politics and became Parliamentary candidate for Gravesend in 1931 and 1935, where his opponent was Irving Albery, a wartime critic of 18B. He organized the local Labour Parties into district associations to provide unity to offset the union block vote, in particular by electing their own representatives to the Executive. This naturally annoyed the party bosses, who included Arthur Greenwood, Herbert Morrison, and Ernest Bevin. He also discovered mishandling of election fund contributions, and an obscure financial scandal.[27] The Executive of the party was then in his view dominated by communists and fellow travellers, and Greene left it in disgust, formally resigning in November 1938 after the Munich agreement, which he naturally supported. He had other quarrels with the party. In 1935 he had acted for the League of Nations as Deputy Chief Returning Officer in the Saar plebiscite. He returned to the Saar in 1936 for the Quakers to investigate stories of atrocities. 'I suggested on my return that a deputation from the Labour Party should go to the Saar and investigate conditions for themselves. This proposal was violently opposed by leaders of the Labour Party and was used to support a frequent accusation that I was a Nazi agent.'[28]

In 1938, according to his own account, he was asked by the Quakers to visit Germany and investigate the treatment of the Jews on *Kristallnacht*,

[27] Connected with 'the great sugar-beet scandal', which involved subsidies to this industry. Greene was proposing to ventilate the matter at the party conference in 1937.

[28] In Greene's affidavit. In his representations to the Home Office (Greene Papers, B/6) he records a visit to Germany in 1936 at the time of the Olympics, when he collected from the Anglo-German Fellowship translations of some of Hitler's speeches and other documents.

the 'Night of the Broken Glass', a pogrom organized by the Nazis after the murder of Ernst von Rath in Paris in November 1938. He found conditions appalling, and on his return he saw Sir Samuel Hoare at the Home Office, and Woburn House, about the establishment of a selective emigration scheme, to be operated in collaboration with German officials. Clearly such a scheme could be viewed as involving collaboration with the Nazis. He returned to Germany and, through John Scanlon, he came into contact with Herr 'Harry' Bohle, who put him in touch with officials in the German Propaganda Ministry.[29] But on his return to England 'the whole issue became political and in view of the storm of protests it was dropped'. It seems obvious from Greene's own account that he was entirely sincere, but that Bohle cultivated him as a person holding views which could be exploited. He saw Bohle again in February or March 1939 at John Scanlon's flat in London; Scanlon had been a sympathizer with the BU and possibly a member, and earlier an ILP journalist. He also had dealings with Jochen Bennemann or Beinemann, originator of the Anglo-German Circle, which organized camps for schoolchildren. Bennemann visited England in 1935 as leader of a Hitler Youth Group holding a joint camp with Berkhamsted Grammar School.

After leaving the Labour Party, and with the threat of war growing, his commitment to pacifism became more intense. He worked for the Peace Pledge Union, and made plans to start a Peace and Progress Information Bureau. He again visited Germany, and saw Bohle. In March 1939 he began to publish a periodical bulletin, the 'Peace and Progressive Information Service', which produced sixteen issues. Since this used German material, it could be viewed as peddling their propaganda. He began to associate indiscriminately with anyone opposed to war, including a group of maverick fascists, anti-Semites, admirers of Hitler and pacifists; Ben Greene was strong on sincerity, but very weak on discretion. Thus in 1938 Lord Lymington, an admirer of Hitler, formed the British Council against European Commitments in Europe, with Beckett and Joyce, both then running the fascist NSL. Lymington and Beckett started *The New Pioneer* in December. Ben Greene joined contributors to it such as Captain Anthony M. L. Ludovici,[30] and H. T. V. ('Bertie') Mills.[31] Then in 1939 Lord Tavistock formed the BPP, which

[29] Ernst-Wilhelm Bohle (on whom see WO 208/4442) was a friend of Rudolf Hess and Gauleiter of the Ausland Organization of the Nazi Party. Bohle was born in Bradford and educated in South Africa, where his father Herman was an engineering professor. He may have been called 'Harry' by English acquaintances, but the reference is more probably to his brother.

[30] 1882–1971. Ludovici wrote many books and was an expounder of Nietzsche's philosophy; he was essentially fascist, but not so far as I know a BU member, though he did belong to the Right Club. He lived in Ipswich and does not seem to have been detained during the war.

[31] See above pp. 142–4, Griffiths, *Fellow Travellers of the Right*, 322 and 325.

incorporated the Campaign against War and Usury. Ben Greene became Treasurer. The party primarily campaigned for peace, but its rag-bag of policies included 'the right to security and social justice', 'the abolition of a financial system based upon usury which perpetuates social and economic injustice and which foments warfare between classes and nations and the establishment of a system whereby British credit is made available for the welfare of the British people on the highest possible level of consumption', and 'safeguarding the employment and integrity of the British people against alien influence and infiltration'.[32] The party, as we have seen, put up H. St John B. Philby as a candidate in the Hythe by-election in 1939, supported by a group of fascists and admirers of Hitler.[33]

In December 1939 the BPP published *The Truth about the War*. It was 'Produced by the Research Department of the British People's Party', in reality by Greene himself. A copy was sent to Attlee, who was godfather to one of Greene's children. He wrote on 22 December 1939 to Greene's sister:

Thankyou for your letter. I have sent Paul a Panda for Christmas. I am so sorry I forgot his birthday. I have glanced through Ben's book. Frankly it strikes me as one of the nastiest pieces of pro-Hitler propaganda that I have met for a long time . . . I can understand the position of the genuine pacifist but I have no use for people who support Hitlerism. When you told me of the formation of your Party I said that I thought its whole tendency was Fascist. This book confirms my view. I think it would be better, if these are the views you and Ben now hold, that we should not meet.[34]

The most provocative aspect of the book was its account of the Polish crisis, which essentially blamed the Poles and the British government, rather than Hitler, for it. Even *Truth* attacked it as a 'dangerous book'.[35]

In his written statement for the committee Greene denied any substantial political activities since 1 November 1939.[36] But this was not entirely true; for example *The Truth about the War* was not published until December 1939. The BPP officially ceased to operate, but in reality simply changed its name, and Greene, as he admitted, attended a number of its meetings. On 25 February 1940 the *Sunday Dispatch* carried a piece by Charles Graves: 'These Men Are Dangerous'. It named Dr Meyrick Booth, then in Eire, John Beckett, St John Philby, Cola E. Caroll, Ben Greene, Captain Robert Gordon-Canning, and Professor A. P. Laurie as all adherents of Hitler, and mentioned Ben Greene's speech on 14 October 1939 at the first meeting of the BCCSE as 'nothing but the most naked German propaganda'. A police report of 30 May 1940 shows that

---

[32] Documents in the Greene Papers. The party also published the People's Charter, with rather different proposals.
[33] See above p. 216.   [34] Greene Papers, B/4.   [35] Issue of 8 December 1939.
[36] Statement to HM Secretary of State by Ben Greene, 4 September 1941 in TS 27/522.

Greene, on 14 March 1940, spoke at a meeting of the council attended by S. F. Darwin-Fox, along with Beckett.[37] He then said he was Treasurer of the London Regional Council. He also spoke at a meeting in March, giving the impression that the BPP was still active; he spoke of the danger of Jewish and American capitalists.[38] It is clear that Greene did not give up politics in 1939; he was quite incapable of doing so. It is also clear that Greene brought suspicion on himself both by his association with fascists and sympathizers with Hitler, and by his own passionate belief that the war with Germany had not been in any sense Hitler's fault. Indeed it is clear that as early as 1936 'a confidential source' reported, quite wrongly, that he was in Nazi employment.[39]

Early in 1940 the Lord-Lieutenant of Hertfordshire, Lord Hampden, raised the question of his suitability as a Justice of the Peace, and Maxwell wrote: 'The British Council appears to be an organization promoted by persons with pro-German and Fascist views, who got on to the council a certain number of genuine pacifists, some of whom are said to have subsequently dissociated themselves from the Council on discovering its Fascist tendencies.' Maxwell advised the Lord Chancellor's Department that he had at the moment no information which would justify removing Greene from the Commission of the Peace.[40]

The Detention of Ben Greene

From about January of 1940 Kell urged the Home Office to take action against the BPP, and both Greene's and Beckett's names, though curiously neither Gordon-Canning's nor Tavistock's, were on the list for detention on 22 May.[41] They were not BU members, but their inclusion was deliberate, MI5 assuming that the party would be covered by the new 18B (1A). Maxwell thought this was unnecessary; they could be detained under the ordinary 18B. Mrs Jenifer Hart, formerly as Miss Fischer Williams Maxwell's private secretary, later, in 1941, recalled that Maxwell thought there should be a note in the files saying why MI5 wanted them detained; she could not recall whether these notes were prepared before or after the orders were made. She could not say if Anderson ever saw them, but thought he did: 'it seems certain if my recollection of events is correct that he directed his mind to Greene's case personally'. Norman Brook, who was then private secretary to Anderson, also recalled that originally it

---

[37] In TS 27/522.

[38] Report in *Northants Evening Telegraph* for 29 March 1940.

[39] Police report in TS 27/522.

[40] LCO 2/1454. The Chief Constable had raised the matter in October 1939.

[41] Recollection of Anderson set out in a report of a conference on 9 March 1943 in TS 27/542, letter of 23 October 1942 from J. Hart in TS 27/522.

was thought they could be interned as members of the BPP, but 'it was found that it was enough to pull them in personally'.[42] The basis, he said, was 'the two statements against them', the reference being, as we shall see, to statements made by two MI5 agents.

Greene's order, which was for 'hostile associations', was signed on 22 May; the recommendation, but not the statement of its basis, is available.[43] Anderson's own recollection played down the importance of the MI5 agents.[44] After explaining Kell's earlier pressure to act against the BPP he went on:

A close watch had been kept on Greene and Beckett for a long time, and he knew all about them. When the emergency arose and Holland was run over, Sir John looked at the whole matter again . . . Greene, though not then a fascist, was that sort of person. Sir John knew all about him, and had quite enough against him to make an order without the allegation about contact with persons believed to be German agents. When the hour struck, orders were made . . . He never bothered about the agents and such stories.

Greene was arrested on 24 May. He heard that the police were looking for him and went to Scotland Yard; he later claimed that he thought the police wanted to see him over a report he had made to Scotland Yard about the odd behaviour of one of the two agents. His own account reads:

I had no copy of the detention order and I was not aware of the reasons of my detention. I was taken before the Governor of the Prison and he told me that I could appeal to an Advisory Committee but I had to hand in my appeal within three days. I said I did wish to appeal and later in the day was given a sheet of foolscap paper suitably headed but I had no means of writing on it. On the third day an officer came round and demanded my paper. There were only two ink pots and two pens for the 60 prisoners and I had not been able to get hold of either. This officer took me down into the cell used by prisoners for shaving and I had to address my appeal there and then under impatient threats of the officer that he could not wait. Other prisoners were actually shaving in the cell at the time . . . I had to address my appeal to the Advisory Committee in ignorance of what I was appealing about.[45] Three or four days after my appeal had been handed in I was given a copy of my detention order whereby I understood that the reasons for my detention was on account of hostile associations.

---

[42] Letter of 24/10/42 in TS 27/542.

[43] HO 45/25698/840166. 'Make order under Reg. 18B for internment of (1) Ben Greene on grounds of hostile associations (2) Beckett on grounds of having been recently concerned in acts prejudicial . . . '

[44] In TS 27/542.

[45] This is confirmed by an account by Edward R. Greene CMG, who saw him in prison, also in the Greene Papers.

The Basis for the Order

The 'Reasons for Order', dated 15 July, were drafted by A. A. Gordon-Clark, and erroneously said the order was for 'acts prejudicial'.[46] The particulars read:

1. As one of those concerned in the management and control of the British People's Party and the British Council for Christian Settlement in Europe you endeavoured in speeches and writings to persuade your auditors and readers that the war was being waged solely for the benefit of financial interests, and could and should be brought to an end by a negotiated peace; that British policy up to and after the outbreak of war had been a policy of bluff and treachery; and that Hitler was justified in his invasion of Poland.

2. You were privy to the activities of John BECKETT, alias John STONE, in the publication of pro-German propaganda in a periodical name 'Headline News Letters' and you have assisted the said John BECKETT in persuading the readers of the said periodical that the interests of the British Empire were not threatened by Hitler.

3. You were, subsequent to the outbreak of war, communicating and/or attempting to communicate with persons in Germany who you knew or suspected to be in association with persons concerned in the government of Germany; and you counselled, assisted and advised others as to the best means of sending messages into Germany by illicit channels.

4. You were, subsequent to the outbreak of war, desirous of the establishment of a National Socialist regime in Great Britain, with the assistance if necessary of German armed forces, and endeavoured to make known your sentiments in this regard to those in control of the German government.

5. You freely associated with persons of German nationality whom you had reason to believe were agents of the German government, and offered to assist them by every means in your power to avoid detention by the authorities in Great Britain and to continue their work on behalf of Germany.

6. There is reasonable cause to believe that, unless restrained, you desired and intended to continue the actions aforesaid and actions of a like nature.

The 'Statement of the Case' started by setting out what it calls 'Greene's official activities': his contacts with Bennemann, the Anglo-German Circle and camps; his work for the Joint Peace Manifesto, organized by the Peace Pledge Union; his approach in January 1939 to Bohle of the German Propaganda Ministry in connection with his Peace and Progress Information Bureau; his seemingly pro-German newsletters, including one setting out the ill-treatment of Arabs by the British police in Palestine; his correspondence in April 1939 with a Herr Hoffmann over obtaining the 'News from Germany' service; his recommendation in August 1939 of Mrs Anne Beckett to Bohle as a good shorthand typist for

---

[46] Later enquiries suggested that a Home Office official misled Gordon-Clark.

work in Germany. The document then dealt with the BPP. Just before the war Greene appealed for money for it 'in order to avoid war and bring about much needed social regeneration'; appeals were sent amongst others to a Fräulein Osterhild and Herr Paul Hopf, both being Germans who returned home before the war began. And on 14 October 1939 he addressed a meeting of the BCCSE, describing British policy as one of bluff and treachery; he sneered at those who said Britons could not trust Hitler, and declared that Hitler had been justified in all he had done; he used such phrases as 'those of us who admire him'.

As if this was not bad enough the document then considered

the far greater question of his secret opinions, actions and intentions . . . In March 1940, Greene came into contact with a young German named Kurtz, who had just been released from an internment camp. Kurtz gave him to understand that his sympathies were entirely with the Nazis, that he was working on their behalf, and that he was anxious to find some means of communicating with Germany. Greene showed the greatest sympathy with him, and gave him advice as to how to avoid being interned again, suggesting that Kurtz should give out that his views had changed since the invasion of Norway. He discussed with him methods of sending communications (which Greene must have believed or suspected to be messages for the use of the German authorities) to Germany by way of Ireland, or through the medium of one of Reuter's correspondents in Switzerland. He suggested that if Kurtz would make his way to Northern Ireland he, Greene, knew many disused roads over the border by which anyone could penetrate into Eire. He further asked Kurtz to tell his friends in Germany that there were 'men in this country ready to take over the government after a German victory, men trained in and filled with the proper spirit of National Socialism—a British National Socialism'. Greene also, according to Kurtz, said he was in communication with his sister, Barbara, the mistress of a high official in the German foreign service; she was about to be naturalized and marry him. Communication with her was 'in a very informal way'.

On 28 April, so MI5 claimed, Greene dined with Kurtz and met one Fräulein Gaertner (or Gärtner), another MI5 agent; he said that in a year's time German soldiers would be marching through London. Only National Socialism could save the British Empire. He stated that he had been persecuted for his views; it was necessary to build up an underground movement to conduct his peace campaign. Communication with Germany was again discussed—he suggested contacting his sister Katherine Gray, whom Kurtz had met; she was working in Beckett's office. Greene also said that he had recently seen a member of the SA in London, but took no steps to tell the authorities. Greene also mentioned a friend of his, Meyrick Booth, an ardent friend of Hitler— Kurtz must meet him when he was next in England. Kurtz should obtain a job in the Ministry of Information, as this would provide excellent cover.[47] Obviously if all this was true then Greene was both a fascist and a traitor. According to Greene, a report was made by him to the police of Kurtz's suspicious behaviour. The police denied this and, according to A. Masters in his life of Maxwell-Knight, the latter persuaded the police to lie about this. This may well be true.[48]

The First Advisory Committee

The committee (Chairman A. T. Miller) saw Greene on 24 July, and Greene explained his pacifist and religious views. The members were not impressed by his forgetting having attended a BCCSE meeting on 18 March, though immediately after the hearing Greene wrote saying he now recalled it. The committee had statements from the two agents, and in its report wrote:

The Committee expressed a desire to see and examine these witnesses in order to test their evidence, in view of the direct conflict between many of their statements, and the evidence given verbally before the Committee by GREENE himself. The Committee have however been informed by letter of 20 August 1940 from MI5 'that it has been decided by the highest authority here that in no circumstances will we consent to agents going before the Committee'.

The report was dated 30 August; the delay must have arisen because of conflict with MI5 over access to the agents.

The Greene papers contain an undated memorandum describing four meetings with the two agents. The first took place in Kurtz's flat in late March; Kurtz had written to Greene about 11 March attempting to set up a meeting. The second took place in April, again at Kurtz's flat. The third meeting, again at the flat, involved a dinner-party attended also by Fräulein Gaertner, and took place near the end of April. The fourth meeting, also involving Gaertner, occurred in May at a lecture given for the BPP in Holborn, after which Greene, Kurtz, and Gaertner went out to supper in a restaurant.[49]

---

[47] The statement Kurtz made for Greene's second legal action is much less dramatic. He then said that he met Greene through Ilse von Binzer, whom he had known at school, and who had worked as secretary to Herr Roesel, Gauleiter of the NSDAP in London. When he was expelled she worked for the Anglo-German Academic Bureau as secretary to B. A. Kunz. Maxwell-Knight told him that the authorities were interested in Greene and the BPP, and he wrote to Greene on 14 March. Greene and a Miss Moorhouse came to Kurtz's flat, where Kurtz gave the impression he was pro-Nazi, which did not seem to worry Greene. Later he met Greene's sister Katherine, alias Grey, and she praised Haw-Haw etc.

[48] Masters, *The Man Who Was M*, 157. A fifth meeting was arranged, but was cancelled by Greene.

[49] LCO 2/1454 contains a letter of 17 August from Jenifer Hart on the case: 'I understand the Committee has had some difficulty in coming to a conclusion in this case.' Maxwell must have become involved, and it is conceivable that the matter went to Swinton's committee.

In the event the committee could only scrutinize the statements, note how they corroborated each other, and note that MI5 vouched for their reliability:

they accept the statements as substantially accurate. They should state also that their view is that GREENE would not have been, and would not be, disposed in any circumstances to assist the German armed forces to defeat the British. GREENE expected the Germans to win, thought a German occupation of this country probable, and the Committee consider it likely that GREENE intended and planned to take advantage of the situation which would then arise. GREENE hoped and believed he might then find his opportunity to secure a position of influence for himself and to further his own peculiar political and religious views.

The conclusion was that: 'the Committee are unable to regard GREENE's assurances and promises as a sufficient safeguard, and accordingly recommend that the detention of Benjamin GREENE should be continued'. It is hard to see what other recommendation was possible.

Greene's own account of his appearance before the committee exists.[50] He noticed, when he received the 'Reasons for Order', that the order was now based on 'acts prejudicial'. Understandably he did not think this was a mistake; the particulars specified acts of treachery.

Five days after I received the communication from the Advisory Committee I was taken to my hearing without any warning . . . I had neither shaved nor had my breakfast . . . I was hurried down to the prison van but all my notes were confiscated and taken to Burlington Gardens where for the whole of the morning we sat downstairs in the dark room. Then I was given a piece of dry bread and corned beef. As soon as I had eaten this I was taken upstairs to the committee . . . I had no idea what the procedure of the Advisory Committee would be. I anticipated some kind of trial. I expected an officer from Scotland Yard or the Home Office to state the case against me and that I would then be given an opportunity to reply to it. I was rather bewildered at being made to sit in a chair in the middle of the room with the members of the Advisory Committee sitting behind a table some considerable distance away. I was asked by the chairman whether I desired to make a statement or whether I chose to be questioned. I asked at once what the evidence was on which these very serious charges were based and the chairman indicated that was why I was there. The procedure then adopted was that I was asked questions. I was asked where I was born, who my parents were and I was asked to give a complete picture of my political activities since 1920. No reference whatever to the actual charges was made in the first part of the hearing . . .

This dealt with his sister Barbara, his pacifist activities, and his Quaker beliefs; he said he knew the first name of Barbara's German friend but nothing else. By lunchtime the committee had dealt with the charges relating to his political activities.

[50] B/6. Handwritten memo drawn up some two years later.

After lunch he was asked about the three treachery charges, which he guessed were based on the evidence of Kurtz (though he did not at this time recall Kurtz's name).

Again to my astonishment I was given no indication whatever upon what evidence they were based. I merely formally denied them and it would have appeared as if that would have ended the hearing. It was quite clear that the committee had not accepted my explanations and they had made it clear that they did not believe in my truthfulness. I thought it was best to work on my theory that Kurtz to save his own skin had denounced me to the police and I thereupon told them my story of Kurtz as set out in another memorandum . . . [51] With regard to the charge that I was working for the setting up of a Nazi regime with the help of German armed forces, I could only deny this and no questions were asked and nothing further was said on this matter.

During the hearing Greene's German contacts with Hoffmann, Bohle, and Bennemann were also explored.

Greene returned to Brixton and spent the night on a bed which was too short and prevented sleep; he was six foot eight and a half inches in height. On his resumed appearance the next day he was in a state of sleepy stupefaction. He was taken through the charges one by one. He only found out at this stage that he could also make representations to the Home Secretary, which he did.[52] He later wrote: 'I felt very dissatisfied with the whole procedure and my weak position. The total absence of legal assistance, the total absence of evidence, documents or anything in the nature of proof. I felt that the confiscation of my notes was most unfair and the sudden last minute changes in my charges.'

Eventually, in October, Greene was told that his detention would be continued.

Greene's Dismissal from the Bench

He was to suffer a further indignity. Jenifer Fischer Williams informed the Lord Chancellor's Department of the decision, correctly saying that Greene was detained for 'hostile associations'. Schuster, who assumed it was for 'acts prejudicial', wrote a long memorandum for the Chancellor advising that he be removed from the Commission of the Peace. This conceded that: 'This is an example of a very difficult class of case. Greene has not been convicted by a court of law.' He summed up the matter by saying that 'the Committee appear to have found that Greene had entered into a conspiracy with the German government or their agents. Such a conspiracy, in time of war, appears to amount to treason'. On 10 October

---

[51] Handwritten memo in unlisted papers in the Greene Papers.
[52] Copy in Greene Papers, B/6.

Greene was told that the intention was to remove him. He protested in vain, refused a suggestion that he resign, and was removed on 8 November.

So Ben Greene, like Robert Liversidge, both viewed as important detainees, remained in Brixton. The administrative mechanisms for their protection had delivered to them nothing of value, and as the year 1940 drew to a close both had been driven to the conclusion that their only hope lay in an appeal to the judges, the traditional if unenthusiastic guardians of British liberty against the over-mighty executive.

17

The Leading Cases in Context

Actions for False Imprisonment and Smeaton-Stuart[1]

Liversidge claimed damages for false imprisonment; he did not apply for habeas corpus. His was not the first such action; Mosley, Ramsay, and the de Lange brothers had issued writs for false imprisonment, and Smeaton-Stuart, after release in November 1940, had brought such an action, and lost on 26 June before Mr Justice Tucker.[2] Since he was at liberty habeas corpus was pointless, and this explains in his case the choice of proceeding.

Liversidge was still in detention, but such an action, as well as leading to damages, had three potential advantages over habeas corpus proceedings. The first was that interlocutory proceedings, decided by judges or lower court officials, were possible. In them the defendant (and for that matter the plaintiff) could be required to give fuller information about the defence (or cause of action), answer questions about it, and produce relevant documents. No such proceedings were possible at this period in applications for habeas corpus.[3] The second was that whereas habeas corpus applications were normally dealt with by judges on the basis of affidavits, actions for false imprisonment were determined by a trial, in which the parties and others would go into the witness-box, and be cross-examined. It might even be possible to question the Home Secretary himself, either on paper in interrogatories before trial, or in open court at trial. The third was that although most civil actions were tried by a judge alone, it was possible to apply for a trial by jury, and a jury might be more sympathetic to a detainee who appeared hard done by than a judge. Hence actions for false imprisonment were extremely alarming to the authorities, raising the appalling spectre of Anderson, or Morrison, or both, being quizzed as to why they had detained the plaintiff. Where evidence is given by affidavit the lawyers control what is said, since they draft these devious documents; once a lawyer's client is in the box this control is lost.

---

[1] See above p. 205 et seq.

[2] TS 27/493, HO 45/25714, *Stuart* v. *Anderson and Another* [1941] 2 All ER 665. HO 144/21995 (Mosley and Ramsay).

[3] See R. J. Sharpe, *The Law of Habeas Corpus* (Oxford, 1989), 61 and 124–5.

Smeaton-Stuart's action asserted that his detention had always been unlawful, since the Home Office knew, or could reasonably have discovered, that he was not a danger; alternatively his detention became unlawful after 9 October, when, so he claimed, he had not been promptly released although his release had been ordered. There was some confusion as to when his release actually had been ordered. His lawyers did not fully exploit the possibilities of the form of proceeding selected; thus his case was tried by Mr Justice Tucker without a jury.

The strategy of the Crown lawyers was to resist Smeaton-Stuart's action by simply producing the detention order. This new strategy was adopted because the action, unlike a habeas corpus application, could not be resisted just by tendering an affidavit, and the only alternative would have been to offer to put Anderson in the witness box, and thereby open him to cross-examination. The only additional information put before the court consisted of two letters of Smeaton-Stuart, neither of which had been available when he had been detained, which tended to show him as a dedicated fascist. So the Crown lawyers' contention was that the production of an 18B order, which did not have to be in any particular form, *could*, by itself, be a sufficient answer to the action, discharging the burden of proof which, at law, rested on the defendant in such an action.

However, the lawyers knew that mere production of the order might not be a *conclusive* answer. The ruling doctrine at this time derived from *Lees*, which said that a court could investigate the basis for an order, so as to see if it was legal. Hence it followed that although producing the order put the ball back in the plaintiff's court, it did not necessarily remain there. If the plaintiff could present evidence to show that the power had not been exercised honestly and in good faith, or show a mistake as to identity, or a failure to follow the requirements set out in the regulation, or if the order had been made 'without the Home Secretary ever having applied his mind to one of the essential matters', then the ball would be back in the defendant's court. The Home Office would then have to present additional evidence—conceivably oral evidence from Anderson himself, or perhaps from Maxwell—to rebut such suggestions in order to win the case. In legal jargon the burden of proof would shift back to the Home Office. This was accepted by the judge as the right approach to the case. The Crown lawyers no doubt prayed that matters would never come to this horrific pass.

So Smeaton-Stuart's counsel made various attempts to shift the burden: the order was formally invalid, as an 'omnibus' order; it rehearsed alternative grounds for detention of the 345 individuals, indicating a lack of careful attention to each case; his client's character was blameless; he left the BU in 1937, so Anderson could not possibly have had reasonable cause to believe that he ought to be detained. All these arguments were dutifully rejected by Mr Justice Tucker, in the spirit of the Reading Presumption of Executive Innocence, but with difficulty, for *Lees*, the leading decision, had never even hinted that mere production of an order sufficed. Tucker particularly relied on a decision by the Court of Appeal, only five days earlier, in the Liversidge case, which was already before the courts. The Court had approved his own decision which supported the general refusal of the Home Office to show the courts the material which led the Home Secretary to make an order.[4] This made the claim that the judges were the protectors of liberty somewhat ridiculous; Tucker conceded as much in rejecting Smeaton-Stuart's claim: 'It is perfectly impossible to express any opinion as to whether or not, in a case of this kind, any injustice has been done to a particular man.' The practical outcome so far as Smeaton-Stuart was concerned was that producing the order won the action, but this might not happen in other suits. It all depended on the particular facts of individual cases; in a different case something more might be needed, especially if the judge was not so protective of the Home Office as Tucker.

Liversidge's Action

Liversidge started his action in March 1941. His counsel were D. N. Pritt KC and G. O. Slade. Pritt, a communist fellow-traveller, was at this stage in the war no doubt nervous lest the regulation be used against communists, and so very ready to be involved. By the time the action was decided his view changed; once Russia entered the war the CPGB was safe and Pritt became an enthusiast for 18B. Liversidge's solicitors were Buckeridge and Braune, Braune having been himself a detainee in both wars. The lawyers attempted to exploit the possibilities of an action for false imprisonment in interlocutory proceedings. The fact that Liversidge, unlike Smeaton-Stuart, was a wealthy man, may have helped in what must have been very expensive proceedings. Slade supplied the Crown lawyers with the 'statement of claim', alleging that Liversidge had been detained under what merely purported to be an 18B detention order. The Crown set out its defence, which conceded that Liversidge had indeed been detained under an 18B order, signed by Anderson. The plan was to defend the action simply by producing the order, and quoting the regulation.[5]

For Liversidge's lawyers this was not enough; they objected to this 'concession' and did not accept that there was an 18B order in force. They could not tell whether Liversidge was lawfully detained under a valid

---

[4] *Liversidge* v. *Anderson and Morrison* [1941] 2 All ER 612, decided 12 June, upholding Tucker's decision on 23 May.

[5] Arguments below the Court of Appeal are not reported.

order unless they were told the grounds upon which the Home Secretary had 'reasonable cause to believe' that Liversidge was 'of hostile associations', and needed to be controlled. So they applied for an order that Anderson should disclose particulars of the grounds upon which he had come to his belief. To be sure Liversidge had been provided with the 'Reasons for Order', but of the eight allegations, six were plainly irrelevant to a 'hostile associations' order, so fuller information was needed.[6] The application came before Master Moseley, who refused it.[7] There was an appeal to Mr Justice Tucker, who upheld Master Moseley. An appeal was then taken to the Court of Appeal, comprising Lord Justices MacKinnon, Luxmoore, and du Parcq; they rejected it. Their decision faithfully accepted the logic of *Lees*—in *some* situations a court might go behind the order. All that they decided was that at this early stage in the litigation no order for disclosure would be made. If, later in the action, the evidence tended to show that the order might be invalid, the burden on the defence might not be satisfied by simply producing the order—'in a proper case, the judge might at that stage make some order by way of particulars of the allegations of the defendants'.

From this decision Liversidge's lawyers, unwisely as it turned out, appealed to the House of Lords, and this appeal was considered in tandem with that of Ben Greene, whose application for habeas corpus had been turned down by the Court of Appeal on 30 July.

Greene's Habeas Corpus *Application*

It was Ben's brother Edward who obtained Hickson's services as solicitor; neither the family solicitors, nor his uncle's, would help. But someone suggested Hickson:

I went to see him. He rather reminded me of a character out of Dickens; big fellow, huge fellow, hair standing all on end. I told him what I came to see him for. First questions was, 'Well, why is he being detained?' I said, 'I don't know, not does Ben.' 'Nonsense, you must know; there must be some reason behind it.' 'No' I said, 'we do not know, although I must be fair and say that Ben had, before the outbreak of war and subsequently, made, with the advantage of hindsight, some rather foolish statements, publicly and privately.' Hickson hesitated a long time; at last he said, 'All right, I'll see what I can do.' He thereupon wrote to the Home Office, and demanded the reason for Ben Greene's detention. I think it was in July [i.e. of 1940] that these [i.e. the 'Reasons for Order'] were given to him. There were eight conditions. Hickson called me up at the office, and said 'You must come immediately, I have got the reasons for Ben's detention.' When I saw them I

---

[6] By way of alternative to a request, which was rejected and is not here discussed, to strike out para. 3 of the defence on a technical ground.

[7] An administrative officer with some judicial powers.

was horror-struck, and said that if there is any foundation of truth in any of these charges, why is he in Brixton Prison, not on trial in the Old Bailey? Hickson said, 'Exactly; that is my opinion too. Now if you agree and Ben agrees, I will write to the Public Prosecutor and demand an immediate trial.' This he did. Within a week we had a reply: 'Nothing doing'. They refused.[8] Hickson thereupon said, 'All right, something smells. We will get down to this.'[9]

Hickson's next action was to write to the committee protesting at the failure of the 'Reasons for Order' to particularize the allegations—for example they did not say who the persons were whom Greene was said to have believed were agents of the German government. He was not at this point successful.

The application for habeas corpus was first made to the Divisional Court on 25 and 26 March, and eventually argued before Justices Humphreys, Singleton, and Tucker on 2 May 1941. Greene's counsel was J. W. Williamson, but Greene wished to argue his own case, and the court, surprisingly, allowed this.[10] The application was peculiarly embarrassing to the Home Office because of the error which had been made in the 'Reasons for Order'. In the Sabini case there had been criticism of the Home Office, and about this time the officials must have known or suspected errors in a number of other cases, though the scale of the problem may not yet have been appreciated.[11] In addition Greene was well connected, and known in political circles, and the allegations were peculiarly grave. Since agents were involved it was vital that no disclosure be made to the court, lest the agents, one of whom was involved in the 'double-cross' operations, be compromised; in any event public revelation of the use of *agents provocateurs* might well cause political trouble.

In its turn the Divisional Court was becoming nervous about a possible rash of applications for habeas corpus from the 800 or so remaining detainees. Conceivably the Lord Chief Justice had been told of preparations being made by many of them on the Isle of Man. At the resumed hearing he said:

I desire to say this. It must not be assumed that anyone who is detained can come to the Court and expect his application to be treated in the same way as if the matter had not been discussed by the Court of Appeal [that is in the Lees case] . . . it might become a farce if everyone who was detained was put in a position to come and call for an affidavit by the Home Secretary.

Greene only got a hearing because his affidavit suggested that the regulation itself was *ultra vires*, a point never raised in *Lees*, and one which, in the event, was never pursued.

[8] This refusal was repeated on 20 June 1941.
[9] Conversation of 2 July 1979 in Greene Papers.
[10] Transcript in TS 27/522. Normally counsel must appear.
[11] Budd won on 27 May, and Campbell's case was then pending.

Greene supported his application with two affidavits. The first gave an account of his life, which, he argued, showed that Anderson could not possibly have believed that he had engaged in 'acts prejudicial'; it made no point about the error in the 'Reasons for Order'. His second affidavit was a reply to one sworn by Anderson, which admitted an error had been made; this did claim that the error prejudiced him, and raised a number of other objections to the way he had been treated—for example it said that he had never been given a copy of the order. But his central argument was that the court could enquire into the basis for his detention, and the court, given the *Lees* decision, could hardly dispute this: 'Mr Justice Humphreys. I must point out that you have been told at least half a dozen times that nobody will dispute in this Court that we have the power to enquire. In the first case which came before the Court, Lees, it was specifically agreed by the Law Officer of the Crown who appeared. So do not argue that.'

Greene suggested that the court could sit in camera, if need be in his absence, to do this:

My point is this, that this court has power to call on the Home Secretary to produce all the evidence upon which he acted and, if necessary . . . it may be that I should have to be excluded. It may be in the national interests that I should not know who the informants against me are. I have no means of knowing, but the court can judge.

This sensible suggestion produced alarm on the bench, concealed by judicial huffing and puffing: 'Mr Justice Humphreys. Are you suggesting that the court . . . would decide a case in the absence of and without the knowledge of the person concerned? If so you are putting forward something which is quite foreign to my mind. I should be very sorry to be a member of such a court.' Greene, whose alternative was the committee, said he was indeed suggesting this, adding, 'I personally prefer the decision of the Court.' Humphreys had no reply.

The Crown lawyers relied upon the order itself, but also put in affidavits from both Anderson and Morrison. The former followed the stereotyped form employed in Lees's case, but went on to admit the error in the 'Reasons for Order', and to claim: 'I am unable to say how the error occurred in the document.' This statement was essentially dishonest; the Home Office knew perfectly well that Gordon-Clark had produced an erroneous document, but there was some reason to suppose that he had been misled by a Home Office official who had not been identified; an honest affidavit would have explained this. It then added: 'The error was an error in the statement of my reasons for making the order and there is no error in the particulars. I submit that the error cannot have prejudiced Mr Greene as he had a copy of the detention order, as he admits in his Affidavit.'

In argument the Attorney-General said that the Home Office accepted responsibility for the error, but claimed it was not possible to discover how it had come about. This was again wantonly misleading; indeed in the course of argument Mr Justice Singleton pointed out that it must be possible to discover who had drawn up the particulars. In the course of the argument the Attorney-General made a number of muddled, misleading, and possibly dishonest statements to the court, one of which indicates that he, at least, knew then that MI5 was drafting the particulars:

We have tried, and we have failed to discover the individual, but what undoubtedly happened was that some individual, whom we have not been able to trace, getting the particulars from those who made those investigations and so on, and drawing up the form which then goes, I am not sure it would be to the Advisory Committee—it would probably be to the Home Office. . . . the Chairman of the Advisory Committee has, before the hearing, to inform the objector of the grounds. Now the Chairman, of course, has to get the grounds from the Home Office; he does not know. Therefore the document giving the particulars emanates from the Home Office.

Later, in response to a comment from Singleton, he did say that 'What happens is the particulars come in from a certain source', which was a reference to MI5, an institution then not to be named amongst Christians. But the court clearly gained no idea of how the system operated, and Somervell never explained the system clearly to the judges. On balance I think he thought it better for them not to understand, and in effect deceived the court; there is other evidence that he was capable of rather unscrupulous behaviour.[12] However, in fairness to him, there is a dishonest practice in the Civil Service of not passing on information to individuals who are better kept in ignorance. They can then deny knowledge of embarrassing facts without actually lying. Conceivably the system was never clearly explained to Somervell by the Home Office officials; if so his ramblings might have been the product of mere incompetent confusion. It seems, however, extremely unlikely that Holmes did not understand.

The error was again considered in conferences connected with litigation by Greene in March 1943. Anderson said that Home Office responsibility for the error should never have been admitted in Greene's case in 1941; he took no responsibility for MI5, which was a department of the War Office. The 'Reasons for Order' were the responsibility of the Chairman of the committee. At another conference the view was taken that MI5 were the servants of the Home Office in matters concerning Regulation 18B, and as they drafted the document, the Home Office was responsible. The notes of these conferences do not shed any clear light

---

[12] See above p. 301 and below p. 379.

on how much the Crown lawyers understood in 1941, though a certain confusion is evident.[13]

The court refused Greene's application, simply accepting the Home Office affidavits as true. But the judges took a serious view of the error, and repeated the remarks made in the Sabini case. But Greene, in their view, had not been prejudiced: 'It is quite obvious that this is no case of an illiterate cowman or agricultural labourer; it is the case of an educated gentleman who had had the advantage of being at one of our great universities, and who is, as he described himself, I think, a polemical politician.' Much was made of Greene's knowledge of the error when he appeared before the committee; in reality he understandably thought the Home Secretary had changed the grounds for the order to 'acts prejudicial'. The court recommended—it could not order—that he be given a new hearing before a different committee.

After the hearing Somervell wrote to Morrison about the case, saying that if Greene had not argued it himself the unsatisfactory features of the matter might have been made clearer. On the error he wrote:

As I submitted and Mr Justice Humphreys accepted there was a good deal of overlap [i.e. between 'hostile associations' and 'acts prejudicial'] and it may be that there was no prejudice in Mr Greene. In form, however, I think it must be recognized as gross carelessness that in a matter affecting the liberty of the subject, the investigation should proceed on a ground different from that of the order.[14] . . . I sometimes feel that in the calm atmosphere of the court the difficulties of administration may not be fully realized. I think however that at any rate in the present emergency judges are very alive to these difficulties, but when the liberty of the subject is in question they will undoubtedly demand the greatest legal attention to the safeguards provided by the regulations.

Given the record of the courts it is difficult to understand this conclusion. Somervell's letter is extremely odd in one respect; it says nothing at all about the system which produced the error. One cannot but suspect that he avoided putting anything in writing on the matter, and my feeling is that the silence in this letter tends to confirm his guilt in the affair.

The Offer of a New Hearing

The Home Office naturally took up the judges' suggestion of a new hearing, and a new 'Reasons for Order' was served on Greene, with the error

---

[13] The Beckett file (TS 27/542) has a note of a conference of 9 March 1943: 'Sir John Anderson said that the particulars were particulars of the Reasons, not particulars of his beliefs . . . it was for the Chairman to make up his mind what Particulars he communicated to the detainee. Sir John took no responsibility for the substance or form in which the Particulars were presented.'

[14] Letter of 5 May 1941, HO 45/863004/17.

corrected.[15] Hickson responded by requesting a trial for the criminal offences alleged, which was refused, and better particulars of the allegations.[16] Jenifer Hart, now secretary of the committee, initially refused to provide these, no doubt on instructions, but on 12 July relented. The habeas corpus application was still pending, for Greene had appealed to the Court of Appeal; the Crown lawyers thought they were more likely to win if Greene, unlike most detainees, had been given a really fair chance to defend himself before the committee; winning the action took precedence over other considerations. The amended particulars named some of the persons Greene was said to have tried to communicate with—his sister Barbara, Fräulein Ilse von Binzer and Herr Roesel, specified dates for the speeches and writings alleged, and, most surprisingly of all, named the two agents as Harold Kurtz and Fräulein Gaertner or Gärtner. These names were provided because of strong pressure brought to bear on Sir David Petrie, the new head of MI5, by the Attorney-General and Treasury Solicitor.[17] The further particulars confirmed Hickson's suspicions that the gravest accusations derived from Kurtz.

Kurtz had also made contact with Edward back in January, apparently in an attempt to compromise him too, and had also called on him after Ben Greene had been arrested.[18] Attempts were made through Searle's detective agency to locate him, but these did not succeed until 21 October, which was after the case had been argued before the House of Lords. Hence they played no part in the legal outcome of the case.

Greene in the Court of Appeal

Hickson declined the offer of a new hearing until his habeas corpus case was concluded. His appeal was heard by Lord Justices Scott, MacKinnon, and Goddard, on 15–16 July. On 30 July it was rejected.[19] The leading opinion in the case was delivered by Scott, whom we have already met as Chairman of the Committee on Ministers' Powers and a friend of the executive, and both he and Goddard adopted an approach to the case which departed radically from *Lees*. Whereas in *Lees* it was laid down that a court could, in suitable circumstances, investigate the reasonableness of the Home Secretary's belief, they now took the line that

---

[15] There were other minor changes; para. 1 now read: 'You were born of a German mother, and your sister has remained in Germany since the outbreak of the war, either being married or engaged to a German official, who either is or has been working for the Germans.'

[16] Letters of 13 and 20 June between Hickson and the DPP.

[17] Letter of Petrie of MI5 to Maxwell, 6 January 1942. SH para. 103.

[18] Letter of Edward Greene to Hickson (24 July 1941), Greene Papers, B/12. Kurtz also contacted Ben's mother. Edward Greene's flat was also searched by the police; he was associated with the BPP.

[19] [1942] 1 KB 87.

he was the final judge in the matter. So long as the Home Secretary honestly thought someone should be detained under the regulation, and the right person was arrested, that was the end of the matter. Hence unless the good faith of the Home Secretary was challenged, the production of an 18B order was all that was normally required to win a case. Somervell had invited the court to take this line, which entailed overruling *Lees*. The two judges argued that since the Court of Appeal in that case had only been concerned with costs, its approval of Humphreys' opinion had been unnecessary (in legal jargon *obiter*, 'by the way'), and was thus not binding on the Court of Appeal. This view changed what was then understood to be the legal position over detention orders; its authors were both by disposition strong supporters of the executive. Goddard had, however, been a member of the court which had approved Humphreys' opinion in *Lees*. The third judge, also a member of that court, did not take this line.

The House of Lords' Decisions

The Crown lawyers presenting the case to the House of Lords took up the position suggested by the opinions of Scott and Goddard, and abandoned the theory which the Solicitor-General, Jowitt, had presented in the Lees case. They no doubt did so because of the alarming risk, in actions for false imprisonment, of orders being made for discovery of documents, and of the cross-examination of the Minister at the trial.

The Scott–Goddard theory, which seemed to surround Home Office decisions with an impenetrable wall of secrecy, was adopted by the majority of the House of Lords, which delivered judgement in both Liversidge's and Greene's appeals on 3 November.[20] An order could only be impugned before the courts by showing that the Home Secretary had acted in bad faith—in practice something virtually impossible to prove—or by showing mistake as to the person arrested. Nor was it even necessary for the Home Secretary to swear an affidavit as to his belief; it would be presumed from the fact that he had made the order. In Liversidge's case this meant that he was not entitled, in connection with litigation in the courts, to be given any information at all about his detention; this would bring before the court material which it had no business to investigate. In Greene's case too the production of a detention order alone was sufficient to defeat the application. The majority of the judges interpreted the regulation as giving the Home Secretary, rather than the courts, the final say over detention.[21] In non-technical terms the Law Lords ruled that it was not for the courts to

---

[20] *Liversidge* v. *Anderson* [1942] AC 206; Liversidge's case was argued on 18, 19, and 22 September. *Greene* v. *Secretary of State for Home Affairs* [1942] AC 284; Greene's case was argued on 23–4 September. See generally G. Lewis, *Lord Atkin* (1983) 132–157.

interfere with the executive in security matters in wartime. They washed their hands of responsibility in the matter.

In a very strongly worded opinion Lord Atkin dissented in Liversidge's case, and as a result suffered some considerable degree of ostracism from his colleagues. The row was even ventilated in the pages of *The Times*.[22] He had, he said, 'listened to arguments which might have been acceptably addressed to the Court of King's Bench in the time of Charles I'. His opinion has come to be celebrated by lawyers as a sermon on the liberty of the subject, but, as I have argued elsewhere, Lord Atkin's passion was inspired not by any special commitment to liberty, but by concern over the relative status in the scheme of government of judges on the one hand, and officials and ministers on the other. His attitude was driven by the same concern for status as that of the other 18B dissenter, Stable. Claud Schuster back in 1929, writing of the conflicts between the Civil Service and the courts, explained them in a similar way as the product of a sort of jealousy, though he does not use the word, and thought the judges were mistaken: 'the deeper and more under-lying truth seems to be that Judges, however subconsciously, desire to retain and obtain for the judiciary problems more fit for executive decision'.[23] But neither Atkin nor Stable went so far as to wish to decide detention cases themselves; they did, however, wish to retain a role in the business sufficient to maintain the superior status of the judiciary in the scheme of government.

Atkin's opinion is quite unconvincing, for it fails to explain with any clarity at all how the supervisory role of the courts was to operate, granted the right, which he conceded, to withhold information of a confidential character. Like the other judges involved he had no idea how the system was operated, and he made no attempt to develop a jurisprudence under which the courts, whilst not usurping the functions of the Home Secretary and his committee, supervised both their procedures and the interpretation placed upon the regulation, providing thereby some protection for detainees. All that he seems to have wanted was for the Home Office to exhibit deference to the judges by being a little more forthcoming about the basis for detention orders. It is ironic that Liversidge's detention was a case in which there was abuse, albeit understandable abuse, of the regulation.

---

[21] For legal discussion see Sharpe, *Habeas Corpus*, 100–8.

[22] See R. F. V. Heuston, '*Liversidge* v. *Anderson* in Retrospect', *Law Quarterly Review*, 86 (1970), 33, and '*Liversidge* v. *Anderson*: Two Footnotes', *Law Quarterly Review*, 87 (1971), 161. After the decision his principal opponent, Lord Maugham, wrote to Churchill poohpoohing critics of the decision, but suggesting detainees should be legally represented before the committee (letter of 14 November 1941 in PREM a/39/4A). In discussions with him and the Attorney Birkett opposed this; see SH para. 165.

[23] LCO 2/1133. My argument is presented in 'Rhetoric, Reality and Regulation 18B', *Denning Law Journal* (1988), 123.

After the Lords' decisions attempts to challenge detention in habeas corpus proceedings became largely futile, but desperate attempts were made by Pitt-Rivers, Beckett, Luttman-Johnson and Vaughan-Henry.[24] Pitt-Rivers's order was attacked as bad on its face, since it did not recite the necessity for controlling the detainee, and because Pitt-Rivers, never at any time associated with the BU, could not be detained by an 18B (1A) order. Both arguments were rejected; the order was ruled good on its face and in consequence the second point could not be investigated. Almost incredibly Lord Caldecote found place in his opinion for the traditional judicial humbug on the liberty of the subject:

Nothing I have said must for a moment be taken to detract one iota from all that has been said by many judges about this historic writ, so jealously guarded and adapted to provide swift and effective remedies in cases of the unlawful invasion of any man's personal liberty. It is just as much a part of the law today as it was in the seventeenth and eighteenth centuries.

Out of him and his colleagues was however squeezed, like blood out of a stone, the dramatic ruling that a written order was essential if detention was to be lawful.

Beckett applied for habeas corpus in April 1943 on the ground that there had been a mistake. Morrison, in a statement in Parliament on 26 November 1941, had enumerated the categories of persons still detained in a way which did not cover Beckett. The application was dismissed on 17 May; courts take no notice of statements in Parliament. An appeal was withdrawn, since he had been released in October.[25] As we shall see, Luttman-Johnson's application was never pursued. Vaughan-Henry applied for habeas corpus and mandamus; his application was refused by the Divisional Court, comprising Humphreys and Cassels, on 3 February 1944. He had originally been arrested under Regulation 18D on 10 June 1940; this permitted temporary detention when a person's identity was in doubt or his presence in a particular place was suspicious. As Vaughan-Henry was in his own home with a brass plate on the door, this arrest was illegal. An 18B (1A) order had been made on 17 June, though he had left the BU in 1935, and in addition a 'hostile associations' order was served on 30 December 1940, since the main case against Vaughan-Henry was his Nazi contacts and sympathies. His case depended in part on his original unlawful arrest, and his counsel, Harold Brown, also argued that he had been given inadequate particulars; the court should make an order (mandamus) that adequate ones be provided. The court briefly ruled that it

[24] See TS 27/514 and *The Times*, 5 December; *R. v. Brixton Prison (Governor) ex parte Pitt-Rivers* [1942] 1 All ER 207; *The Times*, 30 August, 29 November, 2 December, and 19 December 1941; TS 27/533.
[25] *Parl. Deb.* HC 376: 376, 848–9.

had no jurisidiction to go into these matters since he was in custody under two valid 18B orders; he had been given the particulars as required by the regulation. Apparently his case had been before the committee on numerous occasions. He was probably released in late 1944.

The Release of Liversidge

As for Liversidge, his action probably delayed his release, for he was needed in Brixton to create a leading case; however, as late as July of 1941 the RAF still wanted him to be detained. Once the case was won, the views of MI5 and of the Air Ministry were sought, and by 9 November, six days after the Crown had won the right to keep him locked up, it was established that nobody actually wanted him locked up. However, since he had asked for another hearing on 25 October, the day on which he was told he had lost his case, Birkett's committee conducted a charade on 4 December. The same day release was recommended; he was in fact set free on 31 December. One of the minor forms of heartless official behaviour was to be in no hurry even after release was certain.

The report of the committee added:

The committee feel that this is a case where Liversidge should now be released at once. They all entertain the gravest doubt that his detention on the ground of hostile association could ever be substantiated. But now that the real ground of the detention is removed, it is obvious that the only course is . . . immediate release . . . The committee really never had entertained any doubt about the essential loyalty of Liversidge.

The report also emphasized Liversidge's strenuous denials of business frauds, and the absence of any evidence which rebutted these denials. Liversidge made an unsuccessful attempt to secure compensation, and was given an interview at the Home Office, on condition there was no discussion of the reasons for his detention. This simply protected the Home Office from trouble; no security interest whatever was involved. Having failed in the interlocutory proceedings, he did not pursue his action, which never came to trial. He wanted to return to the RAF, but the RAF would not reinstate him. In 1943 an official, presumably from the Home Office, saw him riding in Rotten Row and queried why he was not engaged in war work. His health had suffered badly, and he was declared medically unfit; in the event he joined the Fire Service. Lord Selkirk, his former commanding officer, had a high opinion of his abilities, and about this time offered him work with Transport Command, but this offer came to nothing. So he continued his multifarious business activities, becoming an extremely wealthy man. In 1947 accusations were made against him before the Lynskey Tribunal; he was a friend of John Belcher, the minister who fell from grace over the affair. The report goes out of its way to exonerate Liversidge of any misconduct whatever. Over forty years later he remains distressed over his treatment, for which he never received a word of apology. It is hard to blame him.

The Trapping of Harold Kurtz

Ben Greene was more persistent, and the sequel to his case began when Harold Kurtz was located on 21 October.[26] After Ben's arrest Kurtz had approached his brother Edward, saying he had known Ben, and had just been released from a camp in the Isle of Man. They met twice, and Kurtz tried to set up Edward Greene by getting him to supply letters to Germans to help Kurtz start a new life in Brazil; he said he was going there, and had a visa. Edward suspected Kurtz, checked, and found no visa had been issued. He informed Hickson, who said: 'My God, if you had given him those letters, you would have been in gaol within five minutes. Obviously a trick.' When the further particulars arrived Hickson asked Edward to locate Kurtz. In October 1941 he met Kurtz by chance outside the Café Royal and asked him to lunch in Simpson's on 21 October. At the end of this lunch,

Kurtz said to me, 'By the way, how is your brother's case? How is he getting on?' I said, 'We're very puzzled by the whole thing. We've come to the conclusion there had been some misunderstanding in the Home Office, and it has to do with Ben's work on behalf of the Quakers in regard to the Jews.' I said, 'Just struck me, by the way, that you might be able to help. Now if you can spare me a few moments, I will see if Hickson is in his office and perhaps you would care to come round with me.' He hesitated a moment and said, 'All right.'

Edward pretended to ring Hickson who, by previous arrangement, was waiting.

There was Hickson, sitting behind a big desk; on his left was a secretary and in the other corner sat a clerk. Kurtz and I came in; Hickson stood up, then said, 'Mr Harold Kurtz, my name is Oswald Hickson, Solicitor. I am acting on behalf of Ben Greene, who is detained under Defence Regulation 18B, and I want now to read you the charges under which he has been detained.' I noticed Kurtz had begun to sweat. He read these charges, and said, 'Now,' picking up another, 'we have been told these charges are based on a report made by one Harold Kurtz. Is that you?' Kurtz got very excited, jumped up, and said, 'This is a trap; I refuse to say anything more. I want my solicitor.' 'All right, who is your solicitor?'—He gave a well-known name.[27] 'I will ring him up right away,' Hickson said. 'No,

---

[26] What follows is based on material in the Greene Papers.

leave it; I'll deny everything.' Hickson said, 'Sit down', and thereupon dictated a memorandum, saying exactly what happened, and that Kurtz had denied making these charges. He signed those and gave a copy to Kurtz, who then left.[28]

Three days later, as had been agreed, Hickson delivered this bombshell to the Home Office, where no doubt it caused both consternation and perhaps some pleasure in view of the department's running conflict with MI5.[29] Kurtz reported on the incident to MI5, and on 23 October Petrie wrote to Maxwell enclosing Kurtz's statement and Hickson's memorandum, explaining Kurtz's 'withdrawals' as a desperate reaction to the predicament in which he was placed and, in the spirit of the pot calling the kettle black, strongly criticizing Hickson for adopting dirty tricks.[30] Whether all this was conveyed to the Attorney-General is wholly obscure, and if it was it is not obvious that he would have had any obligation to inform the Law Lords, who had already heard argument; as we have seen, the loss of the appeal was communicated on 25 October, though the opinions were not delivered until 3 November.

Greene's Second Hearing

On 3 June 1941 S. H. Noakes of MI5 had produced a new 'Statement of the Case', not substantially different from the original one, and this, together presumably with the information about Kurtz and MI5's reaction to it, was available when Greene appeared for a second time before the committee on 11 and 12 November.[31] The committee also saw Hickson on the 11 November, Edward Greene on 14 November, and, contrary to normal practice, both Kurtz on 14 and 17 November, and Maxwell-Knight, now a Major, on 5 December.[32] The other agent, Fräulein Gärtner, or Fredericka Stottinger, who was an important double agent, did not appear.[33] The report of the committee, dated 16 December,

[27] Sir Robert C. Witt of Stephenson, Harwood and Tatham. Brief to Counsel, Greene Papers, B/17.
[28] Kurtz did not himself sign.   [29] Copy in the Greene Papers
[30] TS 27/522.
[31] Birkett, Cockburn, Mrs Eveline Lowe, Mr W. Stott.
[32] A letter from Petrie to Maxwell of 6 January 1942 in TS 27/522 indicates that there had been some other occasions on which agents had appeared.
[33] The name Stottinger was used in a statement for Greene's second action, and was her maiden name. Her name by a marriage which took place before she came to England was Gaertner or Gärtner. Her elder sister Lisa (also Lisi and Liesel) also came to England in about 1937 and worked as a floor show dancer at the London Casino. Friedl, according to Joan Miller, *One Girl's War: Personal Exploits in MI5's Most Secret Station* (Dingle, Eire, 1986), 86–9, 153, was sent to England as a German agent, and her name does appear in records associated with the surveillance of pro-German groups before the war. She became the double agent 'Gelatine', her case officer being William Luke. N. West, *MI5* (London, 1983), 250, 258, 305, has her as Friedle Gaertner, aged 27 (in about 1939), Gelatine ('pretty

pointed out that the gravest allegations against Greene depended solely upon the word of Kurtz.

Harold (or Harald) Kurtz, alias Court, alias Courtenay, was born on 2 September 1913 in Stuttgart[34] and was the grandson of a member of the Don (or Don Wauchope) family, Sir John Douglas Don-Wauchope Bt. or, according to Maxwell-Knight, Sir William Don Bt. of Yorkshire.[35] He came to England on holiday in January 1937 whilst a student at Geneva University, and decided to stay, supporting himself with private money, work for a bookseller, and as private secretary to Lord Noel Buxton. He also worked at the Warburg Institute as assistant to Professor Witkoffer.[36] In 1938 he met Maxwell-Knight, and became a salaried agent. On 6 January 1939 he was in touch with Domvile and Pitt-Rivers.[37] Between November 1939 and 8 March 1940, and again from June to November 1940, he was interned as a stool-pigeon. Kurtz was, like Maxwell-Knight, a homosexual, in those days something which invited a risk of blackmail; he also wanted to be naturalized, as he was after the war, and this too no doubt gave Maxwell-Knight a hold over him. Kurtz's main problem was a tendency to live beyond his means, coupled with a craving for drink, which became progressively worse. Although he was a witty and highly intelligent person, he was, I am told by those who knew him, a not very reliable person. Later in the war he worked for the BBC; he was a translator at the Nuremberg trials, and was employed to record the dying words of the Nazi war criminals incompetently hanged by the American executioner, an assignment which did not improve his drink habit. After the war he lived in Oxford, scrounging off his friends, who seem not to have resented this failing; he established something of a reputation as a writer with *The Trial of Marshal Ney* (1957), and *The Empress Eugenie* (1964). Those who then knew him as a historian were

little thing') to MI5 and Ladymay to the Germans; she posed as pro-Nazi to infiltrate German front organizations. J. C. Masterman, *The Double Cross System in the War of 1939 to 1945* (New Haven, Conn., 1972), 86, 96, 109, 138, 140, 149, 176, has her as originally an MI5 agent, and then a double agent. Friedl married an American diplomat in about 1945, and Lisa married Ian Menzies, the brother of the head of MI6. Both are still alive.

[34] Death certificate Oxford, 2 January 1973, recording his death on 20 December 1972. There are obituary notices by Christopher Sykes, J. M. Rogister, and Lord and Lady Longford in *The Times* (23 December, 1 and 2 January. Kurtz's parents were alive in 1941 living in Munich, his father, a publisher, being a Nazi supporter. He had an older brother in the German Civil Service and a younger brother who was probably in the German navy; another brother may have been a Jesuit priest. Amongst other informants I am indebted to Dr Albi Rosenthal, the antiquarian bookseller, who was a friend of Kurtz, though one who fully appreciated his faults. Kurtz tried to recruit Dr Rosenthal for MI5, but failed.

[35] 1859–1951 and 1861–1926.

[36] He had an apartment at 147 Ebury Street. According to Joan Miller this was a boarding-house run by Madame and Miss Titoff; there also lived there another agent, a German Jew and son of a judge who had come to England in the early 1930s, and had a cover job in the BBC.

[37] DOM 55.

entirely unaware of his earlier work for MI5. He died, ultimately of drink, in Oxford, and in his declining days, so I am told on impeccable authority, stole to support his habit.

Birkett's committee formed an extremely unfavourable view of Kurtz, who now denied that he had ever given Ben Greene the impression that he was a German agent. It concluded he was completely unreliable: 'The Committee are profoundly dissatisfied with the evidence of Kurtz. They do not think it is evidence on which they ought to rely.' It is possible that Birkett was particularly irritated because he knew of other cases in which Kurtz's evidence had, in deference to MI5, been relied upon; Kurtz may well have been the agent involved in the Domvile case, and was also involved over Beckett.[38] The report also by implication criticized Maxwell-Knight for adopting unreliable procedures in recording Kurtz's evidence; again there may have been other cases.[39] So far as Gaertner was concerned, they could not accept her written statement without seeing her.[40] In consequence the committee concluded: 'they desire to say in the plainest terms that Greene is entitled to be acquitted of these terrible allegations [ie those of treason], not merely because the case is not proved . . . but because they also believe the evidence of Greene.' As for the other allegations about Greene's open pacifist and political activities the committee accepted the substance of MI5's account.[41] They thought he was in no way disloyal, and accepted his assurances that he would do nothing to hinder the war effort, and keep clear of John Beckett and the Duke of Bedford. There was no need to detain him; he should also be freed from the allegations of treason.

The report was analysed by Newsam, who recommended that Greene be released:

This case illustrates vividly the possibility of injustice being caused to persons who are detained wholly or mainly on the evidence of agents employed by the Security Service and the desirability of ensuring that information supplied by such persons is subjected to the closest examination. This matter ought to be taken up urgently with the Security Service.[42]

Two days later Petrie wrote in tones of outrage to Maxwell urging that Greene's detention be continued, and condemning the whole tone of the report. He particularly objected to this passage: 'If the practice of one's calling necessitates the habit of lying, it is not to be wondered at if the

---

[38] See above p. 139.
[39] Kurtz's report to Maxwell-Knight consisted of an undated statement written some time after 30 April, which was taken down in shorthand and subjected to minor amendments. For Greene's second action Maxwell-Knight said the original handwritten reports of both Kurtz and Gärtner were destroyed in the first invasion scare.
[40] Permission must have been refused.   [41] Those in paras. 1, 2, 6, 7, and 8.
[42] Memo of 4 January in TS 27/522.

evidence one gives in grave matters is looked at with special care.' He pointed out that 'officers employed on security duties often have to live a life which is a complete "lie", but do so from the highest motives, and often at risk of their lives. The same may be said of agents.' Kurtz he thought entirely reliable; he deeply regretted the fact that Hickson had ever been given his name.

The Home Office was not impressed, and on 9 January the decision was taken to suspend the order.

Greene and the BPP (BCCSE)

But this decision was complicated by its relationship to those of two other members of the BPP, Beckett and the Duke of Bedford. Beckett remained in detention, whilst the Duke, as we have seen, had never been detained at all.[43] MI5, relying in part on the evidence of Kurtz—operating as Mr Courtenay—had believed him to be pro-Nazi, to be a self-confessed member of the Fifth Column, to have been trying to make contacts in the services, and to have been in touch with agents of the German government, supplying them with lists of reliable British Fifth Columnists. This was back in June 1940 when the myth was believed in MI5; no doubt Kurtz supplied what was expected of him.[44] Beckett had been detained for 'acts prejudicial' at the same time as Ben Greene.

Beckett appeared before the committee on 10 July 1940; the committee responded to MI5's refusal to let Kurtz appear by ignoring the allegations of contact with the enemy, and the case against Beckett was reduced to his political activities in opposition to the war. With some misgiving the committee recommended his continued detention, plainly being influenced by his instability and his association with Joyce, who by 1940 was public enemy number one. The recommendation was accepted, and when the case was reviewed in October 1941 and again in December 1941 the same recommendation was made. But it was difficult to see any great difference between Greene's case and Beckett's, more particularly because the graver allegations against Beckett depended principally upon the evidence of Kurtz.[45]

Indeed Maxwell thought the cases of the Duke of Bedford, Beckett, and Greene were much the same, but in the event Greene went free, his release being authorized on 9 January 1941; the Duke remained free; and the unfortunate Beckett, detained solely for his propaganda against the

---

[43] See above pp. 211–2.

[44] MI5 report in TS 27/542 and the 'Statement of the Case' of 1 June 1940 by A. A. Gordon-Clark.

[45] There was also evidence from P. G. Taylor, the BU industrial adviser and an MI5 agent. In a further review in April 1943 release was recommended by a committee presided over by Morris, but this was rejected in August 1943. Beckett's order was suspended on 26 October 1943. He remained restricted until the end of the war.

war, spent two more years in detention.[46] His release was opposed by MI5, for whom G. R. Mitchell argued that if it was wrong to detain under 18B for mere propaganda quite a number of detainees were wrongfully imprisoned. Thus Arnold Leese of IFL was detained for 'acts prejudicial' and the 'particulars' provided to him stated: 'The said Arnold Spencer Leese was Director General of the Imperial Fascist League, a pro-German and Fascist organization and in that capacity was responsible for the propaganda produced and disseminated by the League against the prosecution of the war and the Allied cause.' As we have seen, there were other borderline cases.[47]

The Home Office did not simply release Greene. On 16 January Maxwell formally withdrew the charges of treason. Hickson's reaction was not as expected. For the purposes of the habeas corpus proceedings Anderson had sworn that there was no error in the 'particulars' (which contained the allegations of treason) provided originally to Greene, but only in the 'grounds' (that is the reference to 'acts prejudicial' rather than 'hostile associations'). Hickson naturally took this to mean that the Home Office now admitted misleading the courts:

we look upon it very seriously that the Treasury Solicitor allowed an affidavit to be prepared in his office and deposed to by a minister of the Crown containing statements which are now withdrawn. The matter is the more serious because the Divisional Court, the Court of Appeal and the House of Lords all accepted the affidavit of Sir John Anderson as true and founded the decision upon that affidavit.

This caused consternation. Considerable care was therefore devoted to constructing a reply, and the combined efforts of the officials produced something of a masterpiece of equivocation. This explained that Sir John's affidavit had been accurate when sworn, and was quite unaffected by the withdrawal of the treachery charges. There had been no error in the particulars 'because this part of the document correctly set out the information which, in the opinion of the Chairman of the Advisory Committee should—in accordance with para. 5 of Defence Regulation 18B—be given to your client to enable him to present his case to the committee.' Anderson's affidavit, this letter claimed, had thus never asserted the particulars were, or ever had been, true.

Behind the scenes a memorandum from the Treasury Solicitor's office crisply pointed out the absurdity of this letter at the time:

1. Home Secretary must have 'reasonable cause to believe' etc.

2. That belief must obviously be based on grounds which the Home Secretary believes to be true.

---

[46] Memo of 28 May 1943 in HO 45/25698 by W. Lyon.
[47] Letter of G. R. Mitchell of 6 May in HO 45/25698.

3. The Chairman is required to inform the objector of the 'grounds' with 'particulars' etc.

4. The grounds must be the 'grounds' mentioned in 2 above. Does it not follow that the Home Secretary must have believed in the truth of the grounds and particulars given by the Chairman? And shall we not be forced to admit this?

But more Jesuitical counsels had prevailed. Hickson was outraged, and the letter may have encouraged him and his client to make a desperate attempt to secure redress by further litigation.[48]

Greene's Second Action

So in March 1942 Greene sued for damages for libel, for which the claim was hopeless,[49] and false imprisonment. The claim for false imprisonment was based on Anderson's order on 22 May. Before the case came to trial in April 1943 there were elaborate interlocutory proceedings.[50] The Crown lawyers succeeded in confining the issue in the case to one simple question: 'The only thing which in this action can be discussed will be when Sir John Anderson said "I have reasonable cause to believe", was he lying and was it the fact that he did not believe anything of the kind? Unless the Plaintiff can prove that he fails.'[51] So the chance of success was a slim one indeed. Greene had to present his case in such a way as to convince the jury that no honest person could, in May of 1940, have possibly thought that he should be detained.

In order to have any chance Greene needed to prise out of Anderson as detailed a statement as possible as to what was in his mind when he made the order, and what information and reports it was based upon; whatever answers were given could then be made the subject of cross-examination at the trial. What had to be shown was Anderson's bad faith, but this in law included acting recklessly without, as it were, caring whether the order was justified or not. Juries do not always apply the strict law, and I suppose that Greene might have won if the jury had thought Anderson merely silly to have detained him.

So the lawyers concocted a long list of elaborate questions, probing into

---

[48] He also tried, without success, to be reinstated as a Justice of the Peace.

[49] The libel was based on the publication of the 'Reasons for Order' to the Lord Chancellor's department, the committee, and prison officials. It was quite hopeless since Hickson did not know who had drawn it up (in fact A. A. Gordon-Clark of MI5), who had sent it to the Lord Chancellor's Department (in fact Miss Jenifer Williams, now Mrs Hart), nor if any prison official in Brixton had ever read it. The Crown lawyers of course resisted disclosing any of this information, as they were legally entitled to do, and in any event this communication within government was itself privileged, and outside the law of libel. In effect it was abandoned.

[50] My account is simplified.

[51] Lord Clauson in the Court of Appeal, 22 July (Lord Greene MR and Lord Clauson) in the Greene Papers, B/27.

the reasons why Anderson had made the order, and what information he had possessed at the time. Similar probings had been made and refused in Liversidge's case; the Lords there ruled them irrelevant to any question the court might properly consider. However, in Liversidge's case bad faith was not in issue; it had never been alleged. Here it was; and, under a well-established legal doctrine, lack of a reasonable basis for a belief could, in law, be *evidence* of bad faith. It followed that questions relating to the reasonableness of Anderson's beliefs were relevant, and not excluded by the Liversidge decision. The interrogatories consequently caused extreme anxiety to the Crown lawyers: 'any answer to such interrogatories as these would open the way to cross-examination and it might be difficult to refuse to answer interrogatories in other cases or even in previous cases which might be re-opened'.[52]

The trickiest probed into the basis for Anderson's beliefs. In the hearings before the committee, and in the documents supplied to Ben Greene, the principal reason for detention had been the evidence of treason from Kurtz and Gaertner. But Anderson explained to the lawyers that back in May 1940 when he made the order: 'I had no information before me of any communication between the plaintiff and either Kurtz or Fräulein Gärtner. I was informed at the time that the plaintiff had recently been in contact with a man who he had every reason to think was a German agent; but I was not given, nor did I seek, any information about that man.'[53] Anderson's practice, as we have seen, was to take a general view of the sort of person the proposed detainee was; he did not delve into matters of detail.[54] But if it had come out in court that the Home Secretary had been signing detention orders without bothering to investigate the details of each case, there would surely have been a public scandal. As he himself said in a conference on 9 March 1943, 'He never bothered about the agents and such stories—*but that could hardly be put before the Court* [my italics].' Possible suits by other detainees, whose files, in hundreds of cases, had never even passed over the Home Secretary's desk, must surely have caused further nightmares to the Crown lawyers.

They succeeded in reducing the number of questions from twenty to a mere seven, and of these two dealt with the hopeless claim for libel. After a tortuous discussion between Anderson and the lawyers it was decided to answer the more innocuous questions, and refuse to answer the others on the basis of a direction to Anderson from the now Home Secretary, Morrison, that answering them would be contrary to the public interest.[55]

[52] Instructions to counsel in TS 27/522.

[53] Memo of 24 February 1943 for counsel by Norman Brook.

[54] Considerable efforts were made to find out precisely what had taken place in May 1940—for example Jenifer Hart gave her hazy recollections of the matter; it had of course been a busy time, and nobody really knew.

[55] Memo of a conference at the offices of the Lord President in TS 27/542.

In fact the interest involved was exclusively that of the Home Office in concealing how the system had operated. Anderson was also able to resist the production of numerous documents on the essentially absurd ground that since he was no longer Home Secretary he no longer had custody of them, as if he could not have asked his colleague Morrison to oblige.

Anxiety must have been enhanced when the maverick Mr Justice Stable ordered a trial by jury, and Hickson issued subpoenas against, amongst others, the Lord Chancellor, David Lloyd George, and Norman Birkett.

The memorandum prepared for Crown counsel reflects a ruthless determination to win the case; thus of Kurtz it says: 'this man was a trusted agent of the Security Service and is still a trusted agent . . . It is a little obscure why the second Advisory Committee appears so determined to discredit Kurtz.' MI5 were happy for him to appear, but very concerned over Gaertner, alias Stottinger; Ian Wilson of MI5 would bring her to court to appear as Fräulein Schneider or Miss X.[56] MI5 had two other unidentified agents, thought by Greene to be his friends, in readiness; Petrie was also determined to win the case.[57]

In the event Greene's action, which came before Mr Justice Lawrence and a special jury on 8–9 April 1943, collapsed, and was withdrawn on the second day.[58] Greene, who was a poor witness, was presented as a blameless pacifist, whom no reasonable person could believe to be 'of hostile associations'. In cross-examination the Attorney-General had no difficulty in showing that his political activities, both before and during the war, could easily be viewed as showing support for Nazi Germany, and in fact had been so viewed by others. As his brother Edward Greene explained in a conversation in 1979:

Ben, I am sorry to say it, but he was very, well, I can only say, very stupid in some of his utterances . . . I went to see Ben, and we had a long talk and I said, 'Ben, you must get out of this political activity, it is not going to do you any good.' And he hummed . . . but in the end he did; he resigned from the British People's Party; but the damage had been done.[59]

Kurtz was then called as a witness and took his revenge on Hickson; he withdrew his withdrawal, and it became clear that he would repeat his original account of treasonable conversations. Since he was Greene's own witness, his evidence would have to be accepted by Greene's counsel; in litigation you cannot challenge the evidence of a witness whom you have

---

[56] Probably a solicitor in civilian life, David Ian Wilson. An Ian Wilson appears in West's *MI5* as a solicitor recruit to MI5 who ran agents, in particular Dusko Popov, 'Tricycle'.

[57] Report of a conference of 27 March.   [58] Transcript in TS 27/522.

[59] Greene Papers, unlisted, record of conversation of 2 July (present E. R. Greene CMG, Dr F. Greene, E. P. C. Greene, Ben's son, J. T. Munby, T. H. N. Rodrigues, and Mrs Edward Greene) with comments by Mrs L. von Goetz, Ben's daughter.

yourself called just because it turns out to harm your case. If Fräulein Gaertner was called she would presumably support Kurtz. So after an adjournment Greene's counsel withdrew the action. Costs of £1,243 were awarded against Greene, and proceedings were begun to make him bankrupt, but these were abandoned.

Greene never really seems to have recovered from the whole affair; he became obsessed with the idea that he was the victim of persecution, and thought his internment had been the consequence of a plot against him involving the leaders of the Labour Party.[60] A document in the Greene Papers claims that after the war he met a person who had been in MI5, and had interviewed him in Brixton. This person apologized for what he had done in connection with his case, and said that a letter underlying Greene's cross-examination had been forged by MI5; it is impossible to confirm this story, or identify the MI5 officer.[61] But a reading of the transcript of the case makes it obvious that such a forgery would have made little difference to the outcome.

Ben Greene continued to be involved in politics, and to associate with persons of the far right. He apparently left the BPP and formed his own English Nationalist Association,[62] which merged with a neo-fascist group known as The National Front After Victory, formed in 1944.[63] He came to think that fascism was a Marxist bogey; he also developed the idea that the British constitutional system was a disaster; his political views seem to have become increasingly unstable. He died in October 1978. Though in a sense he brought his troubles on himself, it is difficult not to feel sympathy with an individual whose idealism turned him into a victim of Regulation 18B.

Greene was not the last desperate former detainee to turn in vain to the courts. In addition to Beckett's and Vaughan-Henry's applications Thomas Wilson, a War Office clerk detained on 17 April 1940 for 'acts prejudicial'—he was suspected of passing information improperly to a third party—tried in 1943 to have Anderson committed for contempt of court, and also claimed damages. Wilson, who may have been an MI6 agent,[64] had been detained in error—he was released on 9 September 1941 conditionally, and the condition had been removed in December. In July 1940 he submitted a petition to the High Court, which was passed to MI5; an officer, probably one of the lawyers, decided not to send it on. He was

---

[60] His brother in 1979 referred to his persecution mania.

[61] Greene Papers—'The Great Betrayal'.

[62] It is possible that this was the organization he was suspected of being involved with at the time he began his second action; there is a reference in the instructions given to counsel. According to the Duke of Bedford's memoirs Greene at the time of his detention had already formed another organization distinct from the BPP.

[63] See R. Thurlow, *Fascism in Britain: A History, 1918–1985* (Oxford, 1987), 241–2.

[64] See above p. 335. Access to papers in LCO 2/2709 has been refused.

also denied access to a solicitor in August 1940—possibly whilst in Latchmere House. The Home Office conceded that his petition had been improperly kept from the court by an official, but declined to identify who it was, thus making it impossible for Wilson to proceed against him. The judges were not likely to lock up the Lord President of the Council, and his suit predictably failed; the Court of Appeal ruled it had no jurisdiction in such a case, it being criminal in character. In February 1943 he wrote to *The Times*, which applauded the decision under the ridiculous headline *Nulli Negabimus*,[65] bitterly complaining of the lack of remedy, and the fact that he had been ruined by legal costs.[66]

The Outcome of the Lords' Decisions

Although Greene's second action showed that even after the Lords' decisions of November 1941 there remained some risks to the authorities, the outcome of the Liversidge case was generally highly satisfactory to them.[67] What was in issue for the executive was not so much civil liberty, which the Home Office favoured, as open government, which it opposed. This was neatly put in a letter of 3 September by A. C. Newman of the Treasury Solicitor's Department to Kendal: 'the value of a judgement in our favour in the House of Lords would be that we could avoid in the future this probing into reasons in cases in which it is embarrassing to give them'. Liversidge's case was just such a one. His case raised similar issues to *Duncan* v. *Cammell Laird*, an action for negligence arising out of the loss of the submarine *Thetis* on trials in 1939.[68] The submarine incorporated a number of design features which the Admiralty wanted to be kept secret—for example the external torpedo tubes, particulars of the Asdic and wireless, and the fact that all oil fuel was carried inside the pressure hull. The Crown wanted the case to be tried in camera; the lawyers for the plaintiff would not agree, so the Crown claimed privilege for many of the documents involved, and the House of Lords upheld the power of the Crown to withhold the documents in litigation on the ground of public interest, essentially at the Crown's own discretion. The Liversidge decision, in which official secrecy was not necessary to national security, produced much the same result over detention by another route. If the Lords had ruled that the courts had jurisdiction to

---

[65] From Magna Charta—'to no man will we deny right and justice . . . '

[66] See *The Times* for 9 October 1942, 19, 26, 29 January, 6 February 1943; C. K. Allen took part in the correspondence. Some reading between the lines is involved; one can only guess at what was in the affidavits from remarks by the judges in the brief report. Two closed files exist on this case: HO 45/25708 and LCO 2/2709.; I have recently been refused access to the latter. SH para. 141 has further detail and tends to confirm that Wilson had been a spy. The name of the official was in the end revealed.

[67] See below pp. 398–9, for a suit over the conditions of imprisonment.

[68] [1942] AC 642. There is much material on this case in TS 32/101–17.

review 18B orders, the Crown could still have refused to place reports and other documents before the judges in litigation.

The official claim was that secrecy was in the public interest and, as we have seen, the authorities consistently refused to provide detainees with information on this ground, though in litigation the Crown would always change its tune and provide information if this was thought to help to win the case, as happened in Sabini's and Greene's cases. The Crown would even identify an individual Civil Servant if this helped their case, though, as in Wilson's case, the individual would not be identified if the Crown was not going to benefit.[69] The most unscrupulous release of information took place not long after the Liversidge and Greene decisions in habeas corpus proceedings brought by Luttman-Johnson.[70] These had been adjourned to await the Lords' decisions; Luttman-Johnson's brother had sworn an affidavit that he was a loyal person, and there were probably other supporting affidavits. On 5 December Gerald Gardiner appeared before the Lord Chief Justice, sitting with Hilbery and Asquith, to inform the court that he did not propose to proceed further with the application. Apart from the question of costs, which the Crown was awarded, there was nothing further to be done. But Valentine Holmes proceeded to inform the court that 'there seems to be a widespread belief that persons detained under the regulation were deserving of sympathy' and, with of course the consent of the three judges, cynically set about the task of blackening Luttman-Johnson's character by selective use of material from his dossier. He read out passages from an affidavit which had been sworn by Anderson (and no doubt drafted by himself) which suggested that Luttman-Johnson had not tried to obtain war work, and from a letter, written at some point during the phoney war, to a German woman friend. This letter had been obtained after the order had been made, and the passages quoted by Holmes could well be taken to show that Luttman-Johnson's sympathy for Germany amounted to disloyalty, though his counsel did his best to explain that if the letter was read in context it was wrong to read it in this way.[71] It seems extraordinary that Holmes, having only just before been engaged in convincing the House of Lords that information about the reasons underlying a detention order should not be disclosed to the courts, should now go out of his way to present such information to the judges in a case in which it was wholly

[69] The identity would be known.   [70] *The Times*, 5 December 1941.
[71] Luttman-Johnson was obsessively anti-Bolshevik, and could see no difference between German and Russian behaviour over Poland. In 1939 he saw no need for a war with Germany, a country he liked and admired. His counsel explained that his views had changed since the phoney war ended, and my own reading of his surviving letters and diary suggests that he held views typical of numerous other 'fellow travellers of the right' and was entirely patriotic. He must have convinced the committee of this since he was released in 1942, but his Home Office file no longer exists. SH para. 125–6 deals with the incident.

irrelevant to any issue before them, and even more extraordinary that the judges permitted this abuse of legal process to take place.

No doubt Holmes acted on instructions, and the aim of the exercise was political: to discourage other detainees, and quieten critics of the regulation. For the Lords' decision in *Liversidge* was also a source of some embarrassment to the Home Office. It appeared to say that the Home Secretary possessed an entirely uncontrolled power to detain anyone he wished, and it also seemed to many to deprive the change made in Regulation 18B in 1939 of all practical significance. If the decision was correct then Parliament, it was argued, had been misled. The Home Office officials investigated the matter, and managed to convince themselves of the contrary, though Jowitt, as Solicitor-General and participant in the consultations in 1939, had assured the court in Lees's case that there was a power of judicial review. There was demand for a debate, and on 10 November Churchill raised the matter at the War Cabinet; he had to reply to a question asking whether the government intended to change the regulation to conform to the opinion of Lord Atkin. He proposed to say 'No', adding an assurance that the power of detention would be abandoned as soon as possible; it is clear that his own view by now was that 18B should be abolished, but he bowed to Morrison's wish to retain it. The possibility of detaining the Duke of Bedford was at this time before the Cabinet, but a decision was postponed, no doubt in the light of the coming debate.[72] The matter was again discussed by the War Cabinet on 20 November, and Morrison said that he intended to say that the power of detention was still necessary, though it would be given up as soon as possible.[73] He was satisfied that the inclusion of the words 'reasonable cause to believe' was not intended to give rise to any power of judicial review, which would greatly hamper him in his duties.

Not everyone was convinced and, as we have seen, any misunderstanding was entirely the fault of the Home Office.[74] There was extensive correspondence in the press, and on 26 November the matter was raised by Sir Irving Albery and Commander Sir Archibald Southby in debate in the Commons. Southby claimed that he and others had thought that some form of review by the courts on the reasonableness of decisions had been introduced by the change in the wording of the regulation, though not an appeal on the merits. Not being a lawyer he would be unskilled in the subtleties of the matter. Spens, who was a lawyer, never thought any question of judicial review was intended or raised at the consultations, but he never attended.[75]

---

[72] CAB 65/20 WM (41) 115 of 17 November.   [73] CAB 65/20 WM (41) 116 5.

[74] *Parl. Deb.* HC Vol. 367 c.776 ff. See above Ch. 4.

[75] See also the remarks of Earl Winterton, *Parl. Deb.* HC Vol. 367 c.788–9 (26 November 1941). Earl Winterton imagined he had been there. I suspect some other meeting of members took place at which 18B was discussed.

The Attorney-General and Morrison defended the government. Some play was made of the fact that the committee was now chaired by a High Court judge; Birkett had been conveniently appointed to the bench shortly before the debate. Somervell's speech was disingenuous; he had somehow to counter the argument that the changes made in 1939 seemed to have made no difference. So he claimed the words 'have reasonable cause to believe' were inserted in 1939 to emphasize—as if before it had not been thought necessary—that the Home Secretary must give personal attention to each decision; he knew of course that in the summer of 1940 nothing of the sort happened, and in any event the distinction was legal nonsense. But the House was not divided, and the government weathered the storm.[76]

After the decisions Lord Simon, who had not sat on the appeals, wrote an unattractive and silly memorandum for Churchill on the subject; clearly he had been somewhat shaken by the vehemence of Lord Atkin's dissent. After reminding Churchill of the 'glorious' record of the judiciary on the liberty of the subject he argued that it was 'the acme of absurdity' to suggest that the decision over Liversidge made light of fundamental liberties, and ridiculous to suggest that it approved the methods of the Gestapo and the concentration camp. The reality was that the decision had nothing to do with wide questions: 'It is a decision about the correct meaning and application of half a dozen words in a Defence Regulation.' With unconscious contradiction he went on to argue that a wider matter was indeed involved: the whole constitutional structure would collapse if 'judges when called upon to interpret a regulation went outside their province and attempted to control government policy'.[77] And as if to give final confirmation to the view that there is no limit to the hypocrisy of which lawyers are capable he delivered a broadcast on 27 April 1942 contrasting the state of affairs in Germany with that in England, where there existed

a fifth freedom without which no country could truly claim to enjoy liberty. That was the freedom of every citizen, however poor, however uninfluential, however unpopular, however wrongheaded, to appeal to the law and the Courts to protect him from injury or insult, even though the wrong was committed by the misuse of official power. In this country the writ of habeas corpus had not been suspended.[78]

---

[76] For discussion in the press see in particular letters in *The Times* on 5 November 1941 from Albery, arguing that the Home Office ought now always to accept recommendations from the committee; on 7 November from Gerald Gardiner, arguing that the Law Officers were now claiming that the change in the regulation in 1939 had made no practical difference; and on 20 Nov. from Richard O'Sullivan, arguing that it had.

[77] PREM 4/39/4A, Memo of 13 November 1941.

[78] *The Times*, 28 April 1942. Similar rubbish is found in Scott's opinion in the Court of

Indeed it had not, but to the 18B detainees it is hard to see what difference it would have made if it had been.

Appeal in Greene's case (*The Times*, 31 July 1941: 'The liberty of the subject was only one degree less important than the safety of the nation . . . the subject's right to habeas corpus has not been abolished. It remained untouched in the war . . . '. More realistically, Sir William Jowitt in his *Some Were Spies* (London, 1954), 15, conceded that habeas corpus was suspended, and called this, and detention, a 'harsh and hard procedure'. Eric Gibb, a Director of the Economist, prepared a BBC talk on the controversy, but this was cancelled through Home Office and Ministry of Information pressure as not being impartial and accurate. This provoked protest in Parliament where the whole text was read out. See SH para. 150, *Hansard* Vol. 37618 December 1941 cols. 2189–223. It is difficult to see why the authorities were so excited.

18

The Declining Years of Regulation 18B

The Later Detainees

Although most orders were made in 1940, quite a few were made in later years—sixty-six in 1941, twenty-nine in 1942, fourteen in 1943, and five in 1944. A few names are discoverable, such as Thomas Hubert Beckett, detained in 1943 after serving a sentence for improper possession of plans.[1] Some suspended orders were reactivated,[2] and a number who escaped were recaptured.[3] Prominent amongst Morrison's detainees were Cahir Healy, a Republican member of the Ulster Parliament, earlier detained from 1922 to 1924,[4] a Canadian journalist, Erland Echlin, detained from March 1941 to September 1943,[5] and former Squadron Commander Frederick J. Rutland DSC, AM. Former fellow detainees connect him with the Kent affair. Echlin was London correspondent for a number of Canadian papers, and at one time for *Time* and *Newsweek*. On release he was required to remain in London. It seems likely that he fell foul of the authorities through attempts to get to the bottom of the Kent affair.

'Rutland of Jutland's' case was very peculiar.[6] He was detained about 15 December 1941 as a suspected Japanese agent. A distinguished pioneer of naval aviation, his nickname derived from his presence at the Battle of Jutland. In 1933 he became a paid agent for the Japanese government on naval aviation. In June 1941 he was in the USA when one Itaru Tashibana

[1] HO 45/25752. Also Leslie. J. Harrison, John Tedesco, Dennys C. Wace, and Guiseppi Mariconi.

[2] HO 45/25115; 6 cases including Evoy, D. H. Rose (HO 45/25733 and 283/59), A. Marson (HO 45/25736 and 283/49), and Edna Munn alias Harris (HO 45/25752).

[3] A. L. Mason (twice) and J. C. Preen; HO 45/25752.

[4] *Parl. Deb.* HC Vol. 373 c.2110, 7 August 1941. He refused to appeal. See also 374: 2040 ff Healy (1877–1970) represented Fermanagh South. Order dated 8 July 1941.

[5] HO 45/25115 and 45/25752 (arrived Brixton 3 August 1942); 1943 *Parl. Deb.* HC Vol. 387 c.1794; *New York Times*, 8 Mar. 1941, 12 Sept. 1943, 4 Sept. 1951 (obituary). The Luttman-Johnson Papers suggest release in Mar. 1943. His daughter visited England recently in an attempt to discover why her father was detained. He protested against the committee's procedures. His order appears to have been revoked in 1944.

[6] HO 283/60, HO 45/25105; *Daily Telegraph*, 26, 29, 30 August, 9 September 1960; D. Young, *Rutland of Jutland* (London, 1963; written before the Home Office files were released).

was arrested for espionage. The FBI said they could bring grave charges: 'It was agreed that the public prosecution in the autumn of 1941 of a British Squadron Leader on a charge of espionage against the United States would cause an outrageous scandal and must gravely damage British Interests and that the best solution to a highly embarrassing situation would be to send Rutland back to this country.' The US authorities may not have wished to reveal at a trial that they had broken the Japanese 'Purple' code, intercepts being the evidence against him. Rutland returned to England, and offered to become a double agent. He said he had taken money from the Japanese, but done nothing wrong in return. But his offer was rejected and he was detained for 'hostile associations'. The attack on Pearl Harbor took place on 7 December, and the battleships *Prince of Wales* and *Repulse* were sunk by aircraft on 10 December; there is no documentary evidence, but he may have been suspected of giving advice on these attacks, and this was hinted by Admiral Keyes in a debate on 21 July 1942.[7] His release on 20 December 1943 suggests that he was exonerated. Rutland committed suicide in 1949, and his detention belatedly aroused public comment in the 1960s.

Another disagreeable case was that of Duncan A.C. Scott-Ford, a young merchant seaman who supplied information about convoy sailings to German agents in Portugal for money.[8] He was detained under 18B on 24 August 1942 at the request of 'Buster' Milmo of MI5, to be interrogated in Latchmere House and persuaded to reveal accomplices. The Home Office gave permission for one week only, not for as long as it took Milmo to 'bust' him. Hinsley and Simkins record that he made a full confession, but say nothing about accomplices. He pleaded not guilty. He was tried in camera and sentenced to death 'without any emotion at all' by Birkett J. under the Treachery Act on 16 October 1942. Conceivably he was offered his life for information, but had none. The selection of Birkett as trial judge cannot have been an accident. Given the critical state of the Battle of the Atlantic in 1942 his treatment was understandable, if illegal. He was executed in November, by when two other British subjects, four Germans, two Dutch, one Swiss, and one Belgian had suffered the same fate.

The Release of the Fascists

But after 1940 the main task was suspending or revoking orders already made. Once the Home Office won the dispute with MI5 over BU

[7] *Parl. Deb.* HC Vol. 381 c.1475; Keyes had obviously been informed about the background. There is an FBI file, but at the time of writing I have not yet seen a copy because of processing delays.

[8] HO 45/25763, Hinsley and Simkins, 337, note his interrogation but not the move to Latchmere House; see PCOM 9/2121.

detainees about 450 could be released.[9] By the end of 1941 only 200 BU detainees were still in detention; this dropped to just over 130 in April 1942, and remained constant to the spring of 1943.[10] The number of Anglo-Italians fell to between 150 and 200 by November 1941. The number of other detainees who were of British origin (some for 'acts prejudicial', some for 'hostile associations') fell to ninety-two in April 1942, and was probably a little less, say eighty, a year later. The total number of detainees fell from the peak of 1,428 at the end of August 1940 to 718 at the same point in 1941, 515 in 1942, just under 400 in 1943, and 188 in 1944; as time passed a progressively higher proportion would be Anglo-German or Anglo-Italian.

Home Office officials accepted most committee recommendations. At the end of January 1941 recommendations had been accepted in 92 per cent of the thousand or so cases determined. Of these 582 were for release, but 368 were for continued detention. Where recommendations were not accepted this was noted in the reports; over time, however, this became progressively less common. In nineteen cases in all the Home Office released against the advice of the committee.

The Periodic Reviews

The regulation did not require the Home Office to review cases periodically. But in May 1940 Newsam and Birkett agreed that all cases ought to be reviewed annually, though a second hearing might not be required.[11] In April 1941, with the backlog cleared, the matter was again discussed. Birkett's view was set out on 21 April, when he was weary and disillusioned with the friction with MI5:

Numbers of British subjects are in internment, and it is right that there should be as complete an assurance as possible that these internments are necessary and justifiable. The Advisory Committee have recommended release in many cases where their recommendation has not been followed . . . It may well be that the considered opinion of the Advisory Committee is wrong, but in view of the difference of opinion it is naturally a satisfactory thing to feel that such cases can be reviewed. For people who are interned may be there for years, with their homes gone, their businesses ruined, their children handicapped in their education, and with a sense of bitterness which enforced detention must inevitably bring to the person detained.

---

[9] CAB 65/10 WM (40) 293 of 21 Nov.; CAB 67/8 WP (G) (40) 308 of 9 Nov.; HO 45/25756/863032/17, 27; Hinsley and Simkins, 62.
[10] *Parl. Deb.* HC Vol. 379 c.328, 16 April 1942 giving a figure for British born detainees of 229, of whom 135 were BU.
[11] Letter of 25 May in HO 283/21.

He did not think that his committee should conduct reviews; there had been too much contention surrounding its work.

He proposed an entirely new body, presided over by a High Court judge:

the procedure would be that after this body had presented its report, the decision would be left to the Home Secretary without intervention from any quarter . . . All information would be before the new Tribunal including the shorthand notes, the report of the Committee and all subsequent memoranda; and the Tribunal should have power to call any objector before them, or other witnesses, and all representations from the Police or MI5 or other interested bodies should be given to the Tribunal before the final report is made.[12]

Birkett's scheme must have been alarming both to the Home Office and to MI5, and it was not adopted.

In November 1941 the matter came up for decision in the light of the Law Officers' opinion on the right of appeal; this, as we have seen, ruled that rehearings were only appropriate when there was something new to investigate. Automatic review was arranged annually; MI5 would put forward their views, and detainees invited to state their case in writing for release. The committee would decide whether a hearing would be useful. After February 1942 review of Anglo-Italian cases went to Birkett's committee, afforced by O'Sullivan and Scott.

The majority of reviews were in the event apparently conducted in the Home Office without reference to the committee.[13] It is not entirely clear why; possibly the committee did not think there was anything new to investigate, or its members had become disillusioned. Whether many detainees put in written cases, or requested hearings, is obscure, though probably many did not. There were in all five general reviews, involving 781, 503, 295, 112, and 19 individuals, and a number of cases were considered out of turn.[14] The number of outstanding disagreements steadily diminished. Thus by 30 September 1942 there had been sixty-seven over BU detainees, five over 'acts prejudicial', and sixty-three over 'hostile origin/associations' cases. After first review these had been reduced to thirteen, three, and three; after second review to seven, one, and two. But until the end of 1943 there were a significant number of long-term detainees who would have been at liberty if the committee had had its way—twenty-eight out of 266. But by the end of 1944 the number had dropped to a mere three out of sixty-five.

---

[12] HO 45/25754/112162; no papers on the response.
[13] Parl. Deb. HC Vol. 399 c.947–8, 27 April 1944. In the previous 6 months there had been 225 releases; only 28 cases had been reviewed by the committee.
[14] Summary in HO 45/21515.

The Liberalization of Policy

Policy over release became more liberal. General policy decisions are poorly documented, though we know that the Swinton Committee and War Cabinet were directly involved over the fascists; there must also have been a similar decision over the Anglo-Italians, and one dealing with Anglo-Italians under 18 is documented.[15] After 1940 many relaxations came about on a case-to-case basis. Birkett and his colleagues were much influenced by professions of patriotism,[16] assurances of a change of heart since initial detention, promises to avoid political activity, enthusiasm for national service, particularly in the armed services[17] (Louise Irving was asked if she would milk cows[18]), or special family circumstances.[19] Camp reports became available, and conduct and associates in the abnormal conditions of detention became important, as is typically though irrationally the case with prisoners. In one case, that of the 19-year-old J. L. Flockhart, it can be documented that Morrison used detention simply as a punishment. Flockhart had been listed as a ringleader of Peveril riot; the Camp Commandant, Superintendent S. M. Ogden, and the committee thought he should be released. In 1942 Morrison agreed to release him but only after he had spent three more months in detention.[20]

Papers surely saved by devoted weeders for this very reason show Maxwell's benevolent influence. Thus he persuaded Morrison, no natural enthusiast for liberty when fascists were involved, to release Lieutenant Dudley M. Evans.[21] Evans had joined Mosley in 1933. He was Branch Leader in Worthing until 1934 and paid subscriptions until 1938. He visited Germany in 1938 and had been in contact there with Conwell Evans, Secretary of the Anglo-German Fellowship; he had been impressed by some of the Nazi achievements. He helped over the Sark radio concession. He joined the Territorials in 1938, and on being commissioned left the BU. In 1940 he was with the Royal Engineers at RAF Debden. His commanding officer there called him 'an enthusiastic and energetic officer'. But an RAF intelligence officer decided that he must be a member of the Fifth Column—'one of the best men they had got'—and claimed that he was a fanatical pro-Nazi. He was detained under an 18B

---

[15] 24 August 1940, FO 371/25254; also HO 45/25115; 67 persons were released.
[16] Case of Frank Clifford, D/L, HO 45/25754.
[17] Case of E. Harvey Whittleton, a BU speaker and Link secretary, serving in the army and a good soldier. HO 45/25754. Case of Francis Foster, BUF D/T, joined Territorials 1939, serving in the army with good report from Commanding Officer.
[18] Personal information.
[19] Case of Mrs Hudson, WD/L Chichester, who had three teenage children. HO 45/25754.
[20] HO 45/25752, paper of about 23 March 1942.
[21] HO 45/25727 and 283/34. His detention was based on a general policy decision in a Home Office file which is not available, reference GEN 22/5/5.

(1A) order. The committee in October 1940 said he had once been an active fascist, but formed a good impression of him, regarding the accounts of his fanaticism as exaggerated; he should be released and return to the army.

On 23 December Morrison, apparently thinking he deserved punishment, rejected this recommendation, even though it was supported by Hutchinson and Newsam in the Home Office, and by MI5. He minuted: 'Evidently your view is settled by attitude of MI5, but I cannot let release be determined by their view. This is a serious case and detention should be continued. USS [Under-Secretary of State] to see.' Morris, who chaired this committee, wrote to Maxwell for an explanation:

I remember that Evans who was serving in the Army made a favourable impression and this was borne out when we later saw the terms of the many letters which were written about him . . . it would I think greatly help us in the consideration of other cases if we knew what were the principal points which actuated the Secretary of State . . .

Jenifer Hart replied on 29 March; Morrison was not convinced that Evans had given up his sympathies with the Nazi regime, and therefore felt unable to release someone who had high-up Fascist and pro-German contacts. Morris pointed out that Evans had left the BU in 1938, and was wholly patriotic. Maxwell then wrote a long minute for Morrison, concluding: 'I feel it would be difficult to justify the view that the continued detention of this man is necessary for the purposes of public safety.' After further face-saving manœuvring to enable Morrison to climb down, the order was revoked on 10 April. Evans was re-employed by the army in June, and in 1944 had risen to the rank of Captain.

Later cases show Maxwell's influence as conditions changed. Miss Baggaley, a fascist with strong pro-Nazi sympathies, had been detained in June 1940.[22] In October 1940, and again in January 1942, the committee recommended detention; her views had not changed. In April 1942 her case was again reviewed. Markham and Stuart-Bunning favoured detention. Morris regarded her as a stupid person, unlikely to influence others, and favoured release; MI5 agreed. In the Home Office Newsam minuted: 'This lady would cause friction in almost any community other than one of Nazi sympathizers. In my view she is better detained.' Morrison minuted: 'US/S further observations please. Her opinions are poor, but is she dangerous. Check age.' She was in her mid-fifties. Maxwell advised:

The policy now should be, I suggest, in review cases to direct attention mainly to the questions (1) is the individual likely to commit acts of a treacherous character or to engage in secret activities of a dangerous character and (2) has he or she such

---

[22] HO 45/25710, of which only one subfile has escaped destruction. On a 'general' list; not apparently BU.

ability or influence, organizing ability or political experience as to be likely to influence or take a leading part in building up some anti-war movement or Fascist organization or (3) is he, even if he has no special ability, likely to engage in *public* propaganda activities and to try to propagate his Fascist views by speeches, lectures, leaflets etc. I do not think that Miss Baggaley falls under any of the three classes. She is an obstinate and unpenitent Fascist . . . I recommend that she be released.

Morrison was persuaded.

About the same time the curious case of Oddson was being considered.[23] Oddson who, as we have seen, became very depressed during detention, was an Icelander who had been naturalized in 1915. He had joined the BU as an inactive member in August 1939, out of concern over unemployment. He was detained in August 1940 as BU, but the real ground appears to have been suspicions, apparently groundless, that his trawler business was a cover for sinister activities. Naval intelligence regarded Iceland as a centre for the Fifth Column. After over four months his case came before the committee on 10 December, and release was recommended; the recommendation was rejected in May 1941; no doubt Naval Intelligence was involved in enquiries. Oddson was particularly distressed by the American occupation of Iceland in early July 1941, which he viewed as a grave threat to Icelandic culture. His opposition to the war and fascist sympathies hardened; he attributed his detention to a conspiracy involving a commercial rival. His case was reviewed in December 1941 and he was again seen in February 1942. The committee under Morris once more recommended release; MI5 opposed, and the Home Office officials rejected the recommendation, although Hoare minuted: 'I have never felt that there were any very strong security objections in this case, but the man's attitude seems to leave no alternative to his detention.' The policy in 1942 was not to release persons of alien origin who were opposed to the war, particularly if they had a BU background. A report in 1943 from an MI5 officer at Peveril showed him bitterly opposed to the war, viewing himself as an Icelander, disliking Jews, and wanting a negotiated peace. His associates were listed—including De Guerin, Darwin-Fox, Elwyn Wright, and Baker—all viewed as extremists, though to common sense disturbed. MI5 therefore opposed release. In effect his bitter reaction to detention ensured that it would continue.

But on 7 June 1943 Maxwell recommended release; he was both unimportant and not dangerous. It was no longer necessary to detain him merely on account of his attitude. He was not allowed to resume his business, and ended up farming on the Isle of Man at Ballacallin, his farm

---

[23] HO 283/51 and HO 45/25738, in part withheld and much weeded. What looks like a letter from Oddson is quoted in *Parl. Deb.* HC Vol. 381 c.1503.

becoming a meeting-place for former detainees. The change in policy secured him freedom after three years, though the case for detaining him at all had surely been very weak indeed.

The Review of 1943

During the spring and summer of 1943 MI5 analysed the cases of all remaining detainees. About 130 were BU, about eighty British born 'acts prejudicial' or 'hostile association' detainees, and about 240 Anglo-Germans, Anglo-Italians, and other non-enemy aliens. Some records of this have survived.[24] A consequence was a considerable increase in the numbers released. Between January and April 1943 there had been on average seven releases each month; between May and December the average was just over twenty-five. There must have been a policy decision over Anglo-Italians, for in November and December fifty-three were set free. An individual beneficiary of this operation was the BU accountant, Maurice T. Pacey, who had possessed 'sticky-backs' advertising the NBBS.[25] He joined at the age of 19 in 1934, and became a District Leader and District Inspector. In detention his views softened little and in April 1943 detention was maintained. But in August 1943 MI5 said: 'This man is an orthodox follower of BU but he is not of any personal importance and could be released.' His order was suspended on 4 September. In about August the Home Office, using classifications of detainees provided by MI5, applied a policy of releasing individuals such as Pacey who, though still fascists, were 'of no personal importance'. MI5 somewhat grudgingly accepted this policy, in Pacey's case urging that he be kept away from London where an underground fascist group existed. A considerable number of other BU detainees were set free late in 1943 under this policy.

The Release of Mosley

In November 1943 it was decided to release Mosley and his wife Diana.[26]

The cases of very prominent detainees would normally have been reviewed annually; however, a memorandum of 15 March 1942 listing the Mosleys, Domvile, Ramsay, Vaughan-Henry, and Admiral Wolkoff suggested they should be taken off the review list, and a policy decision taken

[24] HO 45/25704 (Pacey, see also 283/55) has reports also C. R. C. Evans and P. J. Fenn; HO 45/25691 (Perry) contains a summary and recommendation dated October 1943 from a review of hostile origin/association cases on a 'List C', with a reference to HO 863005/29.
[25] HO 45/25704 and 283/55.
[26] Principal sources are HO 45/24892 and 24893 and CAB 65/40 WM (43) 156th Concl., Minute 4 Confidential Annexe, 17 November 1943. Morrison's statement to the Commons on 23 November 1943, and his speech on 1 December, *Parl. Deb.* HC Vol. 393 c.1428 and 394: 461.

to maintain detention. Of these only Mosley was a leader; the others were merely detainees particularly badly thought of, though why the aged Wolkoff was included is obscure. Their cases were again considered in March 1943, and Morrison decided to maintain detention.[27]

In August 1943 friends and relatives became anxious over Mosley's health, in particular over a loss of weight from 189 to 157 lb., and depression. Maxwell initially viewed what he called 'agitation' on the matter with some scorn. Nevertheless Mosley was seen by a Lord Dawson of Penn and by Dr Geoffrey Evans in July and August, and on the basis of their reports his solicitors asked that the order be suspended. However, the prognosis was uncertain, and the prison doctors regarded the symptoms as typical of those found in detainees. The request was refused. In October the issue was raised again. Churchill, lobbied by Clementine, in her turn lobbied by 'Muv'—Lady Redesdale, Diana's mother—called for a report; Morrison replied that there was no ground for release.[28]

It chanced that Churchill was interviewed by W. P. Crozier of the *Manchester Guardian* on 22 October, and it is clear that the matter was preying on his mind:

Look at what has happened to the liberties of this country in the war. Men of position are seized and kept in prison for years without trial and no 'have your carcase' rights, and the public and newspapers don't care a hang. Thomas Mosley for instance—I think no good of him, but he's been in prison all this time and he's likely to die in prison this winter, and he has never been accused and never tried— a frightful thing to anyone concerned about English liberties.

Churchill went on to admit his responsibility and justify the decision, but thought 'the necessity is no longer there to the same extent'.[29]

Backstairs pressure continued and Lord Halifax, Anderson, and Brendan Bracken became involved.[30] Dr Methuen, the Medical Commissioner for prisons, suggested that Lord Horder, Dr George Riddock, and Dr Russell Brain be also consulted. Lord Dawson proposed that if there was no agreement there should be a conference. On 6 October Dawson reported that Mosley suffered from phlebitis; the condition was serious, progressive, and life-threatening; prison would not favour recovery. A conference on 9 November was attended by Dawson, Dr Evans, Dr

[27] HO 45/24892.
[28] D. Mosley, *A Life of Contrasts: The Autobiography of Diana Mosley* (London, 1977), 196, gives an engaging account of the British Establishment in action. Clementine Churchill had been bridesmaid for Lady Redesdale. Diana Mosley has kindly let me have copies of a number of letters written by her mother and father on her behalf to a variety of individuals, including Lord Simon and Lord Atkin.
[29] A. J. P. Taylor (ed), *Off the Record: Political Interviews 1933–43* (London, 1973), 381 and 385. Mosley was usually called 'Tom' by acquaintances.
[30] A. Roberts, *'The Holy Fox': A Biography of Lord Halifax* (London, 1991), 269, relying on private information. Randolph Churchill and Beaverbrook may have been involved.

Mathieson (Governor of Holloway), Dr Fenton (the Brixton doctor), and Methuen; all agreed it would be wise to release him. Mosley did indeed suffer from phlebitis, and was in poor health, as were numerous other detainees, some being released in consequence.[31] But less important people did not have such a galaxy of medical talent at their disposal.

Thus Morrison was given little option but to release Mosley, but subjected him to stringent restrictions amounting to house arrest. He also decided to release Diana Mosley both on humanitarian grounds and because the supposed reason for detaining her had been to prevent her acting as a go-between for the BU and her detained husband.[32] The War Cabinet approved on 17 November, but Ernest Bevin, who loathed Morrison, insisted on recording his dissent; the decision would 'weaken morale and would have an unfortunate effect on negotiations and discussions in the industrial field'. Morrison argued in reply that he was not entitled to take such matters into consideration in a judicial decision. The press was told on 18 November, and Mosley and his wife were permitted to live at Rignell House near Banbury with Diana's sister Pamela and her husband Derek Jackson, under conditions which excluded both from all political and public activities. Soon after, because Jackson, a physicist of great distinction, was engaged on secret war work, they were, to his fury, made to leave, and moved to a disused hotel, the Shaven Crown, in Shipton-under-Wychwood. Roger Hollis for MI5 reported the number of Communist Party members living within thirty miles; there was fear of trouble. A benevolent policeman, Sergeant Buswell, kept an eye on things. In 1944 the Mosleys moved to Crux Easton House near Newbury. There were, in the event, no local difficulties.[33]

But the Communist Party organized protests and demonstrations, and Morrison was in serious trouble with the Labour Party, aggravated by the myth that the detention of Mosley had been a price for supporting Churchill's government. There was a risk that Morrison would be forced to resign, or even that the coalition might collapse.[34] Churchill's doctor, Moran, records him saying: '"The government may go over Mosley. Bevin is kicking". Then followed a great diatribe about Labour's folly and stupidity. Much about Habeas Corpus.'[35] Morrison only survived a meeting of the Parliamentary Labour Party by fifty-one votes to forty-three. There was a debate in the Commons on 1 December in which

---

[31] Some are listed in HO 45/25115.

[32] CAB 65/40 WM (43) 156th Concl., Minute 4 Confidential Annexe.

[33] D. Mosley, *Loved Ones: Pen Portraits by Diana Mosley* (London, 1985), 70ff., who also mentions a Detective Jones. SH Appendix 9 gives the conditions imposed on release.

[34] HO 45/25386 (notes for the debate).

[35] Lord Moran, *Winston Churchill: The Struggle for Survival, 1940–1965* (London, 1966), 144. R. Skidelsky, *Oswald Mosley* (London, 1975), 462, with hindsight calls the incident a storm in a tea cup.

Morrison vigorously defended his action.[36] For it the Home Office triumphantly found a precedent; Henry Mack had been released from fourteen days' imprisonment in 1912 on account of phlebitis.[37] Sixty-two members voted against the release, fifty-five of them members of the Labour Party. They included D. N. Pritt who, in spite of his advocacy for Liversidge, had become an enthusiastic supporter of detention without trial, as had the NCCL. But 327 members supported Morrison, and the crisis passed. Someone, discovering that rat poison could cure phlebitis, sent a bottle of it to the Home Office.[38] The department has a history of curious gifts, the oddest perhaps being a dead baby, posted to the Home Secretary by an eccentric parson back in 1884, and marked 'perishable'. Unlike the baby the rat poison was kept as a memento, and for all I know may still exist, no doubt under extended closure.[39]

Churchill's part in the affair is intriguing. He and his wife Clementine, having put pressure on Morrison, felt some responsibility for his difficulties. Churchill was in Cairo when the decision was taken. On 18 November he cabled: 'I highly approve your action.'[40] On 21 November he cabled again:

You might however consider whether you should not unfold as a background the great privilege of habeas corpus and trial by jury, which are the supreme protection invented by the English people for ordinary individuals against the state. The power of the Executive to cast a man into prison without formulating any charge known to the law, and particularly to deny him the judgement of his peers, is in the highest degree odious and is the foundation of all totalitarian government whether Nazi or Communist . . . Extraordinary power assumed by the Executive should be yielded up when the emergency declines. Nothing is more abhorrent than to imprison a person or keep him in prison because he is unpopular. This is really the test of civilization.

Maxwell decided not to circulate this dangerous document, which implied that 18B was ripe for abolition.[41] In a cable of 25 November

[36] *Parl. Deb.* HC 394 c.264 of 30 November (debate on the address) and cols.397–478 of 1 December.

[37] HO 45/25836 (brief for debate). Other releases on medical grounds include John Beckett, released temporarily in May 1942 after an operation for piles, and again in July 1943 because of general debility; Eifflander, released in July 1943 to an epileptic colony; Leese, set free after a prostate operation in February 1944; and Longfellow, released in February 1943 because of tuberculosis of the spine. Claud L. C. de Geurin, a former naval Commander and BU detainee apparently became insane in detention, and may have been released in consequence. Budd was apparently moved to hospital in October 1942 for problems arising from his war wounds.

[38] HO 45/2893.

[39] See my *Cannibalism and the Common Law* (Chicago, 1984), 245 for fuller details.

[40] M. Gilbert, *Winston S. Churchill*, vii. *Road to Victory* (Boston, 1986), 566–7, quotes two of the telegrams, coded Frozen 136 and 145. His account curiously does not mention the fact that the issue which led to the cables was the release of the Mosleys.

[41] Gilbert does not quote it; possibly it has been weeded from the Churchill Papers.

Churchill said: 'I am convinced that 18B should be completely abolished as the national emergency no longer justifies abrogation of individual rights of habeas corpus and trial by jury on definite charges.' But he agreed not to press the matter, whilst exhorting Morrison to make no concessions to totalitarian views: 'Do not quit the heights.'

I suspect that Churchill initially favoured the release of Mosley since the next logical step was to abandon 18B entirely; the regulation was utterly at odds with Churchill's vision of the British constitution and his own place in history. But he backed off from this position for reasons of political expediency. In his *Finest Hour*, the volume of his history of the war which covers 1940, Churchill states categorically that 'No Fifth Column existed in Britain.' This was written in 1948 or perhaps earlier, and Churchill does not explain when he came to realize that the Fifth Column was mythical; in all probability he would know this by late 1940 and, as we have seen, he expressed his scepticism in a Commons speech on 5 November 1940. It is quite inconceivable that he or anyone else in his War Cabinet continued to believe the myth as late as 1943.[42]

The Other Prominent Detainees

With Mosley freed, it was not easy to see why other prominent detainees, particularly his lieutenants, should remain in prison. The idea of releasing 'leaders' now that Mosley was free appears to have been the thinking in the Home Office. At the Cabinet on 17 November Morrison said that under the review he had been conducting a substantial number of detainees had been released, including some of the 'serious' cases—he instanced Christobel Nicholson, Domvile, and Beckett. Nicholson was released in early September, Domvile on 29 July, and Beckett, who was ill, in late October.[43] Some other prominent detainees were released about the same time. Quentin Joyce went free about July.[44] Caroll, secretary of the Link, in November, Gordon-Canning in August,[45] and Prince Henry

[42] The full passage reads: 'No Fifth Column existed in Britain, though a few spies were carefully rounded up and examined. What few Communists there were lay low. Everyone else gave all they had to give.' W. S. Churchill, *The Second World War*, ii. *Their Finest Hour* (London, 1949), 246. This same volume (p. 49) reproduces a memo of Ismay of 18 May 1940 indicating that Churchill then did believe in the Fifth Column. For his speech on 5 Nov. see above, Ch. 11 n. 131.

[43] HO 45/25752 (lists 'leaders'). *The Times* 7 September 1943 (Nicholson); DOM 56 entry for 22 November 1943, *The Times*, 6 December 1943 (Domvile); *The Times*, 30 October 1943 (Beckett).   [44] HO 283/43.

[45] *The Times*, 9 August 1943. By 1945 Gordon-Canning has disappeared from *Who's Who*. I am told that he helped to defray the legal costs involved in the defence of William Joyce for treason in 1945, and he achieved notoriety for purchasing a bust of Hitler at the sale of the contents of the German Embassy. This was to be used in Kingdom House in connection with the worship of Hitler, and he told a reporter after the sale that, like Christ, Hitler would come into his own again. See the *New York Times*, 28 November 1945.

of Pless about 10 October. The de Laessoes, housed with the Mosleys in Holloway, were set free with them. Diana Mosley describes this as an act of 'disgraceful cynicism', motivated by the administrative convenience of closing down the preventive detention block. In view of their age there may have been nervousness lest one or other might die, which would have been extremely embarrassing after the release of Mosley.[46]

Morrison envisaged that most of the remaining regular citizens in detention—not such persons as Anglo-Germans—would soon be set free, including Ramsay. But the Cabinet, mindful of the trouble over Mosley's release, was unhappy at this; it was important clearly to separate release on medical grounds from other cases: 'it would be preferable that a certain period of time should elapse after the release of Sir Oswald and Lady Mosley before the further review took place'. In consequence the release of BU 'leaders' was delayed not for security reasons, but purely for fear of trouble with the illiberal wing of the Labour Party. Nevertheless some prominent detainees were released in late 1943: 'Rutland of Jutland' in December,[47] Cahir Healy late in the year, [48] Leese, who was unwell, in December.[49] Other less prominent individuals were also freed late in the year, some thirty-three Anglo-Italians in November.[50] In the early months of 1944 there were further releases, twelve in January, seventeen in February, and twelve in March, but the only prominent individual was the 72-year-old Admiral Wolkoff, whom the committee had recommended releasing back in August 1942.[51] His must surely have been a case of detention by way of punishment for whatever it was he had done.

Ramsay, the most prominent of all, was still in detention in June of 1944 when a motion was debated condemning his continued incarceration.[52] On 7 September he was discussed in the War Cabinet. Morrison claimed that previously it had not been possible to release him, partly because it was thought impossible to release a Member of Parliament conditionally—presumably Morrison's bizarre point was that you could not require a Member of Parliament to abstain from all political activity. The other was that his 'strange views', which led to the 'indefensible act' (whatever it was), remained unaltered; he might still engage in irresponsible and mischievous actions. But since the war situation had now changed he was

---

[46] *The Times*, 25 November 1943, Mosley, *Life of Contrasts*. 198. In the event both died in 1948. *Comrade*, 14.

[47] Young, *Rutland of Jutland*, 176, suggests a slightly earlier date, but see HO 214/67 (report of 30 November 1943 noting his poor health).

[48] *Parl. Deb.* HC Vol. 395 c.1713, 16 December 1943.   [49] Ibid. 396: 61.

[50] Noted specially in the November report to Parliament.

[51] HO 45/25115. *The Times*, 14 January 1944 (release).

[52] *Parl. Deb.* HC Vol. 406 c.2317–1418, 16 June 1944.

released unconditionally on 26 September 1944.[53] He resumed his seat in Parliament the following day. His release naturally caused some anger; Willie Gallagher MP, whose son had recently been killed in action, made a violent protest in the Commons.[54]

In August of 1944 MI5 came to favour the release of some of the less important remaining fascists; Shelford thought there were advantages in releasing some soon, so that their activities could be monitored; he added: 'It is also preferable for the releases to be spaced out over a period rather than to take place all together at the end of the war.' He mentioned the cases of T. E. Williams, D. H. Rose, R. L. Knott,[55] and P. G. Fenn—'. . . all of them are insignificant.'[56] His advice appears to have been accepted.

Mosley's Lieutenants

The Home Office decision to release the five remaining BU leaders was taken on 29 September 1944, reversing a decision not to release taken in February. They were Francis-Hawkins, Donovan, McKechnie, Raven-Thompson, and Clarke, of whom only the last was now thought to have the ability to cause any trouble.[57] These releases were on conditions; Francis-Hawkins, for example, was not allowed to live in London where his home was; there would be a ban on political activity.[58] Morrison also proposed to release ten other fanatical pro-Nazis who were in detention for 'acts prejudicial'. It is impossible to be sure of the identity of all, but they included 'Jock' Houston,[59] and almost certainly Bernard C. Perrigoe, a detainee viewed with particular suspicion by MI5.[60] Other possible names are Vaughan-Henry (not however an 'acts prejudicial'

[53] CAB 66/55 WP (44) 505. No formal steps had ever been taken to expel him from the House.

[54] Parl. Deb. HC Vol. 403 c.41–8 of 26 September 1944. The Times for 27 and 28 September 1944.

[55] Conservative, then Junior Imperial League; joined BUF 1933, running the Windsor Branch; left at the abdication; joined the IFL; arrested 12 June 1940 when working as a fitter in the Hawker Aircraft Factory at Langley; released 26 August 1944 'four years and three months after arrest which is about equal to a six year prison sentence'. Account in Britons' Archives.

[56] The 1943 report on Fenn is in HO 45/25704. He was a BU detainee of Irish origin; MI5 reported he would fight against Britain if given the chance. Returning him to Ireland was considered but rejected as his home was near the border. See HO 45/25733 (D. H. Rose), also HO 283/59.

[57] Minute of Newsam 7 February, Maxwell 14 February, agreed by Morrison in HO 45/25699 (McKechnie). From HO 45/25700 (Francis-Hawkins) and HO 45/25699 it appears that the cases of the 6 leaders were reviewed in July 1943, the review being completed by 2 September; leaders were placed in a list called Group F, this containing those to be released last. There must therefore have been 5 other categories.

[58] Comrade, March 1988. He appealed, and the conditions were lifted sometime in 1945.

[59] Still in detention in February 1944; HO 283/41.

[60] In HO 283/41 as one of six BU detainees whose release had not been recommended by MI5 by late August.

case), W. A. Crowle, E. C. P. Whinfield, and Professor Serrocauld (or Serocold) Skeels.[61] Royston L. Knott was certainly one; he was set free on 25 August 1944. Some of the ten may have been women.[62]

Ramsay's release could not be concealed, but Morrison prudently kept quiet about the remaining BU leaders, whose release appears to have passed unnoticed by the press and public; they may have left prison on separate days to prevent any joint celebration. Morrison explained to the Cabinet that Ramsay's release was the consequence of yet another Home Office review of the 223 detainees held on 31 July 1944, which led to seventy releases.[63] He did not intend to release all the remaining detainees, but forty more were in fact set free by the end of October, and another eighteen in November. In December 1944 further reviews were conducted and eleven detainees released; three were 'acts prejudicial' cases, and the others 'hostile origin and/or hostile associations'.[64]

The Final Releases

By the end of 1944 sixty-five detainees remained; most were 'of hostile origin or associations', and twenty had German citizenship; quite a number were indeed detained in aliens camps.[65] At the end of March 1945 there were fifty detainees left, three under BU orders, eight for 'acts prejudicial' and the others for 'hostile origin' and/or 'hostile associations'. In April thirty-nine persons were set free.[66] The last detainee held under a BU order was A. J. Schneider, an Anglo-German member nicknamed 'Dozy'; he joined the group which worshipped Hitler as God. Though Morrison tried to suggest that few regular British subjects remained in detention, a

---

[61] Vaughan-Henry and Skeels listed as permanent residents in Brixton in February 1943 and again in April in HO 45/25752. On Skeels, who may have been Australian, see *Parl. Deb.* HC Vol. 397 c.115 (said to have been detained since October 1942); he was then 69, a veteran of the Boer and 1st World War; said to have been a schoolmaster in South Africa; in 1934 prospective candidate for the United British Party in Cambridge; of the Nordic League and White Knights of Britain and United Empire Fascist Party (HO 144/22454). In 1941 he had been convicted of an attempt to communicate with the enemy and imprisoned (HO 45/24968). His case was raised in the Commons without naming him on 14 March 1944, *Parl. Deb.* HC Vol. 398 c.48.

[62] Possibilities are Enid M. Riddell (a friend of Anna Wolkoff and member of the Right Club), and Mary A. G. Stanford. Olive Burdett was still in detention in April 1943 (HO 45/25752).

[63] CAB 66/55 WP (44) 505.

[64] Information from HO 45/25752, which contains subfiles for December 1942, 1943, and 1944, the other subfiles having been destroyed.

[65] *Parl. Deb.* HC Vol. 404 c.950 of 4 November 1944. HO 215/495 notes that four Anglo-Germans were in the German Aliens Camp L at Ramsay, one Anglo-Italian in the Italian Aliens Camp N, and 6 others (Dickson, Darwin-Fox, Findlay, Lockwood, Hepburn-Ruston, and Wright) in Camp X at Port Erin.

[66] Some originally held under BU orders, such as Hepburn-Ruston, had their orders changed to 'hostile associations'.

list shows several of the thirty-nine released in April 1945 were regular citizens: Professor Samuel F. Darwin-Fox,[67] P. Elwyn Wright,[68] T. G. St
Barbe-Baker, W. A. Dickson,[69] Richard F. Findlay,[70] A. T. V. Hepburn-
Ruston,[71] Harold H. Lockwood,[72] T. W. Victor Rowe,[73] Charles R.
Short,[74] possibly A. G. L. Thornton,[75] and perhaps others; these individuals all seem to have been strongly pro-Nazi and to have made no secret
of it.

Between 30 April and 9 May all but one of the eleven remaining
detainees were released; the exception was an alien awaiting deportation,
R. Lyncke. The last ten detainees released after 30 April included some
individuals, for example J. De Graaf, S. E. Lonsdale, Anton Bernardi, A.
A. or R. W. Froebel, and T. C. H. Osborne, who had been in detention
since 1939. Five were in Australia at the time of their release. As we have
seen, a certain number of non-enemy aliens had been held under
Regulation 18B in MI5's prisons, Latchmere House and Huntercombe
Place, and they do not appear to feature in the official 18B statistics for
final release; by 1945 they were probably held under the Aliens Order, on
which figures were not regularly published. But quite what happened to
them is obscure; some, like Dr Branimir Jelić the Croatian fascist, would
remain in detention under deportation orders.[76] And there are mysteries
over some of the German agents—the most notable is the strange case of
the individual, plainly connected in some way with the German secret
service, found walled up in a cave on Ingleborough in 1947 above the village of Clapham, where I then lived.[77]

---

[67] Formerly a Professor of English at Fribourg University, and, he claimed, a grandson
of Charles Darwin. A letter of his of 4 January 1946 to Frank Wiseman (IWM 86/1/1) has
him living in the Isle of Man, idolizing the memory of Hitler about whom he was writing a
book which was being checked by Gordon-Canning and typed by Elwyn Wright. He had
plans to establish a Hitlerian Institute.
[68] Former Secretary of the Anglo-German Union; an associate of extremists.
[69] Detained for 'acts prejudicial'.   [70] HO 214/67; detained for 'acts prejudicial'.
[71] He was the father of the actress Audrey Hepburn, whose mother, Baroness van
Heemstra, had been associated with the BU in the early 1930s. As J. V. A. Ruston he appears
in the Foreign Office List as Consul at Samarang, Java, 1923–4.
[72] HO 45/25717 and 283/46; IFL; detained for 'acts prejudicial'. An article in *People's Post*
for December 1945 which I have not seen is cited by R. Thurlow, *Fascism in Britain: A
History, 1918–1985* (Oxford, 1987), 229.
[73] See above pp. 71–2.   [74] An 'acts prejudicial' case.
[75] Noted in HO 45/25115 as an 'acts prejudicial' case. Mr Row tells me he was regarded as
Anglo-German, and used the name Leuthardt or Leutardt. He had been a cook, had spent
some time in the USA, and had a strong but obscurely based grievance against both the
British and American governments.
[76] See above, pp. 84–5.
[77] See the *Craven Herald and Pioneer*, 29 August, 28 November 1947. He was equipped
with a purpose-made cyanide phial of the type used only by agents, and had died or been
killed between 1940 and 1945. Such enquiries as I have made from persons who ought to
know have produced evasiveness.

Claims for Compensation

Release was one thing, compensation quite another. Any general scheme of compensation would always have been politically impossible.[78] Yet it seems bizarre that even those detained entirely unjustifiably were denied any form of *ex gratia* payment. Some victims of error were promptly reinstated in employment. An example is E. L. Diamond, a Ministry of Supply engineer detained in June 1940 as 'of hostile associations' at the request of Lieutenant-General Sir Maurice Taylor, the senior military officer with the Ministry.[79] Taylor did not wait for an MI5 report. The case against him as a suspected agent amounted to nothing. Walter Hedley KC, somewhat unusually, conducted an enquiry, and explained: 'Belgium and Holland had just been over-run and the British Army was in full retreat to Dunkirk. For the first time it was fully realised how successful Germany had been in placing agents in key positions in foreign countries. In consequence MI5 were inundated with cases requiring close enquiry.' Diamond was even sent a letter of apology: 'he [the Home Secretary] wishes me to express to you his deep regret that you should have been detained and to state that the information now before him makes it clear that there are no reasons for regarding your character and loyalty as having been in doubt'.

This was a unique concession. The unfortunate Alfred Block, detained quite unjustifiably as a member of the mythical spy ring, attempted through his solicitors to obtain a letter which would re-establish his reputation. The Home Office provided one which, if anything, made his position worse: '[the Home Secretary] has indicated that he has satisfied himself, after careful review of all the circumstances, that the loyalty of your client is such as to make his continued detention unnecessary'. Attempts to obtain a more generous document produced a statement that the Home Secretary 'regrets any suffering your client may have been caused owing to the fact of his having been detained in the interests of national security . . . ' These documents were deliberately drafted to imply that the detention had been quite proper; protecting the Home Office from public criticism thus took precedence over any concern for its victims. Of course the more mistakes were made the greater the fear of the consequences of providing apologies.

Hamilton S. L. Knight, who was, as we have seen, another wholly innocent victim of 18B, was similarly badly treated.[80] The Home Office gave him no assistance in his action against the Guildford Corporation for

---

[78] *Parl. Deb.* HC Vol. 370 c.158, 19 March 1941 (Stokes). Ibid. 377: 1256, 5 February 1942, where Morrison said: 'I do not think that His Majesty's government could take the responsibility for providing compensation for the families of detained persons.'
[79] HO 45/25721. SH para. 126.   [80] HO 45/25695.

wrongful dismissal, and Holderness's reaction to the fact that he was angry at his treatment was to describe him as 'an unbalanced and vindictive individual'. Knight argued that he should be compensated, or at least helped to find a job after demobilization. After the war his case was taken up by Flight Lieutenant Challen MP but the Home Office refused to accept any liability whatever, and indeed denied that any mistake had been made in detaining him. Maxwell, advising about a question in the Commons, had suggested this reply: 'Mr K. was one of the victims of the very few errors which occurred as a result of the justifiable view that in cases of reasonable doubt it was better to err on the side of security than in the direction of laxity.' But Newsam, ever protective of his Minister, thought this went too far; no error at all should be admitted, though he went on: 'But Mr K. has suffered great hardship and I think we should do what we can to assist.' What, if anything, was done is obscure, but by February 1946 he was employed by the Alvaney Edge Urban District Council.

In 1942 an attempt was made to achieve by court action what could not be achieved through the political process. A number of actions, financed by Mosley and the Duke of Bedford,[81] were commenced, in which damages were claimed for the conditions in which detainees had been held in prisons in the summer of 1940. Technically the basis was breach of statutory duty arising out of the Prison Rules and the White Paper of January 1939.[82] Curiously no claims were apparently made over Latchmere House where conditions were at their worst; conceivably some sort of compensation was discreetly paid to such detainees. Two actions, those by Frank Arbon, former District Leader in Lincoln,[83] and Major H. H. A. de Laessoe,[84] were treated as test actions. There were elaborate interlocutory proceedings which reached the Court of Appeal in February 1942.[85] Eventually the actions were tried before Lord Justice Goddard, a government lawyer if ever there was one; he predictably held that the Home

---

[81] To the extent of £1,500 (information from Diana Mosley).

[82] Cmd. 6162 of 1940. HO 144/21992 sf. 13 indicates that 13 actions were pending; list of witnesses indicates that the plaintiffs (in addition to Arbon and de Laessoe) probably were E. G. Clarke, C. Cuthbert Smith (formerly a schoolmaster at one time in Germany; after the war became a Catholic priest), F. Ibbetson, Mosley, Domvile, A. E. Baker, F. J. Hamley (a schoolteacher in Sheffield), H. T. V. Mills, Dr Otto Bode, McKechnie (who had been in Latchmere House), and Francis-Hawkins. Baker's case was peculiar in that he suffered from leprosy. D. A. Gourdon (Royal Artillery until arrest) was summoned as a witness but was not a plaintiff (Gourdon MS).

[83] TS 27/512. A hairdresser detained on the omnibus order of 30 May 1940; released on 3 September 1941.

[84] TS 27/511 (habeas corpus 1940) and HO 144/21992 (action for breach of statutory duty, seen on privileged access).

[85] [1942] 1 All ER 264. The point at issue was whether the Home Secretary was vicariously responsible for unauthorized actions of prison officials, and the decision was that he was not.

Secretary was not responsible through the courts for the administration of prisons, and prisoners had no right of action for failure to provide adequate conditions. The White Paper of January 1940 'contains nothing more than administrative departmental instructions which do not and are not intended to confer any rights on prisoners and cannot do so', and the rules made under the Prisons Act of 1898 were in like case.[86] The Crown lawyers resisted access to the Emergency Orders under the doctrine of Crown privilege established in 1942 in *Duncan* v. *Cammell Laird*.[87] There was no conceivable public interest served in refusing disclosure; the motive was simply to conceal the truth to protect the department. Had the action, which naturally caused extreme anxiety, succeeded, it would have opened the way to many other suits, but it would not, of course, have established any general right to compensation.

The Aftercare of Detainees

Release did not end the problems of wholly innocent detainees, much less those associated with extremely unpopular political activities. During detention families of detainees had to rely on private means, national assistance, or private charity; the government did not even keep up their national insurance contributions. George Dunlop, one-time BU District Leader in Limehouse, and never detained, organized a charitable relief fund, the 18B Detainees (British) Aid Fund, registered under the War Charities Act 1940. This gave temporary assistance in 350 cases and sustained assistance in 140; it also helped to find employment, paid medical and legal expenses, and took up cases with the Home Office or Ministry of Labour.[88]

On release many detainees joined the forces, or such organizations as the Auxiliary Fire Service.[89] The news-sheet *Comrade*, which circulates amongst former BU members, dedicated much space to recording the war service of former members of the BU, including former detainees; there is abundant evidence that many served loyally. But ex-detainees could have great difficulty in obtaining employment. One reason was that identity books carried a red record of detention.[90] From 1941 this was not the case if the order was wholly revoked.[91] But many detainees were released con-

[86] Reported [1943] 1 All ER 154.   [87] See above p. 376.

[88] The fund was associated with the 18B Publicity Council. The sum expended was £6,000; see Saunders Papers. See *Parl. Deb.* HC Vol. 404 c.950 for illiberal left-wing protest.

[89] For example R. R. Bellamy. He later worked with the War Agricultural service in Norfolk.

[90] See for example Bellamy MS iii. 212. He notes that forged identity cards could then be had for £30 to £40, and claims that a London BU member, one 'Blackie' Baker (apparently A. E. Baker), escaped and survived the war at liberty on forged papers, which seems incorrect.

[91] *Parl. Deb.* HC Vol.376 c.1240, 4 December 1941.

ditionally—by 9 November 1944 934 had been, but 204 had subsequently had the conditions removed.[92] In December 1944 endorsement was ended in all cases.[93]

The authorities might also block certain forms of employment; thus Second Lieutenant H. V. Crisp, though released after only six months in detention, was excluded from the army, and Oddson was excluded from his fishing business.[94] F. C. Wiseman, a schoolteacher and member of the BU, was released on condition that 'The above named person shall not engage in any teaching or educational work'. The conditions also excluded him from war work, work in communications, on the railways, in military hospitals, in clubs for service persons, and in prohibited places.[95] There could be considerable hostility if a detainee returned to his former place of work, as did Leslie Grundy.[96]

A number of attempts were made to persuade the Home Office to help former detainees to rehabilitate themselves. Thus on 22 April 1941 a question was asked in the Commons suggesting that something should be done to remove the stigma of detention when an order was revoked.[97] On 21 July 1942 it was suggested that they be given some sort of document on release which would assist their rehabilitation. Morrison's reply was: 'It is quite impossible for us to give testimonials to persons who have been released from detention under Regulation 18B. We have been justified in detaining them, and we have been justified in subsequently releasing them in the altered circumstances, or after investigations which we have made.'[98]

The Advisory Committee was especially concerned over young detainees. Desmond Rose had joined the BU at the age of 15.[99] His release was recommended to get him out of bad company, and his order was suspended in March 1941. Unfortunately, as he later admitted, he had hoodwinked the committee over his attitudes, and on release he communicated with other detainees and expressed pro-German views. So he was detained again in August. At Peveril he was flamboyantly pro-German, yet quarrelled with the pro-German group associated with Richard Findlay; the camp report viewed his behaviour as simply a pose, and also recommended release to separate him from bad company. The committee

[92] *Parl. Deb.* HC Vol. 376 c.1240, 4 December 1941, 404: 1525; 819 had been released unconditionally from the outset.

[93] Home Office Circular 279/1944, reference in Britons' Archives.

[94] *Parl. Deb.* HC Vol. 373 c.1777, 5 August 1941. He had been detained on a BU order, but had never been a member.

[95] Wiseman Papers IWM 86/1/1. Wiseman had been detained in June 1940, released 1943. Morrison refused to remove the restrictions. F. Manly (an error perhaps for Hamley) of Sheffield was also prevented from teaching (Charnley MS, 199). Mrs Louise Irvine of the BU was, however, employed on release in her previous teaching post.

[96] David Brown's factory in Huddersfield.   [97] *Parl. Deb.* HC Vol. 371 c.987.

[98] Ibid. 381: 1519, 21 July 1942.   [99] HO 45/25733 and 283/59.

must have agreed. But detention was maintained until 31 August 1944; through the intervention of Newsam he then was allowed to live in Norwich, where his home was. Perhaps the committee, hoodwinked or not, had been right all along.

The file on another young detainee, Arthur Marson, shows that in 1943 Morris actively tried to persuade the Home Office to think about the rehabilitation of young fascists. Marson should never have been detained in the first place.[100] Brought up in deprived conditions, he joined the Hull BU as a non-active member at the age of 18; he worked as a junior clerk for the London and North-Eastern Railway, and was unpopular with his workmates, whose protests may have caused his detention. In no conceivable sense did he fall within the supposed policy of detaining leaders and active fascists; indeed when he was detained in August 1940 there was no evidence that he was a member of the party at all. In February 1941 his release was recommended; on 11 March the order was suspended, one of the conditions being that he notify any change of address. Marson joined a ship, the SS *Chaucer*; when the Captain found out he had been detained, he came near to losing this job. The vessel put to sea, was bombed, and the voyage abandoned. In an attempt to bury his past he moved to Manchester without notifying the police, and used another name; he associated there with BU sympathizers. For the breach of condition he was sentenced to twenty-eight days, and then re-detained. He became embittered and wanted to emigrate. MI5 viewed him as utterly unreliable and, surely absurdly, dangerous, but Morris and his committee, before whom he appeared in October 1943, did not agree with the second claim. The case raised

certain long term issues to which at this stage of the war they feel bound to draw attention . . . The period of twenty five years before the world war was one in large measure of cynicism and frustration. As such it was a fruitful ground for the growth of specious theories especially attractive to the disgruntled and the half educated. Mosley's party undoubtedly owed much of its success to the disillusion and dislocation of the period.

Morris argued that consideration should now be given to helping the rank and file who had been drawn into the movement:

If no effort of any kind is made to restore them to some useful place in the community many of them will remain permanently embittered and consequently easy tools in the hands of mischief makers more experienced and more unscrupulous

---

[100] HO 283/49. The Home Office file 45/25736 has a retained subfile. According to his own account the case made against him initially was that he was anti-British and pro-German, not that he was BU. He had been in touch with a German propaganda organization before the war. Marson emigrated to Canada after the war and later worked in Germany, where he died in December 1990.

than themselves . . . Any person known to have been detained during the war under 18B will be a marked man.

Morris's plea appears to have fallen on deaf ears, though Home Office officials certainly had some sympathy with young detainees. In 1941 there had been some discussion of segregating them; there were then eighty-five detainees aged 21 or less, many of them Anglo-Italians. But the idea was dropped in favour of a policy for releasing as many of them as possible. Superintendent Ogden, Commandant at Peveril, opposed segregation, and thought the young detainees often the worst of all.[101]

The Bond of Martyrdom

It is clear that the effect of detention on at least some members of the BU was to forge a bond of martyrdom between them; thus Domvile's diary for 22 October 1943 recorded 'Quentin Joyce to lunch and stayed to 6.25 bus—these 18Bs do hang on!'[102] One expression of this bond was the organization of reunions. The first, on 27 May 1944, involved a fund-raising concert in the Kingsway Hall; between 500 and 600 attended.[103] There was a Christmas gathering in 1944 and a fund-raising dinner-dance on 24 March 1945, organized by L. A. ('Alf') Lockhart.[104] The second Christmas gathering was in the Royal Hotel in Woburn Place, of all locations to choose, on 15 December 1945; there was a scuffle with a journalist and questions were asked in the Commons.[105] The 'Friends of Sir Oswald Mosley' continue to hold annual gatherings today. To what extent the revival on a small scale of modified fascism after the war was affected by the bonds formed in detention it is not easy to say, but quite a number of former detainees were active in Mosley's Union Movement after the war.[106] Of his principal lieutenants Francis-Hawkins, though apparently involved behind the scenes, was not openly politically active. He took up his earlier employment with a Derby-based medical supply company, but as a result of a strike, said to have been communist-led, lost this job in

[101] HO 215/168, contains lists of young detainees. In December 1941 there were 64 detainees at Peveril Camp under 23, most being Anglo-Italians or BU.

[102] DOM 56. Other examples are a visit from Miss Faulkner on 23 May 1944. On 19 June 1944 Domvile sent £20 to George Sutton, Mosley's former secretary, who had 'written in great distress, poor chap'. There is much similar evidence in the Saunders Papers. Thus former detainees Miss Griffin and Miss Ryder employed Major de Laessoe on their smallholding (letter of 17 December 1944) and for a time Lt. Fane employed P. Davies, a former detainee.

[103] DOM 27 May 1944. Domvile attended and the Hammonds, Joe Beckett, the de Laessoes, and Pitt-Rivers.

[104] The Saunders Papers contain a souvenir programme, from which it appears that 'Blackie' Baker was one of the musicians.

[105] *Parl. Deb* .HC Vol. 417 c.1542.

[106] Generally see Skidelsky, *Oswald Mosley*, 490ff., Thurlow, *Fascism in Britain*, ch. 10.

May 1945, and then set up his own company, Household and Industrial Cleaning. He died aged 47 in 1950.[107] Raven-Thomson took a prominent part as Secretary, and edited *Union* until his death in October 1955. Clarke appears to have given up politics; he had considerable difficulties in finding employment, working for a time on Mosley's farm estate. Donovan had similar difficulties and withdrew from politics; he became an active Roman Catholic; in due course he became a Tertiary of the Lay Order of the Carmelites at Aylesford Priory. He died in 1985.[108]

After the war had ended an attempt was made by Sir John Mellor and Richard Stokes to persuade the Home Office to provide former detainees with a chance to clear their names before a court of law, or to provide the evidence upon which they had been detained, but this was refused.[109] Over the years an uncertain number of former detainees have corresponded with the Home Office directly, or through their Members of Parliament, but without achieving any success; so too have relatives of detainees, understandably concerned about the reasons why their parents or whatever were locked up. The official line taken is that since detainees were never convicted of any offence, 'There is no power by which the Home Secretary can affect or, as it were, "wipe out" the fact that [he] was detained under the exceptional powers of detention in the Defence regulations. I am afraid I can only confirm that there is no action which the Home Secretary could now properly take.'[110] Since the Home Office has destroyed virtually all their files such attempts are now largely futile.

Conceivably MI5 files still survive; there is some evidence that information about detainees has been passed to Commonwealth governments, and if so MI5 is more likely to be the culprit than the Home Office. Arthur Marson lost a job with the Australian Immigration Service in 1972, apparently because it came to light that he had been detained. A Home Office letter of that year concedes that such information has been communicated, without conceding that his job was lost for this reason.[111]

Campaigns against the Regulation

Within the Commons there were always members prepared to take up the cases of individual detainees.[112] A few actively opposed the regulation on

---

[107] HO 45/25700, *Jewish Chronicle*, 4 May 1945 cited Thurlow, *Fascism in Britain*. 228, *Comrade*, 11.

[108] Information from the Bishop of London, *Comrade*, 30.

[109] *Parl. Deb.* HC Vol. 417 c.381–2, 24 October 1945. The matter had previously been raised on 11 October.

[110] Letter from J. Patten to R. Fearn MP of 28 August 1988 dealing with J. W. Charnley.

[111] I have a copy.

[112] HO 45/25758 lists of 121 detainees whose cases had been raised by MPs, 61 by Conservatives, 30 by Labour, 5 by Independents, 4 by Liberals, and 1 by Commonwealth.

principle: in particular Richard Stokes. After the initial debate in 1939 the leading critics—Morrison, Jowitt, Cripps, and Foot—were in due course absorbed into the government, but there were a small number of members who continued to challenge 18B. In the whole course of the war there were eleven debates relating to the regulation in the Commons, and two in the Lords.[113] The next significant debate took place on 10 December 1940 when Stokes launched a general attack on the regulation and its administration, but without dividing the House; what generated support was not so much opposition to the regulation itself, but the administrative collapse caused by the mass arrests of the summer. The following day there was opposition to accepting the report of the Committee of Privileges over the detention of Ramsay. Many questions were asked about individuals at this period.[114] By the end of February 1941 the pressure eased, though particular cases continued to be raised.[115] On 4 March an attempt was made, without success, to persuade the Home Office to provide Parliament with the reasons for Ramsay's detention, and on 23 July opponents of 18B, including P. C. Loftus, the member for Lowestoft, aired their grievances when the Emergency Powers (Defence) Act came up for renewal. The Liversidge and Greene decisions in November 1941 produced a new flurry of activity, with requests that the regulation should be modified to conform to Lord Atkin's dissenting opinion. This produced a debate on 26 November, on a motion of Sir Irving Albery, seconded by Sir Archibald Southby. The House was not divided.[116] So the government weathered the storm, and Morrison made no concessions. The publicity given to the case of Ben Greene caused further activity in the Commons, but there was no debate.[117] The next serious attack was launched on 21 July 1942 by Commander Bower in a motion to reduce the Home Office vote. In the debate D. N. Pritt KC spoke warmly in favour of the regulation, which he thought should be more firmly used.[118] There was a division; the voting was a mere 22 against 222. Morrison continued to resist all suggestions for change. Thus

---

[113] *Parl. Deb.* HC Vol. 351 c.63–110 (24 August 1939), 352: 1829–902 (31 October 1939), 367: 836–83 (10 December 1940), 933–91 (11 December 1940), 369: 864–79 (4 March 1941), 373: 941–1024 (23 July 1941), 376: 776–862 (26 November 1941), 381: 1426–519 (21 July 1942), 386: 1375–412 (10 February 1943), 391: 425–56 (15 July 1943), 400: 2317–418 (16 June 1944), and *Parl. Deb.* HL 115: 27–61 (29 November 1939), and 130: 487–516 (25 January 1944).

[114] For example on 19 December 1940 *Parl. Deb.* HC Vol. 367 c.1367 ff. raising the cases of F.W.O. White, D. S. Lawley, A. W. Scott, and J. C. Preen.

[115] For example the case of Councillor and former Mayor John Sperni JP was raised by Stokes on 18 March, *Parl. Deb.* HC Vol. 370 c.33.

[116] Robert Boothby spoke powerfully in this debate.

[117] For example in the *News Chronicle* 6 February 1942—'The Case of Benjamin Greene. A Public Inquiry Must be Held.' *Parl. Deb.* HC Vol. 377 c.1256 for 5 February, col. 1274 for 12 February 1942.

[118] *Parl. Deb.* HC 381: 1473 ff.

on 17 December 1942 he was asked if members could be given the names of constituents kept in detention against the advice of the committee; he refused.[119] On 10 February 1943 Albery raised the case of Domvile; a letter by him to *The Times*, protesting at the procedures of the committee, had been stopped; Peake for the Home Office explained that it was policy to stop all such letters, whatever their contents.[120] Grumblings surfaced again on 15 July when the Emergency Powers (Defence) Act again came up for renewal.

From time to time there were mild concessions; thus on 28 January 1943 Morrison announced that in future, at least as a general rule, British subjects in detention could have unsupervised consultations with their lawyers.[121] The protests at the release of Mosley in 1943, and the less significant opposition to Ramsay's release in 1944, cannot have encouraged Morrison to risk any further liberal gestures. The last Commons debate took place on 16 June 1944, before his release, when it was argued that his continued detention should be justified to the House in Secret Session, and that the regulation ought now to be reconsidered and the ultimate responsibility transferred to a judicial body. In the division 31 members opposed to government, which had a majority of 103.

In late 1943 the Duke of Bedford gave notice of a motion attacking the regulation in the House of Lords; this was debated on 25 January 1944.[122] It posed no threat, and was the last debate of any significance. All in all Parliamentary opposition to Regulation 18B achieved little in the way of formal concessions at any time during the war; even the changes made in 1939 were largely cosmetic. What is impossible to assess is the degree to which fear of trouble in the Commons exercised a restraining influence on the Home Office, or aided it in its conflict with MI5. Ironically what can be documented is that it delayed the release of Mosley's lieutenants.

Outside Parliament, once the invasion scare was over, there was much criticism of the regulation, particularly at the time of the Liversidge and Greene cases. The Society of Friends in 1941 established a committee for the 18B detainees, and protested against the regulation.[123] An organization known as the 18B Publicity Council, largely deriving its support from BU detainees, published a number of pamphlets.[124] *In Search of Justice*,

---

[119] *Parl. Deb*. HC Vol. 385 c.2053.

[120] The text of the letter is given. Boothby spoke in this debate, and on 15 July 1943.

[121] *Parl. Deb*. HC Vol. 386 c.600; in response to pressure from Hickson (HO 144/21992/840194/22).

[122] The brief for Lord Simon is in HO 45/25106, written by C. Ross. Only one other peer, Lord Morris, spoke.

[123] Records which I have not consulted exist in Friends House in London.

[124] Run by G. Dunlop; the Secretary was a Mrs P. E. Jones and the Treasurer J. Jones. I have not traced a copy of *Magna Carta in the Dustbin* by Jane Zedd, or of *The Case of G. R. Merriman*.

by Henry St George, argued that the regulation was both unconstitutional and unjust.[125] *Shall Injustice Prevail?* by Ernest Dudley BA gives a historical account of British liberty and argues that 18B should be abolished. *Runnymede Reversed: Tyranny Today:—and Tomorrow?* sets out the legal history of 18B, and was a response to the Greene and Liversidge decisions. *Suffer Little Children*, with a foreword by Clifford Woodland, consists of a statement by W. E. Birch of Norwich from Peveril Camp, dated 20 November 1941; it gives an account of the death of his child, born in detention.[126] *Is This Justice? An Examination of Regulation 18B*, by the Duke of Bedford, published in 1943, was a thirty-six page pamphlet which refers to a considerable number of specific cases and concludes with a number of fairly moderate suggestions—for example that the Advisory Committee should include a legal 'prisoner's friend' to protect his interests, and that on release there should be financial compensation for loss, and no obstacles to securing employment.[127] *Persecuted Women in Britain Today* was perhaps written by Olive Burdett; it is severely critical of early conditions in Holloway. In addition the Smeaton-Stuart Memorandum was circulated as a cyclostyled pamphlet.[128] An organization known as the Petition of Right Council was set up by one Sylvia Morris, with Dr Margaret Dix as Treasurer, and presented a petition to the Home Office requesting that detainees should be put on trial; the same organization also published its own short pamphlet, *It Can't Happen Here*. H. G.

[125] It gave an account of the action brought by Hamilton S. L. Knight, and listed 11 'Tragedies': 1. George R. Merriman, about to leave for Dunkirk. 2. Mr C. whose wife was assaulted after his arrest; not identified. 3. C. M. was a veteran of the Boer War who died shortly after release; probably Kiddell-Monroe, a former Conservative agent. 4. D. was Daniel Delargez, see Wiseman Papers. 5. B., whose wife and two small children were then persecuted, and one sent to an approved school; not identified. 6. R. R., probably R. Rix, an ex-service shell-shocked person in the City; he died 1941. 7. H., a crippled ex-serviceman; not identified. 8. P. T., Palmer Thomson, who died of cancer in Walton. 9. W., who was released unconditionally early 1941, unable to get work, wife blind, three children, died 3 months after release; not identified. 10. G. D., in fact Frank Danby, whose family was killed in Belfast. 11. Mr and Mrs W. E. B. (W. E. Birch).

[126] Evelyn Josephine Birch was born 27 Jan. 1941. 'On the death of the baby daughter we applied to the Home Office for her burial at her native town where others of the family are interred. Permission was granted only on the condition that we undertook the whole expense. As detention for more than a year and a half has deprived us of livelihood and earning capacity we have only been able to make arrangements to pay for the burial of our child by selling some of the last remains of our small property.'

[127] They include those of the Domviles, Greene, Beckett, Gordon-Canning, Ramsay, Dickson, Hamilton-Piercy, Budd, Hopkins, Arbon, Shelmerdine, Evans, Foden, Rose, McEvoy, Bowman, and Burdett. The most curious unidentified case is that of the Director of a Shipping Company detained in June 1941 on evidence provided by Owens (SNOW), whom Bedford somehow knew was associated with the secret service. The pamphlet also claims that all but one of those released as a consequence of the Budd case started legal proceedings, were re-arrested, and released only when they dropped legal proceedings.

[128] Other pamphlets may have included one entitled *1914–18(b)* but I have not traced copies.

Wells was a supporter.[129] Another campaigning organization which had protested back in 1939 against the original 18B, and which financed the litigation by Lees, was the Liberty Restoration League, whose President was the very right-wing Duke of Wellington. It published *How Freedom is in Peril: The Revolution of 1 September 1939* and *The Defence Regulations: Was Parliament Misled?*

But all this activity, much of which took place when the regulation was in any event in decline, achieved very little. There never developed widespread sympathy or support in Britain for 18B detainees as people; in so far as there was a popular view it is that they were a crowd of traitors who richly deserved all that happened to them. More surprisingly perhaps there never developed a strong principled objection to the regulation as a gross invasion of civil liberty; no doubt the explanation lies in the desperate conditions in which it was principally employed. Once the war ended and the detainees were all released, the subject died. In legal circles there persists, as part of received legal culture, disapproval of the interpretation placed upon the regulation by the judges in 1941; Lord Atkin's dissent, its significance in my view wholly misunderstood, has contributed to his being viewed as a sort of legal saint in a profession which is rather light on sanctity. But this myth has wholly failed to interest the public at large.

[129] See *The Times* 15 March 1943.

——— 19 ———

Death and Post Mortem

The Death of 18B

In August and September 1943 conferences took place, attended by representatives of MI5, MI6, and the Security Executive, to decide what was to become of Regulation 18B when the war in Europe ended. Kendal seems to have wanted to retain it permanently; more modestly MI5 wanted to be able to detain for 'acts prejudicial' in Japanese espionage cases until Japan was defeated. This was grudgingly accepted both by the Home Office and the Emergency Legislation Committee; Maxwell feared political difficulties, which perhaps might be avoided by severely narrowing the power.[1] By early 1944 it was settled that at the end of hostilities in Europe all detainees connected with the European war would be released.[2] In the event it was decided not to retain 18B in any form, and it was abolished by an Order in Council passed the day after VE Day.[3] I suspect but cannot prove that Churchill's views played a part in this. Regulation 18, however, remained in force until 1947 under the Emergency Laws (Transitional Provisions) Act of 1946, and under it Mosley and four other persons were prevented from travelling abroad; Mosley and Francis-Hawkins were also denied passports after this regulation lapsed.[4] There was even talk after the war of a permanent legal ban on fascism, a nightmare both to anyone trying to draft legislation and to civil libertarians. But the idea was soon abandoned.[5] So 18B died, or perhaps we should say seemed to die, for we can be quite sure that an updated version of the regulation is alive, and well, and living in a file marked 'Secret' in the Home Office, ready for use if there is a next time. We may be equally sure that the officers of MI5, an institution now ten or more times larger than it was back in 1939 in Kell's day, has its little lists ready for use too.[6]

[1] CAB 71/29 EL (43) 6; HO 45/25108/863041, HH 50/25, 27. Those involved included R. S. Wells, A. H. G. Alston, and K. Diplock of the Security Executive, Petrie, Harker, Liddell, Hollis, Lt.-Col. P. R. Parry, D. C. H. Abbott, J. L. S. Hale, and J. R. P. Milmo of MI5.

[2] CAB 71/29 EL (44) 3 of 14 January.

[3] The decision is not recorded in the Cabinet papers or Home Office file; it may be in 863041/6, not available. Cf. HO 45/19770 and 19771 (End of the War in Europe Book).

[4] *Parl. Deb.* HC Vol. 143 c.847. O. Mosley, *My Life* (London, 1968), 417–18.

[5] HO 45/25399, CAB 128/2 Cab. 63 (45) minute 3, CAB 128/5 Cab. 31 (46) 129 CP (46) 137, discussed R. Thurlow, *Fascism in Britain: A History, 1918–1985* (Oxford, 1987), 234.

[6] P. Hennessy, *Whitehall* (London, 1989), 474, estimates 1,500 employees.

Unmuzzling the Ox

In this book I have tried to tell the story of Regulation 18B in a way which enables my readers to form their own conclusions about it and the uses to which it was put. Inevitably my own interpretation of the evidence will have become reasonably clear, and, on the principle of not muzzling the ox, I shall conclude with some general reflections on the matter.

The story of 18B illustrates a problem which faces liberal democracies in times of grave crisis—is it essential to their survival that they should temporarily cease to be liberal democracies until the threat is over? The problem seems particularly acute when the danger comes from an illiberal enemy, believed at the time, though wrongly, to have its whole economy organized exclusively for war. Was General Ironside correct when, on 8 June 1940 he wrote in his diary: 'The fact remains that no democratic nation could ever hope to compete with a nation which has developed its war effort as the Nazis have. You must also become a Nazi nation in order to survive'?[7] Or was Robert Boothby right when, in a letter written many years later to a former detainee, he wrote: 'I fought the monstrous Regulation 18b from start to finish, as I thought it was what we were fighting to prevent.'[8] Not all problems have solutions, and this is surely true of this particular problem; democracies will no doubt continue to do whatever seems necessary at the time to protect themselves, or politically expedient, and witch-hunts can be politically expedient. But in evaluating what was done from a historical point of view we can ask, as those in positions of power should ask at the time, whether the action taken really was necessary. And, with the advantage of hindsight, we may apply common sense to whether it did contribute significantly to survival, and evaluate the extent to which respect for important values such as personal liberty, fairness to individuals, legality, and simple humanity limited the degree to which autocracy was pursued in the name of state security. In any calculus we also need to include the costs involved; it is an expensive business, for example, to hold people in prison, or to allow a security service to absorb a large number of able individuals, who might be more profitably employed elsewhere.

The case for 18B is easy enough to state in terms of generalizations; when the security of the nation is at stake the risks involved in dealing with disloyal people through the regular mechanisms of the criminal law are too great. Disloyal people need to be arrested *before* they do harm, and wrongdoers put away even though there is no proof which would satisfy a regular criminal court, or which can be presented to one. To be sure the use of the regulation was harsh, and violated basic civil liberties. To lock

---

[7] R. McLeod and D. Kelly, *The Ironside Diaries 1937–1940* (London, 1962), 357.
[8] Letter of Lord Boothby to A. W. Swan, 24 February 1982.

up citizens without trial or term set, to deny them legal representation or
the opportunity to confront their accusers, to refuse to reveal either the
case against them, or the conclusions reached after their cases had been
investigated, to make no special provision for the care of their families
and dependants, or for their rehabilitation, to deny them compensation of
any kind, or even an apology where serious errors were made—it is surely
not necessary to go on. All this may be conceded by a defender of 18B, as
well as the fact that many detention orders were quite unjustified. But,
the argument goes, war is a rough business; you cannot make omelettes
without breaking eggs. When the security of the state, and the very survival of British liberty, is at stake, the rights and interests of individuals
simply have to go by the board. The speech for the defence writes itself.

But the very concept of a threat to state security is so vague as to be
largely meaningless; it suggests that some deviant action or other, usually
of a trivial nature, is, unlike some regular crime like bank robbery, or
indecent exposure, likely to bring the whole fabric of society tumbling
down. Even actions which everyone would agree were 'threats to security'—the thievings of Tyler Kent, or the treachery of John H. King—did
not, in the event, bring anything tumbling down. They caused a lot of
trouble; codes had to be changed, and new staff engaged, but life went on
much as before. So general assertions of the paramountcy of state security
are largely rhetorical; they provide no practical guidance as to what prices
must be paid, and by whom, to prevent troublesome acts of disloyalty. So
far as 18B is concerned they largely beg the question, which is whether the
regulation, and the specific uses to which it was put during the war, contributed to the survival of British liberty. And this question in its turn is
unfortunately so general as to be probably incapable of any very convincing answer. Any suggestion that 'necessity' was involved, in the sense of a
sine qua non, is absurd. Nobody could possibly argue that but for 18B
Britain would have lost the war.

Reflection upon the question I have posed, in the light of the detailed
story I have told, does seem to argue in favour of one important general
conclusion, which, although it will not provide automatic guidance as to
what needs to be done, will at least tend to encourage sensible decisions.
The conclusion is that it is wise to be extremely sceptical when security
services, or indeed anybody else, puts forward the claim that drastic
action needs to be taken against an enemy within: a Fifth Column in this
instance, but in other contexts witches, Judmas, commies, or whatever.
Those who were sceptical in 1940, such as Anderson and Maxwell, were
right. MI5 was dramatically wrong. You can never really trust security
services, for they are in the business of constructing threats to security,
and the weaker the evidence the more sinister the threat is thought to be.
And the mechanisms which insulate them from public accountability con-

tribute to their unreliability and perpetuate the sort of silliness which sur-faced over the *Spycatcher* affair.

Common sense applied to what is known about 18B further strongly suggests the conclusion that very many of those detained under the regu-lation were in no sense significantly dangerous, and that the war would not have lasted an extra day if the vast majority of them had been left at liberty. No doubt some would have been troublesome, but both under the regular criminal law and under the Defence Regulations the executive was amply armed with draconian powers to deal with such people. Those who were caught in misconduct could expect little mercy from the courts of wartime Britain. Thus between 1940 and 1943 121 individuals were con-victed before magistrates of what I have called the grotesque offence of spreading 'alarm and despondency'—as anyone who can remember the period will know, this was a universal and therapeutic social activity. No fewer than forty-eight of these wretched people were actually imprisoned.[9]

Had there been no 18B some few individuals would, no doubt, have 'got away with it', but no doubt numerous troublesome people escaped deten-tion under 18B. No system is perfect. That there was never any real need to lock most detainees up is simply common sense.

It is also as clear as such things are ever going to be that the regulation was used to counter general dangers which simply did not exist. There was no elaborate organization of German agents in Britain at the outbreak of war; Kell and his officers were pursuing a phantom. Nor did the orga-nized and lethally dangerous Fifth Column of April and May 1940 ever exist; a few people engaged in wholly unimportant acts of disloyalty, such as publicizing the NBBS, whose existence was in any event easily discov-erable from the regular press. If a few of the tiny number of Britons who owned short-wave radios had turned from Lord Haw-Haw to the NBBS, it would not have mattered in the least. There was no underground BU ready to assist a German invasion; so far as the Anglo-Italians were con-cerned Kell's and Harker's 'desperate characters' were largely imaginary. In late 1940 the Germans did indeed try to set up agents in Britain; virtu-ally all were caught, and Regulation 18B had nothing whatever to do with their capture. What remains obscure is whether there existed a sizeable number of important people, not associated with political fringe groups, who were working towards an accommodation with Hitler; if so then 18B posed no threat to them. As we have seen, hardly any important people were detained.

The case for general scepticism seems to me to be quite unanswerable.

It does not, of course, follow that the regulation itself was unnecessary;

[9] HO 45/25758.

common sense would also suggest that detentions under 18B may have in some instances prevented individuals with pro-German sympathies from attempted acts of espionage or sabotage, and been useful in contributing to the control of the IRA or in preventing leakage of information about the Normandy landings. Regulation 18B may also have saved some individuals from violence, from long prison terms, or even from death sentences. It certainly ensured that a number of weird eccentrics who held unpopular and sometimes vicious views, such as George Pitt-Rivers, were temporarily tucked out of the way. One can only speculate on the part detention would have played had there been a German invasion; all common sense suggests that the outcome of battles, except in occupied countries where there is an organized resistance, is wholly unaffected by the popular police activity of rounding up the usual suspects, which simply wastes resources, though it may help to preserve morale. And in any assessment of the use of 18B the very considerable costs involved need to be kept in mind, though they were dwarfed by the costs of detaining the 28,000 or so 'enemy aliens'. Some of these costs may, however, be difficult to assess; thus it is hard to know whether detention encouraged the revival of forms of fascism after the war. If so the legacy of 18B remains.

There are many more specific questions about the use and administration of the regulation which may be asked. In practical administration it is such particular questions, arising on a case-to-case basis, which require decision. Was it necessary, or desirable, or understandable, to detain Liversidge? To hold detained women in Holloway? To separate mothers and small children? To refuse detainees legal representation before the Advisory Committee? To stop them writing to the press? To keep Mosley's lieutenants in detention long after he was released? To force-feed Bowman as a punishment? There is no general answer to such questions, nor a general theory which provides one, apart perhaps from one part of Acton's claim: that all power corrupts. Particularly is this true over power exercised in secret. Readers will form their own view. The largest such question arises out of the Cabinet decision to cripple the British Union in the summer of 1940; I have tried to bring out the climate of thought in which that decision was taken, one in which there was both widespread belief in the Fifth Column, though always sceptics like Anderson, and a special sort of political necessity—to exhibit a ruthless determination to continue the war against Germany at whatever cost. The critical consideration at the time will often be the alternatives; I have suggested that in May 1940 allowing the BU alone to continue its activities could not have long remained an option for Churchill's government, though this, if true, did not necessarily entail the mass detentions which followed. There were other mechanisms which could have been employed to cripple the party, and the authorities never gave them a chance. Those who are not so deeply committed to the ideals of liberal democracy may argue that stamping out the fascist party, as no doubt the fascists would have stamped out the CPGB, and indeed liberal democracy, was a good thing anyway; this was the view of many at the time. Even Richard Stokes told the Commons that Mosley should be shot, though after a trial. But Mosley's party was, for all practical purposes, dead in 1940 anyway, and at no point in its history remotely approached power. Events would surely have crippled it and excluded Mosley from serious politics, and Mosley's attempt at a comeback after the war was a fiasco.

Some critics of 18B at the time, and today, would go beyond pragmatic scepticism, and view executive detention as simply wrong in principle. It is perhaps worth remembering that any absolute objection to detention without trial runs into problems unless it also excludes the pre-trial detention of persons accused of crimes, and the detention of the mentally ill, or at least explains why these practices may neverthless be justifiable.

The Moderation of the Authorities

The scheme of government, embodied in emergency legislation, under which both the First and Second World Wars were fought, has been called by Clinton Rossiter *Constitutional Dictatorship*. Within a normally liberal and democratic state there is a transfer, through the forms of law, of autocratic power, including law-making power, to an executive government composed of civilians rather than the military, and an accompanying massive diminution in the liberties of individuals. This transfer occurs in response to crisis, and is understood to have as its purpose the restoration of the 'normal' state of affairs which preceded that crisis. It is therefore intended to be temporary only. In analysing British wartime government in the light of this model Rossiter specifically discusses 18B, 'the most radical invasion of a cherished English liberty', and makes the point that it was used with remarkable moderation; he characterizes the peak number of detainees as 'a trifling number considering the state of England's defenses at that time'.[10] In a comparative sense this is true. In the USA, for example, the number of citizens detained, with far weaker justification, if indeed any at all, was around 65,000. In the west, where the detentions took place, there was no risk whatever of an invasion; the detention policy fed on a combination between panic and racialism. There were also extensive 'relocations' in Canada, and, though I have not investigated the matter, many detentions in France before the German attack.[11] What happened in Germany was of course on a wholly different

[10] C. L. Rossiter, *Constitutional Dictatorship: Crisis Government in the Modern Democracies* (New York, 1963), 197, and generally ch. 13.

[11] See my 'Detention Without Trial in the Second World War: Comparing the British

scale. If it is conceded that the scale on which civil liberty was invaded under Regulation 18B was relatively modest, that such ill-treatment as the detainees suffered was mainly not malevolent in design, and that the severe fall from grace was confined to the desperate period between May 1940 and February or so of 1941, there is a problem of explanation. So far as the Communist Party is concerned that explanation was in part fear; the party was too powerful, and there was nervousness of industrial unrest. But communists apart there were many others who might have been detained: what forces and institutions tended to protect civil liberty and restrain the executive from using its draconian powers more freely?

Of the institutions involved Parliament, primarily the Commons, behaved in a somewhat fickle way. Initially hostile to the original regulation, its intervention in 1939 had little practical effect; in the panic time of 1940 it tended to demand repressive action. Thereafter its behaviour broadly supports the conclusion reached by J. Eaves, that 'it was able to act as a fairly effective watchdog', though the number of members prepared actually to vote against 18B was always very small.[12] This, in Morrison's hypocritical view, was its function: 'What the House must do is to keep watch on the Home Secretary . . . to look out for cases where in their judgement he has gone wrong and they can get evidence that he has . . . I agree it is not cricket, but I cannot help it.'[13] The hypocrisy is plain; the whole system was run, so far as possible, in secret so as to prevent the Commons acting as a watchdog. For example members were not told which of their constituents was detained.[14] There was no security reason for this, and throughout the life of 18B there was never candour with the Commons, whose members had extreme difficulty in discovering cases in which the Home Office had gone astray. Nevertheless the pressure from some members must surely have had its influence in producing moderation in the use of the regulation; to this extent it is right to say that the Commons was a *fairly* effective watchdog.

Leaving on one side their absolute hostility to open government the Home Office officials, particularly Maxwell, come out of the story reasonably well; so surely does Anderson. Given the pressures of the time, and the constraints under which they operated, it might well have all been much worse. Anderson's capitulation in May of 1940 perhaps derives from the fact that although he was now a Minister, he remained at heart a civil servant, there to implement policy rather than make it, controlled ulti-

and American Experiences', *Florida State Law Review* 16 (1988), 225. For Canada see K. Adachi, *The Enemy that Never Was: A History of the Japanese Canadians* (Toronto, 1976) and F. E. La Violette, *The Canadian Japanese and World War II: A Sociological and Psychological Account* (Toronto, 1948).

[12] J. Eaves, *Emergency Powers and the Parliamentary Watchdog: Parliament and the Executive in Great Britain 1939–1951* (London, 1957), 187–8.

[13] *Parl. Deb.* HC Vol. 381 c.1509, 21 July 1942.   [14] Ibid. 385: 2053.

mately by his political masters, here the War Cabinet. Until May of 1940 the Home Office was a severe restraint on MI5; after a general loss of control in the summer of 1940, restraint was reimposed, and many detainees were in consequence released. In general Home Office officials seem to have genuinely respected legality, though there was a willingness to stretch things and break the rules when it seemed in the public interest to do so, for example over the detention of Liversidge, or the use of 18B to detain arriving aliens about whom nothing whatever was known, or over Latchmere House. So far as the conditions of detention are concerned the record is more mixed. Much of the apparent inhumanity involved in detention—for example the separation of mothers from young children—was simply typical of the normal repressive activities of government, over which the Home Office presided; no doubt officials, particularly those associated with the prisons, developed a somewhat thick skin as a normal incident of their employment. A great deal of what the Home Office did, or still does, is intrinsically very unpleasant—keeping people locked up, deporting them, refusing them admission to the country, and so forth. At this period the Home Office also organized forced feeding, flogging, birching, and killing. It also licensed what is called surveillance, that is spying on people, as by opening private letters, and listening in on telephone calls. A certain detachment is needed to preside over such things. The heavy weather made of the suggestion that couples should be allowed to live together, for example, derives from this, and from the inevitable isolation of officials from the reality over which they presided. Civil Servants deal with files, not people. Much of the unpleasant treatment of detainees arose through the inability of the officials to cope with the massive increase in the use of detention in the summer of 1940, for which, ultimately, the War Cabinet rather than the Home Office was responsible.

A more serious general criticism of the Home Office is that in spite of the releases of late 1940 and early 1941 it continued to uphold detention of the fascists on a considerable scale long after the original ground for their detention was known to be baseless. To put the point in a different way, the original action against the BU had been based on military grounds; the action was persisted in on purely political grounds—positively to stamp out the fascist party, negatively to fend off trouble with the Labour Party. Once Mosley was set free the continued detention of his lieutenants was a mere act of political expediency. In this it seems to have been the politicians, particularly Morrison, who bear the main responsibility, rather than the officials, and since even Churchill did not feel able to bring about the abolition of 18B, and this long after it seemed to him to be unjustified, we ought perhaps to place the blame on Parliament and public opinion generally. For there was, as Churchill himself lamented, no strong public pressure against the continuance of 18B even after 1941; as the *Manchester Guardian* titled a leader on 27 November 1941, 18B was 'Obnoxious but Inevitable'. And, as late as 1944, the number of members of the Commons prepared to vote for rethinking the system which had kept one of their colleagues in detention for four years on unrevealed grounds was only a miserable thirty-one. The story might make a cynic wonder whether the British do have any strong commitment to civil liberty; perhaps the explanation is that the British—or at least the vocal middle classes—then tended to defer to strong government, and to trust their masters, to whose wisdom they deferred. And certainly a respect for liberty and the legal spirit in the higher Civil Service can go a long way to offset public apathy, and in the Home Office this certainly existed. F. A. Newsam, writing the preface to *The Home Office* after the war, was not, I think, being hypocritical in conceiving of the two functions of his department as being 'the preservation of order and the maintenance of civil liberty'.

A great deal may be said against the advisory committees. Clearly Birkett, and his colleagues too, sailed close to the wind on occasions—for example over the Lees case, over Liversidge, and indeed over Mosley himself. They went along, albeit with grumbling, with such practices as denying the detainee adequate knowledge of the case against him, and favoured the refusal of legal representation. Yet it is quite clear that Birkett and his colleagues—Morris in particular and also Loraine—played an important part in making matters better than they would otherwise have been for detainees. Indeed informants have assured me that Birkett himself detested the whole system; the analogy is with a prison doctor in the days of capital punishment who abominates the practice, but is prepared to do his best for the condemned man, for example by reporting on his mental state, or by providing tranquillizing drugs. Essentially the committees operated within standards of conduct appropriate to Civil Servants; they took the system for granted and operated it as benignly as they could. But participation in the system served to legitimate it, and the fact that lawyers were involved, and from 1941 a real judge, conveyed the impression that in some obscure sense the legal rights of detainees were safe. A public resignation by Birkett, say in 1941, would have greatly strengthened the hands of the critics of 18B, and perhaps ended it, but Birkett was never one to rock the boat. Undoubtedly he and his colleagues, in uneasy alliance with the Home Office against MI5, brought about many releases from detention.

The Security Service

What little is known of the behaviour of the Security Service, or what has come to be called, somewhat ridiculously, 'the intelligence community', for 'the intelligence gang' would surely be a better title, does not inspire confidence, and inspired little in either the Home Office or its committee at the time. The service was inadequately financed before the war, and weakened by a defective system of recruitment. Its archive must have largely comprised ill-digested and unreliable tittle-tattle. What is noticeable too is the way in which it concentrated on deviant groups, such as the Nordic League or Right Club, which possessed about as much significance in the life of the nation as the Flat Earth Society. Had its officers been more competent there would never have been such pressure for detention in 1940, and the administrative confusion of the service was, in part at least, the consequence of the paranoia it had encouraged. With the recruitment of new staff on a very lavish scale, and the appointment of Petrie, the impression one gains, and it can be little more, is that matters improved, and resistance to the release of detainees waned. Victor Cavendish-Bentinck, Chairman of the Joint Intelligence Committee, defending the service in 1940, for example against the claim that its chiefs were 'long retired military officers regarding whose capacities the less said the better', wrote with some justice: 'It is not possible to build up an efficient contre-espionage organization in a few weeks. For years M.I.5 has been starved of funds, and after war broke out they did not succeed in recruiting officers of the calibre a contre-espionage system requires.' It had taken much longer, he added, to bring the Gestapo to its admirable state of efficiency.[15]

Yet the continued support for extensive detention in spite of the fact that its original rationale, the organized Fifth Column, was known to be a myth, is disturbing, as is Petrie's continued support of so flawed a creature as Kurtz. One cannot but wonder what other seedy individuals were relied upon. The process by which MI5 became proprietor of lavishly staffed private and secret prisons is surely extremely worrying. So far as Special Branch is concerned Kendal comes across as a deeply illiberal and somewhat silly person, but the evidence is quite inadequate to enable any assessment to be made of the efficiency of his force.

MI5's chief achievement in 1940 was the detention of the aliens; 18B detentions, justified by the same myth, were on a much smaller scale, and involved individuals for whom, if we except the Anglo-Italians, there was much less natural sympathy. The Foreign Office archives from which I have already quoted contain a diatribe by R. E. T. Latham against MI5 which was provoked by this disaster.[16] Apart from its general criticisms of MI5—lack of experience in weighing evidence, lack of political

[15] FO 371 365ff. Minute of 29 July 1940. V. F. W. Cavendish-Bentinck was a career Foreign Office official.
[16] Latham was a Fellow of All Souls who was employed in the Foreign Office refugee section; remembered for *The Law and the Commonwealth* (1949).

understanding, stupidity and poor organization—it made an important structural point on the relationship between MI5 and the Home Office, which was as relevant to 18B detentions as to the detention of aliens.

[The Home Office] has been placed in the anomalous and humiliating position of having to administer and to acknowledge as its own a policy which it did not desire, the details of which it did not frame, and to which it is not in a position to make exceptions and modifications except by reference to an independent authority whose nature is such that it cannot be made publicly responsible for its actions. Inefficient administration by the Home Office is a natural consequence of this situation.

Thus over 18B, as we have seen, the independent and secret character of MI5 enabled it to withhold information and evidence from the Home Office's committee, and to pressure the Home Office into decisions whose merits the Home Office was unable to check, and for which the Home Office was nevertheless politically responsible. The other side of the same coin, Latham pointed out, was that the Home Office was tempted to defend itself by 'sheltering, as they now do, under the advice of the Security Services'. Placing MI5 under the control of Swinton, not himself a minister, merely added another complication; it was still the Home Office which bore the responsibility. It is perhaps ironic that it was Anderson himself, perhaps the greatest Civil Servant of his time, who had earlier been involved in perpetuating the very system of independence and irresponsibility which led him to preside over the administrative chaos of the summer of 1940. But the fact that MI5 was an organization distinct from the Home Office may have made it easier for Home Office officials to assume a position of conflict with it, which contributed considerably to the protection of liberty.

The Law

Lawyers and legal institutions do not seem to come out of the story at all well. The courts certainly caused considerable nervousness in the Home Office, and some of the judges took pleasure in being rude to the civil servants; thus in Budd's case in the Court of Appeal the Master of the Rolls, Lord Greene, referred to the mistake made as a 'cynical piece of carelessness' which, no doubt, it was not.[17] But the courts did virtually nothing for the detainees, either to secure their liberty, to preserve what rights they did possess under the regulation, to scrutinize the legality of Home Office action, or to provide compensation when matters went wrong. The legal profession too, as a profession, did nothing; I am told that it was not

---

[17] [1942] 1 All ER 377.

easy to persuade lawyers to act for detainees at all. Only a very few lawyers, notably Oswald Hickson and Gerald Gardiner, played any active role. Some would add from the judiciary Stable and Atkin, though I doubt whether concern for detainees was their principal motivation. So far as the government lawyers were concerned, the Treasury Solicitor's Department comes across as unattractive; its ethos was ruthless determination to win cases at the least possible cost. One cannot but be struck by the absence in the papers of any hint of sympathy to those who litigated, or any generosity of spirit to individuals none of whom had been charged or convicted of any crime. Of the Law Officers Somervell seems to have sailed very close to the wind, and both he and Jowitt changed their tune over the relationship between the courts and the regulation. I cannot but suspect that other examples of dubious conduct have been concealed by the accidental loss of Treasury Solicitor's files—for example in the cases of Bowman, Budd, and Wilson; other surviving papers are not obtainable. In Bowman's case the Crown lawyers successfully defended conduct which Holmes at least regarded as illegal, as indeed it surely was. The behaviour of government lawyers is part of a general feature of Civil Service behaviour; protecting the department from outside criticism takes precedence over most other considerations. Newsam's advice that errors should never be conceded is an example that this attitude was in no way special to the lawyers. As for the traditional judicial practice of trumpeting professional solicitude for the liberty of the subject, the less said the better.

But an advocate for the judges might argue in reply at least to part of the indictment that the whole scheme of the defence regulations—whether or not all MPs understood this—placed executive power in detention cases in the hands of the Home Office, indeed in those of the Secretary of State personally. And, except where the regulation expressly provided otherwise, he was to determine the rights of detainees, the conditions of their detention, and the procedures followed over appeals and reviews, all this at his own discretion. The courts were never intended to have any significant role in the business of state security. This general approach was very clearly set out by Lord Denning in *R. v. Secretary of State ex parte Hosenball*, a deportation case, in 1977: 'There is a conflict between the interests of national security on the one hand and the freedom of the individual on the other. The balance between these two is not for a court of law. It is for the Home Secretary. He is the person entrusted by Parliament with the task.' Lord Denning went on to weaken his statement of principle with some rhetorical rubbish to the effect that the Home Office had always got everything right, and caused universal satisfaction, but this does not affect the fact that his statement more or less accurately sets out the reality of the relationship between courts and

executive during the two wars.[18] In particular it states the philosophy
behind the leading case of *Liversidge* v. *Anderson*.

At the time the *Manchester Guardian* summarized that decision as well
as it can be done:[19]

Yesterday's judgement in the House of Lords leaves it clear that the Law Lords
have pretty well washed their hands of any concern in the exercise of Defence
Regulation 18B; it is the Home Secretary's province, and the Lords of Appeal are
not competent to criticise, discuss, or control any action he may take under that
regulation 'provided only that he acts in good faith'. As they must be even less
competent to challenge the good faith of the Secretary of State the field is left to
him, and to him alone.

Yet the doctrines of the courts have never been that the law has no role
whatever to play in controlling the exercise of executive powers simply
because they are powers related to state security. Given commitment to
the ideal of the rule of law, together with the notion that the superior
courts (rather than some other entity, such as the Jockey Club or the
Home Office) have, under British constitutional arrangements, an ultimate responsibility for imposing the rule of law on the institutions of government, it inevitably follows that the courts ought to have some
function. In the history of 18B and its precursor 14B this was never
denied. Indeed outside the particular field of security a massive body of
administrative law has been developed under which courts have an
important role to play in controlling other governmental institutions in
the exercise of power, and in providing remedies in cases in which there
has been a supposed abuse of power, or misconduct of one kind or
another by governmental agencies.[20] Throughout this branch of the law
the persistent problem is one of demarcation between the role of the
courts and their law, and the role of the discretionary power of other governmental institutions, controlled by policy and ultimately at least in theory by Parliament where central government is engaged. Subject to the
fact that Parliament can overrule them, the courts decide what their role
is, and the principles they then formulate to express this role are called
the law.

Thus over 18B the courts, as we have seen, decided that they had the
job of settling the form of legally valid detention orders, and then ruled
that so long as they were written they were valid. This became thus 'the
law' on the matter; other details were, under the law, at the 'discretion' of
the Home Secretary. Obviously the courts could have refused to go so far

[18] [1977] 1 WLR 166. For discussion and fuller quotation see J. A. G. Griffith, *The Politics
of the Judiciary*, 4th edn. (London, 1990), ch. 5.
[19] 4 November 1941.
[20] A clear account is given by P. Cane, *An Introduction to Administrative Law* in the
Clarendon Law Series (Oxford, 1986).

even as this, and left the whole matter to the Home Office. What is noticeable over the behaviour of the courts in both 14B and 18B cases is that, although they had numerous choices to make, the tendency was always to assume a very small role, and thereby increase the area of discretion left under the law to the Home Office. They did, as the *Manchester Guardian* put it, 'pretty well wash their hands of any concern'. Even when, as in Lees's case, the judges asserted the considerable role of deciding whether the Home Secretary had 'reasonable grounds' to make an order or not, they backed off from taking this assertion seriously. Its only fruit was Humphreys' and perhaps Singleton's opinion in Budd's first case, and essentially Budd was released simply to teach the Home Office better manners.

A case can I think be made for saying that the judges did the right thing, and that the decision in *Liversidge* v. *Anderson* was appropriate in a security case where the whole process of executive decision was shrouded in secrecy. How could the judges have any function when they had no idea why the individuals had been detained, and were more or less completely ignorant even over the administrative procedures involved? Given the veil of secrecy 'the law' had nothing to contribute. Thus Liversidge's own order for 'hostile associations' was, at the least, very close to being an example of an order made in bad faith, but the judges were wholly ignorant of this.

If the force of this argument is conceded, as in my view it must be, even if we do not find it compelling, there is a somewhat disturbing conclusion. Imposition of the rule of law upon governmental action through the courts is simply incompatible with secret administration, and in the conflict between secrecy and the rule of law secrecy wins. Of course the courts themselves, as Greene suggested in his habeas corpus proceedings, might join the secret state themselves, as Birkett and his colleagues did, but this hardly solves the problem, for public accountability is integral to the ideal of the rule of law. Furthermore secret administration, as was pointed out at the time, is incompatible with Parliamentary control and sovereignty too.[21] All we are left with is self-regulation within the executive, as occurred in the wartime Home Office under Maxwell and Newsam, with only a very limited degree of public accountability dependent upon the leakage of at least some information about what is going on.

Yet it is not clear that the courts had to wash their hands of responsibility as enthusiastically as they did. They could have carved out for themselves a larger role. Thus had Stable's suggestion in *Budd No. 2* been followed they would have prised more information out of the executive in that and other 18B cases, and thereby empowered themselves to exercise a

---

[21] See the debate of 21 July 1942, *Parl. Deb.* HC Vol. 381 c.1426ff.

greater degree of supervision, for example in the interpretation of the categories employed. By accepting the laconic Home Office affidavits, before *Liversidge* v. *Anderson* made even them redundant, they hamstrung themselves. The claim that they carried out 'the intention of Parliament' is mere rhetoric; on the detailed administration and interpretation of 18B no such thing existed or could exist. No doubt they could never have penetrated far into the secret world without encountering strong resistance both from the Home Office and its lawyers, and ultimately from MI5, and any resulting conflict would have been resolved by the political process; the outcome might have been some form of compromise. But a judiciary which does not champion the rule of law will tend to diminish the respect in which the courts are held, and there is a sense in which judges like Stable and Atkin may have been right in conceiving of the conflict in terms of status: not so much their personal status, but that of the institution to which they belonged.

Government Secrecy

This study has been hampered both by the destruction of about 99 per cent of public records dealing with detention, which is in line with general practice, and by refusal of access to such records as still do exist, which include records dealing with Ramsay, Pitt-Rivers, Greene, Budd, Domvile, Mason, and Nicholson, and no doubt others; there must also exist material on Fuller.[22] The Home Office has also destroyed its own internal history of the regulation.[23] The extent to which MI5 records still exist is itself kept secret. Most destruction is simply, so far as one can tell, random, and designed to reduce bulk.[24] One has only got to look at the Public Record Office at Kew and compare its size to that of a warehouse or aircraft hangar to see that provision for the preservation of British public records is on a pathetic scale. Obviously the records of detention were going to be of interest to historians—those of the fascists in particular—but there is no evidence so far as I am aware that any competent historian was ever consulted; there is indeed a committee but I am told that it does nothing. Some weeding of files and destruction may be inspired by sinister motives, or just by a desire to show the department in a good light. Most is just institutionalized vandalism, driven by parsimony and philis-

[22] Home Office papers do not survive on Luttman-Johnson, Vaughan-Henry, Randall, Durell, or Sherston of those who litigated.

[23] By C. D. Carew-Robinson. See HO 45/25754/86300. The destruction was confirmed by letters to me from the Home Office of 22 April and 11 August 1988; the Departmental Records Officer clearly regretted this, but knew of no explanation.

[24] The system is mercifully full of inconsistency. Thus PREM 4/31 contains Churchill's prominent persons detained; it is closed for 75 years. The same lists are open in HO 45/25747.

tine lack of regard for national history. Given the rooted hostility of the Civil Service to open government it is hardly surprising that it destroys most government records.

Refusal of access to what little does survive after this lapse of time seems quite extraordinary. Prolonged correspondence with the Home Office has, in my case, led to access to a very few files; in general I just gave up. Those I was allowed to see on Greene comprised transcripts of litigation heard in open court in 1943; why they should not be in the Public Records is beyond me. In general the few papers I have seen on privileged access, in both London and Edinburgh, should all have been released under the thirty-year rule. Apart from the historical interest in such material, and the irritation caused by the sheer silliness of the Home Office, Lord Chancellor's Department, and Security Service, there is a point of principle involved, and it concerns accountability for secret executive action in a democracy when it grossly invades civil liberty. Under 18B the Home Office and security service exercised largely uncontrolled power, in secret, over British citizens. The imposition of secrecy made it largely impossible for Parliament to exercise any general supervision at the time; all that members of Parliament could do was to harry. The judges washed their hands of responsibility, and would have encountered serious difficulties if they had not. Accountability was principally left to the individual consciences of the Civil Servants engaged in the business, and they actively concealed their activities at the time. This state of affairs may have been necessary or desirable in the 1940s, though even then Churchill himself had his doubts, once the crisis of 1940 was past. The war has now been over for forty-seven years, and it seems to me at least that officialdom should no longer hinder the provision of historical accounts of how this power was exercised. Were all government departments to follow the spirit of the formal arrangements for the Public Records there would be less cause for complaint, though the problem of mass destruction would remain. We applaud *glasnost* in Eastern Europe not simply because the revelations which follow are entertaining; it is about time it spread to Britain, and I can only hope that this book, necessarily imperfect though it is, may contribute to that end.

APPENDIX I
The Principal Texts

A. The Emergency Powers (Defence) Act of 1939 allowed the executive to make defence regulations which could: 'make provision for . . . the detention of persons whose detention appears to the Secretary of State to be expedient in the interests of the public safety or the defence of the realm.'

B. The original Regulation 18B of 1 September 1939 provided that: 'The Secretary of State, if satisfied with respect to any person, that with a view to preventing him acting in any manner prejudicial to the public safety, or the defence of the realm, it is necessary to do so, may make an order . . . ' (The order could be a detention order.)

C. The amended regulation of 23 November 1939, provided: 'Detention 18B. (1) If the Secretary of State has reasonable cause to believe any person to be of hostile origin or associations or to have been recently concerned in acts prejudicial to the public safety or the defence of the realm or in the preparation or instigation of such acts and that by reason thereof it is necessary to exercise control over him, he may make an order against that person directing that he be detained. (2) At any time after an order has been made against any person under this regulation, the Secretary of State may direct that the operation of the order be suspended subject to such conditions—(a) prohibiting or restricting the possession or use by that person of any specified articles; (b) imposing upon him such restrictions as may be specified in the direction in respect of his employment or business, and in respect of his association or communication with other persons; as the Secretary of State thinks fit; and the Secretary of State may revoke any such direction if he is satisfied that the person against whom the order was made has failed to observe any condition so imposed, or that the operation of the order can no longer remain suspended without detriment to the public safety or the defence of the realm. (3) For the purposes of this regulation, there shall be one or more advisory committees consisting of persons appointed by the Secretary of State; and any person aggrieved by the making of an order against him, by a refusal of the Secretary of State to suspend the operation of such an order, by any condition attached to a direction given by the Secretary of State or by the revocation of such direction, under the powers conferred by this regulation, may make his objections to such a committee. (4) It shall be the duty of the Secretary of State to secure that any person against whom an order is made under this regulation shall be afforded the earliest practicable opportunity of making to the Secretary of State representations in writing with respect thereto, and that he shall be informed of his right, whether or not such representations are made, to make his objections to such an advisory committee as aforesaid. (5) Any meeting of an advisory committee held to consider such objections as aforesaid shall be presided over by a chairman nominated by the Secretary of State and it shall be the duty of the chairman to inform the objector of the grounds on which the order has been made and to furnish him with such particulars as are in the opinion of the chairman sufficient to enable him to present his case. (6) The Secretary of State shall make a report to Parliament at least once in every month as to the action taken under this regulation (including the number of persons detained under orders made thereunder) and as to the number of cases, if any, in which he has declined to follow the advice of any such advisory committee as aforesaid. (7) If any person fails to comply with a condition attached to a direction given by the Secretary of State under paragraph (2) of this regulation that person shall, whether or not the direction is revoked in consequence of the failure, be guilty of an offence against this regulation. (8) Any person detained in pursuance of this regulation shall be deemed to be in lawful custody and shall be detained in such place as may be authorized by the Secretary of State and in accordance with instructions given by him.'

D. 18B (1A) of 22 May 1940 read: 'After paragraph (1) of Regulation eighteen B of the Defence (General) Regulations, 1939, there shall be inserted the following paragraph:–(1A) If the Secretary of State has reasonable cause to believe any person to have been or to be a member of, or to have been or to be active in the furtherance of the objects of, any such organisation as is hereinafter mentioned, and that it is necessary to exercise control over him, he may make an order against that person directing that he be detained. The organisations hereinbefore referred to are any organisation as respects which the Secretary of State is satisfied that either—(a) the organisation is subject to foreign influence or control, or (b) the persons in control of the organisation have or have had associations with persons concerned in the government of, or sympathies with the system of government of, any Power with which His Majesty is at war, and in either case that there is a danger of the utilisation of the organisation for purposes prejudicial to the public safety, the defence of the realm, the maintenance of public order, the efficient prosecution of any war in which His Majesty may be engaged, or the maintenance of supplies or services essential to the life of the community.'

E. Regulation 18AA of 26 June 1940 empowered the Secretary of State to apply the regulation to any organization covered by 18B (1A) and went on to provide that: '(3) No person shall—
(a) summon a meeting of members or managers of an organisation to which this regulation applies,
(b) attend any such meeting in the capacity of member or manager of such an organisation,
(c) publish any notice or advertisement relating to any such organisation,
(d) invite persons to support such an organisation,
(e) make any contribution or loan to funds held by or for the benefit of such an organisation or accept any such contribution or loan, or
(f) give any guarantee in respect of such funds aforesaid.'

(The regulation then provided for the winding up of such organisations by court order.)

F. The British Union had Regulation 18AA applied to it on 10 July. The order stated: 'Whereas I am satisfied with respect to the organisation named below that the persons in control of that organisation have had sympathies with the system of government of a power with which His Majesty is at war and that there is a danger of the utilisation of the organisation for purposes prejudicial to the efficient prosecution of the war: Now, therefore . . . I by this Order direct that the said regulation shall apply to the organisation known as British Union.'

APPENDIX II

Note on Sources

Material from the Public Record Office is referred to by class and piece number; the class number, for example HO 45, indicates the department of origin. The principal departmental records used are **HO** (Home Office), **TS** (Treasury Solicitor's Department), **PCOM** (Prison Commissioners), **FO** (Foreign Office), **MEPO** (Metropolitan Police), **CAB** (Cabinet Papers), **INF** (Ministry of Information), **WO** (War Office), **HH** (Scottish Office), **LCO** (Lord Chancellor's Office), **CRIM** (Central Criminal Court), and **PREM** (Premier; documents associated with W. S. Churchill). Piece numbers do not generally include the original file numbers, which I have usually not given.

The Papers of Sir Alexander Cadogan, including the original **Cadogan Diaries**, are in the archives of Churchill College, Cambridge (**ACAD**), and contain material not, for reasons of delicacy, reproduced in the published edition edited by D. Dilks, *The Diaries of Sir Alexander Cadogan, OM, 1938–1945* (London, 1971). The National Maritime Museum holds the diaries of Sir Barry Domvile, catalogued as **DOM**. The **Loraine Papers** are in the Public Record Office in class FO 1011. The **Luttman-Johnson Papers** have now been deposited in the Imperial War Museum. The Imperial War Museum also has the **Wiseman Papers** of the late F. C. Wiseman and the **Papers of Vernon Kell**. The University of Hull holds the **NCCL** records, and the University of Sheffield the **Saunders Papers**, which were those of Robert Saunders, BU District Leader in Dorset. The Stokes Papers are deposited in the Bodleian Library, Oxford.

I have been given access to a number of unpublished documents and publications which are not easy to obtain; these are mentioned in the notes. Other unpublished accounts apparently exist. I have attempted to secure access to the memoirs of Nellie Driver, but without success. Lord Birkett tells me that there survive no diaries of his father for the wartime period, the biography by H. Montgomery Hyde gives the contrary impression, but is misleading. The **Britons** possess some archives, and I have been given copies of some; these are referred to in footnotes. The **Bleach Papers** comprise copies of documents, principally from the archives of the Britons, made available to me by Mr K. Bleach, and currently in my possession. The **Charnley MS** (copy in my possession) has been published in a virtually complete form as J. W. Charnley, *Blackshirts and Roses* (London, 1990). The **Greene Papers** are in the possession of Mr E. P. C. Greene of Oxford. The **Grundy, Knott**, and **Williams MSS** comprise short accounts of detention by former detainees; copies in my possession. Scholars who wish to consult material in my possession, which includes copies of pamphlets and other ephemera, are welcome to do so, subject to permission being obtained where appropriate.

Amongst the other documents used the autograph book comprises autographs of some 64 BU detainees; signatures and comments seem to have been entered about the time of release. The Board of Deputies of British Jews holds a considerable archive (**BDBJ Archives**) on fascists and anti-Semitic activity before the war, to which I have been given access. The **Beavan Diary** was written by Arthur Beavan, and covers the period 12 May 1941 to 26 October 1941. The **Bellamy MSS** are the work of the late Richard Reynell Bellamy, who became a historian of the BU. His much revised MS now exists in three volumes: 'Mosley in Perspective', 'We Marched with Mosley', and 'Memoirs of a Fascist Beast'. I refer to these works as i, ii, and iii. The **Gourdon MS** is a short account by Denis A. Gourdon of his experiences. The ledger of the **Right Club** is possessed by Professor Richard Griffiths. He has not, however, told me who gave it to him, this being the understanding, though I think I can guess. The **Rowe MS** consists of a short statement by T. W. Victor Rowe. The **Swan MS** comprises a short account by Mr Arthur W. Swan of his life and connection with the BU. The **Watts MS** was written by Charles Frederick Watts, and is entitled 'It Has Happened Here: The Experience of a Political Prisoner in British Prisons and Concentration Camps during the Fifth Column Panic of 1940/41'. The Somervell Papers in the Bodleian Library contain nothing relevant to the legal cases, though Somervell considered writing his account. The Monckton Papers do contain material concerning Mosley, closed until 1999.

Although collections of material connected with the BU exist, it is unlikely that any documents exist which would be relevant. Pre-war fascist newspapers contain much biographical information.

APPENDIX III
Spy Trials

The Foreign Office Papers (FO 371/5084) contain a list prepared for a Parliamentary Question of 18 October 1945 of thirteen persons convicted and sentenced to death under the Treachery Act during the war:

Jose Waldberg	German
Carl Heinrich Meier	Dutch
Charles Albert van der Kieboom	Dutch
George Armstrong	British
Werner Heinrich Walti	Believed German
Karel Richard Richter	Sudeten German
Johannes Marinus Dronkers	Dutch
José Estella Key	British
Alphonse Louis Eugène Timmerman	Belgian
Rogerio de Maghalhaes Peixote de Menenezes	Portuguese
Oswald John Job	British Subject
Pierre Richard Charles Neukermans	Belgian
Joseph Jan Van Hove	Belgian

Nigel West in *MI5* (London, 1983) also lists Duncan Scott-Ford, British, executed 3 November 1942 (OH 337; his Home Office File is HO 45/25763), José Jakobs alias George Rymer, German, executed 14 August 1941 in the Tower of London after trial by court martial (see pp. 326–8), Karl Drucke alias François de Deeker, German, executed 12 June 1941, and Franciscus Winter, Belgian, executed 26 January 1941. He also names two Spaniards executed in Gibraltar on 11 January 1944. West at p. 346 names Wilhem Ter Braak (real identity unknown) as a spy who committed suicide by shooting himself in Cambridge in 1940 or 1941; he appears in the official history (Hinsley and Simkins 91, 312, 326) as Jan Wilhelm Ter Braak. Spellings of the names of these individuals differ in the sources.

Jowitt gives an account in his *Some Were Spies* (London, 1954) of three trials of German agents for espionage. One involved Kieboom (Dutch) and Pons (also Dutch) who landed near Hythe on 3 September 1940, a second Waldberg (German) and Meier (Dutch), who landed at Dungeness, also on 3 September 1940, and a third Drucke and Walti, who landed in company with a woman, Vera Erikson or Eriksen (with various other names), on the coast of Banffshire on 30 September 1940. She was not tried and Jowitt implies that she became a double agent. Hinsley and Simkins (323–5) say she was detained. Pons was acquitted and at once detained under Regulation 18B. Nigel West in his *MI5* gives (without indicating sources) considerably more information. Vera Erikson is identified as

Danish, aged 27, and her real name as Vera de Cottani-Chalbur; he says she was a former agent for Charles Maxwell-Knight, and was detained under Regulation 18B in Holloway. Jowitt implies that she became a double agent. I have found no reference to her being in Holloway.

APPENDIX IV
Tyler Kent and Anna Wolkoff

Kent was dismissed with effect from 20 May; the State Department did not request his deportation to the USA. There is no evidence of lengthy discussions between the British and US government over the incident. The decision was taken by Johnson and agreed by Ambassador Kennedy on 19 May. A State Department telegram confirming the waiver of immunity on 22 May says: 'The purpose of waiving immunity was that the British authorities might proceed against Kent. There is no objection to formally charging the offender with violations of British law. Publicity in connection with such charges might not be helpful under the circumstances.' It would have been embarrassing to have publicity about a spy in their London Embassy, operating on the scale involved. Breckenridge Long wrote in his diary: 'every diplomatic manoeuvre was exposed to Germany and Russia . . . No doubt the Germans will publish another White Book during our political campaign which will have as its purpose the defeat of Roosevelt.' Johnson had been assured that any legal proceedings against Kent and his accomplices would take place in camera. It is puzzling why Kennedy and Johnson so promptly agreed to waive diplomatic immunity, before informing the State Department. Conceivably Kennedy was nervous of what Kent might reveal about his own activities if a trial took place in the USA.

A deportation order of 23 May 1940 enabled Kent to be held whilst investigations proceeded. The fact that Kent, a one-time Embassy official, and Wolkoff were to be tried was not itself kept secret. The decision to prosecute Kent and Wolkoff (but not Ramsay) was formally taken on 30 July, and Kent was informed that he would be charged with offences under the Official Secrets Act. It is possible that charges carrying the death penalty could have been preferred. Kent and Anna Wolkoff were jointly indicted, and their trial began on 23 October before Mr Justice Tucker; he obligingly ruled that they could be tried in camera, but allowed separate trials.

Kent was charged with seven offences relating to four of the documents. The principal charges fell under section 1 of the Official Secrets Act of 1911, and the prosecution had to prove that Kent had acted 'for a purpose prejudicial to the safety or interests of the state'. Apart from technical questions over jurisdiction to try him at all his defence was that he had an innocent motive. The prosecution sought to show that Anna Wolkoff was a foreign agent, and that Kent's contacts with her showed that his purpose was as charged. Hence the trial involved an attack on Anna Wolkoff, then awaiting trial. Kent claimed, and his counsel argued on his appeal, that he did not have a fair trial, since his embassy prevented him tendering in evidence the other abstracted documents: only by looking at the cache as a whole would his innocent motive appear.

Kent was convicted on all the charges except one charge of theft; the jury

retired for half an hour. Anna was also convicted. But the judge deferred sentenc-
ing them—this was in public—until 7 November, two days after Roosevelt had
been re-elected, and after Anna had also been convicted, probably on 1
November. Kent received a sentence of seven years' imprisonment. One cannot
but suspect that the timing was contrived. Whatever the rights and wrongs of the
matter the US State Department had, by waiving immunity, allowed an American
citizen to be tried in secret in Britain, when he could perfectly well have been
deported and tried openly in the USA. Since all this was discoverable before the
Presidential election, some considerable risk was involved. One cannot therefore
but suspect that Kent had some other information which it was desired to conceal.

Apart from two Churchill–Roosevelt telegrams the two other documents
involved in Kent's trial were letters from Captain Guy Maynard Liddell of MI5
to the FBI. One, dated 19 October 1939, provided information about foreign
agents thought to be operating in the USA, and the second, of 7 November 1939,
arose in some way out of a search of a Room 307, presumably a reference to postal
censorship. In it MI5 requested that the home and office of one 'F' (supposed to
be the first letter of his name) be searched; 'F' was thought to be running Russian
military intelligence in Britain, and a search, it was hoped, would identify Russian
agents in Britain.

It is conceivable that there was an ideological component in Kent's Russian
sympathies. He was continuously anxious to stress his opposition to bolshevism,
but in his letter to his fellow smuggler he records that his Legation chief suspected him of pro-bolshevist leanings. More probably Kent was simply after
money. His own story was, naturally enough, different. In his initial interrogation
in the US Embassy Kennedy asked him: 'What did you think you were doing
with our codes and telegrams?' Kent replied: 'It was for my own information . . .
Because I thought them very interesting.' He claimed to have no idea what was in
the locked Right Club volume. To Maxwell-Knight he said he had copied documents 'to preserve for my own use records which I considered of importance
without any specific object in mind'. In evidence at the trial he remained evasive,
but a cipher clerk who has abstracted hundreds of documents from his embassy,
arranged for some to be photographed, and even copied keys to the code room,
has some explaining to do. He came up with the only conceivable justification: he
was a patriotic 'whistle-blower', unhappy about certain aspects of US foreign policy, and considering whether to alert members of Congress or others in the USA
to what was going on. What he said he objected to was a policy which had the tendency of drawing the USA into war. He also was sympathetic to Germany, and
Hitler's anti-Semitic views, though he said he did not approve of anti-Semitic
violence. There was also the ridiculous suggestion that the telegrams involved
some sort of impropriety, or underhand plotting, behind the back of the Prime
Minister. Given the isolationist movement in the USA Kent's story, had it
emerged in a trial in America, would surely have caused embarrassment. But the
decision to allow Kent to be tried in England appears to have been taken before
the 'whistle-blower' defence had emerged; this too makes me suspect that Kent
may have had other information which perhaps Kennedy wanted to conceal.

The aftermath of the affair may be briefly described. The State Department
was forced on to the defensive on the matter; there was litigation in the USA over

his case, and extensive comment in the press; this all continued after Kent's release in 1945, and deportation back to the USA in 1945. Kent's mother campaigned on his behalf; enemies of Roosevelt and isolationist groups associated with the far right of the Republican Party developed the idea that there had been a great cover-up or even frame-up; Kent had discovered a sinister correspondence involving some hundreds of cables between Roosevelt and Churchill, thought by some on the lunatic right, which flourishes in the USA, to include this communication from Churchill: 'I am half American, and if I become Prime Minister and you and I work together, we can rule the world.' Two Foreign Office files, FO 371/38704 and 44628, deal with the aftermath, on which there is much information in R. Bearse and A. Read, *Conspirator: The Untold Story of Churchill, Roosevelt and Tyler Kent, Spy* (London, 1991).

Kent, no doubt in self-protection, posed as a committed anti-communist, a prudent course in America in the 1950s; he indicated that he possessed alarming information, which he might one day reveal. Those unsympathetic to him thought he ought to be prosecuted under American law, and he was in consequence investigated, incompetently so far as can be judged, by the FBI. He talked his way out of being brought before a Grand Jury. The account of his interrogation in 1951 reveals him as an extremely shrewd operator; he gave away virtually nothing which was not already known from the transcript of his trial. The reaction of the naïve FBI officer was to regard him as frank and straightforward. The outcome was that the Churchill–Roosevelt correspondence, which only accounted for a tiny proportion of the 1,500 documents abstracted, came to assume an entirely distorted significance in the affair.

Kent himself, presumably very nervous indeed as to what might be discovered about his activities, became a prominent right-wing activist. He was associated with papers which supported the Ku Klux Klan; nobody could think him a 'commie'.

As for Anna Mr Justice Tucker sentenced her to ten years' imprisonment, claiming, in confirmation of the view that lawyers lack imagination, that, although no naval or military secrets were involved, 'It is difficult to imagine a more serious offence.' In reality the actions for which she was convicted at the trial, though evidencing disloyalty, were in themselves of no importance. What was important was what else she may have done.

Anna Wolkoff was killed in company with Enid Riddell in a car accident in Spain in 1969. Tyler Kent died in Texas in 1988.

APPENDIX V

Mosley's 'Reasons for Order'

Reasons for Order[1]

The Order under Defence Regulation 18B was made against you, Oswald Ernald Mosley, for the following reasons.

1. The Secretary of State has reasonable cause to believe that you have been a member of the organisation now known as 'British Union'; and to have been active in the furtherance of its objects; and that it is necessary to exercise control over you.

2. The organisation known as British Union is subject to foreign influence and/or control.

Particulars.

(a) The constitution of the organisation is influenced by Italian or German political and/or national organisations.

(b) The constitution of the organisation has been and is subject to Italian or German influence in the original name of the organisation, 'The British Union of Fascists', its later name 'The British Union of Fascists and National Socialists', its emblems, its uniforms, its procedure, the form of public meetings, and similar matters.

(c) The policy of the organisation has been and is subject to Italian or German influence; e.g. the anti-semitic campaign of British Union.

(d) There is reasonable cause to believe that between the years 1932 and 1937 the organisation has been in receipt of monies from Italy.

3. That you . . . as one of the persons in control of the organisation have or have had associations with persons concerned in the government of Germany, a power with which His Majesty is at war.

Particulars.

(a) In or about the month of June and July 1938 you entered into close associations with persons concerned in the government of Germany in connection with the erection of a wireless broadcasting station in Germany, to be used by an English Company in which you were closely interested.

(b) German propaganda literature has been received by the organisation for the purpose of distribution by arrangement between the organisation and persons concerned in the government of Germany.

[1] Dated 19 June 1940; HO 283/9.

(*c*) That you . . . have paid visits to Germany, and been received with every sign of honour from Herr Hitler. Your reception by Herr Hitler was in consequence of the affinities existing between your organisation and the Party organisation in Germany.

(*d*) That many members of the British Union have been encouraged by you, as leader, to visit Germany and consider and study the organisation existing in that country, for the purpose of strengthening your own organisation.

4. That you . . . as one of the persons in control of British Union, have sympathies with the system of government in Germany, a power with which His Majesty is at war.

Particulars.

(*a*) In public speeches and writings you have extolled the system of government existing in Germany and condemned the democratic system of government existing in Great Britain.

(*b*) That one of the objects of British Union is to replace the present system of government in Great Britain by the system of government now obtaining in Germany with appropriate modifications.

5. There is a danger of the utilisation . . . [quoting the text of the regulation and giving of course no particulars].

BIBLIOGRAPHY OF PRINCIPAL
WORKS CITED

ADACHI, K., *The Enemy that Never Was: A History of the Japanese Canadians* (Toronto, 1976).

ALLEN, C. K., *Bureaucracy Triumphant* (London, 1931).

——*Law and Orders* (Oxford, 1945).

ALLEN, E. A., *It Shall Not Happen Here: Anti-Semitism, Fascists and Civil Liberties* (London, 1943).

ALLEN, LORD, OF ABBEYDALE, 'In State Service: Reflections of a Bureaucrat', in *The Home Office: Perspectives on Policy and Administration. Bicentenary Lectures 1982* (London, 1983; published by Royal Institute of Public Affairs).

ANDERSON, G., *Fascists, Communists and the National Government* (London, 1983).

ANDREW, C., *Her Majesty's Secret Service: The Making of the British Intelligence Community* (London, 1987). (Originally published in 1985 as *Secret Service: The Making of the British Intelligence Community*.)

BALFOUR, W. A., *Propaganda in War, 1939–1945* (London, 1970).

BAMFORD, F., and BANKES, V., *Vicious Circle* (London, 1965).

BARKER, R. *Conscience, Government and War: Conscientious Objection in Britain 1939–1945* (London and Boston, 1982).

BATTERSBY, J. L., *The Bishop Said Amen* (Poynton, Cheshire, 1947).

BEARSE, R. and READ, A., *Conspirator: The Untold Story of Churchill, Roosevelt and Tyler Kent, Spy* (London, 1991).

BEDFORD, DUKE OF, *Is This Justice? An Examination of Regulation 18B* (Glasgow, 1943).

BENEWICK, R., *The Fascist Movement in Britain* (London, 1972).

BETCHERMAN, L.-R., *The Swastika and the Maple Leaf: Fascist Movements in Canada in the Thirties* (Toronto, 1975).

BEVAN, B., *The Development of British Immigration Law* (London, 1986).

BIRD, J. C., *Control of Enemy Alien Civilians in Great Britain 1914–1918* (New York and London, 1986).

BOELCKE, W. A. (ed.), *The Secret Conferences of Dr Goebbels: The Propaganda War 1939–1943* (New York, 1970).

BRERETON, H. L., *Gordonstoun: Ancient Estate and Modern School* (Edinburgh, 1968).

BREWER, J. D., *Mosley's Men: The British Union of Fascists in the West Midlands* (Aldershot, 1984).

BULLITT, O. H., *For the President–Personal and Secret: Correspondence between Franklin D. Roosevelt and William C. Bullitt* (Boston, 1972).

BULLOCH, J., *MI5: The Origins and History of the British Counter-Espionage Service* (London, 1963).

CANE, P., *An Introduction to Administrative Law* (2nd. edn.; Oxford, 1992).

CARLTON, D., *Anthony Eden* (London, 1986).

CAWELTI, J. W. and ROSENBERG, B. A., *The Spy Story* (Chicago, 1987).

CECIL, R., *A Divided Life: A Personal Portrait of the Spy Donald Maclean* (New York, 1989).

CEADEL, M., *Pacifism in Britain 1914–1945* (London, 1950).

CHAPPELL, C., *Island of Barbed Wire* (London, 1984).

CHARNLEY, J. W., *Blackshirts and Roses* (London, 1990).

CHESTER, N., *The English Administrative System 1780–1870* (Oxford, 1981).

CHURCHILL, W. S., *The Second World War*, ii. *Their Finest Hour* (London, 1949).

COCKERILL, G. K., *What Fools We Were* (London, 1944).

COCKETT, R., *Twilight of Truth: Chamberlain, Appeasement and the Manipulation of the Press* (London, 1989).

COHN, N., *Warrant for Genocide: The Myth of the Jewish World Conspiracy and the 'Protocols of the Elders of Zion'* (London, 1967).

COLE, J. A., *Lord Haw Haw: The Full Story of William Joyce* (London, 1964).

COLVILLE, J., *The Fringes of Power: 10 Downing Street Diaries 1939–1955* (London, 1985).

CONWELL-EVANS, T. P. *None So Blind* (London, 1947).

COOGAN, T. P., *The IRA* (15th impression; London, 1990).

COOKRIDGE, E. H. [pseud], *Secrets of the British Secret Service: Behind the Scenes of the Work of British Counter-Espionage during the War* (London, 1948).

COSTELLO, J. *Mask of Treachery* (New York, 1988).

—— *Ten Days that Saved the West* (London, 1991).

COTTER, C. P., 'Constitutional Democracy and Emergency: Emergency Powers Legislation in Great Britain since 1914'. Harvard University D. Phil. Thesis, 1953.

COWLING, M., *The Impact of Hitler: British Politics and British Policy 1933–1940* (Cambridge, 1975).

CRESCIANI, C., *Fascism, Anti-Fascism and Italians in Australia 1922–1945* (Canberra, 1980).

CROSS, C., *The Fascists in Britain* (London, 1961).

CROFT, BRIGADIER GENERAL THE LORD HENRY PAGE, *My Life of Strife*. [London, 1946]

CROSS, J. A., *Lord Swinton* (Oxford, 1982).

CROUCHER, R., *Engineers at War* (London, 1982).

CROZIER, L. P., *Off the Record: Political Interviews 1933–1943*, ed. A. J. P. Taylor (London, 1973).

DALTON, H. *The Fateful Years: Memoirs 1939–45* (London, 1953).

DEACON, R. [pseud. for D. MacCormick], *The Greatest Treason: The Bizarre Story of Hollis, Liddell and Mountbatten* (London, 1989).

DEARDEN, H., *The Fire Raisers: The Story of Leopold Harris and his Gang* (London, 1934).

DENNING, LORD, *The Family Story* (London, 1981).

DILKS, D. (ed.), *The Diaries of Sir Alexander Cadogan 1938–1945* (London, 1971). (The original diary, not fully reproduced, is in the Churchill College Archives.)

DOMVILE, B., *From Admiral to Cabin Boy* (London, 1947).

DRENNAN, J. [pseud. for W. E. D. Allen], *B.U.F.: Oswald Mosley and British Fascism* (London, 1934).

DUTTON, G., *The Hero as Murderer: The Life of Edward John Eyre* (London, 1962).

EALES, R. and SULLIVAN, D., *The Political Context of Law* (London, 1986).

EAVES, J., *Emergency Powers and the Parliamentary Watchdog: Parliament and the Executive in Great Britain 1939–1951* (London, 1957).

FARAGO, L., *The Game of the Foxes: The Untold Story of German Espionage in the United States and Great Britain during World War II* (London and New York (paperback edition), 1971).

FARSON, H., *Henry: An Appreciation of Henry Williamson* (London, 1982).

FAY, J. *The Helicopter: History, Piloting and How It Flies* (Newton Abbot, 1976).

FELSTEAD, S. T., *German Spies at Bay* (New York, 1920).

FERGUSON, T. G., *British Military Intelligence 1870–1914: The Development of a Modern Intelligence Organization* (Frederick, Md., 1984).

FIRMIN, S., *They Came to Spy* (London, 1947).

FLEMING, P., *Invasion 1940: An Account of the German Preparations and the British Countermeasures* (London, 1957).

FORSYTH, W., *Cases and Opinions on Constitutional Law* (London, 1869).

FOSTER, M., *A Report of Some Proceedings . . . etc. (commonly known as Crown Law)* (London, 1791).

FOX, J., *White Mischief* (London, 1982).

FRY, C. K., *Statesmen in Disguise* (London, 1969).

GARLINSKI, J., *Intercept: The Enigma War* (London, 1979).

GARNER, J. W., *International Law and the World War* (London, 1920).

GATES, E. M., *End of the Affair: The Collapse of the Anglo-French Alliance, 1939–40* (Berkeley, Calif., 1981).

GILBERT, M., *Winston S. Churchill,* vi *'Finest Hour'* (New York, 1986).

GILLMAN, P. and GILLMAN, L., *'Collar the Lot!' How Britain Interned and Expelled its Wartime Refugees* (London, 1980).

GLEES, A., *Exile Politics in Britain during the Second World War: The German Social Democrats in Britain* (Oxford, 1982).

——*Secrets of the Service: British Intelligence and Communist Subversion* (London, 1986).

GOLDMAN, A. L., 'Defence Regulation 18B: Emergency Internment of Aliens and Political Dissenters in Great Britain during World War II', *Journal of British Studies,* 11 (1973), 120–37.

GOOCH, J., *The Plans of War* (London, 1974).

GREENLEAF, W. H., *The British Political Tradition,* iii. *A Much Governed Nation* (London, 1987), Parts 1 and 2.

GRIFFITHS, R., *Fellow Travellers of the Right: British Enthusiasts for Nazi Germany 1933–9* (London, 1980).

GUINNESS, J. (with C. Guinness), *The House of Mitford* (London, 1984).

HAMM, E. G., *Action Replay: An Autobiography* (London, 1987).

HANCOCK, W. K. and GOWING, M. M., *British War Economy* (London, 1949).

HARRISON, T. *Living through the Blitz* (London, 1976).

HENNESSY, P., *Whitehall* (London, 1989).

HEUSTON, R. F. V., *Lives of the Lord Chancellors 1885–1940* (Oxford, 1964).

—— '*Liversidge* v. *Anderson* in Retrospect', *Law Quarterly Review,* 86 (1970), 33.

HEWART, G. (Lord Chief Justice), *The New Despotism* (London, 1929).

HINSLEY, F. H. and SIMKINS, C.A.G., *British Intelligence in the Second World War*, iv (London, 1990).

HIRSCHFIELD, G. *Exile in Great Britain: Refugees from Hitler's Germany* (Leamington Spa, 1984).

HOLMES, C., *Anti-Semitism in British Society 1876–1939* (London, 1979).

—— *John Bull's Island: Immigration and British Society, 1871–1971* (Basingstoke, 1988).

HOLT, E., *Protest in Arms: The Irish Troubles 1916–1923* (London, 1960).

HOOPER, D., *Official Secrets: The Use and Abuse of the Act* (London, 1987).

HOWSIN, H. M., *The Significance of Indian Nationalism* (Madras, 1922; reprint).

HUGHES, D., *The Prison Sonnets of T. E. Nicholas* (London, 1948).

HYAM, R., *Elgin and Churchill at the Colonial Office* (London, 1968).

HYDE, H. M., *Norman Birkett* (London, 1964).

IRVING, D. J. C., *Hitler's War* (New York, 1977).

—— *Churchill's War: The Struggle for Power* (Bullsbrook, W. Australia, 1987).

ISRAEL, F. L. (ed.), *The War Diaries of Breckenrige Long* (Lincoln, 1966).

JAMES, R. R., *Victor Cazalet: A Portrait* (London, 1976).

JONES, G., *Herbert Morrison: Portrait of a Politician* (London 1977).

JONG, L. de, *The German Fifth Column in the Second World War* (Chicago, 1956).

JOWITT, W. A. (EARL), *Some Were Spies* (London, 1954).

KEE, R., *The Green Flag: The Turbulent History of the Irish Nationalist Movement* (New York, 1972).

KEEGAN, J., *The Masks of Command* (London, 1988).

KEIR, D. L. and LAWSON, F. H., *Cases in Constitutional Law* (5th edn.; Oxford, 1967).

KELLY, J. M., *Fundamental Rights in the Irish Law and Constitution* (2nd edn.; New York, 1968).

KELSALL, R. K., *Higher Civil Servants in Britain: From 1870 to the Present Day* (London, 1955).

KENT, H. S., *In on the Act: Memoirs of a Law Maker* (London, 1979).

KIDD, R., *British Liberty in Danger* (London, 1940).

KOCH, E., *Deemed Suspect: A Wartime Blunder* (Toronto, 1980).

KOCHAN, M., *British Internees in the Second World War* (London, 1983).

KOSKOFF, D. E., *Joseph P. Kennedy: A Life and Times* (Englewood Cliffs, NJ, 1974).

LA VIOLETTE, F. E., *The Canadian Japanese and World War II: A Sociological and Psychological Account* (Toronto, 1948).

LAFITTE, F., *The Internment of Aliens* (London, 1940).

LAMB, R., *The Ghosts of Peace 1935–45* (London, 1987).

LAMPLUGH, L., *A Shadowed Man: Henry Williamson, 1895–1977* (Barnstaple, Devon, 1990).

LANGLEY, D. and JONAS, M., *Roosevelt and Churchill: Their Secret Wartime Correspondence* (New York, 1975).

LASH, J. P., *Roosevelt and Churchill: The Partnership that Saved the West* (London, 1977).

LEESE, A. S., *My Irelevant Defence: Being Meditations inside Gaol and out on Jewish Ritual Murder* (London, 1938).

—— *Out of Step: Events in the Two Lives of an Anti-Jewish Camel Doctor* (Guildford, 1951).

LEWIS, D. S., *Illusions of Grandeur: Mosley, Fascism and British Society 1931–1981* (Manchester, 1987).

LYMINGTON, MARQUESS [G. V. Wallop, 9th Earl of Portsmouth], *A Knot of Roots* (London, 1965).

LYONS, F. S. L., *Ireland since the Famine* (London, 1971).

MACLEOD, R. and KELLY, D., *The Ironside Diaries 1937–1940* (London, 1962).

MARKHAM, V. R., *Return Passage* (Oxford, 1953).

MASTERMAN, J. C., *The Double Cross System in the War of 1939 to 1945* (New Haven, Conn., 1972).

—— *On the Chariot Wheel* (London, 1975).

MASTERS, A., *The Man Who Was M: The Life of Maxwell Knight* (Oxford, 1984).

MILLER, J., *One Girl's War: Personal Exploits in MI5's Most Secret Station* (Dingle, Eire, 1986).

MONTGOMERY HYDE, H., *The Quiet Canadian* (London, 1962).

—— *Norman Birkett: The Life of Lord Birkett of Ulverston* (London, 1964).

MOON, H. R., 'The Invasion of the United Kingdom: Public Controversy and Official Planning 1888–1918'. University of London Ph.D. Thesis, 1968.

MORAN, LORD, *Winston Churchill: The Struggle for Survival, 1940–1965* (London, 1966).

MORISON, S., *I Renounce War: The Story of the Peace Pledge Union* (London, 1962).

MORRISON, H., *Herbert Morrison: An Autobiography* (London, 1960).

MOSLEY, D., *A Life of Contrasts: The Autobiography of Diana Mosley* (London, 1977).

—— *Loved Ones: Pen Portraits by Diana Mosley* (London, 1985).

MOSLEY, L., *The Druid* (London, 1982).

MOSLEY, N., *The Rules of the Game* (London, 1982).

—— *Beyond the Pale: Sir Oswald Mosley and his Family 1933–1980* (London, 1987).

MOSLEY, O. E., *The Greater Britain* (London, 1932).

—— *My Life* (London, 1968).

MUIRDEN, B., *Puzzled Patriots* (Melbourne, 1968).

MUNSON, K. G., *Helicopters and Other Rotorcraft since 1947* (London, 1968).

NEWSAM, F., *The Home Office* (London, 1954; revd edn. 1955).

O'BRIEN, T. H., *Civil Defence: History of the Second World War* (London, 1955).

OCCLESHAW, H., *Armour against Fate: British Military Intelligence in the First World War* (London, 1989).

PATKIN, B., *The Dunera Internees* (Stanmore, NSW, Australia, 1979).

PELLEW, J., *The Home Office 1848–1914: From Clerks to Bureaucrats* (London, 1982).

PENROSE, B. and FREEMAN, S., *Conspiracy of Silence* (London, 1987).

PETRIE, D., *Developments in Sikh Politics, 1900–1911: A Report*. (Amritsar, 1972).

—— (ed. M. Saha), *Communism in India, 1924–1927* (Calcutta, 1972).

PHILBY, H. ST JOHN B., *Arabian Days: An Autobiography* (London, 1948).

PLAICE, K. B., *The Home Office 1782–1982* (London, 1981).

POLDEN, P., *Guide to the Records of the Lord Chancellor's Department* (London, 1989).

PONTING, C., *1940: Myth and Reality* (London, 1990).

PORTER, B., *The Origins of the Vigilant State: The London Metropolitan Police Special Branch before the First World War* (London, 1987).

PORTSMOUTH, EARL OF, *A Knot of Roots: An Autobiography* (London, 1965).

PRITT, D. N., *The Autobiography of D. N. Pritt*, 3 vols. (London, 1965–6).

—— *The Mosley Case* (n.d.).

RAMSAY, A. H. M., *The Nameless War* (London, n.d. [1952]).

RAVEN-THOMSON, A., *Civilisation as Divine Superman* (London, 1932).

—— *The Coming Corporate State* (London, 1935).

RICHARDS, D., *The Royal Air Force 1939–1945* (London, 1974–5).

ROBERTS, A., *'The Holy Fox': A Biography of Lord Halifax* (London, 1991).

ROBERTS, C. E. B., *The Trial of William Joyce* (London, 1946).

ROE, E. G. MANDEVILLE, *The Corporate State* (London, 1934).

ROSSITER, C. L., *Constitutional Dictatorship: Crisis Government in Modern Democracies* (New York, 1963).

RUSSELL, H. W. S., Duke of Bedford, *The Years of Transition* (London, 1949).

RUTTER, O., *Portrait of a Painter: The Authorised Life of Philip de Laszlo* (London, 1939).

SCOTT, H., *Your Obedient Servant* (London, 1959).

SEMMEL, B., *Jamaican Blood and the Victorian Conscience: The Governor Eyre Controversy* (Boston, 1963).

SETH, R., *The Spy who Wasn't Caught: The Story of Julius Silber* (London, 1966).

SEWELL, B., *Henry Williamson: The Man, the Writings: A Symposium* (Padstow, Cornwall, 1980).

SHARPE, R. J., *The Law of Habeas Corpus* (2nd. edn.; Oxford, 1989).

SHORT, K. R. M., *The Dynamite War: Irish American Bombers in Victorian Britain* (Atlantic Highlands, NJ, 1979).

SILBER, J., *Invisible Weapons* (London, 1931).

SKIDELSKY, R., *Oswald Mosley* (London, 1975).

SLADEN, N. ST B., *The Real Le Queux* (London, 1928).

SQUIRE, P. H., *Most Generous of Men* (London, 1963).

STAMMERS, N., *Civil Liberties in Britain during the Second World War: A Political Study* (London, 1983).

STANSKY, P., *Churchill: A Profile* (New York, 1973).

STENT, R., *A Bespattered Page? The Internment of His Majesty's 'Most Loyal Aliens'* (London, 1980).

STEVENSON, W., *A Man Called Intrepid: The Secret War* (New York, 1976).

STRACHEY, J., *The Menace of Fascism* (London, 1934).

STUART, C., *Opportunity Knocks* (London, 1952).

TAYLOR, F. (ed.), *The Goebbels Diaries 1939–1941* (London, 1982).

TEMPLEWOOD, VISCOUNT, *Nine Troubled Years* (London, 1954).

THOMPSON, L. V., *1940: Year of Legend, Year of History* (London, 1960).

THOMSON, B., *Queer People* (London, 1922).

—— *My Experience at Scotland Yard* (New York, 1923).

—— *The Story of Scotland Yard* (London, 1935).

THURLOW, R., *Fascism in Britain: A History, 1918–1985* (Oxford, 1987).

TOWNSHEND, C., *The British Campaign in Ireland 1919–1921* (Oxford, 1975).

—— *Political Violence in Ireland: Government and Resistance since 1848* (Oxford, 1983).

TROUP, C. E., *The Home Office* (London, 1925).

TRYTHALL, A. J., *'Boney' Fuller: The Intellectual General 1878–1966* (London, 1977).

TURNBULL P., *Dunkirk: Anatomy of a Disaster* (New York, 1978).

TURNER, E. S., *The Phoney War* (London, 1961).

WASSERSTEIN, B. A., *Britain and the Jews of Europe 1939–1945* (London, 1979).

WATT, D. C., *How War Came: The Immediate Origins of the Second World War 1938–1939* (New York, 1989).

WEBBER, G., 'Patterns of Membership and Support for the British Union of Fascists', *Journal of Contemporary History*, 19 (1984), 575.

—— *The Ideology of the British Right, 1918–1939.* (London, 1986).

WELLS, W. B. and MARLOWE, N., *A History of the Irish Rebellion of 1916* (Dublin, 1916).

WEST, N. [pseud. for Rupert W. S. Allason MP], *MI5* (London, 1983).

—— *Mole Hunt: The Full Story of the Soviet Spy in MI5* (London, 1987).

—— *GCHQ: The Secret Wireless War 1900–1986* (London, 1986).

WEST, R., *The New Meaning of Treason* (New York, 1964).

WEST, W. J., *Truth Betrayed* (London, 1987).

WHALEN, R. J., *The Founding Father: The Story of Joseph P. Kennedy* (New York, 1964).

WHEELER-BENNETT, J. W., *John Anderson, Viscount Waverley* (London, 1962).

WIGHTON, C. and PREIS, G., *Hitler's Spies and Saboteurs* (New York, 1958).

WILLIAMS, D., *Not In the Public Interest: The Problem of Security in Democracy* (London, 1965).

WILLIAMS, R. C., *Klaus Fuchs, Atom Spy* (London, 1987).

WILLIAMSON, H., *The Story of a Norfolk Farm* (London, 1941).

—— *The Phoenix Generation* (London, 1965).

—— *A Solitary War* (London, 1966).

WRIGHT, P., *Spycatcher: The Candid Autobiography of a Senior Intelligence Officer* (New York, 1988).

YOUNG, D., *Rutland of Jutland* (London, 1963).

YOUNGER, C., *Ireland's Civil War* (London, 1968).

ZIEGLER, P., *King Edward VIII: The Official Biography* (London, 1990).

INDEX

Lightning Source UK Ltd.
Milton Keynes UK
UKHW020056311218
334748UK00004B/91/P

9 780198 259497